Studies in Church History

59

(2023)

THE CHURCHES AND RITES OF PASSAGE

THE CHURCHES AND RITES OF PASSAGE

EDITED BY

FRANCES KNIGHT

CHARLOTTE METHUEN

ANDREW SPICER

PUBLISHED FOR
THE ECCLESIASTICAL HISTORY SOCIETY
BY
CAMBRIDGE UNIVERSITY PRESS
2023

Published by Cambridge University Press & Assessment
on behalf of the Ecclesiastical History Society
University Printing House, Cambridge CB2 8BS, United Kingdom

First published 2023

ISBN 9781009421744

ISSN 0424–2084

SUBSCRIPTIONS: *Studies in Church History* is an annual subscription journal (ISSN 0424–2084). The 2023 subscription price (excluding VAT), which includes print and electronic access, is £133 (US $213 in the USA, Canada and Mexico) for institutions and £73 (US $118 in the USA, Canada and Mexico) for individuals ordering direct from the Press and certifying that the volume is for their personal use. An electronic-only subscription is also available to institutions at £91 (US $145 in the USA, Canada and Mexico). Special arrangements exist for members of the Ecclesiastical History Society.

Previous volumes are available online at www.cambridge.org/StudCH

Printed in Great Britain by Henry Ling Limited, The Dorset Press, Dorchester, DT1 1HD

A catalogue record for this publication is available from the British Library

Contents

Contents

Preface

This, the fifty-ninth volume of Studies in Church History, brings together the papers presented at the Summer Conference held in July 2021 and the Winter Meeting held in January 2022 under the presidency of Professor Frances Knight, after the original conferences, planned for 2020–21, had to be postponed due to the COVID-19 pandemic. In a new departure for the EHS, both events were held online as a consequence of lockdown restrictions. The editors are very grateful to all who participated in the conferences and shared their research despite the ongoing challenges caused by the pandemic.

The articles collected here shed new light on the significance of rites of passage in the churches, and on ways of marking them. Importantly, they also broaden the concept of rites of passage to include events and experiences other than those marked by the Church's pastoral offices. The result is a rich collection of articles which demonstrate the importance of this theme. We are grateful to Professor Knight for proposing the theme and for her leadership of the society during this complex period. We wish also to thank the society's Conference Secretary, Professor Elizabeth Tingle, for her careful planning which ensured the smooth running of the Summer Conference and Winter Meeting. Thanks are due also to the society's Secretary and Treasurer, Dr Jacqueline Rose and Simon Jennings, for their ongoing work and support.

This volume would not have been possible without the work of all those who offered contributions and submitted papers for consideration, and those who peer-reviewed the contributions. Dr Tim Grass and Dr Alice Soulieux-Evans provided capable support as assistant editors. We are very grateful to the society for funding both posts during this period of transition. With this volume, his fifteenth, Dr Grass retires as Assistant Editor. On behalf of the EHS Committee, we wish to express our deep gratitude to him for his work on successive volumes of Studies in Church History and for his contribution to the society, not least in his role as business manager.

The Ecclesiastical History Society offers two annual prizes for articles accepted for publication in Studies in Church History. In this volume, the Kennedy Prize, for the best contribution by a postgraduate student, has been awarded to Tim Yung for his article '"Does God Mind?" Reshaping Chinese Anglican Rituals, *c.*1877–1940.' The President's Prize, for the best contribution by an early career scholar, was awarded to Conor O'Brien, 'The Origins of Royal Anointing.' These articles both draw on careful scholarship to offer an innovative exploration of the theme.

Charlotte Methuen
University of Glasgow

Andrew Spicer
Oxford Brookes University

Contributors

Rémy Bethmont
Professor of British History and Culture, University of Paris 8, France; TransCrit Research Group

Clyde Binfield
Professor Emeritus in History, University of Sheffield

Dan D. Cruickshank
Tutor in Church History and Theology, University of Glasgow

Françoise Deconinck-Brossard
Emerita Professor, Université Paris Nanterre, France

Zachary Guiliano
Career Development Research Fellow in Early Medieval History, St Edmund Hall, Oxford

Benjamin Hansen
Postgraduate student, University of Minnesota

Ralph Houlbrooke
Professor Emeritus, University of Reading

W. M. Jacob
Independent scholar, London

Frances Knight
Professor Emeritus in the History of Christianity, University of Nottingham

Chris R. Langley
Staff Tutor in History, The Open University

Fiona McCall
Senior Lecturer in History, University of Portsmouth; Departmental Lecturer in Local & Social History, University of Oxford Department of Continuing Education

Conor O'Brien
Associate Professor, University of Oxford

Thomas O'Loughlin
Professor Emeritus of Historical Theology, University of Nottingham

Calum Platts
Independent scholar, Colchester

Rebecca Probert
Professor of Law, University of Exeter

Salvador Ryan
Professor of Ecclesiastical History, Saint Patrick's Pontifical University, Maynooth

R. N. Swanson
Research Fellow of the Institute for Advanced Study in Humanities and Social Science and Professor in the Institute for Medicine and Civilization, School of History and Civilization, Shaanxi Normal University, Xi'an, China; Emeritus Professor of Medieval Ecclesiastical History, University of Birmingham

Elisabeth van Houts
Emeritus Professor in European Medieval History, University of Cambridge

Alexandra Walsham
Professor of Modern History, University of Cambridge

Peter Webster
Independent scholar and consultant; Managing Director of Webster Research and Consulting Ltd

David L. Wykes
Senior Fellow, Institute of Historical Research, University of London

Tim Yung
Lecturer, The University of Hong Kong

Abbreviations

ActaSS	J. Bolland and G. Henschen, eds, *Acta sanctorum* (Antwerp etc., 1643–)
BIA	Borthwick Institute for Archives
BL	British Library
BM	Bibliothèque municipale
BnF	Bibliothèque nationale de France
Bodl.	Bodleian Library
CChr.CM	Corpus Christianorum, continuatio medievalis (1966–)
CChr.SG	Corpus Christianorum, series Graeca (1974–)
CChr.SL	Corpus Christianorum, series Latina (Turnhout, 1953–)
CERS	Church of England Record Society
ChH	*Church History* (1932–)
CSCO	Corpus Scriptorum Christianorum Orientalium (Paris, 1903–)
CUL	Cambridge University Library
CYS	Canterbury and York Society
EETS	Early English Text Society
EHR	*English Historical Review* (1886–)
ET	English translation
HBS	Henry Bradshaw Society
HC Deb.	House of Commons Debates
HistJ	*Historical Journal* (1958–)
HL Deb.	House of Lords Debates
HR	*Historical Research* (1986–)
JEH	*Journal of Ecclesiastical History* (1950–)
JHC	*Journal of the House of Commons*
LMA	London Metropolitan Archive
LPL	Lambeth Palace Library
MGH AA	Monumenta Germaniae Historica, Auctores antiquissimi, 15 vols (1877–1919)
MGH Conc., Ord.	Monumenta Germaniae Historica, Ordines de celebrando concilio (1996)
MGH Epp.	Monumenta Germaniae Historica, Epistolae (1887–)

MGH LL nat. Germ.	Monumenta Germaniae Historica, Leges nationum Germanicarum (1892–)
MGH Poetae	Monumenta Germaniae Historica, Poetae Latinae Medii Aevi (1881–)
MGH SRG i.u.s.	Monumenta Germaniae Historica, Scriptores rerum Germanicarum in usum scholarum seperatum editi (1871–)
MGH SRM	Monumenta Germaniae Historica, Scriptores rerum Merovingicarum, 7 vols (1884–1951)
MGH SS	Monumenta Germaniae Historica, Scriptores (in folio) (1826–)
n.d.	no date
n.f.	neue folge
n.pl.	no place
n.s.	new series
ODNB	H. C. G. Matthew and Brian Harrison, eds, *Oxford Dictionary of National Biography*, 63 vols (Oxford, 2004), and subsequent online versions
o.s.	old series
Parl. Deb.	Parliamentary Debates
PBA	*Proceedings of the British Academy* (1904–)
PG	J.-P. Migne, ed., Patrologia Graeca, 161 vols (Paris, 1857–66)
PL	J.-P. Migne, ed., Patrologia Latina, 217 vols + 4 index vols (Paris, 1844–65)
P&P	*Past and Present* (1952–)
SCH	Studies in Church History (1964–)
SCH Sub	Studies in Church History Subsidia, 14 vols (1978–2012)
TNA	The National Archives
TRHS	*Transactions of the Royal Historical Society* (1871–)
TTH	Translated Texts for Historians

Illustrations

Introduction

Christians, like all humans, have evolved rituals to mark the key moments of transition in life: rites of passage. The earliest Christian sources mention wedding feasts and allude to burial practices. They discuss baptism, of course, but besides baptism, the only time that the rite itself becomes the subject of the story is the wedding at Cana (John 2: 1–11). This narrative tells us something important about the way rites of passage work. When there is a perilous moment with the wine supply, we pick up the collective sense of the guests wanting to help, to ensure the success of the wedding. Rites of passage change the status of the individual or individuals directly involved, but they also involve the wider community.

The Churches and Rites of Passage was proposed as the theme for Studies in Church History 59 in order to promote sustained reflection on the historical development of those life events to which the churches responded with specific rites and ceremonies. It was intended in part to address current interests in life-cycle history, and in 'rites of passage', both ecclesiastical and secular. The major life-cycle rites of passage, the 'checkpoints in the pilgrimage of life', as Swanson calls them, are all covered in this volume. It includes articles discussing baptism, the churching or 'purification' of women after childbirth, confirmation and first communion, marriage, ordination, and events surrounding death and funerals, with coverage ranging from seventh-century Spain to contemporary America. Several articles explore terrain beyond the widely used life-cycle rites. O'Brien's prize-winning essay discusses early royal anointing, a ceremony obviously much less frequently celebrated. It was the rite that made someone who was not a king, a king, and it was particularly crucial when royal succession was non-dynastic. Guiliano explores the renunciation of wealth as a rite of passage into the religious life, and ultimately the kingdom of heaven. Langley, meanwhile, investigates the officially sanctioned passage into clerical old age, with an account of what transpired when a minister in early modern Scotland became unable to perform his duties due to age and infirmity.

Studies in Church History 59 (2023), 1–7
doi: 10.1017/stc.2023.21

It was Arnold van Gennep (1873–1957) who provided us with the language of 'rites of passage'. His influential anthropological study was published in French in 1909, but not translated into English until 1960. Van Gennep explored how an individual in any society experiences life as a succession of major events, particularly relating to birth, puberty, marriage, parenthood and, finally, old age and death. The term became grafted on to what Anglicans traditionally described as the 'occasional offices' (now more usually described as the 'pastoral offices'), although that term tends to be limited to an understanding of liturgical forms, without the wider social and cultural meanings implied in a rite of passage. In the opening article, O'Loughlin re-assesses van Gennep by placing his anthropological work in the context of the assumptions of the church history of his own day, and by showing how he anticipates, and normalizes, the diversity that we now (mostly) take for granted in the contemporary practice of religious history. Van Gennep's presence hovers over this volume: his ideas are also discussed in the contributions by Cruickshank, Deconinck-Brossard, Guiliano, Hansen, Knight, Langley and Walsham. Even after more than a century, he remains closer to us than we might have supposed.

It goes without saying that each of the rites of passage recognized within historic Christianity has its own particular cultural history and theological significance. Confirmation may have lost its status as a sacrament at the Reformation, but, as Walsham argues, its investigation offers fresh insights into the evolution of theology, liturgy and ecclesiology, as well as into the revolution in ritual theory precipitated by the Protestant challenge. The level of scholarly interest in the different rites has been uneven. Baptism, the threshold of entry into the Christian life, has attracted regular academic enquiry, as has ordination. Marriage and funeral rites have also elicited interest, although sometimes more from the perspective of social and cultural history than ecclesiastical history. In the medieval world, though, the surviving ecclesiastical evidence can be stronger. Van Houts demonstrates this in her discussion of the practice of blessing wedding chambers and beds in medieval north-western Europe, where there is a tantalizing mismatch between the plentiful liturgical and the sparse narrative sources for this intriguingly intimate domestic custom. Churching, the ceremony of reincorporating women into society after childbirth, is another intriguing custom, and one that has remained relatively little explored.

In historically Christian societies, the almost universal engagement of people with the Church's rites of passage has sometimes led to the conclusion that their participation must have been perfunctory. Often, of course, there is no evidence either way. In England, as Swanson shows, the records that pre-date the introduction of parish registers in 1538 document only the financial transactions associated with the rites, telling us nothing about the events themselves, and very little – if anything – about the people involved. As we move through time, we begin to catch glimpses of the little gatherings around fonts and altar rails, and of some of the people whose feelings on these occasions found their way into the written record. In Ottery St Mary during the Interregnum, McCall introduces Nicholas Haydon, whose child was rejected for baptism by the minister Mr Tuchin, because Tuchin insisted on a public demonstration of faith, and Haydon, perhaps confused by the question, responded by saying that some of the articles of his faith, the Trinity and the Incarnation, were 'indemonstrable'. In Malton in 1607, Walsham presents an exhausted Archbishop Matthew, who was struggling to confirm hundreds of people, and exclaimed: 'There were so many candidates, I nearly melted away in the heat'.

The turbulence created by the theological upheavals of the sixteenth and seventeenth centuries could result in a 'grumbling focus of local antagonism' directed towards the rites of passage, as McCall shows in her analysis of baptism during the English Interregnum. Walsham tells of the staunchly Calvinist Elizabethan archdeacon who sarcastically denounced the clergy's use of chrism; it was pointless, he said, 'unless they have shut the Holy Ghost in their grease pot'. It was an outburst of sarcasm that indicated something of the extent of the theological chasm that had opened up. Later, the 'grumbling antagonism' might mutate into a general sense of resentment towards the Church. It could become focused on the clerical enthusiasm for the public performance of baptism and churching, which many new parents considered best done discreetly and in private.

Death in its various stages is discussed in this volume. Ryan investigates it at its earliest intimation: the point when, within Roman Catholic culture, friends and family decide that it is necessary to call for a priest to administer the last rites to the dying person. The drama of the priest on his way to a sick call, hindered or assisted on this vital journey by obstacles or interventions, both human and supernatural, emerges as a recurrent theme in the Irish folk tales that Ryan explores. After death has occurred and the ceremonies surrounding it have been concluded, the universal necessity of disposing of the corpse remains. Jacob's article focuses on the practicalities of dealing with large numbers of dead bodies in the nineteenth-century London metropolis. Then follows the process of remembering the life that had been lived. Binfield and Cruickshank analyse memorial literature produced to honour specific individuals. Binfield discusses Joseph Parker, the celebrated London Congregational preacher, who published a commemoration of his father-in-law, Andrew Common, a year after his death, recapturing 'a vital humanity that surely could not be extinguished'. Cruickshank considers George Bell's eulogy for Dietrich Bonhoeffer, delivered at his memorial service in London in 1945, and broadcast on the BBC. Bell emphasized Bonhoeffer's passage into martyrdom, and the continuing significance of his death in post-war Germany and Europe.

As well as the ink spilled over centuries in attacking, defending and explaining the theology and practice behind each rite of passage for a learned audience, there was also the mass production of ephemeral material, designed to encourage whatever the body producing it considered to be 'right belief'. In England, this material included the little tracts distributed in bulk by the Society for Promoting Christian Knowledge, and in France, the first communion cards that were sent to friends, relatives and teachers by youngsters or their parents, as souvenirs of the child's first communion. The almost chance survival of these tracts and communion cards provides an insight into the changing religious worlds in which they were used. In a different sense, the Irish folk tales can also be seen, in origin at least, as ephemeral survivals. In the late 1930s, the Irish Folklore Commission set about getting school children to gather and write up the folk tales of mainly rural parts of the recently independent Irish state. The material was then carefully preserved in a voluminous archive, ensuring its transition from ephemeral oral survival to carefully curated source.

Ordination sparked relatively little interest amongst the contributors to this volume and its associated conferences. There are two exceptions. The first is Platts's investigation of the sources for the early eighth-century Northumbrian church, with their focus on the ordination and other rites of passage experienced by Wilfrid. The second is Webster's article on Eric Mascall, an Anglican theologian who emerged as a prominent opponent of women's ordination in the second half of the twentieth century. Mascall's opposition arose in part from his intense sense of the orderliness of Christian theology, and the difference in the roles it assigned to men and women. It was an argument that had been widely made in the earlier years of the debate, but by the 1980s and 1990s it was looking progressively less compelling.

If the passage of time brought significant change to rites such as ordination (at least within the Protestant churches), the impact of place has been another key factor. How have rites of passage, forged in the heartlands of Christendom, translated into other cultures? This is topic that would merit much further exploration. In the late seventh century, Anastasius of Sinai formulated a 'discreet and streamlined piety' comprised of what Hansen terms 'rites of maintenance': baptism, eucharist and the sign of the cross, a pared down ritual intended to sustain Christian identity on the boundaries of the Christian and Muslim worlds in the Umayyad Levant. Many centuries later, similar issues emerge in China. Yung's prize-winning article investigates Anglican rites in China, and the complicated interplay between Christian belief and respect for Chinese customs and elders. Wedding practices that seemed unproblematic in the West, such as joining the hands of a bride and groom, were abandoned because they attracted ridicule in the Chinese context. Payment for brides, and petitioning heaven and earth for blessings, were also forbidden as unchristian. The continued use of red sedan chairs in the bridal procession was, however, permitted as a harmless fashion statement. These were all matters of immediate concern for those organizing Anglican weddings in China, and Chinese Christians also had to wrestle with the issue of polygamy until the 1920s. Funeral practices posed further challenges. The Lambeth conferences issued documents on baptism and marriage for 'consideration' by worldwide Anglicanism, but these did not have any legislative authority. Over time, Chinese Anglicans and missionaries began to conclude that rites of passage could not be prescribed at conferences or in publications, but had to accommodate the realities of local life; Yung concludes that Chinese Anglicans became, in the end, 'self-theologizing'.

In her introduction to Studies in Church History 56, *The Church and the Law*, Rosamond McKitterick remarked that her choice of theme had been prompted, in part, by the conflict between the Marriage (Same Sex Couples) Act, passed by the Westminster

Parliament in 2013, and the canon law of the Church of England. Studies in Church History 59 provides further historical reflection on the divergences and debates over the development of marriage law, where permissible practice is defined by statute, the teaching of the churches and the aspirations of some church members. Houlbrooke's article sets the scene with an investigation of early modern England's wedding sermons, a rather sparse and hitherto neglected homiletic genre that seems to have suffered from the enthusiasm of hearers to move on to the next stage of the festivities.

Subsequent articles focus more on the legal context. In the period from 1753 to 1836, English law limited the scope of legal marriage to that offered in the Church of England, with exceptions only for Quakers and Jews. This led, as Wykes explains, to the campaign among Unitarians and other Freethinkers who objected to the Trinitarian language in the marriage service. The law before the 1836 Marriage Act could also be burdensome to clergy, who might be legally obliged to marry couples whilst they protested loudly at this infringement of their religious freedom. 1836 proved to be a turning point with the passing of the Registration Act and the Marriage Act. As Jacob explains, this legislation, and the Burial Acts that followed, remedied some of the grievances of Dissenters, without significantly infringing on the activities of the Church of England. Probert's article picks up the story from 1836, exploring the public perceptions and legal entanglements surrounding early civil marriage ceremonies. In the twenty years after 1836, it was possible to have a wedding in a register office with the religious content of one's choice, but this was outlawed in the Marriage and Registration Act of 1856, which created the enduring separation between civil and religious marriage ceremonies.

In the concluding article in this volume, Bethmont brings the topic up to date with his discussion of the ways in which Anglican same-sex couples have created and adapted ceremonies, as civil same-sex marriage became available to them on both sides of the North Atlantic. Such couples have sometimes used the marriage liturgy creatively as a resource to give meaning and to 'change the fabric of reality' in ways that reliance on the sole power of the law could not. This, Bethmont argues, has unravelled a rigidly legal understanding of Anglican wedding ritual. It is evidence of the continuing potency of the ecclesiastical rites of passage, and their ability to be refashioned for the needs of a new generation of believers.

The contributors to this volume include postgraduate students, early career researchers and senior scholars. Their articles began life as papers delivered at the Ecclesiastical History Society's Summer Conference in July 2021, and its associated Winter Meeting, in January 2022. Both events were held online, as we continued to deal with the effects of the COVID-19 pandemic. They attracted significant numbers of registrations, from all parts of the world. I am very grateful to everyone who participated, and for the new light that was shed on the topic. For many contributors, participation also meant putting up with the postponement of the conference that had originally been scheduled to take place in Nottingham in 2020, and working through the difficulties created by the extended closure of libraries and archives.

The committee of the Ecclesiastical History Society showed ingenuity and resilience as we navigated the COVID years. I am especially grateful to the Conference Secretary, Elizabeth Tingle, who remained unfailingly positive as we went through various permutations of on-campus planning, postponement, cancellation and finally online delivery. Meanwhile, the editorial team of Charlotte Methuen, Andrew Spicer, Tim Grass and Alice Soulieux-Evans produced the excellent and pertinent volume Studies in Church History 58, *The Church in Sickness and in Health*, when the *Rites of Passage* volume had to be rescheduled. I would particularly like to thank Tim: this is his final Studies in Church History, as he lays down a task that he began more than fifteen years ago. Generations of contributors have benefited from his excellent copy-editing, and from his wise and kindly interventions.

Frances Knight

'Rites of Passage' and the Writing of Church History: Reflections upon our Craft in the Aftermath of van Gennep

Thomas O'Loughlin*
University of Nottingham

Van Gennep's work on rites of passage can be viewed as part of the rise of anthropology in the period prior to the First World War, and has been very influential conceptually and on the practice of churches ever since. This article examines how his own historical work, taking baptism as an example of a rite of passage, compares with the practice of church history at the time. It then seeks to assess van Gennep's assumptions in comparison with the assumptions about the past used in church history writing today, acknowledging that the turn to plurality – that uniformity in doctrines, rituals and texts is subsequent to diversity – of recent scholarship is in several respects anticipated by van Gennep.

History was holy because the nation was holy.

Pierre Nora[1]

Arnold van Gennep's most famous work, *Les Rites de passage*,[2] appeared in 1909 and caused, apparently, not a ripple on the serene surface of ecclesiastical history. The Church moved through time, and history was, most simply, the account of that procession. If its history were more positively conceived, then history was an intellectual relic that made the Church's past present. History was sacred because it made the vital connection between the holiness of the past and the actuality of what Christians were doing day by day.

* E-mail: thomas.oloughlin@nottingham.ac.uk.

[1] Pierre Nora, *Realms of Memory: Rethinking the French Past*, ed. Lawrence D. Kritzman, 2 vols (New York, NY, 1996), 1: 5.

[2] Arnold van Gennep, *Les Rites de passage. Étude systématique des rites* (Paris, 1909); translated by Monika B. Vizedom and Gabrielle L. Caffee as *The Rites of Passage* (Chicago, IL, 1960).

Studies in Church History 59 (2023), 8–26
doi: 10.1017/stc.2023.3

The churches looked to their histories as prologue, genealogy guaranteeing origins and (when seen aright) a roughly linear continuity from the clear moment of origin to the present. Within this well-defined narrative, the anthropologists' abstractions based on folk religion and non-Christian cults had seemingly little to offer. By contrast, van Gennep saw religious practices as expressions of the particularities of groups seen in their folklore – he saw himself as an expert in French folklore and, by extension, ethnography – and it was this historically shaped endeavour that would reveal more universal truths about humans and their beliefs.

Given that this volume takes its theme explicitly from van Gennep's classic work, it is worthwhile to see how reading it again can form a basis for historiographical self-reflection on how the discipline of ecclesiastical history has changed over the last century, both in its fundamental assumptions and within the larger subject area of theology and Christian studies. What I seek to offer is not a history of history, much less an overview of key developments during the last century, but rather an examination of some of the ways in which van Gennep utilized Christian historical evidence in his work and a comparison of that with historians' practice then and now. My aim is to show that not only has the framework of rites of passage entered our work as historians, but also that we now share some of van Gennep's most basic assumptions about religious movements.

Context 1: Anthropology

The decades preceding the First World War can be seen as the heroic age of anthropology: the territories of the world were now open to both colonization and study. Scholars turned their attention to the exotic peoples and their customs that were to be met in their colonies with a fascination that was rooted not only in the assumption that they were curiously different 'from us' but also in a conviction that they were 'us' as we used to be. The anthropologist was working in a living museum and might there discover elemental truths about humanity. The apparent 'rawness' (*crudité*) of the cultures encountered by anthropologists showed a human condition without the occluding effect of layers of civilization with its inchoate note of artifice and inauthenticity. Typical of this movement was the now famous 1907 exhibition of African art at the Trocadéro Museum in

Paris. It was there that Picasso 'discovered' African masks and what he wrote about this event – in explicitly religious, indeed liturgical, terms – captures the larger atmosphere:

> Men had made those masks and other objects for a sacred purpose, a magic purpose, as a kind of mediation between themselves and the unknown hostile forces that surrounded them, in order to overcome their fear and horror by giving it a form and an image. At that moment I realized that this was what painting was all about. Painting isn't an aesthetic operation; it's a form of magic designed as mediation between this strange, hostile world and us, a way of seizing power by giving form to our terrors as well as our desires. When I came to that realization, I knew I had found my way.[3]

Whether it was from objects taken from colonized peoples or in recognizing the untutored peasant mind that produced a Breton calvary or a Bavarian votive painting, there was a truth to be uncovered from the time before modernity. The turn to anthropological evidence appeared to offer a direct route to fundamental human understanding. A Chokwe mask (Figure 1), for example, was an encounter with a ritual object that spurred comparative studies of ritual between 'primitive' cultures and those of Europeans. That there could be common features – over a long time span and crossing cultures that were supposed to be in isolation from one another – allowed writers such as van Gennep to see themselves as anthropologists in the strict sense: they were investigating a fundamental aspect of what it is to be human.

This anthropological turn was already to be found in Britain in the work of Sir James Frazer. His *Golden Bough* first appeared in 1890 in two volumes with the subtitle: 'a study in comparative religion'; then again in 1900 in three volumes, now subtitled: 'a study in magic and religion'; and yet again over a span of nine years (1906–15) in twelve volumes, quite apart from a very popular one-volume abridgement (first published in 1922) which avoided frightening its wider readership by omitting many comparisons involving Christian origins. Van Gennep was aware of Frazer's work and not only cites him in *Rites of Passage* as a quarry for material, but also declares him to be the founder of a school of investigation. By this act of classification, he distanced his own methodology from Frazer's.[4]

[3] Cited according to Colin Rhodes, *Primitivism and Modern Art* (London, 1994), 116.
[4] Van Gennep, *Rites of Passage*, 6.

Figure 1. A late nineteenth- or early twentieth-century Chokwe mask, a *Pwo*, from Angola, used in female initiation rites. The cross-like tattoos probably derive from crosses distributed by seventeenth-century Portuguese Franciscan missionaries. © The author.

Another monument to British scholarship spanning this period is the *Encyclopaedia of Religion and Ethics*, whose thirteen volumes were produced under the editorship of James Hastings, an inveterate organizer of reference works, between 1908 and 1926.[5] While focused on religion as universal human category, the choice of topics and the methods employed by very many of its contributors reflected the new interest in anthropology within religious studies, while the work as a whole with its diligent gathering of diverse evidence exhibited the new attention to empiricism that was common to both anthropologists and historians. Hastings, despite his own very explicit biblical and theological interests, showed an appreciation of the value of anthropology, both by treating equally other living religions alongside Christianity and in his desire to attend to religions globally. The detail of popular religion which the *Encyclopaedia* embraces was expansive and included what previous generations would have dismissed as 'magic' and 'superstition': each phenomenon

[5] In the 1960 translation of van Gennep this work is cited on p. 79, but in an additional note by the translators. Van Gennep finished *Les Rites de passage* in 1908, the year that the first volume of the *Encyclopaedia of Religion and Ethics* appeared.

was to be valued as part of the overall description of *homo religiosus*. It is probably this implicit anthropological dimension that has ensured that nearly a century after its production the *Encyclopaedia of Religion and Ethics* can still be useful to scholars today.

Although published after *Rites of Passage*, a work from 1912 is probably the best indicator of the new confidence in the value of anthropology in religion: Émile Durkheim's *Les Formes élémentaires de la vie religieuse* which (unlike van Gennep's work, which took over fifty years to find an English translator) appeared in English in 1915.[6] We tend to think of this work in terms of the philosophy of religion – and it engaged with all the great themes of Western philosophy of the period – or the sociology of religion, but it is also a work of anthropology using historical research as a central investigative tool. While in English it is subtitled '*A Study in Religious Sociology*', we should note that its original subtitle links it directly with the themes of anthropology: '*Le Système totémique en Australie*'.

So, while church historians may not yet have been taking the insights of anthropology into the core of their research, among anthropologists the history of the practices of the Christian churches was now being studied afresh and being brought into the centre of an expanding discourse.

Context 2: Church History

While technically the later long nineteenth century saw a transformation of the landscape of church history – one need but recall the advent of new and more accessible sources, whether in the form of inrush of papyrus fragments or the steady progress of *Monumenta Germaniae Historica*[7] – conceptually very little happened with regard to its place within Christian studies: de facto, it remained a subdiscipline within theology mainly concerned with the training of

[6] Durkheim's work was published in Paris in 1912; it was translated by Joseph Ward Swain and published as *The Elementary Forms of the Religious Life* (London, 1915).

[7] The Gospel of Peter was published by Urbain Bouriant in 1892 and can be seen as marking the beginning of arrival of 'new' material that directly affected understanding of the core of Christian memory seen as a well-defined 'New Testament': cf. Brent Nongbri, *God's Library: The Archaeology of the Earliest Christian Manuscripts* (New Haven, CT, 2018), 91–8; M. D. Knowles, 'Presidential Address: Great Historical Enterprises, III. The Monumenta Germaniae Historica', *TRHS* 5th series 10 (1960), 129–50.

ministers. However, we should begin by noting some voices that anticipate a later time. In 1908 W. C. Bishop, in a review article prompted by the publication of F. E. Brightman's *Liturgies Eastern and Western*, wrote:

> The tendency to approach the consideration of liturgical questions from a hard-and-fast dogmatic standpoint has too often been a stumbling block in the way of historical truth and a right understanding of the problem presented. In order to obtain fruitful results from any investigation of this kind it is an essential condition that we should begin by investigating the historical facts, putting on one side for the purposes of the investigation whatever dogmatic prepossessions or beliefs we may hold, and treating them as non-existent for the moment.[8]

Bishop did not draw out the point that implicit in this *epoché* was the possibility that historical fact might not align with subsequent doctrinal certainty as to the ubiquity, clarity and consistency of the tradition. However, one who did was George Tyrrell. In his 1903 book *Lex Orandi* and its 1906 sequel *Lex Credendi*, he explicitly appealed to the historical practice of different groups of Christians – be that differing formal practices or popular customs and beliefs – as part of the Christian inheritance.[9] But such writers were marginal voices: the debate on the eucharist to which Bishop contributed rumbled on until the 1980s without his insight being taken seriously,[10] while the approach of Tyrrell came almost to a complete stop when he was excommunicated by the Roman Catholic Church; the relationship of the so-called *lex orandi* and the *lex credendi* is still not a settled matter in that church.[11]

[8] W. C. Bishop, 'The Primitive Form of Consecration of the Holy Eucharist', *Church Quarterly Review* 66 (1908), 385–404, at 386.

[9] George Tyrrell, *Lex Orandi (or Prayer and Creed)* (London, 1906); idem, *Lex Credendi: A Sequel to Lex Orandi* (London, 1908).

[10] See Thomas O'Loughlin, 'Reactions to the *Didache* in Early Twentieth-Century Britain: A Dispute over the Relationship of History and Doctrine?', in S. J. Brown, Frances Knight and John Morgan-Guy, eds, *Religion, Identity and Conflict in Britain: From the Restoration to the Twentieth Century. Essays in Honour of Keith Robbins* (Farnham, 2013), 177–94.

[11] See Paul De Clerck, '"*Lex Orandi, Lex Credendi*": The Original Sense and Historical Avatars of an Equivocal Adage', *Studia Liturgica* 24 (1994), 178–200, which explores how the rejection of Tyrrell's work was still an active force in Catholic studies of the liturgy until at least the 1950s.

For most church historians, their work was that of fleshing out in practical detail a grand plan whose essentials were doctrinal certainties: there was one single and largely unambiguous past.[12] While the past might be fiercely contested by each group claiming it as their specific inheritance, the common ground was that anyone who would look at it with sufficient dispassion would come to a singular conclusion: the difficulties lay in the observers, compounded by technical obscurities which were gradually being overcome, rather than in the past itself. As such, the past was 'the secure judge' and an appeal to it was a route to a certainty that would empirically underpin, and perhaps confirm, the known doctrinal certainties. This objective quality of history was pithily expressed by the leading French military historian of the time: 'History alone leads us to solid conclusions which nothing can shake, and whence convictions spring. Therefore, in order to rough out a sketch of military science we shall have recourse to the historical method.'[13] We could substitute 'theology' for 'military science', because the practitioners of both shared a confidence that this method would deliver certain, externally verifiable results that would be beyond sectarian prejudices.[14] There was a single revealed datum within the historical record that industry and care could reveal.[15] This was the very opposite of those more vague generalizations found among anthropologists, with their sometimes eclectic combinations of evidence from different cultures and periods.[16]

[12] See William H. C. Frend, *From Dogma to History: How our Understanding of the Early Church developed* (London, 2003); the chapter on Louis Duchesne (ibid. 108–43) is particularly relevant.

[13] Jean Colin, *The Transformations of War*, transl. L. H. R. Pope-Hennessy (London 1912), xv; the French original appeared in 1911.

[14] See Thomas O'Loughlin, 'Divisions in Christianity: The Contribution of "Appeals to Antiquity"', in Simon Oliver, Karen Kilby and Thomas O'Loughlin, eds, *Faithful Reading: New Essays in Theology and Philosophy in Honour of Fergus Kerr OP* (London, 2012), 221–41.

[15] See Jonathan Z. Smith, *Drudgery Divine: On the Comparison of Early Christianities and the Religions of Late Antiquity* (Chicago, IL, 1990).

[16] Anthropologists such as Durkheim were aware of this problem of generalizing from a limited base of evidence but seemed content to note similarities in distinct cultures as evidence of common human elements. For example, in discussing 'the idea of the soul' and referencing a range of material collected from Australian tribes, Durkheim wrote that 'the bases on which our inference rests may be deemed too narrow', yet he then proceeded to resolve this difficulty thus: 'but … the experiment holds good outside of the societies which we have observed directly. Also, there are abundant facts proving that the same

Turning to histories of those Christian ritual events that can be seen as falling within the bounds of 'rites of passage' – baptism, marriage and ordination – the emphasis is on the history of the doctrine of which the actual ritual is but a visible manifestation. When a ritual variation is noted, it is as an item within the larger wrapping that might reflect a commitment to this or that approach to the doctrine.[17] Religious practice is pared down to a legally understood minimum because this alone had a reality that was greater than the transient wrapping of ceremony. Similarly, the Church is understood as the collection of assenting believers rather than a cultic community with a community's needs for cultic expression. Where practice was important was in providing precedents for issues disputed later. Did they (i.e., some group of Christians in the past) at that time in the past baptize infants? Was that baptism performed by immersion or sprinkling? Was marriage considered a sacrament or not? Did that past group of Christians imagine a specific 'power' conferred in ordination and were there further qualifications on the transmission of that power? Since church historians were asking of earlier evidence a set of precise questions whose existence was a function of a later paradigm, these investigations were rarely conclusive; it could hardly be otherwise. In the face of inconclusive evidence, while some took refuge from the difficulty in 'black box' solutions such as that put forward by John Henry Newman that the evidence was there but in a form that could not yet be seen, most scholars redoubled their efforts to understand the evidence, as witnessed by the constant stream of new and better editions of historical texts.

Accompanying the search for justifying evidence – in the manner of a lawyer seeking out precedents – was the notion that doctrine had primacy in Christian revelation and was, subsequently, manifested in

---

or analogous conceptions are found in the most diverse parts of Australia [thus justifying his opening statement that "all the Australian societies" held certain beliefs] or, at least, have left very evident traces there. They are found even in America [thus justifying his more embracing generalisation]': Durkheim, *Elementary Forms*, 256.

[17] One can see examples of this approach in the bitter controversies that followed the Vatican's statement on the invalidity of Anglican orders in 1896. One of the underlying assumptions among the statement's authors was that changes in ritual were indicative of a shift in theology, an assumption that can be otherwise expressed by saying that ritual is but a manifestation of doctrine: see Thomas O'Loughlin, 'Locating Contemporary Catholicism in Relation to *Apostolicae Curae*: What it can tell Catholics about themselves', *Centro pro Unione Bulletin* 101 (Spring 2022), 30–40.

rites. Consequently, specialists in liturgical history aside, any attention given to ritual evidence was not from interest in the ritual itself and what that manifested about those engaged in it as a primary human reality, but concerned with how that ritual gave expression in a material manner to the doctrine which was the object of faith. While van Gennep and the anthropologists pursued rites for what their actuality told them about societies, Christian historians pursued them as symptoms of doctrines assented to by individuals. Hence there was a belief that beneath the apparent diversity of historical phenomena and conflicting opinions – heresies – there was an original unity: as logically diversity follows unity, so historically the original moment of perfect uniformity in unity, when there was 'one Lord, one faith, one baptism' (Eph. 4: 5), was the starting point. Just as no one doubted that one could, though skill and patience, return to the New Testament in the 'original Greek', so too no one doubted that it was possible to return to the original practice and understanding.[18] The main difficulty was the toll that time and vandalism had taken on the evidence, but the surviving fragments were coherent and mutually coherent, provided one could interpolate the lost material, and it was this act of 'filling the gaps' so that the jigsaw fitted that constituted scholarly brilliance.[19] Such vaults of imagination were made possible by the tacit assumption that the same frameworks of understanding being used by the historians were those of the people or institutions being examined: the present reached back into the past in such a way that the past manifested itself in the present.[20] Since there was confidence in the sequence that rites followed practices which manifested doctrine, many assumed that if one could get the theology rightly understood and agreed upon, then the other problems in practice between Christians could be resolved or eliminated.

[18] The most explicit claim in English to this being the aim of editorial work is to be found in the prolegomena volume to the edition of Westcott and Hort: Brooke Foss Westcott and Fenton John Anthony Hort, 'Introduction' and 'Appendix', to *The New Testament in the Original Greek* (Cambridge, 1881), 1–324 and 1–188.

[19] There is hardly a better example of this in any language than the massive commentary on Acts by F. J. Foakes Jackson and Kirsopp Lake, *The Beginnings of Christianity*, Part 1: *The Acts of the Apostles*, 5 vols (London, 1920–33).

[20] There could surely be no better expression of this than the dictum of Johann Albrecht Bengel (1687–1752): *te totum applica ad textum: rem totam applica ad te* ('apply your whole self to the text, then apply the whole text to yourself'), which prefaced Nestlé-Aland editions of the New Testament prior to the twenty-sixth edition which appeared in 1979.

Thus history was more than a tool in apologetics, but held the promise of resolving disputes by discovering the golden moment underlying differences. In this return *ad fontes* there was the vision also of renewal, and perhaps even of a perfect liturgy.[21] Since there had once been a perfect moment, could there not be one again?

Van Gennep and Baptism

Reading *Rites of Passage* as a text from the first decade of the twentieth century presents us with a world that is the polar opposite of that historians' idyll. This radical divergence in approach is captured in the book's opening sentence: 'Each larger society contains within it several distinctly separate social groupings. As we move from higher to lower levels of civilization, the differences among these groups become accentuated and their autonomy increases.'[22] Van Gennep assumes that diversity is at the heart of human society and that rituals not only reflect this, but that diversification and separation into distinct groupings is what we should expect. While we baulk today at his casual assumption that there is a 'scale of civilizations', a notion he introduces at the very beginning of the book and employs throughout it,[23] it is clear that history is more than sources. Rather, it is a study of distinct societies that differ both from one another and from the society of the researcher: only the subjects' humanity is common.

It is directly from this approach to ritual as an essential part of a social group's cohesiveness that van Gennep first mentions baptism, which he sees as an accessible example of a rite of passage familiar to his francophone readership in 1908: 'Being born, giving birth, and hunting, to cite but a few examples, are all acts whose major aspects fall within the sacred sphere. Social groups in such societies likewise have magico-religious foundations, and a passage from group to group takes on that special quality found in our rites of baptism and ordination.'[24] In this passage baptism is neither an 'outward sign of inward grace', nor an external expression of a doctrinal revelation, but a fact in its own right. Baptism is not taken aside into a

[21] This was the agenda of Sources Chrétiennes, which was established in 1942: see Patricia Kelly, *Ressourcement Theology: A Sourcebook* (London, 2021), 61–71.
[22] Van Gennep, *Rites of Passage*, 1.
[23] The phrase is first found at ibid. 2.
[24] Ibid.

special sphere as a Christian sacrament, but is studied among a set of human phenomena characterized collectively as 'magico-religious' acts. It is this action placed within a social network involving many individuals in one collective endeavour – baptizing and being baptized – that brings about its 'effect' for the participants and it is to be understood as part of their collective story. Baptism does indeed 'effect what it signifies' for the group in that individuals pass from one state to another, they are changed by effecting the ritual, and they move on into the future as new people. We shall note again later that van Gennep starts with the ritual and then looks at what this experience means in its effects among the group, not in terms of a rational abstraction of 'meaning'.

Baptism is next looked upon as one of a sequence of actions by a specific group – Christian Bulgarian women in this case – as they move through a rite of passage: through it they come to terms with the disruption in individual, family and group life that goes hand in hand with childbirth.

> From St Ignatius' day until the calends (*Kolièda*) the expectant mother must neither wash her hair, clean her clothes, nor comb her hair until after nightfall; she must not leave her house during the ninth month. She must not remove for a whole week the clothing she wears at the time of delivery. A fire is kept burning until the christening [*jusqu'au baptême*] and the bed is surrounded with a rope. The cakes are baked; the young mother must eat the first piece and share the rest with her relatives; not a single crumb may leave the house. The relatives bring gifts and all spit on the mother and child (obvious rites of incorporation). They come to see her throughout the first week. On the eighth day the baptism takes place. On the fifteenth day the young mother bakes cakes and invites her neighbours and the women of her acquaintance to come and eat; all of them bring flour.[25]

This account seems hardly remarkable, in that in a historically Christian country like Bulgaria in the late nineteenth century we should expect that the formal ceremony of baptism would be one of the key events after childbirth. This looks like an ethnographic account of the secular customs of a people into which a Christian

[25] Ibid. 45; the presence of Christian liturgical language is more marked in the original (directly translated here) than in the published translation.

sacrament has been interwoven, but such a reading would not do justice to van Gennep's cultural hermeneutic in *Rites of Passage*.

Van Gennep's account is a single whole: he has described a complete and unitary community process, and splitting it into moments, such as secular / religious or sacramental / non-sacramental, would miss his essential point. Through this process, this rite of passage, the community comes to terms with its new member; the mother relates to the community, her own experience and her baby; and the newborn is properly prepared to know that she / he is a fully accepted member of the group. Where does the 'magico-religious' – a favourite term of van Gennep – act begin or end? We have a description of a long series of distinct actions, all in a known sequence which is a *datum* within the community, leading to a known, desired result. The meaning – if the perspective of the investigator is allowed to intrude – of this ritual lies in the awareness of those involved of doing what is needed: their experience is fundamental. This is completely opposite to a focus on the parents bringing the infant to the church to be baptized, and a set of rituals in which they have minimal engagement, where they are told by the minister from out of his study of an academic tradition of theology not only what the experience is 'really about' or means, but also, indeed, what the infant is experiencing.[26] Instead, experience – and this is always a social and bodily reality of common memory as is seen in the precise details van Gennep believes we, the readers, must note – is the basis for understanding. Any extrinsic 'explanation' would be simply one more moment in the process and one additional mythic (albeit in this case verbal) element in the group's reality. In adopting this perspective, van Gennep anticipates several movements in twentieth-century scholarship, all of which have a bearing on the work of church historians. In its focus on community memory, I believe that van Gennep's approach anticipates the work of Maurice Halbwachs (1877–1945) and more recently Pierre Nora, both of whom have impacted on the historical work of New Testament scholars. In his attention to process, he was directly the inspiration for Victor

[26] However, since there is no way of assessing what the infant is actually experiencing (or whether the infant – perhaps asleep – is experiencing anything), this account is an extraneously sourced (usually from a catechism of some sort) account of what baptism means within the group's formal theology. On this distinction of deriving a 'meaning from' and placing a 'meaning upon' ritual, see Thomas O'Loughlin, 'Eucharistic Celebrations: The Chasm between Idea and Reality', *New Blackfriars* 91 (2010), 423–38.

Turner (1920–83), whose work (in my view) increasingly affects the study of the history of liturgy as it moves away from being simply the archaeology of texts. The concern with the intrinsic experience of reality, as distinct from its extrinsic determination, mirrors the theological concerns of Maurice Blondel (1861–1949) and the historical turn of Henri de Lubac (1896–1991) in historical theology, and the incarnational turn of those theologians who engage with the significance of the historical Jesus within theology, such as Edward Schillebeeckx (1914–2009).

Rites of Passage mentions baptism, and the link between baptism and naming, on several occasions, but the next extended reference to it is when the importance of giving a name, or a new name, is examined:

> The rites of naming would merit a monograph to themselves. Though frequently studied, I think they have never been considered in full detail or in their true light. When a child is named, he is both individualized and incorporated into society.
>
> ...
>
> It will be noted that in Gabon the rite of naming coexists with a rite which is strikingly analogous to baptism. Baptism has most often been regarded as a lustration, a purging and purifying rite, i.e., a final rite of separation from the previous world, whether it be a secular world or one that is actually impure. This rite must be evaluated with care, however, for it may also signify incorporation when it is performed with consecrated rather than with ordinary water. In that case the person baptized not only loses an attribute but also gains one. This consideration leads us to examine a new set of ceremonies, ordinarily known as initiation rites.[27]

Here, once more, we see the characteristic elements of van Gennep's approach: begin with the actual ritual and 'read' this within society: the social group remains the primary *locus* of interpretation and meaning. But this passage also draws us into another theme of modern historical research in that, after the mention of baptism, van Gennep places a footnote indicating that 'for baptism as a rite of initiation' the reader should turn to a work of Lewis Richard Farnell

[27] Van Gennep, *Rites of Passage*, 62–3.

(1856–1934).[28] Farnell is now known almost exclusively as a Greek scholar and a classicist, but his 1905 work, subtitled 'an anthropology of religion', puts him among those anglophone anthropologists who influenced van Gennep and stand also in our own background as church historians. Farnell's work appeared in the Crown Theological Library alongside volumes dedicated to bringing historical-critical scholarship to bear on both biblical studies and the historical issues in theology. It is perhaps best studied on the assumption that its readers are historians of Christian practices and beliefs. On baptism, Farnell wrote:

> ... we should probably find, if we followed out the history and origin of infant baptism, that the pre-Christian tradition was a strong efficient force for the settlement of the question: there were reasons why the rite should soon have come to be maintained by the early Church, for analogous rites whereby the new-born child was consecrated to the divinity were probably part of the hereditary tradition of most of the converted races.[29]

Religions exist within cultures for Farnell and to imagine them simply as functions of their formal theology does not enter his landscape. The act of investigating a ritual is much less a theological question than an engagement with a cultural tradition and its needs. The ritual has its own integrity as part of a group's cultural heritage: it is shaped by the group and it reveals the group to the investigator. This becomes clearer in Farnell's more detailed comments on baptism, in which he rejects rationalist explanations of rituals, such as Aristotle's explanation of plunging babies into water as a 'hardening up' process, in favour of a human need to engage with mystery. Thus the baptism of the adult is a 'mystic service' that simulates both death and being born anew, and the historical questions are to be pursued in the light of this observation.[30] Anthropology is here pressed into the service of historical investigation; while theology, conceived of as 'primary ideas and essential beliefs', is to be understood not on its own claims but as subsequent to the activities of a community engaging in

[28] Van Gennep's note is precise: 'see Farnell, *The Evolution of Religion*, pp. 56, 57, 156–58'.
[29] Lewis Richard Farnell, *The Evolution of Religion: An Anthropological Study* (London, 1905), 56.
[30] Ibid. 57.

rituals.[31] Farnell, who acknowledged his debt to historians of liturgy such as Louis Duchesne (1843–1922), saw a clear sequence of investigation: one begins with an anthropological study, then proceeds to examine the diverse historical evidence, then looks at the explanations offered in liturgy and catechetics; only then can one appreciate how interpretation is 'regarded' by theology.[32] His method prepares for that used by van Gennep; indeed, Farnell is arguably the originator both of the notion of 'rites of passage' and of the approach that views baptism as 'initiation'. He thus stands at the origin of the movement that has been so enormously influential in Christian liturgy since the 1950s.

My last example of how van Gennep looked at baptism is taken from his chapter on initiation rites:

> Then came the transitional period: the catechumen, just like those initiated into the lesser mysteries, was permitted to attend religious assemblies and had a special place in the church, but he was required to withdraw before the beginning of the true mysteries (the Mass). He was periodically submitted to exorcism and thus separated more and more from the non-Christian world; he was gradually instructed; his 'ears were opened.' After a last exorcism came the *effeta*: the priest moistened his finger with saliva and touched the top of each catechumen's upper lip; the candidates undressed, and their backs and chests were anointed with consecrated oil; they renounced Satan; swore to ally themselves with Christ; and recited the Credo.
>
> ...
>
> It was followed by rites of the incorporation proper. ... [T]he catechumen ... hence became *regeneratus*, or *conceived again* according to the very terms of the prayer pronounced during the rite which followed.[33]

[31] Ibid. 156.

[32] The key work of Duchesne used by both Farnell and van Gennep was his *Origines du culte chrétien. Étude sur la liturgie latine avant Charlemagne* (Paris, 1889). It went through numerous revisions and enlargements, with probably its most complete expression being the fifth edition in English, translated by M. L. McClure: *Christian Worship: Its Origin and Evolution. A Study of the Latin Liturgy up to the Time of Charlemagne* (London, 1919), which was reprinted many times.

[33] Van Gennep, *Rites of Passage*, 94; the chapter on initiation (ibid. 65–115) contains several sustained examinations of the ritual of baptism, especially at ibid. 93–6, 107–8.

We have already met many of the themes of this passage, such as attention to the ritual itself and the emphasis on sequence and process, but its manner of reference to the liturgical details is noteworthy. Such attention to detail was the preserve of rubricians and those who studied ritual from the standpoint of antiquarians: details to be enjoyed, marvelled at or revived in their reconstruction of an ideal past. Here, without any interest in making a theological point, liturgy is part of human inheritance and this ritual is firmly in the social sphere. Liturgy is examined as a complete unity in experience rather than as ritual gestures tied to formulae – liturgy is no longer a book – and in this van Gennep anticipates the key difference between modern liturgical investigators and the approach, dominant in most Western churches until the 1960s, which was centred in written texts. Here, explicitly, those texts – 'and recited in the Credo' – follow the actual events that initiate and transform. In making this study van Gennep references the work of Duchesne. Duchesne's own engagement with the liturgical past was that of a critical historian rather than the nostalgic gathering of the jewels of an enchanted past in the face of a bitter modernity that characterized so many of Duchesne's contemporaries working in French, such as Fernand Cabrol (1855–1937) or Henri Leclercq (1869–1945).

Because van Gennep took the Christian liturgy so seriously, viewing it as embedded in the human person who in turn was embedded in society, what he wrote was immediately accessible to those theological scholars who interpreted his work in the light of their theological anthropology, and so it could speak seamlessly to their ecclesiology and become manifest in their liturgical reforms. However, while this influence of van Gennep was significant, we should also note that it occurred without fanfare and was very uneven across the Christian churches. This article has given a certain priority to francophone scholarship in deference to van Gennep, but the patchiness of his reception is perhaps best seen in English-language scholarship. For example, it is often remarked that the churches of the anglophone world were least aware of the movements for liturgical reform that swept France and Germany from the 1920s. We see this in the complaint by the Anglican scholar Peter Hammond in 1960 that the work of the continental Liturgical Movement was virtually unknown in Britain.[34] Similarly, Roman Catholics from across the English-

[34] Peter Hammond, *Liturgy and Architecture* (London, 1960), 4–10, 12–16.

speaking world, who might be expected to have a greater awareness of developments in France, Germany and Italy, seem to have been taken by surprise by the liturgical discussions of the Second Vatican Council (1962–5). The English-speaking liturgical churches, as a whole, appear to have begun to engage with the liturgical movement only from the late 1960s.[35] Perhaps this time lag is to be explained, partly, by the fact that van Gennep was only translated into English in 1960.[36]

The Turn to Plurality

One of the most characteristic features of historical writing today across the disciplines falling under the heading of 'religion' is the awareness of plurality. We speak of the diversity of *Judaisms* that were to be found in the period before the destruction of the temple in 70 CE. We speak of the *churches* rather than 'the church' and of early *Christianities* rather than assuming there was a single organizational or doctrinal edifice. We have become suspicious of the ancient heresiologists and are aware that the development of 'orthodoxy' or the canon of the New Testament are as much events in the evolution of the Christian movement as the variations we find in rituals in different places. While this plurality is often not grasped or welcomed as a reality by elements within each church, it is now the assumed norm within the mainstream academy.

However, this interest in plurality has an even deeper foundation. Probably from as early as the second century, one of the unquestioned assumptions of much Christian scholarship has been that there was a

[35] A good example of this is dissatisfaction with the medieval lectionary for use at the eucharist which was taken over, more or less as it stood, into the vernacular liturgies of almost all the Protestant churches (e.g. the Book of Common Prayer of the Church of England); but it was the Evangelical Church in France which was the first to abandon and replace it, in 1953, with a new lectionary with three readings in three cycles, which proved to be the forerunner for the Roman Catholic *Ordo lectionum Missae* (1969) and, thereby, for the now widely used Revised Common Lectionary: see Annibale Bugnini, *The Reform of the Liturgy 1948–1975* (Collegeville, MN, 1990), 415–17.

[36] Significantly, the introductory essay by Solon T. Kimball (pp. v–xix) to the 1960 English translation of van Gennep's *Rites of Passage* presents its importance solely in terms of the sociology of religion and the ongoing work of anthropologists, without any hint that contemporary Western practitioners of religion, such as liturgists, might find it of value to their work.

moment when all was perfectly one, harmonious and singular. The work of Walter Bauer (1877–1960) in the 1930s (once again, note the time lag before this appeared in English in 1971) shattered that cosy illusion once for all.[37] Bauer showed that consistent and explicit doctrines are subsequent to a variety of teaching and a range of acceptable formulae. More recently, Epp and Parker have shown that the quest for the single original form of those texts, such as the gospels, which later achieved canonical status is not only not possible but fails to take account of the diversity inherent in their being 'living texts'.[38] In the actual life of the early churches, the texts were continually being varied – deliberately and not as a result of faulty transmission – as the situations in which they were being used varied. For over a century, exegetes had sought out the ecclesial *Sitz im Leben* as a guide to understanding the formation of the tradition, but the challenge now is to speculate on the whole range of situations in which this text, or one like it, was being used. Likewise, when it comes to practices of the churches, the quest for the original action or pattern has given way to an acknowledgment that diversity preceded uniformity.[39] The uniformity of a common 'shape' (to use Gregory Dix's term) was the result of liturgies seeking to borrow from one another and pattern themselves on one another in response to an earlier diversity, rather than the remnants of an original form progressively diversified by corruption and idiosyncratic development.[40]

The turn to plurality implies a second shift in perspective: a radical acceptance of the incompleteness of our evidence. When, for example, Westcott and Hort set out in detail their method,[41] they were as aware as we are of the fragmentary nature of the evidence. They

[37] Walter Bauer, *Rechtgläubigkeit und Ketzerei im ältesten Christentum* (Tübingen, 1934); the English translation is based on the second edition: *Orthodoxy and Heresy in Earliest Christianity* (Philadelphia, PA, 1971).

[38] See, for example, Eldon J. Epp, 'The Multivalence of the Term "Original Text" in New Testament Textual Criticism', *Harvard Theological Review* 92 (1999), 245–81; David C. Parker, *The Living Text of the Gospels* (Cambridge, 1997); from the many writings of these two scholars. While Epp and Parker approach the question from very different starting points, they come to very similar conclusions: the notion of a single original text – which *ipso facto* would have authority – is a later concern.

[39] Paul F. Bradshaw, *The Search for the Origins of Christian Worship: Sources and Methods for the Study of the Early Liturgy*, 2nd edn (London, 2002).

[40] See Gregory Dix, *The Shape of the Liturgy* (London, 1945).

[41] See Westcott and Hort, *New Testament*, 1–3.

believed that by careful labour they might eventually glimpse the original whole and it inspired their labour: even a partial access to that wondrous moment was their reward. We have no basis for such confidence. We simply know that there were situations earlier than our earliest extant evidence, for it was those situations that produced our fragments.

I began this article by noting that I would not attempt to trace specific influences of the anthropologists of van Gennep's time upon church historians (the academic pursuit of 'spot the source'); nor would I try to write a history of history (a foolhardy endeavour in an article even if I were competent to undertake it). Rather, I wanted to examine van Gennep's assumptions and ways of working in order to facilitate our reflection upon our own situation, for the pursuit of history is always about us and is far more reflective in nature than we often care to acknowledge. Writing of an earlier French historiography, Pierre Nora has remarked that '[t]hrough the past we venerated above all ourselves';[42] he might have been describing the ecclesiastical history of the early twentieth century. The challenge facing us is far more complex. We can no longer imagine ourselves like detectives who assemble the evidence, aiming eventually 'to close the case'. As historical investigators of past religious phenomena our work is akin to that of anthropologists who live with the incompleteness that is a result of human variation. It is enough to understand something of the past's religiosity; veneration is best left to others.

42 Pierre Nora, 'Between Memory and History: Les Lieux de Mémoire', *Representations* 26 (1989), 7–24, at 16.

The Origins of Royal Anointing

Conor O'Brien*

University of Oxford

The anointing of kings emerged as a Christian rite of passage in the early Middle Ages, although the exact circumstances and sequence of events that led to the general emergence of the rite remain controversial. This article argues that royal anointing first became a recognized and repeated practice within two separate societies: seventh-century Visigothic Spain and the eighth-century Frankish kingdom. Whereas previous work has stressed the role of Christian clerics in the emergence of this rite, the article argues that royal anointing had its origins within lay elite political culture and spoke primarily to the needs, not of the clerics who performed it, but of the laypeople who received and beheld it.

In the 1970s, Janet Nelson (later president of the society) read two important communications on medieval royal anointing to the Ecclesiastical History Society. In these she proposed that we should understand anointing in the Western tradition as a rite of passage, a ritual that worked to turn its recipient into a new man: someone who was not a king became a king.[1] This article is inspired by Dame Janet's work to return to the question of royal anointing as a specifically Christian rite of passage and to ask how it came about: what were the forces within the societies in which it first emerged that made it necessary for rulers to go through a special religious ceremony in order to change their status? My argument is that these forces emerged from the lay elite political culture of those times and places where royal anointing first took hold: namely, Visigothic Spain in the seventh century and the Frankish kingdom in the eighth century.

* E-mail: conor.obrien@history.ox.ac.uk.

[1] Janet L. Nelson, 'National Synods, Kingship as Office, and Royal Anointing: An Early Medieval Syndrome', in G. J. Cuming and Derek Baker, eds, *Councils and Assemblies*, SCH 7 (Oxford, 1971), 41–59 (repr. in her *Politics and Ritual in Early Medieval Europe* [London, 1986], 239–57); eadem, 'Symbols in Context: Rulers' Inauguration Rituals in Byzantium and the West in the Early Middle Ages', in Derek Baker, ed., *The Orthodox Churches and the West*, SCH 13 (Oxford, 1976), 97–119 (repr. in Nelson, *Politics and Ritual*, 259–81). Hereafter I cite both articles from the reprint.

Studies in Church History 59 (2023), 27–47
doi: 10.1017/stc.2023.4

There is, of course, a vast quantity of material on early medieval royal anointing, debating its origin, purposes and nature. Most of this is narrowly focused on specific acts of anointing, especially that of Pippin III as the first Carolingian king of the Franks.[2] One of the really impressive things about Nelson's work in the 1970s was that she sought to look at the entire 'early medieval syndrome' of royal anointing and identify the common factors within different societies that embraced the rite of passage. She identified as key the existence of an active culture of episcopal synods, leading to a strong sense of group identity and shared interests amongst the higher clergy; anointing emerged out of 'a crystallization of the clergy's needs and expectations of kingship'.[3] I have been inspired by the ambition of Nelson's analysis to think across different societies where royal anointing emerged; if I come to a different conclusion from hers, that is primarily because I examine different case studies.

Nelson pointed to four contexts in which royal anointing became standard: seventh-century Spain, mid-ninth-century West Frankia, late ninth-century East Frankia and mid-tenth-century England.[4] I look at a narrower range of case studies than Nelson did because, as will become apparent, I believe royal anointing had already become a significant and sustained practice in Frankia before the ninth century, and the example of this Carolingian tradition of anointing clearly provided an authorizing model for the later development of the rite in the post-Carolingian states of the ninth and tenth centuries. While anointing probably became common in England before the tenth century (as Nelson's own work has shown), it was introduced there as a result of eighth-century Carolingian influence.[5] Arguments that anointing was practised or theorized before the eighth century in the British Isles are now generally found unconvincing.[6]

[2] The relevant literature is cited where appropriate in what follows.

[3] Nelson, 'National Synods', 241–8, 254–5 (whence the quotation); eadem, 'Symbols in Context', 265.

[4] Nelson, 'National Synods', 244–8.

[5] Janet L. Nelson, 'The Earliest Royal *Ordo*: Some Liturgical and Historical Aspects', in Brian Tierney and Peter Linehan, eds, *Authority and Power: Studies on Medieval Law and Government* (Cambridge, 1980), 29–48 (repr. in Nelson, *Politics and Ritual*, 341–60); Joanna Story, *Carolingian Connections: Anglo-Saxon England and Carolingian Francia, c.750–870* (Farnham, 2003), 87–8, 157–60, 178–80.

[6] The work of Michael J. Enright argues for an Irish origin for anointing: *Iona, Tara and Soissons: The Origin of the Royal Anointing Ritual* (Berlin, 1985); idem, 'On the Unity of *De Regno* 1–4 of the "Hibernensis": The First Royal Anointing Ordo', *Frühmittelalterliche*

Consequently, I would argue that Visigothic Spain and early Carolingian Frankia are the earliest two contexts in which we can be sure that royal anointing emerged essentially independently and endogenously.[7] I examine these two case studies in turn before briefly comparing them to draw some general conclusions.

Visigothic Spain

By the time the kingdom of Visigothic Spain was swept aside by the Arab Conquest of 711, its kings seem to have been regularly anointed at the start of their reigns, but when this practice began has been a contentious question. Some historians suggest that the point of origin was 589, when King Reccared first became a Nicene Christian.[8] He would have received a confirmation-anointing as part of that process, for this was the standard liturgical accompaniment to an 'Arian' heretic's being restored to Mother Church. But we know that the majority of the Gothic aristocracy converted with Reccared; this does not seem like a very likely context for an explicitly royal connection with anointing to emerge.[9] Others propose 633 as the start date, when the bishops of

---

Studien 48 (2014), 207–35. For earlier work, see Raymund Kottje, *Studien zum Einfluss des Alten Testamentes auf Recht und Liturgie des Frühen Mittelalters (6.–8. Jahrhundert)* (Bonn, 1964), 97–103. For the arguments against, see Jan Prelog, 'Sind Weihesalbungen insularen Ursprungs?', *Frühmittelaterliche Studien* 13 (1979), 303–56; Thomas Charles-Edwards, 'A Contract between King and People in Early Medieval Ireland? *Críth Gablach* on Kingship', *Peritia* 8 (1994), 107–19, at 109–10; Michael Richter, 'Die frühmittelalterliche Herrschersalbung und die *Collectio Canonum Hibernensis*', in Matthias Becher and Jörg Jarnut, eds, *Der Dynastiewechsel von 751. Vorgeschichte, Legitimationsstrategien und Erinnerung* (Münster, 2004), 211–19.

[7] Spanish-born clerics (such as Theodulf of Orléans) came to be influential at the court of Charlemagne, but Carolingian anointing predates the evidence for substantial Visigothic influence.

[8] Michel Zimmermann, 'Les Sacres des rois wisigoths', in Michel Rouche, ed., *Clovis, histoire et mémoire. Le Baptême de Clovis, son écho à travers l'histoire* (Paris, 1997), 9–28, at 15–16; Alexander Pierre Bronisch, 'Die westgotische Reichsideologie und ihre Weiterentwicklung im Reich von Asturien', in Franz-Reiner Erkens, ed., *Das früh-mittelalterliche Königtum. Ideelle und religiose Grundlagen* (Berlin, 2005), 161–89, at 168; Andrew Fear, 'God and Caesar: The Dynamics of Visigothic Monarchy', in Lynette Mitchell and Charles Melville, eds, *Every Inch a King: Comparative Studies on Kings and Kingship in the Ancient and Medieval Worlds* (Leiden, 2013), 285–302.

[9] I agree here with Céline Martin, 'L'Innovation politique dans le royaume de Tolède. Le sacre du souverain', in Corinne Péneau, ed., *Élections et pouvoirs politiques du VIIe au XVIIe siècle* (Pompignac, 2008), 281–300, at 282.

Spain, in council at Toledo, decreed that the king was the Lord's anointed whose life was therefore sacrosanct; hence the suggestion that anointing was introduced as a practice to defend the king against the 'Gothic disease' of regicide.[10] Modern historians have made rather more of the phrase *christus domini* than the bishops themselves did in 633; for them, it served purely to introduce the necessary Old Testament proof texts condemning the killing of a king.[11] The bishops never mentioned unction as a practice. More importantly, in his most famous work Isidore of Seville, who presided at the 633 Council of Toledo and probably had a hand in the writing of its acts, spoke of royal anointing as something that had happened in the Israelite past, but no longer occurred in the present; that he neither knew of, nor showed any interest in restoring, royal anointing is significant.[12]

The earliest evidence we have for an actual practice of royal anointing dates to 672: Julian of Toledo's account of King Wamba's inauguration of that year specifically states that he was anointed on the head with oil. After Wamba we start to see passing references in documentary sources to kings' having been anointed, something that never happened before 672.[13] The balance of scholarship has therefore shifted in favour of Wamba's being the first Visigothic royal anointing, and therefore the first anointing of any Christian king.[14]

[10] P. D. King, *Law and Society in the Visigothic Kingdom*, Cambridge Studies in Medieval Life and Thought, 3rd series 5 (Cambridge, 1972), 48–9; Pablo C. Diaz and M. R. Valverde, 'The Theoretical Strength and Practical Weakness of the Visigothic Monarchy of Toledo', in Frans Theuws and Janet L. Nelson, eds, *Rituals of Power: From Late Antiquity to the Early Middle Ages*, Transformation of the Roman World 8 (Leiden, 2000), 59–93, at 78–80. Cf. Aloys Suntrup, *Studien zur politischen Theologie im frühmittelalterlichen Okzident. Die Aussage konziliarer Texte des gallischen und iberischen Raumes* (Münster, 2001), 240–1.

[11] Fourth Council of Toledo (633), c. 75, in Gonzalo Martinez Diez and Felix Rodriguez, eds, *La Colección Canónica Hispana*, 6 vols (Madrid, 1966–2002), 5: 248–60 (with *christus domini* at 249–50).

[12] Isidore, *Etymologiae* 7.2.2. For close parallels between the acts of the Toledan council and the writings of Isidore, see Pierre Cazier, 'Les Sentences d'Isidore de Séville et le IVe Concile de Tolède. Réflexions sur les rapports entre l'Église et le pouvoir politique en Espagne autour des années 630', *Antigüedad y Cristianismo* 3 (1986), 373–86.

[13] Julian of Toledo, *Historia Wambae regis*, hist. 4 (MGH SRM 5, 503–4); *Laterculus regum Visigothorum*, c. 47 (MGH AA 13, 468); Twelfth Council of Toledo (681), c. 1 (Diez and Rodriguez, eds, *La Colección*, 6: 151–3).

[14] Nelson, 'National Synods', 247; Kottje, *Studien zum Einfluss des Alten Testamentes*, 96–7; Eugen Ewig, 'Zum christlichen Königsgedanken im Frühmittelalter', in Hartmut Atsma, ed., *Spätantikes und Fränkisches Gallien: Gesammelte Schriften (1952–1973)*, 3 vols (Munich, 1976), 1: 3–71, at 33–4; Patrick Henriet, 'Rite, idéologie, fonction. Remarques

Wamba was a middle-aged courtier who had been elected to the kingship by the elite of the realm on the death of his predecessor, King Reccesuinth. To some extent, Wamba's succession to the kingship was a model case, for election by the court aristocracy and higher clergy was the constitutional form established as legal in 633 by the Council of Toledo. It had not been the practical norm in the intervening generation, but by 672 there were strong grounds for such a practice to be put into effect. During Reccesuinth's long reign in particular, an aristocratic elite of palatine officials emerged who would come to dominate Visigothic politics for the remainder of the century, particularly through their attendance at the national councils of Toledo.[15]

Wamba was one of this group: he emerged from the fairly narrow ruling clique that chose him. As will be obvious by now, Visigothic monarchy was non-dynastic: this had essentially been the norm since the beginning of the seventh century, a small number of (usually short-lasting) father-son successions notwithstanding. Direct inheritance of the throne does not reappear after Wamba's succession until the very end of the century. That does not mean that kings were chosen from a wide pool of candidates. A small number of often interconnected families, closely associated with the central royal court, seem to have supplied all the Visigothic kings from Wamba until 711.[16] The leading representatives of this group, as I have mentioned, attended national church councils and, although

sur l'onction des rois wisigoths et hispaniques du Haut Moyen Âge (VIIe–XIe siècle)', in Giles Constable and Michel Rouche, eds, *Auctoritas. Mélanges offerts à Olivier Guillot* (Paris, 2006), 179–92, esp. 180–2; Christoph Dartmann, 'Die Sakralisierung König Wambas. Zur Debatte um frühmittelalterliche Sakralherrschaft', *Frühmittelaterliche Studien* 44 (2010), 39–57, at 45–6. Cf. Martin, 'L'Innovation politique', who argues that Wamba was not anointed but rather his contemporary, the rebel king Paul. Dietrich Claude, *Adel, Kirche und Königtum im Westgotenreich* (Sigmaringen, 1971), 155–7, and Roger Collins, 'Julian of Toledo and the Royal Succession in Late Seventh-Century Spain', in P. H. Sawyer and I. N. Wood, eds, *Early Medieval Kingship* (Leeds, 1977), 30–49, at 48, both argue that anointing was practised before 672 but that greater emphasis came to be laid on it in the late seventh century.

[15] For the rise of the palace aristocracy in the Toledan councils, see Claude, *Adel, Kirche und Königtum*, 135, 145, 161–2, 177–81; Suntrup, *Studien zur politischen Theologie*, 274–5; Roger Collins, *Visigothic Spain: 409–711* (Oxford, 2004), 86–90; José Orlandis and Domingo Ramos-Lisson, *Die Synoden auf der Iberischen Halbinsel bis zum Einbruch des Islam (711)* (Munich, 1981), 335–7.

[16] Claude, *Adel, Kirche und Königtum*, 196–8; Collins, *Visigothic Spain*, 113–16.

laymen, frequently signed the canons that emerged from those councils: these were men with titles from the court administration, such as Count of the Chamberlains or Notaries, but many of them also held the military rank of *dux*.[17] This lay elite seems to have taken part in the Christian spiritual government of the nation. Kings often noted at the later Visigothic councils that Christ or the Holy Spirit was present when bishops gathered in Christ's name; it is possible that this divine inspiration was thought to seep out from the episcopal core to irradiate the palatine officials present on these occasions.[18] While the liturgical ordo for Visigothic church councils specified that kings had to leave before deliberation began, their greatest lay subjects may have become agents of the Spirit through their presence at the gathering.[19]

Wamba's inauguration took place in a context of contestation: he faced a rival king who had been chosen by a different gathering, one that represented the interests of provincial aristocrats in the Gallic parts of the Visigothic kingdom, somewhat distant from the Toledan court. The rebel king, Paul, is also described as having been anointed in Julian of Toledo's account of Wamba, as well as having been crowned with a purloined votive crown. If true, this coronation with a sacred object would also be an innovative rite of passage in a Visigothic context.[20] Julian's text deals entirely with this challenge and how Wamba repressed it, including through the imposition of strict Old Testament purity regulations to ensure divine favour for his army.[21] Mayke de Jong, amongst others, has argued

[17] Eighth Council of Toledo (653), subscriptiones (Diez and Rodriguez, eds, *La Colección*, 5: 447–8); Ninth Council of Toledo (655), subscriptiones (ibid. 5: 514); Twelfth Council of Toledo (681), subscriptiones (ibid. 6: 197–9); Thirteenth Council of Toledo (683), subscriptiones (ibid. 6: 265–7); Fifteenth Council of Toledo (688), subscriptiones (ibid. 6: 343); Sixteenth Council of Toledo (693), subscriptiones, in José Vives, ed., *Concilios Visigoticos e Hispano-Romanos* (Madrid, 1963), 521.

[18] Twelfth Council of Toledo (681), tomus (Diez and Rodriguez, eds, *La Colección*, 6: 142); Thirteenth Council of Toledo (683), tomus, lex (ibid. 6: 223, 270); Fifteenth Council of Toledo (688), tomus (ibid. 6: 292–3); Sixteenth Council of Toledo (693), lex (Vives, ed., *Concilios*, 515); Seventeenth Council of Toledo (694), tomus (ibid. 522–3).

[19] *Ordo de celebrando concilio* 3, c. 14 (MGH Conc., Ord., 213).

[20] Julian of Toledo, *Historia Wambae*, epistola Pauli (MGH SRM 5, 500); ibid. c. 26 (MGH SRM 5, 522). See Martin, 'L'Innovation politique'.

[21] Julian of Toledo, *Historia Wambae*, c. 10 (MGH SRM 5, 510). On Julian's response to the contested circumstances of Wamba's early rule, see now Molly Lester, 'The Ties that Bind: Diagnosing Social Crisis in Julian of Toledo's *Historia Wambae*', in Helmut Reimitz and Gerda Heydemann, eds, *Historiography and Identity II: Post-Roman Multiplicity and*

for this as a sign of a developing Gothic identification as the New Israel, in which the centre of the kingdom and its ruling elites were framed as masculine, ethnically pure and (Old Testament) Israelite, while peripheral groups were understood as feminine, foreign and (New Testament) Jewish.[22] Of course, as metropolitan of Toledo, Julian had an obvious vested interest in emphasizing the importance of the Toledan centre in the making of legitimate Visigothic monarchs; anointing in this context was something that helped put him and his successors at the heart of the king-making process, since Julian was clear that a king could only receive effective unction in the metropolitan church of Toledo itself.[23]

Even allowing for Julian's possible distortion, there remains a plausible context for the emergence of Visigothic royal anointing in the second half of the seventh century. The need for a rite of passage was clear in a case where royal succession could not be presented as a natural, dynastic fact. The king had to leave the group of the palace aristocracy and be separated from them, all the while maintaining the consensus and shared interests which bound him to the politically powerful elite. Anointing made sense in terms of the Israelite group identity that the central aristocracy might have developed at this time, but it also usefully set the king apart as something rather more than just a *primus inter pares*, more than just the leader of equals who, potentially, looked forward to their own day on the throne. In a context in which many of this ruling elite may have regularly bathed in the divine inspiration poured out upon the participants in a church council, their king needed an even closer relationship with divine inspiration in order to be seen as superior: Julian tells us that when the oil touched Wamba's head a shaft of steaming light went up and bees flew out.[24] For Julian, clearly, royal anointing provided an awe-inspiring spectacle, and spectacles only make sense when considered

---

New Political Identities, Cultural Encounters in Late Antiquity and the Early Middle Ages 27 (Turnhout, 2020), 269–96.

[22] Mayke de Jong, 'Adding Insult to Injury: Julian of Toledo and his *Historia Wambae*', in Peter Heather, ed., *The Visigoths from the Migration Period to the Seventh Century: An Ethnographic Perspective*, Studies in Historical Archaeoethnology 4 (Woodbridge, 1999), 373–402. See also Bronisch, 'Die westgotische Reichsideologie', 169–74.

[23] Collins, 'Julian of Toledo', 45–6; Henriet, 'Rite, idéologie, fonction', 183–4; Dartmann, 'Die Sakralisierung König Wambas', 49–50; de Jong, 'Adding Insult to Injury', 379.

[24] Julian of Toledo, *Historia Wambae*, hist. 4 (MGH SRM 5, 504).

in terms of their audience. While undoubtedly the bishop's account stressed the episcopal contribution to king-making as vital, it seems that a need to manage the relationship between different members of the lay elite created this new rite.

One final piece of evidence for Visigothic royal anointing may deserve consideration: the liturgical evidence. All the manuscript records of a Mozarabic liturgy of anointing were created in the kingdom of Asturias / León, centuries after the fall of the Visigothic kingdom. Two bodies of material survive, although they may both derive from a single liturgical tradition: prayers for the office of the 'ordination' of a king are preserved in the Antiphonary of León, while the scriptural readings from the mass for the 'ordination' of a king are preserved in the *liber commicus / comicus* lectionary tradition.[25] The Antiphonary of León (León, Cathedral Library, MS 8) dates from the first third of the tenth century. While it can no longer be taken to be a copy of an exemplar dating from the beginning of Wamba's reign (previously the standard inference from a dating clause early on in the manuscript, which is now thought to have no relationship to the liturgical contents), it probably derives from an earlier (possibly late eighth-century) antiphonary.[26] The earliest manuscript of the *liber comicus* that I know of dates possibly to the ninth century: Toledo, Biblioteca del Cabildo, MS 35.8;[27] recent study of the Lenten readings in the *liber comicus* has concluded that they reflect seventh-century Spanish liturgical practice.[28] We may, therefore,

[25] Thomas Deswarte, 'Liturgie et royauté dans les monarchies asturienne et léonaise (711–1109)', *Cahiers de civilisation médiévale* 58 (2015), 55–67, at 59, believes that these are two parts of a single ceremony derived from that developed by Julian of Toledo.

[26] Manuel C. Díaz y Díaz, 'Some Incidental Notes on Music Manuscripts', in Susana Zapke, ed., *Hispania Vetus: Musical-liturgical Manuscripts from Visigothic Origins to the Franco-Roman Transition (9th–12th Centuries)* (Bilbao, 2007), 93–111, esp. 94–100. Elsa de Luce, 'Royal Misattributions: Monograms in the León Antiphoner', *Journal of Medieval Iberian Studies* 9 (2017), 25–51, which summarizes subsequent scholarship on the dating of the manuscript, agrees with Díaz y Díaz and provides further evidence for an early tenth-century date.

[27] A. M. Mundó, 'La datación de los códices litúrgicos visigóticos toledanos', *Hispania Sacra* 18 (1965), 1–25, at 16, argued for a later date, but most scholarship remains undecided: e.g., H. A. G. Houghton, *The Latin New Testament: A Guide to its Early History, Texts and Manuscripts* (Oxford, 2016), 98–9, 240.

[28] Nathan Chase, *The* Homiliae Toletanae *and the Theology of Lent and Easter*, Spicilegium Sacrum Lovaniense Études et Documents 56 (Leuven, 2020), 65–8; for earlier work on the *liber comicus* reflecting seventh-century liturgy: Paul G. Remley, *Old English Biblical Verse: Studies in Genesis, Exodus and Daniel* (Cambridge, 1996), 212–13.

have access to elements from a Spanish anointing liturgy of the 800s, if not earlier. This is a liturgy which shows no trace of a relationship to Frankish traditions, which were well established by the ninth century and already proving influential elsewhere in Europe.[29] The Spanish manuscripts seem to preserve a liturgy of royal anointing which is entirely the product of indigenous Spanish developments; they are, consequently, probably the closest we can get to how Visigothic royal anointing was performed.

The antiphonary material provides evidence of a self-conscious comparison of the ruler's subjects with Israel, and some striking use of the Psalms to describe the awe-inspiring sight of the king in his regalia which chimes with my comments above on the significance of spectacle in Julian of Toledo's account of Wamba's anointing.[30] The lectionary evidence is more interesting. The three readings (which are Old Latin, not Vulgate) are: Wisdom 9: 1–12 in the voice of Solomon, chosen by God as king, requesting wisdom so that he will rule justly and worthily; Romans 13: 1–8 on obeying all powers because they come from God, with the ruler as a minister of God to punish the wicked; and Luke 4: 16–22 where Christ reads in the synagogue about the Spirit of God anointing the Messiah to preach, help the downtrodden and proclaim the day of judgement.[31] This last lection ends with Christ announcing that this, the anointing of the Messiah, is now fulfilled 'before you'. If we think of Visigothic royal anointing as a rite of passage, as a ritual journey from one status to another, here we have the indication that the king has been transformed from being the weak candidate for the throne, the *homo infirmus* of Wisdom 9: 5, to the anointed one himself. Alongside the king's transformation, the audience of the lections shifts from God himself in Wisdom to the surrounding congregation, whose obedience to the king is demanded by Romans 13, and whose wonder at the miraculous transformation which has occurred is elicited by the Gospel text.

Julian's mention of Wamba's illuminated head conjures up this same sense of wonder. His text may give us a clerical perspective,

[29] Deswarte, 'Liturgie et royauté', 59–60.

[30] Louis Brou and José Vives, eds, *Antifonario visigotico mozarabe de la cathedral de León* (Barcelona, 1959), 450–2. Cf. Collins, 'Julian of Toledo', 44.

[31] Justo Pérez de Urbel and Atilano González y Ruiz-Zorrilla, eds, *Liber commicus*, 2 vols (Madrid, 1950–55), 2: 535–7.

but it nonetheless hints at how the reaction of the lay congregation around Wamba mattered, something the liturgical evidence also suggests.[32] Nelson made an important point in emphasizing the significance of seventh-century Spain's conciliar tradition. This certainly played a role in the process by which Visigothic kingship came to be understood as an office with religious and moral responsibilities that in part limited and constricted the king.[33] But the presence of the laity at Toledan councils means that these ideas cannot have simply expressed clerical opinion, separate from that of the rest of the leading aristocracy. In the lectionary for a royal inauguration, we see a stress on submission to the king, a glorification of him, and a narrative telling us how he is no longer just like other men; the readings say surprisingly little about how a king ought to behave. This may be a liturgy which, rather than simply sending a clerical message to kings, might have been intended to send a royal message to lay subjects, until recently the king's colleagues and equals.

The Carolingians

Frankish anointing is far better known and more extensively studied than its Visigothic predecessor. That the usurping Pippin III exploited anointing to establish himself on a throne held by members of the Merovingian family for the previous two and a half centuries is one of the most repeated facts of early medieval history. Older comments about how the sacrality of the Merovingians could only be replaced by a revolutionary 'piece of church magic' still do the rounds outside specialist scholarship on occasion, but tend not to be taken very seriously by historians now.[34] Indeed, much that was once

[32] For a reading of Julian's account of Wamba as describing essentially a 'secular' king-making: Collins, 'Julian of Toledo', 43–4.

[33] Nelson, 'National Synods'; I explore this development of an office of Christian kingship in Visigothic Spain in my forthcoming book, *The Rise of Christian Kingship*.

[34] J. M. Wallace-Hadrill, 'The *Via Regia* of the Carolingian Age', in Beryl Smalley, ed., *Trends in Medieval Political Thought* (Oxford, 1965), 22–41, at 26, quoted with approval by Francis Oakley, *Empty Bottles of Gentilism: Kingship and the Divine in Late Antiquity and the Early Middle Ages (to 1050)* (New Haven, CT, 2010), 160. Also on anointing and 'sacrality': Marc Bloch, *The Royal Touch: Sacred Monarchy and Scrofula in England and France*, transl. J. E. Anderson (London, 1973), 35–41; David Harry Miller, 'Sacral Kingship, Biblical Kingship, and the Elevation of Pepin the Short', in Thomas F. X. Noble and John J. Contreni, eds, *Religion, Culture, and Society in the Early Middle Ages: Studies in Honour of Richard E. Sullivan* (Kalamazoo, MI, 1987), 131–54.

known about Pippin's anointing has had to be rethought in light of some devastating primary source criticism in recent years, especially by Josef Semmler and Rosamond McKitterick.[35] The old story told how Pippin was anointed twice, once in 751 by St Boniface on the orders of Pope Zacharias (741–52), and again in 754 by Pope Stephen II (752–57) in person, but it is now not clear that any anointing took place in 751 at all: if it did, Boniface certainly had nothing to do with it. His role is mentioned only in the *Annales regni Francorum*, put together in or near Charlemagne's court around the year 790; the much more closely contemporary so-called *Continuation of Fredegar* simply refers to a consecration (*consecratio*) of Pippin by unnamed bishops.[36]

Pippin was certainly anointed in 754 by the pope; plenty of papal evidence, including numerous letters written in subsequent years by the pope himself, shows that Stephen II anointed both the king and his two young sons, Charles (i.e. Charlemagne) and Carloman, on that occasion.[37] Much excellent work has been done showing that the papacy probably developed the ritual of royal anointing out of that of post-baptismal anointing, so that Carolingian anointing could be understood as a kind of spin-off of confirmation, a rite of passage exported from the Roman Church to the rest of Western Europe.[38] Alternative liturgical origins have been suggested: Nelson

[35] Rosamond McKitterick, 'The Illusion of Royal Power in the Carolingian Annals', *EHR* 115 (2000), 1–20; Josef Semmler, *Der Dynastiewechsel von 751 und die fränkische Königssalbung*, Studia Humaniora 6 (Düsseldorf, 2003), 10–56; Olaf Schneider, 'Die Königserhebung Pippins 751 in der Erinnerung der karolingischen Quellen', in Becher and Jarnut, eds, *Der Dynastiewechsel von 751*, 243–75.

[36] *Annales regni Francorum* [hereafter: *ARF*], *s.a.* 749 (MGH SRG i.u.s. 6, 8); *Continuation of Fredegar* (recte *Historia vel gesta Francorum*), c. 33, in J. M. Wallace-Hadrill, ed. and transl., *The Fourth Book of the Chronicle of Fredegar with its Continuations* (London, 1960), 102. On the meaning of *consecratio*: John F. Romano, 'The Coronation of Charlemagne as a Liturgical Event', *Mediaeval Studies* 82 (2020), 149–81, at 161–2.

[37] *ARF*, *s.a.* 754 (MGH SRG i.u.s. 6, 12); *Codex epistolaris Carolinus* [hereafter: *CC*] 6, 7, 8 (MGH Epp. 3, 489, 493, 496); *Liber Pontificalis* [hereafter: *LP*] 94.27, in Louis Duchesne, ed., *Le* Liber pontificalis. *Texte, introduction et commentaire*, 2 vols (Paris, 1886), 1: 448.

[38] Arnold Angenendt, 'Rex et Sacerdos. Zur Genese der Königssalbung', in Norbert Kamp and Joachim Wollasch, eds, *Tradition als Historische Kraft. Interdisziplinäre Forschungen zur Geschichte des früheren Mittelalters* (Berlin, 1982), 100–18; Paul A. Jacobson, '*Sicut Samuel unxit David*: Early Carolingian Royal Anointings Reconsidered', in Lizette Larson-Miller, ed., *Medieval Liturgy: A Book of Essays* (New York, 1997), 267–303; Semmler, *Der Dynastiewechsel*, 46–53.

pointed to the development, within Frankia itself, of priestly anointings in particular; a number of scholars have pointed to how oil rituals, of all sorts, were increasingly common in Western Christianity at this time.[39] This stress on the liturgical context for royal anointing has exacerbated the tendency to see the ritual as a clerical imposition on lay rulers, something rather foreign to kings, reflecting little of the Carolingians' own concerns and priorities. That was Nelson's original interpretation: for her, the anointing(s) of the 750s were a one-off clerical creation that went nowhere, because unrepresentative of Frankish lay interests and concepts; only the episcopate of the ninth century, regularly meeting in synod, eventually ensured that royal anointing became the norm.[40]

Nelson pointed to all the literature we have from the court of Charlemagne, none of it mentioning his anointing at papal hands: 'Don't courtiers write what kings want to hear?'[41] The problem, of course, is that what kings want to hear changes. Literary works, mostly from the 790s, do not necessarily allow us to see lay perceptions of anointing several generations earlier. Charlemagne's anointing seems to have mattered more in the generation after 754 than it did by the end of the eighth century. My contention is that the role of royal anointing changed in Carolingian society over time, and did so within a continuing tradition of royal anointings, from 754 until the early ninth century. Rather than there being a substantial gap in Carolingian anointings between Pippin in 754 and Charles the Bald in 848, there were probably unctions in 768, 771, 781, 800, 816 and 823, as well as an attempted anointing around 772/3. However, we cannot take the reality of all these events for granted, and I therefore need to devote some space to the technical task of setting out the evidence.[42]

[39] Janet L. Nelson, 'Inauguration Rituals', in Sawyer and Wood, eds, *Early Medieval Kingship*, 50–71, at 58 (repr. in Nelson, *Politics and Ritual*, 283–307, at 291) [hereafter I cite the reprint]; Janet L. Nelson, 'The Lord's Anointed and the People's Choice: Carolingian Royal Ritual', in David Cannadine and Simon Price, eds, *Rituals of Royalty: Power and Ceremonial in Traditional Societies* (Cambridge, 1987), 137–80, at 150; Enright, *Iona, Tara and Soissons*, 137–59; Jan Clauß, 'Die Salbung Pippins des Jüngeren in karolingischen Quellen vor dem Horizont biblischer Wahrnehmungsmuster', *Frühmittelalterliche Studien* 46 (2013), 391–417, at 403–4.

[40] Nelson, 'Inauguration Rituals', 289–95; eadem, 'National Synods', esp. 256.

[41] Nelson, 'Inauguration Rituals', 292.

[42] Carlrichard Brühl, 'Fränkischer Krönungsbrauch und das Problem der "Festkrönungen"', *Historische Zeitschrift* 194 (1962), 265–326, at 306, 313–14, and

In 768, Pippin III died and his two sons, Charlemagne and Carloman, succeeded him. In separate ceremonies within their own sub-kingdoms, both kings were raised to their new positions on 9 October 768. To my knowledge, only one Carolingian text described what happened on that date as an anointing: the *Annals of St Amand* declared that 'Charles and Carloman were anointed as kings'.[43] Do we have any reason to give this single source much credence? It is broadly contemporary; this section of the *Annales sancti Amandi* was completed in or shortly after 771, and the text may be strictly contemporary in many of its entries from around this time.[44] Therefore someone in north-eastern Frankia, shortly after the events of October 768, believed that Pippin's two sons had been anointed when they succeeded their father. Also closely contemporary (and much closer to the Carolingian kings themselves) was the *Continuation of Fredegar*, which here again used the word *consecratio*. Presumably, this is a deliberate echo of the terminology used to describe Pippin's inauguration in 751: clearly some sort of episcopal consecration was involved in 768.[45]

We may see the impact of a 768 royal anointing in papal letters to Charlemagne and Carloman. During their father's reign, the two young kings had received numerous letters from Rome which made reference to their anointing by Stephen II, events also mentioned in some letters to their father Pippin.[46] These references almost all take

Enright, *Iona, Tara and Soissons*, 122, accept the reality of the 768 and 771 anointings; Mary Garrison, 'The Franks as the New Israel? Education for an Identity from Pippin to Charlemagne', in Yitzhak Hen and Matthew Innes, eds, *The Uses of the Past in the Early Middle Ages* (Cambridge, 2000), 114–61, at 138, does not; Nelson, 'Inauguration Rituals', 291–2, is undecided.

43 'Karlus et Karlomannus ad reges uncti sunt': *Annales sancti Amandi, s.a.* 768 (MGH SS 1, 12).

44 Norbert Schröer, *Die* Annales s. Amandi *und ihre Verwandten. Untersuchungen zu einer Gruppe karolingischer Annalen des 8. und frühen 9. Jahrhunderts*, Göppinger akademische Beiträge 85 (Göppingen, 1975), 5.

45 *Continuation of Fredegar*, c. 54 (Wallace-Hadrill, ed. and transl., 121).

46 For example, *CC* 6, 7, 26, 33, 35, 99 (MGH Epp. 3, 489, 493, 530, 540, 543, 651–2). Although the last letter (*CC* 99) was actually sent in late 767, around the chronological mid-point of the letters in *Codex Carolinus*, it appears at the end of *CC*'s sole surviving manuscript because it was a letter from the 'anti-pope' Constantine II, on whom see Rosamond McKitterick, 'The *damnatio memoriae* of Pope Constantine II (767–768)', in Ross Balzaretti, Julia Barrow and Patricia Skinner, eds, *Italy and Early Medieval Europe: Papers for Chris Wickham on the Occasion of his 65th Birthday* (Oxford, 2018), 231–48.

the same basic form: God had anointed Charles and Carloman as kings through the apostle Peter, by the hands of the latter's representative. But after Pippin's death these mentions of anointing dry up in papal letters: Charlemagne and Carloman never again received a reminder that they had been anointed as kings by Stephen II. Might this simply reflect changes at Rome at either the papal or the notarial level? There is also a noticeable drop-off in the use of biblical references in papal letters after Pippin's death, noted by a number of scholars.[47] But, as we have seen, there was no particularly biblical overtone to how the popes had referred to anointing, so the one change cannot necessarily explain the other. The disappearance of royal anointing from these letters may also slightly predate the decline of biblical rhetoric. Pope Stephen III (768–72) wrote a famously violent letter to Charlemagne and Carloman, warning them off marriage to a Lombard princess, that relied heavily on biblical imagery and language. Stephen admonished the Franks against setting aside their lawful wives, behaviour unworthy of Christians who 'through anointing with holy oil … have been sanctified with a heavenly blessing by the hands of the vicar of the blessed Peter'. Here the anointing of 754 was not described as a royal anointing, as it always had been before, but as a straightforward post-baptismal / confirmation anointing.[48]

The disappearance of royal anointing from papal letters seems to have derived from a conscious decision: when Pope Hadrian I (772–95) reused one of Stephen II's letters to Pippin to provide him with the words with which to address Charlemagne in 775, all reference to the papal anointing of the king was removed.[49] Charlemagne had, of

[47] Thomas F. X. Noble, 'The Bible in the Codex Carolinus', in Claudio Leonardi and Giovanni Orlando, eds, *Biblical Studies in the Early Middle Ages*, Millennio medievale 52 (Florence, 2005), 61–74, at 71–2; Dorine van Espelo, 'A Testimony of Carolingian Rule: The *Codex epistolaris carolinus* as a Product of its Time' (PhD thesis, University of Utrecht, 2014), 188–94. Arnold Angenendt, 'Karl der Große als *rex et sacerdos*', in Rainer Berndt, ed., *Das Frankfurter Konzil von 794. Kristallisationspunkt karolingischer Kultur*, 2 vols (Mainz, 1997), 1: 255–78, at 269–70, notes that Hadrian I never mentioned royal anointing in his letters.

[48] '[Q]uia oleo sancto uncti per manus vicarii beati Petri caelesti benedictione estis sanctificati': *CC* 45 (MGH Epp. 3, 561). ET: Rosamond McKitterick et al., *Codex Epistolaris Carolinus: Letters from the Popes to the Frankish Rulers 739–791*, TTH 77 (Liverpool, 2021), 285. On the biblical imagery: Walter Pohl, 'Why not to Marry a Foreign Woman: Stephen III's Letter to Charlemagne', in Valerie L. Garver and Owen M. Phelan, eds, *Rome and Religion in the Medieval World: Studies in Honour of Thomas F. X. Noble* (Farnham, 2014), 47–63.

[49] *CC* 57 (MGH Epp. 3, 582), drawing on *CC* 8 (MGH Epp. 3, 496).

course, been anointed by the pope on the very same day as Pippin. Why was that fact no longer relevant and why did it cease to be relevant almost as soon as Pippin died? One explanation would be that in 768 the papal anointing had been superseded by another royal anointing of Charlemagne and Carloman, one in which no pope had participated. If the papacy knew that the Frankish kings were, after October 768, appealing to a more recent liturgical unction for their kingly legitimacy, then it might no longer have been deemed politic to refer to the 754 anointing. This would suggest that royal anointing was not just a papal, or even a clerical, idea. Rather, it suggests that it was a Frankish rite presumably valued by the Carolingian family themselves.

On 4 December 771, Carloman died and representatives from his kingdom swiftly journeyed to meet Charlemagne on the border between the two sub-kingdoms to accept him as their ruler. Once again, most sources do not mention an anointing on this occasion, except one: in addition to the list of dignitaries given in the *ARF* entry, the *Annales Mettenses priores* state that 'they anointed the most glorious king Charles as their lord over them'.[50] Now the so-called 'earlier' *Annals of Metz* are certainly not a contemporary source. The text was written around 805 by someone keen to provide a favourable view of the Carolingian family's history, someone probably close to the (post-800) imperial court who intended to defend the providential nature of the Carolingian ascent to empire, and possibly influence succession plans amongst Charlemagne's sons. Charlemagne's sister, Gisela, has been credited with the inspiration for the text, although her patronage is not universally accepted.[51] If true, of course, Gisela's role would mean that the Metz annalist had access to good quality family information about the recent

[50] 'Ibi venientes ad eum Wileharius achiepiscopus et Fulradus Capellanus cum aliis episcopis ac sacerdotibus, Warinus quoque et Adhalardus comites cum aliis principibus, qui fuerant ex partibus Carlomanni, et unxerunt super se dominum suum Carolum gloriossimum regem': *Annales Mettenses priores*, *s.a.* 771 (MGH SRG i.u.s. 10, 57–8). Cf. *ARF*, *s.a.* 771 (MGH SRG i.u.s. 6, 32). See Janet L. Nelson, *King and Emperor: A New Life of Charlemagne* (London, 2019), 108–9.

[51] See Janet L. Nelson, 'Gender and Genre in Woman Historians of the early Middle Ages', in J.-P. Genet, ed., *L'Historiographie médiévale en Europe* (Paris, 1991), 149–63, at 156–60; Paul Fouracre and Richard A. Gerberding, *Late Merovingian France: History and Hagiography, 640–720* (Manchester, 1996), 330–49; Yitzhak Hen, 'The Annals of Metz and the Merovingian Past', in Hen and Innes, eds, *Uses of the Past*, 175–90.

Carolingians.[52] Olaf Schneider has pointed out a number of striking similarities between the events of 771 and the *ARF*'s account of Pippin's anointing in 751; the latter probably distorted the record to make Charlemagne's recent accession to sole kingship seem in perfect continuity with Pippin's receipt of Frankish kingship.[53] If Charlemagne was anointed in 771, that might explain why the *ARF* felt compelled to state that Pippin had been so in 751: anointing, by the early 770s, may have become the standard way that a Carolingian king was made. Alternatively, Josef Semmler has suggested that the Metz annalist simply used 'anointed' to mean 'appointed'; if so, that was a significant choice of word.[54]

The other evidence we have for Carolingian anointings in the eighth century points to a papal rite. In 781, Charlemagne had his sons Pippin and Louis anointed kings of Italy and Aquitaine respectively by Hadrian I in a grand ceremony in Rome; their elder brother, Charles the Younger, had to wait until 800, when he became a king immediately after his father's imperial coronation. Papal sources state that Pope Leo III (795–816) anointed Charles.[55] There was also a papal anointing that never happened. In 772 or 773, the Lombard king Desiderius attempted to have the pope anoint Charlemagne's two young nephews as kings, presumably as part of an attempt to weaken Charlemagne's position within Frankia by establishing rivals for the monarchy. Within a few years, Charlemagne had invaded Italy and taken over the Lombard kingdom, causing his nephews to disappear in the process.[56] There is an important context here: the difficulty of determining who exactly was a member of the royal family in the early Carolingian era. At regular intervals the dynastic tree had to be rather brutally pruned.

Pippin III spent some years before 754 excluding various close male relatives (including his own brother's son) from power in

[52] Nelson, *King and Emperor*, 36.

[53] Schneider, 'Die Königserhebung Pippins', 249–62.

[54] Semmler, *Der Dynastiewechsel*, 41–3.

[55] *ARF*, *s.a.* 781 (MGH SRG i.u.s. 6, 57); *LP* 98.24 (Duchesne, ed., *Le* Liber pontificalis, 2: 7); Romano, 'The Coronation of Charlemagne', 162–4. Alcuin, *Epistola* 217 (MGH Epp. 4, 360), does not mention anointing in 800 but indicates that Charles had received some coronation ritual at the pope's hands; see Rosamond McKitterick, *Charlemagne: The Formation of a European Identity* (Cambridge, 2008), 96.

[56] *LP* 97.8 (Duchesne, ed., *Le* Liber pontificalis, 1: 488): Pope Hadrian's recognition that to have anointed Charlemagne's nephews would have meant a break with the king indicates that at this time royal anointing was understood to have real meaning and impact in the Frankish world: Nelson, *King and Emperor*, 123, 132–5.

Frankia. Having his sons anointed alongside him indicated that only his branch of the Carolingian family was entitled to rule.[57] Charlemagne not only prevented his nephews from using anointing to assert their membership of the royal family; he also seems to have used anointing to manage his own children. The papal anointing in 781 took care of Charlemagne's two youngest sons, setting them up usefully in sub-kingdoms within their father's larger realm. This left the two older sons in a somewhat ambiguous position at best. The eldest, Pippin 'the Hunchback', did not belong to Charlemagne's second family (the children of his, probably, third wife, Hildegard) and may well have been essentially demoted from the status of a legitimate Carolingian in 781, when one of Hildegard's sons was renamed Pippin.[58] Hildegard's eldest son, Charles the Younger, also, rather oddly, was not anointed in 781, although he seems to have enjoyed paternal favour in the years that followed. There may have been personal issues with Charles that raised doubts about his suitability as a king, or Charlemagne may have preferred to maintain some ambiguity rather than raise up another king of the Franks. Having avoided trouble during the revolt of 'the Hunchback' of 792, Charles the Younger was eventually ritually acknowledged as a king in 800, his status as successor to the lion's share of his father's realm (confirmed by the succession plans Charlemagne published in 806) probably being decided at that point.[59]

[57] Matthias Becher, 'Drogo und die Königserhebung Pippins', *Frühmittelalterliche Studien* 23 (1989), 131–53. Fundamental now on the shaping of the Carolingian family, and the creation of consensus around its right to rule, is Stuart Airlie, *Making and Unmaking the Carolingians: 751–888* (London, 2021), which was published after I completed work on this article.

[58] For a survey of Charlemagne's shifting and complex management of his children, see Jennifer R. Davis, *Charlemagne's Practice of Empire* (Cambridge, 2015), 415–22. Janet L. Nelson, 'Charlemagne – *pater optimus*?', in Peter Godman, Jörg Jarnut and Peter Johanek, eds, *Am Vorabend der Kaiserkrönung. Das Epos 'Karolus Magnus et Leo papa' und der Papstbesuch in Paderborn 799* (Berlin, 2002), 269–82, at 273–4, argues that the 781 anointing did not mean that Pippin 'the Hunchback' had certainly been removed from the succession by this point. For the varying attempts to explain the naming of a second son as Pippin in 781: Courtney M. Booker, 'By any other Name? Charlemagne, Nomenclature, and Performativity', in Rolf Grosse and Michel Sot, eds, *Charlemagne. Les Temps, les espaces, les hommes*, Collection Haut Moyen Âge 34 (Turnhout, 2018), 409–26, at 415–19.

[59] Carl I. Hammer, 'Christmas Day 800: Charles the Younger, Alcuin and the Frankish Royal Succession', *EHR* 127 (2012), 1–23; Nelson, 'Charlemagne – *pater optimus*?', 278–81; eadem, *King and Emperor*, 270–5, 385–6. While there is evidence that Charles

Royal anointing thus functioned as an important tool for controlling and manipulating the shape of the Carolingian family and the eventual succession to power. By the end of the eighth century this may have been its primary function in the Frankish lands. The Frankish memory of the 754 anointing ceremony preserved the idea that Stephen II had declared that the Franks could only choose anointed Carolingians as their kings henceforth;[60] regular re-enactments of the papal anointing of that year served to indicate who was a member of that chosen family of monarchs. But that function does not explain the possible anointings of Charlemagne and Carloman in 768, and of Charlemagne alone in 771. In order to explain those, we need to remember that in its early years the Carolingian dynasty was no such thing. The Carolingians were merely the greatest of the aristocratic families in the Frankish realm. They were members of the elite *gens Francorum*, the ethnically defined warrior aristocracy who were celebrated for their religious excellence in much propaganda of the early Carolingian era. A rich array of evidence survives for the intense group identity of the mid-eighth-century Frankish elite, for their self-conception not just as 'strong in arms' but also as 'immune from heresy', a Christian, an orthodox and a holy people.[61] Sanctity had become a key resource in late Merovingian elite politics, accessed via patronage of monasteries

---

received territory to rule in 789, none exists for him holding a royal title before 800: Davis, *Charlemagne's Practice*, 418.

[60] *Clausula de unctione Pippini* (MGH SRM 1.2, 16). This text describes itself as an account of the 754 anointing ceremony written down in 768, but the dating is controversial: McKitterick, 'The Illusion of Royal Power', 7–8; Alain J. Stoclet, 'La *Clausula de unctione Pippini regis*, vingt ans après', *Revue belge de philologie et d'histoire* 78 (2000), 719–71; Schneider, 'Die Königserhebung Pippins', 268–75.

[61] 'Gens Francorum inclita, auctorem Deo condita, fortis in arma, firma pace fetera, profunda in consilio, corporea nobilis, incolumna candore, forma egregia, audax, uelox et aspera, [nuper] ad catholicam fidem conuersa, emunis ab heresa': *Lex Salica*, (D) prologue (MGH LL nat. Germ. 4.2, 2). For discussion of the evidence for Frankish elite identity: Garrison, 'The Franks as the New Israel?'; Matthew Innes, '"Immune from Heresy": Defining the Boundaries of Carolingian Christianity', in Paul Fouracre and David Ganz, eds, *Frankland: The Franks and the World of the Early Middle Ages. Essays in Honour of Dame Jinty Nelson* (Manchester, 2008), 101–25; Ildar H. Garipzanov, *The Symbolic Language of Authority in the Carolingian World (c.751–877)*, Brill's Series on the Early Middle Ages 16 (Leiden, 2008), 262–71.

and family connections to saintly men and women.[62] Carolingian royal sanctification took place, consequently, against a backdrop of wider aristocratic sanctification.

It was one of Janet Nelson's great insights in the 1980s that early medieval king-making rituals were intended both to separate out the king from his subjects, and to appeal to the aristocratic consensus on which royal power depended in practice. For Nelson, anointing was part of this balancing act, but was still a somewhat foreign one, barely reflecting indigenous Frankish lay ideas.[63] But Frankish records of the 754 anointing also mention that Stephen II blessed the assembled Frankish nobles on that occasion. In other words, a confirmation of the religiously special status of the entire elite provided the setting for royal anointing.[64] The Frankish liturgy for royal anointing that existed by the end of the eighth century (incidentally, evidence that anointings were performed by clerics other than popes) shows little sophisticated clerical thought about what royal anointing meant. It is really just a cut-and-paste job, essentially replicating the liturgical prayers used for earlier oil rituals familiar to local lay audiences.[65] Consequently, Carolingian royal anointing very plausibly had its origins in Frankish lay expectations and needs.

In the first instance, anointing may have been a strategy for setting apart some (and only some) members of the Carolingian family from the rest of the Frankish elite as royal, in a manner that made sense in terms of the self-conception of the aristocracy as a whole. Over time,

[62] Paul Fouracre, 'The Origins of the Carolingian Attempt to Regulate the Cult of Saints', in James Howard-Johnston and Paul Antony Hayward, eds, *The Cult of Saints in Late Antiquity and the Early Middle Ages: Essays on the Contribution of Peter Brown* (Oxford, 1999), 143–65. For a recent re-interpretation of the late Merovingian cult of the saints and its relationship to social elites: Jamie Kreiner, *The Social Life of Hagiography in the Merovingian Kingdom*, Cambridge Studies in Medieval Life and Thought, 4th series 96 (Cambridge, 2014).

[63] Nelson, 'The Lord's Anointed', 146–7, 153–7.

[64] *Clausula de unctione Pippini* (MGH SRM 1.2, 15–16). There is also a ninth-century account of the ceremony that similarly portrays a blessing of the aristocracy: Stoclet, 'La *Clausula*', 751–2.

[65] Robert Amiet, ed., *The Benedictionals of Freising (Munich, Bayerische Staatsbibliothek, Cod. Lat. 6430)*, HBS 88 (London, 1974), 100–1; cf. Leo Cunibert Mohlberg, with Leo Eizenhöfer and Petrus Siffrin, eds, *Missale Francorum (Cod. Vat. Reg. lat. 257)*, Rerum Ecclesiasticarum Documenta Series Maior: Fontes 2 (Rome, 1957), 10; Nelson, 'The Lord's Anointed', 150; eadem, 'Inauguration Rituals', 291; Ernst Kantorowicz, *Laudes Regiae: A Study in Liturgical Acclamations and Medieval Ruler Worship* (Berkeley, CA, 1946), 55 n. 142.

with Charlemagne securely on the throne and his position increasingly accepted by a new generation of nobles, anointing seems to have become restricted to managing succession *within* the Carolingian dynasty. The utility of this function also faded with time, as, with all Hildegard's sons anointed by 800, maternal status could unproblematically become the determining factor of who would be a king and who would not. Anointing, therefore, was no longer needed to single out some of Hildegard's sons and so was no longer a noteworthy feature of the younger Carolingians' biographies, as it had ceased to be a noteworthy feature of their father's some years previously.[66] Royal anointing was next deployed in 816 when Louis the Pious sought to limit Carolingian kingship to himself and his children, in a process that excluded his nephew and other relatives.[67] This revival suggests that the dynastic meaning of anointing had impressed itself on Carolingian memories.

Conclusion

What do our two cases studies have in common? In both seventh-century Spain and eighth-century Frankia we see situations in which the distinction between a new king and the other members of the lay aristocracy was not immediately clear. There was a lack of a dynastic principle that commanded consent: this simply did not exist in the Visigothic context and had broken down in the Frankish, where a new royal dynasty was trying to establish itself. Kings in these societies were passing from one social group (the elite aristocracy) into a new status: a rite of passage was needed to mark this transition. In both cases, the lay aristocracy had a strong religious self-understanding as a Christian elite, and were frequently involved in the religious life of

[66] Much recent work has shown the importance of maternal status to dynastic thinking under the Carolingians: Janet L. Nelson, 'Bertrada', in Becher and Jarnut, eds, *Der Dynastiewechsel von 751*, 93–108; Constance Brittain Bouchard, 'The Carolingian Creation of a Model of Patrilineage', in Celia Chazelle and Felice Lifshitz, eds, *Paradigms and Methods in Early Medieval Studies* (Basingstoke, 2007), 135–51; Sara McDougall, *Royal Bastards: The Birth of Illegitimacy, 800–1230* (Oxford, 2016), 66–93.

[67] Karl Ferdinand Werner, '*Hludovicus Augustus*. Gouverner l'empire chrétien – idées et réalités', in Peter Godman and Roger Collins, eds, *Charlemagne's Heir: New Perspectives on the Reign of Louis the Pious (814–840)* (Oxford, 1990), 3–124, at 31–42. See Ermoldus Nigellus, *In honorem Hludowici*, book 2, lines 439–46 (MGH Poetae 2, 36–7), for the stress on Louis's descendants at the 816 ceremony.

the kingdom. Something more than the usual religious features of early medieval kingship was needed to set the monarch apart from his nobles, while also winning support from them by flattering their sense of 'chosenness'. Royal anointing was a rite of passage that chimed with existing elite identities, while also elevating the king.

In the Carolingian case, where the aim was to create a new royal family, the rite was used to ease the succession of the younger generation. By the ninth century, anointing's main purpose seems to have become family management for the rite's significance had changed over time. Further change helps explain why, by the middle of the ninth century, royal anointing had become a much more clerical rite. A sea change in the self-perception of the Frankish episcopate around the 820s led to the emergence of bishops willing and able, as Nelson skilfully detailed, to shape the liturgy and ideology of anointing.[68] But they modified an existing Christian rite, one whose origins had probably been driven more by the laypeople who received and beheld it than by the clerics who performed it.

[68] Steffen Patzold, *Episcopus. Wissen über Bischöfe im Frankenreich des späten 8. bis frühen 10. Jahrhunderts*, Mittelalter-Forschungen 25 (Ostfildern, 2008) is essential on the changing understanding of bishops in the Carolingian world.

Orthodoxy and Authority: Rites of Passage in the *Vita Wilfridi* and the *Vitae Cuthberti*

Calum Platts*
Colchester

The seventh-century Easter controversy raised questions of orthodoxy and the consequent authority of the clergy to minister rites. References to rites of passage are present in three of the most important sources written in early eighth-century Northumbria: the Vita Wilfridi *and the* Vitae Cuthberti. *This article uses rites of passage to examine two debates, concerning Bishop Wilfrid's continental credentials and the relationship between the* Vita Wilfridi *and the* Vitae Cuthberti. *How the three authors use these important religious moments gives insight into the saintly image they wished to portray. The article argues that rites of passage in the* Vita Wilfridi *are designed to prove Wilfrid's continental (and thus orthodox) credentials but also show the extent to which this is a constructed image. In addition, it suggests that the rewriting of the first* Vita Cuthberti *was prompted by questions of orthodoxy raised in the* Vita Wilfridi *and subsequently weaponized in the febrile atmosphere of early eighth-century Northumbria.*

> Now there are here in Britain many bishops for whom it is not for me to criticize, but I know for a fact they are Quartodecimans like the Britons and Scots; by them were ordained men whom the Apostolic See does not receive into communion.[1]

Such was the reasoning behind Wilfrid's request to be sent to Francia for consecration. Much of Wilfrid's career is defined by the Easter controversy, the debate concerning which method of calculating Easter should be followed and of which the charge of

* 11 West Lodge Rd, Colchester, CO3 3NL. E-mail: chfp3@cantab.ac.uk.

[1] 'Sunt enim hic in Britannia multi episcopi quorum nullum meum est accusare, quamvis veraciter sciam quod quattuordecimanni sunt ut Brittones et Scotti; ab illis sunt ordinati, quos nec apostolica sedes in communionem recipit': Stephen, *Vita Wilfridi* [hereafter: *VW*] 11 (*The Life of Bishop Wilfrid*, ed. Bertram Colgrave [Cambridge, 1927], 24).

Studies in Church History 59 (2023), 48–72
doi: 10.1017/stc.2023.24

Quartodecimanism was a significant and emotive part. The Irish used an eighty-four-year cycle to calculate the date of Easter, known as the *Latercus*, while Wilfrid championed the Dionysiac method used in Rome.[2] A third set of tables, drawn up by Victorius of Aquitaine, was also circulating.[3] In Northumbria, the Ionan mission centred on Lindisfarne followed the *Latercus*, which was erroneously deemed to adhere to the Quartodeciman heresy.[4] Ultimately, the Synod of Whitby (664) resolved the matter in Rome's favour.[5] The significance of the epigraph for a discussion of rites of passage is that the final ritual step of Wilfrid's ecclesiastical career, his consecration as bishop, was intimately linked to a rejection of Northumbria's Ionan heritage.

Such an attitude was not limited to Wilfrid and his supporters. The *Penitentials of Theodore* makes it clear that when Theodore, bishop of Canterbury (669–90), arrived from Rome in 669, he regarded the orders of those associated with the *Latercus* as invalid. His initial view was that those who had been ordained by heretics were to be reordained; he moderated this position later, but nonetheless felt that their orders needed to be completed by a catholic bishop.[6] One of the fault lines in the Northumbrian church in the wake of the Synod of Whitby was consequently centred on the legitimacy of the rite of ordination. The ramifications of such a debate are difficult to overstate. The authority of priests to minister sacraments and rites had enormous implications for the quality of pastoral care, while repudiating the authority of specific bishops to ordain legitimate clergy could destroy the Northumbrian church.[7] It is no wonder

[2] *VW* 10 (*Life*, ed. Colgrave, 20–2); Bede, *Historia Ecclesiastica gentis Anglorum* [hereafter: *HE*] 3.24 (*Bede's Ecclesiastical History*, ed. Bertram Colgrave and Roger Mynors [Oxford, 1969], 294–308).

[3] Erin Dailey, 'To choose one Easter from three: Oswiu's Decision and the Northumbrian Synod of AD 664', *Peritia* 26 (2015), 47–64, at 49–56.

[4] Clare Stancliffe, *Bede, Wilfrid and the Irish*, Jarrow Lecture 46 (Jarrow, 2003), 4–5; Bede, *The Reckoning of Time*, ed. Faith Wallis, TTH (Liverpool, 1988), xxxv–xxxvi, lxi.

[5] *VW* 10 (*Life*, ed. Colgrave, 22).

[6] Arthur Haddan and William Stubbs, ed., *Councils and Ecclesiastical Documents relating to Great Britain and Ireland*, 3 vols (Oxford, 1869–78), 3: 180–2, cf. 3: 197; Stancliffe, *Bede*, 11–17. The use of 'catholic' here is in reference to an orthodox bishop who celebrates the correct date of Easter.

[7] Julia Barrow, 'Grades of Ordination and Clerical Careers, *c*.900–*c*.1200', *Anglo-Norman Studies* 30 (2008), 41–61, at 41; Dailey, 'One Easter', 62; Marilyn Dunn, *The Christianization of the Anglo-Saxons*, c.*597*–c.*700* (London, 2009), 116–19.

that Bede observed that believers were 'fearing lest, in receiving the word of Christianity, they were running or had run in vain'.[8]

Wilfrid's life was recorded both in Bede's *Historia Ecclesiastica* (*HE*) and in Stephen of Ripon's *Vita Wilfridi* (*VW*).[9] Both authors knew Wilfrid, and Stephen probably wrote within four years of Wilfrid's death and was close to his bishop, possibly accompanying him on his final appeal to Rome.[10] Stephen's narrative is far more detailed than Bede's and, while nakedly partisan, does not obscure points of conflict.[11] It is easy to assume that Stephen presents a more straightforward account of Wilfrid's life. However, William Foley observed that Stephen was writing in a model derived from St Augustine of Hippo: Stephen emphasized or embellished aspects of Wilfrid's life in order to provide a more edifying account.[12] On Wilfrid's consecration, Stephen weaponized his account to dismiss the earlier Irish missionaries in Northumbria as heretics, allowing his hero to bring true orthodox Christianity to the Northumbrians. Overall, the rites which mark out Wilfrid's passage through the Christian faith and Church are prominent in Stephen's text, covering Wilfrid's birth, his possible confirmation, his tonsuring, his abbatial ordination, his priestly ordination, his episcopal consecration and his death and the translation of his relics. Stephen also describes Wilfrid performing rites of passage as a bishop: baptizing, confirming and ordaining in his Northumbrian diocese and further afield. Given the nature and function of the text, these apical moments may have been moulded to Stephen's agenda and so are worthy of study.

[8] 'Timentium ne forte accepto Christianitatis vocabulo in vacuum currerent aut cucurrissent': *HE* 3.25 (*Ecclesiastical History*, ed. Colgrave and Mynors, 296).

[9] *HE* 5.19 (*Ecclesiastical History*, ed. Colgrave and Mynors, 516–30); *VW*. Stephen identified himself and his rank as a priest in the preface to his work and explained that he wrote at the request of his abbot, Tatberht of Ripon, and the bishop of Hexham, Acca. Stephen's use of the first person at points in the text suggests that he may have witnessed some of the events he described.

[10] *HE* 4.19 (*Ecclesiastical History*, ed. Colgrave and Mynors, 390–2); *VW* 50 (*Life*, ed. Colgrave, 102); David Kirby, 'Bede, Eddius Stephanus and the "Life of Wilfrid"', *EHR* 98 (1983), 101–14, at 103–4; Walter Goffart, *The Narrators of Barbarian History* (Princeton, NJ, 1988), 282–3.

[11] Alan Thacker, 'Wilfrid: His Cult and his Biographer', in Nicholas Higham, ed., *Wilfrid: Abbot, Bishop, Saint* (Donnington, 2013), 1–16, at 3–4; David H. Farmer, 'Saint Wilfrid', in David Kirby, ed., *Saint Wilfrid at Hexham* (Newcastle, 1974), 34–59, at 36–8.

[12] William Foley, *Images of Sanctity in Eddius Stephanus'* Life of Bishop Wilfrid (Lampeter, 1992), 12–14.

Furthermore, the *VW* is not divorced from the other hagiography of early eighth-century Northumbria, above all the *Vitae Cuthberti.*[13] As such, it is worth extending the discussion into how the *VW* intersects with the two *Vitae Cuthberti*, one written by an anonymous author at Lindisfarne (*VA*) before the *VW* *c.*698–705, the second written afterwards by Bede (*VP*) *c.*720–2.[14] Stephen is infamous for appropriating passages from the *VA*, including the anonymous author's claim that Cuthbert had received the Petrine tonsure, an implausible suggestion for pre-Whitby Northumbria, which may have prompted Lindisfarne to commission Bede's version.[15] In questions of orthodoxy, referencing the Petrine tonsure allowed Stephen to undermine Cuthbert, drawing attention to Cuthbert's Ionan connections.[16] Thus, given the link between Wilfrid's episcopal consecration and orthodoxy, rites of passage provide another avenue to approach the dialogue between the *VW*, *VA* and *VP*.

There are, therefore, three distinct sections to this argument. The first concerns Wilfrid's own rites of passage. This may also be organized into three discrete points. Firstly, the rites proving Wilfrid's continental credentials will be considered: Wilfrid's possible confirmation, his tonsuring and his episcopal consecration. Secondly, those which reveal the constructed quality of Stephen's account are analysed: Wilfrid's birth and the translation of his relics. Thirdly, Wilfrid's ordination as a priest and as an abbot provide the opportunity to access a more nuanced image of the bishop. The second section concerns Wilfrid's carrying out of rites of passage. In the third section the use of rites of passage in the *VA* and *VP* will be analysed

[13] The Whitby *Life of Saint Gregory* may react to Wilfridian themes but shows little interest in rites of passage. Episcopal consecration is mentioned in Canterbury but is not extended to Paulinus, as one might expect if there was a desire to prove an earlier Northumbrian Christian history deriving from Gregory the Great: Anon., *Vita Sancti Gregorii* 11 (*The Earliest Life of Gregory the Great*, ed. Bertram Colgrave, 2nd edn [Cambridge, 1985], 93); cf. Goffart, *Narrators*, 264–7.

[14] Goffart, *Narrators*, 256–7; Alan Thacker, 'Shaping the Saint: Rewriting Tradition in the Early *Lives* of St Cuthbert', in Roy Flechner and Máire Ní Mhaonaigh, eds, *The Introduction of Christianity into the Early Medieval Insular World: Converting the Isles I* (Turnhout, 2016), 399–429, at 404; Clare Stancliffe, 'Disputed Episcopacy: Bede, Acca and the Relationship between Stephen's *Life of Wilfrid* and the early Prose Lives of St Cuthbert', *Anglo-Saxon England* 41 (2012), 7–39, at 10.

[15] Anon., *Vita Cuthberti* [hereafter: *VA*] 1.2, 2.2 (*Two Lives of Saint Cuthbert*, ed. Bertram Colgrave [London, 1940], 62–4, 76); cf. *VW*, Preface 6 (*Life*, ed. Colgrave, 2, 14).

[16] Stancliffe, 'Episcopacy', 15, 19.

with reference to how this relates to themes present in the *VW*. In so doing, it may be possible to unpick Stephen's hagiographic presentation and uncover a more nuanced image of Wilfrid, also providing greater insight into the disputes within the early eighth-century Northumbrian church.

Historiography

There are two particular threads to this discussion, Wilfrid's relationship with the Ionan heritage of the Northumbrian church and the interplay between the texts written in the explosion of literature in Northumbria in the first three decades of the eighth century; both have received significant scholarly attention. Wilfrid is typically portrayed as divorced from the Northumbrian church before the Synod of Whitby. His background lay in the education he received within the Frankish and Roman churches. His career was then dominated by his appeals to the papacy against the authority of the archbishops of Canterbury, Theodore (669–90) and Berhtwold (692–731), and the kings of Northumbria, Ecgfrith (670–85) and Aldfrith (*c.*686–705).[17] It is little wonder that Alan Thacker summed Wilfrid up as 'pugnaciously pro-Roman'.[18]

The most significant shift in determining Wilfrid's ecclesiastical identity concerns his attitude towards the Irish. Clare Stancliffe has observed that Wilfrid was not anti-Irish and in fact had positive relations with individuals and areas within Ireland. His antipathy was motivated by opposition to the Quartodeciman heresy perceived to be rampant within the Ionan confederation.[19] Theology, not race, dictated Wilfrid's hostility towards Lindisfarne and the heirs of the Ionan mission, although Stancliffe still keeps Wilfrid firmly separate from Irish Christian culture.

[17] Henry Mayr-Harting, *The Coming of Christianity to Anglo-Saxon England*, 3rd edn (London, 1991), 129–47; Farmer, 'Wilfrid', 40–3; Paul Fouracre, 'Wilfrid and the Continent', in Higham, ed., *Wilfrid*, 186–99; Ian Wood, 'The Continental Journeys of Wilfrid and Biscop', ibid. 200–11; Éamonn Ó Carragáin and Alan Thacker, 'Wilfrid in Rome', ibid. 212–30; Richard Bailey, 'St Wilfrid: A European Anglo-Saxon', ibid. 112–23; Jesse Billet, 'Wilfrid and Music', ibid. 163–85, at 168–76; Foley, *Sanctity*, 71–105; Nicholas Brooks, *The Early History of the Church of Canterbury* (London, 1984), 74, 79.

[18] Alan Thacker, 'England in the Seventh Century', in Paul Fouracre, ed., *The New Cambridge Medieval History*, 1: c.*700*–c.*900* (Cambridge, 2000), 462–85, at 481.

[19] Stancliffe, *Bede*, 2–4; cf. Thomas Charles-Edwards, *Early Christian Ireland* (Cambridge, 2000), 320–1.

Two scholars, Henry Mayr-Harting and Erin Dailey, have argued against such a complete divorce. Dailey has suggested that Wilfrid had come into contact with Columbanian monasticism in Francia and so was sufficiently 'Celtic' for Oswiu to side with him at the Synod of Whitby without creating a fatal split in the Northumbrian church.[20] Mayr-Harting has gone further, locating evidence of Irish influence upon Wilfrid's spirituality and Stephen's hagiography.[21] While not finding much support, their arguments are useful reminders that the dominance of Roman Christianity in the *VW* may be designed to further Stephen's agenda and may not be the full picture.

The dialogue in which the *VA* and the *VW* engage was noted by the texts' modern editor, Bertram Colgrave, although he did not suggest any link between Stephen's borrowings and Bede's rewriting.[22] The theory of tension in the Northumbrian church between pro- and anti-Wilfridians first emerged with David Kirby in 1983.[23] Towards the end of the decade, both Walter Goffart and Alan Thacker developed Kirby's arguments and suggested that debate with Wilfridians provoked the recasting of Cuthbert's life by Bede.[24] Other explanations for the rewriting have been proposed but Alan Thacker in particular has kept the question of Wilfrid at the forefront of the historiography.[25] However, Stancliffe again has suggested a modification, observing that there is a gap of several years between the *VW* and *VP*; the latter is hardly an immediate reaction to the former. Instead, she moots that Acca

[20] Erin Dailey, 'Reappraising the Synod of Whitby', *History Studies* 10 (2009), 31–44, at 38–9.

[21] Mayr-Harting, *Coming*, 139–44.

[22] *Life*, ed. Colgrave, 150.

[23] Kirby, 'Stephanus', 106–10; idem, 'The Genesis of a Cult: Cuthbert of Farne and Ecclesiastical Politics in Northumbria in the Late Seventh and Early Eighth Centuries', *JEH* 46 (1995), 383–97, at 396–7.

[24] Goffart, *Narrators*, 283–5; Alan Thacker, 'Lindisfarne and the Origins of the Cult of St Cuthbert', in Gerald Bonner, David Rollason and Clare Stancliffe, eds, *St Cuthbert, his Cult and his Community to AD 1200* (Woodbridge, 1989), 103–22, at 117–22.

[25] See Walter Berschin, '*Opus deliberatum ac perfectum*: Why did the Venerable Bede write a Second Prose Life of St Cuthbert?', in Bonner, Rollason and Stancliffe, eds, *St Cuthbert*, 95–102, at 84–5; William Foley, 'Suffering and Sanctity in Bede's Prose Life of St Cuthbert', *Journal of Theological Studies* 50 (1999), 102–15; Catherine Cubitt, 'Memory and Narrative in the Cult of early Anglo-Saxon Saints', in Yitzhak Hen and Matthew Innes, eds, *The Uses of the Past in the Early Middle Ages* (Cambridge, 2000), 29–66, at 39–46; cf. Thacker, 'Cult', 11–16; idem, 'Bede and History', in Scott DeGregorio, ed., *The Cambridge Companion to Bede* (Cambridge, 2010), 170–89, at 185–6; idem, 'Lindisfarne', 418–25.

(710–31), Wilfrid's successor as bishop of Hexham, may have sought to suppress the see of Lindisfarne, a crisis which prompted the need for the new life of Lindisfarne's great saint addressing criticisms based upon Cuthbert's suitability as a bishop and his attempts to avoid episcopal office.[26] The theme of 'rites of passage' provides an excellent new means to test both aspects of the historiography, providing new insights into Stephen's hagiographic purposes and the length of the shadow Wilfrid and his hagiographer cast upon Northumbrian literature.

Wilfrid's Rites of Passage (1): Proving Continental Credentials

Stephen delayed describing Wilfrid's first formal engagement with Christian ritual. Only in the fifth chapter does the reader find Wilfrid kneeling before the pope, being prayed over by him and receiving his blessing.[27] Stephen's description is not explicit, but Wilfrid conceivably received the rite of confirmation during his first visit to Rome. The rite of confirmation involved anointing and the laying on of hands by a bishop, thereby confirming the candidate's baptism.[28] The obvious problem with Stephen's account is the lack of reference to oil. However, since Stephen later describes Wilfrid confirming simply by 'the laying on of hands',[29] Stephen may simply have regarded the imposition of hands as more important than anointing and so focused on it in his account. The clinching evidence comes from the *VA*, which describes Cuthbert anointing individuals and placing his hands above their heads, a clear description of confirmation, with phrasing which matches that of Stephen.[30] Stephen's account reads *ponens manum suam benedictam super caput eius*,[31] while the anonymous author described Cuthbert as confirming with *manum ponens super capita singulorum*.[32] This is fairly compelling evidence that the two authors were describing the same

[26] Cubitt, 'Episcopacy', 7–39, especially 11–12, 24–32.
[27] *VW* 5 (*Life*, ed. Colgrave, 12).
[28] H. Banting, 'Imposition of Hands in Confirmation: A Medieval Problem', *JEH* 7 (1956), 147–59, at 150–2.
[29] 'Cum manus impositione': *VW* 18 (*Life*, ed. Colgrave, 38).
[30] Joseph Lynch, *Christianizing Kinship: Ritual Sponsorship in Anglo-Saxon England* (Ithaca, NY, 1998), 102.
[31] 'He placed his blessed hand on [Wilfrid's] head': *VW* 5 (*Life*, ed. Colgrave, 12).
[32] 'He placed his hand on the head of each of them': *VA* 4.5 (*Two Lives*, ed. Colgrave, 116).

ceremony. Certainly, the distinction between the pope's prayers and his blessing indicates that more was going on in Wilfrid's meeting with the pope than a simple papal blessing, and confirmation is a logical alternative.

This importance of this encounter is that it is a significant moment in Wilfrid's Christian journey. It marks the first time Stephen describes Wilfrid engaging with any form of Christian ritual. Wilfrid spent his early life in Northumbria as it was being evangelized by Irish missionaries, presumably receiving baptism from their hands. He ended up in the monastery of Lindisfarne, serving Cudda, a royal retainer who had retired there.[33] Stephen stresses that Wilfrid remained 'untonsured', but also that he chose of his own volition to live the monastic life as fully as possible.[34] As Stephen presents it, Wilfrid therefore lacked formal ties to the pre-Whitby Northumbrian church: his own piety drove him to live a holy life. What is curious is that this absence of engagement continues when Wilfrid appears in other Christian centres on his pilgrimage to Rome, including Canterbury (where once again Wilfrid's personal piety is stressed) and, perhaps surprisingly, Lyons.[35] Bearing in mind Foley's comments that Stephen's Augustinian model prompted him to create an edifying rather than historical account, this shows the extent to which this is a constructed image.[36] It is telling that Wilfrid's first narrative engagement with Christian rites appears in Rome. We may assume that Wilfrid was subject to, and engaged with, other rites during his time at Lindisfarne and Canterbury and on his journey through Francia and Italy to Rome. Most notably, he was presumably baptized by Irish missionaries. Nevertheless, as far as Stephen was concerned, Wilfrid's formal engagement with the Christian church began in Rome, kneeling before the pope. This is certainly a powerful image and arguably one that is designed to place Wilfrid beyond reproach, something that would be undermined by reference to his baptism by Quartodecimans. In short, Wilfrid's Christian journey began in the centre of orthodoxy and authority: Rome.

[33] *VW* 2 (*Life*, ed. Colgrave, 6).
[34] 'Laicus capite': ibid.
[35] *VW* 3–4 (*Life*, ed. Colgrave, 8–10).
[36] Foley, *Images*, 12–14.

Stephen then hastens on, describing Wilfrid's tonsuring by Aunemundus of Lyons in the subsequent chapter.[37] This was presumably the occasion of Wilfrid's reception as either a monk or a cleric.[38] The significance of this passage lies not so much in the ritual progression of Wilfrid's career, as in the parallels that may be drawn with his papal confirmation. In Rome, Wilfrid's encounter with the pope had been preceded by his education in the four gospels, *computus* and other matters of ecclesiastical discipline.[39] In Lyons, Stephen is frustratingly vague, simply observing that Wilfrid spent time learning 'from the most learned teachers'.[40] Unlike his description of Rome, where Wilfrid was clearly confirmed after his studies with Boniface, Stephen is not specific about the timing of Wilfrid's studies and his tonsuring in Lyons. However, the impression is that after three years studying, Wilfrid received the tonsure from Aunemundus. Consequently, Wilfrid's learning is stressed by Stephen before he describes Wilfrid's first formal engagement with Christianity and then his entry into the ecclesiastical hierarchy. Significantly, in both instances Stephen associates Wilfrid with famous Christian centres: Rome and Lyons.[41]

Wilfrid's episcopal consecration makes Stephen's agenda in describing these rites of passage more comprehensible. It is the final step of Wilfrid's ecclesiastical career and, as the introduction makes

[37] *VW* 6 (*Life*, ed. Colgrave, 14).

[38] On why the latter may be more likely, see Stancliffe, 'Episcopacy', 30 n. 108; Catherine Cubitt, 'The Clergy in Early Anglo-Saxon England', *HR* 78 (2005), 273–87, at 277; cf. *Life*, ed. Colgrave, 154.

[39] *VW* 3 (*Life*, ed. Colgrave, 12).

[40] 'A doctoribus valde eruditis': ibid.

[41] Lyon: Elias Lowe, *Codices lugdunenses antiquissimi. Le Scriptorium de Lyon, la plus ancienne école calligraphique de France* (Lyons, 1924); Rosamond McKitterick, 'The Scriptoria of Merovingian Gaul: A Survey of the Evidence', in Howard Clarke and Mary Brennan, eds, *Columbanus and Merovingian Monasticism* (Oxford, 1981), 173–207, at 182; Hubert Mordek, *Kirchenrecht und Reform im Frankenreich* (Sigmaringen, 1975), 79–82. Rome: Farmer, 'Wilfrid', 41; Ó Carragáin and Thacker, 'Rome', 218–22; Thomas F. X. Noble, 'Rome in the Seventh Century', in Michael Lapidge, ed., *Archbishop Theodore: Commemorative Studies on his Life and Influence* (Cambridge, 1995), 68–87, at 83–6; Éamonn Ó Carragáin, 'The Periphery rethinks the Centre: Inculturation, "Roman" Liturgy and the Ruthwell Cross', in Claudia Bolgia, John Osborne and Rosamond McKitterick, eds, *Rome across Time and Space: Cultural Transmission and the Exchange of Ideas,* c.*500–1400* (Cambridge, 2011), 63–83, at 63–6; Michael Reeve, 'Rome, Reservoir of Ancient Texts?', in Bolgia, Osborne and McKitterick, eds, *Rome across Time and Space*, 52–60, at 52.

clear, is intimately linked to a rejection of Northumbria's Ionan heritage. Arguably, however, it goes further. Stephen's comment that Rome rejected 'those who have fellowship with schismatics'[42] is intriguing. Naturally, Wilfrid could not be consecrated by supposed Quartodecimans, but Stephen implies that the orders of the other bishops available to Wilfrid were rendered invalid by their association with the Ionan mission. As the British and Ionan churches both adhered to the *Latercus*, this concern with fellowship can only plausibly refer to the other bishops of the English church, Wine of London (*fl.* 660–72), Berhtgisl of East Anglia (*c.*652–69) and, if he was still alive, Deusdedit of Canterbury (655–64). With backgrounds in Francia and the Roman mission at Canterbury respectively, none followed the eighty-four-year cycle of calculating Easter.[43] Nevertheless, both Wine personally and the Roman mission centred on Canterbury in general seem to have been comfortable working alongside members of the 'schismatic' British and Ionan churches. Wine, for example, was willing to consecrate Chad with the support of two British bishops.[44] Canterbury's attitude is less clear cut. However, Bede notes that Deusdedit's predecessor, Honorius (*c.*627×31–53) honoured Aidan (*c.*635–51), the leader of the Ionan mission in Northumbria and founder of Lindisfarne.[45] This attitude appears to have been generally held within the Roman mission; Felix of East Anglia (*c.*630–47), a Burgundian and evangelizing East Anglia at the behest of Honorius, shared his positive opinion of Aidan.[46] This might also explain why Wilfrid wrote off Berhtgisl.[47] Furthermore, a statement Wilfrid made at the Synod of Austerfeld (*c.*703) suggests that he detected a change in Canterbury's attitude towards the Easter controversy. He observed that he was the first 'after the death of the first elders, who were sent by St Gregory to root out the poisonous weeds of the Scots'.[48] The Roman mission's initial orthodox zeal had lapsed, apparently to the point that they

[42] 'Eos qui scismaticis consentiunt': *VW* 12 (*Life*, ed. Colgrave, 24).
[43] *HE* 3.7, 20 (*Ecclesiastical History*, ed. Colgrave and Mynors, 234, 278).
[44] *HE* 3.28 (*Ecclesiastical History*, ed. Colgrave and Mynors, 316).
[45] *HE* 3.25 (*Ecclesiastical History*, ed. Colgrave and Mynors, 296).
[46] *HE* 2.15, 3.25 (*Ecclesiastical History*, ed. Colgrave and Mynors, 190, 296).
[47] *Life*, ed. Colgrave, 159.
[48] 'Post obitum primorum procerum, a sancto Gregorio directorum, Scotticae virulenta plantationis germina eradicarem': *VW* 47 (*Life*, ed. Colgrave, 98).

honoured a schismatic. Wilfrid could not countenance this and so had to seek episcopal consecration elsewhere.

Stephen draws a deliberate contrast between the flawed nature of the bishops available to Wilfrid and the 'catholic' nature of the Frankish bishops, a word used twice within three sentences.[49] He also introduces Agilbert as one of Wilfrid's twelve consecrators, whose orthodox credentials had already been established by his presence on the Roman or Dionysiac side at the Synod of Whitby.[50] As a result, Stephen appears to be using Wilfrid's consecration to denigrate earlier English Christian tradition, clearing the stage for Wilfrid, with his true orthodoxy and consequent authority, to take centre stage in establishing the true faith amongst them. With this in mind, Stephen's stress upon Wilfrid's education and confirmation in the Roman church and then his education and tonsuring in the Frankish church acquires new significance. Stephen took care to prove that Wilfrid's continental credentials took precedence over any links Wilfrid had with Lindisfarne and Canterbury, which Stephen presents as more informal. At a time when a lack of orthodoxy could remove all ecclesiastical authority from an individual, it was imperative to render Wilfrid unimpeachable.

Wilfrid's Rites of Passage (2): Identifying a Constructed Image

Stephen therefore sought to use rites of passage to emphasize Wilfrid's orthodoxy, separating him from the English church and the confusion created by the Easter controversy and the outcome of the Synod of Whitby. Stephen's description of Wilfrid's birth and the ceremony surrounding the translation of Wilfrid's body to the abbey church of Ripon upon his death both contain details which hint that such an image is Stephen's own construction. Neither are conventionally considered to be 'rites', akin to confirmation or baptism. However, the translation of Wilfrid's body seems to have been the crucial act in establishing his sainthood and so is a ritual steeped in significance. Likewise, Stephen presents Wilfrid's birth as a momentous spiritual occasion.

[49] *VW* 12 (*Life*, ed. Colgrave, 26).

[50] *VW* 10 (*Life*, ed. Colgrave, 20); *HE* 3.25 (*Ecclesiastical History*, ed. Colgrave and Mynors, 298–300); Dailey, 'One Easter', 60–1.

Stephen described the moment of Wilfrid's birth as being accompanied by flames, akin to the burning bush in Exodus 3. The interpretation Stephen placed upon it was as follows: 'Now, brethren, we frequently read that the Holy Spirit has appeared in the form of fire ... This light the Lord commanded to be set, not under a bushel, but on a candlestick and through our blessed bishop it shone openly upon almost all the churches of Britain'.[51] Stephen wished to present Wilfrid's birth as an event divinely marked out as significant, heralding the appearance of the man who would reform the churches of Britain with his knowledge of the Dionysiac Easter. What is noteworthy is the date of Wilfrid's birth, traditionally placed in 634.[52] Stancliffe has used calendar evidence to place Wilfrid's death in 710.[53] Stephen notes that Wilfrid was in his seventy-sixth year when he died; put in more straightforward fashion he was seventy-five.[54] As such, the year of his birth is more likely to be 635. Immo Warntjes has observed that the majority of the evidence points to Lindisfarne's foundation in 635.[55] The Irish annals and the Lindisfarne annals both give 635 as the date of foundation, while Bede is ambiguous, providing relative dates which suggest either 634 or 635.[56] This elision of dates is significant in light of Stephen's comments about the churches of Britain. Wilfrid's birth

[51] 'Nos autem fratres, frequenter legimus spiritum sanctum in igne apparuisse ... quod lumen non sub modio sed super candelabrum Dominus poni iussit. Et hoc per beatum pontificem nostrum omnibus paene Brittanniae ecclesiis palam effulsit': *VW* 1 (*Life*, ed. Colgrave, 4).

[52] Catherine Cubitt, 'Appendix 2: The Chronology of Stephen's *Life of Wilfrid*', in Higham, ed., *Wilfrid*, 334–47, at 342; Farmer, 'Wilfrid', 40; Alan Thacker, 'St Wilfrid', in Michael Lapidge et al., eds, *The Wiley-Blackwell Encyclopedia of Anglo-Saxon England*, 2nd edn (Chichester, 2014), 495–6, at 495; but contrast Mayr-Harting, *Coming*, 107.

[53] Clare Stancliffe, 'Dating Wilfrid's Death and Stephen's *Life*', in Higham, ed., *Wilfrid*, 17–26, at 17–22.

[54] *VW* 66 (*Life*, ed. Colgrave, 142).

[55] Immo Warntjes, 'Victorius vs Dionysius: The Irish Easter Controversy of AD 689', in Pádraic Moran and Immo Warntjes, eds, *Early Medieval Ireland and Europe: Chronology, Contacts and Scholarship. A Festschrift for Dáibhí Ó Cróinín* (Turnhout, 2015), 33–98, at 43 n. 36.

[56] *The Annals of Ulster to AD 1131*, ed. Seán Mac Airt and Gearoid Mac Niocaill (Dublin, 1983), *s.a.* 632; *The Annals of Tigernach*, ed. Whitley Stokes, *Revue Celtique* 16–18 (1895–7), *s.a.* 635; *HE* 3.17 (*Ecclesiastical History*, ed. Colgrave and Mynors, 262–4); Wilhelm Levison, 'Die Annales "Lindisfarnensis et Dunelmenses" kritisch untersucht und neu herausgegeben', *Deutsches Archiv für Erforschung des Mittelalters* 17 (1961), 447–506, at 480, 492.

is arguably portentous not simply because Stephen sought to give his hero a grand entrance, but because Stephen implied that the saviour of the Northumbrian church came into the world at the same time as its corruptor.

This gives a hint at the constructed nature of Wilfrid's image in the *VW*, which is furthered by the translation of Wilfrid's body and the establishment of his saintly cult.[57] Alan Thacker has discussed the origins of this ritual, involving the washing of a body and removal of it into the church itself for burial. It certainly derived from the Frankish church, with Eligius, bishop of Noyon, probably the central figure, who developed the rite in the 640s.[58] Thacker has commented that 'almost certainly, those who devised Wilfrid's funeral ceremonies had Gaulish episcopal translations in mind'.[59] The association is certainly Frankish but the context is another matter. The Wilfridians did not introduce the practice into the English church. Two individuals were translated before Wilfrid: Æthelthryth of Ely (*c*.695) and Cuthbert of Lindisfarne (*c*.698).[60] Furthermore, Bede notes Wilfrid's presence at Æthelthyrth's translation.[61] This means that when Wilfrid's followers removed his body for burial in Ripon, they may have had an English, rather than a Frankish, exemplar. It is a compelling hint that Wilfrid and his followers may not have been as sundered from the rest of the English church as Stephen's account may lead the reader to believe.

Wilfrid's Rites of Passage (3): Nuancing Wilfrid's Background

Wilfrid's birth and translation thus give good grounds for believing that the image Stephen presented was carefully engineered to set Wilfrid up as the saviour of Northumbrian Christianity, grounding him in the indisputably orthodox Roman and Frankish churches. It is at this juncture that Wilfrid's priestly and abbatial ordinations become relevant, as they provide a means of picking apart Stephen's carefully crafted image.

[57] *VW* 66 (*Life*, ed. Colgrave, 142).
[58] Alan Thacker, 'The Making of a Local Saint', in idem and Richard Sharpe, eds, *Local Saints and Local Churches in the Early Medieval West* (Oxford, 2002), 45–73, at 54–62.
[59] Ibid. 62.
[60] Bede, *Vita Cuthberti* [hereafter: *VP*] 42 (*Two Lives*, ed. Colgrave, 290–4); *VA* 4.14 (*Two Lives*, ed. Colgrave, 130–2); *HE* 4.19, 30 (*Ecclesiastical History*, ed. Colgrave and Mynors, 392–6, 442–4).
[61] *HE* 4.19 (*Ecclesiastical History*, ed. Colgrave and Mynors, 394).

Wilfrid's priestly ordination by Agilbert is described in great detail by Stephen, not least to predict Wilfrid's subsequent episcopal consecration.[62] The point to focus on is how Stephen presents Agilbert; he is described simply as a 'foreign bishop'.[63] Agilbert's background is contextualized a few chapters later, when he participates in Wilfrid's episcopal consecration in Francia.[64] Reading the *VW*, one would assume that Agilbert was a random orthodox Frankish bishop who had made his way to Northumbria for some reason. Fortunately, Bede provides a fuller description of Agilbert's career, specifying his time in Wessex and (more intriguingly) that Agilbert had received episcopal consecration in Ireland.[65] Naturally, it is necessary to be cautious about textual silences. However, the lack of any description of Agilbert's career is an interesting silence on Stephen's part.

Agilbert was clearly a significant figure in Wilfrid's life, ordaining Wilfrid priest and then bishop in quick succession.[66] Wilfrid had significant links with the kingdom of Wessex, forming friendships with at least two of its kings, including Cenwalh, whose bishop Agilbert was, and who commended Wilfrid to Alhfrith, sub-king of Deira.[67] During his first exile, Wilfrid came to associate himself with Cædwalla, receiving significant grants of land from him.[68] With these links, can Stephen plausibly be thought to have been ignorant of Agilbert's West Saxon career? Wilfrid's objections to episcopal consecration in Britain are worth revisiting because it is necessary to stress that the Quartodecimans were not the only people causing Wilfrid anxiety. Those who had fellowship with schismatics were not received into communion by the papacy.[69] This aspect of the objection must refer to any surviving bishops of the English church, such as Wine, who was comfortable to consecrate Chad to Northumbria with two

62 *VW* 9 (*Life*, ed. Colgrave, 18).
63 'Episcopus transmarinus': ibid.
64 *VW* 12 (*Life*, ed. Colgrave, 26).
65 *HE* 3.7 (*Ecclesiastical History*, ed. Colgrave and Mynors, 234).
66 Wood, 'Journeys', 202; Fouracre, 'Continent', 191–4.
67 *VW* 7 (*Life*, ed. Colgrave, 15–16).
68 Ibid. 42 (*Life*, ed. Colgrave, 84); *HE* 4.16 (*Ecclesiastical History*, ed. Colgrave and Mynors, 382; P. H. Sawyer, *Anglo-Saxon Charters: An Annotated List and Bibliography* (London, 1986), no. 235 (printed in *Cartularium Saxonicum*, ed. W. de Gray Birch, 3 vols [London, 1883–94], no. 72); Richard Sharpe, 'King Ceadwalla and Bishop Wilfrid', in Scott DeGregorio and Paul Kershaw, eds, *Cities, Saints and Communities in Early Medieval Europe* (Turnhout, 2020), 195–222.
69 *VW* 12 (*Life*, ed. Colgrave, 24).

British bishops.[70] Stephen's silence may have been an attempt to separate Agilbert from an English church that could be considered corrupt. By stressing Agilbert's foreignness and ultimately locating him in the catholic Frankish church, the validity of Agilbert's orders could not be questioned and so, in turn, Wilfrid's orders and indeed his orthodoxy were assured. A comparison of the *VW* and *HE* often reveals discreet Bedan silences, to hide inconvenient truths that disrupted the golden age of Christianity Bede wished to portray.[71] Perhaps here the reverse is detectable; the *HE* demonstrates an uncomfortably close link between Wilfrid and the pre-Whitby English church that Stephen sought to obscure.

This is confirmed by the first ordination in the *VW*, Wilfrid's abbatial ordination. While the establishment of an abbot is not normally deemed ordination, this is the term used by Stephen.[72] It also appears in the *Penitentials of Theodore*, which discusses the ordination of an abbot in a section dedicated to ordination, including that of bishops, priests and deacons.[73] The ritual to ordain an abbot involved the bishop celebrating the eucharist, blessing the new abbot and handing him his staff and sandals.[74] The abbatial ordination follows on from a detailed description of Alhfrith's gifts to Wilfrid. Stephen notes that after giving him ten hides at *Stanforda* Alhfrith 'granted him the monastery at Ripon, together with thirty hides of land and [Wilfrid] was ordained abbot'.[75] The voice of the sentence shifts from the active when Alhfrith's gifts are discussed to the passive when Wilfrid is ordained. This suggests that this is not some form of investiture ceremony involving Alhfrith; indeed, the use of the word 'ordained' implies an ecclesiastical ceremony.[76] While the *Penitentials of Theodore* is a later document, it provides the sole insight into this ceremony and it gives the central role to a presiding

[70] *HE* 3.28 (*Ecclesiastical History*, ed. Colgrave, 316).

[71] Stancliffe, 'Episcopacy', 11; Kirby, 'Stephanus', 102; Goffart, *Narrators*, 307–24; James Campbell, 'Bede II', in idem, *Essays in Anglo-Saxon History* (London, 1986), 29–48, at 41–2.

[72] *VW* 8 (*Life*, ed. Colgrave, 16).

[73] Haddan and Stubbs, eds, *Councils*, 3: 192–3.

[74] Ibid.

[75] 'Coenobium Inhrypis cum terra XXX mansionum … concessit ei, et abbas ordinatus est': *VW* 8 (*Life*, ed. Colgrave, 16).

[76] Cf. Thomas Charles-Edwards, 'A Contract between King and People in Early Medieval Ireland? *Críth Gablach* on Kingship', *Peritia* 8 (1994), 107–19, at 109–11.

bishop.[77] Significantly, Wilfrid's abbatial ordination occurs before Agilbert comes north and there is no credible reason why Stephen would neglect to attribute this to Agilbert if he had been involved.[78] The context for Wilfrid at this point in time in Northumbria is the Ionan mission centred on Lindisfarne. The bishops in the vicinity of Ripon would have been the bishop of Lindisfarne, either Finan (d. *c.*661) or Colmán (661–4), and the bishop of Mercia, Trumhere (*c.*658–62).[79] In that case, Stephen could not identify the person who ordained Wilfrid abbot because to do so would be to ritually associate Wilfrid with someone condemned as a Quartodeciman heretic.

Thus the very questions that Wilfrid raised at the Synod of Whitby had ramifications upon how Stephen was able to develop Wilfrid's hagiography. Stephen had to manage Wilfrid's pre-Whitby career, when the majority of his rites of passage occurred, with intense care. Wilfrid's significance to the English church hinged upon his reforming zeal and rejection of the Scottish weeds, as Wilfrid expressed at the Synod of Austerfeld.[80] Any formal association with them undermined this image. Furthermore, Wilfrid's claims to have been the first since the early Gregorian mission to have eradicated the Scottish weeds are conceivably a claim to primacy in the English church. As the *Penitentials* reveals, such an association risked tainting the legitimacy of an individual's ecclesiastical rank and his consequent authority to act in that capacity.[81] For all Wilfrid's Romanizing tendencies, it is important to remember Mayr-Harting's comment that 'it is easy to underrate the influence on Wilfrid of the four happy years which he spent at Lindisfarne'.[82] Stephen provides a constructed image, not a complete one, in which Wilfrid acts within a corrupt church in need of reform.

[77] Haddan and Stubbs, eds, *Councils*, 3: 192–3. It also derives from a Roman centre, although for Irish influence upon it, see John McNeill and Helena Gamer, eds, *Medieval Handbooks of Penance* (New York, 1968), 181–2; Allen Frantzen, *The Literature of Penance in Anglo-Saxon England* (New Brunswick, NJ, 1983), 62–9; Thomas Charles-Edwards, 'The Penitential of Theodore and the *Iudicia Theodori*', in Lapidge, ed., *Theodore*, 141–74, at 143, 162–3.

[78] *VW* 8 (*Life*, ed. Colgrave, 16–18).

[79] *HE* 3.17, 24 (*Ecclesiastical History*, ed. Colgrave and Mynors, 264, 292–6); S. Keynes, 'Appendix 2', in Lapidge et al., eds, *Encyclopedia of Anglo-Saxon England*, 539–66, at 555, 565.

[80] *VW* 47 (*Life*, ed. Colgrave, 98).

[81] Haddan and Stubbs, eds, *Councils*, 3: 180–2, 197.

[82] Mayr-Harting, *Coming*, 142.

Wilfrid's Performance of Rites

It is in this light that Wilfrid's performance of rites of passage should be viewed. As a priest and then a bishop, whose career stretched across numerous kingdoms and sees, Wilfrid would have conducted a wide range of rites that marked individuals' progression through both the Christian faith and the Christian church. As a hagiography of an individual who lived in a missionary period and indeed pioneered the evangelization of two kingdoms, Sussex and Frisia, there are several references to baptism, with large numbers of converts cited.[83] Curiously, there is only a single reference to Wilfrid baptizing and confirming while he was acting as a diocesan bishop. Stephen refers in passing to Wilfrid carrying out these rites in order to set up a miracle: recalling a young boy from death.[84]

Stephen seems to have been far more interested in Wilfrid's ordinations. He stressed that Wilfrid 'ordained many priests … and not a few deacons'[85] in Kent before Theodore's arrival in 669. Likewise, when claiming that Wilfrid diligently fulfilled his episcopal duties in Northumbria, Stephen evidenced this by citing that 'in every part he ordained numbers of priests and deacons'.[86] There is also a reference to Wilfrid's episcopal duties in Mercia, presumably including ordinations, but Stephen does not make this explicit.[87] In terms of episcopal consecrations, the only one that Stephen specifically references is that of Chad, although Bede notes Wilfrid's involvement in two more.[88] The importance of these acts to Stephen is evidenced by the fact that when narrating Wilfrid's death, Stephen asked: 'who can tell how many bishops, priests and deacons he had ordained and how many churches he had dedicated during the forty-six years of his episcopate?'[89] While Stephen spoke on a local level regarding this latter

83 *VW* 26, 41 (*Life*, ed. Colgrave, 52, 82–4).

84 Ibid. 18 (*Life*, ed. Colgrave, 38–40).

85 'Presbiteros multos … et non paucos diacones ordinavit': ibid. 14 (*Life*, ed. Colgrave, 30).

86 'In omnibus locis presbiteros et diacones sibi adiuvantes abundanter ordinavit': ibid. 21 (*Life*, ed. Colgrave, 44).

87 Ibid. 14 (*Life*, ed. Colgrave, 30).

88 Ibid. 15 (*Life*, ed. Colgrave, 32); *HE* 4.23, 5.11 (*Ecclesiastical History*, ed. Colgrave and Mynors, 410, 484).

89 'Quantos vero per quadraginta sex annos episcopatus sui episcopos et presbiteros et diacones ordinaverat et quantas ecclesias dedicavit, quis enumerare potest': *VW* 66 (*Life*, ed. Colgrave, 142).

point – the foundation of local churches – it offers a prism through which to approach Stephen's agenda concerning Wilfrid's performance of rites of passage.

Wilfrid's performance of rites of passage are primarily related to the church in a structural sense. Two of the three references to baptism are evangelistic in context and so are foundational in nature. Through his evangelism and subsequent baptisms, Wilfrid established the South Saxon church and the Frisian church (although this latter claim is certainly over-optimistic).[90] References to ordination and episcopal consecration relate to the church's ability to carry out its ministry. The stress laid on the latter by Stephen upon Wilfrid's death means that serious thought needs to be given to Stephen's occasional references to ordinations.

It seems likely that Stephen viewed these in a foundational sense too and was extending the theme begun with Wilfrid's apparently Frankish priestly and episcopal ordinations. Stephen's descriptions highlighted that Wilfrid's orders could not be associated with the questionably orthodox English church. Consequently, Wilfrid's activities in ordaining clergy across numerous kingdoms, including Kent, renewed and reinvigorated the English church.[91] There is an additional thread, which demonstrates the scale of Stephen's ambitions for Wilfrid. A very similar sentiment about the orthodoxy of the English clergy is visible in Bede's *HE*. Bede noted that Oswiu and Ecgberht sought consecration for Wigheard in Rome so that 'he could consecrate catholic bishops for the English church throughout the whole of Britain'.[92] Wigheard's death meant that Theodore was sent to fulfil this need to ensure the catholic nature of the English church.[93] The ordinations that Wilfrid carried out in Kent were done before Theodore's arrival. As a result, Stephen gave Wilfrid primacy over Theodore in reforming the post-Whitby English church, an idea continued in the consecration of Chad, which sees Wilfrid, rather

[90] James Palmer, 'Wilfrid in Frisia', in Higham, ed., *Wilfrid*, 231–42, at 241–2.
[91] Brooks, *Canterbury*, 71.
[92] 'Catholicos per omnem Brittaniam ecclesiis Anglorum ordinare posset antistites': *HE* 3.29 (*Ecclesiastical History*, ed. Colgrave and Mynors, 318); Brooks, *Canterbury*, 69–70; cf. Richard Shaw, 'Bede, Theodore and Wigheard: Why did Pope Vitalian need to appoint a new Bishop for the English Church in the 660s?', *Revue d'histoire ecclésiastique* 113 (2018), 521–43.
[93] *HE* 4.1 (*Ecclesiastical History*, ed. Colgrave and Mynors, 328–32).

than Theodore, as the prime mover in his reordination and translation to Lichfield.

Wilfrid's performance of rites of passage, while less detailed in Stephen's account, is therefore no less important. They show Wilfrid as a foundational figure, establishing Christianity in both Sussex and Frisia, but more importantly reimbuing orthodoxy into the English church in the wake of the Easter controversy. Wilfrid's 'Frankish' ordinations meant that he was not caught up in questions of legitimacy visible in the *Penitentials of Theodore*. Moreover, Wilfrid's actions preceded Theodore's arrival in Kent; he consequently had primacy in guiding the English back to orthodox Christianity.

The *Vitae Cuthberti*

Whether reacting directly to Wilfrid or not, it is clear that the author of the *VA* was sensitive to the same questions of orthodoxy. The reference to Cuthbert's receiving the Petrine tonsure implied that Cuthbert was Roman in practice and consequently acted with legitimate authority within the Northumbrian church; he was not to be tainted by the label of schismatic.[94] Not only was the Celtic tonsure associated with the perceived Quartodeciman heresy of Iona, but it was also said to derive from Simon Magus and was consequently linked to simony, raising further questions about legitimacy.[95] The Petrine tonsure allowed the anonymous author to introduce Cuthbert's pastoral work with the confidence that it was orthodox and the sacraments he ministered were legitimate. The anonymous author provides two descriptions of Cuthbert ministering to the laity while in the house of Melrose, baptizing converts to Christianity.[96] He then proceeded to describe Cuthbert's episcopal election and consecration by Theodore and a synod of the English church, which set up descriptions of rites which only a bishop could conduct: the blessing of the chrism and confirmation.[97]

[94] *VA* 2.2 (*Two Lives*, ed. Colgrave, 76); Stancliffe, 'Episcopacy', 15; eadem, 'Cuthbert and the Polarity between Pastor and Solitary', in Bonner, Rollason and Stancliffe, eds, *St Cuthbert*, 21–44, at 23, 27.

[95] *HE* 5.21 (*Ecclesiastical History*, ed. Colgrave and Mynors, 546–8).

[96] *VA* 2.5 (*Two Lives*, ed. Colgrave, 84–6).

[97] Ibid. 4.5 (*Two Lives*, ed. Colgrave, 116).

In many respects the *VA* is unremarkable in its description of rites of passage, mentioning them in an incidental manner while describing Cuthbert's devout ministry in Northumbria, both as a monk and as a bishop. They acquire significance when placed alongside Bede's reworking of the account.

How Bede chose to rewrite the *VA* in these specific places is striking, as Table 1 demonstrates. There is not a precise concordance between the two *Vitae*, but there are similarities. Bede seems to have taken Cuthbert's episcopal election and consecration as a significant moment. References to baptism, which the anonymous author placed before this event, have been removed, with Cuthbert simply preaching, while the one to confirming has been kept.

The reference to Theodore at Cuthbert's episcopal election is a useful guide to Bede's thinking. Bede notes Theodore's role earlier in his narrative of the election, suggesting he was eager to associate Cuthbert with the great archbishop.[98] Theodore's orthodox credentials were impeccable, with Pope Vitalian certainly consecrating him bishop and potentially ordaining him through the other orders in preparation for that.[99] Moreover, Bede observed the request for papal consecration of a new archbishop of Canterbury was made so that he 'could consecrate catholic bishops for the English church'.[100] In short, orders derived from Theodore were entirely orthodox. Once Cuthbert was made a bishop at the hands of Theodore there could be no question about the legitimacy of rites that he enacted.

This provides a useful context for Bede's rewriting of the anonymous author's references to baptism. The circumstances in which a baptism was deemed invalid were unclear and the writer of the *Penitentials* observed that in two places what had been handed down as Theodore's teachings differed from œcumenical or papal decisions.[101] What is consistent, however, is that baptism should ideally be performed by a priest and that if the priest's orders were suspect, it caused questions about the legitimacy of any baptism he had conducted.[102] Cuthbert is never described as receiving priestly ordination, but Bede notes in the *HE* that at Lindisfarne 'those of them

[98] *VA* 4.1 (*Two Lives*, ed. Colgrave, 110); cf. *VP* 24 (*Two Lives*, ed. Colgrave, 238).

[99] *HE* 4.1 (*Ecclesiastical History*, ed. Colgrave and Mynors, 330).

[100] 'Catholicos per omnem Brittaniam ecclesiis Anglorum ordinare posset antistites': ibid. 3.29 (*Ecclesiastical History*, ed. Colgrave and Mynors, 318).

[101] Haddan and Stubbs, eds, *Councils*, 3: 181, 185.

[102] Ibid. 3: 185, 192.

Table 1. Rites of Passage in the two *Lives of Cuthbert*

VA		*VP*	
		9	'he would tarry in the mountains, summoning the rustics to heavenly things by the word of his preaching as well as by the example of his virtue'.[103]
2.5	'he was going along the river Teviot and making his way southward, teaching the country people among the mountains and baptizing them … Then they set out according to God's will to the mountains, as we have said above, teaching and baptizing.'[104]	12	'he had left the monastery to preach as was his wont … having resumed their journey, they set out to reach those whom they purposed to teach'.[105]
2.6	'while baptizing there among the mountains'.[106]	13	'when he was preaching the word of life to a crowd of people'.[107]

103 'Demoratus in montanis plebem rusticam verbo predicationis simul et exemplo virtutis ad coelestia vocaret': *VP* 9 (*Two Lives*, ed. Colgrave,186).

104 'Proficiscebat iuxta fluvium Tesgeta tendens in meridiem inter montana docens rusticanos et baptizabat eos … in voluntate Dei, ad montana ut supra diximus proficiscebant docentes et baptizantes': *VA* 2.5 (*Two Lives*, ed. Colgrave, 84–6).

105 'Predicaturus iuxta consuetudinem suam populis, de monasterio exiret … resumpto itinere, ad docendum eos, quos proposuere profecti sunt': *VP* 12 (*Two Lives*, ed. Colgrave, 194–6).

106 'Ibi inter montana baptizans': *VA* 2.5 (*Two Lives*, ed. Colgrave, 86).

107 'Dum congregatis … perplurimis verbum vitae praedicaret': *VP* 13 (*Two Lives*, ed. Colgrave, 198).

4.1	'he was elected to the bishopric of our church at Lindisfarne … he was led away unwillingly … while the council together with Archbishop Theodore still awaited him'.[108]	24	'when no small synod had gathered together, in the presence of the most pious King Ecgfrith beloved of God over which Archbishop Theodore of blessed memory presided, he was elected to the bishopric of the church at Lindisfarne with the unanimous consent of all'.[109]
4.4	'anointing her with chrism consecrated by his blessing'.[110]		
4.5	'he placed his hand on the head of each of them and anointing them with consecrated oil he blessed them'.[111]	29	'laying his hand on those who had been lately baptized'.[112]

108 'Ad episcopatum nostrae aecclesiae Lindisfarnensium electus est … invitus … abstractus est expectante etiam adhuc senatu, cum archiepiscopo Theodoro': *VA* 4.1 (*Two Lives*, ed. Colgrave, 110).

109 'Congregata sinodo non parva sub praesentia piissimi ac Deo dilecti regis Egfridi, cui beatae memoriae Theodorus archiepiscopus praesidebat unanimo omnium consensu ad episcopatum ecclesiae Lindisfarnensis electus est': *VP* 24 (*Two Lives*, ed. Colgrave, 238).

110 'Unguens eam crisma': *VA* 4.4 (*Two Lives*, ed. Colgrave, 116).

111 'Manum ponens super capita singulorum, liniens unctione consecrata benedixerat': *VA* 4.5 (*Two Lives*, ed. Colgrave, 116).

112 'Nuper baptizatis … manum imponeret': *VP* 29 (*Two Lives*, ed. Colgrave, 252).

who held the rank of priest administered the grace of baptism'.[113] There is also a miracle in the *VA* that could be read as Cuthbert holding priestly orders. A woman was very sick, afflicted with a demon, and her husband, Hildmer, asked Cuthbert, then prior of Lindisfarne, to supply a priest to administer the last rites. Cuthbert ordered a priest to depart but changed his mind, stating that he should go instead. Only while journeying to Hildmer's wife, Cuthbert revealed that the cause of the woman's illness was a demon and that she did not need the last rites. The passage could be read as implying that Cuthbert originally intended to carry out priestly functions.[114]

Bede removes any possibility of such a reading. While the general narrative of Hildmer's wife's sufferings and cure is the same, Bede explicitly states that before he chose to go himself Cuthbert 'suddenly realised in his spirit that the wife for whom the man was praying was afflicted by no ordinary infirmity but by the attack of a demon'.[115] By reworking the casting out of this demon and removing references to baptism, Bede prevents any suggestion that Cuthbert was a priest and so, through his association with the *Latercus* and its questionable dating of Easter, had orders that were either incomplete or invalid. In essence, what Bede's recasting of rites of passage reveals is how threatening Stephen's lifting of the anonymous author's description of Cuthbert's Petrine tonsure actually was. Stephen did not simply catch Lindisfarne in a lie about an embarrassing association.[116] By undermining the credibility of this claim to orthodoxy, he raised questions about the authority with which Cuthbert performed baptismal rites, which in turn raised questions about his ecclesiastical rank and its legitimacy.[117] In terms of Acca's designs upon the see of Lindisfarne, it would have been an excellent means by which to denigrate Lindisfarne's great episcopal hero and patron.[118] It is perhaps a mark of the seriousness of the position Lindisfarne found itself in that Bede did not respond directly to these questions. Instead, Bede

113 'Gratiam baptismi, quicumque sacerdotali erant gradu praediti, ministrare': *HE* 3.3 (*Ecclesiastical History*, ed. Colgrave and Mynors, 220).
114 *VA* 2.8 (*Two Lives*, ed. Colgrave, 90–2).
115 'Cognovit repente in spiritu quia non communi infirmitate sed demonis infestatione premeretur coniux, pro qua supplicabat': *VP* 15 (*Two Lives*, ed. Colgrave, 204).
116 *VW* 6 (*Life*, ed. Colgrave, 14).
117 Cubitt, 'Clergy', 277 n. 19.
118 Stancliffe, 'Episcopacy', 32–3.

sidestepped them, removing any suggestion that Cuthbert was bound to the Lindisfarne mission by ordination, only acknowledging rites of passage once Cuthbert was elected and consecrated bishop by Theodore and no questions could be asked about the validity of his orders. Furthermore, by giving Theodore greater prominence in Cuthbert's succession to the episcopate, Bede could associate Cuthbert with a source of orthodoxy equal to Wilfrid. In so doing, he shored up Cuthbert's legitimacy and suitability as an example of episcopal conduct. Bede was doing for Cuthbert what Stephen did for Wilfrid; constructing an image of orthodoxy upon which to ground the legitimacy of Cuthbert's ritual actions.

Conclusion

At the outset, it is striking how similar the *VW*, *VA* and *VP* are in their use of rites of passage to prove the orthodoxy of their subjects and their consequent right to hold positions of authority within the seventh-century English church. The questions of legitimacy raised at the Synod of Whitby and stamped upon the *Penitentials of Theodore* cast long shadows that reached into the eighth century. In light of this, Wilfrid's rites of passage demonstrate three specific points. Firstly, one of Stephen's priorities in describing them was to prove Wilfrid's ritual links to the Frankish and Roman churches. This is fundamental to the image of Wilfrid that Stephen wished to present: a man whose orthodoxy was beyond doubt in the febrile atmosphere in the wake of the Synod of Whitby. Secondly, this concern was not limited to the Northumbrian church; rather the entire pre-Whitby English church was suspect. Thirdly, this was a constructed image. Through what Stephen does not say about Wilfrid and his rites of passage, it is possible to associate Wilfrid with the pre-Whitby Northumbrian church specifically and the English church generally. Wilfrid may not have been as sundered from his peers as Stephen may lead readers to believe. Stephen also used Wilfrid's performance of rites of passage to create a foundational authority for him, which would have been impossible had Wilfrid been tainted through formal association with Christianity corrupted by 'Quartodecimanism'.

Bede and the anonymous author were both similarly sensitive to the problems of legitimacy raised by the *Latercus*. The anonymous author sought to reassure readers that Cuthbert had always adhered to Roman practice by reference to the Petrine tonsure. Bede instead avoided ritual questions in his account of Cuthbert's monastic career, focusing on his episcopal consecration at the hands of Theodore, an act to which no one could object. In terms of the dispute with Acca and Hexham, it confirms that questions of orthodoxy were part of the threat to Lindisfarne's position in the Northumbrian church and that Bede, in rewriting the *VA*, did not seek to attack Wilfrid but to rehabilitate Cuthbert. Evidently, rites of passage were rendered highly charged issues by the questions of orthodoxy in the Northumbrian church after the Synod of Whitby, being used to grant authority to, or dispute the authority of, saintly figures associated with both sides of the Easter controversy. They provide a means to cut through the hagiographic propaganda and access the concerns of the authors and in so doing provide a fuller understanding both of Wilfrid and of the debates between Lindisfarne and Hexham in the wake of his death.

The Renunciation of Wealth as a Rite of 'the poor' and 'perfect': Bede and his Successors

Zachary Guiliano*

St Edmund Hall, Oxford

The renunciation and abandonment of wealth are rarely described as Christian rites of passage. Yet, for many medieval commentators on Scripture, such as the Venerable Bede and his successors, they were necessary rites, preliminaries to entry into the kingdom of heaven and into the class of 'the perfect'. This article explores Arnold van Gennep's description of rites of passage in conjunction with the discussion of poverty in the Western exegetical tradition, centred in particular on Jesus's statements about poverty in Luke. It focuses on Bede's models of renunciation and abandonment of wealth which influenced Latin theology at least until the Reformation. The renunciation and abandonment of wealth provide an excellent test case for exploring van Gennep's ritual framework and its utility within the discipline of ecclesiastical history.

'If you would be perfect: go, sell what you have and give to the poor, and you will have treasure in heaven. And come, follow me.' Jesus addressed a rich man with these words in Matthew 19: 16–30; they are recorded with small differences in Mark 10: 17–31 and Luke 18: 18–30. This exhortation inspired many in the earliest centuries of the Church to relinquish their property and seek an intense life of ascetic discipline. Some went to Syria, the Holy Land or the Egyptian desert. Others sought perfection closer to home, in repurposed country estates or inner *sancta* within city houses, or as hermits in a local wilderness.[1] In doing so, they became, in the eyes of some contemporaries, living fulfilments of the gospels, signs of endless potential. The perfection held out by Christ is within reach; the impossible is possible with

* St Edmund Hall, Queens Lane, Oxford OX1 4AR. E-mail: zachary.guiliano@seh.ox.ac.uk.

[1] For the range of practice, see Peter Brown, *Through the Eye of a Needle: Wealth, the Fall of Rome, and the Making of Christianity in the West, 350–550 AD* (Princeton, NJ, 2012), 72–90, 135–47, 224–58, 273–88, 528–30; more briefly, Elizabeth A. Clark, *Reading Renunciation: Asceticism and Scripture in Early Christianity* (Princeton, NJ, 1999), 33–8.

Studies in Church History 59 (2023), 73–97
doi: 10.1017/stc.2023.25

God, as Martin of Tours wrote, speaking of Paulinus of Nola and his dramatic conversion.[2]

The dispersal of wealth, however, brought various difficulties, both for followers of ascetic discipline and for commentators on Scripture. The hyper-wealthy, late Roman elite, such as Paulinus of Nola or Melania the Younger, often found it hard to divest themselves of far-flung estates or goods not readily transferred into glittering gold and silver coins for distribution to the poor or filling church coffers. They might frame their renunciation as a matter of 'salvation economics', trading earthbound material goods for splendid spiritual treasure, kept safe beyond the stars,[3] but it was rarely so simple. Practical problems arose; other people and their interests stood in the way (in Melania's case, even the Roman senate).[4]

Would-be seekers of perfection had to reckon, too, with the popularity of their asceticism, and with money and land acquired by their institutions, later to be managed by them. Sometimes, as in the case of Benedict Biscop in late seventh-century Northumbria, a warrior departing royal service might relinquish a claim on ancestral land, honours and dignities, or on property rewarded to martial prowess, only to acquire far more as a venerable and austere figure, a demonstration of Christ's promise that 'a hundredfold' reward came 'in this time' to those who gave up everything for the gospel: 'houses and brothers and sisters and mothers and children and lands' (Mark 10: 30).[5] Those abandoning wealth generally found they still had to live with it, and to continue to make their way in the economic order of their times.

From Late Antiquity to the Middle Ages, authors of biblical commentaries had to deal with problems of exegesis and ambiguities in scriptural teaching. Was a one-time relinquishment of wealth what it meant to 'renounce' possessions, as Jesus had commanded? Was this gospel 'perfection'? Or was more required? And how many had to renounce wealth? These problems could become acute when individual interpreters wrestled with the diverse witness of patristic exegesis and the examples in their community. Bede, for example,

[2] Brown, *Eye of a Needle*, 216–17, citing Sulpicius Severus, *Vita Sancti Martini* 22.

[3] Dennis E. Trout, *Paulinus of Nola: Life, Letters, and Poems* (Berkeley, CA, 1999), 133–59.

[4] Ibid. 216–18, 226–7, 295–300.

[5] See Bede, *Homily* 1.13 (CChr.SL 122); idem, *History of the Abbots* 1.1 (C. W. Grocock and Ian Wood, eds, *Abbots of Wearmouth and Jarrow* [Oxford, 2019], 21–5).

undertook his work in the company of various abbots and monastic contemporaries, often of noble birth, and in a landscape of diverse approaches to ascetic life in early medieval Northumbria and Western Europe.

Renunciation and 'Rites of Passage'

Such issues and questions may seem peculiar in relation to *The Churches and Rites of Passage*. Rites of passage are generally regarded as significant life events shared and ritualized by most human beings throughout history. We may think of them as a natural category, indeed, a necessary and useful one, providing a 'fundamental clue to the essence of religion'.[6] A whole area of law sprang up in response to the COVID-19 pandemic reflecting such an assumption. In order to regulate religious practices and render them safe – or, at least, less prone to increasing viral transmission – government guidance divided them into 'private prayer', 'communal worship', 'festivals', 'voluntary or public services' and 'significant life events'. The guidance also regulated the actions, environments and objects that could surround or be used in every kind of religious observance.[7] The urgency of the moment required vast areas of commonality, a set of categories that could apply across and within religious traditions. It found one close at hand, due to the long-standing influence of anthropologists such as Arnold van Gennep and Victor Turner.

The reason I have taken the renunciation of wealth as a topic is that it could trouble or affirm an understanding of Christian practices across time as fundamentally comprising recognizable sets of activities, whether they be forms of worship and prayer, methods of structuring and inhabiting time, models of service, or, indeed, rites for managing or effecting transitions from one stage of life to another. A rite may appear to be necessary in one time or within one community, and superfluous in another time and place. Even within a single time and place, like Northumbria in its monastic 'Golden Age',

[6] John Milbank, *Theology and Social Theory: Against Secular Reason* (Malden, MA, 1990), 123.

[7] See 'Places of Worship Guidance' (19 July 2021), online at: <https://www.gov.uk/government/publications/covid-19-guidance-for-the-safe-use-of-places-of-worship-during-the-pandemic-from-4-july/covid-19-guidance-for-the-safe-use-of-places-of-worship-from-2-december>.

accounts of the requirements of certain rites or states of life could differ, based on differing assessments of scriptural and patristic teaching. For this reason, any historical approach to the churches and rites of passage should not focus too strongly upon commonalities, but must also consider sporadic, specific and time bound instances of ritual invention or redefinition. The renunciation of wealth may be one of these: one way in which 'Christian communities were increasingly stratified and hierarchalized by an axiology … of "difference" centered on ascetic renunciation', and then, just as increasingly, were not.[8] Renouncing wealth was a significant, and increasingly dominant, part of Christian reading strategies and revered forms of life from Late Antiquity onward. It received dramatic validation in the early Middle Ages and was just as forcefully revised in the Reformation and afterwards.

My inspiration for this topic arises, too, from ambiguities in the work that originated the term 'rites of passage' and the difficulties in using its concepts for contemporary work in ecclesiastical history. Van Gennep's *Les Rites de passage* (1909) rarely placed Christian rites within the same framework as those of other cultures. He explicitly contrasted Western European Christianity, and its limited number of formal rituals, with the patterns of life in cultures he deemed more primitive, those further 'downward on the scale of civilizations':

> We see that in the least advanced cultures the holy enters nearly every phase of a man's life. Being born, giving birth, and hunting, to cite but a few examples, are all acts whose major aspects fall within the sacred sphere. Social groups likewise have magico-religious foundations, and a passage from group to group takes on that special quality found in *our rites* of baptism and ordination.[9]

Van Gennep worked within the social and religious imaginary of early twentieth-century Christianity, upholding cultural simplicity as a sign of civilizational progress. Yet, he said, 'to the semi-civilized mind no act is entirely free of the sacred', and consequently all of life must be enveloped in ceremonies.[10] Civilization and modernity, he thought,

[8] Clark, *Reading Renunciation*, 5, but see ibid. 3–13; and compare David C. Fink, 'Unreading Renunciation: Luther, Calvin, and the "Rich Young Ruler"', *Modern Theology* 32 (2016), 569–93.
[9] Arnold van Gennep, *The Rites of Passage*, transl. Monika B. Vizedom and Gabrielle I. Caffee (Abingdon and New York, 2004; first publ. 1960), 2, emphasis added.
[10] Ibid. 3.

are freed from such complications. For van Gennep, this had practical outworkings. He analysed rites of passage in faraway lands or on peripheries: at the farthest, South Asia, sub-Saharan Africa, Madagascar and Oceania; at the closest, the Savoy or the Balkans, the outer regions and small places of 'civilized' nations and continents, rather than larger centres such as Paris, London or Berlin. Rites of passage were usually confined to other religions, or to an ambiguous category of semi-pagan survivals within Christianity. At times, van Gennep noted analogies between the rites he was discussing and those of the churches, but he refused to draw the latter fully into his analysis, suggesting for example that ordinations in Roman Catholicism or Orthodoxy are 'systematized in their own ways', even if they shared some commonalities with modes of consecration or ordination in other religions and cultures.[11] One must analyse them on their own terms. He did not always acknowledge similar systems in other cultures or religions, however long-standing or systematic their approaches (such as the Brahmanical priesthood).

An interesting comparison lies in van Gennep's examination of rites in Savoy, where he partly grew up and later worked. *De Quelques Rites de passage en Savoie*, a shorter work published only two years after *Les Rites de passage*, tended to treat popular and local observances associated with an individual's life stages, rather than the universal, institutional or sacramental forms of Christianity as they were expressed in the area.[12] It made few connections between the 'systematized' understanding of a rite like baptism and local customs surrounding it. The closest moment comes in the opening pages, when van Gennep described how Christianity took in and transformed local customs, replacing 'les temples gallo-romains' with sanctuaries dedicated to the Holy Virgin and other saints.[13] Despite declaring such overlaps to be numerous, van Gennep rarely drew connections.

[11] Ibid. 106. References to baptism are relatively more frequent in *Rites of Passage* (e.g. 93–7, 107–8). This is for a specific reason: van Gennep analyzes the extensive preliminaries to baptism in the Latin West because he was confident they were 'borrowed so extensively from the Egyptian, Syrian, Asian, and Greek mysteries': ibid. 88. See also, in this volume, Thomas O'Loughlin, '"Rites of Passage" and the Writing of Church History: Reflections upon our Craft in the Aftermath of van Gennep', 8–26, at 17–19, 20, 22–3.

[12] Arnold van Gennep, *De Quelques Rites de passage en Savoie* (Paris, 1910).

[13] Ibid. 2–4.

The prejudices or peculiarities in his writings may appear obvious, but some of them are worth exploring briefly. First, we should query his suggestion that Christian rites are reasonably limited and identifiable (such as baptism and ordination) and that 'the sacred' is approached only at specific times. No historian could cast their eye over the Christian past and suggest that ecclesiastical cultures in numerous times and places have been largely free of ceremonial or, indeed, a sense of the all-pervading presence of the divine. Christian centres of culture (cathedrals, monasteries, royal courts, universities, parishes), have regularly been sites of elaborate and time-consuming ritual observance: places of encountering, but not containing, numinous presence. To set aside such a history, or to regard elaborate ceremony or a pervasive sense of holiness as less than 'Christian' or 'ours', is to work within an ideological frame. Moreover, the frame appears to be one stamped by the influence of sacramental theologies developed in the thirteenth and sixteenth centuries, since gone secular and decadent.

Before the advent of scholasticism, the identification of the sacraments was not focused narrowly on those rites commonly identified as such in modern Catholic and Protestant teaching. Words like *sacramenta* or *mysteria* or *figura* had varied meanings into the High Middle Ages. As Dominique Poiret notes with regard to Hugh of St Victor, 'the Hugonian idea of the sacrament is larger, more complex, and more supple than ours'.[14] Peter Lombard's *Sentences*, however, with its reduction of primary sacraments, in which salvation was regarded as principally consisting (*sacramenta salutaria*), to seven, had lasting influence. It helped define a new theological imaginary, to which Protestant and Catholic reformers would respond in confessional statements and canonical definitions that continue to shape churches worldwide. These approaches would eventually affect nascent anthropological disciplines and other developing realms of inquiry. 'Sociology is the heir of theology', as Philippe Buc affirms,[15]

[14] Dominique Poiret, 'Sacraments', in Hugh Feiss and Juliet Mousseau, eds, *A Companion to the Abbey of Saint Victor in Paris*, Brill's Companions to the Christian Tradition 70 (Leiden, 2017), 277–97, at 277; Hugh Feiss, *On the Sacraments: A Selection of Works of Hugh and Richard of St Victor, and of Peter of Poitiers*, Victorine Texts in Translation 10 (Turnhout, 2020), 61–2.

[15] Philippe Buc, *The Dangers of Ritual: Between Early Medieval Texts and Social Scientific Theory* (Princeton, NJ, 2001), 194, referencing Émile Durkheim, Robert Nisbet and John Milbank, among others.

and the social sciences can seem at times 'doomed to repeat the self-understanding of Christianity' arrived at in the late Middle Ages and early modernity.[16] For those reasons alone, we should observe caution in applying the idea of 'rites of passage' to earlier times, and recognize that contemporary historical inquiry is more theological than many would imagine. Moreover, where van Gennep excluded 'our rites' from his consideration of rites of passage, due to their systematized and limited character, this volume broadens his category in a significant way, by suggesting that rites of passage appear in the churches.

The identification of rites of passage is only one of the ambiguities present in van Gennep's work, which remain relevant to this volume. There are others, not least around the definition of a 'ritual', 'ceremony' or 'rite'. As Buc argued some time ago: 'historians have, collectively at least, piled a vast array of motley practices into the category', freely enriching their inquiries with piquant insights from anthropology or sociology, without fully interrogating the origin and genealogy of their methods.[17] Van Gennep's primary examples were major events marking or effecting movement from one age to another, one state of life to another, one community to another, one time to another. The impetus of such a focus would drive us to look for analogies in Christian cultures. But van Gennep's definition of 'rites' or 'ceremonies' encompassed much more than this, perhaps an unacknowledged inspiration for the 'hazy laundry list' of rituals identified by historians.[18]

For van Gennep, a rite required no formal words or elaborate actions; it could happen in an instant and still be 'a rite'.[19] He cites examples of a woman 'abstaining from eating mulberries for fear her child would be disfigured' and a sailor 'in danger of perishing in a shipwreck' making a vow 'to Our Lady of Vigilance'.[20] These customary actions emerge in particular moments; they would have formal and informal precedents in their cultures, interacting with differing understandings of cosmic or divine order. Despite their

16 Milbank, *Theology and Social Theory*, 9.

17 Buc, *Dangers of Ritual*, 1, 5.

18 '[T]he baptism of rulers, coronations and crown-wearings; princely funerals; entries in cities (or churches) and other processions or parades; civic games; banquets; the hunt; relic translations and elevations; oath-takings; acclamations or laudes; knightings; ordeals; public penances; and acts of submission or commendation': ibid. 5.

19 Van Gennep, *Rites of Passage*, 9.

20 Ibid.

lack of formalism or their rational incorporation into a broader set of rites, in both instances the subjects of these rites invite or prevent significant life-altering. But, truly, when are such customs or senses of agency absent? Taken to their logical extreme, van Gennep's examples make it difficult to see what is and what is not a rite, unless we accept his civilizational and hierarchical definition of rites and ceremonies as features of 'primitive' cultures pervaded by 'the holy'. In such a case, a rite of passage could hardly exist within a secular or highly literate culture.

These ambiguities have broader relevance in relation to the renunciation of wealth. The examples I will explore could be seen either to affirm or to trouble such ritual categories. The renunciation of wealth could be understood within the framework of rites of passage, and particularly as a preliminary to other rites. Whether one sought rebirth or the recognition of Christian maturity, the renunciation of wealth might play a part. For many medieval exegetes grappling with the gospels, it did. Beginning with Bede and his influential gathering of patristic traditions, a common exegetical framework emerged, which retained significant impact until the Reformation. Guided by such texts, we might label renunciation a rite of passage. On the other hand, we might want to label the renunciation of wealth as a rite or ceremony of some kind, but still hesitate to set it alongside rites of passage. I will return to these points in the conclusion, noting how renunciation appears to relate to other rites like baptism, ordination or monastic profession.

Bede and Renunciation in Christian Liturgy and Economy

I limit myself primarily to statements by the Venerable Bede, particularly his *Exposition of the Gospel of Luke* (hereafter: *On Luke*).[21] It is a useful text for this discussion, not only because it deals with many scriptural passages which were significant in the history of asceticism, but also because of its gathering of earlier traditions and its influence

[21] I have used the following editions: Bede, *On Genesis* (CChr.SL 118); *On Samuel* (CChr.SL 119); *On the Tabernacle* (CChr.SL 119A); *On the Temple* (CChr.SL 119A); *On Ezra* (CChr.SL 119A); *On the Song of Songs* (CChr.SL 119B); *On Proverbs* (CChr.SL 119B); *On Mark* (CChr.SL 120); *On Luke* (CChr.SL 120); *Exposition of the Acts of the Apostles* (CChr.SL 121); *Retraction on Acts* (CChr.SL 121). All translations are mine unless indicated otherwise.

on later exegesis. Bede's interpretations were cited in gospel commentaries and homilies throughout the Middle Ages, so there are important commonalities here.[22] Firstly, I will consider his suggestion that the renunciation of wealth is a universal commitment required for salvation. Secondly, I will examine those passages that discuss the relinquishing or dispersal of wealth as an action incumbent upon all those who would be 'perfect'. These suggest that renunciation or dispersal is a one-time action, so, thirdly, I will consider a few passages which show that the paradigm is not so simple.

The clearest statements on renunciation come in Bede's comments on Luke 14, where Jesus describes the kingdom of God as a 'banquet' to which many are invited. He describes 'the cost' of being his disciple. God's house must be filled, but Jesus says:

> If any man come to me, and hate not his father, and mother, and wife, and children, and brethren, and sisters, yea and his own life also, he cannot be my disciple. And whosoever doth not carry his cross and come after me, cannot be my disciple. … So likewise every one of you that doth not renounce all that he possesseth, cannot be my disciple. (Luke 14: 26–7, 33, Douay-Rheims)

For Bede, this is a clear teaching. The Christian must be ready to give up everything: loved ones, neighbours, possessions, even life, that is, 'the soul'. This is what it means 'to count the cost' of discipleship.[23] However, it may not actually be necessary to leave things behind. He comments on Luke 14: 33, finding a distinction in the works of Augustine and Gregory: 'Clearly there is a difference between "renounce all things" and "relinquish all things".'[24]

> It is for all of the faithful to 'renounce all things that they possess', that is, *so to hold those things of the world, that they might not be held in the*

[22] See Zachary Guiliano, 'Holy Gluttons: Bede and the Carolingians on the Pleasures of Reading', in Naama Cohen-Hanegbi and Piroska Nagy, eds, *Pleasure in the Middle Ages*, International Medieval Research 24 (Turnhout, 2018), 281–308; idem, *The Homiliary of Paul the Deacon: Religious and Cultural Reform in Carolingian Europe*, Studies on Patristic, Medieval and Reformation Sermons 16 (Turnhout, 2021). I am currently preparing a monograph, provisionally entitled *Bede's Economy: The Commentary on Luke in the Temple Society of the Latin West.*

[23] Bede, *On Luke* 4.2113–16 (CChr.SL 120: 283).

[24] 'Distat sane inter renuntiare omnibus et relinquere omnia': Bede, *On Luke* 4.2122–3 (CChr.SL 120: 283–4). Bede responded to the difference in terminology in Augustine, *Questions on the Gospels* 2.31; and Gregory the Great, *Homilies on the Gospels* 36.

world through them, to hold *the temporal thing in use, the eternal in desire*; thus to *conduct* earthly affairs so *that, still, with the whole mind they stretch toward* the celestial.[25]

The renunciation of wealth on this model is dramatic and fundamental, but primarily a re-orientation of desire, intent and use, a preliminary step with enduring consequences. Just as one must be ready to take up the cross and follow Jesus in martyrdom – but may not actually die for the faith, because one lives in a time of peace – so one must be ready to leave all things behind, even if one retains wealth. This is how 'so many rich people' in the Old Testament, including Abraham and David, retained their wealth while entering the kingdom of heaven: they learned to 'hold riches as nothing', even as their possessions multiplied. David exhorted his hearers in Psalm 61: 11: 'If riches increase, set not your heart upon them'. But, Bede claims, 'I believe he did not dare to say, "Do not take them."'[26]

In Bede's mind, there is a clear preliminary to entering the kingdom of heaven: acquiring the right attitude to property, kinship and even one's soul, renouncing 'carnal desires'.[27] This applies across times and places, as well as across the Old and New Testaments. It was exemplified by Abraham, even as he wandered through the Ancient Near East and acquired ever more 'sheep and oxen, and he asses, and menservants and maidservants, and camels' (Gen. 12: 16, Douay-Rheims). The father of faith serves as a figure of renunciation to all the faithful, despite his great wealth.[28]

When does this renunciation of loved ones, possessions and life take place? At first, it is not clear. In this part of his commentary, Bede does not remark explicitly on the relationship between this preliminary to salvation and the formal rites of baptism, by which the Christian faithful receive rebirth. Nonetheless, in his discussion of John the Baptist and the 'fruits worthy of repentance' (Luke 3), he makes it clear that repentance and renunciation at baptism are

[25] Bede, *On Luke* 4.2125–39 (CChr.SL 120: 284). Words in italics are Bede's combination of phrases from Gregory, *Homilies on the Gospels* 36.292–3, 297, 309–10 (CChr.SL 141: 342–3).

[26] Bede, *On Luke* 5.1288–94 (CChr.SL 120: 328).

[27] Bede, *On the Song of Songs* 1.1.245–6 (CChr.SL 119B: 196); cf. 'we teach those new peoples of the Church to renounce the devil and to believe in and confess the true God': *On Ezra* 2.1400–2 (CChr.SL 119A: 322).

[28] Bede, *On Genesis* 3.1232–44 (CChr.SL 118: 176–7).

inextricably tied to particular financial practices like almsgiving.[29] 'After the washing of baptism', entry into the 'hall of heaven' is gained, not by leisure, but 'by fasts, prayers and alms'.[30] Moreover, Bede's narrative examples (Abraham, John the Baptist's call to repentance, and Jesus's statements on renunciation) involve dramatic moments of decision, making the connection to baptism clear. Bede's language also evokes the formal renunciations made at baptism, which since early days had included renunciation of Satan, 'all his works' and 'all his pomps'.[31] For example, Bede makes a direct connection between baptism and Abraham's abandonment of family and land in his commentary *On Genesis*:

> For it is certain that the fact that he went out from his country and from his kindred and from the house of his father when he was commanded to do so should be imitated by all the sons of that promise, among whom we too are included. Certainly we go out from our country when we renounce the pleasures of the flesh, from our kindred when we strive to strip ourselves of all the vices with which we were born (insofar as this is possible for men!), and from the house of our father when we struggle out of love for the heavenly life to abandon this world with its prince the devil. For we are all born into the world as sons of the devil on account of the sin of the first transgression; but by the grace of rebirth all of us who belong to the seed of Abraham are made the sons of God.[32]

'All the elect' follow this example of Abraham 'by renouncing the custom of the vices'.[33] Bede's explicit reference to 'the grace of rebirth' makes it clear that he has in mind the moment of baptism, and suggests that his other descriptions – renouncing pleasures, stripping off the vices, abandoning the world – are in themselves examples of both pre-baptismal intentions and post-baptismal life, at least ideally. His *Homily* 2.6 confirms this, suggesting that the meaning of one of the pre-baptismal rites, the 'Effeta' (or 'Ephphatha'), was the casting off

[29] For example Bede, *On Luke* 1.2340–57, 2369–74 (CChr.SL 120: 78–9, 79).
[30] Ibid. 1.2556–9 (CChr.SL 120: 84).
[31] Maxwell Johnson, *The Rites of Christian Initiation: Their Evolution and Interpretation*, rev. edn (Collegeville, MN, 2009), 111, 132, 148, 240, 260, 322, 327, 331, 340, 343, 403, 405, 418.
[32] Bede, *On Genesis* 3.1008–22 (CChr.SL 118: 170–1; transl. Calvin Kendall, *Bede: On Genesis*, TTH 48 [Liverpool, 2008], 247).
[33] Ibid. 3.1026–32 (CChr.SL 118: 171).

of harmful desires (*abiectis delectationibus noxiis*).[34] The desire for wealth may safely be included amongst these, for, in Bede's view, 'he who bends himself to multiplying wealth here scorns to seek the joys of the other life',[35] and 'they who are arrogant, glorying in earthly riches … shall be left emptied of the light of truth'.[36] In this way, renouncing wealth is not only a preliminary to salvation, but Bede appears to have, mentally at least, nested this category of renunciation within the broader renunciations of baptism.

It is impossible to establish the precise sequence or form of the preliminaries to baptism in Bede's milieu to shed light on how renunciation was integrated into them, not least because no full baptismal liturgy from Bede's Northumbria is extant. His own comments on the rites are minimal and normally come in passing as part of his practice of preaching or commentary; he mentions aspects such as the *apertio aurium* ('the opening of the ears'), the *traditio euangeliorum* ('the handing on of the Gospels') and the Effeta, along with the custom of baptizing at Easter and Pentecost.[37] Baptismal rites contemporary to Bede, however, reveal a variety of links to the memory of Abraham. Sixth-century rites, such as those in the Veronese sacramentary, mentioned Abraham during the blessing of milk and honey used in the baptismal rites. In the Bobbio Missal, a seventh-century Frankish text, he is briefly mentioned as Christ's progenitor during the practice of the *traditio euangeliorum*, and the priest also prays at the Easter Vigil that God might 'bless and sanctify' those about to be baptized, as 'you blessed the house of Abraham, Isaac,

[34] Bede, *Homily* 2.6.86 (CChr.SL 122: 222). In the Latin West, the 'Effeta' or 'Ephphatha' took place before baptism, inspired by Mark 7: 31–7. The rite has undergone numerous transformations during the Middle Ages, the early modern period and since the Second Vatican Council: Johnson, *Rites*, 170, 222–3, 240–3, 259–60, 312–13, 366–9, 393–405; David Andrew Pitt, 'Revising the Rite of Adult Initiation: The Structural Reform of the *Ordo Initiationis Christianae Adultorum, Ordo Catechumenatus Per Gradus Dispositus*, 1964–1972' (PhD thesis, University of Notre Dame, 2007).

[35] Bede, *On Luke* 5.1268–70 (CChr.SL 120: 327).

[36] Bede, *Homily* 1.4.271–4 (CChr.SL 122: 28).

[37] Mary T. A. Carroll, *The Venerable Bede: His Spiritual Teaching*, Catholic University of America Studies in Medieval History n.s. 9 (Washington DC, 1946), 104–5. See, for the *apertio* and *traditio*, Bede, *On the Tabernacle* 2.1844–94 (CChr.SL 119A: 89–90); for the Effeta, Bede, *Homily* 2.6.80–96 (CChr.SL 122: 222); *On Mark* 1433–1502, especially 1461–3 (CChr.SL 120: 525–26); for baptizing at Easter and Pentecost, *Homily* 2.6.93–7, 2.17.254–69 (CChr.SL 122: 222, 307–8).

and Jacob'.[38] Notably, the Bobbio Missal's renunciations include Satan's 'luxuries' and further baptismal rites include a foot-washing ceremony that commits the baptized to wash the feet of 'pilgrims, guests, and the poor'.[39]

Most substantively, the Gelasian sacramentary, reflecting seventh-century practice in Rome and elsewhere, witnesses to a general invocation of 'the God of Abraham, Isaac, and Jacob' during a prayer of exorcism. Abraham appears here, too, in the rite of the *traditio euangeliorum* as part of the explanation of Jesus's genealogy.[40] The most explicit link, however, comes in the sacramentary's final set of rites to be performed on Holy Saturday, including, like Bede, the Effeta ritual, here preceding the Easter Vigil. The Gelasian sacramentary links the Effeta to an anointing with oil and the renunciation of Satan, all his works and all his pomps, as Bede had done. Later in the liturgy, a biblical lesson about Abraham is mentioned (but not identified), along with a prayer to be said after the lesson is read. God is said to be making children of Abraham through 'the Paschal sacrament', and the priest prays that 'your people … may worthily enter into the grace of your calling.'[41] Antoine Chavasse has suggested, based on the evidence of other early medieval sacramentaries and lectionaries, that the reading was Genesis 22: the binding and near-sacrifice of Isaac.[42] Abraham is kept from losing his son only by the miraculous provision of a ram. God safeguards the divine promise of countless offspring. Linked with its prayer in the vigil, this lection offers a significant suggestion: God honoured Abraham's willingness to give up all, including his child; so too, will the renunciations of the baptized result in untold rewards, if they retain, and enter fully into, their high calling. We might remember, too, that the primary eucharistic prayer of the Western tradition and the Roman rite (past and present) particularly links the sacrifices of the faithful – in praise, in bread and wine – with

[38] *The Bobbio Missal: A Gallican Mass-Book (MS Paris. Lat. 13246)*, ed. Elias A. Lowe, HBS 53 (Woodbridge and Rochester, NY, 1991), 55, 71.

[39] Ibid. 74–5.

[40] E. C. Whitaker, *Documents of the Baptismal Liturgy*, ed. M. E. Johnson, 3rd edn (Bristol, 2003), 207, 217, 219.

[41] Ibid. 229–31.

[42] Antoine Chavasse, *Le Sacramentaire gélasien, Vaticanus Reginensis 316. Sacramentaire presbyteral en usage dans les titres romains au VIIe siècle* (Paris, 1958), 115–23.

'the gifts of your servant Abel the just, and the sacrifice of Abraham our patriarch, and what your high priest Melchizedek offered'.[43]

We have here a liturgical counterpart to Bede's thought, linking the renunciations and sacrifice of Abraham with the baptismal renunciations of the faithful. Further corroboration appears in Bede's commentary *On Genesis*, where the connection between baptism and the sacrifice of Isaac as 'the son of promise' is clear.[44] Later liturgical texts include similar evocations of the God of Abraham in scrutinies or baptism, and varied discussions of baptismal renunciation – including the renunciation of greed – but these are not easily mined for information on the liturgy at the time that Bede was writing.[45]

Bede on the Abandonment of Wealth by 'the perfect'

Renunciation, of course, was only a first step in Bede's mind. What did he say about those who 'relinquish all things'? He follows Gregory the Great by saying that the abandonment of possessions is a step for the spiritually mature: 'It is for *the few* and perfect *to relinquish everything, to set aside the cares of the world, to gasp for eternal desires only.*'[46] This distinction mirrors a division Bede frequently draws between typical Christians and the *perfecti*, often in regard to possessions. He writes in his commentary *On the Song of Songs*: 'And indeed it is for all Christ's sheep to be purified by the washing of life, because "unless someone be reborn from water and the Spirit" (and the rest); but it is for the perfect to renounce all which they possess, and especially for those to whom care is given for feeding the sheep.'[47] His *Homily* 1.13 carried the image further. The present distinction between the 'two orders of the elect' is their handling of possessions,

43 '[M]unera pueri tui iusti Abel, et sacrificium Patriarchae nostri Abrahae, et quod tibi obtulit summus sacerdos tuus Melchisedech': *Missale Romanum*, Editio typica (Vatican City, 1970), 453.

44 For example, Bede, *On Genesis* 4.1521–1761 (CChr.SL 118: 236–42).

45 Such as *Ordo Romanus* 12 or the numerous baptismal tracts from the Carolingian period: see Whittaker, *Documents*, 244–51; Susan Keefe, *Water and the Word: Baptism and the Education of the Clergy in the Carolingian Empire*, 2 vols (Notre Dame, IN, 2002), 2: 211, 235. These suggest avenues for future research.

46 Bede, *On Luke* 4.2123–5 (CChr.SL 120: 283–4), with Gregory's words italicized: see Gregory, *Homilies on the Gospels* 36.289–90 (CChr.SL 141: 342).

47 Bede, *On the Song of Songs* 2.4.113–16 (CChr.SL 119B: 246). We should not be confused by Bede's choice of words; by 'renounce' he clearly means 'relinquish', as the preceding lines make clear: ibid. 2.4.110–13.

and it will be carried into the future judgment: some took care to give alms to the poor, and Christ will let them enter life; others abandoned all and followed Jesus in strict obedience; they, 'the perfect', will join him in judging the Church and the world.[48]

The 'perfect' or 'mature' have an exalted place in Bede's economy of knowledge and salvation.[49] He has many names for them, such as 'the truly poor' or 'the rulers' of the church. He finds symbols of them hidden everywhere in Scripture: the eyes of the Beloved in the Song of Songs, the golden crown on the altar of Moses, the soaring angels of Revelation. The 'perfect' have many tasks, not least to teach and preach. At the most fundamental level, however, they are those who have heard Jesus's dialogue with the rich young ruler and obeyed: 'If you would be perfect: go, sell all that you have and give to the poor. And, come, follow me.'[50] Bede's mind gravitates to this passage of Scripture regularly, citing it explicitly in at least ten commentaries and in his homilies.[51] It also serves as a model of holiness in his historical and hagiographical writing.[52]

In Bede's comments on the story of the rich young ruler in Luke 18: 18–30, he quotes a long and revealing section of Jerome's *Commentary on Matthew*:

> Whoever wants to be perfect ought to sell what he has and not a part of it, as Ananias and Sapphira did, but everything. And when he has sold it, he must give everything to the poor, and thus prepare for himself treasure in the kingdom of heaven. Nor is this sufficient for perfection, unless after wealth has been despised, one follows the Saviour, ... For a wallet is more easily despised than the will. Many who abandon wealth

[48] Bede, *Homily* 1.13.42 (CChr.SL 122: 89).

[49] See Zachary Guiliano, 'Hierarchies of Knowledge in the Writings of the Venerable Bede', in Michael Champion, ed., *The Intellectual World of Late Antique Christianity* (Cambridge, forthcoming).

[50] For the history of interpretation of this passage, see Clark, *Reading Renunciation*, 94–9; Fink, 'Unreading Renunciation'.

[51] For example, Bede, *On Genesis* 2.1151–64, 4.284–307 (CChr.SL 118: 105, 202); *On Samuel* 1.521–51, 2.701–10 (CChr.SL 119: 25, 85); *On the Tabernacle* 1.748–70 (CChr.SL 119A: 24); *On the Temple* 2.1330–45 (CChr.SL 119A: 225–6); *On Ezra* 1.703–39 (CChr.SL 119A: 258–9); *On Proverbs* 1.3.175–81 (CChr.SL 119B: 43); *On the Song of Songs* 3.4.379–404, 5.7.465–87 (CChr.SL 119B: 254, 329); *Retraction on Acts* 4.130–41 (CChr.SL 121: 127); *Homily* 1.13, 2.2.56–79 (CChr.SL 122: 88–94, 194–5). References in *On Samuel, On Luke* and *On Mark* are too abundant to cite here.

[52] For example, Bede, *Ecclesiastical History* 3.5, 19, 26, 27, 4.3, 5.12, 5.19; *History of the Abbots* 1.1.

> do not follow the Lord. But he follows the Lord who imitates him, and walks in his footsteps. For 'whoever says he believes in Christ ought to walk just as he walked'.[53]

Bede repeats the same quotation in his later commentary on Mark.[54] Like renunciation, Bede regards the abandonment of wealth as ideally a singular event, a rite accomplished before one follows Christ in acts of great obedience, before becoming a teacher or preacher. This is the only way of life that is 'safe', he says, in which one may rejoice to be crucified to the world, neither 'having nor loving' possessions.[55] The tax collector Zacchaeus entered this way, an improbable 'camel' threading the eye of a needle 'after dropping the burden of his hump .... That is, a rich tax collector, having left behind the burden of riches, scorned the value of fraud.'[56] He thus entered the company of 'the perfect':[57]

> This is wise, that foolishness, which the tax collector gathered from the sycamore tree like the fruit of life: to return what was stolen, to give up one's possessions, to despise visible things for invisible, also for him to desire to die, to deny himself, and for him who was not yet seen to follow the footsteps of the Lord, to long to do so.[58]

Wealth must be abandoned all at once.[59] The seriousness and rigidity with which Bede held this view is demonstrated well in his interpretation of both the Gospel of Luke and the Acts of the Apostles, with regard to the example of St Barnabas. He argues that some, like Eusebius of Caesarea in his *Ecclesiastical History*, thought Barnabas was among the seventy-two disciples commissioned by Jesus to preach (Luke 10: 1–23). This could not be, Bede says, because they must have renounced all they had in order to preach, while

[53] Bede, *On Luke* 5.1251–63, quoting Jerome, *Commentary on Matthew* 3.868–77 (CChr.SL 72: 170–1).
[54] Bede, *On Mark* 3.740–50 (CChr.SL 120: 562–3).
[55] Bede, *On Luke* 5.1274 (CChr.SL 120: 327).
[56] Ibid. 1501–4 (CChr.SL 120: 333).
[57] Ibid. 1585 (CChr.SL 120: 335).
[58] Ibid. 1592–6 (CChr.SL 120: 335).
[59] Cf. Bede, *Exposition of Acts* 20.103–5 (CChr.SL 121: 84). Bede enjoins constant manual labour in implicit appeal to the lifestyle of St Paul (2 Thess. 3), explicitly citing his instruction to thieves (Eph. 4: 28).

Barnabas clearly possessed a field at a later point (Acts 4: 36–7).[60] For Bede, the requirement for 'the perfect' to abandon wealth screened out other ways of resolving this question. Ritual abandonment must precede preaching.

It may be helpful to pause and note how unusual Bede's view was in his time. In the early eighth century, giving up wealth (or abandoning kin) was not a preliminary to ordination, nor was it necessarily a preliminary to entering self-described ascetic or monastic life. Late antique and early medieval clerics routinely retained their property after ordination, even as they came to manage ecclesiastical holdings.[61] In time, kings and nobles might grant land and other wealth to monasteries and churches precisely for their own use or that of their kin, or even to 'acquire the privileges associated with ecclesiastical land'.[62] Such churches were often founded near lordly dwellings or within their bounds. Bede himself mentions these problems in his *Letter to Ecgbert*, even as he deplores them: clerics accumulating wealth and secular lords or 'thegns' retreating to their estates, well served by a monastic retinue to chant and pray for them as they enjoyed food, drink and company in a sort of Christianized and Northumbrian version of late Roman *otium*.[63] Bede complained that his attitudes were not more common:

> After all, God's command is 'sell what you own and give alms', and 'unless a man renounces everything he owns he cannot be my disciple'. But the modern custom of some who proclaim themselves as the servants of God is not only not to sell what they own but even to acquire what they did not have! What a cheek it is for a man who is about to enter the service of the Lord to dare to keep back what he had in his worldly life, or, in the guise of a holier life, to heap up riches he never possessed? And this despite the well-known condemnation of the apostles, which did not restore Ananias and Sapphira.[64]

60 Bede, *Retraction on Acts* 4.130–41 (CChr.SL 121: 127); compare *On Luke* 3.1114–69, 1921–44 (CChr.SL 120: 194–6, 215).

61 See the extensive discussions in Julia Barrow, *The Clergy in the Medieval World: Secular Clerics, their Families, and Careers in North-Western Europe,* c.*800*–c.*1200* (Cambridge, 2015); Ian Wood, *The Christian Economy in the Early Medieval West: Towards a Temple Society* (Binghamton, NY, 2022), 79–105.

62 Sarah Foot, *Monastic Life in Anglo-Saxon England,* c.*600–900* (Cambridge, 2006), 80–7.

63 Bede, *Letter to Ecgbert* 1.6, 10–12 (Grocock and Wood, eds, *Abbots*, 134–5, 144–9).

64 Ibid. 1.16 (Grocock and Wood, eds, *Abbots*, 156–7), referring to Luke 12: 33, 14: 33.

Churches and monasteries could control vast estates, collect revenue and serve as centres of economic exchange and transformation, an expression of the 'Temple society' of the early medieval West.[65] Such trends in early England regarding 'proprietary churches' matched those elsewhere in Europe and their link to local revenues.[66] It is even possible that Bede's own monastery began as a family monastery, or was at least 'seen [by others] as a family monastery in the decades after its foundation'.[67] Its independence from family bonds may have been achieved only after some struggle.

Bede would have known differing examples of ascetic life and ministry through personal contact with other clerics and religious, and through the sources he read from Late Antiquity, which mentioned varied models: from praise and blame assigned to married clergy and to rich, holy laypeople in Jerome's *Against Jovinian* and *Letters*, to quite different assessments in Julian of Eclanum's commentary on the Song of Songs; from the simple abandonment of the world by early Egyptian hermits (at least in the accounts of Jerome and Athanasius), to the more complex descriptions of renunciation and the management of episcopal households in Possidius's *Life of St Augustine* and Venantius Fortunatus's *Life of St Martin*.[68] Even the patterns praised by Bede's sources were broad, let alone those they denigrated. It is clear, then, that Bede was arguing for a new rigorous position, based on a particular reading of biblical and Christian traditions. His position was refracted primarily through selections of patristic exegesis and through monastic literature like John Cassian's *Collations* or the Rule of Benedict, rather than reflecting clear practices inherited from the past or exemplified in his milieu.

Bede's own historical works could, however, be seen to mask both this fact and the diversity of practice in his time. The outstanding clerics and monks of the *Ecclesiastical History* are most often praised for particular attitudes to wealth: the early monastic missionaries with

[65] See, for example, Ian Wood, 'Creating a "Temple Society" in the Early Medieval West', *Early Medieval Europe* 29 (2021), 462–86; idem, 'Entrusting Western Europe to the Church, 400–750', *TRHS* 6th series 23 (2013), 37–73.

[66] See Sarah Wood, *The Proprietary Church in the Medieval West* (Oxford, 2006), especially 92–108.

[67] Ian Wood, 'The Gifts of Wearmouth and Jarrow', in Wendy Davies and Paul J. Fouracre, eds, *The Languages of Gift in the Early Middle Ages* (Cambridge, 2010), 89–115, at 96.

[68] Michael Lapidge, *The Anglo-Saxon Library* (Oxford, 2006), Appendix E, 191–228.

Augustine of Canterbury, imitating 'the way of life of the apostles' by living moderately (*HE* 1.26); Gregory the Great, urging Augustine to institute a common life among the English clergy (*HE* 1.27); Aidan of Lindisfarne, who had no possessions and gave away any gift he received, while exhorting King Oswald and others to great moderation, and eventually dying in a tent (*HE* 3.5, 6, 17); Sigebert, who saw 'the love of riches' as one of the fires consuming the world, and so left behind all (*HE* 3.19). Beside these, Bede ranks his own abbots and their lives: Benedict Biscop renounced high rank, Eosterwine was willing to get his hands dirty at any kind of manual labour, and Ceolfrith ate lightly and exhibited a moderation in dress 'rarely found' among rulers (*History of the Abbots* 1.1, 8, 16). The glow of such virtues cast others in a dimmer light.

We should see Bede's comments – in his exegesis, his historiography and his *Letter to Egbert* – as an intervention in his society, part of a larger attempt at reforming the church's structures to conform them more closely with what he saw as the commands of Jesus, the example of the early church and the nature of Christian maturity. This explains his consistent return to the story of the rich ruler and the call of Jesus ('If you would be perfect'). He saw faults in contemporary practices and rites, and he had seen an example of living holiness in his own community, in the willingness to abandon all for the sake of the kingdom. Bede's attempt to amend the church of his day probably took many forms, but among them was his attempt to insist on two preliminary rites to baptism, ordination and monastic profession: giving up wealth, spiritually and practically.

A final note: Bede discusses the renunciation of wealth and its material abandonment as dramatic one-time actions that potentially brought a person into the kingdom of God or the company of the spiritually mature. However, other comments suggest that he recognized that managing one's attitude and practices toward wealth was far more complicated. For example, the everyday Christian's life after baptism might include freedom to 'enjoy the world' (*fruuntur hoc mundo*), although that life was meant to be marked by continual patterns of merciful giving to the needy and to the church.[69] If one's desires and practices were not perpetually oriented toward reaching heaven, a single promise, intention or rite made little difference.

[69] See Bede, *On the Song of Songs* 4.6.103–10 (CChr.SL 119B: 302).

Similarly, abandonment of wealth had to be accompanied by continual work, what Bede affirmed as 'work with one's hands' to provide for those in need. One had to attend to the state of one's soul if it had been lacerated by riches, and to one's mind, suffocated by the privileges and ease of wealth. 'It is the greatest labour for those having money or trusting in money to enter the court of the heavenly kingdom, casting off the bonds of greed' (*filargiria*).[70] Passage into the class of 'the perfect' committed each teacher or preacher to a state of continual progress and moral purification. And this progress was marked practically: did they continue to give away to the needy and poor anything they acquired? To renounce or relinquish wealth could be both a 'rite of passage', then, and a perpetual state of being, requiring varied 'rites of maintenance'.[71] For 'the poor' or 'the perfect', renouncing wealth and abandoning it were acts to be done once and always.

Conclusion

It would be tempting to conclude that Bede's views were idiosyncratic, limited to his time and place. That may be partly true. However, the popularity of his work ensured that his understanding of poverty and perfection became embedded within Western exegesis. When Bede first expressed these ideas, they may have been strange or extreme; they became widespread. His commentaries, including *On Luke*, were among the standard patristic texts from the Carolingian period onwards, attested in library catalogues, extant manuscripts and many citations.[72] Like Bede's other works, *On Luke* was a major source for liturgical and homiletic collections like the Homiliary of Paul the Deacon, Ælfric's *Catholic Homilies* and

[70] Bede, *On Luke* 5.1280–2 (CChr.SL 120: 327).

[71] See, in this volume, Benjamin Hansen, 'Making Christians in the Umayyad Levant: Anastasius of Sinai and Christian Rites of Maintenance', 98–118.

[72] Rosamond McKitterick, 'Kulturelle Verbindungen zwischen England und den fränkischen Reichen in der Zeit der Karolinger. Kontext und Implikationen', in Joachim Ehlers, ed., *Deutschland und der Westen Europas im Mittelalter* (Stuttgart, 2002), 121–48; Joshua Westgard, 'Bede and the Continent in the Carolingian Age and Beyond', in Scott DeGregorio, ed., *The Cambridge Companion to Bede* (Cambridge, 2010), 201–15; Hannah Matis, *The Song of Songs in the Early Middle Ages*, Studies in the History of Christian Traditions 191 (Leiden, 2019), 22–3, 219–21. This conclusion draws on material from my forthcoming *Bede's Economy*.

many other compilations or translations of patristic and early medieval material.[73] Each year, Charlemagne would listen to Bede's comments on the renunciations of Zacchaeus, likely at the annual dedication feast of St Mary's, Aachen.[74] A commentator like Rabanus Maurus would import nearly all of Bede's commentary on the rich young ruler and other passages into his own *Exposition of Matthew*,[75] while others, like Paschasius Radbertus or Sedulius Scottus, were more selective.[76] Other writers of homilies and gospel commentaries, such as Haimo and Heiric of Auxerre, Abbo of Saint-Germain and many anonymous authors, would find *On Luke* an invaluable resource, including for their comments on poverty and renunciation.[77] Such works helped direct and shape numerous later 'glosses' and related works, including the *Ordinary Gloss*, the *Golden*

[73] Guiliano, *Homiliary*, 107–13, 163–97.

[74] It is among the texts assigned in Charlemagne's homiliary *On the Dedication of a Church*: see Réginald Grégoire, *Homéliaires liturgiques médiévaux* (Spoleto, 1980), 477 (entry for Paul the Deacon, 2: 129; renumbered to 2: 128 in Guiliano, *Homiliary*, 65).

[75] Rabanus included material from Bede's works on Mark and Luke and *Homily* 1.13: *Exposition of Matthew* 5 (on 19: 16–30; CChr.CM 174A: 513–22).

[76] Sedulius Scottus, *On the Gospel of Matthew* 2.3 (*Sedulius Scottus. Kommentar zum Evangelium nach Matthäus*, ed. Bengt Löfstedt, 2 vols [Freiburg, 1989–91], 2: 445–6); 'Index auctorum', in Paschasius Radbertus, *Expositio in Matheo*, vol. 3 (CChr.CM 56B), 1543–4.

[77] For example, Haimo, *Homilia* 2.18 (PL 118: 589D, 592C–D, 596B–C, 597A–D), drawing on Bede, *On Luke* 5.242–460 (CChr.SL 120: 302–7); ibid. 2.51 (PL 118: 776C–777C, 778D, 779B–D), drawing on Bede, *On Luke* 2.1415–31, 1478–9, 5.1218–63, 1542–8 (CChr.SL 120: 136, 138, 326–7, 334). There are 227 Bedan quotations in 'Index auctorum', *Heirici Autissiodorensis Homiliae*, vol. 3 (CChr.CM 116B), 529–33. For Abbo, compare Bede, *On Luke* 2.1865–70, 4.448–51 (CChr.SL 120: 157, 242) with *Estote misericordes*, in *Abbo von Saint-Germain-des-Prés. 22 Predigten, kritische Ausgabe und Kommentar*, ed. Ute Önnerfors (Frankfurt am Main and New York, 1985), 194, 196–7. Compare also *Sermonary of Beaune* 2 with Bede, *On Luke* 2.2087–8, 2091–3, 2060–3, 2098–2104, 2126–38 respectively, and *On Luke* 2.25–161 (CChr.SL 120: 71–3, 100–4). See also Michael T. Martin, 'The Italian Homiliary: Texts and Contexts' (PhD thesis, Western Michigan University, 2005), especially *Homilies* 53, 56, 62, 65, 70, 78, 99, 113; Raymond Étaix, 'Le Sermonnaire carolingien de Beaune', *Revue des études augustiniennes* 25 (1979), 105–49; Henri Barré, 'L'Homeliaire carolingien de Mondsee', *Revue bénédictine* 71 (1961), 71–107, at 83–90. Also compare Paul Mercier, *Quatorze homélies du IXe siècle d'un auteur inconnu de l'Italie du Nord*, Sources Chrétiennes 161 (Paris, 1970), 155 (Homily 2.1), with Bede, *On Luke* 1.1026–36, 1049–55, 1166–9 (CChr.SL 120: 45, 48). Another unedited Bavarian homiliary used Bede: for example, compare Bamberg, Staatsbibliothek, Msc. Patr. 156 (s. ix), fols 9^r^, 10^r^ with Bede, *On Luke* 1.1064–1120, 1240–1, 1281–4, 1296–1328 (CChr.SL 120: 46, 50, 51, 52).

Chain of Thomas Aquinas, and the Wycliffite *Glossed Gospels*.[78] These ensured that Bede's rigorist positions were put before varied eyes and into many ears, due to the central place of such glosses in late medieval exegesis and scholarship. To provide a few examples: Bede's comments on Luke 14: 33, about the necessity of renunciation by all the faithful and relinquishment by the perfect, were regularly quoted or adapted.[79] Other comments on Luke 18: 24 – on the distinction between 'having wealth and loving wealth' and the 'safe' status of abandoning all – were also commonly referred to until the Reformation.[80] It would be easy to show other examples of Bede's exegetical influence.

Were there any direct consequences? A consideration of monastic profession may be the simplest, since (by and large) the abandonment of personal wealth gradually became a *sine qua non* of the monastic or religious life, though it took hundreds of years of development and no small amount of royal and imperial intervention to make it so. Diverse ascetic experiments existed before Bede's day; later they came to centre on a particular model. Whilst we can hardly argue that Bede alone brought about such a change, his exegesis permeated the places where these discussions were held.

The consequences for the preliminaries to ordination or baptism were not the same. Clerical wealth was a source of uneasiness right

[78] On the latter, see Andrew Kraebel, *Biblical Commentary and Translation in Later Medieval England: Experiments in Interpretation* (Cambridge, 2020), especially 133–75.

[79] See Bonaventure, *Commentary on the Gospel of St Luke* 14.33; idem, *Questiones disputatae de perfectione euangelica* 2.1.6; Henry of Ghent, *Quodlibet VII*, Q.29; Thomas Aquinas, *Golden Chain on Luke* 14.33; idem, *Contra impugnantes Dei cultum et religionem* 5.1; Zacharias Chrysopolitanus, *In unum ex quattuor* 2.67. Condensed version: *Ordinary Gloss on Luke* 14.33; Denys the Carthusian, *Enarratio in euangelium secundum Lucam* 14.33; Petrus Iohannis Olivi, *Lecture on Luke* 2.14.33. Paraphrased: John Wycliff, *Tractatus de ciuili domino* 3.14.

[80] Quoted in full by Rabanus Maurus, *Exposition of Matthew* 6 (on 19: 23); Sedulius Scottus, *On the Gospel of Matthew* 2.3.20 (on 19: 23); Claudius of Turin, *Exposition of Matthew* 19.23; Aquinas, *Contra impugnantes Dei cultum et religionem* 6.207–8. Quoted in part: *Ordinary Gloss on Matthew* 19.23; Zacharias Chrysopolitanus, *In unum ex quattuor* 3.106; Aquinas, *Golden Chain* 19.23; Bonaventure, *Luke* 18.24. Also Iohannes Pecham, *Quaestio de perfectione euangelica*; Petrus Cantor, *Summa quae dicitur Verbum adbreuiatum*, Franciscus de Marchia siue Franciscus de Esculo, *Improbatio contra libellum domni Iohannis qui incipit 'Quia uir reprobus'*; Marsilius de Padua, *Defensor Pacis* 2.13.20. Condensed: *Ordinary Gloss on Luke* 18.24. Paraphrased: Christian of Stavelot, *Commentary on the Gospel of Matthew* 19.23; perhaps also Alcuin, *Letter* 182: 'It is one thing to hold the world, and another to be held by it'.

through the Middle Ages; and Bede's comments became part of the war over gospel poverty waged in the thirteenth and fourteenth centuries between the mendicant orders and secular clerics. Bede's comments also became part of the critique of church wealth and of the papacy, not least by John Wycliff and Marsilius of Padua. Still, Bede and others failed to make the abandonment of wealth a universal characteristic of preachers and a preliminary to ordination. The rites of Christian initiation also remained without any formal or explicit renunciation of wealth. Candidates for baptism might be exorcized, anointed with oil, rubbed with saliva or given the salt of wisdom; they would renounce the devil, his works and his pomps; they would be catechized. But if there was a baptismal rite that explicitly included renouncing wealth, it has yet to emerge.

Perhaps this tells us something about rites of passage in relation to this framework of Christian exegesis. Within the religious culture of the Latin West, no single attitude toward the renunciation or management of wealth was dominant. Bede's views were specific and stringent, and he was among the authors most likely to be studied, quoted and followed. His views no doubt inspired some to renounce or abandon possessions, but they did not and could not attain universal observance. There were formal preliminaries to baptism, ordination and monastic profession. Learned exegetes like Bede hoped for more, and found existing rites wanting; they thought this precisely because of their participation in the centuries-long tradition of scriptural commentary. Their heightened literacy brought an intense sense of the demands of Christian obedience and its ideal expression in ritual form. For that reason, what they regarded as the true form and requirements of a rite or ceremony were not always shared with their contemporaries.

Baptism, ordination and monastic profession may have been designed to mark or effect the passage from sin to salvation, from youth to maturity, from one state of consecration to another; yet they did not always grant what they promised. In this way, to Bede and many others, they might serve *merely* as rituals: the ceremonies of a particular culture, marking an individual's stages in life, rather than providing the doorway to the heavenly kingdom or a necessary step along the path to perfection. This was not because the medieval Latin West lacked a commitment to rites and ceremonies or a pervading sense of the holy. Nor did it lack literacy or the systematization of rites. But its members had not, in the eyes of some contemporaries, undergone the transformations expected. We have an echo here of Buc's contention regarding ineffectual solemnities: the moral and social status of practitioners could result in the loss of *mysteria*.[81]

For historians looking back on the Middle Ages or considering the validity or usefulness of van Gennep's model, this has no little significance. The model of the sacred and profane presented in *Les Rites de passage* was highly eurocentric and bound to the early twentieth century. Its mode of analysis relied in part on a hierarchical view of cultures and religions that many today would find distasteful. It possessed hidden debts to Christian theology. Nonetheless, some of its observations provide fruitful sites for interaction. The observation of a culture's major rituals, undertaken without explicit commitment regarding their ability to achieve what they promise, is not necessarily a position requiring the eyes of a twentieth-century anthropologist or a commitment to secular modernity. One need not be a van Gennep making observations about a culture deemed foreign or primitive. A Bede or a Bonaventure could observe Christian rites and subject them to analysis, regard them with a critical eye and question their purpose. So can we. For historians of our day, on the other side of the development of anthropology and other social studies, this is an important point, whatever our confessional position. Anthropologists and folklorists like van Gennep often chose to focus on the local and the specific, the strange and idiosyncratic, and this has opened up greater possibilities and interest for historical work ever since. What we may wish to remedy or fill in, however, is the gaps they left: to reconsider, say, Savoyan baptismal or marriage customs alongside formal church rites; to place the apparently unique in its broader setting.

For the topic explored here, the renunciation of wealth, this remains a task of significance and interest. Clearly, the Church has long been imbricated in the economic transformations of broader European society. It produced a vast array of positions regarding wealth, some justifying and some undercutting many economic orders. These positions filled the highest and most common products of Christian literary culture: biblical commentaries and sermons. The stances taken in such works were not abstract or merely theoretical but arose in particular institutional settings and had material manifestations. How many thousands, if not millions, of people sought gospel perfection through renunciation? How many Christian

[81] Buc, *Dangers of Ritual*, 175–6.

foundations were richly endowed or maintained as a result? In positing preliminaries to the Church's rites of passage, Bede helped fashion a self-critical and often tumultuous ecclesiastical culture, ready to castigate the wealthy and powerful and seek economic purity. These may not be qualities we associate with him, with biblical exegesis or with church rites, but that is only because we have yet to attend closely to the turnings of this history.

Making Christians in the Umayyad Levant: Anastasius of Sinai and Christian Rites of Maintenance

Benjamin Hansen*
University of Minnesota

Toward the end of the seventh century, Anastasius of Sinai took it upon himself to offer advice to lay Christians facing a new Umayyad world. For Anastasius, Christian identity needed simplification. In his Edifying Tales *and* Questions and Answers, *he would de-emphasize theology, arguing that Christian identity was a more basic affair, involving baptism, the eucharist and the sign of the cross. For him, these were 'rites of maintenance', acts which sustained Christian identity in a fluid world of religious alternatives. Such actions warded off the demonic and drew a clear boundary between Muslim and Christian. This was important for Anastasius, who considered it his pastoral duty to offer uneducated Christians a tangible sense of their own identity (and superiority). His ritualistic simplification bears witness to an important shift in Palestinian-centred Christianity, as intra-Christian disputes were set aside in an attempt to maintain a ritualistic boundary between Christian and non-Christian.*

Anastasius of Sinai is an indispensable witness to the shifting fortunes of Christians in Syria-Palestine and the greater Levant during the second half of the seventh century. His assumptions concerning the place of Chalcedonian Christian communities under Islamic rule mark a distinct change. In the 630s, for example, Jerusalem's patriarch Sophronius could assure his audience that the Arab armies were God's temporary chastisement, and that repentance would shortly bear the fruit of political liberation.[1] Anastasius tells a different story. His was a world in which early Islam was not simply a matter of

* E-mail: hanse848@umn.edu.

[1] See Sophronius, *On the Nativity of Christ* 25, in the recently edited Greek edition of John M. Duffy, *Sophronios of Jerusalem: Homilies* (Cambridge, MA, 2020), 51. Translations are my own unless otherwise noted.

Studies in Church History 59 (2023), 98–118
doi: 10.1017/stc.2023.6

armies but a matter of neighbours as well.[2] He would encourage prayers for the Islamic caliphate, however begrudging.[3] This was not the first time, he reminded his audience, that the faithful had been called to learn how to live under such uncomfortable arrangements.[4] Indeed, Anastasius was keenly concerned to adjudicate this transition, serving as privileged midwife for a nascent Umayyad Christianity.[5]

Anastasius lived a busy life.[6] Born on Cyprus in the 630s,[7] his name would become associated with his residency at the Mount Sinai monastery now known as St Catherine's. He enjoyed travel. His stories offer a tour of the eastern Mediterranean from Egypt to

[2] For evidence of lives lived 'shoulder to shoulder', see *Questions and Answers* 9, 26, 76, 99, 102 (*Questiones et responsiones*, ed. Marcel Richard and Joseph Munitiz, CChr.SG 59).

[3] Ibid. 60, 65.

[4] Ibid. 101.

[5] I borrow the paradoxical label 'Umayyad Christianity' from the provocative work of George Najib Awad, *Umayyad Christianity: John of Damascus as a Contextual Example of Identity Formation in Early Islam* (Piscataway, NJ, 2018).

[6] The sole monograph on Anastasius's work is Karl-Heinz Uthemann, *Anastasios Sinaites. Byzantinisches Christentum in den ersten Jahrzehnten unter arabischer Herrschaft*, 2 vols (Berlin, 2015). See also John Haldon, 'The Works of Anastasius of Sinai: A Key Source for the History of Seventh-Century East Mediterranean Society and Belief', in Averil Cameron and Lawrence I. Conrad, eds, *The Byzantine and Early Islamic Near East*, 1: *Problems in the Literary Source Material* (Princeton, NJ, 1992), 107–47; Robert G. Hoyland, *Seeing Islam as Others saw it: A Survey and Evaluation of Christian, Jewish, and Zoroastrian Writings on Early Islam* (Princeton, NJ, 1997), 92–103. Rich with biographical material is André Binggeli, 'Anastase le Sinaïte: "Récits sur le Sinaï" et "Récits utiles à l'âme". Édition, traduction, commentaire', 2 vols (PhD thesis, Université Paris IV, Sorbonne, 2001), esp. 330–59. On Anastasius's approach to lay piety, see Nicholas Marinides, 'Anastasius of Sinai and Chalcedonian Christian Lay Piety in the Early Islamic Near East', in Robert G. Hoyland, ed., *The Late Antique World of Early Islam: Muslims among Christians and Jews in the East Mediterranean* (Princeton, NJ, 2015), 293–311. While much of Marinides's account is relevant to this article, my notion of 'rites of maintenance' offers a novel approach to his evidence.

[7] Following the argument of Binggeli, 'Anastase le Sinaïte', endorsed by Joseph A. Munitiz, ed, *Anastasios of Sinai: Questions and Answers*, Corpus Christianorum in Translation 7 (Turnhout, 2011), 9–11. Stephen Shoemaker's argument concerning the dating of the Dome of the Rock may suggest that Anastasius was born earlier in the seventh century: 'Anastasius of Sinai and the Beginnings of Islam', *Journal of Orthodox Christian Studies* 1 (2018), 137–54, at 147–8. Haldon seems to presume an earlier birth and a very long life: 'Works of Anastasius', 113–14. The argument here does not depend on a secure dating of his birth and death. There is a general consensus among scholars that Anastasius died around 700/701 CE. The *Synaxarion* of Constantinople (10th c.) calls him a 'very old man', as noted by Munitiz, *Anastasios of Sinai*, 11 n. 11; cf. Uthemann, *Anastasios Sinaites*, 3–14.

Palestine and Syria, and at times beyond.[8] Anastasius's interests were not confined to the monastery, however; he showed a compassionate (if at times self-important) enthusiasm for the concerns of lay people, particularly evident in his *Questions and Answers*. He was shrewd in his advice, combining his own biblical exegesis with the rich patristic tradition as well as a substantial amount of medical and scientific speculation.[9] His anti-Miaphysite writings, moreover, may have served as a how-to guide for middle-brow Chalcedonian Christians who lived as minorities in Syria and Egypt and who showed interest in theological disputation.[10]

Two of Anastasius's collections seem particularly directed to a popular audience: the *Questions and Answers* and two sets of pious stories, the so-called *Tales of the Sinai Fathers* and the *Edifying Tales*.[11]

[8] See Binggeli, 'Anastase le Sinaïte', 357–9. Like the travels of John Moschus several decades earlier, Anastasius's itinerary highlights the tight link between Sinai and the monastery of Mar Saba in the eastern Judean desert as well as the continued importance of Chalcedonian Christian communities even in the heart of Miaphysite Egypt. The writings of Anastasius and Moschus 'bear witness to an interconnected and mobile monasticism of the Eastern Mediterranean in which monks moved from Egypt to Palestine with ease and frequency, the Sinai Peninsula an open door to both': Benjamin Hansen, 'Bread in the Desert: The Politics and Practicalities of Food in Early Egyptian Monasticism', *ChH* 90 (2021), 286–303, at 289. Note also Binggeli's sense of the 'openness' of the Sinai peninsula: 'Anastase le Sinaïte', 443–7.

[9] See Binggeli, 'Anastase le Sinaïte', 354–6. Medical references and references to contemporary scientific theory are found throughout his *Questions and Answers*. He seems to imply that he had at least witnessed medical dissection (Q. 22.8). If we accept the *Sinai Fathers* as a genuinely Anastasian text, we learn that Anastasius served as a warden of the infirmary in the Mount Sinai monastery at some point: *Sinai Fathers* 1.3, 19 (following Binggeli's numbering). For medicine, health, and healing in Anastasius, see Marie-Hélène Congourdeau, 'Médecine et théologie chez Anastase le Sinaïte, médecin, moine et didascale', in V. Boudon-Millot and B. Pouderon, eds, *Les Pères de l'église face à la science médicale de leur temps. Actes du troisième colloque d'études patristiques, Paris, 9–11 septembre 2004* (Paris, 2005), 287–97.

[10] Most importantly his *Hodegos (Viae Dux)*, ed. Karl-Heinz Uthemann, CChr.SG 8. See Uthemann, *Anastasios Sinaites*, 20–215, for an exhaustive analysis.

[11] Binggeli's dissertation offers the most up-to-date Greek edition of these *Tales* along with a French translation. He is currently working on a critical edition. His work follows upon that of François Nau, 'Les Récits inédits du moine Anastase. Contribution à l'histoire du Sinaï au commencement du VIIe siècle', *Revue de l'Institut Catholique de Paris* 1–2 (1902), 1–70; idem, 'Le Texte grec des récits du moine Anastase sur les saints pères du Sinaï', *Oriens Christianus* 2 (1903), 58–89; idem, 'Le Texte grec des récits utiles à l'âme d'Anastase le Sinaïte', *Oriens Christianus* 3 (1903), 56–75. An English translation of the *Sinai Fathers*, as well as a few entries from the *Edifying Tales*, is found in Daniel F. Caner et al., *History and Hagiography from the Late Antique Sinai*, TTH 53 (Liverpool, 2010), 171–98. Whilst I am well persuaded by Binggeli's argument that

The *Sinai Fathers* is an account of monastic life written for monastics and those lay Christians with a special enthusiasm for monks and miracles; the *Edifying Tales* serves as a sort of rousing pamphlet, promoting and reinforcing Christian religious superiority while tarring the competition. These texts are a treasure trove for the social historian, offering a precious glimpse into the socio-historical world of Levantine Christians under the early Umayyad caliphate. Questions of religious competition and religious neighbourliness are to the fore, combined with matter-of-fact discussions of sex, slavery, plague and money.[12]

Anastasius died around the year 700. The work he left behind, especially his *Edifying Tales* and *Questions and Answers*, bears witness to the extraordinary effort he put into a fundamental pastoral project. For Anastasius, in the novel and at times disheartening Umayyad world, Christian identity needed certain simplifications. In these works, Anastasius, quite a capable theologian, downplays sophisticated theology, arguing that Christian identity was a more basic affair, determined by baptism, the eucharist and the sign of the cross.[13] For Anastasius, these three actions not only warded off the demonic, but they also drew a clear boundary between Muslim and Christian. This was important, as he considered it his pastoral duty to offer uneducated Christians a tangible sense of their own identity (and superiority), in spite of recent political and economic misfortune.[14]

Anastasius of Sinai was the author of both *Tales*, others have cast doubt on the *Sinai Fathers* as a genuinely Anastasian text. This article will therefore rely primarily on the *Edifying Tales* in addition to his *Questions and Answers*, making supplementary references to the *Sinai Fathers*. For an argument against attributing *Sinai Fathers* to Anastasius, see most recently Uthemann, *Anastasios Sinaites*, 456–63.

[12] As argued by Haldon, 'Works of Anastasius', 129–47.

[13] As Jack Tannous has argued, the shared religious worlds of the early medieval Middle East were primarily those of ritual and rite. While religious elites promoted exquisite theologies, most 'simple believers' concerned themselves with basic and effective religious practices. Anastasius is exceptional in this respect, able to play to both audiences depending on the text and context: see Jack Tannous, *The Making of the Medieval Middle East: Religion, Society, and Simple Believers* (Princeton, NJ, and Oxford, 2018).

[14] I certainly do not want to argue that the late seventh century was a time of widescale persecution and discrimination. Archaeological studies have shown that the 'Byzantine-Islamic' transition in the Holy Land was, all things considered, remarkably non-destructive: see Gideon Avni, *The Byzantine-Islamic Transition in Palestine; An Archaeological Approach* (Oxford, 2014); Robert Schick, *The Christian Communities of Palestine from Byzantine to Islamic Rule: A Historical and Archaeological Study*

This pastoral concern led Anastasius to search for a discreet and streamlined piety, tacitly acknowledging the relative theological illiteracy of much of his flock. Anastasius expressed caution over what he understood to be the relative 'weakness of the majority' of his audience when it came to speculative theology.[15] Certainly he was willing to address the learned among his fellow Christians, not least in his *Hodegos*.[16] However, a late antique pastor needed to use more than one approach.[17] This demand for pastoral flexibility when it came to a largely uneducated flock was nothing new. As Jack Tannous has shown, many Christian leaders between the fourth and the seventh centuries realized that circumstances required them to make accommodations for the 'simple believers' in their congregations.[18] Moreover, that much of Anastasius's teaching was directed towards

(Princeton, NJ, 1995). But even from the 630s, sermons such as those of Sophronius of Jerusalem mark a real sense of panic and disappointment. Moreover, Charlemagne's embassy to the Holy Land *c.*800 bears witness to a church greatly diminished in clergy and finances: see Michael McCormick, ed., 'The *Basel Roll*: Critical Edition and Translation', in idem, *Charlemagne's Survey of the Holy Land: Wealth, Personnel, and Building of a Mediterranean Church between Antiquity and the Middle Ages* (Washington DC, 2011), 5–22. The concern elicited by the construction of the Dome of the Rock should tell us something about the state of unease in certain Christian communities: Anastasius, *Edifying Tales* 7; Ps-Shenute, *Apocalypse* (Émile Amélineau, ed., *Monuments pour servir a l'histoire de l'Égypte chretienne aux IVe, Ve, VIe, et VIIe siècles*, 2 vols [Paris, 1888–95], 1: 341). For the place of the Dome of the Rock in Anastasius's work, see Uthemann, *Anastasios Sinaites*, 357–64. For the effect that the building of the Dome of the Rock may have had on Christian communities more broadly, see G. J. Reinink, ed., *Die Syrische Apokalypse des Pseudo-Methodius* (CSCO 541), xxiv–xxv.

[15] 'τῶν πολλῶν ἀσθένειαν': Anastasius, *Edifying Tales* 20.14 (Binggeli, 'Anastase le Sinaïte', 249). This concern for the 'simple', however, was not limited to the *Tales* and *Questions and Answers*. Anastasius notes that expositions of contemporary Christological debates risked scandalizing 'the simple' (τοῖς ἁπλουστέροις) when not done with appropriate care: *Hodegos* 1.2.17–18.

[16] As Jaclyn Maxwell has argued, one must be cautious in driving too deep a wedge between 'theology' and 'popular religion': 'Popular Theology in Late Antiquity', in Lucy Grig, ed., *Popular Culture in the Ancient World* (Cambridge, 2017), 277–95. Maxwell's analysis is largely based on fourth- and fifth-century sources and it is unclear whether popular debate concerning Arianism had an appropriate seventh-century parallel. Still, we might approach Anastasius's *Hodegos* as an effort to gain 'complete control over the discussions' at hand, reflecting Maxwell's estimation of episcopal sermons on complex theological matters: 'Popular Theology', 284.

[17] A fine introduction to pastoral care in Late Antiquity is Pauline Allen and Wendy Mayer, 'Through a Bishop's Eyes: Towards a Definition of Pastoral Care in Late Antiquity', *Augustinianum* 40 (2000), 345–97.

[18] Tannous, *Medieval Middle East*, 46–110.

lay Christians by means of written questions and answers likewise reflected a venerable Christian practice.[19] The letter collections of sixth-century figures such as the Gazan monks Barsanuphius and John or the patriarch Severus offer precious glimpses into the religious concerns of lay Christians, both Chalcedonian and non-Chalcedonian.[20] While Anastasius's *Questions and Answers* and *Edifying Tales* owe much to this tradition, he nevertheless radicalized and reshaped this emphasis in response to the pressing concerns which Islam presented to Christian audiences.

Anastasius's 'ritualistic simplification' bears witness to an important shift for Umayyad Christians. While he was clearly competent in (and enthusiastic about) intra-Christian Christological disputes, *Questions and Answers* and *Edifying Tales* downplay these in an attempt to create and fortify a ritual boundary between Christian and non-Christian. He was concerned with keeping Christians Christian, with the maintenance of Christian identity. Indeed, he laid particular stress on what I call 'rites of maintenance', simple actions accessible to the widest variety of lay people, regardless of their theological literacy.

RITES OF PASSAGE OR RITES OF MAINTENANCE?

I have chosen this somewhat clumsy term 'rites of maintenance', calling to mind 'rites of passage' while at the same time making a key

[19] 'Questions and Answers' is a genre which raises a variety of scholarly problems concerning audience, interpretation and composition, none of which have found fully satisfactory answers. In Anastasius's case, a key clue is found at the end of Q. 81, where he presumes that at least some of his answers are being read aloud in churches. For a preliminary discussion of this genre, see Annelie Volgers and Claudio Zamagni, eds, *Erotapokriseis: Early Christian Question-and-Answer Literature in Context* (Leuven, 2004). See Munitiz, *Anastasios of Sinai*, 11–12, for a brief discussion of Anastasius's audience.

[20] For lay concerns in the epistolary corpus of Barsanuphius and John, see Jennifer Hevelone-Harper, *Disciples of the Desert* (Baltimore, MD, 2005), 79–105; eadem, 'The Letter Collection of Barsanuphius and John', in Cristiana Sogno, Bradley K. Storin and Edward J. Watts, eds, *Late Antique Letter Collections: A Critical Introduction and Reference Guide* (Berkeley, CA, 2016), 418–32, at 418–20; for a discussion of genre more broadly in these letters, see François Neyt, Paula de Angelis-Noah and Lucien Regnault, eds, *Barsanuphe et Jean de Gaza: Correspondance*, 1/1, Sources Chrétiennes 426, 50–3. Pauline Allen and C. T. R Hayward highlight Severus's correspondence with concerned lay people: *Severus of Antioch* (Abingdon, 2004), 53–4; Tannous also emphasizes Severus's concern for lay participation: *Medieval Middle East*, 48 n. 7, 68–9.

distinction. We associate 'rites of passage' with the ground-breaking work of Arnold van Gennep, although his well-known *Les Rites de passage* (1909) largely failed to attract scholarly attention in the English-speaking world until its elaboration and amplification in the work of Victor Turner.[21] Both authors emphasize the threefold structure, or three stages, of all rites of passage: the pre-liminal, the liminal and the post-liminal. We might also call these the break, the transition and the final incorporation.[22]

In this line of thinking, the pre-liminal demands a break with the past. Here, for example, we may think of the exorcism preceding baptism. The liminal is a stage marked by openness to transition and contains within itself an inherent and necessary vulnerability. The neophyte is naked, a *tabula rasa* for the ensuing ritual (van Gennep and Turner both draw our attention to the nakedness of early Christian baptism).[23] As the final stage, the post-liminal is an incorporation or welcoming into the new community. Here it makes sense to think of rites such as confirmation or chrismation and first communion.

The phrase 'rites of passage' presumes a movement from beginning to end; its connotations are those of completion. I wish to contrast this sense of completion with 'rites of maintenance' in the thinking of Anastasius.[24] For him, such rites were key to maintaining differentiation between one community and the other. As Catherine Bell has argued in her discussion of the nature and purpose of ritual, these rites are, among other things, 'a strategic way of acting' which effect differentiation between those who perform the rite and those who do not.[25]

[21] See now Arnold van Gennep, *The Rites of Passage*, transl. Monika B. Vizedom and Gabrielle L. Caffee, 4th edn (Chicago, IL, 1966); Victor Turner, *The Ritual Process: Structure and Anti-Structure* (Ithaca, NY, 1969). Arpad Szakolczai offers a succinct account of the reception of van Gennep's work and the concept of 'liminality' in other disciplines: 'Liminality and Experience: Structuring Transitory Situations and Transformative Events', *International Political Anthropology* 2 (2009), 141–72, at 141–6; Catherine Bell offers a discussion of van Gennep's lasting contributions to ritual theory: *Ritual: Perspectives and Dimensions* (Oxford and New York, 1997), 35–8.

[22] Helpfully summarized in Szakolczai, 'Liminality and Experience', 147–8.

[23] Van Gennep, *Rites of Passage*, 93–5; Turner, *Ritual Process*, 103.

[24] Though it should be noted that van Gennep observed that many 'rites of communion' wear off and must be repeated: *Rites of Passage*, 29.

[25] Catherine Bell, *Ritual Theory, Ritual Practice* (New York and Oxford, 1992), 7. Bell emphasizes the stability (we might say 'maintenance') of identity which these rites provide for distinct communities in her discussion of van Gennep: *Ritual: Perspectives and Dimensions*, 37.

She notes that 'ritualization is the production of this differentiation' between a host of binaries, marking the body with one identity while denying (or at least ignoring) another.[26] For Anastasius, ritual not only created difference, it constantly sustained it.

Indeed, in reading *Tales* and *Questions and Answers*, it becomes clear that Anastasius was especially concerned with keeping his audience in something akin to van Gennep's notion of the post-liminal, serving as what Turner would call a 'ritual elder'.[27] Anastasius was well aware that religious competition in the form of Islam, sorcery or Judaism held the potential to pull Christians away from their post-liminal state back into the ambiguous arena of liminality, making these Christians potential blank slates for alien rites and rituals.[28] It was ritual, therefore, which Anastasius decided was essential for Christian identity in the Chalcedonian Levant, a distinct shift from his emphasis elsewhere on intra-Christian credal competition.[29]

[26] Ibid. 90; see also 101–7.

[27] Turner, *Ritual Process*, 96. Of course, Anastasius's work also addresses rites of passage as such. His *Sinai Fathers* is particular concerned with death and burial (e.g. 1.8, 9, 14–16, 29); he addresses the when, whom and how of baptism in *Questions and Answers* (e.g. QQ. 9, 14, 28). His advice on marriage is, as a rule, more pastoral than ritual in *Questions and Answers*. Whether the *Hexaemeron* attributed to Anastasius is genuine is a subject of much debate: see the discussion in *Anastasius of Sinai: Hexaemeron*, ed. Clement A. Kuehn and John D. Baggarly, Orientalia Christiana Analecta 278 (Rome, 2007), xiii–xxiii. In *Hexaemeron* 9–10, the author emphasizes marriage primarily as the union between Christ and his church.

[28] Space precludes addressing Anastasius's portrayal of Jews and Judaism. Along with anti-Jewish rhetoric in *Questions and Answers* and *Edifying Tales*, he may have been the author of a *Disputatio adversus Iudaeos* (Clavis Patrum Graecorum 7772). Uthemann dedicates a substantial portion of his monograph discussing this possibility: *Anastasios Sinaites*, 583–714. The sermons of Sophronius of Jerusalem likewise bear witness to virulent opposition to Palestine's Jews in the seventh century. It seems more plausible that this virulence sprang from real religious competition rather than being merely a rhetorical ploy against heretics and Muslims, *pace* David Olster, *Roman Defeat, Christian Response, and the Literary Construction of the Jew* (Philadelphia, PA, 1994).

[29] Especially in his *Hodegos*. The latter presumes a context in which Chalcedonians would have been in the minority but in which public debate was possible (we might presume especially in Egypt). Still, it is important to note that in the *Hodegos* Anastasius mentions debates with (among other non-Christians) Muslims: *Hodegos* 1.1.43; 7.2.117–18; 10.2.4.9. See the preliminary remarks of Sidney Griffith, 'Anastasios of Sinai, the *Hodegos*, and the Muslims', *Greek Orthodox Theological Review* 32 (1987), 341–58, at 347–58.

Ritual as Synecdoche: Basic Christian Actions

Throughout Anastasius's writings, but especially in his *Edifying Tales*, Christian ritual served as a synecdoche for the faith as a whole. Anastasius tells us, for example, of a certain Theodore the sailor who had renounced the Christian faith. What did such a renunciation entail? Theodore left the faith, Anastasius writes, by 'renouncing both the cross and baptism'.[30] We find a more explicit link between ritual and Christian identity, however, in Anastasius's descriptions of Christian interaction with the demonic.[31] Thus Anastasius tells of one Moses, an on-again, off-again Christian: at times apostate, at times pious. Moses explained the troubles he had when a Christian, namely, demonic harassment. In fact, his demon was looking for a deal; the harassment would cease, the demon told Moses, if he would cease acting like a Christian.

The demon's instructions were straightforward, telling Moses: 'Do not bow down to Christ and I will let you be. Do not confess him as God and son of God, and I will not hinder you. Do not take communion, and I will not bother you; do not seal yourself [i.e., with the sign of the cross], and I shall be kind to you.'[32] The stark simplicity of the credal content of Christianity in this story is striking, especially if we compare it to Anastasius's Christological polemics. A basic confession of the deity and sonship of Christ is thus here more concerned with nascent Islam than it was with Miaphysites. The emphasis on the practices of Christianity, that is, the sign of the cross and the eucharist, merits even more attention.

This ritual simplification is quite conspicuous when Anastasius takes his readers into a prison which housed, among others, several sorcerers awaiting trial. He tells us that one particularly forthright sorcerer gave friendly advice to his Christian interlocutor: the would-be interrogator of sorcerers should 'never do so without having first taken communion and without wearing a cross around your neck

[30] 'ἀρνησάμενος καὶ τὸν σταυρὸν καὶ τὸ βάπτισμα': Anastasius, *Edifying Tales* 10.4 (Binggeli, 'Anastase le Sinaïte', 230).

[31] See Binggeli, 'Anastase le Sinaïte', 395–7. Tannous discusses many of the following episodes: *Medieval Middle East*, 142–4.

[32] 'Μὴ προσκυνήσῃς τὸν Χριστὸν, καὶ οὐ σιαίνω σε, μὴ ὁμολογήσῃς αὐτὸν Θεὸν καὶ ὑίον Θεοῦ, καὶ οὐ προσεγγίζω σοι. μὴ κοινωνήσῃς, καὶ οὐ παρενοχλῶ σοι. Μὴ κατασφραγίσῃ, καὶ ἀγαπῶ σε': *Edifying Tales* 13.20–3 (Binggeli, 'Anastase le Sinaïte', 233).

[ἐάν μὴ πρότερον κοινωνήσῃς καὶ φορέσῃς σταυρὸν ἐπὶ τοῦ τραχήλου σου]. For indeed my companions are wicked men and wish to do you harm. But if you do as I have told you, neither they nor others will be able to harm you.'[33] Anastasius later returns his audience to prison, introducing us to another sorcerer who made this confession before his looming execution: 'My spells never worked against a Christian who had received communion that same day; for the demonic power of sorcery is rendered useless by communion.'[34]

A final example is the most explicit endorsement of the apotropaic power of Christian praxis. Anastasius writes of a certain holy John from Bostra in southern Syria.[35]A local official recruited John to confront four young women, each demonically possessed. Before the exorcism itself, Anastasius describes an idiosyncratic (if not bewildering) interrogation,[36] including this exchange:

> Then the blessed one ended the conversation by asking [the demons] the following: 'What Christian things do you fear?' They answered him: 'Truly there are three important things. One is that which you wear around your necks. Another is that place in which you bathe in the church. Then there is that which you eat in your gathering.' The slave of God John perceived that they had spoken of the honourable cross and of holy baptism and of holy communion. And then he asked them another question, saying: 'Which one of these three things do you fear the most?' They answered him and said: 'If you guard well that with which you commune among yourselves, it is not possible to harm even one of you Christians.'[37]

[33] Ibid. 14.14–17 (Binggeli, 'Anastase le Sinaïte', 235).

[34] 'οὐδεπότε ἴσχυσαν αἱ φαρμακεῖαι μου εἰς ἄνθρωπον Χριστιανὸν κοινωνοῦνται τὸ καθ' ἡμέραν: κατηργεῖτο γὰρ ὑπὸ τῆς κοινωνίας πᾶσα μου ἡ ἰσχὺς ἡ δαιμονικὴ τῆς φαρμακείας': ibid. 16.6–9. A contextual background for Anastasius's portrayal of the power of the eucharist can be found in Vincent Déroche, 'Représentations de l'eucharistie dans la haute époque byzantine', *Travaux et Mémoires* 14 (2002), 167–80; Marinides, 'Chalcedonian Christian Lay Piety', 306–8.

[35] Anastasius tells us that this John held the office of χαρτουλαρίος (an official archivist) in Damascus: see Binggeli, 'Anastase le Sinaïte', 564 n. 2.

[36] Anastasius writes that other topics included the demonic fall from the angelic state; the nature of Eden; the type of fruit which caused Adam to sin; a discussion of the serpent and 'many other topics which it is not necessary to report here, due to the weakness of the majority' of his audience: *Edifying Tales* 20.10–14 (Binggeli, 'Anastase le Sinaïte', 249). This is the 'weakness' discussed above.

[37] 'Εἶτα διακόψας τὸν περὶ τούτου λόγον ὁ μακαρίτης, ἠρώτησεν αὐτοὺς λέγων· Ποῖα πράγματα φοβεῖσθε ἐκ τῶν Χριστιανῶν; Λέγουσιν ἐκεῖνοι πρὸς αὐτόν·

These examples, though representative and not exhaustive, lay the foundation for understanding Anastasius's promotion of the very basics of Christian ritual. This notion of 'ritual maintenance', however, was part of a larger project which touched on Christian identity in the Umayyad Caliphate (especially Palestine) and centred on frequent lay communion with an eye toward religious competition, in the form of Islam or otherwise.

A Renaissance of Lay Piety: Anastasius and the Eucharist

Anastasius's concern with frequent communion comes at the end of a hundred-year reform movement to that end. As Phil Booth has shown, seventh-century Palestine bears witness to a sustained pastoral effort to redefine ecclesiastical community and to encourage lay participation.[38] John Moschus and his companion, Sophronius (later patriarch of Jerusalem) began this pastoral effort, constructing a new Chalcedonian literary republic, one notably inclusive of lay piety and optimistic about the potential of Christian society.[39] Maximus the Confessor worked toward the same end, providing a dense metaphysical coherence to what he argued was a symphony of church, world and sacrament.[40] This reform movement, in Booth's words, was one primarily of 'sacramental reorientation' – a firm emphasis on participation in the church's rites – which marked 'a seminal shift in emphasis within the Roman East', one centred now more than ever on 'sacramental mediation'.[41] From Moschus to

῎Εχετε ὄντως τρία πράγματα μεγάλα· ὃν ὃ φορεῖτε εἰς τοὺς τραχήλους ὑμῶν, καὶ ὃν ὅπου λούεσθε εἰς τὴν ἐκκλησίαν, καὶ ὃν ὅπερ τρώγετε εἰς τὴν σύναξιν. Νοήσας οὖν ὁ τοῦ Χριστοῦ δοῦλος Ἰωάννης, ὅτι περὶ τοῦ τιμίου σταυροῦ εἰρήκασι καὶ περὶ τοῦ ἁγίου βαπτίσματος καὶ περὶ τῆς ἁγίας κοινωνίας, πάλιν ἠρώτησεν αὐτοὺς λέγων· Εἶτα ἐκ τούτων τῶν τριῶν πραγμάτων, ποῖον φοβεῖσθε πλέον; Τότε ἐκεῖνοι ἀπεκρίθησαν αὐτῷ καὶ εἶπαν· ῎Οντως εἰ ἐφυλάττετε καλῶς, ὅπερ μεταλαμβάνετε, οὐκ ἴσχυεν εἷς ἐξ ἡμῶν ἀδικῆσαι Χριστιανόν': Anastasius, *Edifying Tales* 20.24–33 (Binggeli, 'Anastase le Sinaïte', 250).

[38] See Phil Booth, *The Crisis of Empire: Doctrine and Dissent at the End of Late Antiquity* (Berkeley, CA, 1999). Booth's argument in part builds on that of Olster in *Roman Defeat*.

[39] See Brenda Llewellyn Ihssen, *John Moschos' Spiritual Meadow: Authority and Autonomy at the End of the Antique World* (Abingdon, 2014); Booth, *Crisis of Empire*, 90–139, 241–50; Olster, *Roman Defeat*, 99–115. The themes of Sophronius's sermons are also discussed in Jeanne de la Ferrière, *Sophrone de Jérusalem. Fêtes chrétiennes à Jérusalem* (Paris, 1999).

[40] See Booth, *Crisis of Empire*, 170–85.

[41] Ibid. 4–6.

Anastasius, authors centred this vision of the church on lay piety. It was, furthermore, inclusive of monastics who were willing to commune and submit to episcopal authority;[42] and conspicuously ambiguous about (if not implicitly hostile to) the spiritual relevance of the Roman Empire.[43] It was a heady and delicate reorientation.

Yet we cannot include Anastasius in this 'reform movement' without noticing a striking discontinuity. Booth rightly places the eucharistic focus of Sophronius and John Moschus's *Miracles of Cyrus and John*, for example, into the context of intra-Christian disputes.[44] Proper eucharistic piety (and consequent eucharistic miracles) codified boundaries between Chalcedonian and non-Chalcedonian Christians.[45] This was, in short, a eucharistic practice that bore the weight of continual Christological competition. Anastasius, however, directs his audience to the power of eucharistic piety over against non-Christian communities. Thus, for Anastasius, the power of the eucharist was not simply that it clarified Chalcedonian orthodoxy, but rather that it codified Christian supremacy.

Fundamental to all this was frequent communion, and Anastasius is exemplary in this regard. As for monks, a cohort which included many great teachers often ambiguous about the need for communion, he tells his audience in his *Sinai Tales* that even severe ascetics who had achieved a sort of bodiless invisibility in this life still sneaked into the church to communicate.[46] But the *Questions and Answers* best

[42] We find a special emphasis on submission to bishops and monastic-ecclesial harmony in Cyril of Scythopolis's late sixth-century *Lives of the Monks of Palestine*. For Cyril, however, the role of empire is still prominent, not least in the Origenist controversy. For Cyril's hagiography and its Palestinian context, see Lorenzo Perrone, *La chiesa di Palestina e le controversie cristologiche* (Brescia, 1980); more recently, Daniël Hombergen, *The Second Origenist Controversy: A New Perspective on Cyril of Scythopolis' Monastic Biographies as Historical Sources for Sixth-Century Origenism* (Rome, 2001). On the relationship between the monks of the Judean desert monasteries and the Jerusalem patriarchate, see also Christopher Birkner, 'Kirche und Kellion. Zum Verständnis von "Kirche" bei Kyrill von Skythopolis', in Peter Gemeinhardt, ed., *Was ist Kirche in der Spätantike? Publikation der Tagung der Patristischen Arbeitsgemeinschaft in Duderstadt und Göttingen (02.–05.01.2015)* (Leuven, 2017), 163–76.

[43] See the argument in Olster, *Roman Defeat*, 99–115.

[44] See Booth, *Crisis of Empire*, 54–9.

[45] See the rich discussion of eucharistic competition in Tannous, *Medieval Middle East*, 156–9.

[46] Anastasius, *Sinai Fathers* 1.2 (Binggeli, 'Anastase le Sinaïte', 172); cf. ibid. 1.20 (communion before death); 1.33 (distributing communion in the Sinai desert). The *Hexaemeron* 10.4.2, however, allows for advanced ascetics who in fact do not need to communicate by receiving the eucharist in church. If this is a genuinely Anastasian text, this

reveal Anastasius's ardent endorsement of frequent lay communion, along with the disquieting concerns that could keep a lay person from communicating. Two examples are particularly salient:

> *Question 38*: Is it a good thing for somebody who has been in bed with his own wife or who has had nocturnal emission of seed, to wash himself with water and then go straight to church?[47]
>
> *Question 40*: If somebody involuntarily drinks water when washing out one's mouth or when in the bath, should such a person go to communion or not?[48]

These two examples have corollaries elsewhere in Anastasius's collection.[49] His pastoral instincts and visceral grasp of the nature of lay piety allow him to address these concerns with creativity (and some degree of playfulness). As for sexual activity and the need to bathe, Anastasius admits that it would be far better for the questioner to bathe himself in tears on account of his wicked capitulation. Yet, given that this rarely occurs, Anastasius suggests that a simple bath will suffice, 'and then certainly partake of the holy mysteries'.[50] Moreover, whilst getting water into one's mouth was a technical violation of a pre-eucharistic fast, Anastasius still urges his audience to take communion under these circumstances. Otherwise, he writes, Satan will make it his aim to get a little water into a Christian's mouth on a regular basis, having 'found the occasion for preventing such a person from taking communion'.[51] Elsewhere Anastasius allows for the fact that some may communicate daily while others may be wise to abstain for a while on account of their sins.[52] He

concession would reinforce our perception of Anastasius as a pastor willing to offer simpler as well as more complicated explanations depending on the composition of his audience.

[47] 'Ἆρα καλὸν τὸ ἀπὸ τῆς ἰδίας γυναικὸς ὄντα, ἢ πάλιν ἀπὸ ἐνυπνιασμοῦ λούσασθαι ὕδατι καὶ εἶθ' οὕτως ἐν τῇ ἐκκλησίᾳ εἰσέρχεσθαι;': Q. 38 (translation from Munitiz, *Anastasios of Sinai*, 142).

[48] 'Ἐάν τις νιπτόμενος τὸ στόμα ἢ πάλιν ἐν βαλανείῳ καταπιεῖ ὕδωρ μὴ θέλων, ὀφείλει κοινωνῆσαι, ἢ οὔ;' Q. 40 (Munitiz, *Anastasios of Sinai*, 146).

[49] See, for example, QQ. 39, 64, 67.

[50] Q. 38 (Munitiz, *Anastasios of Sinai*, 142).

[51] Q. 40 (Munitiz, *Anastasios of Sinai*, 146).

[52] Q. 41. Though Anastasius errs on the side of frequent communion, he allows a great deal of flexibility in his elaborate answer, arguing that much depends on the conscience of the individual.

proposes, however, that a sinner can bridge the cavern between his own failings and the need to receive communion with acts of almsgiving.[53]

Anastasius's *Edifying Tales* offer further insight into his thinking on lay concerns and the eucharist. The collection begins with an account which assures his readers that the eucharist remains the eucharist even in the hands of an unholy and tainted priest.[54] Anastasius recounts a surprising story, moreover, concerning a pious woman who kept a bit of eucharistic bread in her hand after communicating and took it home to ward off a demon, who straight away ran off and disappeared.[55] What is surprising about this story is not the woman's impulse, for the eucharist's purported apotropaic powers are evident in other late antique Christian texts. Rather, what is surprising is Anastasius's tacit endorsement of her actions; other Christian authorities of late antiquity condemn similar expressions of lay piety without reserve. Jacob of Edessa (*c.*640–708), for example, provides an exhaustive list of dos and don'ts concerning the eucharist.[56] His *Canons and Questions* allow that the eucharist be taken home only for the sick and then only with permission.[57] Anastasius, however, lets the story stand, prefacing it with the simple observation that this woman's boldness stemmed from an intimate relationship with the divine.[58]

'Great is the God of the Christians': Ritual Maintenance and Polemic

We have thus far approached Anastasius in his *Tales* and *Questions and Answers* as a man concerned with describing Christians as those who take communion (as well as using other signs and rituals),

[53] Ibid. He notes that God forgave even Emperor Zeno's sexual misconduct on account of the emperor's magnanimous charity to the poor, following the story in John Moschus, *Spiritual Meadow*, 175.

[54] Anastasius, *Edifying Tales* 1, in which the question is quite explicit. Binggeli notes similar concerns in Anastasius's corpus at ibid. 1.5.38–41 and *Homilia de sacra synaxi* (PG 89, cols 825–49): Binggeli, 'Anastase le Sinaïte', 528 n. 11.

[55] Anastasius, *Edifying Tales* 4.

[56] See Tannous, *Medieval Middle East*, 137–42.

[57] *Questions which Addai the Priest and Lover of Labors asked Jacob, the Bishop of Edessa* 3 (François Nau, *Les Canons et les résolutions canoniques de Rabboula, Jean de Tella, Cyriaque d'Amid, Jacques d'Edesse, Georges des Arabes, Cyriaque d'Antioche, Jean III, Théodose d'Antioche et des Perses* [Paris, 1906], 39).

[58] 'μητέρα ἐκέκτητο τῷ θεῷ οἰκειουμένην': Anastasius, *Edifying Tales* 4.1–2 (Binggeli, 'Anastase le Sinaïte', 222).

rather than relying on dense Christological formulae. As such, he was not simply a theologian or exegete, but played the role of what Turner called the 'ritual elder', overseeing the communion and community of those who practice the rites he endorsed.[59] But to what end? If 'rites of maintenance' served to differentiate Christians, then clearly there was an 'other' from which Christians (in Anastasius's eyes) needed strict differentiation. As we have seen, he was certainly concerned with assuring his audience that these rites offered protection from the demonic.[60] But his demonology goes further, highlighting the alliance of demons with two distinct groups: 'Arabs' or 'Saracens' (he does not use 'Muslim')[61] and sorcerers or magicians. In doing so, he betrays his own concern with the state of religious competition in the late seventh-century Levant. For Anastasius, Christianity was, in spite of its veracity, one option among others.[62]

This comes across most clearly in his *Edifying Tales*, a text with two primary goals.[63] The first, clearly, was to encourage Christians who found themselves discouraged by their novel status in an Umayyad world. The second was simply to slander the opposition in tabloid-like hit pieces. The target of this slander was very often Islam. In

[59] Turner, *Ritual Process*, 96.

[60] The Christian sense of the demonic threat, while evident in the New Testament, received enthusiastic emphasis in the literature of the early Christian monks: see David Brakke, *Demons and the Making of the Monk: Spiritual Combat in Early Christianity* (Cambridge, MA, 2006). For the popularity of this literature and the development of demonology thereafter, see now Eva Elm and Nicole Hartmann, eds, *Demons in Late Antiquity: Their Perception and Transformation in different Literary Genres* (Berlin, 2020).

[61] He does use the term μαγαρίτης at *Edifying Tales* 10.10 (Binggeli, 'Anastase le Sinaïte', 230), a word which connotes defilement but becomes a slur for those who have abandoned Christianity for Islam. Cf. Leontius, *Life of Stephen Sabaite* 52.3: in the early tenth-century Arabic translation of the *Life*, we read *muqmis*; the later medieval Greek translation uses μαγαρίτης (*ActaSS*, July 3, 531–613). John C. Lamoreaux offers alternative explanations in *Leontius of Jerusalem: The Life of Stephen of Mar Saba*, CSCO 579 (Leuven, 1999), 81 n. 223. See further Charles du Fresne du Cange, *Glossarium ad scriptores mediae et infimae graecitatis* (Lyon, 1608), cols 849–50; E. A. Sophocles, *Greek Lexicon of the Roman and Byzantine Periods (From B.C. 146 to A.D. 1100)* (New York, 1900), 725.

[62] By 'religious competition' I mean evidence in Christian texts of the temptation of religious alternatives. From the eastern Levantine milieux of the sixth and seventh centuries, examples abound, such as *Life of George of Choziba* 4.15, 18; 10.50, 52; John Moschus, *Spiritual Meadow* 26, 30, 36, 47, 48, 85, 177, 199; Sophronius of Jerusalem, *On the Annunciation*, 10.3–6. Whilst some of these episodes and Sophronius's homiletical rhetoric may be merely tropes, they nevertheless betray a marked anxiety.

[63] Binggeli notes this bifurcation: 'Anastase le Sinaïte', 395.

fact, Anastasius ends several *Tales* with series of exclamations expressing a similar sentiment: the superiority of the Christian faith. These exclamations include: 'Great is the faith of the Christians',[64] 'Great is the God of the faith of the Christians'[65] and, simply, 'Great is the God of the Christians'.[66] They conclude some of Anastasius's stories like a catchy political slogan or a rhythmic chant or mantra. Acclamations as such, whether political or theological (if we dare distinguish these), were certainly commonplace in the late antique world.[67] Yet given the context and purpose of Anastasius's *Edifying Tales*, it seems quite possible that such acclamations were meant to hold a special meaning for an audience probably familiar with another very similar confession: *Allāh Akbar*, the Islamic *Takbir*, 'God is great!'

If so, Anastasius was giving his audience a pithy riposte, something of a Christian *shahada*.[68] Ritualization of the tongue and voice would therefore go hand in hand with physical action in tracing the sign of the cross or approaching with hands open to receive the sacred

[64] 'μεγάλη ἡ πίστις τῶν Χριστιανῶν': Anastasius, *Edifying Tales* 15.38 (Binggeli, 'Anastase le Sinaïte', 237).

[65] 'μέγας ὁ θεὸς τῆς πίστεως τῶν Χριστιανῶν': ibid. 9.19 (Binggeli, 'Anastase le Sinaïte', 229).

[66] 'μέγας ὁ θεὸς τῶν Χριστιανῶν': ibid. 15.37 (Binggeli, 'Anastase le Sinaïte', 237); cf. 10.16–17; 17.173–4; 27.1.

[67] See Charlotte Roueché, 'Acclamations', in G. W. Bowersock, Peter Brown and Oleg Grabar, eds, *Late Antiquity: A Guide to the Postclassical World* (Cambridge, MA, 1999), 274–5.

[68] Binggeli briefly claims as much, but offers no elaboration: 'Diegēmata psychōphelē kai steriktika genomena en diaphorois topois epi tōn hēmeterōn chronōn', in David Thomas and Alex Mallett, eds, *Christian-Muslim Relations Online*, 2010, online at: <https://referenceworks-brillonline.com.ezp3.lib.umn.edu/entries/christian-muslim-relations-i/diegemata-psychophele-kai-steriktika-genomena-en-diaphorois-topois-epi-ton-hemeteron-chronon-COM_23478>, accessed 26 January 2022. Yet a tentative case can be made. There is archaeological evidence for the use of the *Takbir* in the second half of the seventh century, albeit limited: Tareq A. Ramadan, 'Religious Invocations on Umayyad Lead Seals: Evidence of an Emergent Islamic Lexicon', *Journal of Near Eastern Studies* 78 (2019), 273–86, at 280–1. For an analysis of later Byzantine misunderstanding concerning the *Takbir*, see Tarek M. Muhammed, 'The Concept of *al-takbīr* in Byzantine Theological Writings', *Byzantinoslavica* 1 (2014), 77–97, which presumes that an author such as John of Damascus misunderstood the Arabic of the *Takbir*. I find this unlikely and assume that John was not above distorting the *Takbir* for polemical purposes. As for Anastasius, we may guess that he heard the cry of the *Takbir* in his travels and probably knew enough simple Arabic (even from Arabic-speaking Christians) to grasp its basic meaning.

communion meal. To Mary Douglas's assertion that 'ritual is preeminently a form of communication'[69] we might respond that many forms of (spoken) communication are likewise pre-eminently a form of ritual. In this light, it is no surprise that the so-called *Pact of Umar*, however far back we date it, should seek to regulate the ritual soundscape of the Levant, implicitly acknowledging that ritual contagion is not only tangible and visible, but aural as well.[70] Elsewhere Anastasius describes Christian psalmody as an effective riposte to demonic cacophony.[71]

Returning to the *Edifying Tales*, we catch Anastasius also emphasizing the thinly veiled alliance between Islam and the demonic.[72] After describing demonic aversion to the image of the cross, for example, he makes an obvious allusion to other contemporary 'enemies of the cross' who seem to pose a pressing problem for his audience.[73] Such allusions are completely unveiled when we return to John of Bostra, and to his exchange with the demons. John, Anastasius tells us, followed up his first set of questions with a question which served as a complementary opposite: if demons hated the cross, baptism and the eucharist, what sort of religion did they prefer? '"That of our companions", they answered. "And who are they?" John asked. They answered: "Those who have none of what we have just spoken [i.e., the three

[69] Mary Douglas, *Natural Symbols* (New York, 1973), 41; cf. Frits Staal, 'The Sound of Religion', *Numen* 33 (1986), 185–224, at 213: 'In ritual we are primarily dealing with sounds and acts, and these correspond to each other'.

[70] Traditionally dated toward the end of the seventh century, the *Pact of Umar* contains regulations governing a number of non-Islamic ritual activities, including sounds. Scholars debate how far back this tradition goes, many dating the composition of something like the *Pact* to the eighth or ninth centuries: see, inter alia, Milka Levy-Rubin, *Non-Muslims in the Islamic Empire: From Surrender to Coexistence* (Cambridge and New York, 2011), 58–87; Mark R. Cohen, 'What was the Pact of 'Umar? A Literary-Historical Study', *Jerusalem Studies in Arabic and Islam* 23 (1999), 100–57; Ibn 'Asākir, *Ta'rīkh madina Dimashq*, 80 vols (Beirut, 1995), 2: 120, 174–9 (includes five different versions); translated in A. S. Tritton, *The Caliphs and their non-Muslim Subjects* (London, 1930), 5–6; A. Noth, 'Abgrenzungsprobleme zwischen Muslimen und nicht-Muslimen. Die "Bedingungen 'Umar's" (*ash-shurūṭ al-'umariyya*) unter einem anderen Aspekt gelesen', *Jerusalem Studies in Arabic and Islam* 9 (1987), 290–315.

[71] Anastasius, *Edifying Tales* 7.

[72] Briefly discussed in Uthemann, *Anastasios Sinaites*, 529–32. A broader overview is Bernard Flusin, 'Démons et Sarrasins. L'Auteur et le propos des *Dièjmata stèriktika* d'Anastase le Sinaïte', *Travaux et Mémoires* 11 (1991), 381–409.

[73] Anastasius, *Edifying Tales* 14.21–2 (Binggeli, 'Anastase le Sinaïte', 235).

Christian things – BH]. Those who do not recognize the son of Mary as God or as the Son of God.'"[74]

For Anastasius, then, Islamic identity is something completely negative. 'Islam', by this definition, is to be without the cross, baptism and the eucharist, and thus a Muslim is one who lives outside the order of Christian ritual. Likewise, Anastasius presents the credal content of Islam in a completely pessimistic light. Islam, in this account, is a series of negations, a nihilistic un-belief. Of course, Anastasius may have also had in mind the very concrete inscriptions of the Dome of the Rock; he was aware of 'Abd al-Malik's monumental shrine and very conscious of the anxiety it caused some of the Christian faithful.[75] But regardless of the role of this architectural novelty in the crafting of such a story, the sharp rhetorical critique remains. Anastasius's demons emphasize simple Christian ritual in contrast to simple Islamic belief (or disbelief, as it were).[76]

Yet Islam was not the only temptation Anastasius's audience faced. We conclude with a brief observation on the place of sorcery or magic in his thinking. The vocabulary in the *Edifying Tales* includes roles such as φάρμακος (sorcerer / poisoner / magician) or even φάρμακος πρεσβυτέρος (priest-turned-sorcerer), as well as terms relating to the content of their craft such as φαρμακεία (drugs, medicine, poison or witchcraft).[77] It is beyond the scope of this article to explore concepts of magic and sorcery in the late antique world.[78] For

[74] 'τὴν τῶν ἑταίρων ἡμῶν. Λέγει πρὸς αὐτούς· Καὶ τίνες εἰσὶν οὗτοι; Λέγουσι πρὸς αὐτόν· οἱ μὴ ἔχοντες μήτε ἓν πρᾶγμα ἐκ τῶν τριῶν, ὧν εἴπαμεν πρός σε, μήτε ὁμολογοῦντες θεὸν ἢ υἱὸν θεοῦ τὸν υἱὸν τῆς Μαρίας': ibid. 20.36–9 (Binggeli, 'Anastase le Sinaïte', 250); discussed in Tannous, *Medieval Middle East*, 360; cf. Anastasius, *Edifying Tales* 7.

[75] Anastasius addresses the issue of the Dome of the Rock in *Edifying Tales* 7; see n. 14 above. I refer to the inscriptions on the Dome emphasizing that Jesus is the son of Mary and deny that he is divine or the Son of God: see the translation in Fred Donner, *Muhammad and the Believers: At the Origins of Islam* (Cambridge, MA, 2010), from the transcription in Christel Kessler, "Abd Al-Malik's Inscription in the Dome of the Rock: A Reconsideration', *Journal of the Royal Asiatic Society* 10 (1970), 2–14.

[76] Anastasius tells a lurid story concerning crude Islamic sacrifices: *Edifying Tales* 11. The following story is an elaboration on the Christian liturgy as a pure and effective alternative: ibid. 12.

[77] See Uthemann, *Anastasios Sinaites*, 525–9.

[78] See Matthew W. Dickie, *Magic and Magicians in the Greco Roman World* (Abingdon, 2001); Henry McGuire, ed., *Byzantine Magic*, 2nd edn (Cambridge, MA, 2009); David Frankfurter, 'Beyond Magic and Superstition', in Virginia Burrus, ed., *A People's History of Christianity*, 2: *Late Ancient Christianity* (Minneapolis, MN, 2005), 255–84, 309–12.

our purposes, it is sufficient to point out that for Anastasius, to practise sorcery was to engage in an illicit rite, one which risked compromising Christian identity at its very core. Thus his ritual-based approach to maintaining communal boundaries over against Islam paralleled a venerable tradition of Christian polemic against a host of magical practices.[79]

The problem of what we would call sorcery is present in the *Edifying Tales* and the *Questions and Answers*.[80] Other Christian texts from seventh-century Palestine share this concern.[81] Illicit rites were very much a live option for Anastasius's Christian audience, an old problem which continued alongside novel forms of Islamic piety. His community, like so many others, was very much willing to mix and match rituals, preferring what was effective to that which was strictly canonical. Even his 'sorcerer-priest' appears notably creative in his synthesis of disparate rituals.[82]

However, this attraction to non-Christian ritual would have presented an existential problem for someone like Anastasius. If Christian ritual maintained Christian identity, alien rituals would, practically speaking, be tantamount to apostasy. Using van Gennep's categories, we might say that non-Christian rites snatched the participant from their post-liminal state back into the relative fluidity (and vulnerability) of religious liminality. Here one risked becoming again a cultic *tabula rasa* and a potential candidate for inclusion into some other form of ritual community. As Turner noted, unsanctioned liminal activity is 'almost everywhere attributed with magico-religious properties', and is thus 'regarded as dangerous, inauspicious, or polluting to persons, objects, events and relationships'.[83] Paradoxically, this blurring of boundaries which Anastasius was so concerned to prevent may well have been the very source of

[79] See, inter alia, Joseph E. Sanzo's 'Magic and Communal Boundaries: The Problems with Amulets in Chrysostom, *Adv. Iud.* 8, and Augustine, *In Io. tra.* 7', *Henoch* 39 (2017), 227–46.

[80] See Q. 57; cf. Q. 62, which addresses 'signs' or 'wonders' performed by non-Christians or heretics.

[81] For example, *Life of George of Choziba* 4.15, 18; 10.50, 52.

[82] Anastasius, *Edifying Tales* 15. Jacob of Edessa condemns the resort of his flock to non-Christian 'demonic' practices in their care for fields and cattle: *Questions which Addai asked Jacob* 46 (Nau, *Les Canons*, 58); cf. Tannous, *Medieval Middle East*, 148.

[83] Turner, *Ritual Process*, 108. Of course, in this sense, magic is in the eye of the beholder, religion (in some sense) being sanctioned magic by another name (and magic, following van Gennep, simply unsanctioned religion).

magic's appeal. To combine diverse rites, as Vicky Foskolou has suggested, appeared sophisticated and also held out the promise of being more effective (like visiting several doctors and taking several treatments for the same set of symptoms).[84]

Anastasius of Sinai and the Christians of the Umayyad Levant

Anastasius of Sinai was many things to many people. To the Chalcedonian minorities in Syria and Egypt, he was a fierce promoter of Christological orthodoxy and a thoughtful, if idiosyncratic, theological polemicist. To the monks of Mount Sinai, he was especially a storyteller, a man steeped in the tradition of monastic travelogues and *apophthegmata*, providing a sort of literary charter for the monks who walked in Moses's footprints. His three homilies on the creation and nature of human beings betray Anastasius as a sophisticated theological communicator, trained to offer an elaborate and nuanced anthropology for those with learned interests.[85] For many, however, especially perhaps for the Christians of the largely Chalcedonian lands of Palestine, he had another project in mind.[86]

As a 'ritual elder' or 'ritual specialist', Anastasius sought to offer his audience a simple and coherent form of Christianity consisting of basic credal content combined with familiar rituals which he invested with special significance for their pressing contemporary concerns. As Bell has argued, ritual power, although often tailored by literate specialists, is not primarily concerned with the power and prestige of the specialists themselves. Rather, rituals empower communities as communities.[87] Here, in Bell's words, 'ritual does not control; rather, it constitutes a particular dynamic of social empowerment'.[88] To put it

[84] Vicky A. Foskolou, 'The Magic of the Written Word: The Evidence of Inscriptions on Byzantine Magical Amulets', *ΔΧΑΕ* (2014), 329–48, at 346.

[85] *Homilia i, ii, iii de creatione hominis* (Clavis Patrum Graecorum 7747–9). See Karl-Heinz Uthemann, ed., *Anastasii Sinaïtae: Sermones duo in constitutionem hominis secundum imaginem Dei necnon opuscula adversus monotheletas*, CChr.SG 12.

[86] On the eventual triumph of Chalcedonian Christianity in Palestine, see Lorenzo Peronne, '"Rejoice Sion, Mother of All Churches": Christianity in the Holy Land during the Byzantine Era', in Ora Limor and Guy G. Stroumsa, eds, *Christians and Christianity in the Holy Land: From the Origins to the Latin Kingdoms* (Turnhout, 2006), 141–73, at 164–8; Lorenzo Peronne, 'Christian Holy Places and Pilgrimage in an Age of Dogmatic Conflicts', *Proche Orient Chrétien* 48 (1998), 5–37, at 22–33.

[87] Bell, *Ritual Theory*, 182–93.

[88] Ibid. 181.

another way, Anastasius was giving his audience tools with which they could build and sustain their own Christian identity as a ritually coherent community. As such, he was surprisingly open to certain charismatic impulses, which were evident, although often condemned, in other pastoral authors.[89] Certainly his work furthers our understanding of laity in late antique Christian contexts, not as passive recipients of theology, but rather, as Georgia Frank has argued, as 'religious agents'.[90]

Anastasius's primary concern, then, was to contrast the effective and licit rituals of Christians with the (purportedly) nihilistic confession of Islam and the illicit ritualization of sorcery. In doing so, he provided a straightforward way of being Christian for an audience which included very few theological connoisseurs. In this literature (and in contrast to his other works), Christological formulations – debates on natures, persons, wills and energies – all took a back seat to public, practical and physical acts: truth codified in a democratic simplicity. This is how Anastasius went about making and maintaining Christians in the Umayyad Levant.

[89] As can be seen in his treatment of the woman: *Edifying Tales* 4. Note also his cautious endorsement of the use of the Bible as an omen text: Q. 57.

[90] Georgia Frank, 'Laity Lives: Reclaiming a "Non-" Category', *Studies in Late Antiquity* 5 (2021), 119–27, at 119.

The Blessing of the Wedding Bedchamber in North-Western Europe, *c.*950–*c.*1200

Elisabeth van Houts*
University of Cambridge

This article addresses two specific problems. First, between c.*950 and* c.*1200 there appears to be a mismatch between liturgical manuscripts and narrative sources on the Christian blessing of the wedding bedchamber and bed, with the former recording the ritual but the latter scarcely mentioning it. The second concerns the question as to whether the ritual was expected to take place at home or in the church. In order to shed light on the development of the ritual, where it took place and how frequently, the article is divided into four parts. A discussion of liturgical manuscripts for the blessing of the wedding bedchamber and bed is followed by an analysis of the prayers to establish why the wedding bedchamber and the bed warranted a blessing. We then turn to an evaluation of the sparse evidence for the priest's liturgical role at home weddings. Finally, the liturgical evidence is linked to historical and fictional evidence. The article concludes that ambiguity about where the ritual should take place allowed for discretion on the part of those involved, and that the great majority of the laity may have been ignorant of the ritual altogether.*

The blessing of the wedding bedchamber and bed is a practice with a long history, going back to Greek, Roman and Jewish traditions.[1]

* E-mail: emcv2@cam.ac.uk. I am very grateful for initial discussions with David Ganz and Susan Rankin before embarking on this article. Pawel Figurski and Susan Rankin read versions of the text and gave me extremely useful guidance, for which I thank them most warmly. I am deeply indebted to the two anonymous reviewers of this article for their advice on further reading and some corrections. Any mistakes that remain are my own.

[1] Korbinian Ritzer, *Formen, Riten und religiöses Brauchtum der Eheschließung in den christlichen Kirchen des ersten Jahrtausends*, ed. Ulrich Hermann and Willibrord Heckenbach, 2nd edn, Liturgiewissenschaftliche Quellen und Forschungen 38 (Münster, 1982), 206–8; Protais Mutembe and Jean-Baptiste Molin, *Le Rituel du mariage en France du XIIe au XVIe siècle* (Paris, 1974), 27–8, 35–6, 326–7 (this book was also published in the same year in Paris, for a different series, with the names of the authors reversed; the pagination in both issues is the same); Cyrille Vogel, 'Les Rites de la célébration du mariage. Leur

Studies in Church History 59 (2023), 119–141
doi: 10.1017/stc.2023.5

Taking place within the bedchamber, it was a ritual whereby the newly wed couple would be wished a happy life, fertile marriage and offspring. In the early church, the secular event gained a religious character. Avitus, bishop of Vienne (*c.*494–518), alluded to the practice in a letter, in which he implicitly contrasted the blessing of a virgin *in sancti altaris thalamo* (in the bedchamber or bed of the holy altar, i.e. in a church) with a marriage blessing *in thalamo*, in the home.[2] Another mention of this practice appears in the *Vita sancti Amatoris* of Stefanus 'Afer', written *c.*570. In it, he describes an instance in which Bishop Valerianus of Auxerre was invited into the bedchamber (*thalami*) to read prayers for the couple (*coniugali preces*) from a prayer book held in his right hand (*libellum sacrarum precum dextera arriperet*).[3] Both texts mention a domestic setting for the ritual. The next piece of evidence relating to this blessing appears over a hundred years later in the Bobbio Missal (Paris, BnF lat 13246), a late seventh- or early eighth-century liturgical book from south-western France.[4] This is one of the oldest European liturgical manuscripts in existence and has generated much scholarly interest.[5] Amongst an assortment of blessings, there are two relating to marriage. The first begins with the rubric *Benedictio talami super nubentes* ('blessing of the bedchamber / bed of the couple') which is followed by the prayer *Deum qui ad multiplicandum humani genere prole* ('[we pray that] God, by offspring, multiply the human race'). The second

Signification dans la formation du lien durant le haut moyen age', in *Il matrimonio nella società altomedievale 22–28 aprile 1976*, Settimane di studio del centro italiano di studi sull'alto medioevo 24, 2 vols (Spoleto, 1977), 1: 397–472, at 452–3; Kenneth Stevenson, *Nuptial Blessing: A Study of Christian Marriage Rites*, Alcuin Club Collections 64 (London, 1984), 51–2, 56–7, 59, 63–4, 71–8; Philip L. Reynolds, 'Marrying and its Documentation in pre-Modern Europe: Consent, Celebration and Property', in idem and John Witte, eds, *To Have and to Hold: Marrying and its Documentation in Western Christendom, 400–1600* (Cambridge, 2007), 1–42, at 21–5.

[2] '[S]i sponsam Christo devotam et in sancti altaris thalamo benedictione dotatam': Avitus of Vienne, Letter 55 to Ansemund (MGH AA 6.2, 84), lines 8–11; cf. Ritzer, *Formen,* 207; Vogel, 'Les Rites', 424.

[3] Stefanus 'Afer', *Vita sancti Amatoris*, ActaSS Mai I (1860), 52; cf. Ritzer, *Formen,* 207; Vogel, 'Les rites', 427.

[4] E. A. Lowe, ed., *The Bobbio Missal: A Gallican Mass-book: Ms Paris. Lat. 13246*, HBS 53, 58, 61, 3 vols (London, 1917, 1920, 1924), 2: 167–8; cf. Ritzer, *Formen,* 208 n. 20, 354–5; Mutembe and Molin, *Le Rituel du mariage*, 224; Vogel, 'Les Rites', 428.

[5] Yitzak Hen and Rob Meens, eds, *The Bobbio Missal: Liturgy and Religious Culture in Merovingian Gaul* (Cambridge, 2004).

one is rubricated as *item alia*, followed by *Te deprecamur* ('we beseech you'). Their contents will be discussed below in section two. Importantly, these prayers occur without a mass, a pattern which later became customary. As this article focuses on north-western Europe, the next set of surviving examples after the Bobbio Missal come from England, followed by Normandy, and finally elsewhere in northern France.

Before turning to England, however, we need briefly to consider the suggestion of an Iberian tradition of the blessing of the wedding bedchamber. According to Reynolds, the bedchamber rite was 'conspicuous in nuptial liturgies in Visigothic and Mozarabic Spain', although, in these cases, it took place before, rather than after, the wedding mass, and salt was sprinkled in the bedroom.[6] As such, this Iberian ritual differs quite substantially from the wedding ritual and prayers with which I am concerned, not only in terms of timing, but also in the content of the prayers themselves.[7] Moreover, although the evidence comes from eleventh-century liturgical manuscripts from the bishopric of Tarragona (the Roda Pontifical, Catedral de Lleida, Codex 16, dating to *c.*1000; and the Sacramentary of Vich, Museu Episcopal Vich, Codex 66, dating to *c.*1030), liturgists have assumed, but cannot prove, that it represents a much older Visigothic tradition. The argument for an older, unproven, Visigothic ritual lies behind the suggestion that it is possible that the maker of the Bobbio Missal received his inspiration from the Iberian peninsula. However, given the similarity of the Bobbio prayers with those of the north-western European tradition, and the distinctiveness of both from the Iberian ones, I will leave the supposed Visigothic tradition to one side.

This article will address two specific problems. First, between *c.*950 and *c.*1200 there seems to be a mismatch between liturgical manuscripts and narrative sources on the Christian blessing of the wedding bedchamber and bed, with the former recording the ritual but the latter scarcely mentioning it. The second problem concerns whether the ritual was expected to take place in the home or in the

[6] Reynolds, 'Marrying and its Documentation', 23, who refers to Brian Bethune, 'The Text of the Christian Rite of Marriage in Medieval Spain' (PhD thesis, University of Toronto, 1987), which I have been unable to consult.

[7] Ritzer, *Formen*, 356–64, appendix 5; Mutembe and Molin, *Le Rituel du mariage*, 27–8; Stevenson, *Nuptial Blessing*, 48–52, 54–5.

church. Non-liturgical narrative sources such as chronicles, saints' lives and fictional texts are mostly silent on this issue, a silence that corresponds with a similar lack of evidence for the celebration of weddings more generally. Indeed, in numerical terms, references to weddings in narrative sources before 1200 are mostly to domestic festivities – eating, singing and dancing – with scarcely any mention of a priest's liturgical involvement. Admittedly, there are plenty of references to the presence of priests at weddings, but mostly as guests in their capacity as kin to either the bride or groom.[8] Apart from a few exceptions, the narrative image of wedding celebrations is that of a mostly secular affair. Given the mismatch between liturgical evidence and narrative texts relating to this ritual, scholars have been reluctant to surmise whether the blessing of the wedding bedchamber or bed, mentioned in liturgical manuscripts as following a mass, would be recited in church or in the home.[9] This article seeks to shed light on the development of the ritual, and where it took place, and will be divided into four parts. It will begin with a discussion of the evidence for the blessing of the wedding bedchamber and bed to be found in liturgical manuscripts. This will be followed by an analysis of the prayers themselves, in order to establish what it was about the wedding bedchamber and bed that warranted their blessing. There then follows an evaluation of the (sparse) evidence for the priest's liturgical role at home weddings. Finally, the article connects the liturgical sources to historical and fictional evidence, to argue that the ambiguity about where the ritual should take place allowed discretion for those involved in it.

The Evidence of Liturgical Manuscripts

Before discussing the liturgical manuscripts in question, it is important to address some methodological points relating to this type of evidence.[10] Liturgical manuscripts can be divided into various genres,

[8] Elisabeth van Houts, *Married Life in Medieval Europe, 900–1300* (Oxford, 2019), 40–1, 68, 82.

[9] Ritzer, *Formen,* 315, 318 (domestic ritual); Vogel, 'Les Rites', 453 (home ritual); Stevenson, *Nuptial Blessing,* 67 (in church); Reynolds, 'Marrying and its Documentation', 23 (a home setting); Helen Gittos, *Liturgy, Architecture and Sacred Places in Anglo-Saxon England* (Oxford, 2013), 271 (a home setting).

[10] Helen Gittos, 'Researching the History of Rites', in eadem and Sarah Hamilton, eds, *Understanding Medieval Liturgy: Essays in Interpretation* (London, 2016), 13–30, at 17–19.

of which, for my purpose, priests' books – such as sacramentaries and missals, as well as pontificals and benedictionals – are the most important.[11] By the eleventh century, each liturgical manuscript was normally designed for a person with specific responsibilities, usually a priest.[12] It may have contained only parts of a service. For these reasons, liturgical manuscripts are very diverse in terms of content and as such we cannot extrapolate from them 'rules' issued by a universal church. On the contrary, liturgical manuscripts attest to the ways in which individual institutions looked after their own liturgical traditions. Nevertheless, despite differences in the ordering and positioning of prayers in relation to the celebration of a mass, there is a remarkable uniformity in the prayers relating to the wedding bedchamber and bed. Yet this apparent uniformity may be misleading in suggesting a straightforward narrative of development of the blessing, since the prayers are only one isolated part of the ritual. Finally, as will become clear in this article, the collection of prayers concerning the wedding chamber should not be read as a blueprint or template for a standardized set of actions in practice. It is often unclear whether the prayers associated with any ritual were meant as a practical guide to an actual service or were merely intended to be read privately. With this in mind, we can now turn to the manuscripts themselves, beginning in England, where the earliest examples of the wedding bedchamber ritual in north-western Europe can be found.

One of the earliest English testimonies to the wedding bedchamber blessing in pre-conquest England appears in the Durham Collectar (Durham Cathedral Library MS A.IV.19). Dating to the first third of the tenth century, it was written in the south, perhaps the south-west, of England, before being taken to Chester-le-Street around 970, where substantial additions were made in the later tenth century.[13] Most of the bedchamber blessings occur in the

[11] Richard W. Pfaff, 'Massbooks: Sacramentaries and Missals', in idem, ed., *The Liturgical Books of Anglo-Saxon England*, Old English Newsletter Subsidia 23 (Kalamazoo, MI, 1995), 7–34; Janet L. Nelson and Richard W. Pfaff, 'Pontificals and Benedictionals', ibid. 87–98.

[12] For secular priests and the variety of their liturgical books, see Gerald P. Dyson, *Priests and their Books in Late Anglo-Saxon England*, Anglo-Saxon Studies 34 (Woodbridge, 2019).

[13] Alicia Corrêa, ed., *The Durham Collectar*, HBS 107 (London 1992), 220–3 (mass) and 224 (prayers nos 626–30), with the suggestion that the blessings were 'recited by the priest over the marriage bed at night'; Mutembe and Molin, *Le Rituel du mariage*, 29 (by the

original part of the manuscript in the form of a nuptial mass and five prayers, of which one is a blessing of the bedroom (*Benedic Domine thalamum hoc*), as encountered in the Bobbio Missal, followed by four prayers under the rubric 'In the bedroom' (*in thalamo*). This includes a blessing for the couple (*istos adhulescentulos*), one for procreation (*creator et conservator humani generis*), and one for 'the bed and those who lie in it' (*lectum istum et omnes habitantes in eo*), asking God's blessing that 'they will be full of holiness, chastity and tenderness' (*ut sit in eis sanctitas, et castitas et laenitas et pleni*).[14] Although the Durham Collectar is undoubtedly an early English priest's book, its continental exemplar for the original contents (including the wedding chamber blessings) came probably from northern France.[15]

The second set of English liturgical sources are bishops' books. One example is the Egbert Pontifical (Paris, BnF lat 10575), a tenth-century manuscript that contains wedding material.[16] Instead of a set of mass prayers, it contains a number of blessings (introduced with rubrics or titles), including one for the bedchamber (rubric: *Benedictio thalami*; incipit: *Benedic domine thalamum hoc et omnes habitanter in eo*); one for the couple (rubric: *Alia*; incipit: *Benedic domine istos adulescentulos*); one for the ring (rubric: *Benedictio annuli*; incipit: *Creator et conservator*); one for the bed and for those in it (rubric: *Benedictio lecti*; incipit: *Benedic domine lectum istum et omnes habitantes in eo*); and one for the couple's parents and offspring across four generations.[17] According to Andrew Prescott, it has many

---

priest at home); Stevenson, *Nuptial Blessing*, 63–4; Richard W. Pfaff, T*he Liturgy in Medieval England: A History* (Cambridge, 2009), 65–6.

[14] Corrêa, ed., *Durham Collectar*, 76. For *adolescens* as a sexually mature person, see Isidore of Seville, *The* Etymologies *of Isidore of Seville*, transl. Stephen A. Barney et al. (Cambridge, 2010), 241.

[15] Corrêa, ed., *Durham Collectar*, 110–11.

[16] H. M. J. Banting, ed., *Two Anglo-Saxon Pontificals (The Egbert and Sidney Sussex Pontificals)*, HBS 204 (London, 1989), 133–4; Vogel, 'Les Rites', 427, 452; Stevenson, *Nuptial Blessing*, 67.

[17] Incipit: 'Benedictio domini sit super uxorem tuam et super parentes vestros ut videatis filios vestros, et filios filiorum vestrorum usque in tertiam et quartam generationem et sit semen vestrorum benedictum a deo Israel qui regnat in secula seculorum' (cf. Tob. 9: 10–11): Banting, ed., *Two Anglo-Saxon Pontificals*, 134. There is a further blessing of the couple (Banting, ed., *Two Anglo-Saxon Pontificals*, 140) referring to Abraham, Isaac and Jacob (cf. Tob. 7: 15), for the groom's seed, and further prayers for the bedroom / bed (*thalamum*) and those in it. These ask that they may live in God's peace and continue according to his will (*tua voluntate*), that they may live in love (*in amore*) and grow old together

traits in common with other early English bishops' books, although these, interestingly for us, do not contain the wedding chamber ritual.[18] The so-called Benedictional of Archbishop Robert (Rouen, BM 369/Y7), for instance, dates from the last quarter of the tenth century.[19] It contains a mass with prayers for the ring and its conferral, as well as the blessing of the bride and the groom (*Benedictio sponsi et sponsae*). However, it does not include a blessing for the bedchamber or the bed, despite containing the 'blessings for the young people' (*benedictiones super adholescentes*) normally associated with the ritual of the bedchamber. While Reynolds has claimed that these blessings 'seem to have been intended for the bedchamber rite', with the implication of a home setting,[20] Stevenson believes they were said in church.[21] Two other early English bishops' books which contain the *Benedictio sponsi et sponsae*, but not the wedding chamber blessing, are the Sherborne Pontifical (Paris, BnF lat 943), dating to 960×988 in its original layer from Christ Church Canterbury; and the Lanalet Pontifical (Rouen, BM 368/A27), dating from the first half of the eleventh century, and probably originating from Winchester for Lyfing, monk of Winchester and bishop of Crediton (1027–46).[22] The final piece of evidence for pre-conquest England is a priest's book, the so-called Red Book of Darley (Cambridge, Corpus Christi College MS 422) written *c.*1060, perhaps at Sherborne. It

(*senescant*), and multiply throughout the length of their days (*multiplicentur in longitudine dierum*) (cf. Gen. 1: 28).

18 Andrew Prescott, 'The Structure of English pre-Conquest Benedictionals', *British Library Journal* 13 (1987), 118–58, at 128–9.

19 H. A. Wilson, ed., *The Benedictional of Archbishop Robert*, HBS 24 (London, 1903), 149–51. Regarding its dating, see Prescott, 'Structure', 124; but note that Nicholas Orchard, in *The Leofric Missal*, HBS 113–14, 2 vols (London, 2002), 1: 70–1, dates it to 980x88; Ritzer, *Formen*, 365–8 (text of blessings); Stevenson, *Nuptial Blessing*, 66–7; Pfaff, *Liturgy*, 81 n. 53.

20 Wilson, ed., *Benedictional of Archbishop Robert*, 151, for the blessing of the adolescents; Reynolds, 'Marrying and its Documentation', 23.

21 Stevenson, *Nuptial Ritual*, 66–7; cf. also Mutembe and Molin, *Le Rituel du mariage*, 30 n. 24.

22 Prescott, 'Structure', 126–8. See also ibid. 147, where the prayer 'Benedictio sponsi et sponsae' is identified as that found in E. Moeller, ed., *Corpus Benedictionum Pontificalium*, CChr.SL 162 A–C (Turnhout, 1971–9), 1: 678–9 (no. 1657), 735 (no. 1798). The difference between the two versions is very slight indeed. For the dating of the Lanalet Pontifical as after 1020, see Orchard, ed., *Leofric Missal*, 1: 76.

contains a set of mass prayers together with blessings of the couple, of the ring and of the bedchamber.[23]

In summing up the pre-conquest English evidence, it can be suggested that a mass (itself a set of prayers) became a standard component of the solemnization of weddings in churches. The mass was coupled with a variety of associated prayers for the couple, the wedding bedchamber and bed, occasionally in combination with blessings for the ring, and for food or drink, and for the couple's families. The wedding bedchamber prayers are present in books made for priests and their communities (such as the Durham Collectar and the Red Book of Darley) and for bishops (such as the Egbert Pontifical).[24] The scant rubrication in the manuscripts as to where the prayers are to be read, however, is inconclusive. A prima facie case can be made that the blessings are meant for a domestic setting, and certainly the Durham Collectar suggests as much with the rubric *in thalamo* referring to the bedroom, alongside a prayer for the bed. The Egbert Pontifical is more restrained in its rubrics, but distinguishes between bedroom and bed. The other manuscripts do not have rubrics with specific indications of location.[25] However, both here and in what follows, the evidence of rubrication cannot be taken as proof for the location, if any, where the prayers were meant to be said.

More English liturgical manuscripts become available in the twelfth century. They also become more expansive with regard to the liturgy and, crucially, contain explicit rubrication with guidance for the priest as to where the constituent parts of the wedding ceremony should be said. The clearest example of this is the so-called Bury St Edmunds Missal, probably dating from the 1120s or

[23] Cambridge, Corpus Christi College, MS 422, available online at: <https://parker.stanford.edu/parker/catalog/fr610kh2998>, last accessed 25 January 2023, with the marriage rite at 276–84; Pfaff, *Liturgy*, 94–6; Mutembe and Molin, *Le Rituel du mariage*, 284, 286; see also Helen Gittos, 'Is there any Evidence for the Liturgy of Parish Churches in Late Anglo-Saxon England?', in Francesca Tinti, ed., *Pastoral Care in Late Anglo-Saxon England* (Woodbridge, 2005), 63–82, at 77, where she notes that the Red Book of Darley has a rubric at p. 280 for the blessing of the marriage (*bletsung.benedictio*) which is in Old English and Latin. Stevenson, *Nuptial Blessing*, 67, erroneously refers to this rubric as 'the blessing of the brides'.

[24] I am most grateful to one of the reviewers of this article for this point.

[25] The Leofric Missal contains a nuptial mass and prayers, but none for the wedding chamber: see Orchard, ed., *Leofric Missal*, 1: 72; 2: 435–6; Pfaff, *Liturgy*, 131–2. Vogel, 'Les Rites', 439–40, is superseded by these two works.

1130s, and written at the monastery of St Edmund, although soon after transferred to Laon (now Laon, BM MS 238).[26] Scholars agree that the form in which these wedding blessings and mass prayers were copied would become the standard service in England and north-western France.[27] The Bury St Edmunds manuscript helpfully includes rubrics which indicate where the blessings should be read. It begins with the blessing of the ring just 'before the church door' (*ante hostium templi*), with the priest verifying the groom's and bride's consent.[28] Then comes the assignment of 'the dowry and other gifts' (*dos et alia dona*), followed by the giving of the bride to her husband-to-be. The priest then presents the ring and other gifts to the groom, who in turn gives them to the bride while reciting prayers: he first puts the ring on her right thumb, then on her index finger, before finally placing it on her middle finger – the thumb and fingers representing the Trinity. The bride, now with ring and gifts, prostrates herself before her husband, presumably as a sign of submission and obedience. The rubrics then describe how the couple and priest enter the church, where another blessing takes place before the altar. The priest celebrates mass for the Holy Trinity as if it is a Sunday. After the mass, there follows yet another set of blessings: first, that of a drink (*potum*, presumably wine), then that of the bedchamber or bed (*thalamum*). Crucially, there is no guidance, in the form of rubrics, as to the location for these post-mass blessings.[29]

[26] The marriage rite with its variations, each printed as a numbered 'ordo', are printed in Mutembe and Molin, *Le Rituel du mariage,* 289–91 (Ordo V); Stevenson, *Nuptial Blessing,* 68–9; Pfaff, *Liturgy*, 184–6, 192–9. This manuscript descends from Rouen, BM MS 274, the so-called Missal of Robert of Jumièges: H. Wilson, ed., *The Missal of Robert of Jumièges*, HBS 11 (London, 1896). It dates from between 1014 and 1023, has a wedding blessing (ibid. 269–70), but none for the bedchamber or bed. In fact, Rouen, BM MS 274, is a sacramentary from Peterborough or Ely given to the abbey of Jumièges by its former abbot, Robert, when he was bishop of London (1044–51). Furthermore, the Peterborough or Ely scribe used an exemplar from Flanders. See Nicholas Orchard, 'An Anglo-Saxon Mass for St Willibrord and its later Liturgical Uses', *Anglo-Saxon England* 24 (1995), 1–10, at 4 n. 12; Pfaff, *Liturgy*, 88–91.

[27] Reynolds, 'Marrying and its Documentation', 21–5.

[28] Stevenson, *Nuptial Blessing,* 68 erroneously refers to rings as plural.

[29] For other twelfth-century English liturgical manuscripts without rubrics for the post-mass blessings, see H. A. Wilson, ed., *The Pontifical of Magdalen College with an Appendix of Extracts from other English Manuscripts of the Twelfth Century*, HBS 39 (London 1910), 205 (the Magdalen Pontifical) and 226 (the pontifical now at Cambridge, Trinity College, MS B.11.10).

Due to the relative lack of study of liturgical manuscripts from northern France before 1100 for the blessing of the wedding chamber and bed,[30] it has generally been assumed that the practice of this ritual was transmitted from England to France, via Normandy, in the eleventh century, although whether this happened before or after the Norman Conquest remains unclear. Vogel argues for a date connected to the transfer of the Egbert Pontifical to Evreux in Normandy, which he places in the eleventh century.[31] Given the more recent study of liturgical manuscripts in pre-conquest England, several of which contain texts that may go back to continental exemplars, we have to keep an open mind about the direction of influence in the process of criss-crossing of liturgical books and their owners across the Channel during the tenth and eleventh centuries. Yet there are signs of receptivity to some liturgical aspects of the English reform movement in early eleventh-century Normandy.[32] More explicit evidence of liturgical practice (including the blessing of the wedding bedchamber and bed), comparable to that in England, can be found in several Norman liturgical manuscripts dating from the twelfth century. They include the blessing of the ring, as well as the blessing of the bedchamber and bed, but, like the English manuscripts, there is no explicit guidance as to where these should be read.[33] Three Norman liturgical manuscripts lack rubrics for the setting of the post-mass blessing of the wedding bedchamber and bed: the Bayeux Missal (Paris, Bibl. Mazarine 404) from the first half of the twelfth century;[34] the twelfth-century missal (now Paris, BnF lat 14446) from Normandy, which has not been identified as belonging to a specific monastery or cathedral;[35] and the Avranches Pontifical, dating to the first half of the twelfth century (Paris, BnF lat 14832). The Avranches Pontifical contains the same blessings as

30 Note that, according to Duby, *The Knight, the Lady and the Priest*, 152, the eleventh-century Soissons Missal (Laon, BM 237) contains the blessing for the bedchamber.

31 Vogel, 'Les Rites', 428, 453, where he argues that the bedchamber blessing is the ritual referred to in the Rouen Synod of 1072, which he erroneously dates to 1012, see below, p. 134.

32 Pierre Bauduin, 'Du Bon Usage de la *dos* dans la Normandie ducale (Xe–début du XIIe siècle)', in F. Bougard, L. Feller and R. le Jan, eds, *Dots et douaires dans le haut Moyen Âge* (Rome, 2002), 429–55, at 434.

33 Ritzer, *Formen*, 319.

34 Mutembe and Molin, *Le Rituel du mariage*, 284 (Ordo I), with the assumption that the blessings after mass are said at home; they record Ritzer's text (*Formen*, 382) as unreliable.

35 Ritzer, *Formen*, 380–1, at 381.

Mazarine 404 and BnF Lat 14446, although not immediately following the mass:[36] sandwiched between them is a blessing of a drink (*Benedic domine hunc potum*: 'bless, Lord, this drink'), also found in some English liturgical manuscripts.[37] According to Orchard, the Avranches manuscript is a copy of a Canterbury exemplar, and is thus heavily indebted to English liturgical practice.[38] Unlike the three other Norman manuscripts, one other, seemingly idiosyncratic, twelfth-century manuscript from the abbey of Lyre (later preserved at Evreux but unfortunately now lost) was published by Edmond Martène, the eighteenth-century liturgist.[39] The lost Lyre manuscript contained rubrics with unambiguous direction as to where the prayers over the wedding bedchamber and bed ought to be recited: 'In the evening / night when the couple go to bed the priest will come and bless the bed, saying …' (*Nocte uero cum ad lectum pervenerint accedat presbyter et benedicat thalamum dicens*). This is followed by another rubric: 'Then he makes this blessing over them, saying …' (*Deinde faciat super eos benedictionem dicens*). These indications suggest that, according to the compiler of the manuscript (if not the eighteenth-century editor Martène), the priest was expected to enter the bedroom with the couple and that, therefore, the prayers were expected to be said at home, in a domestic environment.

The evidence gathered by Mutembe and Molin for northern France (apart from Normandy) before *c.*1200 is rather limited. It suggests that the Bury St Edmunds manuscript that was transferred to Laon was one of the earliest liturgical manuscripts with the rite of the wedding bedchamber in use in northern France. We may recall that this manuscript contains an extensively rubricated wedding rite, which, although containing blessings for the wedding bedchamber and bed after the mass, does not include rubrics for the location of this particular ritual. This aligns the Bury St Edmunds manuscript with most of the Norman ones containing the rite. What is

[36] Mutembe and Molin, *Le Rituel du mariage*, 288–9 (Ordo IV), again with the assumption that the blessing of the wedding bedchamber / bed is a domestic rite performed at home; Stevenson, *Nuptial Mass*, 70.

[37] Mutembe and Molin, *Le Rituel du mariage*, 324–5; cf. also p. 127 above.

[38] Orchard, ed., *Leofric Missal*, 1: 77–8.

[39] As quoted in Mutembe and Molin, *Le Rituel du mariage*, 35–6, 286–7 (Ordo III). The text for the bedchamber and bed is also given in Adolph Franz, *Die kirchlichen Benediktionen im Mittelalter* (Freiburg im Breisgau, 1909), 181. I am very grateful to David Ganz for this reference.

particularly interesting in this regard is a so-called 'rituale' from the monastery of Saint-Maur-des-Fossés near Paris (Paris, BnF lat 13317), dating from the first half of the thirteenth century.[40] This contains explicit guidance for the priest regarding where to recite the blessings:

> After the mass, when the groom and bride have returned home, the priest will bless the bedchamber before they enter the chamber, saying this prayer 'Benedic domine thalamum hunc…'. Then the priest guides them into the chamber, saying 'Deus Abraham…'. Thereafter the priest blesses them seated on the bed, saying 'Benedic domine hos famulos [Bless, Lord, these servants]'.

These rubrics suggest that in the early thirteenth century, at least near Paris, priests were expected to conduct this part of the marriage service in the home.

What does the liturgical manuscript evidence tell us about the ritual's development in north-western Europe?[41] On the whole, there is ambiguity as to location of the ritual for England, Normandy and northern France before 1200. There is also growing evidence for a liturgical celebration in three parts: firstly, prayers at the church door concerning the handing of the bride to the groom (later with expressions of consent) and the assignment of the dowry; secondly, a mass in the church; followed, thirdly, by prayers. However, the location for the post-mass prayers for the blessing of the wedding bedchamber, bed and couple is ambiguous.

The Prayers for Blessing the Wedding Bed and Bedchamber

The purpose of the ritual was to bless the bedchamber and bed, as well as the couple, but what was its meaning? Rituals which mark important events associated either with the human life cycle or with the public life of a community are common in all societies.[42]

[40] Mutembe and Molin, *Le Rituel du mariage,* 298–300 (Ordo XI).

[41] Cf. Gittos, 'Researching the History of Rites', 27.

[42] The literature on rituals is vast; for a selection, see Geoffrey Koziol, 'How does a Ritual Mean?', in idem, *Begging Pardon and Favor: Ritual and Political Order in Early Medieval France* (Ithaca, NY, 1992), 289–324, 414–21. For an influential, though controversial, critique of using the concept of 'ritual' in the early Middle Ages, see Philippe Buc, *The Dangers of Ritual: Between Early Medieval Texts and Social Scientific Theory* (Princeton, NJ, 2001), 248–61.

They are often associated with religion and, in the case of Christianity, recorded in liturgical evidence.[43] It is worth noting that although liturgical rituals might seem long-standing or even static, they were often incredibly varied and experienced change over time.[44] If explicit evidence regarding the purpose of a ritual is lacking, as seems to be the case for the blessing of the wedding bedchamber or bed, it has to be deduced. A closer analysis of the three most common wedding prayers for the bedchamber or bed is therefore essential and to this we now turn. In most surviving sources for this blessing, in the first prayer the priest asks God that the couple might live in the knowledge of his love,[45] and in the second that God might bless the couple just as he blessed Tobias and Sara, daughter of Raguel.[46] The biblical couple's exemplary conduct – they fasted for three days before they consummated their marriage – is presented as a Christian role model. Both prayers end in the same manner, namely with the request that God will consider the couple to be worthy of God's love, that they may live and grow old together, and 'multiply throughout the length of their days'.[47] This last phrase in particular encapsulates Christian thinking about marriage as the indissoluble union of two people for the purposes of companionship and procreation.[48] With procreation of children seen as the most essential reason for marriage, the apostle Paul had expounded the

[43] Gittos, 'Researching the History of Rites', 27–8.

[44] Ibid. 27; for more general context, see Gerd Althoff, 'The Variability of Rituals in the Middle Ages', in idem, Johannes Fried and Patrick J. Geary, eds, *Medieval Concepts of the Past: Ritual, Memory, Historiography* (Cambridge, 2002), 71–88; idem, *Family Friends and Followers: Political and Social Bonds in Early Medieval Europe*, transl. Christopher Carroll (Cambridge, 2004), 136–59.

[45] 'Benedic, domine, thalamum hoc, et omnes habitantes in eo, Per Dominum': Mutembe and Molin, *Le Rituel du mariage*, 326 (no. 33).

[46] 'Benedic domine istos adolescentes sicut benedixisti Tobiam et Saram filiam Raguelis ita benedicere digneris Domine' ('Bless, Lord, this couple as You blessed Tobias and Sara, daughter of Raguel whom you Lord deem worthy to bless'): Mutembe and Molin, *Le Rituel du mariage*, 326 (no. 36). The story is told in the Old Testament Book of Tobit. For its use in the marriage liturgy, see Philip L. Reynolds, *Marriage in the Western Church: The Christianization of Marriage during the Patristic and Early Medieval Periods* ((Boston, MA, and Leyden, 2001), 334–7, 370–4; Christopher Brooke, *The Medieval Idea of Marriage* (Oxford, 1989), 43; Reynolds, 'Marrying and its Documentation', 20–1.

[47] '[U]t in amore tuo vivent, et senescent et multiplicentur in longitudine dierum': Mutembe and Molin, *Le Rituel du mariage*, 326 (no. 33); 'ut in nomine tuo vivent et senescent et multiplicentur in longitudine dierum': ibid. (no. 36); cf. Gen. 1: 28.

[48] David L. d'Avray, *Medieval Marriage: Symbolism and Society* (Oxford, 2008), 74–98.

notion of the conjugal debt, according to which the married couple owed each other sexual intercourse.[49] The stress on multiplication, that is, producing children, as the only means to propagate humanity, is the most important reason for marriage.[50] While the prayers speak of love and of growing old together, they also act as a reminder of the importance of procreation. Apart from the reference to Tobias and Sara, there is a third blessing based on the story told in the Book of Tobit that refers to the three generations of Abraham, Isaac and Jacob, where each man blessed the son of the next generation.[51] This prayer illustrates the notion of multiplication expressed in the earlier prayers. The Abrahamic blessings are then likened to God's blessing of the couple. The emphasis lies on the role of the father as the head of the family, who through his seed becomes the progenitor of the new generation, a sentiment to which I return in section four. The three prayers based on the Book of Tobit are the most frequently used ones for the bedroom, bed and couple. The prayers have no commentary attached to them, so it is unclear how they would have been interpreted. Set in the context of contemporary theological discussions regarding the purpose of marriage as procreation, and the belief that intercourse was unavoidable and that the enjoyment of the sexual act was sinful, it is tempting to see these prayers as reminding the couple, on the day of their wedding, of these Christian precepts.[52]

[49] 'The husband should give to his wife her conjugal rights, and likewise the wife to her husband. For the wife does not have authority over her own body, but the husband does; likewise the husband does not have authority over his own body, but the wife does. Do not deprive one another except perhaps by agreement for a set time, to devote yourselves to prayer, and then come together again, so that Satan may not tempt you because of your lack of self-control': 1 Cor. 7: 3–5 (NRSV).

[50] See Rüdiger Schnell, *Sexualität und Emotionalität in der vormodernen Ehe* (Cologne, Weimar and Vienna, 2002), 97–116; van Houts, *Married Life*, 88–102, for a discussion based on texts by authors ranging from Augustine of Hippo to Peter Abelard.

[51] 'Deus Abraham, Deus Isaac et Deus Jacob benedic adolescentos istos, et semina semen vite eterne in mentibus eorum ut quicquid pro utilitate sua didicerint facere cupiant per Ihesum Christum recuperatorem hominum filium tuum unigenitum qui tecum et cum Spiritu Sancto vivit et regnat et nunc et semper per aeterna saecula saeculorum Amen': Mutembe and Molin, *Le Rituel du mariage*, 327 (no. 39). Tob. 7: 15 reads: 'et adprehendens dexteram filiae suae dexterae Tobiae tradidit dicens Deus Abraham et Deus Isaac et Deus Iacob sit vobiscum et ipse coniungat vos impleatque benedictionem suam in vobis' (Douay-Rheims: 'And taking the right hand of his daughter, he gave it into the right hand of Tobias, saying: The God of Abraham, and the God of Isaac, and the God of Jacob be with you, and may he join you together, and fulfil his blessing in you').

[52] On the theological discussions and other medieval texts on the subject, see Schnell, *Sexualität und Emotionalität*, 97–116; van Houts, *Married Life*, 88–102.

Why then the blessing of the bedroom and bed? What follows is my interpretation of the prayers. Clearly the priest's moral message was deemed most effective if it was said aloud in the very bedchamber and near the bed in which the couple would have sex. The blessings would have been understood to fill the bedchamber, the bed and those in it with divine grace, a theological belief recently explored by Pawel Figurski.[53] It is almost as if the bedchamber and bed were seen as a site of memory, to remind the couple every time they slept together of the Christian message: to have sex for procreation only. The pastoral care offered to married couples, with its emphasis on chaste living – in the sense of sleeping together and having sex for procreation only – led to difficulties when some couples took the advice on chaste sleeping to mean sharing a bed, but not engaging in sex, and thus not producing children. This extreme interpretation of a sexless married life was a recurring theme in medieval hagiography.[54] Anxiety about fertility was real. Herein lies, I think, the origin of the ritual of blessing the bedchamber, bed and couple as an old fertility rite going back to a pre-Christian past, perhaps involving charms and amulets.[55]

The contents of the wedding bedchamber blessings present a prima facie case for a home setting, as the ritual only makes sense in a domestic context where bedchambers and beds can be found. Yet, at the same time, since most of the prayers are based on biblical texts, they could have been used more symbolically, after the end of the mass in church, as a means of foreshadowing the intimacy of a couple's first time in bed. A church ritual would also avoid any awkwardness on the part of the couple. The absence of explicit rubrics in the liturgical manuscripts, indicating that the priest ought to leave the

[53] Pawel Figurski, 'Sacramental Kingship, Modern Historiography versus Medieval Sources', in idem, Johanna Dale and Pieter Byttebier, eds, *Pontifical Liturgies in the High Middle Ages: Beyond the Legacy of Ernst H. Kantorowicz* (Turnhout, 2021), 25–60, at 53–4.

[54] For chaste sleeping as a theme in medieval hagiography that was implemented in real life by some married couples to the consternation of their families worried about the absence of children, see Dyan Elliott, *Spiritual Marriage: Sexual Abstinence in Medieval Wedlock* (Princeton, NJ, 1993), esp. ch. 4, 'The Conjugal Debt and Vows of Chastity: the Theoretical and Pastoral Discourse of the High and Later Middle Ages', 132–94.

[55] Richard Kieckhefer, *Magic in the Middle Ages* (Cambridge, 1989), 69–80 (on the use of charms and amulets for fertility reasons, amongst other objects). For anxiety about fertility and practical help and advice from *matronae* (experienced women), involving 'pagan' rituals for married couples who did not conceive, see van Houts, *Married Life*, 88–103.

church after mass and perform certain rituals in the home, is especially striking. The very lack of specificity may have enabled the priest and family to decide where the blessing of the wedding bedchamber and bed should take place. If there was a preference for blessing the bedchamber and bed at home, it is worth asking how common it was for priests to perform other rites (connected with weddings) in a domestic setting.

The Priest and Wedding Rites at Home

To answer this question, we will now consider the priest's ritual wedding activity in the home, rather than in a church. Early eleventh-century England produced the vernacular *Wifmannes Beweddung*, an Old English text containing details for a marriage arrangement dated to the episcopacy of Wulfstan of York (1002–23).[56] It contains a clause regarding the wedding ceremony: 'At the wedding, there shall be a priest authorized to say mass, who should arrange their union with God's blessing for all prosperity.' The reference to a priest suggests a solemnization of the wedding with a mass and prayers, as recorded in liturgical manuscripts. However, the presence of the priest and couple in a church is hinted at, though not made explicit. Given the evidence from the pre-conquest liturgical English manuscripts discussed above, it is important to stress that the advice expressed in this document leaves open the option for a priestly blessing at home, including the blessing of the wedding bedchamber or bed. In Normandy, the earliest hint we have of a couple marrying in a domestic setting in the presence of a priest comes not from a liturgical text, nor from a chronicle or saint's life, but from the canons of a provincial synod that took place in Normandy in 1072.[57] In that year,

[56] F. Liebermann, ed., *Die Gesetze der Angelsachsen*, 3 vols (Halle, 1903–16), 1: 442–4, at 442; Patricia Skinner and Elisabeth van Houts, transl., *Medieval Writings on Secular Women* (London 2011), 70–1 (no. 33). For the date, see Patrick Wormald, *The Making of English Law: King Alfred to the Twelfth Century* (Oxford, 1999), 385–6.

[57] Ritzer, *Formen*, 314–15, indirectly quotes Dom Bessin, *Concilia Rothomagensium provinciae* 1 (Rouen, 1717), and dates the synod to 1012. In this he is followed by all other liturgical scholars. The correct date is 1072: see Orderic Vitalis, *The Ecclesiastical History of Orderic Vitalis*, ed. and transl. Marjorie C. Chibnall, 6 vols (Oxford, 1969–80), 2: 284–93, at 288–9: 'Item. Ne nuptiae in occulte fiant neque post prandium sed sponsus et sponsa ieiuni a sacerdote ieiunio in monasterio benedicantur, et antequam copulentur progenies utrorumque diligenter inquiratur' ('Again: Marriages are not to be celebrated in secret or after dinner: the husband and the wife, both fasting, shall be united in a church

Archbishop John of Rouen (1067–79) issued guidance on marriage and consanguinity.[58] He ordered that no weddings take place in private (*in occulte*) or after a meal (*neque post prandium*), but that the fasting bride and groom (*ieiuni*) be blessed in a church by a fasting priest (*ieiune*). The implication of this decree is that weddings too often took place at home after a festive meal, either with a priest who had taken part in the festivities, or without a priest at all. These new regulations required the presence of a priest, who would ensure that the occasion was public, and demanded abstinence from food, guaranteeing the occasion was a sober and orderly affair, to take place probably in the morning and preferably in a church. Again, there is no reference to the blessing of the bedchamber or bed.[59]

From twelfth-century Hainaut (in modern-day Belgium) originates a little-used text which throws some light on a priest's ritual practice in the home.[60] It concerns the *Life of the Blessed Virgin Oda* (d. 1158) by Philip Harveng (d. 1183), abbot of the Premonstratensian monastery of Bonne Espérance in the diocese of Tournai (at Vellerelle-les-Brayeux, thirteen kilometres south-east of Mons).[61] It is important to note that this belongs to a sub-genre of saint's life which concerns saintly women who escaped arranged marriages.[62] Other examples include the Life of Christina of Markyate in England, written by Robert de Gorron, monk at St Albans, in the 1140s or 1150s; and the Life of Yolande of Vianden in Luxembourg, written by Brother Hermann in the early thirteenth century.[63] Oda's life falls, chronologically, between these two. The

by a priest who is also fasting, and before the marriage is consummated careful enquiry shall be made into the ancestry of both'). Orderic is the only source for the text of this Rouen synod printed by Bessin.

58 David Bates, *William the Conqueror* (London, 2015), 356–7.

59 Both Ritzer, *Formen*, 313–14, and Vogel, 'Les Rites', 453, assumed that the synod referred to ritual of the blessing of the bedchamber / bed.

60 Mutembe and Molin, *Le Rituel du mariage*, 65–6, note that the passage refers twice to custom, which they identify as the custom of the archdiocese of Reims and of the neighbouring region of the Pas-de-Calais.

61 PL 203, cols 1359–74, esp. 1362–6 (ET: Theodore J. Antry and Carol Neel, eds and transl., *Norbert and Early Norbertine Spirituality* [New York, 2007], 219–42, at 227–33).

62 Van Houts, *Married Life*, 74–5, 94–6.

63 Charles H. Talbot, ed. and transl., *The Life of Christina of Markyate, a Twelfth-Century Recluse*, rev. Henrietta Leyser and Samuel Fanous (Oxford, 2008); for the attribution to Robert Gorron, see Katie Ann-Marie Bugyis, 'The Author of the Life of Christina of Markyate: The Case for Robert de Gorron (d. 1166)', *JEH* 68 (2017), 719–46;

protagonist's struggle to remain a virgin and become a bride of Christ fuels the narratives about marriage, with an emotive language that we have to bear in mind. Nonetheless, it contains important evidence regarding medieval wedding ceremonies and rituals.[64] Oda's story is that of an arranged marriage that failed dramatically *c.*1130, before the wedding was even concluded. Philip, the author of her Life, recounts how he was present at Oda's funeral and collected his information from those who knew her.[65] The most interesting aspect of Oda's wedding ceremony, for our purposes, is the fact that it did not take place in a church at all, but the priest was summoned to the bride's home. According to Philip, the wedding took place there because 'the church was too far away'.[66] The specific circumstances of a reluctant bride may well explain the domestic arrangement of a priest attending at the bride's home, rather than at a church. With the church at a distance, the bride might have tried to escape en route to it. There is one further intriguing aspect in this story about the reluctant bride Oda: the prominent place of the bedchamber at the end of the narrative. After the withdrawal of Simon, the jilted groom, the bride flees to her mother's bedchamber (*matris thalamum*). Alone in the room, Oda takes the sword hanging at the end of the bed, intending to cut off her nose, but fails.[67] This attempted self-mutilation was a drastic way of avoiding ever being married off again.[68] What is particularly interesting is the link between the failed wedding celebration and the presence of the bride, on her own, in the bedchamber which had conceivably been

---

Brother Hermann von Veldenz, *Bruder Hermann von Veldenz, Leben der Gräfin Yolanda von Vianden*, ed. Claudine Moulin (Luxembourg, 2009); idem, *Brother Hermann's Life of Yolande of Vianden*, transl. R. H. Lawson (Columbia, SC, 1995).

[64] Van Houts, *Married Life*, 46–7, 49–51, 131–2, 224–5 (Christina); ibid. 35–6, 40–1, 100–5, 128–9, 233–6 (Yolande).

[65] *Vita s. Odae*, cols 1373–4 (Antry and Neel, eds and transl., *Norbert and Early Norbertine Spirituality*, 241); G. P, Sijen, 'Les Oeuvres de Philippe de Harveng, abbé de Bonne Espérance', *Analecta Praemonstratensia* 15 (1939), 129–66, at 163.

[66] 'Et quia ecclesia haud prope erat': *Vita s. Odae*, col. 1364 (Antry and Neel, eds and transl., *Norbert and Early Norbertine Spirituality*, 230).

[67] '[A]rrepto gladio quem ad caput lectuli videt derendum nasum suum festinet praecidere': *Vita s. Odae*, col. 1366 ('seizing the sword hanging at the head of the bed, she tried to cut off her nose': Antry and Neel, eds and transl., *Norbert and Early Norbertine Spirituality*, 232).

[68] For a recent discussion of disfigurement as (self-inflicted) punishment, see Patricia Skinner, *Living with Disfigurement in Early Medieval Europe* (New York, 2017).

prepared as the wedding chamber and was potentially where the priest would have said his blessing. However, this is speculation, as the text does not refer to it. We are not told what happened to the priest; presumably he went home. While there is scant evidence of priests (potentially) officiating in the home as part of wedding celebrations, it is worth considering whether any other non-liturgical narratives refer to blessings of the wedding bedchamber or bed.

The Blessing of the Wedding Bed(chamber) in Non-Liturgical Narratives

By far the most elaborate description of the blessing of the wedding bedchamber is that by the chronicler Lambert of Ardres *c.*1200. It is also one of the most neglected by historians of liturgy.[69] In his history of the counts of Guines and Ardres, two medieval counties south of Flanders (now in France), Lambert gives an important description of the blessing of the marriage bed of Arnold V of Guines (d. 1220) and Beatrice of Boubourg, which he himself had attended as chaplain.[70] This is therefore a first-hand account of liturgical practice.[71] According to Lambert, it was 'on the first evening' after the solemn nuptials, presumably in the church, that Count Baldwin II (1169–1206), the father of the groom, demanded the ceremony of the blessing of the bed and couple. For this reason, he called his chaplain Lambert, together with Lambert's sons, William and Robert, who was the priest at Audruick (Pas-de-Calais). They blessed the bed, along with the couple lying in it, by sprinkling them with holy water and wafting incense, and by commending the couple to God. Surprisingly, however, it was the count who read out the prayers, which were addressed to 'God, who blessed Abraham and his seed

[69] None of the historians of liturgy mentioned in this article refers to Lambert's testimony. Amongst historians of the Middle Ages, only Georges Duby discussed it, see notes 70, 73 below.

[70] Lambert of Ardres, *Historia comitum Ghisnensium*, c. 149 (MGH SS 24, 550–642, at 637–8); Leah Shopkow, transl., *The History of the Counts of Guines and the Lords of Ardres* (Philadelphia, PA, 2001), 185–7; Georges Duby, *The Knight, the Lady and the Priest: The Making of Modern Marriage in Medieval France*, transl. Barbara Bray (New York, 1983), 258–9; van Houts, *Married Life*, 70.

[71] Lambert's elaborate description of the wedding festivities of Arnold II of Ardres (d. *c.*1138) and Gertrude does not mention the blessing of the bedchamber and bed: see van Houts, *Married Life*, 70.

… so that they may live in your divine love and persevere in concord and their seed may be multiplied throughout the length of their days for an unending eternity.' Count Baldwin then turned to bless his eldest son Arnold:

> I give to you the same grace in a father's blessing upon his son, if any bounty and grace of benediction has been passed down to me by the patriarchs, I give to you the same grace of benediction that God the Father once granted our father Abraham, Abraham gave his son Isaac, Isaac then conferred upon his son Jacob and his seed, to the extent that this devotion pertains to our faith.

As we have seen above, the reference to the three generations from Abraham to Isaac, taken from the Book of Tobit, along with the petition to be blessed in turn, was a standard prayer for the blessing of the wedding chamber.[72] As has long been recognized since the discussion of this passage by Georges Duby in the 1980s, this is a very rare example from north-western Europe suggesting that *c.*1200, marital beds were actually blessed in the home.[73] While Lambert's eyewitness account appears trustworthy, its unusual inclusion in a dynastic chronicle raises questions. A possible clue regarding its inclusion in this work lies in Lambert's description of the final blessing. As everyone prepares to withdraw from the bedchamber to leave the bride and groom alone, Count Baldwin and his son Arnold join hands, whereupon the father bends his head and whispers to him: 'I bless you, if indeed I have the power to do so saving the right of your brothers [to be blessed by me], and I leave to you here [the power to bless] for ever and ever.'[74] Since Arnold, as the eldest son, would continue the dynastic line, combining those of the counties of Guines and of Ardres, his father is reminding him of his duty to procreate. Count Baldwin felt it was his responsibility, in an Abrahamic fashion, to bless his eldest son in the hope of begetting offspring, thus safeguarding his landed possessions for future generations. This is a good illustration of elite fathers' anxiety about infertility, as discussed earlier.[75]

[72] See above, section two.
[73] Duby, *The Knight, the Lady and the Priest*, 258–9; van Houts, *Married Life*, 70–1.
[74] 'Tibi benedico, salvo iure fratrum tuorum; tibi, si quam habeo benedictionem, relinquo hic et in secula seculorum' Lambert of Ardres, *Historia comitum Ghisnensium*, c. 149 (MGH SS 24, 637). I am most grateful to one of the reviewers for advice on the translation.
[75] See above, pp. 131–2.

Lack of offspring had fuelled intergenerational strife in the families of Ardres and Guines in the past.[76] The occasion of the wedding night, prior to the conception of a new generation, was a solemn occasion on which to pass on this stern message to his son. At the same time, however, he also handed over the father's right to bless his son, so that he, in due course, could pass it on down to future generations. No doubt the count and his chronicler-chaplain used the liturgical ritual of the blessing of the wedding bedchamber, bed and couple to highlight the significance of procreation for the continuation of the dynasty in the eldest son's line. According to Lambert, the initiative for the bedchamber rite was taken by the count himself, who presumably wanted to recite the prayers for maximum effect. This is a striking example of lay participation in liturgical rites nominally reserved for priests.[77]

Apart from Lambert of Ardres's quite elaborate description of the blessing of the marriage bed, the only other non-liturgical source to contain such an allusion is both fictional and tantalizingly vague. Chrétien of Troyes, who wrote in the 1170s at the court of either Marie, countess of Champagne or Philip of Flanders, included in his vernacular romance *Erec et Enide* a lengthy description of wedding celebrations, stretching out over many days. The wedding night proper followed the first day of festivities. In one line, he situated the couple in their bedchamber 'with bishops and an archbishop', albeit without any reference as to what their presence signified.[78]

All this is a surprisingly meagre collection of evidence for the blessing of the marriage bed in non-liturgical sources, given the impressive number of detailed prayers for such an occasion in liturgical manuscripts. However, what Chrétien of Troyes and Lambert of Ardres have in common is that they unambiguously present officiating priests in the bedroom of the newly wed couple. In Lambert's case, they explicitly blessed the couple in bed, although the majority of prayers were said by the count, the bridegroom's father, a layman.

[76] Jean-François Nieus, 'Les Conflits familiaux et leur traitement dans *l'Historia comitum Ghisnensium* de Lambert d'Ardres', in M. Aurell, ed., *La Parenté déchirée. Les Luttes intra-familales au Moyen Age*, Histoires de famille. La Parenté au Moyen Ages 10 (Turnhout, 2010), 343–58.

[77] Carol Symes, 'Liturgical Texts and Performance Practices', in Gittos and Hamilton, eds, *Understanding Medieval Liturgy*, 239–67, at 263–6, with a brief discussion of marriage ceremonies at 264.

[78] 'Eveques et archeveque i furent': Chrétien de Troyes, *Erec et Enide*, ed. and transl. Carleton W. Carroll (New York, 1987), 90–1, line 2036; cf. van Houts, *Married Life*, 67.

Chrétien is silent as to what the archbishop and bishops actually did in the bedroom.[79]

In conclusion, liturgical evidence traces the development of the blessing of the wedding bedchamber in north-western Europe, across the Channel from England to northern France, including Normandy and Flanders, and vice versa. Importantly, we should note that among those historians of liturgy mentioned here, Ritzer, Mutembe and Molin, Stevenson and Reynolds, only Mutembe and Molin followed up on any evidence for these rites in sources other than liturgical manuscripts, although they ignored Lambert of Ardres's testimony. The evidence presented here suggests that there was ambiguity as to where the blessing of the wedding chamber, bed and couple actually took place. The liturgical evidence provides a prima facie case for a domestic ceremony, though the general lack of rubrication in liturgical manuscripts for the post-mass prayers from *c.*1100 onwards, if taken at face value, suggests discretion on the part of those involved – priest, couple and kin – as to the place where this should take place. I have argued that this lack of precision opened up the possibility for the post-mass prayers to be recited in church, though in the few cases where the manuscript rubrication is explicit, it seemingly gives the priest directions to perform the blessing in the home. The sparsity of reports of actual domestic celebrations in non-liturgical sources is difficult to explain. We could argue that their authors and readers considered the ritual in the home to be too common an event to warrant a mention; this seems a rather feeble explanation. Alternatively, we might argue that the domestic ritual was a rare event, in which case the testimonies of Chrétien de Troyes and Lambert of Ardres are the exceptions that prove the rule. In all likelihood, it seems that the ambiguity regarding the location of the blessing of the wedding bedchamber, bed and couple in the sources does not allow for a definite answer as to whether it was an exclusively domestic or an exclusively

[79] For a priest forcing a married couple to sleep together in the same bed covered by liturgical vestments, in an attempt at reconciliation after a fall-out, see the famous description by John of Salisbury of Pope Eugenius as marriage counsellor to King Louis VII of France and Queen Eleanor of Aquitaine in Rome, on their return journey from the disastrous Second Crusade in October 1149. According to John, the pope had the bed made up with his own precious vestments ('Fecit eos in eodem lecto decumbere, quem de suo preciosissimis vestibus fecerat exornari'): see John of Salisbury, *Historia Pontificalis*, ed. and transl. Marjorie Chibnall (London, 1966), 61.

church event.[80] The ambiguity itself is testimony to the church's openness in allowing it to happen in either the church or the home. The liturgy offered the possibility for a ritual of blessing of the wedding bedchamber, bed and couple, but for the period under consideration, on the basis of the evidence collected, it seems that the ritual, as contained in a significant number of liturgical manuscripts, did not find its way into practice amongst the laity, except for a small number of elite families. The great majority of the laity may have been entirely ignorant of this ritual's existence.

[80] One of the reviewers plausibly suggested that whether blessings took place at home or in a church might have depended on whether an elite household comprised a priest who could officiate at home; a village priest might more naturally have performed blessings in a local church.

Recording Liturgical and Sacramental Rites of Passage in Pre-Reformation English Parishes

R. N. Swanson*
Shaanxi Normal University, Xi'an, China

The introduction of parochial registers in England in 1538 was a milestone in the recording of (some) liturgical and sacramental rites of passage. Limited evidence reveals an earlier and superficially similar system incorporating detailed recording of offerings and other receipts among parochial 'altarage' income in benefice accounts. The material is examined and contextualized, to establish its relationship with the system introduced in 1538 and its value for appreciating the experience of liturgical rites of passage in pre-Reformation England.

Introduction

In 1975, in Beijing, a Chinese student learning English and 'unaware of the sprinkling of French idioms in modern English … translated *rite de passage* as "the ceremony of entering into traffic".'[1] Parishioners in pre-Reformation England would probably have appreciated that rendering; certainly for baptism, which one Middle English text described as the 'firste passage of alle goode pilgrimage'.[2] Duly modified, it can be applied to the subsequent liturgical and sacramental checkpoints experienced by parishioners on 'The Pilgrimage of the [Christian] Lyfe'; primarily baptism, marriage, the 'purification' or 'churching' of mothers after childbirth, extreme unction conferred in anticipation of death, and the funeral which followed it. Those checkpoints provide the focus for this discussion, addressed through

* E-mail: r.n.swanson@bham.ac.uk. This article is a side-shoot of a continuing research project, 'The English Parish, *c*.1290–*c*.1535', funded as a Leverhulme Trust Major Research Fellowship (MRF-2012-016) in 2013–16. That support is gratefully acknowledged.

[1] Frances Wood, *Hand-Grenade Practice in Peking: My Part in the Cultural Revolution* (London, 2000), 45.

[2] Guillaume de Deguileville, *The Pilgrimage of the Lyfe of the Manhode, translated anonymously into Prose from the First Recension of Guillaume de Deguileville's Poem*, Le Pèlerinage de la vie humaine, ed. Avril Henry, EETS o.s. 284, 292, 2 vols (Oxford, 1985–8), 1: 6.

Studies in Church History 59 (2023), 142–163
doi: 10.1017/stc.2023.7

the evidence for their systematic recording (or absence) within surviving parochial records. The end-point is set by Thomas Cromwell's mandate requiring the nationwide introduction of parochial registration of baptisms, marriages and burials in England in 1538. The key sources date mainly from the fifteenth and early sixteenth centuries, but the practices extend back into the thirteenth. Most of the affected parishioners were laypeople under the spiritual oversight and jurisdiction of their parochial incumbent; their experience unavoidably dominates the records. For the clergy, ordination created an alternative cycle culminating in priesthood, experienced within a different framework. While clergy were not totally abstracted from the parochial cycle (they would all eventually die and be buried), their ordination was not technically part of the standard series. Specific liturgical commemoration of promotion to the priesthood does, however, leave occasional traces within parochial records, and accordingly requires some discussion here.

Cromwell's injunction, issued as vicegerent in spirituals for King Henry VIII, laid the burden of compliance firmly on the parochial 'parson, vicar, or curate'. He was to supply the necessary book and weekly record (in the presence of the churchwardens) 'all the weddings, christenings, and buryings made the whole week before'. The wardens were required to provide a 'coffer with two locks and keys' for the book's safekeeping.[3] Despite being issued within the broader context of the programme of church reform of the early Henrician Reformation, this was not intrinsically an ecclesiastical measure. Its introduction lacked a declared rationale, although plausible validations can be postulated.[4] The requirement is not overtly based on previous practices, but it is unsurprising that one early twentieth-century scholar was provoked to seek precedents and analogues among earlier records (not all of them English).[5] That hunt was misguided, tracing similarities but overlooking differences, and tinged by a desire to prove that the novelty was not merely following foreign fashions. Analysis and limited contextualization of one cache of parochial records within that framework generated the firm conclusion

[3] Henry Gee and William J. Hardy, eds, *Documents Illustrative of English Church History, compiled from Original Sources* (London, 1921), 275–81, at 279.

[4] As, e.g., in Nicholas Orme, *Going to Church in Medieval England* (New Haven, CT, 2021), 357–9.

[5] Andrew Clark, ed., *Lincoln Diocese Documents*, EETS o.s. 149 (London, 1914), 29–30, 35.

that '[the] Injunctions of 1538, did no more than impose on all parish churches a registration-system which had long been (regularly, if somewhat laxly) in use in many'.[6]

That conclusion was faulty, although a few of the earliest surviving 'Cromwellian' registers do contain entries dated before 1538, suggesting some kind of precedent, although not necessarily a precise one.[7] Reconsideration of the specific records from which the false equivalence was derived – from the parishes of All Saints and St Michael at the North Gate, Oxford – provides the springboard for this article. They are annual statements of receipts for liturgical activities within those churches compiled for submission to the Rector and Fellows of Lincoln College as the churches' corporate rectors, and meshed into the college's annual accounting process.[8] Their most immediately relevant feature is their inclusion of key life-cycle spiritual events (purifications of women after childbirth, solemnizations of marriages and funeral celebrations) listed under precise dates in a calendrical order.[9] The differences between these records and the parochial registration imposed in 1538 are fundamental, and critical. Baptism is completely absent (and purification no substitute for it), while a funeral does not place a corpse as precisely as a burial does. Most strikingly, and most importantly, these records do not routinely record names: the *dramatis personae* usually remain anonymous. At heart, these records do not reflect a concern or requirement to catalogue events as such. Their basic purpose is financial: they record receipts from events, not the events themselves; why income was generated, not who paid or the individuals at the centre of the rites. They cannot be addressed and interpreted in the same way as post-1538 parish registers.

The recording of life-cycle rites of passage in these and similar accounts challenges any expectations and preconceptions of pre-Reformation practices based on the Cromwellian registration

[6] Ibid. 30.

[7] See J. Charles Cox, *The Parish Registers of England* (London, 1910), 236–9.

[8] Fuller discussion in R. N. Swanson, 'Town and Gown, Nave and Chancel: Parochial Experience in Late Medieval Oxford', in David Harry and Christian Steer, eds, *The Urban Church in Late Medieval England: Essays from the 2017 Harlaxton Symposium held in Honour of Clive Burgess*, Harlaxton Medieval Studies 29 (Donington, 2019), 301–31.

[9] Representative entries extracted in Clark, ed., *Lincoln Diocese Documents*, 29–34. For an overview of the ecclesiastical ceremonial of life-cycle rites of passage, see Orme, *Going to Church*, 302–49; for a broader social assessment, see Katherine L. French, *The Good Women of the Parish: Gender and Religion after the Black Death* (Philadelphia, PA, 2008), 50–84.

requirements. It merits attention and comment as a distinctly different phenomenon. This first requires some discussion of the available sources and their basic utility as evidence for the rites. The approach can then be reversed to consider the rites themselves, as dealt with in the sources. Goals here are deliberately limited, with the focus very firmly on the parochial events and their records. This avoids the traps and diversions which threaten any attempt at broader contextualization within the administrative structures and records of royal and diocesan governance and oversight. The outcome is essentially descriptive, becoming argumentative only when necessary to explain the character and content of the sources.

Sources

Among parochial records, the basic split within parishes between 'chancel' and 'nave' is crucial. On the chancel side lies the clerical benefice centred on the cure of souls, sacramental authority and priest-directed liturgical performance under the jurisdictional authority of the local incumbent or rector. The nave side embraces the semi-autonomous community of parishioners – not exclusively lay – with their own financial administration geared primarily to funding maintenance of the parish church, and usually directed by churchwardens. Both regimes can be complicated by the existence of subsidiary units, with their own subject administrations and varying degrees of financial and fiscal autonomy. The division between the 'clerical' and 'communal' (or 'lay') versions of 'the parish' was physically symbolized by the chancel arch, but the performance of the rites, and the benefice accounts which reflect them, transcend this notional separation. That transcendence potentially integrates transients and short-term residents, rich or poor, into the records of both chancel and nave, falling under the incumbent's spiritual jurisdiction as parishioners, and mentioned in nave accounts in relation to costs or payment for rites.[10]

While the core evidence considered here derives from the chancel side, recording liturgical performance and its integration into the duties of pastoral care, and detailing elements of the associated

[10] As with an unnamed 'man from London', whose funeral is mentioned in both the benefice and churchwardens' accounts for St Michael at the North Gate, Oxford, in 1475: Swanson, 'Town and Gown', 326.

miscellaneous and varying income gathered by the rector or his substitute under the broad heading of 'altarage', the nave cannot be ignored. The parishioners maintained their own financial records, in the varied forms and formats of surviving pre-Reformation churchwardens' accounts. These significantly outnumber the detailed chancel accounts, but are still relatively rare. Like the chancel accounts, their purpose was essentially fiscal; but their recording is more haphazard. Nothing within them amounts to a formal registration of lifecycle rites of passage, regarding which their concern is not primarily the liturgical events themselves, but the use and consumption of parochial resources. What matters is the revenue generated by the burning of wax and torches, the ringing of bells and the hiring of other liturgical accessories, and finally burial fees (usually for intramural graves). Their listing is rarely explicitly calendrical; the amount of detail reflects the whims of their compilers and local accounting practices. For our immediate purposes, the nave material is supplementary to the chancel evidence, and generally of secondary value and utility. It has greater value in the extremely rare instances where surviving records allow complementary insights from both sides of the chancel arch, with St Michael at the North Gate in Oxford being possibly the best example.[11] Beyond the accounts, additional material survives incidentally in a wide range of contexts. Litigation records perhaps add the most, to the point that one batch of chancel accounts is known only by its survival among the file of court documents relating to a dispute over a vicar's income.[12]

Surviving calendrical lists of liturgical events like those for the two Oxford parishes of All Saints and St Michael at the North Gate are extremely rare.[13] That rarity in part reflects their place in the accounting cycle: the detail was relevant only for the accountant compiling a statement for transmission and incorporation into a higher layer

[11] Others, with less informative chancel accounts, are noted in Swanson, 'Town and Gown', 328–9 n. 122. More may await detection.

[12] The Hornsea accounts are discussed and edited in Peter Heath, *Medieval Clerical Accounts*, St Anthony's Hall Publications 26 (York, 1964), 5–11, 25–59. These are now at York, BIA, CP.F.306.

[13] The closest match to the Oxford accounts is Salisbury, Salisbury Cathedral Archives, FA/2/1-24 (others undated in FA/2/2), from St Thomas's Church, Salisbury. Very similar are those for Scarborough, now at Kew, TNA, E101/314/31-2: see Heath, *Medieval Clerical Accounts*, 3–4; the calendrical statement of liturgical income for 1435–6 is translated in R. N. Swanson, ed., *Catholic England: Faith, Religion, and Observance before the Reformation* (Manchester, 2014), 151–7.

within an institutional financial administration. At that system's apex, the detail is usually reduced to a mere summary. The detailed statements for both Oxford parishes thus appear in the itemized booklets of income and expenditure prepared annually by the bursars of Lincoln College, but not in the final summary balance sheets.[14] The production and survival of detailed records usually reflects a specific organizational context for the benefices, without automatically meaning that they were created only in that context. Survival is obviously essential. Many of the known examples relate to appropriated parishes, in which the cure of souls was delegated to chaplains who compiled the initial lists. These were then fed into the appropriators' accounting process (possibly with some editing, and sometimes via intermediary agents). The detailed lists had evidential value to validate the totals, but presumably soon became disposable ephemera.[15] These fully calendrical accounts can be supplemented by others, such as those from Hornsea (Yorkshire) and Topsham (Devon), which give less detail, breaking the year into terms, or organizing the rites by category.[16] (Events may still be noted in chronological order, but without dates.) At the highest accounting levels, summary annual balance sheets may still indicate annual income from the rites, but that is variable: within extended runs, practice can change over time.[17]

Even if normally retained by an appropriator, the post-Reformation survival of these sources usually requires that institution's own survival and archival continuity: Lincoln College, Oxford, for the two Oxford parishes; Salisbury's cathedral chapter

[14] Oxford, Lincoln College Archives [hereafter: LCA], Bursary Papers, Miscellaneous Bundles, 1–3 and Charters 39.

[15] Totals in some of the Durham proctors' accounts (see n. 17 below) have the validating comment: 'ut patet in papirum computantis' ('as is shown in the accountant's paper').

[16] For Hornsea, see n. 12 above; for Topsham, see Exeter, Exeter Cathedral Archives, 4647.

[17] For sample material from Great Yarmouth and Bishop's [now King's] Lynn (both Norfolk), see Swanson, *Catholic England*, 157–63; for discussions, see idem, 'Standards of Livings: Parochial Revenues in Pre-Reformation England', in Christopher Harper-Bill, ed., *Religious Belief and Ecclesiastical Careers in Late Medieval England* (Woodbridge, 1991), 151–96, at 164, 168, 190; idem, 'Urban Rectories and Urban Fortunes in Late Medieval England: The Evidence from King's Lynn', in T. R. Slater and Gervase Rosser, eds, *The Church in the Medieval Town* (Aldershot, 1998), 100–30, at 108, 110, 122–3. Totalling at an intermediate point appears in the proctors' accounts for the churches at Norham (Northumberland) and St Oswald and St Margaret, Durham, all appropriated to Durham Cathedral Priory: Durham, Durham University Library, Archives and Special Collections, DCD-St Mar. acs; DCD-St Os. acs; DCD-Norh. acs.

for similar calendrical material from St Thomas, Salisbury; Exeter Cathedral chapter for the Topsham records. Comparable accounts may have been much more common, even in unappropriated parishes, possibly within the 'Easter books' (alternatively identified as Easter or Lenten rolls) often mentioned in medieval sources. Their precise character and content are elusive, but they appear in several entries in the *Valor ecclesiasticus* of 1535, implicitly associated with altarage income.[18] They may have been compiled by vicars in appropriated parishes and rectors in unappropriated ones, but a more likely background is their creation by the stipendiary parochial chaplains who undertook the basic donkey work of pastoral and liturgical care (especially for absentee incumbents), and presumably had to account to their employers for the revenues they received (and, possibly, failed to receive) on their behalf. Two detailed accounts from Blunham (Bedfordshire) were probably prepared for the rectory's lay farmer, indicating the privatization of such ecclesiastical revenues when rectorial resources were leased out (to clerical or lay holders); but no accountant is named.[19] The surviving Hornsea accounts were compiled for the vicar by the parochial chaplain.[20] Some chaplains officiating in dependent chapels which enjoyed some autonomy compiled their own Easter books to account to the parochial incumbent; similar arrangements are also conceivable in some of the 'extra-parochial' areas associated with monastic houses.[21]

However speculative imagination and enthusiasm may shape attitudes and readings of the initial stages of the receiving process, the end results, even if seemingly detailed, are not always useful for

[18] For example, [John Caley and Joseph Hunter], eds, *Valor ecclesiasticus*, 6 vols (London, 1810–34), 3: 180–1, 268–9; 5: 57–61, 213–15; 6: xlii–xliii.

[19] John S. Thompson, ed., *Hundreds, Manors, Parishes and the Church: A Selection of Early Documents for Bedfordshire*, Publications of the Bedfordshire Historical Record Society 69 (Bedford, 1990), 125, 145–69 (esp. 145–6, 161–3; also mention of 'th'Eyster book' at 144).

[20] Heath, *Medieval Clerical Accounts*, 27–8. Several of the accounts name no accountant, so could have been compiled by the vicar.

[21] For example, BIA, CP.G.247 (from 1536), discussed in R. N. Swanson, 'Fissures in the Bedrock: Parishes, Chapels, Parishioners and Chaplains in Pre-Reformation England', in Nadine Lewycky and Adam Morton, eds, *Getting Along? Religious Identities and Confessional Relations in Early Modern England: Essays in Honour of Professor W. J. Sheils* (Farnham, 2012), 77–95, at 90–1. See also [Caley and Hunter], eds, *Valor ecclesiasticus*, 3: 269. Distribution may be suggested by references to chapels 'used as a parish church' in the Yorkshire chantry surveys of the 1540s: Swanson, 'Fissures', 83, 87; see also 84, 90. St Margaret, Durham, was an autonomous chapelry of St Oswald (see n. 17 above).

present purposes. A brief run of accounts from [Santon] Downham (Suffolk) includes itemized purifications, marriages and burials scattered among the disorderly entries, with other notes seemingly as annual totals. The paucity of precise entries suggests that they cannot record all such occurrences (perhaps confirmed by a mortuary entered with no sign of an associated funeral); but it is impossible to be sure.[22]

Checkpoints and Toll Stations

The fiscal imperative behind the creation of the pre-Reformation chancel material establishes the basic functional distinction between such sources and the Cromwellian registers. The rites noted in the pre-Reformation records were ones which generated income for the relevant cleric; what mattered was the money generated by liturgical performance, not the performance itself. That affects how the records were constructed and how they can be interpreted. The life-cycle rites of passage can be imagined as checkpoints in the pilgrimage of life; the character of the benefice accounts almost makes negotiating some of them equivalent to negotiating going through a tollbooth.

Entering Traffic: Births, Baptism and Purification

Perhaps surprisingly, baptism does not usually appear as the first tollbooth, despite its critical role on the road to salvation. None of the examined accounts itemize baptisms, presenting a stark contrast with the stipulations of Cromwell's injunctions. One explanation may be that payment would reek of simony, the illicit purchase of a sacrament, although ways could have been found around that obstacle. A financial statement from Kirkby Malhamdale (Yorkshire) in 1454–5 does mention a fee charged there (¼*d.*), but this stands alone.[23] Lack of accounting need not mean lack of recording, potentially among the information collected in Easter books. Recurrent statements by witnesses in secular legal proceedings to prove the

[22] TNA, E101/517/27, fols 1^r, 2^r, 3^{r}–^{v}, 4^v–5^r, 6^r.

[23] London, BL, Add. Roll 32957. The totals entered in this account cannot be converted into separate events. Income from *baptisteria* appears in the proctors' accounts for the churches of St Oswald and St Margaret at Durham, and at Norham (see n. 17 above); what they mean is uncertain, but they may indicate payments for chrisom cloths used at baptism. (See also below, p. 151 [at notes 30–1].)

ages of minors seeking to enter inheritances on attaining their majority declare that a baptism had been entered in a mass book or other liturgical volume; although this cannot have been normal for all baptisms (even if it had happened in the stated instances).[24] The urgency of baptism and the likelihood of neonatal death may lie behind the absence: baptism had, in these cases, to be performed speedily. In really urgent instances, that might be by a midwife, lest a priest did not arrive in time; but with subsequent priestly ratification by conditional rebaptism if he did. The frequency of such midwife-baptisms cannot be assessed, for lack of evidence. They may lie behind some of the complaints against clergy who had allegedly allowed newborns to die unbaptized, if a Devonshire case from the mid-1530s is representative. That baby died before the priest arrived, 'unchristened except that [which] the midwife did to it'.[25]

The first recorded rite which suggests a new life-cycle centres, however, on the mothers, not the babies: their purification (or 'churching'), performed around forty days after the birth (but not always that long after) to reintegrate the mother into the parochial community after surviving the ordeal of childbirth.[26] It seems a reasonably safe assumption that any purification which produced income would be recorded where accounts were kept; but the rite was sometimes celebrated illicitly or clandestinely, and some women may have evaded it or been denied access.[27]

[24] The credibility of proofs is debated. Despite doubts about their detailed reliability, they are plausible guides to contemporary practice at a general level. For varying assessments, see Sue Sheridan Walker, 'Proof of Age of Feudal Heirs in Medieval England', *Mediaeval Studies* 35 (1973), 306–23; Joel T. Rosenthal, *Telling Tales: Sources and Narration in Late Medieval England* (University Park, PA, 2003), 1–62; Matthew Holford, '"Testimony (to Some Extent Fictitious)": Proofs of Age in the First Half of the Fifteenth Century', *HR* 82 (2009), 635–59.

[25] French, *Good Women*, 57–8; Joyce Youings, ed., *The Dissolution of the Monasteries* (London, 1971), 139–40, at 140.

[26] French, *Good Women*, 61–3. For evidence from proof of age proceedings, see L. R. Poos, *A Rural Society after the Black Death: Essex, 1350–1525* (Cambridge, 1991), 122 and n. 28.

[27] See BIA, CP.G.222 (duplicated at CP.G.240), for an illicit purification celebrated at a chapel. Purifications are among those actions specifically banned at one chapel in Philippa M. Hoskin, ed., *Robert Grosseteste as Bishop of Lincoln: The Episcopal Rolls, 1235–1253* (Woodbridge, 2015), no. 1871, 'nisi in articulis necessariis' ('other than at the points of urgent need'), but allowed at another (no. 2062), with licence from the parochial rector and vicar.

While a purification was often a positive celebration, its character was frequently tempered by the reality of a stillbirth or neonatal death (the latter sometimes evident – or strongly suggested – from funeral entries).[28] As a 'rite of passage', purification was not necessarily a unique lifetime event. Repetition and normality may explain why the income it generated was rarely significant: in the Oxford parishes, it was usually only a few pence. This could also be a sign of maternal or familial poverty, or an indication that most celebrations produced only a customary fee. At Kirkby Malhamdale, the expected payment was 2*d.* (halved if the purification occurred in conjunction with a marriage).[29] It is likely that at least 1*d.* of that was a 'mass penny'. The payment for the chrisom cloth used at baptism was also handed over at the purification, in effect a deferred baptismal fee. Purifications are rarely mentioned in nave records, but several appear in fifteenth-century churchwardens' accounts from Saffron Walden (Essex).[30] Their analysis is challenging, and few are itemized. Sums received were minimal and, where indicated, varied between ½*d.* and 2*d.*; at least two women paid nothing as paupers. What the payment was actually for is not revealed; it may have been for hire of a special purification pew.[31]

The manner of recording purifications varies. At Scarborough, they are listed simply as impersonal events. At Hornsea, itemized purifications are all of wives (identified only as appendages to their husbands), but others, unspecified, are combined in collective totals

[28] Stillbirths cannot be detected because such children could not receive baptism and full funeral rites. The collocation of a child's funeral and the mother's purification (linked by shared surname) allows for the assumption of a neonatal death, without actually establishing it. For example, among the accounts for the two Oxford parishes, we have: 1495 – funeral of Asley's child (February) and his wife's purification (March) (LCA, Computus 1, Calc. 7, p. 1); 1509 – purification of Hugh Hynd's wife and child's burial (February) (ibid., Computus 1, Calc. 9, p. 1). The proximity of funerals for a child and wife also suggests the deaths of a newborn and its mother, for e.g., in 1507, the funerals of Schappe's child and wife (April) and Collyn's child and wife (June) (ibid., Computus 2 Calc. 4, pp. 4, 5). For a firmly neonatal funeral, see n. 47 below.

[29] See n. 40 below. The reduction may reflect the fact that the mass penny was 'saved' by celebrating a single mass for the two rites.

[30] Poos, *Rural Society*, 123–4. No mention appears in Beat Kümin, *The Shaping of a Community: the Rise and Reformation of the English Parish, c.1400–1560* (Aldershot, 1996).

[31] French, *Good Women*, 63.

'from others' (*de diversis*).[32] Whether, or how, the distinction between itemized and collective entries matters is unclear. It may be mirrored in the Oxford records, which likewise identify some of the women as wives, but leave others with no indication of marital status. In context, the differences may simply reflect status, with the wives of parochial leaders being indicated, while the impersonal labels suggest women of lower status and poverty. Some of the latter are identified merely as *muliercula* or *paupercula*,[33] for which the formal translations as respectively 'little woman' and 'poor little woman' may be inadequate. Inherited linguistic overtones of immorality in the designations of *muliercula* and *paupercula* could indicate a prostitute, not simply a poor woman of low status, but this cannot be tested.[34] Innumerable babies must have been born to prostitutes or unmarried mothers, or to pregnant vagrants whose marital status and child's legitimacy were unknown. However, explicit indications of bastardy are strikingly absent, the only obvious instance in consulted material being the purification at Topsham of a woman identified as John Mayner's concubine.[35] Interpretation of the purifications which occurred on the same day as the (presumed) parents' marriage complicates the picture, but they probably reflected delayed solemnizations of a preceding marital contract. That the threat of denial was used against some women, as moral blackmail or policing, is occasionally reported in other sources. The raft of accusations against one Yorkshire vicar in the early fifteenth century included the charge that he had refused to baptize the children of single mothers unless they publicly named the fathers. He denied the charge as framed, but admitted that he had demanded denunciation

32 Swanson, *Catholic England*, 151–6; Heath, *Medieval Clerical Accounts*, 28–30, 35–6, 42–3.

33 For example, LCA, Computus 1, Calc. 8, pp. 8–9; Computus 2, Calc. 4, p. 6.

34 *Muliercula* carried such associations in classical Latin: J. N. Adams, 'Words for "Prostitute" in Latin', *Rheinisches Museum für Philologie* n.f. 126 (1983), 321–58, at 354. The few citations in the *Dictionary of Medieval Latin from British Sources* (online at: <http://clt.brepolis.net/dmlbs/>, last accessed 19 January 2022) do not extend the meaning that far. One associates the word with *paupercula*, but without clear sexual imputation. *Paupercula* appears as the feminine form *s.v. pauperculus*, likewise without the negative sexual connotations. *Pauperculus* is applied to some men in LCA, Computus 2, Calc. 4, pp. 5, 7.

35 Exeter Cathedral Archives, 4647, fol. 1r. A servant's purification, with no husband named, may be another: ibid.

when the mothers sought purification.[36] This makes his action a disciplinary act against the mother, rather than a punishment against the child and a threat to its soul. From one standpoint, the charge could indicate that the vicar was being unduly harsh in his treatment of these women. Alternatively, his demand for public revelation may have been feared as socially disruptive. The women had clearly concealed their babies' paternity throughout their pregnancies; the fathers' naming may have been the real threat, potentially undermining reputations and status within the parish.

Marriage

Marriages appear less often in the accounts than purifications, for the fairly obvious reasons that not all mothers were married, and wives often produced several children. Although not always unique life-cycle events, their repetition was limited, but is sometimes detectable in benefice accounts when mentioned after a deceased spouse's funeral.[37]

Formally, the liturgical rites noted in the chancel records were not the actual marriage – the exchange of vows – but its solemnization at a nuptial mass. The two often – probably usually – coincided, but that was not a technical or legal requirement. Unless performed clandestinely (implying secrecy, and perhaps payments which did not go through the parochial books), solemnization would normally succeed a public exchange (or restatement) of vows at the church door; an event intended to be noticed and remembered, and usually preceded by advance notices in church (banns) to give objectors opportunities to allege impediments.[38] In some circumstances, the solemnization

36 J. S. Purvis, *A Mediaeval Act Book, with Some Account of Ecclesiastical Jurisdiction at York* (York, [1943]), 38. Priests were expected to ask about paternity when baptizing the child of an unmarried mother: David Wilkins, ed., *Concilia Magna Britanniæ et Hiberniæ*, 4 vols (London, 1737), 2: 132.

37 For example, at All Saints, Oxford, 1477, Philip Glover's burial (February) and his widow's remarriage (September): LCA, Computus 1, Calc. 3, pp. 1, 3.

38 R. H. Helmholz, *The Oxford History of the Laws of England,* 1: *The Canon Law and Ecclesiastical Jurisdiction from 597 to the 1640s* (Oxford, 2004), 523–4, 531. For clandestine celebrations, see, e.g., Ian Forrest and Christopher Whittick, eds, *The Visitation of Hereford Diocese in 1397*, CYS 111 (Woodbridge, 2021), nos 252–3, 306. A secular link between church marriage and conferral or confirmation of rights of dower reinforced its public significance: Sir John Baker, *Collected Papers on English Legal History*, 3 vols (Cambridge, 2013), 3: 1371–5.

was understood as the formal public completion and ecclesiastical ratification of a pre-existing union; sometimes mistakenly so, if procured in an attempt to validate one which was potentially illicit and void under canon law.[39]

The legal and practical complexities surrounding pre-Reformation marriages are ignored in the accounts. As financial records, their prime concern is with the offerings made and payments for wax used during the ceremony, with a mass penny presumably incorporated into the total. As elsewhere, the Kirkby Malhamdale statement provides firmer guidance, but not a template, and indicates that a marriage there was expensive. The fee for the church door ceremony (the exchange of vows) was 8*d.* (of which 2*d.* went to the parish clerk); altar candles cost another 2*d.* If the woman was purified at the same time (instances are suggested in the Topsham accounts), the sum was reduced to 1*d.*[40] Standardization of fees and offerings – both probably customary rather than formally regulated – is occasionally suggested elsewhere, but not always detectable.[41]

Unlike the Cromwellian registers, the benefice accounts do not normally identify the marital partners. The parish's social hierarchy may be exposed here, in the distinction between those named and those left anonymous, but that does not always apply. Brides are often left nameless, identified only as their fathers' daughters. Any movement across parochial boundaries by either party (or both) was irrelevant in the accounting process, and is invisible within it.

Exiting Traffic: Death, Burial and Beyond

The final sacramental life-cycle rite of passage was extreme unction, the last communion and absolution before death and burial. Like baptism, but for different reasons (it was not conferred in church; the anticipated death might not occur; and no mass was celebrated),

[39] For 'completion', see Stafford, Staffordshire Record Office, LD30/3/3/1, fol. 7[r]. For attempted validation, see Forrest and Whittick, eds, *Visitation*, nos 306, 1014, 1071, 1076. See also Helmholz, *Oxford History*, 531.

[40] BL, Add. Roll 32957. A couple of entries in the Topsham accounts record receipts for purification and marriage (in that order) *in eadem die* ('on the same day'): Exeter Cathedral Archives, 4647, fol. 3[v]; similar entries without that precision at ibid., fol. 1[r], and purification after or at the wedding (*post nupcias* or *in nupciis*) at ibid., fols 3[v], 8[v].

[41] Swanson, 'Town and Gown', 311.

extreme unction is absent from the records.[42] Socially, what mattered was the funeral; spiritually (and within that), what mattered was the requiem mass which signalled the soul's transit into the afterlife.

The entries for funerals are perhaps the most problematic element in parochial recording of rites of passage, enmeshed in jurisdictional complexities amidst which the concept of 'parishioner' itself became blurred. While parishioners might be expected to be buried in their home parish, they retained the right to choose burial elsewhere. The mortuary due at death was payable to the incumbent of the parish where the death occurred, even if the deceased was only a transient; the incumbent could legitimately claim that the funeral be held there also. Numerous variables created conflicting rights and expectations, further complicated by uncertainties about geographical boundaries and local customs. Contested claims concerning funerals and burials generated innumerable court cases centred on corpses and their resting places.[43]

Parochial recording would be affected by these uncertainties and conflicts, but demonstrating this from the available benefice accounts becomes an argument from silence, pierced only by insights obtained from other sources with little direct overlap and of uncertain applicability. The occasional indications of formal local tariff arrangements have questionable general validity, and clearly are not universal templates. At Kirkby Malhamdale, everyone dying above the (unstated) age at which they would receive sacramentals paid 7*d.* as 'nythewax'; maybe implying that there were no charges for infants and young children. A flat rate of 1*d.* was charged for each candle burning around the bier (*feretrum*).[44] Meanwhile, in 1525 at Bodmin (Cornwall), the parishioners asserted that their vicar received 6*d.* 'for every direge and masse, for ev[er]y man, woman, and chylde,

[42] Canonically, any priest could confer extreme unction on anyone qualified to receive it who appeared to be at the point of death (*in articulo mortis*), although it was normally expected to be conferred by the incumbent or his stand-in as a component of the spiritual jurisdiction of the parochial cure of souls. Alleged breaches of that prerogative sometimes feature in cases in the ecclesiastical courts, with chaplains accused of acting without authorization, or of usurping occupation of a subsidiary chapel. For examples of court cases, see BIA, CP.G.222 (duplicated at CP.G.240); Margaret Bowker, ed., *An Episcopal Court Book for the Diocese of Lincoln, 1514–1520*, Lincoln Record Society 61 (Lincoln, 1967), 4–6: in both, the accused chaplain claimed that he acted *in articulo mortis.*

[43] For cases illustrating some of the tensions and critical points, see n. 50 above.

[44] BL, Add. Roll 32957. The 'nythewax' payment may include a mass penny, without actually saying so.

dedde', although this may refer to post-funeral commemorations.[45] The possibility that funerals of children below a certain age occurred without payments may explain the apparent paucity of child burials in some accounts.[46] It is, however, immediately challenged by the obvious child and infant funerals noted at Oxford, most strikingly those following the neonatal deaths of a set of triplets.[47] A more worrying possibility is that accounts are misleading in not revealing all of the funerary rites performed within the parish. Going to law, incumbents sought recompense for revenue lost at allegedly adulterine funerals and burials outside their parish, or (within it) at chapels which lacked authorized burial rights.[48] Burials at friaries were particularly problematic. Canon law stipulations sought to protect incumbents' and parochial rights by requiring a funeral-like 'last farewell' (*ultima vale*) at the parish church and guaranteeing the incumbent a 'canonical quarter' of the offerings and legacies at the burial church, whatever its status.[49] Other battles were fought between incumbents of rival parishes (sometimes because the deceased lived in an enclave of one within the other), or when incumbents or their parishioners, or chaplains and their chapelry's inhabitants, resisted the monopolies of burial rights claimed by some cathedrals (in the first scenario) or their parish church (in the second).[50] If such crises erupted in any of the

[45] [John Wallis], ed., *The Bodmin Register* (Bodmin, [1838]), 37 (in the context of a dispute with the vicar over his financial claims on the parishioners). The quotation is followed by the words quoted below, n. 69, which do relate to post-funeral commemorations. Reference to 'dirige' with the mass prompts association with the funeral (Orme, *Going to Church*, 341), but may not be conclusive.

[46] None are obviously visible at Hornsea; only a few at Topsham (Exeter Cathedral Archives, 4647, fols 1^{v}, 4^{r}–^{v}), most of them in a distinct cluster.

[47] LCA, Computus 2, Calc. 7, p. 8.

[48] For cases, see n. 50 below.

[49] Thomas M. Izbicki, 'The Problem of Canonical Portion in the Later Middle Ages: The Application of "Super cathedram"', in Peter Linehan, ed., *Proceedings of the Seventh International Congress of Medieval Canon Law, Cambridge 23–27 July 1984*, Monumenta iuris canonici, Series C: Subsidia 8 (Vatican City, 1988), 459–73. For receipts from the canonical quarter at Bishop's Lynn, see Swanson, 'Urban Rectories', 120–1. The friars aggressively defended their own claims to perform funerals and burials, resisting the claims of parochial clergy in the courts of their own papal conservators: R. N. Swanson, 'The "Mendicant Problem" in the Later Middle Ages', in Peter Biller and Barrie Dobson, eds, *The Medieval Church: Universities, Heresy, and the Religious Life*, SCH Sub 11 (Woodbridge, 1999), 217–38, at 221–4, 238; BL, Add. MS 32089, fols 108^{v}–110^{v}.

[50] For relevant disputes, see Forrest and Whittick, eds, *Visitation*, no. 179; R. N. Swanson, 'Parochialism and Particularism: The Disputed Status of Ditchford

parishes for which benefice accounts survive, they are undetectable in them. Only one *ultima vale* is mentioned in the Oxford accounts; its singularity is as noteworthy as its appearance. Where the corpse actually ended up is not indicated.[51]

If there were standardized payments for funerals, their standardization is also undetectable in the surviving parochial statements. These only record the total received, normally amalgamating the receipts from offerings and / or dues with payments for wax provided by the incumbent. Wax purchases were not necessarily compulsory, or charged at the Kirkby Malhamdale rate: more likely wax was sold by weight. Purchases, or payments for the hire or waste of torches, also appear in churchwardens' accounts, as do payments for bell-ringing and the hire of the hearse.[52] At Scarborough, the wax income is noted separately, sometimes exceeding the offerings. There, also, some families are noted as using their own wax, producing no receipts.[53] (The church may then have received the leftover wax, as is noted for one Oxford funeral.[54])

Looking beyond the benefice accounts, funerals are the most likely of all the life-cycle rites of passage to leave traces within churchwardens' accounts and related sources, either by explicit mention of receipts associated with the ceremony, or indirectly by payment of burial fees. In both categories, the recording is usually incomplete or uninformative, but for differing reasons. The direct references, and the gaps, obviously reflect wealth and relative concerns for social status, as well as, in some cases (imaginable, but not overtly detectable

Frary, Warwickshire, in the Early Fifteenth Century', in M. J. Franklin and Christopher Harper-Bill, eds, *Medieval Ecclesiastical Studies in Honour of Dorothy M. Owen* (Woodbridge, 1995), 241–57; idem, '"*Liber de practica advocatorum, non utilior in Anglia*": A Canonist's Compilation from the Fourteenth-Century Court of Arches', forthcoming in Travis Baker, ed., *Christian Culture and Society in Later Catholic England* (Leiden, 2023); Ian Forrest, 'The Politics of Burial in Late Medieval Hereford', *EHR* 125 (2010), 1110–38.

51 LCA, Computus 3, fol. 53r. The *ultima vale* of a fellow of Pembroke Hall, Cambridge, appears in the Peterhouse accounts of 1464–5 'because he died within our parish' (St Peter without Trumpington Gate): Cambridge, Peterhouse Archives, Computus Roll 25.

52 For example, David Dymond, ed., *The Churchwardens' Book of Bassingbourn, Cambridgeshire, 1496–c.1540*, Cambridgeshire Record Society 17 (Cambridge, 2004), xlvi, xlix–lvii, 292 *s.v.* 'burials'; Reginald C. Dudding, ed., *The First Churchwardens' Book of Louth, 1500–1524* (Oxford, 1941), 3–6, 45–6, 48–51, 60–3.

53 Swanson, *Catholic England*, 152, 155.

54 Swanson, 'Town and Gown', 311 and n. 49.

in accounts), a desire to reduce ostentation for spiritual reasons.[55] Pauper funerals, almost by definition, would be very different from elite ones. If recorded, burial fees might provide a fuller census, but equivalence to a Cromwellian burial register is unlikely. The Westminster churchwardens' accounts of 1460 to 1510 – with some gaps in their series – have been described as amounting to 'a mortuary register … as the name of the person interred is always entered [regardless of] whether [the burial occurred] in the spacious churchyard or within the church'; but that assessment may be over-confident.[56] Unless funded by charitable collections or grants, pauper funerals might produce no income;[57] delayed receipts could be hidden unitemized in the next year's (or years') arrears; even an 'elite' funeral might not be recorded, its dues wiped out to cancel an earlier debt.[58] As already noted, the life-cycle events recorded in benefice accounts are chiefly those of lay parishioners. Recording for the clergy is much sparser and more elusive. In the mainstream sequence, they would only appear at their funerals: the distinctively clerical adult rites of passage marked the progression through the successive stages of ordination (as acolyte, subdeacon and deacon) to its completion in admission to priesthood. Ordinations were not inherently parochial events, even if they were sometimes celebrated in parish churches.[59] (The same argument applies to ordinations to first tonsure, which marked initiation into clerical status, usually conferred in childhood or adolescence.[60])

[55] See general discussion of funerals and burials in Sally Badham, *Seeking Salvation: Commemorating the Dead in the Late-Medieval English Parish* (Donington, 2015), 187–97, 209–14, 241–3.

[56] J. Charles Cox, *Churchwardens' Accounts from the Fourteenth Century to the Close of the Seventeenth Century* (London, 1913), 27. It has not been possible to consult the original accounts, now London, City of Westminster Archives Centre, SMW/E/1/1.

[57] Dymond, ed., *Bassingbourn*, 94; William Hale, *A Series of Precedents and Proceedings in Criminal Causes, extending from the Year 1475 to 1640; Extracted from the Act-Books of Ecclesiastical Courts in the Diocese of London, Illustrative of the Discipline of the Church of England*, ed. R. W. Dunning (Edinburgh, 1974), 95.

[58] As in Dudding, ed., *Louth*, 39, 45.

[59] For ceremonies in parish churches, see, e.g., Warwick P. Marett, ed., *A Calendar of the Register of Henry Wakefield, Bishop of Worcester, 1375–95*, Worcestershire Historical Society n.s. 7 (1972), nos 874–983 (intermittently); John C. Bates, ed., *The Register of William Bothe, Bishop of Coventry and Lichfield, 1447–1452*, CYS 98 (Woodbridge, 2008), nos 317, 320, 336–9, 342.

[60] For such ordinations in parish churches, see, e.g., R. C. Fowler and C. Jenkins, eds, *Registrum Simonis de Sudburia, diocesis Londoniensis, A.D. 1362–1375*, CYS 34, 38, 2 vols

A different ambiguity affects an associated rite, the celebration of a priest's first mass. If it was indeed his first exercise of his newly received power to transubstantiate wafers and wine into the body and blood of Christ, its identification as a rite of passage does seem justified. In some cases, it was a 'parochial' event, at least to the extent that it generated income entered in a benefice account. However, firm evidence that a first mass was considered special is elusive; its seeming appearance as such in a benefice account may be deceptive. Among the consulted accounts, relevant entries appear only in those from Oxford, suggesting that its highlighting indicates deliberate choice.[61] The sums recorded are comparatively high (12*d.* or 20*d.*). Described as 'compositions', what they represent is unclear. They possibly covered payment to the rector (in this case, Lincoln College) for the wafer(s) and wine used at the new priest's first consecration. Such payments, made by visiting or subsidiary priests, are occasionally noted elsewhere.[62]

More significantly absent from available benefice accounts are references to an incumbent's funeral. In general, that is only to be expected: if the records derive from appropriated parishes served by chaplains, there was no individual incumbent.[63] Elsewhere, the situation was more complicated. Formally, at an incumbent's death the benefice income during the subsequent vacancy would normally lapse to the parish's jurisdictional superior. Information about the funeral receipts for the deceased incumbent should then appear in the vacancy accounts later submitted to that superior by the caretaker

(Oxford, 1927–38), 2: 10, 27, 63; G. R. Dunstan, ed., *The Register of Edmund Lacy, Bishop of Exeter, 1420–1455: Registrum Commune*, CYS 60–3, 66, 5 vols (Torquay, 1971), 4: 80–229, for numerous examples. For discussion of these minor orders, conferred before the major, holy, orders and known as 'first tonsure' (by this period usually conflated into a single ordination rite), which infused a potentially lifelong clerical 'character' without requiring celibacy, see R. N. Swanson, *Church and Society in Late Medieval England* (Oxford, 1989), 40–3; David Robinson, 'First Tonsures in England in the First Half of the Fourteenth Century', *JEH* 73 (2022), 505–24, esp. 505, 507, 510, 520, 523–4.

[61] LCA, Computus 2, Calc. 3, p. 7; Computus 4, pp. 48–9.

[62] LCA, Computus 3, fols 94^{v}–95^{r} (and elsewhere in the full run); cf. Peterhouse Archives, Computus Rolls 24, 25.

[63] The situation with 'collective incumbencies', exercised by colleges of secular priests, nuances this statement. Funerals of individuals within the undying collectivity might then appear in the benefice accounts, as they do for the Fellows of Lincoln College, Oxford.

administrators appointed for the interval. Relevant entries appear in early sixteenth-century archidiaconal accounts from Lincoln diocese, although not for all parochial vacancies caused by an incumbent's death.[64]

Thus far, the notion of 'rites of passage' has been confined to the terrestrial life cycle, as the Christian *viator* – whether a mere 'traveller' or consciously a 'pilgrim' – journeys from birth to death, paying the required dues to the parochial toll collector en route. But if funeral offerings represent toll payments, the journey remained unfinished: death was itself but a staging post in the soul's continuing pilgrimage into and through the afterlife. 'Rites of passage' there would be very different in quality and function from those of the earthly life, and applying the label 'post-mortem' may be open to challenge. Yet, if the living who made the funding arrangements for the rites thought they were paying part of the fare for a soul's journey to salvation (often their own), and those attending and participating in them believed that they were assisting it towards that destination, the label does seem valid.

Its application must, however, be strictly limited, and exclude many aspects of the arrangements for post-mortem liturgical commemorations, designed to assist souls through purgatory.[65] Many such commemorations were organized as autonomous foundations, frequently beyond a parochial context and beyond the pale of parochial records, even when the stipulated rites occurred within a parish church. They accordingly fall beyond the remit of the present discussion, or only uncertainly within it. The daily masses of salaried or beneficed chaplains with short- or long-term chantry obligations are too routine to count as 'rites of passage', although the specific celebration of an annual obit or anniversary which signalled another year off a soul's journey through the afterlife would. Perpetual chantries established as autonomous benefices in parish churches fall between the stools; but endowed anniversaries celebrated by paid priests probably should count, especially if the endowment was administered by parochial wardens or created a subsidiary parochial entity. The

[64] Lincoln, Lincolnshire Archives, Bp. Accts/6; Add.Reg.7, fols 135r–136r, 139v, 140v, 142r, 143r. The incomplete recording has numerous possible explanations, which need not be detailed here.

[65] There is no comprehensive general survey of the practices of post-mortem liturgical commemoration of the dead in pre-Reformation England. Badham, *Seeking Salvation*, 135–62, offers a useful indicative summary.

uncertain status of similar foundations in chapels within the parish is more problematic.

Some of those challenges emerge in the records relating to the two Oxford parishes of All Saints and St Michael at the North Gate. Several endowed obits were celebrated within the chapel of Lincoln College, the corporate rector of both churches. However, no record of their celebration appears in the benefice accounts, although they are noted elsewhere within the bursar's accounts. Until taken over by the college in 1475, the chantry of St Anne was an independent (and sometimes disruptive) benefice situated within All Saints Church, its incumbent administering his own endowments and accounts. He functioned within the parochial framework, yet without meriting mention in the benefice accounts. Even after 1475, the chantry's administration remained distinct within the bursar's accounts.[66]

Within benefice accounts, the key stages in the presumed journey into the afterlife are marked by the specific commemorations of the month's mind and the anniversary, usually held at those intervals after the death or funeral. While a week's mind is sometimes noted as a first waymarker on the journey, it appears rarely in benefice accounts.[67] The month's mind, the 'thirtieth day', appears more often, with the obvious caveat that its celebration presupposes the ability to pay for it, and so limits the number of souls which could benefit. The same limitation applies to the annual commemorations of obits and anniversaries, whose perdurance depended on the scale of their endowment, or the willingness of heirs to fund them voluntarily.[68]

That rectorial rights did not include a monopoly of post-mortem commemorations restricts evaluation of their significance and impact as parochial rites of passage, as might the freedom for individuals to establish anniversaries in several parishes. Only commemorations which contributed to the altarage would be recorded in benefice

[66] Such ambiguity is evident in Lincoln College's Oxford parishes: Swanson, 'Town and Gown', 318–20.

[67] Some appear in BL, MS Add. 34786 (not consulted in person): references in Orme, *Going to Church*, 457 n. 234). Orme, ibid. 347, seems to treat the week's and month's minds as alternatives. Badham, *Seeking Salvation*, 150, adds the 'sennight (15th day)', without references. I am not aware of having encountered it.

[68] Clive Burgess, 'A Service for the Dead: The Form and Function of the Anniversary in Late Medieval Bristol', *Transactions of the Bristol and Gloucestershire Archaeological Society* 105 (1987), 183–211; Badham, *Seeking Salvation*, 150–4.

accounts.[69] Others were financially independent, and parishioners could attend and participate wherever the rites were celebrated. The entries in benefice accounts merge into a broader regime of masses for souls within that 'cult of the living in support of the dead' which was a central feature of late medieval Catholicism.[70] The personalized and emphasized commemorations of month's minds and anniversaries punctuated that broad current; but where they became merely part of an annual round, or acquired other associations from links to annual hand-outs and charitable distributions, or to fraternity loyalties, their significance specifically as rites of passage may have been reduced.

Conclusion

The recording of spiritual rites of passage in pre-Reformation English chancel accounts precedes the innovations of 1538, but is not a precedent for them. As records of liturgical celebrations of life-cycle rites of passage (and their afterlife analogues), they have only accidental similarities to the Cromwellian registers. Even the calendrical character of some of the pre-Reformation sources must be treated carefully. They record events in date order by choice, not to satisfy official requirements; their formal standing is no greater than that of accounts which list events without dates, or arranged by categories. Moreover, the dates relate not to the events themselves, but to the handing over of the money. Event and payment may well have coincided (it is certainly convenient to assume so), but sometimes they clearly did not.[71] Some liabilities may not have been entered in the account for the year they fell due, with payment delayed for years, or permanently evaded.[72] Delayed handovers were perhaps accounted for among 'arrears', outside the detailed annual record and beyond comment.

[69] At Bodmin, in 1525, it was said that the vicar claimed *6d.* 'for ev[er]y monyth mynde and twelfe monyth mynde': [Wallis], ed., *Bodmin Register*, 37.

[70] A. N. Galpern, 'The Legacy of Late Medieval Religion in Sixteenth-Century Champagne', in Charles Trinkaus and Heiko A. Oberman, eds, *The Pursuit of Holiness in Late Medieval and Renaissance Religion: Papers from the University of Michigan Conference*, Studies in Medieval and Renaissance Thought 10 (Leiden, 1974), 141–76, at 149.

[71] Swanson, 'Town and Gown', 56.

[72] A composition at Oxford for wedding dues from 1507 was still owed in 1517: LCA, Computus 3, fol. 69^{v}.

Neither, similarly, can the real scale of compliance with these fiscal regimes, nor the level of resistance to charges which obviously caused some resentment, be realistically assessed. There was a long history of lay criticism of, and resistance to, the payments expected at purifications, marriages and funerals, and hostile clerical reaction to it. The rites were desired; the costs were not, other than a basic 1*d.* at each event. This suggests a willingness to pay the mass penny, but no more.[73]

The Cromwellian registers introduced in 1538 marked a break in the documentary culture of English parishes; but did not automatically make the earlier arrangements obsolete, or inherently obsolescent. They were a state-mandated addition to existing practices, not a replacement for them. The old rites survived, and mutated, within the new liturgical regime of the Book of Common Prayer. They still generated altarage, its scale changing in the new context of devotional and doctrinal transformation, and changing institutional structures set against a backdrop of increasingly complex and fragmented confessional identities and allegiances.[74]

The character and limited survival rate of the pre-Reformation evidence for the parochial recording of liturgical and sacramental rites of passage limits broad interpretation and analysis, and precludes extrapolation into countrywide generalizations regarding practice. Even with those limitations, the sources offer valuable insights into the daily reality of parochial experience in late medieval England. They make a real contribution to the reconstruction of the broader sociology of parochial devotional regimes and personal religiosity. Those collective regimes and individual engagements were each shaped and punctuated by the unending succession of liturgical rites of passage celebrated by and for the constant flow of human traffic through this world and into the next.

[73] Charles Drew, *Early Parochial Organisation in England: The Origins of the Office of Churchwarden*, St Anthony's Hall Publications 7 (York, 1954), 15–18; for a later case (from 1399), see R. N. Swanson, ed., *Calendar of the Register of Richard Scrope, Archbishop of York (1398–1405): Part 1*, Borthwick Texts and Calendars: Records of the Northern Province 8 (York, 1981), no. 669. See also Arthur Brandeis, ed., *Jacob's Well: An English Treatise on the Cleansing of Man's Conscience, Part 1*, EETS o.s. 115 (London, 1900), 19.

[74] For survival, see David Cressy, *Birth, Marriage, and Death: Ritual, Religion, and the Life-Cycle in Tudor and Stuart England* (Oxford, 1997), 210–12, 348–9, 459–60; John H. Pruett, *The Parish Clergy under the Later Stuarts: The Leicestershire Experience* (Urbana, IL, 1978), 82, 90, 94, 100.

Coming of Age in Faith: The Rite of Confirmation after the English Reformation

Alexandra Walsham*
University of Cambridge

This article explores confirmation as a ritual of Christian initiation in the context of the English Reformation. It examines how this rite of passage, which was demoted from its traditional status as a sacrament, survived and evolved in the wake of the theological, liturgical and ecclesiological changes associated with the advent of Protestantism. It traces the permutations of the practice of laying on of hands that both united and fractured people within the Church of England and its evangelical outer rings between the sixteenth and eighteenth centuries. It also considers the social history of a ritual that increasingly coincided with the transition from childhood to puberty, and its capacity to shed light on the formation of collective religious identity, bodily habitus and lived experience. Finally, it briefly discusses the Counter-Reformation of confirmation and its transformation into a marker of the confessional militancy of a minority faith.

The stained-glass window in the parish church of St Michael's, Doddiscombleigh, in Devon (Figure 1) is a remarkable late medieval survival. Part of a larger scheme depicting the seven sacraments, it was installed around 1495. In this panel, we see the sacrament of confirmation. A mitred bishop is shown laying his hands upon a tiny child presented by his sponsor on the left, behind whom stands a woman cradling an infant in her arms. The cleric in the background holds a casket containing the holy oil or 'chrism' with which the child is anointed as part of this rite of Christian initiation, whereby the young were made full members of the Catholic Church. The bishop's thumb is clearly visible, tracing the sign of the cross on his or her forehead.

* Emmanuel College, Cambridge, CB2 3AP. E-mail: amw23@cam.ac.uk.

Studies in Church History 59 (2023), 164–197
doi: 10.1017/stc.2023.8

Figure 1. Panel depicting confirmation in the seven sacraments window, St Michael's parish church, Doddiscombleigh, Devon (*c.*1495). Reproduced by permission of the rector and churchwardens. Photograph credit: David Cook.

Two other conventional aspects of the pre-Reformation ritual are not present in the picture. One is the gentle blow on the cheek, which the bishop gave to each confirmed person as a reminder to be brave in defending the faith. This symbolic gesture was a mnemonic of the body. The second was the tying of a linen band around the child's head, which they were required to wear for three days in order to protect the sacred substance, and as a token of the fact that they had been strengthened against the assaults of the devil and the world. Many believed that it was unlucky to remove this prematurely. This part of the ritual is clearly depicted in a mid-fifteenth-century altarpiece painted for Jean Chevrot, bishop of Tournai, who is the figure administering the sacrament (Figure 2). To his right, a deacon or priest binds the head of the boy in blue who has just received it; in the foreground, three other children of various ages walk away from the scene. Their white headbands clearly indicate that they too have been blessed by the bishop.

A Flemish tapestry panel dating from the 1470s, now in the Victoria and Albert Museum, captures one further element of the ritual of confirmation, or 'chrismation' (Figure 3). It shows the bishop using a large pair of shears to cut the hair of the child kneeling before him with his hands raised in prayer. Next to him stand two other children, whose heads have already been clipped and shaved for anointing. This is an act of holy barbering that deliberately evokes the tonsuring of those about to be ordained as priests.[1] A practice that continues for newly baptized members of the Orthodox Churches, in the medieval West it signified that the children being confirmed were entering the second stage of the spiritual life cycle. It was a religious rite of passage.

The Reformation demoted confirmation from its status as one of the seven sacraments. Reduced to a mere ceremony, it had a contested existence in sixteenth- and seventeenth-century England. It nevertheless survived in modified form and retained its place in the liturgy of the Church of England. Today, it usually takes place in a person's mid- to late teens. The early modern history of confirmation in England has been comparatively neglected since Canon Ollard's extensive study of it, published in an SPCK volume in

[1] For a discussion of which, see Adolpho S. Cavallo, *Medieval Tapestries in the Metropolitan Museum of Art* (New York, 1993), 169–70. Adult religious were the subject of similar rituals: as a symbol of religious renunciation and humility, monks were tonsured and nuns had their hair cut when they entered the convent or took their final vows. On religious rituals of hair cutting, see Alexa Sand, 'Religion and Ritualized Belief, 800–1500', in Roberta Milliken, ed., *A Cultural History of Hair in the Middle Ages* (London, 2019), 19–36. I owe these references to Stefan Hanß.

Figure 2. Rogier van der Weyden, *The Seven Sacraments* (*c.*1448), Royal Museum of Fine Arts, Antwerp, inv. no. 393-395. Photograph credit: Dominique Provost, Collection KMSKA – Flemish Community (CC0).

Figure 3. Tapestry panel depicting confirmation (Tournai, 1470–5), © Victoria and Albert Museum, London, T.131-1931.

1926.[2] Susan J. Wright provided a brief treatment of the topic in an essay on the role of the young in the post-Reformation church in 1988.[3] Patrick Collinson devoted a page and a half to it in *The Religion of*

[2] S. L. Ollard, 'Confirmation in the Anglican Communion', in *Confirmation or the Laying on of Hands,* 1: *Historical and Doctrinal* (London, 1926), 60–245. For a shorter treatment of the early period, see F. J. Taylor, 'The Anglican Doctrine of Confirmation in the Sixteenth Century', *The Churchman* 60 (1946), 3–14.

[3] Susan J. Wright, 'Confirmation, Catechism and Communion: The Role of the Young in the Post-Reformation Church', in eadem, ed., *Parish, Church and People: Local Studies in Lay Religion 1350–1750* (London, 1988), 203–28.

Protestants, remarking on 'the considerable obscurity of an important subject'.[4] David Cressy excluded it from his book on religion and the life cycle, *Birth, Marriage and Death,* in 1997, along with other 'petty rituals' which lacked the degree of 'structure, scripting, and coherence' that marked these major milestones.[5] There is no entry to it in the index to Judith Maltby's *Prayer Book and People*, while Alec Ryrie makes only incidental reference to confirmation in his evocative study on *Being Protestant,* suggesting that, though a source of 'some limited controversy', it 'hardly registered' in devotional life after the Reformation.[6] Recent work on the later seventeenth and eighteenth centuries is beginning to fill the lacuna in our knowledge of this rite, but it remains an overlooked aspect of religious culture in the wake of the Protestant schism.[7]

This article contends that historians have underestimated confirmation's capacity to illuminate the twists and turns, tensions and frictions, within England's long and troubled Reformation. Close investigation of this rite and its various afterlives offers fresh insight into the evolution of theology, liturgy and ecclesiology in this period, within and beyond the established church and its porous outer rings. As we shall see, this is not simply a story about the origins of the entity anachronistically referred to as 'Anglicanism' in this era.[8] Confirmation also affords an opportunity to explore the revolution in ritual theory precipitated by the Protestant challenge and the role of formal ceremony and habitual gesture, as well as doctrine and belief, in the process of religious change. It complements Arnold Hunt's forthcoming study of the English Reformation as a movement that reconfigured social relations in

[4] Patrick Collinson, *The Religion of Protestants: The Church in English Society 1559–1625* (Oxford, 1982), 51–2.

[5] David Cressy, *Birth, Marriage and Death: Ritual, Religion, and the Life-Cycle in Tudor and Stuart England* (Oxford, 1997), 6–7.

[6] Judith Maltby, *Prayer Book and People in Elizabethan and Early Stuart England* (Cambridge, 1998); Alec Ryrie, *Being Protestant in Reformation England* (Oxford, 2013), 337 n. 91.

[7] See Robert Cornwall, 'The Rite of Confirmation in Anglican Thought during the Eighteenth Century', *ChH* 68 (1999), 359–72; James F. Turrell, '"Until such time as he be Confirmed": The Laudians and Confirmation in the Seventeenth-Century Church of England', *The Seventeenth Century* 20 (2005), 204–22; Phillip Tovey, *Anglican Confirmation 1662–1820* (Farnham, 2014).

[8] This remains a strong tendency in the literature. See, e.g., Ruth A. Meyers, 'By Water and the Holy Spirit: Baptism and Confirmation in Anglicanism', *Anglican Theological Review* 83 (2001), 417–25.

and through the transformation of bodily routines and dispositions, such as bowing at the name of Jesus, using the sign of the cross, and kneeling to receive communion.[9] It is a chapter in the history of human touch.

Finally, I seek to reconstruct confirmation as a species of lived religion, through the quasi-ethnographic lens of contemporary observers of this collective public ritual. In adopting the stance of a historical anthropologist, I am conscious of the long shadow cast by Arnold van Gennep's *Rites of Passage*. Ranging widely across many cultures, his chapter on initiation rites treats them as a sequence of processes of separation, transition and incorporation which loosely, but never exclusively, coincides with the onset of puberty.[10] In what follows, I explore what it meant to come of age in faith in the post-Reformation period. I investigate the complex and unpredictable ways in which the biological, social and spiritual life cycles both intertwined and diverged in early modern England.

Medieval Chrismation and the Reformation of Confirmation

In the early church, baptism and confirmation were part of a single integrated ceremony of Christian initiation, which was closely followed by the administration of communion. The ritual admission of adult neophytes or catechumens to its ranks was a process orchestrated by bishops, who baptized, confirmed and administered the eucharist in rapid succession. A combination of factors led to the gradual disentangling of these elements from each other: the rising number of infants born to Christian parents and the logistical difficulties that this presented to the increasingly busy episcopal officials who presided over these rituals. Baptism was devolved to the parish priest, but chrismation was reserved to bishops as a residue of their pastoral mission to the laity, and delayed until they were able to visit to confer it upon the faithful. Simultaneously, growing emphasis on original sin fostered a tendency for baptism to occur as soon as possible after birth, lest the child perish without receiving the regenerating grace of the sacrament.[11]

9 Arnold Hunt, *Protestant Bodies: Gesture and the English Reformation* (Cambridge, forthcoming).

10 Arnold van Gennep, *The Rites of Passage,* transl. Monika B. Vizedom and Gabrielle L. Caffee (London, 2004; first publ. 1960), 65–115.

11 For the early history, see A. J. Maclean, 'The Theory and Practice of the Confirmation in the Church up to the Reformation', in *Confirmation or the Laying on of Hands,* 25–59.

The interval between baptism and confirmation grew over the course of the Middle Ages. In Anglo-Saxon England, the rite became known as 'bishopping'. It was envisaged as a process by which the candidates reached a higher level of religious maturity and, through the infusion of the Holy Spirit, became more perfect Christians, fit to participate in the holiest mystery, the eucharist. In addition to the rituals described earlier, it was not uncommon for a new name to be given to the confirmed child as a further mark of their movement into a new phase of their lives as Christian believers. As in baptism, they were presented for the rite by a godparent.[12]

In the thirteenth century, church councils recommended that confirmation take place when a child was aged between one and three; by the later part of the period, seven was considered the optimal age. From Cuthbert of Lindisfarne in the seventh century to Wulfstan of Worcester in the eleventh, bishops carried this out as they toured their dioceses in the course of visitation, often in the open air, in fields and cemeteries, and on remote hillsides.[13] The thirteenth century saw greater episcopal efforts to ensure that baptized children were presented for confirmation. Concern that some reached puberty or even old age without receiving it led several bishops to prescribe punishments for negligent parents, such as fasting or exclusion from church. Overwhelmed by the sheer number requiring the rite, others employed suffragans to help them. The scale of the task remained daunting given the size of some of England's dioceses.[14] In the 1520s and 1530s, Cardinal Wolsey confirmed large crowds of children at St Oswald's Abbey in Yorkshire in two shifts, from 8 to 11 in the morning and from 1 to 4 in the afternoon, where, according to his biographer George Cavendish, he was 'at the last constrained for weariness to sit down in a chair'. The next morning, he confirmed many more before departing for the village of Cawood. En route he dismounted from his mule to confirm some two hundred children assembled at a stone cross on a green near Ferrybridge.[15]

[12] Joseph H. Lynch, *Christianizing Kinship: Ritual Sponsorship in Anglo-Saxon England* (Ithaca, NY, 1998), 99–121.

[13] Ibid. 102–3.

[14] For late medieval confirmation, see Nicholas Orme, *Going to Church in Medieval England* (London and New Haven, CT, 2021), 317–23.

[15] George Cavendish, *The Life and Death of Cardinal Wolsey*, in Richard S. Sylvester and Davis P. Harding, eds, *Two Early Tudor Lives* (London and New Haven, CT, 1962), 1–193, at 148.

Some – especially those of royal and aristocratic blood – were still confirmed at a much earlier age in private ceremonies. The future Elizabeth I, for instance, was baptized by Bishop Stokesley and confirmed by Archbishop Cranmer at Greyfriars Church in Greenwich on 10 September 1533, just three days after her birth on 7 September.[16]

The Reformation represented a significant threat to rites such as confirmation that had no explicit foundation in Scripture. John Wycliffe had already savagely attacked it as a 'frivolous rite', invented 'at the prompting of the devil' to delude the laity; later Lollards alleged that it was 'nother profitable ne necessarie to the salvacion of mennys sowlis'.[17] Martin Luther was equally dismissive, scorning it as a form of fraudulent juggling designed to bolster the false charisma of the episcopate.[18] Early English evangelicals such as William Tyndale and Thomas Becon denounced it as a 'dumb ceremony' which fostered an array of superstitious delusions, including the view that 'if the bishop butter the child in the forehead' it would be safe from all spiritual peril. The notion that unloosing the cloth tied around their head or neck was a recipe for trouble was no more than a silly taboo. Such 'reliques of Rome' were rooted in fake decretals.[19] John Calvin was even more vehement, declaring that this 'abortive mask of a sacrament' was 'one of the most deadly wiles of Satan'. He scorned the opinion that, until children were 'besmeared' by the 'rotten oil' that was chrism, they were only 'half

[16] John Stow, *The annales, or a generall chronicle of England,* ed. Edmund Howes (London, 1615), 568.

[17] John Wycliffe, *Trialogus* (1383), in J. C. C. Fisher, ed., *Christian Initiation: The Reformation Period. Some Early Reformed Rites of Baptism and Confirmation and other Contemporary Documents* (London, 1970), 165–6; J. Patrick Hornbeck II, '"A Prophane or Hethyn Thing": English Lollards on Baptism and Confirmation', *Mediaeval Studies* 74 (2012), 283–306, at 291–3, 295, 303–4.

[18] Fisher, *Christian Initiation,* 171–3. For Henry VIII's response to the relevant passages in Luther's *Babylonian Captivity* (1520) in his *Assertio Septem Sacramentorum* (1521), see ibid. 206–7. Nevertheless, Lutheranism retained the rite of confirmation, transferring its administration to the parish priest. Confirmation became (and remains) an important ecclesiastical and social ritual for young people in the Lutheran tradition.

[19] Fisher, *Christian Initiation*, 230–3; William Tyndale, *The Obedience of a Christian Man,* in idem, *Doctrinal Treatises and Introductions to Different Portions of the Holy Scriptures,* ed. H. Walter (Cambridge, 1848), 127–344, at 225; Thomas Becon, *An Humble Supplication unto God for the Restoring of his Holy Word,* in idem, *Prayers and Other Pieces,* ed. John Ayre (Cambridge, 1844), 223–50, at 224; Thomas Becon, *The reliques of Rome* (London, 1563), fols 105^r–106^r.

Christians'. These were 'nothing but theatrical gesticulations, and rather the wanton sporting of apes without any skill in imitation'.[20] According to the staunchly Calvinist early Elizabethan archdeacon of Colchester, James Calfhill, this ritual had no efficacy 'unless', he wrote sarcastically, 'they have shut the Holy Ghost in their grease pot'.[21]

In short, in the eyes of the reformers, confirmation was not a true sacrament. Its removal restored baptism to its proper place as a sign of God's everlasting promise to the seed of Abraham and their reception into the congregation of Christ's flock. The wider reconceptualization of the very meaning of ritual that the Reformation inaugurated – from a mechanism for creating a holy presence, to an outward representation of a divine decision or event – also emptied it of sacred significance. At best, it fell into the category of things indifferent or adiaphora, the use of which was constrained by the rules of Christian edification and by the danger of scandalizing weaker brethren. Tainted by association with popish idolatry, it ran the risk of nurturing attachment to past error and impeding the advance of the gospel.[22]

Yet Protestants were obliged to admit that one component of the rite did have scriptural precedents. Jacob's blessing of Joseph's children in the Old Testament (Genesis 48: 9–22) prefigured a powerful passage in the New: the Apostles laying their hands upon new believers so that they might receive the Holy Spirit (Acts 8: 17), as the conduits of a kind of personal Pentecost. Accordingly, while fiercely criticizing the adulterated form into which confirmation had degenerated during the Middle Ages, the reformers yearned to revive the practice in what they imagined to be its primitive purity. Calvin did not 'mislike' the ancient custom of bringing young children to attest their religious knowledge and make a profession of lively faith when they came to years of discretion, noting that the imposition of hands had no supernatural power in and of itself, but simply invested the process with greater solemnity and reverence.[23] An order for confirmation drawn up in Strasbourg in 1550 reflects the influence of Martin Bucer, who encouraged adolescents to make a

[20] Fisher, *Christian Initiation,* 254–60; John Calvin, *Institutes of Christian Religion,* transl. Henry Beveridge, 2 vols in 1 (Grand Rapids, MI, 1989; first publ. 1845), 2: 625–32 (4.19.4–13).

[21] James Calfhill, *An aunswere to the treatise of the cross* (London, 1568), 97.

[22] Edward Muir, *Ritual in Early Modern Europe* (Cambridge, 1997), 155–84.

[23] Fisher, *Christian Initiation,* 258–9; Calvin, *Institutes,* transl. Beveridge, 2: 626–7 (4.19.5–6).

conscious act of voluntary submission to their religion, in order to combat the anabaptist charge that children baptized in infancy were too young to understand the vows made on their behalf.[24] Bucer's arrival in England the previous year coincided with the first edition of the Book of Common Prayer. This incorporated a translated and modified version of the Sarum office, which dropped the anointing with oil and the linen band, but retained the sign of the cross and the laying on of hands 'after the example of thy holy Apostles ... to certify them (by this signe) of thy favour and gracious goodnes toward them'. The revised liturgy of 1552 quietly dropped the offensive sign of the cross, setting the standard for the Elizabethan Prayer Book of 1559.[25]

Critically, the rite for confirmation was prefaced by a short catechism, which the child was to digest and internalize. Having done so, they would also be able to recite the Lord's Prayer, the Apostles' Creed and the Ten Commandments in their mother tongue, imploring God in his mercy to 'kepe us from al sinne and wickedness, and from our gostly enemy, and from everlastyng death'. The rubric instructed that confirmation was to be administered to 'them that be of perfecte age' and mature enough to comprehend the core beliefs of their faith. It concluded 'No manne shall thynke that anye detrimente shall come to children by differryng [i.e. deferring] of theyr confirmacion' until they had reached this stage. If they died in infancy, but had been baptized, Scripture provided assurance that they were 'undoubtedly saved'.[26] The rite discharged their godparents from the responsibility of ensuring the child's religious education and laid it upon the shoulders of the young themselves. As Keith Thomas remarked, the Reformation had the effect of raising the age of religious adulthood, though this was understood less as a numerical gauge than a sliding scale dependent upon the intellectual capacity and spiritual attainment of the individual in question.[27] In the process it became aligned with biological puberty rather than the earlier years of childhood, that is, with a

[24] Fisher, *Christian Initiation,* 174–8. For Bucer's *Censura,* see ibid. 244–50.

[25] Brian Cummings, ed., *The Book of Common Prayer: The Texts of 1549, 1559, and 1662* (Oxford, 2011), 58–63, 150–6. See also Peter J. Jagger, *Christian Initiation 1552–1969: Rites of Baptism and Confirmation since the Reformation Period* (London, 1970), 19–21.

[26] Cummings, ed., *Book of Common Prayer,* 58–63, 150–6.

[27] Keith Thomas, 'Age and Authority in Early Modern England', *PBA* 62 (1976), 205–48, at 224.

Figure 4. Minister or layman catechizing children: woodcut in John Day, *A booke of Christian prayers* (London, 1578), p. 46 (sig. Nii^{r}), Cambridge University Library, shelfmark SSS.24.13. Reproduced by permission of the Syndics of Cambridge University Library.

time when by 'the frailtye of theyr awne fleshe' and the temptations of Satan they were liable to lapse into sin.[28]

The close connection between confirmation and catechizing turned the rite into a kind of graduation exercise, as well as an entrance test for admission to holy communion, at least theoretically (Figure 4). Catechisms for 'children in years and in understanding' prepared by godly ministers index the disillusionment that set in as the Reformation moved from its illicit protest phase to the status of an institutionalized church, and as the laity failed to display the requisite zeal. They reflect the perception that many needed remedial instruction to bring them up to speed. The 'babes' for which these ministers prepared nourishing 'milk' were older adults as well as young people.[29] Directed towards parents and heads of households, these catechisms were part of a campaign for religious education that was seen as key to nurturing the next generation of Protestants: those who had been born into the true church rather than chosen to convert to it. If they encapsulated the conviction that rote learning and

[28] Cummings, ed., *Book of Common Prayer*, 150–1.

[29] See Ian Green, '"For Children in Yeeres and Children in Understanding": The Emergence of the English Catechism under Elizabeth and the Early Stuarts', *JEH* 37 (1986), 397–425; idem, *The Christian's ABC: Catechisms and Catechizing in England, c.1530–1740* (Oxford, 1996).

memorization of the Prayer Book catechism was insufficient to make real Christians, they themselves were instruments of the same process of confessionalization.[30] The rite of confirmation had become the formal endpoint of a process of indoctrination, which the godly regarded as a hollow and unsatisfactory substitute for feeling the workings of the Holy Spirit within one.

Those on the more radical left wing of the Reformation movement remained squeamish about confirmation for these and other reasons. In Edwardian Worcester, Bishop John Hooper refused to carry it out, and it was likewise a sticking point for some of the Marian exiles in Frankfurt in the 'troubles' that erupted among English brethren in the mid-1550s.[31] In puritan circles, it continued to be the target of vicious polemic, not least because of its umbilical link with the disputed institution of episcopacy. The 'bishopping of baptized children' was regularly included in the roll call of 'stinking' customs and ceremonies which the Romanists had allegedly devised to bedazzle their followers: 'anoynting, annoyling, absolving, kneeling, knocking, whipping, crouching, kissing, crossing, shaving, greasing, and ten thousand such tri[n]ckets mo[r]e'.[32] The abrogation of those ceremonies that had been retained within the liturgy of the Elizabethan church remained a priority for the hotter sort of Protestants. The Admonition to Parliament of 1572 described confirmation as 'popish and pevish' and the presbyterian leader Thomas Cartwright complained that the imposition of hands by the bishop led country people to go to considerable expense and unnecessary inconvenience in travelling half a score miles or more to obtain this false blessing for their offspring.[33] A bare ordinance of man, at best it was a superfluous

[30] On the comparable development of confirmation in the Lutheran context, see Susan C. Karant-Nunn, *The Reformation of Ritual: An Interpretation of Early Modern Germany* (London and New York, 1997), 66–71.

[31] Diarmaid MacCulloch and Pat Hughes, 'A Bailiff's List and Chronicle from Worcester', *Antiquaries Journal* 75 (1995), 235–53, at 247; Patrick Collinson, *Archbishop Grindal 1519–1583: The Struggle for a Reformed Church* (London, 1979), 74.

[32] Arthur Dent, *The opening of heaven gates, or the ready way to everlasting life* (London, 1610), 111.

[33] John Field and Thomas Wilcox, 'An Admonition to the Parliament', in W. H. Frere and C. E. Douglas, eds, *Puritan Manifestoes: A Study of the Origins of the Puritan Revolt* (London, 1924), 5–39, at 27–8; Thomas Cartwright, *A replye to an answere made of M. Doctor Whitgifte against the admonition to the parliament* ([Hemel Hempstead], 1573), 199–200.

appendix; at worst it led many to doubt the all-sufficiency of baptism.[34] Never one to mince words, the puritan Anthony Gilby regarded it as a remnant of the 'olde beaste', one of the 'filthy dregges' that turned the church from the 'chast spowse of Christ' into a 'romish harlot'.[35] Henry Barrow and the Brownists listed it among other Antichristian 'abominations' and 'trumperies' that justified their schismatic separation from the Church of England.[36] At the Easter quarter sessions in Devizes in 1588, the Wiltshire villager Thomas Baslyn, presented for having had his daughter baptized privately at home, declared that the confirmation of children was an unwritten tradition that lacked biblical sanction, like the 'Juysh cerymonie' of the churching of women.[37] Some editions of the Geneva Bible were bound with bowdlerized versions of the Prayer Book that omitted these contested rites to cater for the tastes and accommodate the scruples of England's self-styled godly people.[38]

The Revival of Confirmation

Enquiries about confirmation were not a prominent feature of visitation articles in the Elizabethan period.[39] John Whitgift's letter to his fellow bishops in 1591 urging the renewal of this 'auntient and laudable ceremonie' bears out suggestions that it had been generally neglected in the preceding decades. Whitgift was eager to resurrect it as a strategy for remedying the 'dissolute' manners of the youth of the realm, who through 'the negligence both of natural and spiritual fathers, are not (as were meete) trayned up in the chiefe and neacessarye principells of Christian religion … especially in their tender

[34] Albert Peel, ed., *The Seconde Parte of a Register being a Calendar of Manuscripts under that Title intended for Publication by the Puritans around 1593, and now in Dr Williams's Library, London*, 2 vols (Cambridge, 1915), 1: 200, 259.
[35] Ibid. 1: 141.
[36] Henry Barrow, *The Writings of Henry Barrow 1590–1591*, ed. Leland H. Carlson (London, 1966), 41, 84; Henry Ainsworth, *A true confession of the faith, and humble acknowledgement of the alegeance* ([Amsterdam?], 1596), sig. A4^{r}.
[37] H. C. Johnson, ed., *Wiltshire County Records: Minutes of Proceedings in Sessions 1563 and 1574 to 1592*, Wiltshire Archaeological and Natural History Society 4 (Devizes, 1949), 123.
[38] Collinson, *Archbishop Grindal*, 232.
[39] Most of the few articles relating to confirmation ask about it as a precondition for admission to communion. See W. P. M. Kennedy, *Elizabethan Episcopal Administration*, 3 vols (London, 1924), 2: 71, 3: 140.

yeres'. Encouraging bishops to perform it not merely during their visitations but 'also at other fit opportunities', Whitgift followed in the footsteps of those Calvinists for whom confirmation, preceded by diligent catechizing, was a tool for fostering the spiritual edification of the young.[40] But his enthusiasm for it must also be understood in the context of the positive apology for the rite that he was obliged to mount in answer to its hotter sort of Protestant critics. This was elevated to another level by Richard Hooker in Book 5 of his *Lawes of Ecclesiasticall Politie* published in 1597, in which he accused puritans of 'sponging out' a good Christian custom and insisted that the ceremony now practised was not only free from popish error, but bore the imprint of a venerable patristic tradition.[41]

Hooker's text was a straw in the wind of the renewed emphasis on confirmation that became a feature of what Peter Lake has called avant-garde conformity.[42] Puritan calls for its abolition in the Millenary Petition of 1603 were answered by the ecclesiastical canon of the same year that made it a requirement for bishops to carry out this 'solemn' and 'holy action', 'continued from the apostles' times', in their triennial visitations.[43] Jacobean bishops were more assiduous than their predecessors in enquiring about the diligence of ministers in preparing and presenting candidates for confirmation. Bishop John Howson was particularly insistent in his articles for the diocese of Oxford in 1619.[44] A sermon on Acts 8: 17 preached by his chaplain, Edward Boughen, strongly enjoined its use as a means of strengthening Christians to fight in the battle of life. Reflecting the influence of Arminian opinions gaining ground within the upper ranks of the Church of England, Boughen claimed that confirmation

[40] Edward Cardwell, ed., *Documentary Annals of the Reformed Church of England*, 2 vols (Oxford, 1844), 2: 42–4.

[41] Richard Hooker, *Of the Lawes of Ecclesiasticall Politie. The fift booke* (London, 1597), 166–73.

[42] The phrase was coined in his 'Lancelot Andrewes, John Buckeridge, and Avant-Garde Conformity at the Court of James I', in Linda Levy Peck, ed., *The Mental World of the Jacobean Court* (Cambridge, 1991), 113–33. See also Peter McCullough, '"Avant-Garde Conformity" in the 1590s', in Anthony Milton, ed., *The Oxford History of Anglicanism,* 1: *Reformation and Identity,* c.*1520–1662* (Oxford, 2017), 380–94.

[43] Gerald Bray, ed., *The Anglican Canons 1529–1947*, CERS 6 (Woodbridge, 1998), 817–19, 351 respectively.

[44] Kenneth Fincham, ed., *Visitation Articles and Injunctions of the Early Stuart Church*, 1: *1603–25*, CERS 1 (Woodbridge, 1994), 17, 29, 53, 176. For Howson, see ibid. 190. See also Kenneth Fincham, *Prelate as Pastor: The Episcopate of James I* (Oxford, 1990), 123–9.

could serve to increase the believer in grace. He invoked the simile of an 'infant newly borne' who could not perform the part of a man 'unlesse age and strength make the addition', and insisted that although the miraculous powers bestowed upon the apostles at the time of Pentecost were now a thing of the past, their capacity to convey 'the inward gifts of sanctification' continued through the ministry of bishops in confirmation. In some sense, therefore, this rite was indeed necessary for salvation and contempt for it would 'cut off our passage to everlasting blisse'. Boughen lashed out against Reformed churches on the Continent that had 'pulled downe the Aristocracie of Bishops' and 'erected the Anarchie of a confused lay-presbyterie' and 'so consequently cast off the sacred use of Confirmation'. Current practice was not compromised by the abuses of the popish sacrament. Its attendant gestures were sanctioned by antiquity: even the use of the sign of the cross was left to the bishop's discretion. Boughen noted that this had been allowed in the 1549 Prayer Book and could find no evidence that it had ever been revoked.[45]

Boughen's celebration of confirmation indexed two developing tendencies. The first was a growing emphasis on the elevated status of those who administered it; the second, a renewed appetite for ceremonialism and sacred gesture. Both were features of the concurrent reassertion of episcopacy north of the border in Scotland. The Perth Articles of 1618 required episcopal confirmation, alongside kneeling to receive the Lord's Supper, private baptism and communion, thereby precipitating protests that culminated in the Bishops' Wars twenty years later. This stirred renewed debates about the significance of the imposition of hands and whether it was permissible to make use of things indifferent, or whether this should be omitted because it was 'still abused to make up a bastard Sacrament'. Its opponents insisted that the blessing of the bishop amounted to 'but a prophanation with his fingers'. Too often administered to children who could give no 'serious confession of their faith' but merely 'utter some few words of a short catechisme like parrets', the whole rite was a mockery of true apostolic practice.[46]

[45] Edward Boughen, *A sermon of confirmation, preached in Oxford, at the first visitation of the right reverend father in God, John Lord Bishop of Oxford. September, 27. 1619* (London, 1620), 14, 24, 47, 57, 11.

[46] [David Calderwood], *Perth assembly* ([Leiden], 1619), 87–95, at 89; idem, *A re-examination of the five articles enacted at Perth anno 1618* ([Holland?], 1636), 209–21, at 210,

The impulses behind the renewed emphasis on confirmation in some reaches of the established churches of England and Scotland came to fuller fruition in the Laudian campaign to restore the beauty of holiness in the 1630s. Leading Laudians, such as Richard Montagu and John Cosin, increasingly recast confirmation in quasi-sacramental terms, dialling down the earlier emphasis on catechetical instruction and highlighting the external actions that lent it reverence and gravity. Cosin also advocated the reanimation of elements of the medieval rite that had been discarded at the Reformation: the symbolic blow on the cheek, the sign of the cross, the anointing with chrism and the appointing of godparents.[47] The actions of the bishop's hands were reimagined as critical to the process of receiving the Holy Spirit. As James Turrell has argued, this amounted to an attempt to change 'the official gate to church membership from knowledge to ritual'.[48] Although these reforms were never fully implemented in practice, it is perhaps telling that Bishop Robert Wright dwelt upon confirmation in his visitation articles for Bristol in 1631, which also asked about unlawful conventicles, private fasts and 'impugners' of innocent rites and ceremonies.[49]

Yet if confirmation was steadily harnessed as an arm of the conformist and Laudian agenda to reform the Church of England, its significance for the rival, evangelical strand of churchmanship that ran alongside it cannot be ignored. The overt ceremonialism of Cosin contrasts with the preoccupations of prelate-pastors eager to ensure that it was only administered to those who were properly instructed in the principles of the reformed religion. This was the gist of Thomas Ravis's enquiries about parishes in Gloucester deanery in 1605 and it also characterized the practice of Arthur Lake, bishop of Bath and Wells in the 1620s.[50] The preaching diary of Tobie Matthew,

220. For a defence of the articles on this point, see David Lindsay, *A treatise of the ceremonies of the church* (London, 1625), 97–104.

[47] *The Works of the Right Reverend Father in God John Cosin, Lord Bishop of Durham*, 5: *Notes and Collections on the Book of Common Prayer*, ed. J[ohn]. B[arrow]. (Oxford, 1855), 149. See also John Cosin, 'On Confirmation', ibid. 526–8.

[48] Turrell, 'Laudians and Confirmation', 217.

[49] Kenneth Fincham, ed., *Visitation Articles and Injunctions of the Early Stuart Church*, 2: *1625–42*, CERS 5 (Woodbridge, 1998), 58–9. For Laud's articles for Lincoln in 1634, see ibid. 88. See also Richard Montagu's articles for Norwich in 1638: ibid. 202.

[50] Fincham, ed., *Visitation Articles and Injunctions, 1603–25*, 53; idem, *Prelate as Pastor*, 126.

successively bishop of Durham and archbishop of York, provides a record of his diligence in this department. He confirmed thousands in the course of his visitations, laying hands on 'many, both young and old' at Stillingfleet in 1614. At Malton in 1607 there 'were so many candidates, I nearly melted away with the heat, and did indeed earn the right to go to bed'.[51] Whether many of these children met the high standards of spiritual understanding idealized by Calvin and his disciples is perhaps doubtful, but Matthew's assiduous commitment to the task both reflects the compatibility of confirmation with an alternative vision of the Jacobean and Caroline Church of England and attests to the capaciousness of that institution.

The example of Joseph Hall, bishop of Exeter and later Norwich, also calls into question any suggestion that confirmation became a monopoly of the Laudians, even as he illustrates its capacity to co-opt theological moderates with some priorities in common. In his visitation articles, Hall was insistent that 'none doe offer themselves to confirmation, but such as both for yeares and instruction are fit for that institution'.[52] His book on 'apostolicall confirmation', *Cheirothesia,* published during the Interregnum in 1651, lamented the lapse of this 'worthy practice' and argued that its revival would be 'infinitely advantageous'. 'How happy it were', he wrote, 'if in this case, we could walke with an even foot in the mid-way betwixt Romish Superstition, and profane neglect'. He pushed back against those who 'cryed down' and 'hooted at' it as an odious remnant of popery. But he was equally determined to strip it of the various 'fopperies' that had been added to the 'plaine and holie dresse' it had worn in the primitive era: 'clapping on the cheek, the crosse of the thumb, treading on the toe, filleting the forehead for seven days, and the like', which were 'no lesse vaine then new' and served 'onely to confirme us in the lightnesse and indiscretion of their founders'. If this 'trash' was removed, confirmation still had value and utility, provided the children to whom it was administered went beyond a mere 'verball learning' of the articles of their religion. In retaining it, the Church of England was 'more eminent in this point then her other sisters'.

51 '[I]sc ut pene contabesecram prae calore adeoque Lectum consendere mortibus': York, York Minster Library, Additional MS 18, 85. See Rosamund Oates, *Moderate Radical: Tobie Matthew and the English Reformation* (Oxford, 2018), 201. Matthew also spoke in support of the imposition of hands on children at the Hampton Court Conference: ibid. 145.

52 Fincham, ed., *Visitation Articles and Injunctions, 1625–42*, 10.

Greater fidelity in carrying it out, he alleged, would have 'prevented many foul and monstrous exorbitances in matter of Doctrine' and the 'many horrible enormities', 'woefull distractions' and 'Paradoxes of contradiction' with which the commonwealth was 'now miserably pestred and over-run'. Quoting Hooker, he said that it would foster true godliness in young children, preserve the seed of the church of God, maintain the unity of the faith, and exclude the ignorant and scandalous from the 'sacred Ordinance' of the Lord's Supper.[53] Hall wrote as if the Church of England had not been disestablished, and his treatise gave expression to the self-conscious identity that was being forged in the crucible of its sufferings as a beleaguered minority. Henry Hammond, the Royalist archdeacon of Chichester and canon of Christ Church in Oxford, was another champion of this ancient Christian custom. His learned Latin tract on the topic, composed during these dark years, appeared posthumously in 1661.[54]

These examples encourage us to avoid boxing confirmation into the overly rigid ecclesiastical taxonomies that have bedevilled our understanding of English Protestantism in the first half of the seventeenth century. They encourage us to avoid seeing it simply as a strand of what later became known as 'Anglicanism', and to recognize the coexistence of several overlapping strands of feeling about 'bishopping' in the post-Reformation era. Hall's hope that confirmation would serve as a mechanism for healing the divisions created by the events of the 1640s was shared by those who repudiated episcopacy. Presbyterians and Independents likewise perceived it as a solution to the evils unleashed by the Civil Wars. These had placed intolerable strain on the ideal of an inclusive national church and catalysed the radicalization and fragmentation of puritanism and the explosion of sectarianism. The Prayer Book rite of confirmation was a casualty of the liturgical reforms overseen by the Westminster Assembly and found no place in the *Directory for Publick Worship*.[55] But in the 1650s figures such as Jonathan Hanmer and Richard Baxter called

[53] Joseph Hall, *Cheirothesia: or, a confirmation of the apostolicall confirmation of children: setting forth the divine ground, end, and use of that too much neglected institution* (London, 1651), sigs A2^{v}, A3^{r}–^{v}, 19, 33–4, 41–2, 75, 49, 50, 69–73.

[54] Henry Hammond, *De confirmatione, sive benedictione, post batpismum solenni, per impositionem manuum episcopi celebrata, commentarius ex sententia ecclesiæ Anglicanæ* ([London, 1661?]).

[55] *A directory for the publick worship of God throughout the three kingdoms of England, Scotland and Ireland* (Edinburgh, 1645). Quakers were unremittingly hostile towards

for its 'restauration' as a means of effecting the reconciliation of the 'disordered Societies' of Christians that these troubling decades had brought into being. Baxter, who quoted Hammond approvingly, presented it as an effectual 'Medicine' to bind up these breaches and wounds, and for Hanmer too it was 'an Expedient to promote Peace and Unity among Brethren', whether puritan or episcopalian. Reclaiming it from the degenerate state into which it had descended in the age of Antichrist and reinstating its 'Primitive pattern' was essential to effecting a 'right Reformation'. This rite of investiture was not the preserve of bishops, but, as in continental Protestant churches, an office of regular ministers and pastors.[56]

One imperative for reviving confirmation was to ensure that the children of believing parents who enjoyed baptism as a birth-right made an active and public profession of the personal faith that qualified them for its higher privileges, especially access to the eucharist. If it was a ritual of inclusion and incorporation, paradoxically it was also one of exclusion and separation. Technically, confirmation had long been a qualifying condition for admission to communion in the Church of England, though in practice many communicants had not been blessed by a bishop. The version of it recommended within mid-seventeenth-century puritan circles was designed to sift out the reprobate and ensure that only the worthy received the Lord's Supper.[57]

A second and related incentive was the need to 'compleat' church membership. Confirmation was a vital rite of transition to spiritual adulthood. What it entailed was the growth of religious infants and catechumens into mature believers and elders in faith, their evolution from what Hanmer called 'imperfect Embryoes' to fully fashioned

---

the rite. See George Fox, *Something in answer to the old common-prayer-book* (London, 1660), 18–19; Francis Howgill, *The glory of the true church* (London, 1661), 40–2.

[56] Richard Baxter, *Confirmation and restauration, the necessary means of reformation and reconciliation* (London, 1658); Jonathan Hanmer, *Teleiosis: or, an exercitation upon confirmation, the antient way of completing church-members* (London, 1658), title page, sigs A5^{r}, A6^{v}, 52. Baxter wrote a commendatory preface to this book: ibid., sigs A8^{r}–B6^{r}. See also Philip Stubs's account of Presbyterian support of the rite in *Of confirmation: A sermon preach'd at St Benedict Grace-Church, March 14th 1693* (London, 1693), 10–11.

[57] On exclusion from communion on the grounds of religious ignorance, see Christopher Haigh, 'Communion and Community: Exclusion from Communion in Post-Reformation England', *JEH* 51 (2000), 721–40; idem, *The Plain Man's Pathway to Heaven: Kinds of Christianity in Post-Reformation England, 1570–1640* (Oxford, 2007), 60–2.

organisms. This involved an inner process of regeneration: an evangelical experience of conversion or second birth whereby, in an echo of their initial christening, they cast off the old Adam and became new creatures in Christ.[58] Some dated their birthdays not from their biological, but from their spiritual nativities. The most elaborate exposition of this conception of the religious life cycle was the Congregationalist Ralph Venning's *Christs School*, which categorized four classes of Christians, noting how few people graduated to the highest rank of 'fathers'. Most, even those who seemed precocious saints, were mere babes in understanding, however advanced they might be in temporal years. This was a mode of coming of age that was not necessarily tied to a particular stage of human development.[59]

Once again, internal squabbles ensued regarding the form of the external ritual that accompanied the internal metamorphosis these writers delineated. Echoing Calvin, Hanmer said that if the ceremony of confirmation was 'drained from these mixtures of humane interventions', reduced to prayer and the laying on of hands, and administered by every pastor, it would be found to be very commendable.[60] By contrast, Francis Fulwood, minister at West Alvington in Devon, concluded that though the rite of imposition of hands could be sanctioned once stripped of formality and superstition, it was probably best omitted given that it might 'grate upon popular prejudice' and hinder its main objective of reconciling differences. Its superficial similarity with the format of the popish sacrament might drive away those with scruples.[61]

Ironically, similar disputes erupted within the ranks of the Baptists. The puritan revival of apostolic confirmation was partly designed to answer their stinging allegation that people baptized as infants had no understanding of the Christian faith into which they were incorporated.[62] Only when men and women became adults

58 Hanmer, *Teleoisis,* 147, 133.

59 Ralph Venning, *Christs school: consisting of four classes of Christians, I. Babes, II. Little children, III. Young men, IV. Fathers* (London, 1675). See Alexandra Walsham, 'Second Birth and the Spiritual Life-Cycle in Early Modern England', in Caroline Bowden, Emily Vine and Tessa Whitehouse, eds, *Religion and Life Cycles in Early Modern England* (Manchester, 2021), 17–39.

60 Hanmer, *Teleoisis,* 51.

61 Francis Fulwood, *A discourse of the visible church* (London, 1658), sigs Tt14^{v}–Uu1^{r}.

62 On confirmation as a counterpoint to anabaptism, see Hanmer, *Teleoisis,* sig. B3^{v}, 156; John Priaulx, *Confirmation confirmed, and recommended from scripture, antiquity, & reason* (London, 1662), 31; Baxter, *Confirmation and restauration,* 216.

could they be admitted to the church of Christ. The practice of laying on of hands in believers' baptism precipitated serious schisms within and between Baptist congregations in the mid-seventeenth century. For some this savoured of the 'popedom of Rome'; for others it was vindicated by its scriptural and apostolic precedents. Acrimonious conflicts about its validity continued to divide the movement, cutting across the boundary between the General and Particular Baptists.[63] Henry Danvers's 1674 treatise condemning it was countered the following year by Benjamin Keach's *Darkness Vanquished* which vigorously defended it as a divine institution. Their books rehearsed familiar arguments about whether this ceremony should be discarded as 'an Excrement of Antichrist' because of its connection with 'superstitious' and 'popish' 'bishopping' ('as if that old-fashioned Garment had but a piece of new-nam'd Cloth put to it, and drest up in another Mode'), or acknowledged as 'a standing or perpetual Administration' and used after it had been restored to its pristine purity.[64] Baptist practice reintegrated baptism and confirmation into a single rite of religious passage, reversing the process that had steadily separated it over the course of the Middle Ages. Adult believers were regenerated by the water of baptism and infused with the gift of the Holy Ghost at the same time, like the early Christians whom they revered.

THE RESTORATION OF CONFIRMATION

With the Restoration of the Church of England in 1662, the liturgical rite for confirming those who had 'come to years of discretion' was reinstated. In a departure from previous practice, the rubric of the

[63] See Ernest A. Payne, 'Baptists and the Laying on of Hands', *Baptist Quarterly* 15 (1953–4), 203–15; K. J. Parratt, 'An Early Baptist on the Laying on of Hands', *Baptist Quarterly* 21 (1965), 325–7; J. F. McGregor, 'The Baptists: Fount of all Heresy', in idem and B. Reay, eds, *Radical Religion in the English Revolution* (Oxford, 1984), 23–63, at 42–43; Stephen Wright, *The Early English Baptists, 1603–1649* (Woodbridge, 2006), 100–1, 138–41. For an early publication on this 'great controversy', see John Gosnold, *Of laying on of hands* (London, 1656).

[64] Henry Danvers, *A treatise of laying on of hands, with the history thereof* (London, 1674), 31; Benjamin Keach, *Darkness vanquished: or, truth in it's primitive purity* (London, 1675). Quotations are from the second edition entitled *Laying on of hands upon baptised believers* (London, 1698), sigs A4^{r}, 75. This was prescribed in *The Articles of the Faith of the Church of Christ, or congregation meeting at Horsley-down, Benjamin Keach, pastor* (London, 1697), 23–4.

revised Book of Common Prayer now insisted that individuals kneel before the bishop before he laid his hands upon each of them in turn.[65] The introduction of this bodily gesture of reverence signals the influence of Laudian sacramentalism, especially as articulated by John Cosin, as does the fact that the catechism was no longer presented as part of the liturgy for confirmation, but included in a separate section of the Prayer Book. However, the restored rite also bears the imprint of renewed puritan efforts to reform the ritual, not least in the guise of the concession at the end, that not only those who had been confirmed, but also those 'ready and desirous' to be, could be admitted to communion. A by-product of the Savoy Conference of 1661, at which puritan objections to the Prayer Book rite were aired and discussed, this was one small victory for the cause of comprehension. By conceding that confirmation per se was not a strict necessity for admission to the sacrament, it provided a small loophole for those who sought to evade the ritual.[66]

Phillip Tovey's recent overview of *Anglican Confirmation* between 1662 and 1820 obviates the need for an extended exposition of its history in this period, but the resurgence of this rite of Christian initiation within the Restoration and Hanoverian Church of England must be underlined.[67] Jeremy Taylor's 1664 treatise on the topic, dedicated to James, duke of Ormonde and viceroy of Ireland, powerfully restated the case for confirmation as a 'never ceasing ministry' rooted in apostolic practice that bestowed graces and benefits on those that received it, as well as 'an effective Deletery to Schism'. This was 'the earnest of our inheritance' and 'the seal of our Salvation'.[68] A flurry of confirmation sermons likewise dilated on this milestone in the life cycle of faith. John Riland, archdeacon of Coventry, swapped the conventional trope of the ages of man for a botanical metaphor that compared the young Christian to a small slip or graft that, duly watered, would grow into a sturdy, fruit-bearing tree and 'arrive to a well-rooted and Confirm'd steadiness in God's Paradise'.[69] Anticipating the van Gennepian concept of the

65 Cummings, ed., *Book of Common Prayer,* 426–33. For Cummings's comments on the practice, see ibid. 778–9.

66 Ollard, 'Confirmation', 143–4, 147–8.

67 Tovey, *Anglican Confirmation.*

68 Jeremy Taylor, *Chrisis Teleiotike: A discourse of confirmation* (London, 1664), sigs A2^{r}, 52.

69 John Riland, *Confirmation revived: And doom's-day books opened* (London, 1663), 5.

threshold, the Leicestershire rector Benjamin Camfield described baptism as 'the door or entrance of Christianity', and confirmation as a further stage of initiation into the community of the faithful.[70]

Others chose the texts of Acts 8: 17 and Hebrews 6: 2 about the laying on of hands for exegesis, upholding this practice as the prerogative of bishops, the 'superior Servants' and 'principal Stewards' of the Lord's household.[71] This rite of sacred touch thus helped to rebuild episcopal authority in the Restoration church, just as the royal touch augmented the restored Stuart monarchy: sacerdotalism was the handmaiden of Erastianism and aspiring absolutism, as well as reascendant episcopacy. As Stephen Brogan has shown, the tradition of charismatic healing survived the Reformation for much the same reason: trimmed of its superstitious elements, a ritual that evoked Christ's own thaumaturgic ministry of touch could not easily be completely dismissed. Touching for the king's evil or scrofula was another manifestation of the biblical practice of laying on of hands, albeit one that, with this exception, was widely said by Protestants to have ceased, along with miracles, prophecy and speaking in tongues.[72] The influence exercised by Valentine Greatrakes, the so-called 'Stroker', who allegedly cured thousands of men, women and children suffering from acute diseases and chronic conditions in the mid-1660s, further attests to its resilience.[73]

The religious and political semiotics of bodily gesture were closely intertwined in this period. It is telling that confirmation had been regularly celebrated at the English court since the reign of James I. His children, Henry, Charles and Elizabeth, were confirmed by the dean of the Chapel Royal in splendid ceremonies. Fashionable courtiers such as the duke of Buckingham followed suit in obsequious deference to a rite that the crown evidently regarded as a crucial appendage to monarchical power.[74] In the later part of the period, the rituals

70 Benjamin Camfield, *Of episcopal confirmation: in two discourses* (London, 1682), 4.

71 John Savage, *The sacred rite of confirmation* (London, 1683), 12. For other sermons on confirmation, see Stubs, *Of confirmation*; Francis Prowde, *A sermon preached in the parish-church of Bridgewater, July 16. 1693* (London, 1694).

72 Stephen Brogan, *The Royal Touch in Early Modern England: Politics, Medicine and Sin* (Woodbridge, 2015).

73 See especially Peter Elmer, *The Miraculous Conformist: Valentine Greatrakes, the Body Politic, and the Politics of Healing in Restoration Britain* (Oxford, 2013).

74 Fincham, *Prelate as Pastor*, 124. For a sermon preached at the confirmation of Charles, see George Hakewill, *The auncient ecclesiasticall practice of confirmation* (London, 1613).

associated with the divine right of kings and of bishops remained mutually reinforcing. Some nonjurors sought to restore the practice of anointing the confirmed with holy oil and making the sign of the cross on their foreheads, keen to underscore the solemnity of the occasion on which they received the gift of the Holy Spirit. They also favoured confirming infants with chrism, returning to the medieval tradition in which the symbolic rite of passage to spiritual maturity occurred soon after birth or in early childhood.[75]

Once again though, confirmation was not confined to high church circles. If it offers insight into the afterlives of Laudianism, it also helps to illustrate the current of latitudinarianism that flowed alongside it. The prelate-pastor remained a familiar figure in the Church of England, committed to ensuring that this rite of religious progression was preceded by adequate instruction through catechizing and a true understanding of the baptismal vows they were about to renew. Gilbert Burnet, bishop of Salisbury, who saw confirmation as 'the most effectual means possible for reviving Christianity', is perhaps the best example. His practice was to catechize the children of the parish himself before admitting them. The conscientious diligence of Burnet and other bishops, documented by Norman Sykes in his Birkbeck Lectures for 1933, belies the lingering impression that the Church of England was stagnant and worldly in the eighteenth century.[76] As Robert Cornwall and Phillip Tovey have recently underlined, the picture of perfunctory performance and neglect painted by Canon Ollard requires qualification.[77] In many ways, this was the heyday of confirmation as a collective public ritual. Confirmation could be privately administered in the domestic chapels of the gentry and aristocracy, but it was also a key embodiment of Christian *communitas* in the early modern period.[78]

[75] Ollard, 'Confirmation', 201–4.

[76] Norman Sykes, *Church and State in England in the XVIIIth Century,* The Birkbeck Lectures 1931–3 (Cambridge, 1934), 115–46. For Burnet, see ibid. 117.

[77] Cornwall, 'Rite of Confirmation'; Tovey, *Anglican Confirmation.*

[78] At Sir John Strode's private chapel at Chantmarle (Dorset), children of the family were confirmed in the morning and, after dinner, another 400 or 500 people 'young and old' from the local community: John Hutchins, *The History and Antiquities of the County of Dorset,* ed. William Shipp and James Whitworth Hodson, 4 vols (Westminster, 1873), 4: 6.

Holy Fairs

In the penultimate section of this article, changing gear from ecclesiastical history to ethnographic analysis, I turn to the significance of confirmation as a social rite of passage. Most of what we know about it is mediated through the distorting lens of elite and literate observers, whether through the recollections of bishops themselves, or their biographers, or the critical reflections of hostile commentators. A repeated theme is the immense popularity of the ritual and the teeming crowds that came to receive the blessing of bishops as they visited their dioceses. Like their medieval predecessors, they sometimes administered the rite in the open air, though this may have been the exception rather than the rule. When Bishop Gervase Babington of Exeter came to Barnstaple in 1595, for instance, he was greeted by the mayor and bailiffs in their scarlet gowns and confirmed a number of boys and girls on the Castle Green. The 'multitude' that flocked in from the surrounding countryside on the second day of his visit was such that Babington could 'scarce pass the street'. On an impulse, he escaped from the throng and left the town 'forthhence'. Bewailing that they had abandoned their fields to undertake a fruitless journey to obtain confirmation for their children, the people 'lamented that they had lost a fine harvest day'.[79] As this example reveals, confirmation was a seasonal event, confined for practical reasons – better weather and the greater passability of roads – to the late spring and summer months. It was organized around the rhythms of agricultural labour and frequently took place on market days. The atmosphere on these occasions was sometimes carnivalesque. In the West Country, Joseph Hall was struck by the 'overeager and tumultuous affectation' of the local people for this rite, and the 'fervour and violence of desire' with which they sought it out for their children. He regretted that it was not possible to administer it 'otherwise than in a breathlesse and tumultuary way'.[80] Richard Corbet, who became bishop of Oxford in 1628, was said to have warned the country folk 'pressing in to see the ceremony': 'Bear off there, or I'll confirm

[79] Todd Gray, ed., *The Lost Chronicle of Barnstaple 1586–1611* (Exeter, 1998), 74–5, and see 38–40.
[80] Hall, *Cheirothesia,* 16–17, 82.

you with my staff'.[81] If Laudian bishops were particularly perturbed by the lack of sacred solemnity that surrounded confirmation, Presbyterians such as Baxter worried that it had become a mere charade or 'custom'. He recalled running from school with his classmates at the age of fifteen to receive it 'with a multitude more, who all went to it as a May-game', lamenting the fact that none of them were properly prepared and that the bishop 'dispatched' them at speed and without assessing whether they were truly Christians in either inward disposition or belief.[82]

One consequence of the large numbers that came to receive it was the exhaustion of the often elderly episcopate, whose aches, pains and ailments were exacerbated by the marathon sessions of confirmation in which they engaged over one or more days, sometimes working late into the evening and clocking up impressive figures in the hundreds and thousands. During the summer months of 1709, for instance, William Wake confirmed some 12,800 people, including 5,200 in Lincolnshire: beginning with 1,200 at Grantham on 7 June and ending with another 1,000 at Boston on the 28th, with visits to Lincoln Cathedral, Caister, Louth and Horncastle in between.[83] One is left with the impression of a factory production line (not to say a vaccination queue!). The issuing of tickets to candidates deemed to have qualified for the rite by receiving catechetical instruction was designed to ensure that those unprepared did not slip through, as was the requirement that they bring a certificate signed and sealed by their parish minister. But it was also a response to the disorder that not infrequently ensued. This was only partially effective: some forged the necessary documentation and others resorted to gate-crashing. John Priaulx, canon of Salisbury, worried that tickets were being given to those of 'notorious Ignorance and Profaness', without due attention to the level of Christian knowledge the recipients possessed.[84] Churchwardens were employed to hold back the throngs

[81] John Aubrey, *Brief Lives,* ed. Richard Barber (Woodbridge, 1982), 81.

[82] Richard Baxter, *Reliquiae Baxterianae: or, Mr Richard Baxters narrative of the most memorable passages of his life and times,* ed. Matthew Sylvester (London, 1696), 250.

[83] Sykes, *Church and State,* 429.

[84] Ibid. 134; W. J. Brown, 'Confirmation in Other Days', *Church Quarterly Review* 146 (1948), 246–9; Priaulx, *Confirmation confirmed,* 28. For the recommendation that ministers supply candidates with a certificate and the bishop with a list, see F. W., *A second letter to a bishop from a minister of his diocess* (London, 1692), 26–7. This writer complained that the rite 'hath been often huddled over, and with little Fruit': ibid. 26.

with staves and control 'the indiscreet forwardness of parents' who thrust forth their offspring, sometimes at too young an age.[85] A printed form dating from 1700 provided directions to ministers so that the rite might 'be done to the more Edification, and greater Advantage of your flock'.[86] Another issued by Francis Atterbury, bishop of Rochester, said that children should be charged 'to behave themselves decently and reverently, while it is performing'.[87] It was evidently an uphill battle to invest the ceremony with an appropriate air of decorum. Occasionally things descended into complete chaos, with young people in high spirits struggling for precedence on their way to the chancel, all the while laughing, talking, scuffling and mischief-making. Writing in 1766, William Cole, parson of Bletchley in Buckinghamshire, complained that confirmations were 'done in such a Hurry, with such Noise & Confusion, as to seem more like a Bear ba[i]ting than any Religious Institution'.[88]

Phillip Tovey speaks of confirmation as 'part of the social package' of being Anglican in eighteenth-century England, a form of 'folk religion', the theology of which is for the most part elusive.[89] It is hard to enter the mental world of those who sought and received it. But snippets of evidence are suggestive. Some, including Nicholas Ferrar, later of Little Gidding, did not scruple to seek it more than once, convinced that there could be no harm in getting a double dose. 'By his own contrivance', he was confirmed for a second time in 1598, when his schoolmaster presented him.[90] The bald and bearded adult men who came to be confirmed by Bishop Corbet in the early seventeenth century were probably not first-time confirmands.[91] Philip Stubs, chaplain to the bishop of Chichester, thought it a 'pious Errour … in a great many, who thinking they can't have the Blessing

85 Sykes, *Church and State,* 121.
86 Anon., *Good brother, intending, by God's blessing …* ([London, 1700?]).
87 [Francis Atterbury], *Directions for confirmation* (Rochester, 1716).
88 William Cole, *The Blecheley Diary of the Rev. William Cole M.A. F.S.A. 1765–67,* ed. Francis Griffin Stokes (London, 1931), 22–3. See the graphic description of the 'disorder and prophaneness' at a confirmation in St Michael's, Cambridge, in 1833 by William Cecil, in Ollard, 'Confirmation', 213–16.
89 Tovey, *Anglican Confirmation,* 167, and see also 136–7.
90 John Ferrar and Dr Jebb, *Nicholas Ferrar: Two Lives,* ed. J. E. B. Mayor (Cambridge, 1855), 4.
91 Aubrey, *Brief Lives,* ed. Barber, 81.

of a Holy Man too often, follow the Bishop almost wheresoever he goes'.[92]

In 1784, a foreign visitor noted that many people he spoke to did not think that the ritual stamped them with 'an indelible character'. At Bury St Edmunds, he encountered three or four old women who were confirmed every time their diocesan bishop came to town. 'Their plea is that you cannot have too much of a good thing'.[93] Such episodes highlight the tension between the clerical understanding of confirmation as a unique and unrepeatable rite of passage, and lay perception that its efficacy was not confined to a single occasion. They illustrate the frictions between formal theology and popular practice.

Some also supposed the rite to have therapeutic effects: in the nineteenth century a Norfolk woman claimed to have been 'bishopped' seven times because she found it helped her rheumatism.[94] Here laying on of hands is conceived of as curative. Confirmation becomes a kind of faith healing, akin to the royal touch and Greatrakes's gift of stroking. Others believed that at the moment of blessing 'a special Angel-Guardian is appointed to keep their Souls from the assaults of the Spirits of darkness'. Jeremy Taylor thought this supposition was 'not disagreeable to the intention of this Rite' and did not explicitly condemn it.[95] Nor should the possibility be dismissed that some, inspired by the rhetoric of preachers, saw it as an agent of religious regeneration and perfection that enhanced their hopes of reaching heaven. Assessing these opinions against the yardstick of doctrinal 'orthodoxy' is unhelpful. It effaces the creative and organic character of lived religion and of rite as a human fact. The extent to which confirmation was a spiritual event for individual laypeople should not be underestimated.

However, it is also important to recognize the ways in which confirmation was combined with commensality. Bishop Gilbert Burnet of Salisbury assiduously catechized children himself prior to confirming them, presenting each candidate with a silver crown and

92 Stubs, *Of confirmation*, 25–6.

93 See François de La Rochefoucauld, *A Frenchman in England, 1784 being the Mélanges sur l'Angleterre of François de la Rochefoucauld*, ed. Jean Marchand, transl. S. C. Roberts (Cambridge, 1933), 86.

94 Cited in Keith Thomas, *Religion and the Decline of Magic* (Harmondsworth, 1973; first publ. 1971), 42.

95 Taylor, *Chrisis teleiotike*, sig. A1^{v}.

concluding the proceedings by inviting them to a Sunday meal.[96] Food and drink flowed in the towns to which parents brought their children to be bishopped, and a mood of festivity and conviviality abounded.[97] Striking continuities with the medieval past are clear: confirmation remained a lively rite of passage. It was usually shunted forward in time from childhood to adolescence, but could happen at any point in the life cycle.

It is tempting to see confirmations as the 'fair days' of the Church of England, a phrase evocative of that used to describe the mass communions that took place in Presbyterian Scotland and which, imported across the Atlantic, laid the foundations for American revivalism and the Great Awakening. Leigh Eric Schmidt has provided a rich Geertzian thick description of these sacramental events in the reformed calendar, in which 'religion and culture, communion and community, piety and sociability commingled'. Confirmations present many parallels. Occasions on which the 'sacred and the social were inextricably combined', they too question assumptions about the role of the Reformation in the repudiation and devaluation of ritual.[98] They supply insight into the mixture of theology, liturgy, custom, culture and emotion that surrounds the marking of rites of passage.

The Counter-Reformation of Confirmation

I cannot close without a brief discussion of the role of confirmation within the post-Reformation English Catholic community. The evangelical and Protestant assault upon this sacrament provoked resistance from the beginning. In 1549, the Prayer Book rebels in Devon and Cornwall defended traditional bishopping alongside the Latin mass and 'all other ancient old ceremonies used heretofore by our mother the holy Church'. Following Edward VI's death, the demand for confirmation was apparently high, with people running to churches and churchyards in such numbers that there was insufficient

96 H. C. Foxcroft, ed., *A Supplement to Burnet's history of my own time* (Oxford, 1902), 499–500.
97 Sykes, *Church and State,* 132.
98 Leigh Eric Schmidt, *Holy Fairs: Scotland and the Making of American Revivalism,* 2nd edn (Grand Rapids, MI, 2001; first publ. 1989), 3, 215–16, 218.

space to hold them. Forced to confirm in the fields, the bishop of Chester feared that he would be trodden to death by the importunate crowd.[99] Bishop Bonner's visitation articles for London for 1553 reproved laypeople who refused to bring their own children for confirmation and who dissuaded others from doing so.[100] The rite in its traditional form was already becoming a litmus test of confessional identity. In its seventh session in 1547, the Council of Trent declared anathema upon heretics who dismissed confirmation as an empty ceremony, denied that it was a true sacrament that imprinted an indelible mark on the soul, denigrated chrism as blasphemous, and said that any simple priest could administer confirmation.[101] Rome's premier controversialist Robert Bellarmine buttressed Trent's declarations in 'De Sacramento Confirmationis', adding to confirmation's status as a shibboleth of Counter-Reformation belief.[102]

Dispensing this sacrament was especially challenging for a missionary church like England's. The amputation of its episcopal hierarchy necessitated concessions and emergency measures: casuists conceded that, in these conditions, the eucharist could be ministered to the unconfirmed if this was due to a lack of bishops. They were also told that Gregory IX had granted the faculty of conferring confirmation to priests, and that the Pope could solve the problem by consecrating some of them as titular bishops, assigning them either to some English diocese or other dioceses *in partibus*.[103] This was precisely what happened with the appointment of William Bishop as vicar apostolic and bishop of Chalcedon in 1623, at around the same time as the revival of ceremonialism was starting to take off in the Church of England. He spent the summer after his arrival confirming Roman Catholics in the vicinity of the capital, conferring 'Christes badge and cognisance' upon at least two thousand people before

[99] Robert Whiting, *The Blind Devotion of the People: Popular Religion and the English Reformation* (Cambridge, 1989), 34. For the demand for confirmation following Mary's accession, see Taylor, *Chrisis teleiotike,* 6–7; Nicholas Sander, *Vera et sincera historia schismatis Anglicani* (Cologne, 1628), book 2, 246.

[100] Cardwell, ed., *Documentary Annals,* 1: 161–2.

[101] *The Canons and Decrees of the Council of Trent,* transl. H. J. Schroeder (Rockford, IL, 1978), 52, 54–5, 161–2.

[102] Robert Bellarmine, 'De sacramento confirmationis', in idem, *Opera omnia*, ed. Joseph Giuliano, 6 vols (Naples, 1856–62), 3: 212–34.

[103] P. J. Holmes, ed., *Elizabethan Casuistry,* Catholic Record Society 67 (N.pl., 1981), 81.

winter set in. The Protestant polemicist John Gee mercilessly mocked this 'puffe-paste Titulado' to whom people flocked in large numbers: 'what gadding, what gazing, what prostration, to receive but one drop of that sacred deaw'. Bishop's intention to visit the remote parts of the kingdom the following spring was prevented by his death less than a year later, at the age of seventy.[104] His successor, Richard Smith, published a treatise showing 'the necessitie, spirituall profit, and excellencie of this Sacrament' in 1629, explaining that as in 'our corporall life, wee bee first Children, and after perfect or compleate men', so in spiritual life did people proceed from being like newborn infants to children, and from thence to fully-grown men. Failure to be confirmed was a mortal sin. Turning the devout believer into 'a Souldier of Christ', this sacrament was a shield to resist Rome's enemies in 'time of persecution'. It was 'temeritie to enter into a daungerous Combat without Armour'. In describing the different parts of the ritual, he said that the stroke on the cheek was to admonish the confirmed party of his obligation 'to beare blowes if neede bee for the profession of Christs faith'.[105] Confirmation thus became an emblem of the tribulations Roman Catholics suffered and of the resilience and militancy of the English Counter-Reformation.

This experiment in instituting a Tridentine episcopate in England was short-lived, but in the later seventeenth century it acquired a second wind under the Roman Catholic monarch James II. It is significant that in 1686 Henry Hills, printer to the king's chapel and household, issued a short catechism and account of the holy sacrament of confirmation. This too stressed its status as a kind of sword and buckler for those in the midst of trials and tribulations. It explained that the sign of the cross was designed 'to teach us that we never ought to be asham'd to confess Christ crucifi'd', and that the little slap on the face was 'to shew that we ought to be ever ready to suffer all Affronts and Injuries from Men' without quailing, even to

[104] Philip Caraman, ed., *The Years of Siege: Catholic Life from James I to Cromwell* (London, 1966), 34–5; Michael Questier, *Catholicism and Community in Early Modern England: Politics, Aristocratic Patronage and Religion, c.1550–1640* (Cambridge, 2006), 404–7; John Gee, *John Gee's Foot out of the Snare*, ed. T. H. B. M. Harmsen (Nijmegen, 1992), 122.

[105] [Richard Smith], *A treatise of the sacrament of confirmation wherein is shewed the necessitie, spirituall profit and excellencie of this sacrament* (Douai, 1629), 2, 57–8, 81, 76, 123–4.

the extent of dying for the sake of Christ.[106] Roman Catholics were given permission for the public exercise of their religion, and one the first priorities of John Leyburn, consecrated bishop of Adrumentum in 1685, was a provocative confirmation tour of the country which took him from London to the north, and back again through the Midlands. The surviving register of Leyburn's episcopal progress records 20,859 confirmands.[107] This conspicuous Counter-Reformation spectacle both reflected and fuelled the high hopes of the faithful for the reconversion of England.

Conclusion

Confirmation has proved to be a flexible tool for exploring the theological and liturgical upheavals inaugurated by the English Reformation and its ongoing repercussions over two centuries. Its plural histories have helped to illuminate the ways in which a movement that fundamentally redefined the very meaning of ritual selectively retained and remodelled ceremonies designed to mark the initiation of individual Christians as full members of the Church in heaven and on earth. The debates that this process set off turned around the Church's apostolic heritage and bodily gestures that had their roots in the Bible. This engendered a multiplicity of modes of confirmation that reflected, as well as facilitated, the splintering of Protestant Christianity and its differentiation from Roman Catholicism. Yet if this rite of passage was a fillip to schism and separation, it was also an agent of solidarity and group cohesion. Reformed ambivalence about this ritual did not prevent it from becoming and remaining the focal point of popular piety in Tudor and Stuart society, as well as a ceremony of initiation valorized by clergy of different persuasions, even if they disagreed about its outward form and inward significance. Creating occasions that fused spirituality with senses of belonging and community, confirmation brought people together to celebrate the transition from religious immaturity to knowledge. It was the moment at which, whether

[106] Anon., *A summe of Christian doctrine … with the holy sacrament of confirmation explain'd at large* (London, 1686), 13–22.

[107] London, Archives of the Archdiocese of Westminster, A series, vol. 35; transcribed and edited by J. A. Hilton et al. as *Bishop Leyburn's Confirmation Register of 1687* (Wigan, 1997).

they were children in years or understanding, confirmands symbolically came of age and became adults in faith. For contemporaries, this was a potent metaphor for the religious conversion of institutions and systems as well as individuals. It was a way of conceptualizing the momentous ecclesiastical transformation initiated in the early and mid-sixteenth century. In this sense, the Reformation itself may be seen as a rite of passage.

'The Child's blood should lye at his Door': Local Divisions over Baptismal Rites during the English Civil War and the Interregnum

Fiona McCall*

University of Portsmouth

By the 1640s, Prayer Book ritual had marked rites of passage in England for over eighty years. It formed a reassuring continuum with older Catholic rites and gave communality to parish religion. However, puritans disliked its ceremonial elements, which were banned by Parliament in the 1640s. Anecdotal evidence suggests that parishioners continued to demand old-style rites of passage, and some clergy to offer them. This has led historians to suggest that traditionalist practice was condoned by the regime. This article uses loyalist memories of antagonisms between puritan and non-puritan clergy and parishioners over baptism, as well as evidence from legal prosecutions and other sources, to complicate such presumptions, showing how, with opinion sharply divided on their practice, rites of passage led to clashes and confrontations within parishes and remained a focus for local antagonism.

By the 1640s, Book of Common Prayer ritual had been used for rites of passage in England for over eighty years. Retaining elements of older rites, such as the idea of spiritual regeneration through ritual washing at the font, or familiar words of the liturgy (largely based on the Sarum manual of the medieval Catholic Church), gave a sense of continuity and commonality to parish religion.[1] However,

* E-mail: fiona.mccall@port.ac.uk.

[1] See Katherine Krick-Pridgeon, '"Nothing for the godly to fear": Use of Sarum Influence on the 1549 Book of Common Prayer' (PhD thesis, Durham University, 2018), 196. Other continuities with Catholic practice included the idea of contest with the devil, the making of the sign of the cross, the baptism of infants and the use of godparents.

Studies in Church History 59 (2023), 198–221
doi: 10.1017/stc.2023.9

puritans in the church objected to the ceremonial elements of the Book of Common Prayer, and in 1645 these were banned by parliamentary legislation.[2] Evidence from diaries suggests that some members of the elite, notably the diarist John Evelyn, continued to demand old-style rites, and some clergy to offer them.[3] Because of this, historians have assumed that continuing use of traditionalist practice remained largely unquestioned during this period.[4] Using loyalist memories of antagonisms between puritan and non-puritan clergy and parishioners, as well as evidence from legal prosecutions and other sources, this article complicates such presumptions, showing how, with opinion sharply divided on their practice, rites of passage led to clashes and confrontations within parishes.

The focus here is on baptism, as the rite of greatest importance within the Christian religion. Deriving from the Gospels, it was one of only two of the seven Catholic sacraments retained by Protestants.[5] A very familiar ritual, commonly performed in the context of the gathered Sunday congregation, as David Cressy has shown, it also generated the most post-Reformation controversy over its precise theological meaning, as well as the way, time and place in which it should be conducted. If, as Anna French argues, the sacraments were 'some of the most heavily debated aspects of reformed worship' due to their 'close connection to beliefs about salvation', then in this period baptism was more contentious than the eucharist.[6]

David Cressy cites both theological polemic and parochial confrontations surrounding baptism over the longer post-Reformation period. Yet despite increased interest among religious anthropologists

[2] 'January 1645: An Ordinance for Taking Away the Book of Common Prayer, and for Establishing and Putting in Execution of the Directory for the Publique Worship of God', in C. H. Firth and R. S. Rait, eds, *Acts and Ordinances of the Interregnum, 1642–1660* (London, 1911), 582–607, at *British History Online*: <http://www.british-history. ac.uk/no-series/acts-ordinances-interregnum/pp582-607>, accessed 1 September 2021.

[3] John Evelyn, *Diary and Correspondence of John Evelyn*, ed. William Bray (London, n.d.), 193, 195. Richard Drake, the ejected rector of Radwinter, Essex, lists baptisms, funerals and his own marriage using traditional rites in his diary: Oxford, Bodl., Rawlinson MS D 158, fols 13^{v}, 14^{r}, 15^{v}, 16^{r}, 17$^{r–v}$, 19^{r}.

[4] See Robert S. Bosher, *The Making of the Restoration Settlement* (London, 1951), 5, 12; Paul Lay, *Providence Lost* (London, 2020), 70.

[5] Alec Ryrie, *Being Protestant in Reformation Britain* (Oxford, 2013), 329.

[6] Anna French, 'Disputed Words and Disputed Meanings: The Reformation of Baptism, Infant Limbo and Child Salvation in Early Modern England', in Jonathan Willis, ed., *Sin and Salvation in Reformation England* (Farnham, 2015), 157–72, at 158.

in the role of religion within revolutionary contexts in recent years, Cressy notes the absence of research to substantiate patterns of response, within parishes, to the sharp change of official attitudes towards baptism in the mid-seventeenth century. 'The demography of religious affiliation in this period has so far resisted scholarly investigation', he writes, querying 'how typical were the strategies' of diarists like Evelyn or how attached people were to the new – post-Book of Common Prayer – style of worship.[7]

The tendency in recent years, following the arguments of John Morrill, has been to emphasize the continuing vitality of traditional practice in the 1640s and 1650s.[8] Judith Maltby has argued convincingly for the existence of a 'set of religious attitudes, practices and beliefs which found authenticity, comfort and renewal' in traditional Church of England ritual while it was suppressed, although she and others rightly remind us not to see this as preserving a uniform, single strand equivalent to what we now think of as 'Anglicanism' within the pre-Civil War church.[9] Anthony Milton argues that the content of the Prayer Book petitions of 1641–2 was 'hotly contested', rather than deriving from an unchanging 'Anglican' orthodoxy.[10] Considering the example of Elizabeth Isham, Isaac Stephens warns against an oversimplified division between Maltby's 'prayer-book Protestants' and puritans: individual religious practice such as Elizabeth's might combine elements of both traditional ritual and

[7] David Cressy, *Birth, Marriage, and Death: Ritual, Religion, and the Life-Cycle in Tudor and Stuart England* (Oxford, 1997), 125–134, 180; Ramon Sarró, Simon Coleman and Ruy Llera Blanes, 'Introduction: One Hundred years of the Anthropology of Religion', *Religion and Society: Advances in Research* 3 (2012), 1–3, at 2.

[8] John Morrill, 'The Church in England 1643–9', in idem, ed., *Reactions to the English Civil War 1642–1649* (London, 1982), 89–114; Derek Hirst, 'The Failure of Godly Rule in the English Republic', *P&P* 132 (1991), 33–66; Christopher Durston, 'Puritan Rule and the Failure of Cultural Revolution, 1645–1660', in idem and Jacqueline Eales, eds, *The Culture of English Puritanism* (Basingstoke, 1996), 210–33; Judith Maltby, *Prayer Book and People in Elizabethan and Early Stuart England* (Cambridge, 1998).

[9] Judith Maltby, 'Suffering and Surviving: The Civil Wars, the Commonwealth and the Formation of "Anglicanism", 1642–60', in Christopher Durston and eadem, eds, *Religion in Revolutionary England* (Manchester, 2006), 158–80, at 159.

[10] Anthony Milton, 'Unsettled Reformations: 1603–1662', in idem, ed., *The Oxford History of Anglicanism*, 1: *Reformation and Identity, c.1520–1662* (Oxford, 2017), 63–83, at 71. These were petitions from the counties defending the use of the Book of Common Prayer against proposals to abolish it: see Maltby, *Prayer Book*, especially 23–4, 83–129.

puritan piety.[11] Eclectic practices before the English Revolution should prime us against making assumptions about how individuals and parishes responded to the religious changes that accompanied it, or assuming that any particular pattern of beliefs or practices, traditionalist or otherwise, had the support of the majority.

Although a number of historians have written about religion during this period, most substantively Christopher Durston and Bernard Capp, the reception and impact of the religious changes of the 1640s and 1650s within parishes has yet to be fully investigated. Since 'social historians have long learned not to expect complete consistency between theological precept and practice', as Susan Karant-Nunn observes, understanding the parochial context is at least as important as comprehending the doctrinal issues discussed in print or state policy.[12] Writing about the reception of the Reformation in Gloucestershire, Caroline Litzenberger alerts us to how the enforcement of ritual change on society results in a two-way process of 'complicity, struggle and negotiation' with official policy. 'New or modified rituals not only changed people's pious practices, but were in turn changed by those same practices'.[13] At a statistical level, this response appears both as a rise in private baptism in the 1640s and 1650s, and as a decline of at least ten percent in the number of baptisms overall, according to Kitson, Wrigley and Schofield.[14] If, as Kitson suggests, 'there was a fundamental shift in the nature of religious observance' in the mid-seventeenth century, it was qualitatively different to the one originally envisaged by puritan reformers, and requires further examination.[15]

[11] Isaac Stephens, 'Confessional Identity in Early Stuart England: The "Prayer Book Puritanism" of Elizabeth Isham', *Journal of British Studies* 50 (2011), 24–47.

[12] See also Christopher Durston, '"Preaching and sitting still on Sundays": The Lord's Day during the English Revolution', in Durston and Maltby, eds, *Religion*, 205–25; Bernard Capp, *England's Culture Wars* (Oxford, 2012); idem, 'Introduction: Stability and Flux: The Church in the Interregnum', in Fiona McCall, ed., *Church and People in Interregnum Britain* (London, 2021), 1–18; Ronald Hutton, *The Rise and Fall of Merry England* (Oxford, 1994), 210–16; Claire Cross, *Church and People 1450–1660*, 2nd edn (Oxford, 1999), 175–95; Susan Karant-Nunn, *Reformation of Ritual* (London and New York, 1997), 60.

[13] Caroline Litzenberger, 'Communal Ritual, Concealed Belief: Layers of Response to the Regulation of Ritual in Reformation England', in James Tracy and Marguerite Ragnow, eds, *Religion and the Early Modern State* (Cambridge, 2004), 98–120, at 100.

[14] Will Coster, *Baptism and Spiritual Community in Early Modern England* (Farnham, 2002), 53.

[15] P. M. Kitson, 'Religious Change and the Timing of Baptism in England, 1538–1750', *HistJ* 52 (2009), 269–94, at 292; E. A. Wrigley and R. S. Schofield, *The Population*

Evidence of divisions over baptism appeared in many of the accusations against so-called 'scandalous' clergy made to Parliament and its committees in the early 1640s, which prefigured the changes introduced in 1645. Some reflect long-standing puritan opposition to making the sign of the cross in baptism as too reminiscent of Catholic gestures. Although Luther's baptismal rites of 1523 and 1526 had retained the sign, Martin Bucer's Strasbourg ritual of 1524 removed it and this influenced later Protestant groups, including Calvinists.[16] The Millenary petitioners of 1603 had asked that instructions to use this gesture be removed from the Book of Common Prayer rubric, but this request was firmly denied in the church canons of 1604.[17] The issue resurfaced in the 1640s, when several ministers were denounced for using the sign of the cross even before it had been officially banned by the parliamentary legislation of 1645.[18]

In this period, parishioners seem to have felt that they had the right to determine how baptism was performed for their children. In 1644 it was reported that Richard Peacock, minister of Swaffham Prior in Cambridgeshire, when asked to baptize a child without using the sign of the cross, refused to do so without an order from a higher authority.[19] Cuthbert Nicholson, rector of Newbold Verdon in Leicestershire, was accused of baptizing a child with the sign of the cross 'notwithstanding their fathers standing their forbade

History of England 1541–1871 (London, 1981), 28, 540, quoted in Durston, 'Puritan Rule', 227.

16 Karant-Nunn, *Reformation*, 52–3, 55; see Martin Bucer, *A Review of the Book of Common Prayer*, ed. Arthur Roberts (London, 1853), 19, 21–2. When asked by Archbishop Cranmer to critique King Edward VI's first Prayer Book, which had been published in 1549, before its revision in 1552, Bucer commented unfavourably on the 'delight' of the common people with signs and 'scenic exhibitions' they did not understand; however, he did not at this time express disapproval of the signing with the cross, as long as it was performed religiously and without superstition.

17 Cressy, *Birth, Marriage, and Death*, 126–7.

18 London, BL, MS Add. 15672, Articles Exhibited to the Commissioners for Examining Scandalous Ministers in Cambridgeshire, 1643–4, fols 39r, 46r, 55r. It is often unclear who raised such issues and how – or indeed whether – they were related to the baptismal family. In Cambridgeshire, the names of those testifying are known, but usually they are not; see also Bodl., Rawlinson MS D 158, fols 43r–55v, where Richard Drake chronicles several interventions during baptisms that were not led by the families.

19 BL, MS Add. 15672, fol. 4r.

him'.[20] Thomas Newcomen, rector of Holy Trinity Church, Colchester, 'not being suffered' to cross a child, apparently retaliated by perverting the liturgy, saying, 'We doe not receive this Child into the Congregation'.[21] Gentleman George Salter of King's Lynn testified that Thomas Holt, minister of All Saints in Stamford, had refused to christen his child except with the sign of the cross, 'nor would suffer' another minister to baptize without it. Salter's wife's puritan leanings perhaps swayed him; he also stated that she had 'fallen out' with Holt over the question of kneeling at the altar to receive communion.[22]

Sometimes such concerns were long-standing and had previously been handled with some flexibility by church ministers. In 1646 Nicholas Hall of Loughborough, challenging his sequestration, claimed never to have used the sign of the cross in baptism, despite the church canons.[23] At Saddington in the same county, however, antipathy to the use of the cross was apparently a newly generated scruple. It was said that William Wood, 'an honest godly man', after taking the Solemn League and Covenant of 1643, desired rector Bernard Flesher to omit the sign in baptizing his child, but Flesher refused, causing Wood 'great grief'.[24] Although the Covenant itself makes no mention of baptism, it probably encouraged further religious debate amongst those taking it.[25]

Charles Hefling argues that the Prayer Book has long been a 'primary carrier' of meanings and values within Anglicanism, educating and informing its listeners, long before it was understood by philosophers 'that language is what bestows meaning' on the 'human mind and heart'.[26] The Prayer Book words taught parents to conceptualize baptism as the crossing of a highly significant threshold: baptized infants were 'born again', made 'dead unto sin', 'received into' and

[20] Bodl., MS J. Walker [hereafter: WMS], C11, Proceedings of the Leicester Sequestration Committee, 1646, fol. 65^{r}.

[21] BL, MS Add. 5829, Acts of the Committee against Scandalous Ministers in Essex, 1643–4, fols 71–2.

[22] F. Hill, ed., 'The Royalist Clergy of Lincolnshire', *Reports & Papers of the Lincolnshire Architectural & Archaeological Society* n.s. 2 (1941 for 1938), 34–127, at 80.

[23] Bodl., WMS, C11, fol. 76^{r}.

[24] Ibid., fol. 29^{r}.

[25] *A Solemne League and Covenant, for Reformation, and Defence of Religion* (Edinburgh, 1643).

[26] Charles Hefling, 'Introduction: Anglicans and Common Prayer', in idem and Cynthia Shattuck, eds, *The Oxford Guide to The Book of Common Prayer* (Oxford, 2006), 1–6.

made 'lively members' of 'Christ's holy church', 'regenerated with the holy Spirit', utterly abolishing 'the whole body of sin'.[27] Yet in the early 1640s, while the Prayer Book was still officially the form of service required by the church, a number of clergy had been denounced for expressing this very doctrine, including George Kindleton of Magdalen Laver in Essex, London ministers Benjamin Spencer and William Quelch, and Nicholas Felton at Stretham in Cambridgeshire.[28] Theodore Crosland, vice master of Trinity College, Cambridge, was blamed for the 'debayst drunken man' he employed as his substitute at Bottisham who preached that 'Children that are Baptized are absolutely regenerate'.[29] Hugh Reeve, parson of Ampthill in Bedfordshire, supposedly held 'popish doctrines', claiming that 'the outward act of Baptism ... pronounced by the meanest or silliest priest' was sufficient to 'conferre grace on the child'.[30] A logical, if unacceptable implication of such theology, in the puritan mind, was the belief, supposedly held by Suffolk rector Jeremiah Ravens, that the rite itself conferred salvation.[31] To these cases may be added, if we believe the sensationalized clerical denouncements in John White's *First Century of Scandalous Malignant Priests* (1643), those of Sussex ministers John Wilson and Richard Gough, and of Essex ministers Edward Cherry and William Osbalston.[32]

More distressing, if true, was the claim made by James Buck of Stradbroke in Suffolk that unbaptized children were 'undoubtedly damned' and the complaint that Thomas Bayly, of Brasted, Kent, refused to bury them.[33] Catholic theology postulated the idea of limbo for unbaptized infants, from which they would eventually be released, but, as Protestants, these clergy conceptualized a more

27 *The Booke of Common Praier* (London, 1559), unpaginated.

28 Leicester, Leicester University, MS 31, Reformation of the University of Cambridge and Essex Ministers, 1644, fols 13–14, where his first name is given as Francis; *Articles Exhibited Against Benjamin Spencer* (London, 1642), 2; London, Parliamentary Archives [hereafter: PA], HL/PO/JO/10/1/75, 23 December 1641; BL, MS Add. 15672, fols 1–2.

29 BL, MS Add. 15672, fol. 3^{r}.

30 PA, HL/PO/JO/10/1/47, 16 January 1641; HL/PO/JO/10/1/120, 30 April 1642.

31 Clive Holmes, ed., *The Suffolk Committees for Scandalous Ministers 1644–1646*, Suffolk Records Society 13 (Ipswich, 1970), 39.

32 John White, The *First Century of Scandalous, Malignant Priests* (London, 1643), 1, 3, 12, 14, 20, 32, 37, 44.

33 Ibid. 40, 43.

clearly defined separation between the elect, destined for heaven, and the reprobate, headed for hell.[34] Another Kent minister, Dr Vane at Crayford, was said to have taught that children who died unbaptized could not be saved.[35] The reported doctrine of Richard Dukeson of St Clement Danes, that children dying before baptism are saved by the faith of their godparents, was perhaps an attempt to ameliorate a distressing circumstance, albeit not one which was appealing to puritan sensibilities.[36] All these charges reveal that puritan polemicists were determined to make an issue of the precise theological implications of baptism.

The introduction to the *Directory for Publique Worship* of 1645 gave parliamentary reformers at Westminster the chance to replace Prayer Book orthodoxy with their own. The *Directory* is often thought a rather anodyne document, but on baptism it represents a profound shift in the way the rite was supposed to be conducted and perceived.[37] Godparents were no longer involved and the use of the font was outlawed.[38] Where the Prayer Book normalized public baptism in the context of the gathered congregation, the *Directory* insisted on it.[39] Where the Prayer Book held 'parents' responsible for baptism (although in practice lying-in mothers did not usually take part), the *Directory* involved only fathers.[40] This masculine

34 The Catholic Church has recently described limbo as merely a possible theological hypothesis: see The International Theological Commission, *The Hope of Salvation for Infants who die without being Baptized* (2007), online at: <https://www.vatican.va/roman_curia/congregations/cfaith/cti_documents/rc_con_cfaith_doc_20070419_un-baptised-infants_en.html>, accessed 22 November 2022.

35 L. B. Larking, ed., *Proceedings, Principally in the County of Kent*, Camden Society o.s. 80 (1862), 118.

36 White, *Century*, 40. Martin Luther employed similar arguments: see Madeleine Gray, 'Ritual Space and Ritual Burial in the Early Modern Christian Tradition', in Joan Allen and Richard C. Allen, eds, *Faith of our Fathers* (Newcastle upon Tyne, 2009), 11–25, at 17.

37 J. F. Merritt, 'Religion and the English Parish', in Milton, ed., *Anglicanism*, 122–47, at 142; Judith Maltby, '"Extravagencies and Impertinences": Set Forms, Conceived and Extempore Prayer in Revolutionary England', in Natalie Mears and Alec Ryrie, eds, *Worship and the Parish Church in Early Modern Britain* (Farnham, 2013), 221–43, at 225.

38 *A Directory for the Publique Worship of God* (London, 1645), 20.

39 Ibid. 19–20; Kitson, 'Religious Change', 273–5.

40 *Directory*, 20; Ryrie, *Being Protestant*, 329; Cressy, *Birth, Marriage, and Death*, 149. The inclusion of mothers in the spiritual responsibility for a child dates back to at least 1536: see Will Coster, '"From Fire and Water": The Responsibilities of Godparents in Early Modern England', in Diana Wood, ed., *The Church and Childhood*, SCH 31 (Oxford, 1994), 301–11.

bias perhaps derived from the Scottish or Genevan English baptismal rites, which involved fathers and godfathers but not mothers or godmothers.[41] More significantly, the *Directory* removed much of the power attached to the ritual itself, particularly the idea that it was anything more than symbolic. The baptismal water, it stated, merely 'representeth and signifieth' the taking away of original sin by Christ. Baptized children were received only into the visible church, thereby distinguishing between the baptized and the elect. By baptism, they received a 'Seale of the Covenant of Grace', an endorsement of a state existing separately from the rite itself: the 'inward Grace of Baptisme' was not tied to the moment wherein it was administered, 'the fruit and power thereof reacheth to the whole course of our life', and 'outward Baptisme is not so necessary; that through the want thereof the Infant is in danger of Damnation or the Parents guilty'. While this wording seemed to offer comfort to parents whose children had died unbaptized, the *Directory* refused any guarantees: all that could be done was to pray that, if a child died in infancy, the Lord would be merciful and 'receive him up into glory'; and if he lived to 'years of discretion', his word and Spirit would 'make his Baptisme effectual to him'.[42]

Even if, as Alec Ryrie argues, this downgraded conception of baptism was commonplace in puritan circles – Stephen Dennison was charged before the High Commission in 1634 for preaching that 'Baptisme without the word is like a seal without writinge, … the word is the principall, and the Sacrament is the accessory' – it was unfamiliar to parishioners whose doctrinal ideas were conditioned by the Book of Common Prayer.[43] Even amongst the puritan-inflected clerical accusations of the 1640s, complaints are found which revolved around more traditional concerns, notably that baptismal rites be performed as soon as the parents desired, and performed properly. In 1641 Bryan Walton was accused of refusing to baptize infants presented on a holy day before divine service, 'for what cause, your petitioners know not, other than their parents were not in

[41] Coster, *Baptism*, 85; *The Service, Discipline and Forme of the Common Prayers and Administration of the Sacraments, Used in the English Church of Geneva, … approved by … M. John Calvin, And the Church of Scotland* (London, 1641), 35.
[42] *Directory*, 20–3.
[43] Kew, TNA, SP 16/261, High Commission Minute Book, October 1635, fol. 283.

his favour'.[44] Similar complaints were made to Parliament in 1641 against Andrew Sandiland of Great Waldingfield, Suffolk, for refusing to baptize children presented to him in the forenoons.[45] In August 1644 three working men complained that William Underwood, minister at Hareby in Lincolnshire, had not administered the 'sacrament of Baptisme' once since coming to the church in the Spring.[46]

Such concerns echo earlier objections from the church courts of the 1630s, complaining of clerical neglect causing children not to be baptized when requested, or worse, to die unbaptized. In 1633 William Warmington was cited before the Exeter church courts for refusing to baptize a child brought into church on a Sunday, despite being told it was weak, forcing the parents to travel two miles to another church.[47] Such cases continued to trouble parents years later. Similar allegations against William Churton of Hartland in Devon in 1638 harked back to an incident eight or nine years previously, when his neglect had led to a child's dying unbaptized.[48]

Other accusations in the early 1640s, as well as earlier cases in the church court records of the 1630s, concerned baptisms improperly conducted: Robert Guyon, minister of White Colne in Essex, was said to have confused the marriage and baptism services; Henry Wright of Brampford Speke in Devon was cited in 1636 for baptizing while drunk; Edward Jeffry of Southminster in Essex was accused of baptizing in 1638 while himself excommunicate.[49] Complaints to Parliament against Dr Richard Etkins, vicar of Kensington, in 1641 included his 'carelesse ... fashion of performing the divine offices', including 'omissions of no lesse moment' than forgetting the child's name in baptism.[50] A Harwich lecturer, Thomas Wood, was accused of inventing his own baptism service, to the 'great disturbance' of the inhabitants.[51]

44 *The Articles and Charge Proved in Parliament against Doctor Walton, Minister of St. Martins Orgars in Cannon Street* (London, 1641), 4.
45 PA, HL/PO/JO/10/1/51, 9 February 1641.
46 Hill, 'Royalist Clergy', 65–70.
47 Exeter, Devon Heritage Centre [hereafter: DHC], CC 178, Complaints against William Warmington of Yarnscombe, 1634.
48 DHC, CC 178, Complaints against William Churton of Hartland, 1639.
49 BL, MS Add. 5829, 9 April 1644, fol. 24^{r}; DHC, CC 178, Complaint against Henry Wright, 1636; Chelmsford, Essex Record Office [hereafter: ERO], D/AB/A9, Commissary of the Bishop of London Act Book, 1638–41, fol. 30^{v}.
50 PA, HL/PO/JO/10/1/57, 13 May 1641.
51 Bodl., Tanner MS 62, fols 343–6.

Mock baptisms, soon to be an offence associated with soldiers and sectarians, were said to have been performed by Essex minister John Fenwick and Leicestershire minister Francis Squire in local alehouses.[52] David Cressy gives other examples, although he perhaps underplays the significance and prevalence of such inversion rituals during the Civil War and Interregnum.[53] Blanford Parker writes that each period has its own characteristic modes of satire, involving the 'constant assimilation and displacement of generic norms'.[54] Keith Thomas argues that, for the early modern period, mockeries of ecclesiastical rituals were 'stock methods'.[55] Indeed, James Mawdesley highlights their role in the confessional conflicts of the period.[56] The set forms of traditional religion were also often parodied in printed satire during the 1640s and 1650s: there were mock litanies, mock catechisms, mock sermons, and satires on the Ten Commandments, the Creed, the Lord's Prayer and on biblical verses.[57] Such forms were mimicked precisely because they had such 'serious and solemn Significations', which the parody might critique, but also reinforce.[58] Repeated reports of mock baptisms in the mid-seventeenth century therefore suggest both the importance of the

[52] Leicester University, MS 31, 1644, fols 1–2; Bodl., WMS, C11, fol. 69A; John Gauden, *Hinc Illae Lachrymae* (London, 1648), 12; Thomas Edwards, *The First and Second Part of Gangraena* (London, 1646), 58, 94; Cambridge, CUL, Ms.Mm., 1.45, Baker Transcripts, 'Observat:, Occasionall & Emergent Acts &c: in Parliament tyme', 1640–41, 37; William Dugdale, *Short View of the Late Troubles in England* (Oxford, 1681), 560.

[53] David Cressy, 'Baptized Beasts and Other Travesties: Affronts to Rites of Passage', in idem, *Travesties and Transgressions in Tudor and Stuart England* (Oxford, 2000), 171–85.

[54] Blanford Parker, 'Modes of Mockery: The Significance of Mock-Poetic Forms in the Enlightenment', in Ruben Quintero, ed., *A Companion to Satire* (Oxford, 2007), 493–509, at 495.

[55] Keith Thomas, 'The Place of Laughter in Tudor and Stuart England', *Times Literary Supplement,* 21 January 1977, 77–81, at 77.

[56] James Mawdesley, 'Antrobus the Cleric and Peter the Cock: Civil War, Ministry and Animal Baptism in Mid-Seventeenth-Century Cumberland', *Local Historian* 46 (2016), 15–26.

[57] TNA, ASSI 45/2/2, 23 March 1647; George de Forest Lord, ed., *Anthology of Poems on Affairs of State*, 7 vols (London, 1975), 5: 218; Adam Fox, 'Religious Satire in English Towns', in Patrick Collinson and John Craig, eds, *The Reformation in English Towns, 1500–1640* (Basingstoke, 1998), 221–40, at 235; Chippenham, Wiltshire Heritage Centre, 865/587; Malcolm Jones, 'The Parodic Sermon in Medieval and Early Modern England', *Medium Aevum* 66 (1997), 94–114.

[58] Anon., *A Letter … Concerning the Abuse of Scripture Terms* (London, 1743), quoted in Michael F. Suarez, 'Secular Lessons: Biblical Satire, Parody, Imitation, and Emulation in Eighteenth-Century Chronicles of British Politics', *Age of Johnson* 19 (2009), 69–128, at

ritual in popular consciousness and the degree to which its conduct and meaning were disputed.

Such antics were only one of the ways in which conflicting ideas about baptism led to turbulence in churches during and after the Civil War. Although there were contemporary complaints that most of the congregation left the Sunday service at the start of a baptism, as part of the regular service of public worship it was open to anyone who wished to remain.[59] At a time of civil war and accompanying social unrest, this risked the possibility of interventions from soldiers, unrelated parishioners or strangers less likely to be present at other rites. Sometimes the conduct of the rite itself was at the heart of the dispute. Chaos erupted at Saddington Church in Leicestershire when a parishioner pressurized the rector Bernard Flesher to use the *Directory* for the first time during a baptism. 'Much molested' at the font by one married couple, Flesher had to abandon the baptism until the afternoon.[60] Charges made in July 1644 against Lincolnshire minister Hugh Barcroft refer to an apparent stand-off between Barcroft and 'Captaine Moodies Troope', temporarily in the town, over the lawfulness of Barcroft baptizing with the sign of the cross.[61] In August 1647, assize depositions were taken against Richard Dunwell, clerk, for baptizing with the sign of the cross using the Prayer Book at two churches in York. Three female parishioners testified against him. Ann Bird deposed that she 'tooke notice' of Dunwell's failure to use the *Directory* and told him there and then 'that he would answere it'.[62] The public nature of the rite had facilitated her involvement; no doubt a desire to avoid such scenes encouraged the observed trend towards private baptism. From about 1649 onwards, public baptisms became vulnerable to disruption by Quakers, with two incidents reported in quarter sessions records for Somerset and one in Essex.[63] At Croscombe in

69; idem, 'Mock-Biblical Satire from Medieval to Modern', in Quintero, ed., *Companion*, 525–49, at 525.

59 Ryrie, *Being Protestant*, 333–4.

60 Bodl., WMS, C11, fol. 30^{v}.

61 Hill, 'Royalist Clergy', 44–57.

62 TNA, ASSI 45/2/1, 16 August 1647, nos 80–1.

63 ERO, Q/SBa 2/101, 20 November 1657; Taunton, Somerset Heritage Centre [hereafter: SHC], Q/SR/91/59, 10 September 1655; for the chronology of prosecutions for disrupting church services during the Interregnum, see Fiona McCall, 'Tolerable and Intolerable Local Practices of Religion during the English Interregnum', in Mariëtta

Somerset in July 1653, minister John Whitborne complained that one George Hicks came into the church very irreverently, wearing his hat, and argued loudly concerning his son's baptism. He called for an officer to take Hicks away, but Hicks kept arguing and the congregation was dismissed. There is no specific indication of what the dispute was about.[64]

Baptisms were also disrupted during disputes between clergy over titles to livings in the context of widespread clerical ejections. At Aldenham in Hertfordshire in 1643, the ejected vicar Joseph Soane reportedly waited until after the sermon and the start of the baptism to interrupt his replacement John Gilpin, who was 'kneeling downe to pray' at a font not yet made obsolete by the *Directory*. The violence of Soane and his supporters, including 'many women', halted the baptism.[65] In December 1646, Anthony Lapthorne was forced to baptize in the church porch after having the church doors at Sedgefield in Durham shut against him on two successive Sundays, in a contest with parishioners who wished their existing minister to continue to serve the living.[66]

Similar conflicts within parishes, sometimes even violence, are described in loyalist sources relating to Interregnum religion in the Bodleian Library's John Walker Archive. Such sources, collected in the early eighteenth century, are based on personal memories, oral tradition within families or parishes, and some documentary evidence. As I have argued previously, these were collected with a concern for truthfulness, and not often found to be seriously in error, although they were naturally selective in what they chose to share.[67] They recall the forcible prevention of traditionalist baptisms. The son of curate Philip Goddard, citing legal documents in his possession, related how his father was arrested by soldiers at Durley in Hampshire in 1644 for baptizing with the sign of the cross.[68] Another undated confrontation with soldiers was said to have occurred during a baptism at Barton Blount in Derbyshire, soldiers

van der Tol et al., eds, *Toleration and Religious Freedom in the Early Modern and Contemporary World,* (Oxford, 2021), 57–86, at 75–81.

64 SHC, Q/SR/98/93, 18 February 1658/9.

65 PA, HL/PO/JO/10/1/150, 24 May 1643.

66 PA, HL/PO/JO/10/1/220, 17–31 December 1646.

67 Fiona McCall, *Baal's Priests* (Farnham, 2013), 41–50.

68 Bodl., WMS, C5, fol. 16^{r}.

tearing the leaves of the Book of Common Prayer out of the rector Emmanuel Haywood's combined Prayer Book and Bible.[69] The nephew of John Ferebee, minister of Woodchester in Gloucestershire, described his arrest by Colonel Massey's soldiers while 'at the font baptising a child'. Given the dates of Massey's commands, this probably occurred in 1643–4, before the introduction of the *Directory*.[70] Also described was a failed attempt by one Captain Hitch to arrest the vicar of Childwall in Lancashire, William Lewis, during a private baptism.[71]

'The Protestant Reformation', writes Madeleine Gray, 'was a compromise between the ideas of the more radical reformers and the traditionalism of a large number (possibly a majority) of the population'.[72] The implications of further reformation in the 1640s came as a shock to many ordinary parishioners and clergy. Copies of accusations against clergy within the Walker archive add to the considerable number known to have been denounced for maintaining traditionalist rites, such as Derbyshire rector George Holmes, who used the Book of Common Prayer liturgy and the sign of the cross in baptism 'long after they were abolished'.[73] However, the desire to maintain traditional ways did not just originate with the clergy. Loyalists remembered traditionalist parents being just as forceful as puritans in dictating the terms of their children's baptism. Daniel Whitby recounted how at his wife's baptism in 1642 the incumbent, Mr Strickland, was already demurring at using the liturgy and the sign of the cross, but that her mother, Mrs Margaret Swanton, 'a strict Observer of the Rules of the church' overruled him; in the end he conducted the baptism privately in her house.[74]

After 1645, traditionalists continued to press for baptisms to be performed in the way and by the person they preferred. At Everley in Wiltshire, parishioners were said to have taken their children to neighbouring ministers 'rather than suffer them to be touch't by

[69] Ibid., fol. 83^{v}; presumably the Bible and Book of Common Prayer had been bound together for Haywood's convenience.

[70] Bodl., WMS, C1, fol. 123^{r}; Andrew Warmington, 'Massey [Massie], Sir Edward (1604x9–1674)', *ODNB*, online edn (2004), at: <https://doi.org/10.1093/ref:odnb/18297>, accessed 12 August 2022.

[71] Bodl., WMS, C3, fol. 253^{r}.

[72] Gray, 'Ritual Space', 18.

[73] Bodl., WMS, C5, fol. 52^{r}.

[74] Bodl., WMS, C1, fol. 149^{r}.

the Hands' of the 'illiterate' 'Mechanick', Mr Eastman, a former brasier.[75] At Pontefract in Yorkshire, it was said, the 'Loyal Town', 'mightily disaffected' from Interregnum incumbent Joshua Ferret, took their children to nearby Featherstone and Darrington to be baptized.[76] After his sequestration from Cruwys Morchard in Devon, William Frank arranged for his son-in-law, Jonas Holmes, to serve the living in his stead, but according to Holmes 'his father Frank baptiz'd all the children', probably because Holmes was not then ordained, something that parishioners probably felt crucial for performing baptismal rites.[77] Ejected loyalist clergy who recalled making a meagre income from illicit baptisms included Samuel Forward of Gillingham in Dorset, who 'entertained … now and then at Christenings', and William Seddon in Lancashire, who baptized at the request of loyalists 'according to the antient forms of the church'.[78] This was not without personal risk: 'it gave him sometimes the trouble of musquetiers to guard him into Preston as a Prisoner', but, by the mediation of neighbouring gentry, 'he was soon dismiss'd and returned to his family to recount his hazards'.[79] George Forster at Bolam in Northumberland was similarly said to have been sustained after sequestration by 'the Tokens and presents which he got for Baptisms', but when discovered 'was severely reprimanded' and 'sent to Newcastle to be imprisoned' before being bailed by two friendly JPs.[80]

Legal records provide some evidence of tensions over the use of traditionalist rites. A study of over four thousand records of religious offences tried at assizes, quarter and borough sessions between 1645 and 1660 finds two dozen citations for the use of the Prayer Book, nearly half of them from Yorkshire.[81] The arrests of Seddon and Forster, and the assize prosecution of Richard Dunwell would therefore fit with a greater willingness to prosecute in northern counties,

[75] Bodl., WMS, C8, fol. 163^{v}.
[76] Ibid., fol. 11^{r}.
[77] Ibid., fol. 57^{v}.
[78] Bodl., WMS, C5, fol. 23^{r}.
[79] Bodl., WMS, C2, fol. 217^{v}.
[80] Bodl., WMS, C3, fol. 171^{v}.
[81] For the counties included, see Fiona McCall, '"Breaching the Laws of God and Man": Secular Prosecutions of Religious Offences in the Interregnum Parish, 1645–60', in eadem, ed., *Church and People*, 137–70, at 140. These have been augmented with records from Devonshire, Wiltshire, Staffordshire and Shropshire.

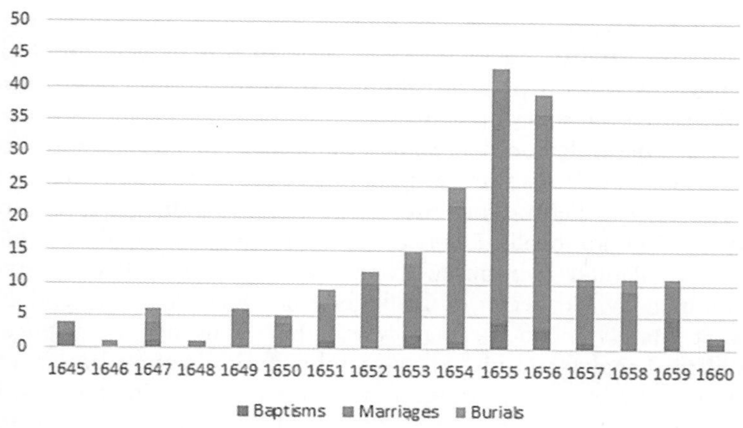

Figure 1. Prosecutions related to rites of passage, 1645–60.

which also had higher rates of clerical sequestration.[82] Out of the whole set of records studied, nearly two hundred cases were found relating to rites of passage, including cases which do not mention the Prayer Book (Figure 1). Cases rise to a clear peak under the Major-Generals (1655–6) before declining. Cases relating to marriage predominate, because permissible practice was clearly defined after 1653 by the Marriage Act, but twenty-one relate to baptism.[83]

Forster was eventually offered a low-valued living where he apparently continued to perform Church of England rites according to the Book of Common Prayer, suggesting the possibility that severity towards traditionalism waned towards the end of the Interregnum.[84] Also undisturbed in a low-valued living was the minister at Slapton in Devon, who, it was said, 'used the service book as often as desired', letting parents decide whether baptism should take place in the basin or the font.[85] On the other hand, continued use of

[82] McCall, *Baal's Priests,* 130–1.
[83] 'August 1653: An Act touching Marriages and the Registring thereof; and also touching Births and Burials', in Firth and Rait, eds, *Acts and Ordinances of the Interregnum,* 715–18, at *British History Online*: <http://www.british-history.ac.uk/no-series/acts-ordinances-interregnum/pp715-718>, accessed 24 November 2022; Christopher Durston, '"Unhallowed Wedlocks"': The Regulation of Marriage during the English Revolution', *HistJ* 31 (1988), 45–59, at 45.
[84] Bodl., WMS, C3, fol. 171^{v}.
[85] Bodl., WMS, C8, fol. 45^{r}.

traditional rites of baptism was still used as grounds to deprive clergy in the late 1650s: Walter Bushnell, vicar of Box in Wiltshire, was charged in 1656 with habitually baptizing using the Prayer Book and making the sign of the cross.[86]

Much depended on the zeal of local puritans to stir up trouble for traditionalists. Wiltshire clergy were subject to renewed attention following the Penruddock Rebellion of 1655; Bushnell, a non-associating traditionalist in a relatively rich living, was an obvious target and blamed Humphrey Chambers, minister at Pewsey, and Adoniram Byfield, rector of Collingbourne Ducis, for his ejection.[87] At St Mary's Lichfield, there was a notorious dispute between William Langley and his colleague John Butler because Butler was found to be baptizing using a false certificate of ordination, but it was Langley who ended up being removed.[88] Robert Bowber, rector of Stockleigh Pomeroy in Devon, was unfortunate that his neighbour was the officious Presbyterian Nathaniel Durant, rector of Cheriton Fitzpaine.[89] Bowber's son related that a 'loyal' 'person of quality', Sebastian Isaac, requested Bowber to baptize his child 'at his house called Combe' using the liturgy and the sign of the cross. The problem was that Isaac's house was in Durant's parish. Durant became 'so incensed against my Father', that he 'fought by all wayes and meanes to turn him out of his place, which at length he effected'.[90] Elizabeth Bentham related how a minister in a nearby living 'complained to Major General Packer' when her husband Samuel Bentham, rector of Knebworth in Hertfordshire, baptized his own son by his first wife, born in 1653, using the Book of Common Prayer rite, 'but

86 Walter Bushnell, *A Narrative of the Proceedings of the Commissioners Appointed by O. Cromwell, for Ejecting Scandalous and Ignorant Ministers* (London, 1660), 3, 13, 25, 87.

87 Ibid., preface, 208.

88 William Langley, *The Persecuted Minister* (London, 1655), 48–70; Bodl., WMS, C3, fols 57^{r}–^{v}; C5, fol. 317^{v}; TNA, SP 18/67, 3 March 1653/4, fol. 30; SP 25/78, 25 May 1658, fol. 633; A. G. Matthews, *Walker Revised* (Oxford, 1648), 324. In this factional struggle, Langley was accused in turn of celebrating Christmas and allowing communions to resume, without ensuring that sufficient mechanisms were in place to hold back the scandalous from receiving. It seems that Butler's faction prevailed, although Langley was approved by the Triers as eligible of holding another living.

89 Durant was particularly active against swearers: see DHC, QS/1/9, 4 October 1653; QS/4/58, Michaelmas 1656.

90 Bodl., WMS, C2, fol. 231^{r}.

by the means of An Lightfoot who had an interest in Packer … was not prosecuted any further'.[91]

The keenest reforming ministers sought to rip fonts out of churches altogether. The royal injunctions of 1561 had prohibited removing the font or using a basin, showing that there was already debate over this issue in the Elizabethan church.[92] By the 1570s, some London churches were baptizing with basins placed near the pulpit, to stress the link between the sacraments and preaching.[93] Following the *Directory*'s ban on using the font in 1645, churchwardens' accounts record fonts being removed in parishes across the country: at St Thomas in Salisbury by order of the committee in April 1647, at Pittington in Durham in 1651, and at St Petrock in Exeter in 1655.[94]

Loyalist narratives challenge the idea that this was always an 'orderly' and consensual process, describing the font as 'torn down' at Modbury in Devon, and other places where the task of removal proved difficult due to unenthusiastic parishioners and the solidity of the workmanship.[95] At Bovey Tracey in Devon, the minister Tucker reportedly tried to dispose of the font with his own hands. He managed to saw halfway through it, 'but being weary, and no one helping him in so ill a work, he was forced to desist, and so it remains half saw'd to this day'.[96] A fifteenth-century font, with a font cover installed around 1660, seemingly in an attempt to restate its importance, survives in the church.[97] At Bedwas in

[91] Bodl., WMS, C2, fol. 97^{v}; Knebworth Baptismal Register, online at: <https://www.ancestrylibraryedition.co.uk/>, accessed 17 September 2021, records the baptism of Samuel Bentham, son of Samuel Bentham, on 19 January 1653.

[92] W. H. Frere and William Paul M. Kennedy, eds, *Visitation Articles and Injunctions of the Period of the Reformation Church of England*, 3 vols (London, 1910), 3: 109.

[93] Kenneth Fincham and Nicholas Tyacke, *Altars Restored* (Oxford, 2007), 48–51.

[94] Henry James Fowle Swayne, *Churchwardens' Accounts of S. Edmund and S. Thomas Sarum 1443–1702* (Salisbury, 1896), 217, probably referring to the parliamentary committee for Wiltshire; James Barmby, ed., *Churchwardens Accounts of Pittington …* , Surtees Society 84 (London, 1888), 304; Robert Dymond, 'The History of the Parish of St. Petrock, Exeter, as shown by its Churchwardens' Accounts and Other Records', *Transactions of the Devonshire Association* 64 (1882), 402–92.

[95] Coster, *Baptism*, 62; Bodl., WMS, C2, fol. 411^{r}.

[96] Ibid., fols 384–6.

[97] Described as 'Usual Octagonal Perp[endicular] type' in Nicholas Pevsner, *The Buildings of England: South Devon* (London, 1952), 56, online at: <https://britishlistedbuildings.co.uk/101334077-church-of-st-peter-and-st-paul-and-st-thomas-of-canterbury-bovey-tracey>, accessed 7 September 2021.

Monmouthshire, it was said that the Anabaptist Watkin Jones, who served the parish, attacked 'a very fine font of stone' and 'when himself and his men cou'd not break it into pieces' used it as a horse and cattle trough.[98] At Carsington in Derbyshire, parishioners remembered that a basin on the side of the pulpit had been used 'after the mode of those times'; the font was removed to the parsonage yard where the incumbent fed his swine, but afterwards returned to the church.[99] With passive resistance to their removal, Fincham and Tyacke are probably right to suggest, on the evidence of the survival of many medieval fonts, that many were left *in situ* and ignored as the cheapest and least controversial option.[100] Some churchwardens' accounts record the introduction of the basin, but not the removal of the font: at Aldeburgh in Suffolk in 1645, at Shepton Mallet in Somerset in 1647–9, and at Hartland in Devon in 1646–7.[101] All three fonts survive.[102] This, combined with the varying dates of font removal elsewhere, suggests that it often needed the personal impetus of active reformists to effect a font's removal, against a backdrop of parochial inertia.

Yet there was more Interregnum font disturbance than font survival might suggest. Some fonts were restored soon after the Restoration, as early as January 1660 at St Thomas's in Salisbury.[103] At Ackworth in Yorkshire, the restored rector Dr Thomas Bradley re-erected the font in 1663 with a Latin inscription attacking the 'bile' of the 'fanatics' who had demolished it.[104] Other surviving fonts have a chequered history, latterly retrieved from all sorts of misappropriations, including being used as wells, sinks and

[98] Bodl., WMS, C4, fol. 66^{v}.
[99] Bodl., WMS, C5, fol. 81^{v}.
[100] Fincham and Tyacke, *Altars Restored*, 281.
[101] Arthur T. Winn, ed., *Records of the Borough of Aldeburgh: The Church* (Hertford, 1926), 50; SHC, D/P/she/4/1/1 1617–1704; I. L. Gregory, ed., *Hartland Church Accounts, 1597–1706* (Frome, 1950), 199.
[102] Church of St Peter and St Paul, Aldeburgh, National Heritage List for England, online at: <https://historicengland.org.uk/listing/the-list/list-entry/1269731?section=official-list-entry>, accessed 24 November 2022; R. W. Cramp, *The Corpus of Anglo-Saxon Stone Sculpture in Britain*, 13 vols (Oxford, 2006), 7: 38; Church of St Nectan, British Listed Buildings, online at: <https://britishlistedbuildings.co.uk/101333125-church-of-st-nectan-hartland#.YhzjFOjP02w>, accessed 24 November 2022.
[103] Swayne, *Churchwardens' Accounts*, 333.
[104] E. Tyrrell-Green, *Baptismal Fonts* (London, 1928), 156.

cisterns, as sundials and for feeding farm animals.[105] A tradition of reverence for redundant fonts against profane uses (or destruction) may perhaps explain how often they have been found in nearby churchyards or gardens, or even in the church itself.[106] If only a minority of parishes removed fonts during the Commonwealth era, where this happened it was as an intentional signal of the new religious order. Loyalists blamed such actions on fanatical factions and depicted the clergy involved as isolated and unpopular.

Interregnum ministers did not help their cause by quibbling about children's rights to receive baptism. There was contemporary debate amongst reformist clergy over the concept of 'believers' baptism', the idea that, for baptism to be effective, the candidate must understand the essentials of the faith it signified.[107] Equally, if baptism were, as the *Directory* implied, not essential for salvation, refusing it now seemed acceptable.[108] Some Independents would only baptize amongst their select congregation: a set of 1660 articles against Henry Butler of Yeovil charge him with denying the sacraments to anyone of 'what quallity soever' not amongst his 'particular' congregation, hindering infants from being baptized for years.[109] Parishioners at St Bartholomew's Exchange in London refused to pay tithes to the curate appointed by the Independent Philip Nye because he refused to 'crissen children … except wee would bee joyned in Communion with his Church'; in twelve months none of the regular congregation had done so.[110]

Sometimes there was rigidity over where and when baptism could take place. A set of 1660 articles against Richard Herring at

105 Francis Bond, *Fonts and Font Covers* (Oxford, 1908), 275–9; Tyrrell-Green, *Baptismal Fonts*, 39–42.

106 David Stocker, '*Fons et Origo*: The Symbolic Death, Burial and Resurrection of English Font Stones', *Church Archaeology* 1 (1997), 17–25; Tyrrell-Green, *Baptismal Fonts*, 39–40.

107 Rachel Adcock, 'Believers' Baptism, Commemoration and Communal Identity in Revolutionary England', in Alexandra Walsham et al., eds, *Memory and the English Reformation* (Cambridge, 2020), 388–402.

108 *Directory*, 20–1.

109 SHC, DD/PH/221/56, Articles against Henry Butler, 'Pretended' Vicar of Yeovil, 1660; Crawford Gribben, 'Defining the Puritans? The Baptism Debate in Cromwellian Ireland, 1654–56', *ChH* 73 (2004), 63–89, at 83, 85.

110 Cross, *Church and People*, 217; Edwin Freshfield, ed., *The Vestry Minute Books of the Parish of St. Bartholomew Exchange in the City of London: 1567–1676* (London, 1890), xxxii.

Drewsteignton in Devon, copied in the Walker archive, claim that he refused to baptize except on Sunday afternoons, forcing parishioners to 'repaire to strangers (much to theire greife)'.[111] The diary of Philip Henry records, in November 1658, his unease over a private baptism which he conducted reluctantly when the father was absent and the mother lying-in.[112] Francis Drake's account characterized Mr Walker, minister at Wakefield, as 'a very Rigid man' in religious practice. He refused to baptize even sick children, Drake said, 'unless brought to Church', leading to an exchange of letters with a Mr Rogers over his refusal to baptize his sick child, but 'Mr. Rogers got the better of him', pleading necessity in this case of private baptism. Another parishioner, Drake recalled, had a seven weeks premature child, 'weak, but yet alive', and 'besought' Walker to christen it; Walker refused unless it was taken to the church. The father warned him that in bad weather this would hazard the child's life; if it died 'the Child's blood should lye at his Door'. The child died while being carried over the church stile.[113]

At Ottery St Mary in Devon, the incumbent Mr Tuchin apparently set public interrogations for the parents, causing a dispute that was just as devastating for the family concerned. According to local people, gentleman Mr Nicholas Haydon brought his child to be baptized. Tuchin first asked Haydon to give a demonstration of his faith before the congregation. This was not unusual in the Reformed churches of Europe, but evidently unfamiliar to Haydon who, apparently not quite able to understand the question, replied that 'several Articles of my faith are indemonstrable, as the Doctrine of the Trinity the Incarnation'.[114] Haydon's answer being deemed unsatisfactory, the child was brought home unbaptized, the trauma of which was blamed for the death of Haydon's wife soon after.[115]

The baptizing of children born out of wedlock had previously been encouraged by the Church of England. Even Calvin had been willing to baptize infants of the wicked and the idolatrous, as long as faith still

[111] Bodl., WMS, C4, fol. 166^{v}.
[112] Philip Henry, *Diaries and Letters of Philip Henry*, ed. Mathew Henry Lee (London, 1882), 42–3, 64–5.
[113] Bodl., WMS, C8, fol. 87^{v}.
[114] Hannah Cleugh, 'Teaching in Praying Words? Worship and Theology in the Early Modern English Parish', in Mears and Ryrie, eds, *Worship*, 11–30, at 18.
[115] Bodl., WMS, C2, fol. 246^{r}.

existed within the community: the parents were reproved, and there were sponsors to vouch for the children. But others thought differently and, in England, this now became a contentious issue.[116] In an extraordinary story related by John Walker's correspondent John Kemble, it was said that neighbours, out of charity, brought an illegitimate child to be baptized by the minister at Minchinhampton in Gloucestershire, Mr Herne. He 'made a scruple to baptise it, but at last took up water in his hand, and basely struck the child in the face, and with Invocation of the Blessed Trinity baptized it Whoresbrat', seemingly in echo of the use of exorcism in the older Catholic rite.[117] In November 1652, John Lake, then minister at Oldham in Lancashire, was removed by the Manchester Presbyterian classis. The charges against him included baptizing 'bastards' from his own and other congregations, including a 'child begotten in adultery' without the parents' 'giving satisfaccion' to the congregation, 'very much' discouraging the 'harts of the Godly'. Lake, later a bishop, defended his actions, saying 'Christ is all in all', and that 'not only bastards but children of heathens and excommunicated persons' should be baptized.[118] Legal cases relating to Interregnum clergy restricting baptism include a Cheshire minister, John Brereton, who in 1653 refused to baptize the child of a woman accused of adultery.[119] In Staffordshire in 1659, two ministers were accused of refusing to baptize 'natural' sons, one also being quoted as saying 'it is not lawfull to baptise Children'.[120]

Parishioners sometimes acted against what they perceived as poor service provision. Complaints were made to the Sussex quarter sessions in October 1653 that the minister of Heyshott, Richard Garret, refused to 'execute the function of minister' in baptizing

[116] Cressy, *Birth, Marriage, and Death*, 104–5, cites parish records registering the baptism of illegitimate children, and cases of ministers or parents threatened with punishment for failure to perform the rite, dating from the 1570s to the 1620s; see also G. W. Bromiley, 'The Elizabethan Puritans and Indiscriminate Baptism', *The Churchman* 62 (1948), 30–3, citing the arguments of Archbishop John Whitgift (1530–1604) and Richard Hooker (1554–1600).

[117] Bodl., WMS, C7, fol. 36r; French, 'Disputed Words', 161.

[118] William A. Shaw, *Minutes of the Manchester Presbyterian Classis*, 3: *1646–60*, Chetham Society n.s. 24 (Manchester, 1891), 386–9.

[119] Chester, Cheshire Archives, QJF 81/2, Trinity 1653, fol. 283; QJF 81/3, Michaelmas 1653, fol. 14.

[120] Stafford, Staffordshire Record Office, Q/SR/308/6, 22 May 1659; Q/SR/306/57, 10 July 1659.

the children of the parish.[121] According to the 'ancient inhabitants' at High Halden in Kent, 'one Web … refused to Baptize Children saying he was sent to preach, not to Baptize', but was removed after a petition to the authorities.[122] In November 1658, Judge Wyndham reportedly pronounced to a Western Circuit assize jury that they should pay ministers who refused to baptize only the minimum 'agreeable to the Law'.[123]

What should we conclude from the conflicts over rites of passage discussed here? Loyalist accounts express the outraged sensibilities of traditionalists towards the new ritual practices of the 1640s and 1650s. They do not suggest that traditional rites carried on blithely through the Interregnum but that, given the virulence of reformist opposition to them from the early 1640s onwards, they often required evasive tactics to proceed. If authorities rarely sanctioned the gentry involved, for the clergy it was a different matter. They might be arrested and potentially lose their livings, but this simply left a large necessitous cohort of ejected clergy willing to meet the demand. Baptism was a rite at the centre of mid-seventeenth-century people's experience and consciousness. It provoked strong emotions and disagreement in its every aspect: where and when it should take place; the conduct, form and meaning of the ceremony; and who should be baptized. The reduced incidence of baptism and the rise of private baptism during this period may have been influenced, at least in part, by a desire to avoid such controversies.[124] Ministerial rigidity over the issue is depicted in loyalist accounts as counter-productive. So was the *Directory*'s emphasis on masculine authority: loyalist accounts and other sources tell stories of women's active desire for involvement in a rite reframed to exclude them, hardly surprising given women's role in childbirth. Private baptism facilitated this. With legal processes disrupted by civil war, many of the earlier confrontations described by loyalists went unrecorded elsewhere. As legal record-keeping recovered after 1645, some clergy were prosecuted for performing Prayer Book rites, although more usually for solemnizing illicit marriages. Faced with acute sensitivities and earlier clashes over baptisms or burials, authorities rarely chose to inflame tensions

121 Chichester, West Sussex Record Office, QR/78, 1 October 1653, no. 6.
122 Bodl., WMS, C1, fol. 386^{r}.
123 TNA, SP 18/183, 25 November 1658, fol. 235.
124 Kitson, 'Religious Change', 275, 279–80.

further by resorting to formal prosecution, which were of doubtful legality in any case after the Instrument of Government of December 1653 abrogated the legal requirement to use the *Directory*.[125] None of the recorded prosecutions after 1656 cite the use of the Prayer Book for rites of passage. Yet rites of passage remained a sensitive issue, and a grumbling focus of local antagonism.

[125] William Sheppard, *A View of All the Laws and Statutes of this Nation Concerning the Service of God or Religion* (London, 1655), 22; Nancy L. Mathews, *Cromwell's Law Reformer* (Cambridge, 1984), 117.

Wedding Sermons in Early Modern England

Ralph Houlbrooke*
University of Reading

This article draws on wedding sermons published in England between the 1580s and the 1740s. The main interest of these sermons lies in the ways in which doctrine based on the scriptural texts, especially those cited in the Form of Solemnization of Matrimony, was refracted through the prism of the various concerns and priorities of preaching clergy. Their exposition of marriage duties was often enriched by personal experience. Yet the number of wedding sermons published in England between the 1580s and the 1740s was small compared with the quantity of those reaching print after delivery at a funeral, another of the foremost rites of passage. It seems likely that many fewer of them were preached at weddings in the first place. Wedding congregations probably made a less receptive audience. The already limited publication of wedding sermons underwent a long-term eighteenth-century decline.

Early modern English sermons have been the subject of much recent research. Prominent topics of this research have included those sermons' themes, delivery, audiences and role in promoting religious change. Sermons preached at court, before parliament, in the universities and parishes, on anniversaries and festival days, and during assizes, fasts and funerals, have all been discussed.[1] Little attention has, however, been given to wedding sermons.[2] This article is based

* Department of History, School of Humanities, University of Reading, PO Box 217, Reading, RG6 6AH. E-mail: r.a.houlbrooke@reading.ac.uk.

[1] See especially Peter McCullough, Hugh Adlington and Emma Rhatigan, eds, *The Oxford Handbook of the Early Modern Sermon* (Oxford, 2011); Lori Anne Ferrell and Peter McCullough, eds, *The English Sermon Revised: Religion, Literature and History 1600–1750* (Manchester, 2000); Arnold Hunt, *The Art of Hearing: English Preachers and their Audiences, 1590–1640* (Cambridge, 2010); Peter McCullough, *Sermons at Court: Politics and Religion in Elizabethan and Jacobean Preaching* (Cambridge, 1998); Mary Morrissey, *Politics and the Paul's Cross Sermons, 1558–1642* (Oxford, 2011).

[2] But see Jacqueline Eales, 'Gender Construction in Early Modern England and the Conduct Books of William Whately (1583–1639)', in R. N. Swanson, ed., *Gender and Christian Religion*, SCH 34 (Cambridge, 1998), 163–74; Erica Longfellow, '"the office of a man and

Studies in Church History 59 (2023), 222–243
doi: 10.1017/stc.2023.10

on some forty wedding sermons published between the 1580s and the 1740s. Occasioned by actual weddings, they were the ones most readily identifiable by means of a title search. The majority purported to be versions of what had been preached at the wedding itself, soon afterwards, or in one case at a contract beforehand.[3] Some sermons celebrating royal weddings have been included. The article will first examine the relationship between the wedding sermon and the nuptial rites. It will then consider the preachers of wedding sermons and their motives for publishing such sermons. Analysis of the content of sermons will show that despite most preachers' consensus with regard to fundamental doctrines of marriage, individual differences of approach, theme and emphasis introduced considerable variety as well as changes over time. A tentative explanation of the relative paucity in numbers of surviving sermons will be offered.

The Wedding Sermon and the Marriage Service

The principal source text for the Form of Solemnization of Matrimony in the 1549 Book of Common Prayer was the *Ordo ad faciendum sponsalia* according to the use of Sarum, the most widely employed marriage rite in late medieval England. The partners' mutual commitment to lifelong love, honour and support, with the wife's pledge of obedience, had been signified by the response '*volo*' ('I will'), to the officiant's question (in Latin in the published version of the rite, but presumably spoken in English in practice). The words of trothplight, 'I N. take thee N … and thereto I geve thee my trouth', had been in English in the earlier rite, with only minor differences in wording. So too had been the man's placing of the ring on the woman's left hand accompanied by his affirmation that he worshipped her with his body and endowed her with all his worldly goods. One of two alternative psalms included in the Prayer Book, Psalm 128, also came from the pre-Reformation service. It promises the God-fearing man that his wife shall be like a fruitful

wife" in John Donne's Marriage Sermons', *John Donne Journal* 29 (2010), 17–32; Robert Matz, ed., *Two Early Modern Marriage Sermons: Henry Smith's* A Preparative to Marriage *(1591) and William Whately's* A Bride-Bush *(1623)* (Abingdon, 2016).

[3] Henry Smith, *A Preparatiue to Mariage. The Summe whereof was spoken at a contract, and inlarged after* (London, 1591), 1–2.

vine and his children like olive branches. Several prayers came from the Sarum rite. One, shortly before the close of the new service, conveyed a warning that that it would never be lawful to put asunder those whom God had made one by matrimony.[4]

In the new service Thomas Cranmer rearranged and added to the materials taken from the Sarum rite. A notable addition was the celebrant's preliminary reminder of the origin, nature and purposes of holy matrimony. It was an honourable estate instituted by God in paradise, and signified the mystical union between Christ and his church (as the sacramental blessing in the nuptial mass had declared). Christ adorned it with his presence at Cana, where he performed his first miracle. It was not to be undertaken lightly, but in the fear of God. It had been ordained for three causes: the procreation of children, as a remedy against sin and (as is implicit in the pledges exchanged by the marriage partners before and after the Reformation) for the partners' mutual society, help and comfort in prosperity and adversity.[5]

The Sarum marriage rite did not include a sermon. The Augustinian canon John Mirk, a prolific author of sermons, described in his *Sermo de nupciis*, probably in the later 1380s, the creation of marriage in paradise by the Holy Trinity, whose votive mass was celebrated at weddings. Mirk's sermon is largely a commentary on the marriage rite, with anecdotal warnings against adultery.[6] A different account of marriage appears in *Dives and Pauper*, an early fifteenth-century treatise on the Ten Commandments, probably written by a Franciscan friar. It represented the sacrament of unity and endless love between God and man, between Christ and Holy Church, between Christ and the Christian soul. Following Paul, the author wrote that every man should love his wife as himself; women must be subject to their husbands as the church is to Christ. God made Eve of Adam's rib because that was next to his heart; not of his

[4] *Manuale ad vsum percelebris ecclesie Sarisburiensis* (Rouen, 1543), fols xlvii^{r}–lvi^{r}; F. E. Brightman, *The English Rite*, 2 vols (London, 1915), 2: 802–13; Eric Josef Carlson, *Marriage and the English Reformation* (Oxford, 1994), 44–6; David Cressy, *Birth, Marriage, and Death: Ritual, Religion, and the Life-Cycle in Tudor and Stuart England* (Oxford, 1997), 336–47.

[5] Brian Cummings, ed., *The Book of Common Prayer: The Texts of 1549, 1559, and 1662* (Oxford, 2011), 64, 157, 434–5.

[6] Susan Powell, ed., *John Mirk's Festial, edited from British Library MS Cotton Claudius A.II*, 2 vols, EETS original series 334–5 (Oxford, 2009, 2011), 2: 252–6, 442–8.

foot to be his thrall, nor of his head to be his master, but to be his fellow and helper.[7]

The first three Prayer Books of 1549, 1552 and 1559 envisaged that a sermon declaring 'the office of man and wife' would normally be included in a communion service immediately following the celebration of marriage. There is scant evidence to show how widespread nuptial communions were in practice. According to one observer 'This custome was [rarely] used, by the better sort of people before the Civill warrs'.[8] The 1662 book merely declared it convenient that the couple should receive communion when they were married or at the first subsequent opportunity, but still allowed for the possibility that there might be a sermon.[9] It seems quite likely, but is impossible to demonstrate, that sermons were sometimes preached without a communion, even when communion was compulsory in principle.

If there were no sermon, the minister was to read prescribed passages from the epistles of the apostles Paul and Peter setting out the most important duties of husbands and wives. The husband's obligations came first. St Paul had commanded them to love their wives as Christ loved the church; 'So ought men to love their wives as their own bodies'. For this cause a man was to leave his parents, and be joined to his wife, and they would become one flesh (Eph. 5: 25–33). Husbands were forbidden to be bitter towards their wives (Col. 3: 19). St Peter, himself a married man, had told married men to dwell with their wives 'according to knowledge', that is, understanding, giving honour to the wife as to the weaker vessel, and as heirs together of the grace of life, that is, their shared Christian life (1 Pet. 3: 7). For their part, wives were to submit to their husbands as to the Lord; they were to be subject to their own husbands in all things (Eph. 5: 22–4; Col. 3: 18). Husbands who did not obey the word, St Peter had added, might be won by their wives' chaste behaviour and fear (or reverence). He reminded them that their ornament should be that of a meek and quiet spirit, not outward adornment (1 Pet. 3: 1–6).

[7] Priscilla Heath Barnum, ed., *Dives and Pauper*, vol. 1/2, EETS original series 280 (Oxford, 1980), 60–2, 65–6.

[8] John Aubrey, *Remaines of Gentilisme and Judaisme*, in idem, *Three Prose Works*, ed. John Buchanan-Brown (Fontwell, 1972), 127–304, at 185.

[9] Cummings, ed., *Book of Common Prayer*, 69–71, 162–4, 440–1.

The work of official marriage guidance that reached the largest audience in early modern England may have been 'An Homily of the State of Matrimony' (1563). It was included in the second volume of *Sermons or Homilies* primarily intended for non-preaching clergy to read to their congregations.[10] Most of it consisted of loose translations of passages from an exhortation by the preacher Veit Dietrich of Nuremberg (1506–49) and St John Chrysostom's twenty-sixth homily on 1 Corinthians.[11] Passages from Dietrich sought to arm couples against the devil's 'principal craft, to work dissension of hearts of the one from the other'. There were few marriages without 'chidings, brawlings, tauntings, repentings, bitter cursings, and fightings'. The husband 'ought to be the leader and author of love', making allowances for the wife's weakness. It was hard for women to 'relinquish the liberty of their own rule'. Nevertheless, Chrysostom had insisted, they must obey even harsh husbands, and resist the temptation to remind those husbands of their duty to them. A wife might even have to endure being beaten, although Chrysostom had absolutely forbidden husbands to beat their wives. The worst of wives were to be 'admonished and holpen' but also treated with forbearance. Prayer was the best remedy for all the trials of marriage.[12]

The official provision for sermons to be preached at English weddings helps to explain the first print publication of such sermons in the late sixteenth century. They formed part of a burgeoning literature of pastoral advice for a lay readership concerning 'Domesticall Duties'.[13] Broadly speaking, historians have subscribed to one of four views, or a combination of them, about the nature and effect of this literature. Some have stressed what they see as its enhanced appreciation of marriage, including sexual fulfilment, compared with pre-Reformation teaching; others have emphasized its patriarchal character and its promotion of the authority of husbands and fathers. A third view underlines the continuity of the most important elements of advice through the Reformation, while a fourth, although

[10] Ashley Null, 'Official Tudor Homilies', in McCullough, Adlington and Rhatigan, eds, *Oxford Handbook of the Early Modern Sermon*, 348–65, at 359–60; Cummings, ed., *Book of Common Prayer,* 683.

[11] John Griffiths, ed., *The Two Books of Homilies Appointed to be read in Churches* (Oxford, 1859), xxxvi–xxxviii, 500, 506.

[12] Ibid. 500–15.

[13] William Gouge, *Of Domesticall Duties eight treatises* (London, 1622).

conceding substantial continuity of ideals, emphasizes important differences between pre-Reformation and Protestant writing. The sixteenth-century Protestant reformers inherited and developed an ideal of marriage that combined husbandly authority with love and close companionship. They also made Scripture the foundation of their teaching to an extent unequalled in medieval guidance. They brought to bear in their advice to the laity the lessons of their own experience of marriage, now open to the clergy through the abolition of compulsory priestly celibacy. They addressed the problems of marriage in greater detail and more exhaustively than had previous writers.[14]

Preachers and Publication

The wedding sermon was never the preserve of men who belonged to a particular position on the religious spectrum. Between the 1580s and the civil wars, wedding preachers included both distinguished conformists and notable puritans. Among the former were men favoured by James I, royal connoisseur of sermons, such as Robert Abbot, John King, Anthony Maxey and Robert Wilkinson.[15] The most famous of these preachers was John Donne, the author of three surviving wedding sermons. His exceptional distinction has ensured his wedding sermons a large share of scholarly attention. They were however atypical of the genre. A penetrating analysis has shown how Donne equivocated, adopted a tone of dry irony, largely evaded some questions customarily posed in wedding sermons, and used humour to offset potentially unpalatable advice.[16] Puritan authors included Henry Smith and William Whately, whose wedding sermons, greatly expanded in their published form, became famous and oft-reprinted works of marriage guidance, as well as William Crompton, Thomas Gataker and Thomas Taylor.

Some of the better known authors of sermons printed after 1650, Nathaniel Hardy, Richard Meggot and William Secker, published

[14] Kathleen M. Davies, 'Continuity and Change in Literary Advice on Marriage', in R. B. Outhwaite, ed., *Marriage and Society: Studies in the Social History of Marriage* (London, 1981), 58–80; Eales, 'Gender Construction', 164–6; Matz, ed., *Two Early Modern Marriage Sermons*, 'Introduction', 1–14.

[15] McCullough, *Sermons at Court*, 7, 106, 117, 124, 128, 130, 138, 192, 210–11.

[16] Longfellow, 'Donne's Marriage Sermons', 17–32.

their work during the Interregnum, but made successful careers in the Restoration church. However, few clergy of the established church published wedding sermons between 1660 and 1750; they were not well-known preachers. Nonconformist wedding preachers included Benjamin Aycrigg, William Harris, Thomas Manton and John Shuttlewood. The great majority of Nonconformists, save for the Quakers, complied with the legal requirement that marriages be celebrated by a minister of the established church.[17] Some Anglican clergy may have been prepared to allow Dissenting colleagues to preach at a wedding celebrated in their churches. Alternatively, a sermon could have been preached after the marriage had taken place.

It was presumably one or more of the couple's 'friends', including parents, or perhaps in some cases the couple themselves, who typically decided whether a sermon should be given and, if so, who should deliver it. Sermons were often preached from notes and might then be written out in full.[18] After Matthew Lawrence had preached at the wedding of Sir William Armyne's son at Chilton (Suffolk) in August 1649, Sir William, Lawrence's 'Singular good Friend, and Patron', asked to see his notes. Instead Lawrence had his sermon beautifully written and decorated in imitation of a printed book by a professional scribe, and dedicated it to Sir William.[19] Some of the wedding sermons that survive in print, including those delivered by John Donne, never got beyond the stage of private manuscript circulation during their authors' lifetimes, and were published posthumously, either for profit or in tribute to their authors. There was a widespread reluctance on the part of preachers to embrace print until the early seventeenth century.[20]

The titles or dedications of roughly sixty per cent of the wedding sermons in print identify the couple whose nuptials had occasioned their preaching. Besides members of the royal family, most of the partners belonged to the gentry or, in a few cases, to London merchant families. Sermons that their authors designed or adapted for

[17] Rebecca Probert, *Marriage Law and Practice in the Long Eighteenth Century: A Reassessment* (Cambridge, 2009), 145–51, 160; John Shuttlewood, *Marriages Made in Heav'n: A Wedding Sermon*, 2nd edn (London, 1712), 7.
[18] Hunt, *Art of Hearing*, 133–4; Morrissey, *Paul's Cross Sermons*, 36–8.
[19] Los Angeles, UCLA William Andrews Clark Memorial Library, MS 1951.018, fols ix–x, online at: <http://www.calisphere.org/item/ark:/21198/n14g8t/>, accessed 22 July 2022; compare also Hunt, *Art of Hearing*, 135–7.
[20] Hunt, *Art of Hearing*, 120–6.

a larger audience were less likely to convey such information. Several of the prefatory epistles that precede the majority of printed wedding sermons were addressed to the couple at whose marriage the sermon had been preached, a partner in the marriage or a close relative of one spouse, as in the case of Sir William Armyne. A few were addressed to other couples known to the preacher in recognition of their happy or exemplary marriages. Occasionally the author chose one or more of his own relatives. An actual or potential patron of his might belong to any of these categories. A few were simply addressed to the 'Christian reader' or the 'courteous reader'. Publication seems to have been due to the preacher's initiative in the majority of cases. Some authors attributed it to a request from a patron or one of the couple concerned, or to importunate friends.[21]

Few authors indicated clearly how they had altered the text of their sermon between original composition and publication.[22] Some clearly added new material. Henry Smith's tract *A Preparatiue to Mariage* (1591) was explicitly described as having been 'inlarged' after first delivery. William Whately claimed in a preface to the first authorized version of his *Bride-Bvsh* (1619) that he had given a copy to a friend, and found it published the previous year without his privity. 'Hence I was occasioned', he continued, 'to peruse certaine larger notes, which I had lying by me of that subiect'.[23] As a result he produced a treatise four times as long as the sermon published in 1617. Smith's and Whately's works had expanded from sermons into what we would regard as larger tracts. Even in the first surviving version of his *Bride-Bvsh,* published without his privity but already designed for a wider readership, Whately wrote that he would have preferred to preach without a text: 'No one place of Scripture doth either directly containe, or plainly expresse the full dutie of the married couple: which yet from many places may well bee collected into

21 William Secker, *A Wedding Ring Fit for the Finger: Or, the Salve of Divinity on the sore of Humanity. Laid open in a Sermon at a Wedding in Edmonton* (London, 1658), 6–7; Richard Meggot, *The Rib Restored: or, The Honour of Marriage, A Sermon Preached in Dionis-Back-Church, occasioned by a Wedding* (London, 1656), sigs A2^{r}–^{v}.

22 See Hunt, *Art of Hearing*, 147–63, 'Revising the Sermon'.

23 William Whately, *A Bride-Bvsh: or, A Direction for Married Persons. Plainely describing the Dvties Common to both, and peculiar to each of them. By performing of which, marriage shall prooue a great helpe to such, as now for want of performing them, doe finde it a little hell* (London, 1619), sig. A1^{r}.

the body of one discourse.'[24] Given the wedding preacher's brief to declare 'the office of a man and wife', it is difficult to draw a hard and fast distinction between wedding sermons and other forms of marriage guidance.[25] A chosen text nevertheless allowed preachers to focus on a particular aspect of the subject.

The majority of printed wedding sermons had probably undergone some revision or elaboration between delivery and publication. Some of them were nevertheless short enough to have been delivered during the hour that was an acceptable duration for an early modern sermon.[26] In 1658, William Secker could claim that what his *A Wedding Ring* had been in preaching, so it was in publishing. Nothing had been added to it. The first edition of 1658 was 'Printed for the Authour, onely to be disposed of to his friends.' Secker's was one of the pithiest yet most comprehensive of wedding sermons, and this no doubt helps to explain why it was frequently reprinted in England, Scotland and North America, and translated into Welsh and German, while most wedding sermons were printed only once or twice.[27]

Defence of Marriage

Early modern wedding sermons most commonly followed the pattern approved by the celebrated preacher William Perkins: the explication of the chosen text, the extraction from it of 'a few and profitable points of doctrine' and their application to the 'life and manners' of his audience.[28] Authors cited in their sermons several additional scriptural texts that reinforced the doctrines educed from the verse or passage on which the sermon had been preached, and usually referred to other authorities, which might include medieval and contemporary writers as well as fathers of the church. Many preachers,

[24] William Whately, *A Bride-Bvsh, or A Wedding Sermon: Compendiously describing the duties of Married Persons* (London, 1617), sig. A3.

[25] Compare Hunt, *Art of Hearing*, 161.

[26] Ibid. 157; Morrissey, *Paul's Cross Sermons*, 36.

[27] Secker, *Wedding Ring*, 6; H. R. French, 'Secker, William (d. 1681?)', *ODNB*, online edn (2004), at: <https://www.oxforddnb.com/view/10.1093/>, accessed 20 September 2021; see also an eighteenth-century miscellany, *Conjugal Duty: set forth in a Collection of Ingenious and Delightful Wedding-Sermons*, 2 vols (London, 1732, 1736), 1: 33–50.

[28] Greg Kneidel, '*Ars Praedicandi:* Theories and Practice', in McCullough, Adlington and Rhatigan, eds, *Oxford Handbook of the Early Modern Sermon*, 3–20, at 13–16.

more especially in the early seventeenth century, also delighted in simile, metaphor and allegory as means of enlivening their sermons and holding their hearers' attention.

Wedding preachers drew both on passages suggested by the *Form of Solemnization* and ones found elsewhere in both testaments. The account of marriage duties in Ephesians 5, the description of marriage as honourable in Hebrews 13: 4, the narrative of Eve's creation in Genesis 2, the report of Christ's first miracle at Cana in John 2, and Psalm 128, with its comparison between the wife of the God-fearing man and the fruitful vine, were all employed by more than one preacher. So too was the praise of the good wife in Proverbs 31: 10–31. The *Form of Solemnization* instructed preachers to declare 'the office of man and wife'. Besides the duties of spouses two recurrent themes of wedding sermons from the sixteenth century to the eighteenth were the defence of marriage as an institution and the criteria held to be important in the choice of marriage partners.

The defence of marriage was especially important for the Protestant clergy, many of whom were married. Some preachers did not simply rely on the highly positive scriptural passages cited in the marriage service but addressed the more mixed messages sent by St Paul in 1 Corinthians 7, where in verse 8 he advised the unmarried and widows to remain celibate, as he himself was.[29] A broad consensus emerged. It was right for most men to marry, but also good for those with the special gift of continence to remain single. Celibacy was appropriate for some men, but marriage was necessary for society, of which it was the essential basis.[30] Throughout the period, preachers rejected the Roman Catholic Church's insistence on clerical celibacy. To forbid marriage was, as described in 1 Timothy 4, a doctrine of devils. It was also hypocritical, as the same passage claimed. Many of the Roman clergy could not contain themselves.[31] Nonetheless,

[29] For example, Meggot, *Rib Restored*, 7–8; Edward Creffield, *A good Wife a great Blessing: or, the Honour and Happiness of the Marriage State in Two Sermons* (London, 1717?), 15–18.
[30] See Secker, *Wedding Ring*, 17–25, for a particularly well-balanced discussion; John King, *Vitis Palatina. A Sermon appointed to be preached at Whitehall vpon the Tuesday after the mariage of the Ladie Elizabeth her Grace* (London, 1614), 3–8.
[31] Smith, *Preparatiue to Mariage*, 15–17; Thomas Taylor, *A Good Hvsband and a Good Wife: Layd Open* (London, 1625), 7; Samuel Wright, *A Sermon on Marriage Preached at Black-Fryers* (London, 1734), 16–19.

John Donne insisted, the Roman Church injured the Church of England in saying that the latter preferred marriage to virginity.[32]

From the later seventeenth century, some felt it necessary to defend marriage in the face of a different challenge: a devaluation of the institution and its obligations. Joseph Fisher identified some causes of that devaluation in a sermon that he dedicated to his friend and former pupil Thomas Lambard. In that profane and profligate age, Fisher claimed, men generally clamoured against God's institutions on the ground of reason among other things. He specifically mentioned 'Audacious and Ungodly Dealers with the Word of God' (i.e. authors of controversial works of biblical exegesis). 'The trifling and jesting humour that prevails in talking of this Subject', the Presbyterian Samuel Wright thought in 1734, 'has often prov'd the reason of keeping it out of religious Discourses'. A few years later Thomas Humphreys, vicar of Driffield (Gloucestershire), held a similar opinion. The dignity of marriage had been more depreciated and vilified in the past century than in any previous age. It had shared this fate with the most excellent and worthy things, 'to be burlesqu'd and droll'd upon by a set of empty fops and profane debauchees'.[33]

Humphreys differed from earlier wedding preachers in the extent to which he relied on rational and utilitarian arguments. After emphasizing in conventional fashion that God himself had instituted marriage, he described how it had been practised all over the habitable world by people of different religions. Its 'mighty usefulness' had been apparent even to the unenlightened part of mankind who had no positive command from God. He also gave a new prominence to the value of marriage in promoting individual happiness. It contributed to everything desirable in life, including health, wealth, credit and pleasure. He pictured the delights of a union in which the

[32] John Donne, 'Number 17, Preached at Sir Francis Nethersole's Marriage', in *The Sermons of John Donne,* ed. G. R. Potter and E. M. Simpson, 10 vols (Berkeley and Los Angeles, CA, 1953–62), 2: 335–47, at 340.

[33] Joseph Fisher, *The Honour of Marriage: or, the Institution, Necessity, Advantages, Comforts, and Usefulness of a Married Life: Set forth in a Sermon January 27. 1694 at Seven-Oak in Kent* (London, 1695), sigs A2^{r}–A3^{v}, 1, 15; Wright, *Sermon on Marriage*, 4; Thomas Humphreys, *Marriage an honourable estate. A Sermon preached at Driffield in Gloucestershire on Occasion of the Happy Marriage of Gabriel Hanger Esq and Mrs Elizabeth Bond* (London, 1742), 3. For further light on the context, see David Fletcher, 'The Clergy and Marriage in Restoration Comedies', in Caroline Bowden, Emily Vine and Tessa Whitehouse, eds, *Religion and Life Cycles in Early Modern England* (Manchester, 2021), 154–72.

partners 'interchangeably express undissembled kindness, and by a frank and honest comportment, adjust themselves to each other in the most tender, obliging, though familiar manner. They reciprocally impart their pleasing ideas, transfuse their satisfactions into each others [*sic*] souls, exchange their joys and divide their griefs.'[34] The marriage pictured by Humphreys is more intimately companionate and closer to equality between the spouses than that presented by any other wedding preacher.

Choice of Marriage Partners

The right choice of partner was the first prerequisite of a good marriage. Shared religious belief was a fundamental criterion. Some preachers had in mind piety contrasted with profanity or indifference, others more specifically a sincere adherence to Protestantism. William Massie delivered the sermon at the marriage of a daughter of Sir Edmond Trafford in the notoriously conservative county of Lancashire in 1586. He emphasized that the husband must fear God and serve him aright, and have a right and righteous faith. Massie would have both partners Protestants, whose sound religion was not that of a Jew, a Turk or a superstitious papist. He went on to describe the essential points of sound religion. The epistle dedicatory described how Sir Edmond, Massie's 'very good patrone', had been a principal protector of God's truth, and had hunted out Jesuits and seminary priests to the uttermost of his power.[35] In 1607, Robert Abbot, elder brother of the future archbishop, preached at the wedding of Sir John Stanhope, son of his patron of the same name and rank. Answering Amos 3: 3, 'Can two walk together except they be agreed?', he asserted the need to walk according to the will and law of God as revealed in Scripture; on the path chalked out for us by the apostles and prophets, 'we neither find the Pope, nor his pardons, nor his masse, nor his images, nor his reliques'.[36] The development of divisions within Protestant ranks attracted

34 Humphreys, *Marriage an honourable estate*, 6–7, 10–19.

35 William Massie, *A Sermon Preached at Trafford in Lancashire at the Marriage of a Daughter of the Right Worshipfull Sir Edmond Trafforde Knight the 6 of September Anno 1586* (Oxford, 1586), sigs A2^{r}–^{v}.

36 Robert Abbot, *A Wedding Sermon preached at Bentley in Darby-shire, vpon Michaelmasse day last past Anno Domini, 1607* (London, 1608), 12–13.

comparatively little comment in marriage sermons. However, Richard Meggot, who was later to be a staunch defender of the Church of England, felt it especially appropriate to emphasize the importance of religious compatibility in view of the divisions, schism and factions then so evident in England, in a sermon he preached in 1655.[37] Edward Creffield may have thought that some Protestant Dissenters belonged in the category of 'Heterodox or Schismaticall' when around 1717 he alluded to the dangers arising from a match between partners of different religions. Some foolish women, he added, had squandered money among their 'dissenting Teachers'.[38]

Some preachers eloquently welcomed Protestant royal weddings. George Webbe was quick off the mark in greeting Elizabeth Stuart's marriage to the Elector Palatine on 14 February 1613, the very day of the wedding, with a sermon delivered at Steeple Aston (Wiltshire), where he was vicar. His text, Psalm 45: 13–15, supposedly celebrated Solomon's marriage. He praised Elizabeth's 'hatred of Popery and Superstition, her zeale to Gods glory, and sincere profession of the Gospell'. Now she had been granted her wish to be 'matched with a Prince, in Religion, in education, in yeeres, in vertues fit, and fit for none but for her selfe'.[39] Preaching at Whitehall shortly afterwards, John King, bishop of London, forecast that Elizabeth would, in the words of Psalm 128: 3, be a fruitful vine by the sides of Frederick's house, a sanctuary for piety and religion built on the rock of true faith.[40] In 1736, the Nonconformist minister Benjamin Atkinson placed the recently celebrated marriage of Frederick Prince of Wales and Augusta of Saxe-Gotha third in a chain of providential unions, following those of Elizabeth Stuart with Frederick V in 1613 and Mary Stuart with William of Orange in 1677. Taking Isaiah 49: 23 as his text, he hoped that Frederick and Augusta would prove true nursing parents to the church.[41]

Piety and virtue had to take precedence in choosing a marriage partner over beauty, wealth and kinship. The lust that drove many, especially younger people, into precipitate marriages, and avarice, a

[37] Meggot, *Rib Restored*, 25.

[38] Creffield, *A good Wife a great Blessing*, 54–7.

[39] George Webbe, *The Bride Royall, or The Spirituall Marriage betweene Christ and his Church* (London, 1613), 76–8.

[40] King, *Vitis Palatina*, 29–30.

[41] Benjamin Atkinson, *Good Princes Nursing Fathers and Nursing Mothers to the Church* (London, 1736), 11–21.

calculating greed of gain, were both likely to produce unhappy unions. Henry Smith, writing around 1591, thought that 'where there can be no hope of children, for age and other causes', marriage seemed rather to be sought for wealth or lust. God made unequal matches of old and young ridiculous everywhere.[42] Matches between partners of markedly unequal social status were also to be avoided.[43]

Several scriptural passages spoke of parents bestowing their children (especially daughters) in marriage or finding partners for them. However, some preachers warned, matches inspired by purely material calculations, without consideration of the inclinations of the couple concerned, caused matrimonial misery. Men of wealth may be deceived in the choices they make for their children, warned the famous puritan minister Thomas Gataker around 1620, and even if the parents of the parties agree, 'yet it may be, when they have done all they can, they cannot fasten their affections'.[44] His text was Proverbs 19: 14: 'Houses and Riches are the Inheritance of the Fathers: But a prudent Wife is of the Lord'. As Anthony Maxey put it when preaching at the marriage of Edward Coke's daughter Anne in 1601, 'The band will neuer hold where money knitteth the knot'.[45]

The consent of prospective marriage partners was essential. It was 'a practice dangerous and intolerable in a well-gouerned *State*', William Crompton insisted in a sermon composed around 1630, 'to force an vnion betweene young yeeres; where there is no actuall power to chuse, nor iudgement to discerne'.[46] Affection could not be compelled. Robert Abbot condemned as 'barbarous and wicked' the counsel to marry first and love after, whereby marriages often drew after them a long cord of misery and sorrow.[47] Henry Smith in 1591 and Richard Meggot in 1655 emphasized the need for

[42] Smith, *Preparatiue to Mariage*, 11–12; Bartholomew Parsons, *Boaz and Ruth Blessed* (Oxford, 1633), 34–6.

[43] Meggot, *Rib Restored*, 26; Secker, *Wedding Ring*, 46.

[44] Thomas Gataker, *A Good Wife Gods Gift. A Mariage Sermon on Prov. 19: 14*, separately paginated in idem, *Two Mariage Sermons* (London, 1620), 10–11.

[45] Anthony Maxey, 'A Sermon Preached at the Mariage of the Right Worshipful Ralfe Sadleir Esquier, and Anne Coke, Eldest Daughter of Edward Coke Esquire, Attorney Generall', in idem, *Certaine Sermons Preached before the Kings Maiestie, and else where* (London, 1619), 389–419, at 413.

[46] William Crompton, *A Wedding-Ring fitted to the Finger of every Paire that have or shall meete in the Feare of God* (London, 1632), 26–7.

[47] Abbot, *Wedding Sermon*, 62.

personal compatibility. Smith likened the well-matched couple to a pair of gloves or hose.[48] 'Divers Men', according to Meggot, 'though in themselves unblameable, are not fit, for Some Women; and divers Women, though in themselves commendable, are not fit for some Men.'[49]

Marriage Duties

The exposition of marriage duties in accordance with the instruction in the Order of Solemnization was naturally the most prominent theme of wedding sermons.[50] Shared religious faith and practice provided the best foundation for marriage. The preachers who said most about domestic religious observance were puritan or Nonconformist divines. William Whately advised that there were two things that would cement and glue the souls of man and wife together: gratitude to God as the matchmaker who had brought them together and their joint practice of 'priuat prayer, good conference, singing of Psalmes, and other like religious exercises'. Such exercises would dig fountains of spiritual love that would still run when 'youthfull & violent affections' had dried up.[51] Thomas Manton (d. 1677), a Presbyterian divine, echoed much of Whately's advice. Both partners had to remember to glorify God for giving each of them a good companion. Awareness of God's hand at work would make it possible the more patiently to bear the crosses incident to marriage and make spouses readier to part with each other when God willed it. The love between married couples should show itself by sincere and real endeavours to bring about one another's spiritual and eternal good.[52] John Shuttlewood, a London Independent minister, exhorted his audience in 1711 to be worshippers of God in their closets and families. Every house should be 'a little Church and Oratory, and the Master the Priest to call on God'. 'Let it be your great Concern', he urged them, 'to promote the Salvation of one anothers Souls'.[53]

48 Smith, *Preparatiue to Mariage*, 26.
49 Meggot, *Rib Restored*, 24.
50 Cummings, ed., *Book of Common Prayer*, 440.
51 Whately, *Bride-Bvsh* (1617), 9–10.
52 Thomas Manton, 'A Wedding Sermon', in *Several Discourses Tending to promote Peace & Holiness among Christians. To which are added, Three other distinct Sermons* (London, 1685), 65–95, at 78–86, 94–5 (pagination refers to the three additional sermons).
53 Shuttlewood, *Marriages Made in Heav'n*, 22–3.

There was general agreement throughout the period that mutual fidelity was especially important. Henry Smith cited Christ's response to the Pharisees in Matthew 19 to show that only adultery could dissolve marriage. William Whately gave chastity, 'the chaste keeping of each ones body each for other' and cohabitation in house and bed, a paramount status as 'main' duties. He believed that adultery and persistent desertion entitled the wronged spouse to marry another partner. The Church of England, however, unlike several continental Protestant churches, did not sanction the dissolution of the marriage or allow remarriage in either of these cases. In 1621, Whately was to be forced to retract his opinion by the High Commission.[54]

Some of the most eloquent passages in wedding sermons were devoted to an ideal of married love. Paul's advice made it natural to dwell at greater length on the husband's love, but the need for mutual affection was recognized. Unless there was a 'ioyning of hearts, and a knitting of affections together' the marriage existed only in 'shew and name'. Love between man and wife must not be superficial, but entire and inward. It ought to exceed all other kinds of amity and love.[55] The body of each partner belonged to the other, but matrimonial love was not the same as physical passion. Inordinate passion had not existed in paradise.[56] 'Let there be a wise and judicious Love; a *respectful Kindness,* founded in a real Value, and expressed by a tender Care', wrote the Presbyterian minister William Harris in 1700. 'Not a fond or unhallowed Passion, that like a Blaze of Fire, glares and expires in an Instant; but a pure Flame of fervent Love that will burn clear and last long.'[57]

To begin matrimonial concord well, Henry Smith wrote, it was necessary for the couple to learn one another's natures, affections and infirmities. Almost all quarrels in marriage had arisen from the failure of one partner 'to hit the measure of the others heart, to apply themselues to either nature', so that when either was offended, one (as he put it) sharpened the other. He commended the example of a couple who never fell out, despite their choleric dispositions. The husband had explained that 'when her fit is vpon her I yeeld to her, as

[54] Smith, *Preparatiue to Mariage*, 84; Whately, *Bride-Bvsh* (1617), 2–5; Eales, 'Gender Construction', 168.

[55] Smith, *Preparatiue to Mariage*, 44; Maxey, *Certaine Sermons*, 403; Abbot, *Wedding Sermon*, 60–1.

[56] *Sermons of Donne*, 2: 339.

[57] William Harris, *A Wedding Sermon Preach'd On March the 7th, 1699* (London, 1706), 43.

Abraham did to Sara, and when my fit is vpon me she yeelds to me, and so we neuer striue together'.[58]

The advice given in wedding sermons throughout this period was based on a fundamental assumption of husbandly superiority, as indeed the oft-cited comparison between the couple on the one hand and Christ and the church on the other implied. This superiority included the quality of the husband's love. His responsibility for the government of the family in both religious and worldly regards had to preclude the excessive fondness that might lead him to betray his command. Given the will to mastery common among women, this was all too real a danger. But he was expected to show the tender regard and understanding that would help him to honour the weaker vessel, especially, some preachers emphasized, given her painful and testing experiences in childbirth and the upbringing of children. Husbands should spread a 'mantle of charity' over their wives' infirmities.[59]

God had created Eve from Adam's rib as a helpmeet for him. This implied a close partnership. Since they were of one flesh, it was natural that the husband should love his wife as himself. It was unthinkable that he should beat her, several preachers emphasized: this was the action of a madman. There was one exception to this consensus: William Whately, in the 1619 edition of his *Bride-Bvsh*, very reluctantly came to the conclusion that a husband might beat an exceptionally recalcitrant wife as a last resort.[60]

One duty that belonged more especially to the husband was that of material provision for the family. There was a conventional distinction between the husband's sphere of work, primarily outside the household, and the wife's within it. In any event, the husband was bound to share all his substance with his wife, in accordance with his undertaking during the marriage service. It was the wife's responsibility to make the best use of the common stock in household management.[61]

The wife's foremost duties were reverence and obedience as well as love. While loving her husband, the wife had at the same time to

58 Smith, *Preparatiue to Mariage*, 46–8.

59 *Sermons of Donne*, 2: 345–6; Crompton, *Wedding-Ring*, 30; Taylor, *A Good Hvsband*, 25–6; Nathanael Hardy, *Love and Fear the inseperable Twins of a Blest Matrimony* (London, 1653), 5–6, 8–10, 16; Secker, *Wedding Ring*, 42.

60 Whately, *Bride-Bvsh* (1619), 169–73.

61 Smith, *Preparatiue to Mariage*, 51–3; Meggot, *Rib Restored*, 17–18.

honour, respect and obey him. The wife's performance of her obligations had to be underpinned by an inward conviction of her inferiority. King David's first wife Michal had despised him in her heart when she saw him dancing, and she had suffered the punishment of barrenness as a result.[62] The female role in the procreation and nurture of children was crucial. Nothing strengthened the love between husband and wife so much as children.[63] Their procreation was the essential means of renewing and continuing church and society. A wife might advise her husband or even remind him of neglected duties. However, she was bound to obey him in all things not contrary to God's word, and even to put up with ill-treatment. William Secker reminded his readers that 'If thou wouldst have thy wife's reverence, let her have thy respect.'[64] Several preachers warned husbands not to provoke their wives with petty interference or overbearing, insensitive, foolish or discourteous behaviour. For such faults the husband would be answerable to God. The wife had no direct means of redress.

Description of the common and separate duties of husband and wife remained a favoured pattern throughout the period. Some preachers nevertheless focused primarily on the qualities and duties of one partner. The Old Testament, and particularly Proverbs, provided a useful mine of texts for sermons on the good wife. In 1607, at the Anglo-Scottish court marriage of Lord and Lady Hay, one of particular interest to James VI/I, Robert Wilkinson preached on Proverbs 31: 14: 'She is like a Merchants ship, she bringeth her foode from a farre [*sic*].' Soundly built for all life's storms, the wife, like the ship, must be steered by her husband. She must not be borne by the wind or carry too much rigging, in the shape of extravagantly fashionable dress. Wilkinson developed the simile in exhaustive detail.[65] Around 1632, William Loe, vicar of Wandsworth,

[62] John Sprint, *The Bride-Womans Covnseller. Being a Sermon Preach'd at a Wedding* (London, 1700), 12.

[63] Maxey, *Certaine Sermons*, 408.

[64] Secker, *Wedding Ring*, 39.

[65] Robert Wilkinson, *The Merchant Royall. A Sermon Preached at White-Hall before the Kings Maiestie, at the Nuptials of the Right Honourable the Lord Hay, and his Lady* (London, 1607), 6–11, 14–15. For discussion of this sermon's political context, see Lori-Anne Ferrell, 'The Sacred, the Profane and the Union: Politics of Sermon and Masque at the Court Wedding of Lord and Lady Hay', in Thomas Cogswell, Richard Cust and Peter Lake, eds, *Politics, Religion and Popularity in Early Stuart Britain: Essays in Honour of Conrad Russell* (Cambridge, 2002), 45–64.

responding to Proverbs 31: 10, 'Who can finde a vertuous Woman? for her price is farre above Rubies', affirmed that a gracious and virtuous wife was indeed a rare and choice jewel. His sermon sets out 'the matchless worth of a vertuous wife' and 'the hatefull company and hellish condition of a vitious'. He addressed the latter topic with particular gusto. Loe could not see any great reason why a man should woo a woman. Masculine virtue far outstripped that of women.[66] Much more warmly positive was William Crompton's exposition, around 1630, of Proverbs 31: 29: 'Many daughters haue done vertuously, but thou excellest them all.' Such women deserved high commendation, and their husbands should show their appreciation of their qualities.[67]

In 1699, a Dissenting minister, John Sprint, used 1 Corinthians 7: 34, 'But she that is Married careth for the things of the World, how she may please her Husband', to insist on the wife's subordinate position in the most forthright terms. It was right that woman, created for man's comfort and benefit, but soon the means of his ruin, should actively seek to please and comfort him. Sprint had heard some women say that they had never undertaken to love, honour and obey their husbands. If Sprint had been responsible for marrying them, they would have had to wait until they were ready to do so. He claimed that his sermon had been 'so unhappily represented to the World by some ill-natur'd Females' that he had been compelled to publish it. He imagined that many women might ask why he could not have pitched on the immediately preceding verse 33, taking occasion to tell married men their duties to their wives, or at least brought in husbands to share with wives. He had addressed women largely because they were less able to learn than men and needed more help with a difficult lesson.[68]

If the husband was the superior partner, he must be first in performance of his duty. Expounding Ephesians 5: 33, 'Neverthelesse, let every one of you in particular so love his Wife even as himself, and the Wife (see) that she reverence her Husband',[69] about 1653, Nathanael Hardy devoted about twice as much space to the husband's duties as

[66] William Loe, *The Incomparable Jewell Shewed in a Sermon* (London, 1632), 3–5, 9, 14–17, 31–9.

[67] Crompton, *Wedding-Ring*, 1–24.

[68] Sprint, *Bride-Womans Covnseller*, 1–9.

[69] Brackets in the original.

to the wife's. The husband's prime duty, Hardy emphasized, was 'first *affection,* secondly *affection,* thirdly *affection*'. This was the mainspring for the performance of his other conjugal duties.[70] The marriage of John Sprint's daughter Mary in 1715 was the occasion for a very different sermon from the one her father had preached in 1699. Benjamin Aycrigg, Dissenting minister at Shepton Mallet, preached at her request, choosing precisely the verse that Sprint had passed over, 1 Corinthians 7: 33. It was 'the Duty of all Husbands', Aycrigg declared, 'diligently and industriously, to ... seek all Occasions, to please their Wives' by means of honour, love, tenderness and courtesy. Honour would include the kind reception of an admonition from her. Love meant behaving towards her in marriage as in courtship, showing the same delight in her company and sympathizing in all her troubles.[71]

Relative Paucity of Printed Sermons

Relatively few wedding sermons were published. The numbers in print came nowhere near matching those published after funerals.[72] The chief reason for the contrast is not far to seek. The account of the deceased person attached to a funeral sermon or woven into it was a valued medium of commemoration. It gained additional importance with the growth of religious division and the rise of party during the seventeenth century. The number of wedding sermons known to have been published in print was largest in the early seventeenth century and declined thereafter. We can now begin to take manuscript sermons into account, thanks to the Gateway to Early Modern Manuscript Sermons (GEMMS) database. This project began only recently and is as yet far from complete; so far, however, it has scarcely altered the picture of the relative numbers of known funeral and wedding sermons.[73] The numbers of surviving sermons in print or manuscript do not provide a reliable indication of how many were actually

[70] Hardy, *Love and Fear*, 6.

[71] Benjamin Aycrigg, *The Bridegroom's Counseller, and Bride's Comforter* (London, 1715), 12, 22–33.

[72] For the estimated total of over 1,300 funeral sermons printed *c.*1550– *c.*1750, see Ralph Houlbrooke, *Death, Religion and the Family in England 1480–1750* (Oxford, 1998), 386–7.

[73] At the time of consultation, 559 funeral sermons and 32 marriage or wedding sermons had been included in the database, which spans the years 1530–1715. This is far from giving a complete picture of surviving material, but it gives an idea of the relative numbers

preached. Reasonably full lists of the sermons preached by individual clergymen are rare. Whilst Ralph Josselin, the conscientious vicar of Earl's Colne in Essex (d. 1683) recorded in his diary several funeral sermons that he preached, he rarely mentioned weddings.[74] The Dissenting minister John Shuttlewood remarked in 1711 that it was a 'usual Custom' to preach a funeral sermon, but not so common to address those who were assuming adult responsibilities.[75]

The eager anticipation of the customarily convivial feast on the part of many wedding guests probably militated against their readiness to hear a long sermon. Preaching early in the seventeenth century on the account in John 2 of Christ's first miracle at the wedding feast at Cana, the puritan minister William Bradshaw emphasized that Christ was no enemy to 'honest mirth & delight, at such meetings and solemnities as this'.[76] He nevertheless condemned the utterly unfitting celebration of marriage feasts all too common in England, with 'laughing and scoffing … beastly and profane Songs, Sonnets, Jiggs, indited by some hellish Spirit'.

In 1775, the Unitarian preacher Richard Elliot remarked that 'though funeral discourses are common from most pulpits, a wedding sermon is very rarely heard of'. There are good grounds for thinking that such sermons had never gained more than limited acceptance. If indeed they had suffered a further decline since the Restoration, they may have suffered from the facetious spirit of which various preachers complained. John Ford, Dissenting minister (possibly an Independent) at Sudbury, declared in 1735 that the topic of marriage was 'very commonly treated in a ludicrous manner in conversation'. Publishing two discourses on the subject, he felt obliged to assure his readers that he had endeavoured to 'guard against everything indecent and ludicrous, not being willing to excite a blush or a smile'.[77] Such

involved: Gateway to Early Modern Manuscript Sermons, online at: <https://gemmsorig.usask.ca>, accessed 8 July 2022.

74 *The Diary of Ralph Josselin 1616–1683*, ed. Alan Macfarlane (Oxford, 1976).

75 Shuttlewood, *Marriages Made in Heav'n*, 7–8.

76 William Bradshaw, *A Mariage Feast*, separately paginated in Gataker, *Two Mariage Sermons*, at E2^{r}–E3^{v}, 3–6, 13–15. Gataker provided the epistle dedicatory to this sermon by his deceased friend Bradshaw. Compare Cressy, *Birth, Marriage, and Death*, 350–76, 'Wedding Celebrations'.

77 R. Elliot, *A Wedding Sermon: being the Substance of a Discourse delivered at Glass-House Yard on May 14. 1775* (London, 1776), iv; Humphreys, *Marriage an honourable estate*, 3;

sensitivity to the possibility of seeming ridiculous might have deterred many less determined men from broaching the subject of marriage.

Conclusions

The reformed marriage service of the Church of England included from 1549 onwards the new requirement that the 'office of man and wife' be declared either in a sermon or by the reading of passages from Scripture. Printed wedding sermons contributed to the growing volume of Christian advice literature addressed to the laity by the Protestant clergy. Authors published their sermons for a variety of reasons, ranging from the desire to please a friend or patron to the belief that their counsel could be useful to a wider audience. The wedding sermon was more particularly favoured in certain milieux: Jacobean court circles, the London parishes of godly ministers and post-Restoration dissenting congregations. Preachers achieved with different degrees of success the balance between husbandly love and wifely submission that the apostolic guidance required. Within the outlines that that guidance provided, individual preachers applied the different colours, the various combinations of light and shade that their own experiences of marriage and the wider society suggested. There were some striking contrasts of emphasis between different preachers in their handling of marriage duties. The defence of marriage as an honourable estate was an important theme. From the later seventeenth century onwards, some preachers saw marriage as an institution under threat from irreligion and libertinism. Wedding sermons were never published in numbers that came anywhere near those of printed funeral sermons. There is some evidence that far fewer were preached in the first place, perhaps because of a generally lower level of receptivity among wedding congregations.

Wright, *Sermon on Marriage*, 4; John Ford, *Two Discourses concerning the Necessity and Dignity of the Institution of Marriage* (London, 1735), ii–iii.

Clerical Old Age and the Forming of Rites of Passage in Early Modern Scotland

Chris R. Langley*

The Open University

This article investigates the rites that marked the end of a clerical career in early modern Scotland. It discusses what would take place when a minister had accepted that he was too old for his charge. It explores the ways in which ministers described their aging bodies, the impact of age on their vocation and how parishioners observed them. The article argues that the bureaucratic machinery devised to address the challenges of clerical old age created personal and professional rites of passage.

In 1712, Robert Wodrow, minister of Eastwood, in the Presbytery of Paisley, wrote a note about Patrick Simson, minister of Renfrew, a parish some fifteen kilometres away. Wodrow reported how Simson, 'the oldest minister in office in this Church' at 'near eighty-four' years old, was 'in a suddain … seized with a palsy in the half of his body'. The same day, Simson had attended the meeting of the Paisley Presbytery, and had seemed 'very hearty' before travelling home. Simson's condition lasted several days, until, 'a little worn off', he was able to 'walk throu the room again, with a litle grip'. Wodrow concluded his short record with the note 'I suspect he will never be able to come abroad', despite his partial recovery.[1] A cursory glance at the attendance lists for Paisley Presbytery confirms Wodrow's fears. Simson's condition resulted in his being absent from all subsequent presbytery meetings; his absence was accepted by his colleagues but (as is typical) the clerk chose not to record the reasons behind it.[2] Wodrow had an

* School of Arts and Humanities, 18 Custom House St, Cardiff, CF10 1AP. E-mail: christopher.langley@open.ac.uk.

[1] Robert Wodrow, *Analecta: Or, Materials for a Story of Remarkable Providences; Mostly relating to Scottish Ministers and Christians*, 2 vols (Edinburgh, 1842), 2: 80.

[2] Edinburgh, National Records of Scotland [hereafter: NRS], CH2/294/7, 144–58. Unfortunately, there is a gap in the kirk session minutes of the parish of Renfrew between 1700–31, so we cannot ascertain how Simson's health affected his pastoral responsibilities: see NRS, CH2/1596/1/1.

Studies in Church History 59 (2023), 244–264
doi: 10.1017/stc.2023.12

acute interest in elderly ministers, conversing with them and recording their recollections in his notebooks. When Simson died in October 1715, Wodrow noted that he and Thomas Warner, minister at Balmaclellan in Kirkcudbright Presbytery, had been the longest-serving ministers in the Church and lamented the loss of Simson's 'clearest judgments' and 'most exact and tenaciouse memorys'.[3] Elderly ministers were Wodrow's connections to the past and could offer lessons for the church in which he lived. To Wodrow, elderly ministers like Patrick Simson offered something unique.

Scholars have recently accepted age as a distinct category of historical analysis.[4] Contrary to the findings of Philippe Ariès, who argued that old age was largely ridiculed, rather than revered, in the medieval and early modern periods, historians now stress that the elderly could elicit sympathy and respect, as well as being the subjects of disdain, jealousy or hatred.[5] The elderly were recipients of alms, supported by friends and kin and respected as holders of communal memory or knowledge.[6] Conversely, those who were considered elderly were expected to behave differently and accept the impact of age on their bodies.[7]

Early modern concepts of what constituted old age were remarkably variable and usually related to an individual's bodily condition or mental acuity. Early modern readings of old age were dominated on the one hand by the remnants of Galenic understandings of the body, according to which the body became colder and drier as it aged as a result of humoral changes, and on the other by the ages of man

[3] Wodrow, *Analecta*, 2: 305.

[4] Elizabeth Ewan and Janay Nugent, 'Introduction: Adding Age and Generation as a Category of Historical Analysis', in Janay Nugent and Elizabeth Ewan, eds, *Children and Youth in Premodern Scotland* (Woodbridge, 2015), 1–12.

[5] Philippe Ariès, *Western Attitudes towards Death: The Middle Ages to the Present* (London, 1976); Allison P. Coudert, 'The Sulzbach Jubilee: Old Age in Early Modern Europe and America', in Albrecht Classen, ed., *Old Age in the Middle Ages and the Renaissance* (Berlin, 2007), 533–56.

[6] Margaret Pelling, 'Old Age, Poverty and Disability in Early Modern Norwich: Work, Remarriage and other Expedients', in eadem and Richard M. Smith, eds, *Life, Death and the Elderly: Historical Perspectives* (London, 1991), 74–10, at 78; David Thomson, 'The Welfare of the Elderly in the Past: A Family or Community Responsibility?', in Margaret Pelling and Richard M. Smith, eds, *Life, Death and the Elderly: Historical Perspectives* (London, 1991), 194–221.

[7] Susannah R. Ottaway, *The Decline of Life: Old Age in Eighteenth Century England* (Cambridge, 2004), 31–5.

model, which divided life on earth into four, six or seven distinct periods, each with a different set of characteristics.[8] Moreover, contemporaries in this period were not entirely comfortable with 'the language of figures' or even clear about how one might calculate one's age with absolute precision.[9] Chronological age was 'largely meaningless' to pre-modern European cultures.[10] In the absence of a chronological understanding, Lynn Botelho has urged scholars to consider the physical manifestations of age that became apparent at certain stages in the life cycle to understand how old age was constructed. These visible changes would affect the perception of others and one's own perception of self.[11] Old age was judged according to the bodies of relatives, friends and neighbours, rather than by arbitrary numbers.

The transitions between different stages of the early modern life cycle were punctuated by rites of passage. Heavily influenced by Arnold van Gennep's idea that certain ritualized actions would 'enable the individual to pass from one defined position to another' in their community, Edward Muir referred to such moments as 'passages of status', reflecting on how the performance of ritual acts could cement, sometimes legally, a person's new position in their community.[12] Victor Turner described such performances as forming distinct 'life crisis' rites.[13] Early modern historians have long focused on the Christian rites and rituals around birth, baptism, churching,

[8] Anthony Ellis, *Old Age, Masculinity and Early Modern Drama: Comic Elders on the Italian and Shakespearean Stage* (Farnham, 2009), 4–5.

[9] Keith Thomas, 'Age and Authority in Early Modern England', *PBA* 62 (1976), 205–48, at 205–6.

[10] Shulamith Shahar, *Growing Old in the Middle Ages: 'Winter clothes us in Shadow and Pain'* (London, 1997), 12.

[11] A. C. L. Beam, '"Should I as yet call you old?" Testing the Boundaries of Old Age in Early Modern England', in Erin J. Campbell, ed., *Growing Old in Early Modern Europe: Cultural Representations* (Aldershot, 2006), 95–116; Lynn Botelho, 'Old Age and Menopause in Rural Women of Early Modern Suffolk', in eadem and Pat Thane, eds, *Women and Ageing in British Society since 1500* (Harlow, 2001), 43–65, at 60–4; Steven R. Smith, 'Growing Old in Early Stuart England', *Albion* 8 (1976), 125–41.

[12] Edward Muir, *Ritual in Early Modern Europe* (Cambridge, 1997), 27–31; Arnold van Gennep, *The Rites of Passage*, transl. Monika B. Vizedom and Gabrielle L. Caffee (Chicago, IL, 1960), 9–11.

[13] Victor Turner, *The Ritual Process: Structure and Anti-Structure* (Chicago, IL, 1969), 167.

communion, marriage and (especially) death.[14] Scholars have been particularly interested in the ways in which the meanings behind these rites subtly shifted in response to the Protestant and Catholic Reformations. Often, however, the rites of passage that marked a separation into old age have either been collapsed into considerations of dying or have escaped historians' attention altogether.

This article will explore the passage of status experienced by the clergy of early modern Scotland as they entered old age. In the absence of similar studies, such an endeavour may offer a model for historians assessing clerical careers, especially relating to old age, in other national contexts. What follows focuses exclusively on Lowland parishes due to the greater volume and consistency of surviving source material produced by church courts in that area. The article argues that, contrary to the findings of Shulamith Shahar, the bureaucratic machinery of the Reformed Church of Scotland and the emphasis on a minister's ability to perform his role created distinct phases of separation, transition and (finally) incorporation into a new status as an elderly member of the clerical profession.[15] The rites of passage experienced by aging clerics in Reformation Scotland were not solely religious rituals, but fused the religious and the social, were often deeply personal and above all were products of the Reformed church's desire to protect the status of the ministry.[16] Unlike many figures experiencing rites of passage, Scotland's early modern ministry had considerable leeway to negotiate the terms of their new status. Nevertheless, old age, and the activities surrounding it, represented a key transition for Scotland's early modern clergy, one that was acknowledged by the bureaucratic machinery of the church, congregations across the country and ministers themselves.

[14] David Cressy, *Birth, Marriage and Death: Ritual, Religion and the Life-Cycle in Tudor and Stuart England* (Oxford, 1997); Arnold Hunt, 'The Lord's Supper in Crisis in Early Modern England', *P&P* 161 (1998), 39–83; Susan C. Karant-Nunn, *The Reformation of Ritual: An Interpretation of Early Modern Germany* (London, 1997); Christine Peters, 'Gender, Sacrament and Ritual: The Making and Meaning of Marriage in Late Medieval and Early Modern England', *P&P* 169 (2000), 63–96; Elizabeth Tingle and Jonathan Willis, eds, *Dying, Death, Burial and Commemoration in Reformation Europe* (London, 2016).

[15] Shahar, *Growing Old*, 14.

[16] Van Gennep, *Rites of Passage*; Victor Turner, 'Betwixt and Between: The Liminal Period in *Rites de Passage*', in idem, ed., *The Forest of Symbols: Aspects of Ndembu Ritual* (Ithaca, NY, 1967), 93–111.

The first stage of the Gennepian rite of passage was a moment in which one separated from one's previous state.[17] In their preaching, Reformed theologians appreciated old age as a distinct category or moment in the life cycle. In *The Institutes of Christian Religion*, John Calvin urged his readers to 'respect those in years as the Lord has been pleased to make that age honourable'. Those who had reached their dotage also had the obligation 'by their prudence and their experience (in which they are far superior)' to 'guide the feebleness of youth'.[18] To Calvin, those who failed to respect their elders were guilty of theft, by withholding honour that was owed.[19] The trope of the elderly served a didactic function in Calvin's thought as older people reminded younger parishioners of the limited, imperfect, nature of life on earth and gestured towards the afterlife. For Calvin, humankind was oblivious to the short-term nature of life on earth: 'we flatter ourselves that life is long', when 'the term of seventy years is short', and especially so when compared to the infinite nature of God. Armed with the realization that life is short, people 'see that they are dragged and carried forward to death with rapid haste and that their excellence is every moment vanishing away'.[20] Old age should remind believers of their obligations in their mortal lives and of the destiny of their souls after they die.

Following Calvin, Scottish preachers impressed on their listeners the reverence in which they should hold their elders. In 1608, the young preacher William Guild recommended: 'When thou commest to appeare before thy betters or elders, in a comely fashion shew the reverence of thy heart towards them, by bowing the knee of thy bodie before them.'[21] The idea of honouring the wisdom of the aged remained widespread in Reformed preaching in early modern Scotland. In the first half of the seventeenth century, David Lindsay told his parishioners in Belhelvie, Aberdeenshire, that 'honorable age is not that quhich standeth in the lenth of tyme nor is measured of the number of yeirs, bot wisdom is gray haires unto men and

[17] Van Gennep, *Rites of Passage*, 21.
[18] John Calvin, *The Institutes of Christian Religion*, transl. Henry Beveridge (London, 1845), 477 (2.8.46).
[19] Ezra Lincoln Plank, 'Creating Perfect Families: French Reformed Churches and Family Formation, 1559–1685' (PhD thesis, University of Iowa, 2013), 65.
[20] John Calvin, *Commentary on the Book of Psalms*, ed. James Anderson, 5 vols (Edinburgh, 1845–9), 3: 471.
[21] William Guild, *A Yong Mans Inquisition, or Triall* (London, 1608), 196–7.

ane unspoilled lyf'.[22] In a sermon in 1638, Alexander Henderson, preacher at Leuchars, Fife, told parishioners:

> 'Thy youth'. That is, thy young men. Those that are renewed by grace they are called young, albeit they were never so old, because their age is not reckoned by their first, but by their second birth. Ay, moreover, still the older that the children of God grow in years and the weaker in the world, they grow younger and stronger in grace. Secondly, they are caled young, because of the strength that they have to resist temptations.[23]

Henderson, himself around fifty-five when delivering this sermon, urged his parishioners to understand that while the body necessarily decayed the elderly held accumulated wisdom as they advanced in years. Those renewed by grace had a youth wholly separate from the age of their bodies.

Beyond this general respect, preachers agreed with Calvin that the physical tokens of age reflected the finite nature of life on earth.[24] In aging, humanity is forced to reckon with its mortality and, consequently, its creator. William Wishart lamented how 'there is no creature on earth, so naked and indigent as man: for naked hee was borne and naked shall he returne againe: and hee hath no peculiar or proper thing in the world, that hee can justly call his, but sinne and infirmity'. Beyond all of humankind's achievements lay 'age and wrinkles and the lineaments of death'.[25] Ultimately, even the wisdom of the elderly accumulated over time paled in comparison with God's infinite knowledge. In 1635, Ninian Campbell told his readers that 'where there is one come to fiftie years, there are ten not come; but to see a man passe his climacterick and then 80 years, it is a rara avis in terris. Never man yet lived a 1000 years, which are but one day in the sight of God.'[26] Preachers used the spectre of aging to remind parishioners of the fallibility of the human body and of its weakness before God, as well as the need to repent effectively before death. Old age

22 NRS, CH2/32/23, 96.

23 Alexander Henderson, *Sermons, Prayers and Pulpit Addresses*, ed. R. Thomson Martin (Edinburgh, 1867), 26.

24 See Steven R. Smith, 'Death, Dying and the Elderly in Seventeenth-Century England', in Stuart F. Spicker, Kathleen M. Woodward and David D. Van Tassel, eds, *Aging and the Elderly: Humanistic Perspectives on Gerontology* (Atlantic Highland, NJ, 1978), 205–20, at 207.

25 William Wishart, *An Exposition of the Lords Prayer* (London, 1633), 373.

26 Ninian Campbell, *A Treatise upon Death* (Edinburgh, 1635), unpaginated.

should spur devotion. In a tract published in 1673, preacher and principal of the University of Edinburgh, William Colvill, stressed how 'such who are in their decrept old age, stouping toward the earth and the grave, let them not imploy their short time and their affections wholly upon the things of the earth, when by the course of nature, they are near to be removed from it: Let them not be busie in the things of the world and careless of the work of their own salvation'.[27] The changes one's body experienced in old age should serve as the ultimate reminder of the immortality of the soul.

Preachers opining on the subject held a particularly lofty view of clerical old age, separating elderly ministers from their younger associates. An eighteenth-century publication by William Wishart told its readers that elderly ministers 'should have great Reverence and Respect paid to them by young Ministers' by 'rising up before them and giving Place to them in Speech and Discourse'. Wishart recommended that less experienced ministers should 'shew great modesty and Respect' to their older colleagues, 'even when they themselves cannot bring themselves to be of their mind'. There was more to admire in elderly ministers than 'gray haires', as Wishart concluded, echoing Calvin by saying that an elderly minister's 'Knowledge, Wisdom, Prudence and Experience, demand this Reverence and Respect'.[28]

This separation between elderly and younger ministers can also be seen in practice. Ecclesiastical courts regularly made alterations to their meetings to accommodate the needs of elderly colleagues, accepting that some older ministers could no longer participate in the same way. In 1623, ministers in the Synod of Fife agreed that 'such brethren as are aged' should be 'disburdened' of having to preach in front of colleagues and 'their place supplied by younger brethren' at future synod meetings.[29]

In most other cases, ecclesiastical courts would accept that elderly colleagues could not be present at all due to concerns over their mobility. In 1639, William Scott, the elderly minister at Cupar, Fife, wrote to his neighbouring ministers to inform them that 'the

[27] William Colvill, *The Righteous Branch growing out of the Root of Jesse and healing the Nations* (Edinburgh, 1673), 375–6.

[28] William Wishart, *Gospel Ministers the Strength of the Nation* (Edinburgh, 1725), 8.

[29] *Selections from the Minutes of the Synod of Fife*, ed. George R. Kinloch (Edinburgh, 1837), 98.

daylie decay of my naturall strenth maks me to dowbt if ever I sall sie yow face to face'.[30] Scott's acceptance that he would no longer appear at ecclesiastical court meetings was shared by other aging ministers. In 1640, the Synod of Moray heard how William Reid, minister at Gartly, excused his absence from the meeting because of 'his unabilitie to travell pairtlie throughe weacknes and old aige'.[31] Further south, similar considerations may have led John Kerr, the sixty-four-year-old minister of Prestonpans, to ask colleagues that his absences from presbytery meetings fifteen kilometres away in Haddington should not be marked in the record book.[32] Travelling on church business during the winter was particularly difficult for elderly ministers and drastically changed how they performed their roles. William Dickson, minister of Glenholm, struggled to attend presbytery meetings in Biggar, some twelve kilometres away from his manse, throughout the 'very stormie' winter of 1660-1 'in respect of his aige'.[33] Historians have encountered such descriptions of immobility in the petitions of the elderly elsewhere in early modern Europe, reflecting how a minister's experience of old age shared many traits with his lay neighbours.[34] However, the physical burden of the administrative machinery of the Reformed Church could weigh profoundly on ministers who were elderly, separating them from the work of their colleagues.

Parishioners' perceptions of their minister would change as his body struggled with the intensity of his vocation. Parishioners in Skene, Aberdeenshire, complained in 1599 that their minister, John White, 'delyvers nocht the doctrine of salvatioun'.[35] Such petitions show lay appreciation and understanding of what was expected from a Reformed minister, but also offer an assessment of his body's changing condition. Commissioners from Burntisland petitioned Kirkcaldy Presbytery in August 1638 requesting a minister to give the communion in their parish 'in respect of thair minister's age

30 NRS, CH2/154/2/2, 8–9.

31 NRS, CH2/271/1, 136.

32 NRS, CH2/185/5, 60.

33 NRS, CH2/35/2, 19.

34 Louise Marsha Gray, 'The Self-Perception of Chronic Physical Incapacity among the Labouring Poor: Pauper Narratives and Territorial Hospitals in Early Modern Germany' (PhD thesis, University College London, 2001), 181–3.

35 NRS, CH2/1/1, 35. My thanks to Dr Catherine E. McMillan for drawing my attention to this example.

and weaknesses'.[36] Age prevented ministers from fulfilling other functions of their office, gradually removing them from certain aspects of their role. By 1646, William Scott, the elderly minister of Cupar, was unable to sign testimonials describing the behaviour of parishioners leaving his parish, forcing him to employ two notaries to sign documents on his behalf.[37]

Perhaps unsurprisingly, previously powerful preachers were separated from their former selves by the effects of age. In August 1640, the elders of Innerleithen told Peebles Presbytery that their minister, Patrick Sanderson, did 'not edifie them as he wes want' in his preaching and was 'not able for the function' due to 'his age and infirmitie'.[38] While the need for mental acuity may have driven Sanderson's parishioners' comments, it was far more common for neighbours to notice how age affected the strength of their minister's voice, shifting their experience of his sermons and risking his reputation among his congregation. In 1643, ministers in Ayr Presbytery visited the parish of Straiton because of reports of the 'age and great infirmitie of … voice and body' of the local minister, John McCorne.[39] This was no isolated example. In 1646, the clerk of Biggar Presbytery described Thomas Campbell, the octogenarian minister of Biggar, as 'not aibill (this long tyme by past and now als) to preache or exerceise [his] ministeriall functione' due to his 'great aige and weaknes'.[40] The elders of Balfron, Dunbartonshire, complained to the local presbytery during a routine visitation of the parish in 1650 that their minister, John Norwell, was 'very much weakened' through 'infirmitie of age'. The elders reported that Norwell was not able to preach effectively, as 'these that sitts nearest to him can heardly somtymes discerne what he sayes'.[41] For ministers like Norwell, their old age was framed by showing how the effects of bodily decay had affected their performance as preachers, that yardstick of the Protestant Reformation.[42] This marked a clear

[36] NRS, CH2/224/1, 439.
[37] NRS, CH2/532/1, 35.
[38] NRS, CH2/295/2, 103–4.
[39] NRS, CH2/532/1, 104.
[40] NRS, CH2/35/1, 55 (parenthesis original).
[41] NRS, CH2/546/1, 169–70.
[42] Michelle D. Brock, 'Exhortations and Expectations: Preaching about the Ideal Minister in Reformation Scotland', in Chris R. Langley, Catherine E. McMillan and Russell Newton, eds, *The Clergy in Early Modern Scotland* (Woodbridge, 2021), 15–31;

separation from the zealous preaching of their earlier lives and started a process by which parishioners' assessments of their performance would change.

The separation from fully active minister to elderly incumbent was also a deeply personal one, as ministers had to confront the very real change in how they devoted themselves to God with a failing body. While the pains incurred in worshipping with an aging body may have been 'meat and drink' to those 'seeking to emulate Christ's bloody sweat in Gethsemane', as Alec Ryrie has stated, such bodily aches and pains underlined a shift in a minister's devotional life.[43] Towards the end of his life, John Welsh, minister of Ayr, was unable to kneel comfortably to pray.[44] Ministers recorded that their aging bodies began to struggle to fulfil tasks that they had found relatively straightforward in their younger years. Lucas Sonsie, the minister of Carrington, told colleagues at a meeting of Haddington Presbytery in May 1618 that the 'weightie burden of the ministrie' was becoming increasingly difficult for him to fulfil considering his 'old age now drawne on'.[45] In January 1629, Adam Colt told the archbishop of St Andrews, John Spottiswoode, that he struggled to fulfil his duties as minister of Musselburgh in Dalkeith Presbytery, 'in respect of his grit burden and aige'.[46] Elderly ministers expressed such problems in remarkably similar terms throughout the period and across the country. In August 1650, Patrick Stewart, minister of Rothesay in Dunoon Presbytery, told his colleagues that he was 'unable to stand under the burthen' of the ministry 'by reason of his age and daylie infirmities growing upon him'.[47] And to the north, John Brodie, minister of Auldearn in Forres Presbytery, informed his colleagues in 1652 of his 'old age and bodilie infirmitie, hardlie able to beare the whole burden of such a weightie charge'.[48] Descriptions of the duties of the ministry emphasized their metaphorical weight but also the very real strain this could have on the aging

Neal Enssle, 'Patterns of Godly Life: The Ideal Parish Minister in Sixteenth- and Seventeenth-Century English Thought', *Sixteenth Century Journal* 28 (1997), 3–28.

43 Alec Ryrie, *Being Protestant in Reformation Britain* (Oxford, 2013), 175.

44 *The History of the Life and Death of Mr John Welch* (London, 1735), 32.

45 NRS, CH2/424/1, 449.

46 NRS, CH2/424/1, 557.

47 NRS, CH2/111/1, fols 16^{r}–16^{v}.

48 NRS, CH2/162/1, 53.

clerical body.[49] Acknowledging that the form of one's devotion was changing marked an important shift in a minister's career.[50]

Ministers and parishioners might mark this separation in a cleric's identity by entering a supplication to the local presbytery or synod. This small act marked a distinct moment in the cycle of a minister's career. The nobility from the parish of Dirleton approached Haddington Presbytery in 1637 with a petition lamenting that the impact of old age had made their minister unable 'to defray the care as befor tymes'.[51] The Dirleton petitioners' comparison with their minister's previous performance was common, even in petitions from ministers themselves. In 1640, Duncan Omey, minister at Southend in Kintyre Presbytery, resigned his office 'out of tenderness of conscience least the people should want service'.[52] Similarly, the octogenarian John Wemyss, minister of Kinnaird, told members of the Presbytery of Brechin in 1658 that 'be reason of his weaknes of body and great age he is unhable to discharge all the dueties of his ministrie … as he was wont'.[53] Such language was common. William Jaffray, minister of Kinedward in Turriff Presbytery, had expressed himself in similar terms in 1650.[54] These moments represented official recognition and acknowledgement from both parish and minister of a cleric's old age.

A key part of an elderly minister's separation from his former role was having to accept the need for a younger minister to help him fulfil his responsibilities. Most elderly ministers would continue to serve in the parish in some capacity until their death, delegating most of their responsibilities to a younger incumbent. In 1653, John Brodie, minister of Forres, told colleagues at his presbytery how he was 'privie to his owne bodilie weaknesse' and wished 'to sie god honoured' with the appointment of a young minister to help him fulfil his responsibilities.[55] Such statements acknowledged the challenges of the clerical

[49] This accords with Susannah Ottaway's findings that early modern men were likely to 'mourn the general loss of strength' in their bodies: Ottaway, *Decline of Life*, 33–5.

[50] Robert W. Daniel, 'Godly Preaching, in Sickness and Ill-Health, in Seventeenth-Century England', in Charlotte Methuen and Andrew Spicer, eds, *The Church in Sickness and in Health*, SCH 58 (Cambridge, 2022), 134–49.

[51] NRS, CH2/185/4, fol. 109^{v}.

[52] *Minutes of the Synod of Argyll 1639–1651*, ed. Duncan C. MacTavish (Edinburgh, 1943), 19.

[53] NRS, CH2/40/1, 411 (emphasis mine).

[54] NRS, CH2/1120/1, 203.

[55] NRS, CH2/162/1, 54.

vocation, but also made clear how ministers felt duty bound to step aside partially when they could no longer perform the task. The connection between bodily infirmity and clerical vocation was made clear in 1658, when John Fife, minister at Navar in Brechin Presbytery, acknowledged 'be reason of weaknes of bodie his willingnes to tak a young man to be a fellow labourer to assist him in the work of the ministrie'.[56] These public utterances formally marked the threshold of old age and a diminution of a minister's role as the person solely responsible for his cure of souls. It also marked the entrance into a liminal state, in which the terms of the cleric's new settlement could be openly discussed.[57]

The second stage of van Gennep's rites of passage is transition: a liminal state in which the individual sits between their new status and their former position. In practical terms, a minister who had accepted that he was too old to fulfil his charge existed in such a liminal space. Before formally appointing a younger assistant minister, local presbyteries frequently diverted other preachers to deputize for the elderly minister, thereby acknowledging his clerical status while also underlining that he was physically no longer fully fit to fulfil the office. In 1628, Archibald Oswald, minister of Pencaitland, 'crave[d] the help' of colleagues in Haddington Presbytery every Sunday until his health had recovered or a helper was appointed.[58] Ministers living in Edinburgh supplied the place of William Arthur in 1649 'out of their brotherlie care' due to his 'great age' and declining health.[59] Neighbouring clerics expended considerable effort on behalf of their aging colleagues. In 1673, ministers from across Dalkeith Presbytery preached every fortnight at the conjoined parish of Fala and Soutra as John Logan, minister of the parish, was no longer able to fulfil his preaching duties. They did so until Logan died the following year.[60]

[56] NRS, CH2/40/1, 402.

[57] There are parallels with pre-Reformation practice, in which the terms of an elderly monastic superior's retirement would only be discussed following formal acknowledgement that he could no longer perform the role: see Martin Heale, '"For the solace of their advanced years": The Retirement of Monastic Superiors in Late Medieval England', *Journal of Medieval Monastic Studies* 8 (2019), 143–67, at 143–50.

[58] NRS, CH2/185/4, 23.

[59] NRS, CH2/718/6, 23.

[60] NRS, CH2/424/5, 7.

Such efforts reflect a widespread belief that a minister's orderly transition into old age protected the dignity of the church. The *Second Book of Discipline* was explicit in recommending that elderly ministers 'ought not to be deposed' and that 'honour should remain to them, their kirk should maintain them; and others ought to be provided to do their office'.[61] Such arrangements may not have been feasible in the immediate aftermath of the Reformation, but a proliferation of trained ministers and improvements to parish finances made outsourcing some of an elderly minister's duties to a younger assistant viable by the early years of the seventeenth century.[62] In 1642, Alexander Henderson, then minister in Edinburgh, reiterated that ministers who 'through old age, sicknesses, or other infirmitie' could not fulfil their pastoral responsibilities should 'still retain the honour of their office and comfort of maintenance during their lifetime. And they performing what they are able in teaching, government, visitation and catechising, others are joined with them by the Presbytery and with the consent of the people to be their fellow labourers and to undergo the main charge.'[63]

While reflecting deferential attitudes towards age, Henderson's comments were also driven by a desire to protect the functioning of the church during a minister's transition into old age. An act of the General Assembly the previous year made similar claims, stating that elderly ministers 'shall not by their cessation from their charge … be put from injoying their old maintenance and dignity'.[64] Elderly ministers sat in a liminal space, continuing to serve as important role models for the local community and the ministry at large, without being able to participate fully in their original responsibilities.[65]

[61] *The First Book of Discipline*, ed. James K. Cameron (Edinburgh, 1972), 32–9.

[62] W. R. Foster, '"A constant platt achieved": Provision for the Ministry, 1600–38', in Duncan Shaw, ed., *Reformation and Revolution: Essays Presented to the Very Reverend Principal Emeritus Hugh Watt* (Edinburgh, 1967), 124–40; Robert M. Healey, 'The Preaching Ministry in Scotland's "First Book of Discipline"', *ChH* 58 (1989), 339–53, at 353; Margaret H. B. Sanderson, 'Service and Survival: The Clergy in Late Sixteenth-Century Scotland', *Records of the Scottish Church History Society* 36 (2006), 74.

[63] Alexander Henderson, *The Government and Order of the Church of Scotland* (Edinburgh, 1642), 13.

[64] Alexander Peterkin, ed., *Records of the Kirk of Scotland, containing the Acts and Proceedings of the General Assemblies* (Edinburgh, 1838), 293.

[65] Janay Nugent, 'Reformed Masculinity: Ministers, Fathers and Male Heads of Households, 1560–1660', in Lynn Abrams and Elizabeth L. Ewan, eds, *Nine Centuries of Man: Manhood and Masculinity in Scottish History* (Edinburgh, 2017), 39–52, at 40–2.

While most figures undergoing some form of cultural or social transformation tend to have little agency, ministers themselves played a vital role in negotiating their transition into old age, especially in details relating to financial questions.[66] At the root of this agency was the expectation that the minister would give up some of his stipend voluntarily and redirect it to his prospective helper. One of the most detailed examples of this desire can be seen in the case of Patrick Simpson, minister of Stirling in 1611. Simpson lamented that 'his manifauld infirmities' threatened 'ane heftie dissolutione of his earthlie tabirnacjaill'.[67] Despite accepting his aging body, Simpson needed to be persuaded to agree to the financial aspects of accepting an assistant minister. Unsurprisingly, aging ministers like Simpson were particularly anxious about their income and their family's financial security into their old age.[68] In East Lothian, James Carmichael, minister of Haddington, excused the lack of preaching in his parish in 1621 because of his 'infirmitie and age', but warned that while committed to 'doe all the gude everie way he culd', he was 'not bund by anie law to give supplie' to sustain another minister and that forcing him to do so would financially ruin him.[69] Similarly, John Logan, the minister of Fala and Soutra mentioned above, told colleagues in Dalkeith Presbytery in 1673 that he would struggle to fund an assistant, 'his stipend being very small and his familie great'.[70] Elderly ministers who had accepted the need for a younger minister to help them continued to consider the security of their own family into their dotage.

Younger ministers from neighbouring parishes were often deputed to broker a deal with their elderly colleagues, asking them to relinquish more of their stipend. Upon hearing about the difficulties experienced by Andrew Playfair, the seventy-one-year-old minister of Aberdalgie, Perth Presbytery sent a neighbouring minister to 'signifie' its concerns (and presumably devise a settlement) in 1650.[71] William

[66] Turner, 'Betwixt and Between', 93.

[67] For similar phrasing, see William Morray, *A Short Treatise of Death in Sixe Chapters* (Edinburgh, 1620), 20.

[68] One sees similar problems in the pre-Reformation diocese of Exeter in England: see Nicholas Orme, 'Sufferings of the Clergy: Illness and Old Age in Exeter Diocese, 1300–1540', in Pelling and Smith, eds, *Life, Death and the Elderly*, 62–73, at 65–8.

[69] NRS, CH2/185/3, 151.

[70] NRS, CH2/424/5, 7.

[71] NRS, CH2/299/3, 134.

Petty, the minister of Petty in Inverness Presbytery, was in his mid-seventies when the bishop informed him in 1682 that his 'great infirmity through old age' made him unable to discharge the duties of a minister. The bishop implored ministers living nearby to 'concurr' with Petty to persuade him to accept some outside help and the reduction in his stipend it would entail. Elderly ministers in these parishes wanted assurances that they would receive sufficient maintenance and care once the assistant minister was in place. In the case of John Norwell in Balfron, noted above, the elderly minister was ordered to accept an assistant minister to help him serve his charge but could maintain possession and use of the manse and glebe land for the rest of his life. Such negotiations were quite common for ministers entering their old age in relatively humble rural parishes and represented a key moment in their transition to their new role.

Authorities were aware of such difficulties and worked hard to negotiate with local patrons temporarily to augment the parish stipend in order to cover both the costs of the new, younger, minister and the ongoing expenses of the aging incumbent until the latter's death. In 1611, ministers in neighbouring parishes in Dunfermline Presbytery visited the parish of Orwell and discovered that the most significant landowners of the village were happy to augment the stipend to obtain an assistant minister to the seventy-nine-year-old incumbent Patrick Geddes.[72] While the end result looked harmonious, the process of persuading the landowners of Orwell took five months to complete.[73] Such intricate negotiations underline how aging ministers continued to hold considerable influence in a parish despite their liminal status.

In some rural parishes, landowners closed ranks to prevent any augmentation of the stipend, usually allowing their aging minister to continue to hold the full value of the stipend, but also forcing him to work into his dotage. The patrons and parishioners of Inverkeithny in Strathbogie Presbytery insisted in 1647 that 'they had satisfaction of their minister', Robert Irvine and under no circumstances would desire an assistant minister. Irvine continued, alone, in post for over a decade despite a routine visitation in 1650 reporting that his lack of teeth made it difficult for his congregation to

[72] NRS, CH2/105/1/1, 81.
[73] NRS, CH2/105/1/1, 99.

comprehend his preaching.[74] In April 1651, ministers in the Synod of Aberdeen complained that nothing had been done to find a helper for Robert Forbes, the seventy-seven-year-old minister of the rural parish of Echt, because of some unspecified 'difficulties', presumably in finding enough lay support from parish landowners to enable Forbes to change status.[75] Such lay input (or the lack of it) could have a considerable influence over the minister's changing status. One clergyman's experience of entering old age could be fundamentally different from another due to the context of the parish in which he found himself. The size of a cleric's stipend could affect how he experienced the transition into old age.

Occasionally, elderly ministers nominated their sons to act as assistant ministers in the parish, which served both to underline the former's influence over this process of negotiation and to emphasize how his role was changing. In 1630, Harry Wilkie petitioned Kirkcaldy Presbytery asking for 'libertie to supplie his father's place in preaching' in the parish of Portmoak during his father's old age.[76] Wilkie's choice to petition the presbytery directly was unusual, as it was customary for the father or someone of standing in the parish to initiate such petitions. When Gideon Penman was preaching in his elderly father's stead in the late 1630s in the Midlothian parish of Crichton, the senior Penman, William, asked the presbytery if Gideon might be 'admitted helper' to him in May 1639.[77] William told his colleagues that 'his age and infirmitie' prevented him from fulfilling some aspects of his ministry.[78] These agreements offered the younger minister an opportunity to learn from his father, while securing the elderly minister's right to live out his life in the parish manse. Such arrangements would have also offered some additional security to the aging minister's wife.[79] By accepting his son as assistant, however, the aging minister's role shifted.

This complex set of financial negotiations was an important component in the liminal state in which elderly ministers found

74 *Extracts from the Presbytery Book of Strathbogie*, ed. John Stuart (Aberdeen, 1843), 74.
75 NRS, CH2/840/1, 37.
76 NRS, CH2/224/1, 33.
77 NRS, CH2/1120/1, 204.
78 NRS, CH2/424/2, fol. 135v.
79 For more on the financial concerns of clerical wives, see Chris R. Langley, 'Clergy Widows in Early Modern Scotland', *Scottish Church History* 51 (2022), 111–32, at 123–6.

themselves. Once a minister had been recognized as no longer able to fulfil the rigours of his vocation, an almost ritualized set of actions were set in motion to negotiate the terms of his transition. Both the elderly cleric and influential lay people in his parish held considerable influence over this process, meaning the experience of becoming an elderly minister could vary widely between different parishes. In most cases, an aging minister had to accept some reduction in his financial status in order to move out of this liminal phase.[80] Authorities in general were eager to ensure that this transition was a smooth as possible to protect the dignity of the clerical estate and to keep local tensions to a minimum. This process of negotiation had quickly become standardized by the end of the sixteenth century and became a permanent fixture in the clerical life cycle. This was an administrative, as well as a personal, rite of passage.

Like other examples of rites of passage, the aging minister's incorporation into his new role brought with it a new set of obligations.[81] The change in his status was clearly marked and would have been visible to his congregation. Nevertheless, the minister's new role was not static, but should be viewed as a starting point of a longer process in which the incumbent slowly ceded more control over parish affairs to his new colleague. While this accords with the idea that reintegration rites could be lengthy, it is here that aging ministers diverge most obviously from van Gennep's model, in holding considerable influence to negotiate the terms of their incorporation into their new status.[82]

The admission of the elderly minister's assistant represented the first act through which the minister's new status was confirmed. During the service, the elderly minister vacated his pulpit and watched with the rest of the congregation as another minister preached the admission sermon for his helper.[83] The sermons that opened the admission ceremony for an assistant minister were

[80] There was no guarantee that this complex process would conclude before the elderly minister died. John Fife in Navar, discussed above, died in May or June 1658, before the appointment of his would-be assistant, Hercules Skinner, who was appointed as sole minister of the parish on 22 July 1658: NRS, CH2/40/1, 408.

[81] Jean Holm, 'Introduction: Raising the Issues', in eadem and John Bowker, eds, *Rites of Passage* (London, 1994), 1–9, at 8–9.

[82] Van Gennep, *Rites of Passage*, 41–2.

[83] See also the admission of Robert Semple as assistant to John Hume at Lesmahagow in May 1648: NRS, CH2/234/1, 365.

based around scriptural texts which emphasized the assistant minister's clerical authority, placing him on an equal footing with his older colleague. In 1638, at the admission of Robert Kerr as assistant to his father in Prestonpans, Adam Blackhall, minister of nearby Aberlady, instructed those present on 'the dewties of pastors and people', encouraging the congregation to be obedient to its new minister.[84] At the admission of Archibald Turner as assistant to James Porteous at Borthwick in 1648, the minister who commenced the service preached on Hebrews 5: 4, expounding the duties of the clergy.[85] Such sermons underscored the new minister's authority and subtly changed the older minister's role.

The elderly minister's incorporation into his new role was a gradual process, as the responsibilities he continued to perform would reduce as his body aged. This flexibility is exemplified by the petition of John Bell, the elderly minister of Glasgow, to the General Assembly in 1638. The moderator of the assembly told those present:

> There is heir a reverend and aged brother, whom we should all honour – for gray haires, for a crowne of glorie – that hath approven himselfe to God in his Church and to the people of this cittie in a speciall manner; and now, finding his natural weaknes increasing, though he hath vigour of mynd as yet and fearing his dissolution drawes near, he hes represented to yow heir a supplication for a helper in the ministerie.[86]

Bell acknowledged the effects of age on his ministry, but felt he still had something to offer his parish due to his 'vigour of mynd'. The specific duties to be undertaken by Bell's prospective assistant were not explicitly described but remained flexible. The minister's relationship with his younger helper would also change according to his need. In December 1647, John Durie, appointed as the helper to the aging minister of Dalmeny, John Gibson, complained that his senior colleague found preaching 'such a burthen unto him that he could scarselie any longer heare him'. Gibson was told to preach 'onleie when he finds himselfe any wayes disposed for it' and to request Durie's help more often.[87] Many ministers saw continuing their ministerial duties as a key part of living out their vocation. While the sixty-

[84] NRS, CH2/185/4, 111.
[85] NRS, CH2/424/3, 237.
[86] *Records of the Kirk of Scotland*, 184.
[87] NRS, CH2/242/3, 281.

nine-year-old minister of Dunbar, Andrew Stevenson, promised to serve with a helper 'in all the points of his ministeriall calling' for as long as he possibly could, his responsibilities had been severely reduced before his death in 1664.[88] The minister's incorporation into his new role would continue to evolve until his death.

Ecclesiastical courts enforced the change in the elderly minister's status. Church authorities moved quickly to protect the interests of elderly ministers who were perceived to be vulnerable to exploitation. In 1651, the Synod of Fife received a petition from Patrick Geddes, the elderly minister of Orwell. After having an assistant appointed to help him the previous year, Geddes told his colleagues 'that some elders of his paroche have of late violentlie and unjustlie stoppit some of his mentinance dew to him and that they ar going about to depyrve him of much of that mantinance quhich is his just right'.[89] The ministers of the synod immediately intervened to ensure 'the aged and reverend brother may live and close the remanent of his days in quyetnes', and to prevent a potentially embarrassing scandal between Geddes, his successor and his neighbours.[90] Maintaining the integrity and reputation of the ministry in general meant protecting elderly ministers' incorporation into their new role.

One can observe this desire to protect the dignity of elderly clerics in the unusually detailed case of Colin Rynd, a minister who had served in Perthshire from 1588 before moving to Ireland in the 1610s. With Ireland gripped by rebellion from the end of 1641, Rynd returned to the place of his birth in search of safety. Unfortunately, his brother Patrick died in early 1641, leaving only a modest estate, meaning that Colin needed to find other forms of support.[91] Upon his petitioning for assistance in 1644, Perth Presbytery appointed ministers across the region to collect money to support Rynd, but added the proviso that ministers should 'distribut the same by pairts as he sall stand in neid'. Rynd settled in the area but his difficulties in obtaining money to support himself increased. In 1648, the region's ministers again tried to collect financial support for him, the clerk describing Rynd as 'aged and distressed'. Rynd's case was so desperate that the Synod of Perth and

88 NRS, CH2/99/1, 132.
89 NRS, CH2/154/2/1, 236.
90 NRS, CH2/154/2/1, 237.
91 NRS, CC20/4/9, 1056.

Stirling intervened and ordered that every parish pay twenty shillings each year to support him. Rynd based himself in Perth and tapped into the networks of patronage and friendship established by his father William Rynd, former schoolmaster of the burgh.[92] Rynd was not, however, surviving alone. In 1651 and again in 1655, Thomas Irvine, a merchant in Perth, petitioned the synod, revealing that he had 'manteind' Rynd 'in bed and burd diverse yeires before the said act wes maid and sensyne' but was yet to receive any payment from the synod for having done so. The matter was still ongoing the following year when some in the synod complained that Irvine was aggressively soliciting them for payment. In April 1657, the synod's moderator implored ministers to pay Irvine after he had told the ministers that Rynd was 'not weill payed therof and that he is now become verie old and is in great necessitie'.[93] Rynd, who was almost ninety by the time of Irvine's last petition, gained access to these support networks through his status as a former minister and through the intervention of ecclesiastical courts who were eager to maintain the public reputation of elderly ministers and to ensure their well-being.

The process by which an elderly minister was incorporated into his new role was not always smooth. Indeed, on occasion, an elderly minister could dissent from his new status and continue to intervene in parish affairs. In 1642, John Cockburn, elderly minister of Humbie was asked to 'abstaine from any such speaches or cariage as might justlie procure a dislyk' of any minister who agreed to be his helper. Similarly, in 1649, ministers in Peebles Presbytery found that Richard Powrie, the elderly minister at Dawyck, 'did not walke answerablie' or in accordance with his new role.[94] Such warnings policed the margins of the minister's incorporation into his new status, while reflecting his continuing influence in parish business.

Old age was accepted as a distinct stage in the life cycle of ministers in early modern Scotland. Accepting their duty as preachers, teachers and parish leaders, ministers understood the challenges of their calling, but the weight of these burdens invariably increased as ministers grew older. While there was no single point that defined old age in this period – these definitions were based purely on ability to fulfil

[92] John Row, *The Historie of the Kirk of Scotland*, ed. William Fleming (Edinburgh, 1842), 211–12.
[93] NRS, CH2/449/2, 267.
[94] NRS, CH2/295/4, 2.

the role, rather than a predetermined age – clerics had to acknowledge the impact of age and decrepitude on their ministry. This involved a series of personal, bureaucratic and communal actions that allowed a minister to move from one role to another. This process maps quite neatly onto van Gennep's three stages of separation, transition and incorporation, but with the minister holding considerable power along the way. This process of transition represents a distinct bureaucratic and personal passage of status that every long-serving minister in early modern Scotland would experience.

The Impact of Legislative Reform on Baptisms, Marriages and Burials 1836–52, with particular reference to London

W. M. Jacob*
London

This article considers, with particular reference to London, the impact of legislation during the second quarter of the nineteenth century on the churches' practice of rites of passage in relation to births, marriages and deaths. It investigates the religious, political and social reasons for legislation relating to these rites which many contemporaries and subsequent historians considered an attack on the Church of England and evidence of advancing secularization. It shows that despite significant constitutional, social and religious changes during these years, religiously motivated politicians, sympathetic to the established church, achieved legislation introducing general registration of births, marriages and deaths, and providing for more satisfactory burial of London's rapidly growing population in the context of a high death rate. While satisfying some grievances of religious Dissenters, this protected the established church's interests, and evidence suggests that a high proportion of London's population continued to access its rites of passage for baptism, marriage and burial.

In the mid-nineteenth century, legislation was passed that had the most significant impact on rites of passage of births, marriages and burials in England and Wales since parish registers had been introduced for recording baptisms, marriages and burials in 1538.[1] The Registration and Marriage Acts 1836 introduced a national registration system apart from the Church of England's parish registers and

* E-mail: wmjacob20@gmail.com.

[1] Lord Hardwicke's Marriage Act of 1753 and Sir George Rose's Act of 1812 had made modifications to requirements for registration and introduced printed registers. For a detailed discussion of the 1753 Marriage Act, see R. B. Outhwaite, *Clandestine Marriage in England 1500–1850* (London, 1995), 75–167; Keith A. Francis, '"An Absurd, a Cruel, a Scandalous and a Wicked [Bill]": The Church of England and the (Clandestine) Marriage Act of 1753', in David J. B. Trim and Peter J. Balderstone, eds, *Cross, Crown and Community: Religion, Government and Culture in Early Modern Britain 1400–1800* (Bern, 2004), 277–307.

Studies in Church History 59 (2023), 265–288
doi: 10.1017/stc.2023.11

provided for marriages elsewhere than in churches, and a series of acts from the 1830s onwards provided for burials in other than parish burial grounds. Many contemporaries – like subsequent historians – considered this a successful attack by Dissenters and secularists on the Church of England's monopoly on providing these rites of passage and a first step towards disestablishment.[2] This article, referring particularly to London, will show that, although the legislation marked further adjustments in the relationship between church and state, it did much to safeguard the interests of the established church, which subsequently continued to provide a high proportion of these rites of passage for a rapidly growing urban population.

In order to demonstrate this, the article will explore the complex interaction of religious, political, legal, economic and social factors involved in securing legislation affecting rites of passage in a changing world. It will show that, despite Anglican fears and Dissenters hopes that the steps taken to remedy the Dissenting community's grievances about the provision of rites of passage would lead to the disestablishment of the Church of England, this did not happen. While partially relieving Dissenters' grievances, a still very largely Anglican parliament and government ministers took into account Anglican anxieties and achieved Registration Acts and burial legislation that largely protected the established church's interests.

The issues involved in achieving this legislation and its impact on the provision of rites of passage have not previously been considered synoptically by historians of nineteenth-century English religion. Owen Chadwick and G. I. T. Machin in their major studies briefly discussed the significance of the 1836 Registration Acts, and Robert Rodes Jr considered legislation in relation to burials, also briefly.[3] M. J. Cullen offered a more extensive discussion of the background to the Registration Acts and the emergence of the statistical

[2] See, for example, Julie Rugg, 'The Rise of the Cemetery Company in Britain 1820–53' (PhD thesis, University of Stirling, 1992), 260; Peter C. Jupp, *From Dust to Ashes: Cremation and the British Way of Death* (Basingstoke, 2006), 9–10.

[3] Owen Chadwick, *The Victorian Church,* Part One: *1829–1859* (London, 1966), 143–6; G. I. T. Machin, *Politics and the Churches in Great Britain 1832–68* (Oxford, 1977), 43–56; Robert E. Rodes Jr, *Law and Modernization in the Church of England: Charles II to the Welfare State* (Notre Dame, IN, 1991), 142–8. For the wider context of religion in London during this period, compare also W. M. Jacob, *Religious Vitality in Victorian London* (Oxford, 2021), 33–58.

movement,[4] and Olive Anderson discussed the impact of provision for civil marriage following the Marriage Registration Act 1836.[5] In an article on Bethnal Green, Arthur Burns noted the impact of the creation of new parishes on rites of passage.[6] Studies of religion in poor districts in late-nineteenth and early twentieth-century London have also noted the continuing high rates of baptisms and marriages in Anglican churches at the end of the nineteenth century.[7] As will be seen, civil registration was comparatively easily achieved, contrasting with the complexity of issues around burial legislation, which will occupy the greater part of this article. Discussion of these has chiefly focused on joint-stock cemeteries and their design. James Stevens Curl's *The Victorian Celebration of Death*[8] was a pioneer study, discussing funerals and burial in London, and F. H. W. Sheppard considered the origins of London's first joint-stock cemetery at Kensal Green in the *Survey of London* volume on North Kensington.[9] Since the 1980s there has been considerable interest in the origins and developments of London's cemeteries.[10] The

[4] M. J. Cullen, 'The Making of the Civil Registration Act of 1836', *JEH* 25 (1974), 39–59; idem, *The Statistical Movement in Early Victorian Britain: The Foundations of early Empirical Research* (Hassocks, 1975).

[5] Olive Anderson, 'The Incidence of Civil Marriage in Victorian England and Wales', *P&P* 69 (1975), 50–87; eadem, 'The Incidence of Civil Marriage in Victorian England and Wales: A Rejoinder', *P&P* 84 (1979), 156–61

[6] Arthur Burns, '"My Unfortunate Parish": Anglican Urban Ministry in Bethnal Green 1809–*c.*1850', in Melanie Barber and Stephen Taylor with Gabriel Sewell, eds, *From the Reformation to the Permissive Society: A Miscellany in Celebration of the 400th Anniversary of Lambeth Palace Library*, CERS 18 (Woodbridge, 2010), 269–393, at 281, 292–3, 328, 365–88.

[7] S. C. Williams, *Religious Belief and Popular Culture in Southwark,* c.*1880–1939* (Oxford, 1999), 87–104; Jeffrey Cox, *The English Churches in a Secular Society: Lambeth 1870–1930* (New York, 1982), 98.

[8] James Stevens Curl, *The Victorian Celebration of Death* (Newton Abbot, 1972).

[9] F. H. W. Sheppard, ed., *Survey of London*, 37: *North Kensington* (London, 1973), 333–9.

[10] Chris Brookes and Elliot Brent, *Mortal Remains: The History and Present State of the Victorian and Edwardian Cemetery* (Exeter, 1989); Ralph Houlbrooke, ed., *Death, Ritual and Bereavement* (London, 1989); Deborah Elaine Wiggins, 'The Burial Acts and Cemetery Reform in Great Britain 1815–1914' (PhD thesis, Texas Technical University, 1991); Julie Rugg, 'Rise of the Cemetery Company'; John Pinfold, 'The Green Ground'; Peter C. Jupp, 'Enon Chapel: No Way for the Dead'; Julie Rugg, 'The Origin and Progress of Cemetery Establishment in Britain', all in Peter C. Jupp and Glennys Howarth, eds, *The Changing Face of Death: Historical Accounts of Death and Disposal* (Basingstoke, 1997), 76–89, 90–104, 105–19; Mary Elizabeth Hotz, 'Down among the Dead: Edwin Chadwick's Burial Reform Discourse in Mid-Nineteenth-Century England', *Victorian Literature and Culture* 29 (2001), 21–38;

major study of burial practices is Thomas W. Laqueur's *The Work of the Dead: A Cultural History of Mortal Remains*.[11] However, none of these has considered the religious dimension of this legislation in its political and social context.

The Registration and Marriage Acts 1836

Until the late 1820s England and Wales remained essentially a confessional state. The legislation introducing the registration of baptisms, marriages and burials by the parish priest in 1538 had imposed a financial penalty for failure to register them. In 1653, under the Commonwealth, responsibility for registering baptisms and burials was transferred to elected 'Parish Registers', and that for conducting and registering marriage to justices of the peace. The previous arrangement was restored in 1660, all citizens being assumed to be Anglicans. After 1689 Trinitarian 'Dissenters' from the established church were permitted to register their meeting houses for the purpose of public worship, but not for the conduct and registration of legally valid marriages. The Clandestine Marriages Act 1753 required that to be valid marriages must take place in a church before an Anglican clergyman, after banns had been published or a licence obtained. Quakers and Jews, however, were exempted from its provisions.[12] Between 1800 and 1830 numbers of Methodist and Dissenting congregations increased significantly, especially in rapidly growing provincial towns. Dissenters' and Roman Catholics' growing numbers and increasing political influence led to repeal of legislation imposing Anglican tests for holding public office in 1828, and Irish unrest led to emancipation for Roman Catholics in 1829.[13] The 1832 Reform Act increased numbers of non-Anglican voters, making

Jupp, *Dust to Ashes*; James Stevens Curl, ed., *Kensal Green Cemetery: The Origins and Development of the General Cemetery of All Souls' Kensal Green, London 1824–2001* (Chichester, 2001); John M. Clarke, *London's Necropolis: A Guide to Brookwood Cemetery* (Stroud, 2004); Catherine Arnold, *Necropolis: London and its Dead* (London, 2006); Darren Beach, *London's Cemeteries* (London, 2006).

[11] Thomas W. Laqueur, *The Work of the Dead: A Cultural History of Mortal Remains* (Princeton, NJ, 2015).

[12] See W. E. Tate, *The Parish Chest: A Study of the Records of Parochial Administration in England* (Cambridge, 1960), 44–50.

[13] Machin, *Politics and the Churches*, 8, 21–2.

governments susceptible to their interests. Dissenters, most of whom believed that the state's role should be restricted to maintaining order, protecting property, promoting prosperity and resisting enemies, objected to state-enforced rates payable by all occupiers of land in a parish to fund parish churches and burial grounds, and tithes to fund clergy. They wanted the Church of England to be financed by members' voluntary contributions, as their chapels were. They were irked by the Church of England's role in registering baptisms and deaths, and by the fact that the 1753 Marriage Act recognized only marriage in church as legal marriage. Parish registers were usually also the only evidence courts accepted as evidence in inheritance and property disputes, and a number of court cases in the 1820s held Dissenting chapel registers to be inadmissible as evidence. Dissenters also objected to the parish clergy's monopoly on officiating in parish burial grounds, and to the fact that, under canon 68 of the Church of England's canons of 1604, clergy might decline to bury unbaptized Baptist children or Unitarians baptized without a Trinitarian formula.[14]

After 1829 the Protestant Dissenting Deputies, who represented Baptists, Independents, Presbyterians and Unitarians, the major denominations of Old Dissent, began pressing for 'General Registration' of births, marriages and deaths. When nothing happened following the 1832 Reform Act, in 1833 they formed a United Committee on Dissenting Grievances which began pressing for general registration of births and legislation to permit marriages in their chapels. Lord John Russell as home secretary, while friendly, was not particularly responsive.[15]

In addition, interest in demography, aroused by Thomas Malthus, and concerns about population growth led the British Association for the Advancement of Science to establish a Statistical Section, also in 1833. They and the London Statistical Society began campaigning for more accurate registration of births, marriages and deaths.[16]

[14] See: <https//www.anglican.net:doctrines:1604-canon-law>, last accessed 7 December 2022. Canon 68 forbade clergy to refuse burial to any except suicides, excommunicates and the unbaptized, as in the rubric of the Book of Common Prayer Order for the Burial of the Dead.

[15] See Bernard Lord Manning, *The Protestant Dissenting Deputies* (Cambridge, 1952), 261–75.

[16] The British Association was founded in 1831 by William Vernon Harcourt, a canon residentiary of York and a distinguished geologist: see Jack Morrell, 'Harcourt, William

Complaints about inadequacies of church registers for reliable statistical evidence were made to a House of Commons select committee. Following the 1831–2 cholera epidemic, there was also pressure, largely from newly emerging medical journalists, for causes of death to be recorded in the registration of deaths.[17]

Episcopal opposition in the House of Lords in 1831 to the first and second Reform Bills and to the eventual 1832 Reform Act had provoked much anti-clericalism. This was fuelled by the republication of John Wade's *Black Book*, identifying the established church with 'Old Corruption'. Many bishops, clergy and lay Anglicans feared that the minority government following the first general election after the Reform Act (based on the new franchise), dependent on votes of Anglican members of the House of Commons feared to be sympathetic towards Dissenters, would place the established church in danger of radical political intervention. The Irish Church Temporalities Act passed in 1833 and the Ecclesiastical Commission established in 1835 to investigate the church's property fuelled these anxieties about the survival of the church's establishment and endowments.[18]

Dissenters, however, differed in their attitudes and strategy towards the established church. Wesleyan Methodists generally accepted establishment. While Independent and Baptist leaders favoured an immediate campaign to disestablish and disendow the church, Unitarians advocated a gradualist approach to dismantling establishment. Petitions were presented in parliament from numerous Dissenting congregations airing their grievances but although politicians were receptive to some reform, achieving a bill about registration acceptable to all parties that might achieve a majority in both houses proved difficult.[19]

Although minority post-reform ministries needed to be sensitive to Dissenting voters, the great majority of government ministers and members of both houses were thoughtful Anglicans who recognized

Venables Vernon (1789–1873)', *ODNB*, online edn (2004), at: <https://doi-org.lonlib.idm.oclc.org/10.1093/ref:odnb/12249>.

[17] Cullen, 'Making of the Civil Registration Act', 46–9.

[18] For the Ecclesiastical Commissions see G. F. A. Best, *Temporal Pillars: Queen Anne's Bounty, the Ecclesiastical Commissioners, and the Church of England* (Cambridge, 1964), 296–347.

[19] Cullen, 'Making of the Civil Registration Act', 50–6; Richard Brent, *Liberal Anglican Politics: Whiggery, Religion and Reform 1830–1841* (Oxford, 1987), 252–62.

the need to respond to some of the Dissenters' grievances by adjusting the church's establishment without endangering it.[20] Lord John Russell as Whig home secretary was strongly criticized by Dissenters when he introduced a bill which made no provision for general registration of births, marriages and deaths apart from church or meeting house registers.[21] When the Whig ministry fell, the devout Tory churchman Sir Robert Peel introduced a bill proposing a form of civil marriage preceding a religious rite.[22] After his government fell, Russell took it up. These early proposals exposed the complexities of the issues. In the general context of suspicion of governmental power and patronage, increased government expenditure and higher taxes, there was opposition to a central national registration system. There were also criticisms of the proposals for requiring civil marriage prior to a religious rite of the parties' choice. Much anxiety was expressed that if banns of marriage were not read in parish churches, which remained a major focus of communal life and information, the lack of community publicity would increase the risk of clandestine marriages. There were also concerns that poor people, having registered a child's name with a registrar, would forgo baptism, thus endangering a child's immortal soul (and eligibility for Christian burial).[23] Anglican clergy petitioned against the proposals. The bishops in the House of Lords sought to defend the Anglican ideal of marriage, and with it the 1753 Marriage Act, although Archbishop Howley and six other bishops, while opposing provision for civil marriages, did not object to marriages in registered non-Anglican places of worship.[24]

The Registration Act in 1836 established national registration of births and deaths. No penalty was imposed for not giving information

[20] See Brent, *Liberal Anglican Politics*, 65–103.

[21] For Russell's religious sympathies see John Prest, 'Russell, John [*formerly* Lord John Russell], first Earl Russell (1792–1878)', *ODNB*, online edn (2004), at: <https://doi-org.lonlib.idm.oclc.org/10.1093/ref:odnb/21764>; Brent, *Liberal Anglican Politics*, 56–63, 137.

[22] For Peel's strong Anglican sympathies, see Machin, *Politics and the Churches*, 48–9.

[23] For reports of the numerous parliamentary debates about registration bills, see Parl. Deb. (3rd series), 25 February 1834 (vol. 21, cols 776–89); 3 March 1834 (vol. 21, cols 994–9); 17 March 1835 (vol. 26, cols 1073–1180); 15 April 1836 (vol. 32, cols 1087–92, 1093–1101); 13 June 1836 (vol. 34, cols 130–45, 490–4); 11 July 1836 (vol. 35, cols 79–89); 21 July 1836 (vol. 35, cols 375–6); 28 July 1836 (vol. 35, cols 604–6); 1 August 1836 (vol. 35, cols 689–92).

[24] Nicholas Dixon, 'The Activity and Influence of the Established Church in England, *c.*1800–1837' (PhD thesis, University of Cambridge, 2019), 83–5.

to a registrar about a birth within forty-two days, a concession to the Church of England which was reversed in 1874; in contrast, registration of death, including recording the cause, was compulsory. This largely satisfied Dissenters but disappointed statisticians. Registration was achieved economically and locally, with registrars based in the new Poor Law unions, and most people continued to seek baptism for their children and funerals for their dead in parish churches or Dissenting places of worship. The accompanying Marriage Act retained parish clergy as registrars for marriages in churches, and permitted marriages in registered non-Anglican places of worship in the presence of a registrar, as well as marriage before a registrar without a religious rite. Politicians thus preserved the role of the clergy of the established church as registrars for marriages and partially resolved Dissenters' grievances by permitting marriages in their meeting houses in the presence of a registrar, and providing a civil form of marriage for those who desired no religious rite. This model of adapting existing practice to new circumstances without significantly infringing on the established church's role was subsequently followed in adapting arrangements for the burial of the dead.

Forebodings among church people that civil registration would lead to a falling away (especially of poor people) from faith to infidelity and secularism, and bring divine judgement on the nation, were not fulfilled. There are, however, at least two reasons why it is not possible to provide accurate estimates of the impact of the legislation on numbers of baptisms and marriages in central and east London's densely populated poor parishes. First, rapid population growth in such parishes renders comparisons difficult. Second, the subdivision during the 1830s and 1840s of most populous central and east London parishes makes comparisons impossible. However, limited evidence from one of the most populous central London parishes and comments from incumbents of newly subdivided parishes suggest that parish churches continued to be very busy with baptisms and marriages. At St Giles-in-the-Fields in Holborn, with a population of around forty thousand, curates conducted 617 baptisms and 212 weddings in 1840.[25] In Bethnal Green, which was subdivided during

[25] London, LMA, P82/GIS/A/02/012–013, St Giles-in-the-Fields, Baptism Registers, February 1837 – March 1840, March 1840 – May 1841; P82/GIS/A/03/012–013, St Giles-in the-Fields, Marriage Registers, July 1837 – May 1840, May 1840 – April 1842.

the 1820s, 1830s and 1840s into eleven new parishes,[26] it was claimed that numbers of baptisms increased from 768 in 1840 to 2,030 in 1850.[27] In 1858, a leading Anglican philanthropist, William Cotton, in evidence to a House of Lords select committee, noted that in one district of Bethnal Green when a new church had been opened, eight hundred men, women and children were baptized in the course of a year.[28] The incumbent of St Peter's, Stepney, in evidence reported 538 baptisms in the previous year.[29] The rector of St Matthew's, Bethnal Green, reported thirty or forty baptisms every Sunday.[30] In 1859, he also alleged that his neighbour at St Philip's had reduced his fee for conducting weddings to 2*s*. 6*d*., attracting people from all over London and frequently marrying fifty couples a day.[31] Thomas Dale, vicar of St Pancras parish, where marriages were reserved to the parish church, reported 1,522 marriages in 1857, including forty-two on Christmas Day.[32] The evidence does not suggest that in London during the decades after the passage of the Registration Act there was a significant falling away in poor districts from seeking rites of passage in parish churches.

Burial Legislation 1832–53

The achievement of civil registration of births, marriages and deaths in the context of the tensions between Anglicans and Dissenters was relatively simple compared with the complexities of solving the problem of providing for the burial of the dead in London, in this context and that of London's rapid population growth and high death rate,

26 See M. H. Port, *Six Hundred New Churches: The Church Building Commission 1818–1856* (London, 1961), 25–6, 37.

27 London, Tower Hamlets Local History Library, LC2203, *Bethnal Green Churches and Schools Fund Report, 1854* (n.pl., 1854), 94.

28 *Report of the Select Committee of the House of Lords appointed to inquire into the Deficiency of Means of Spiritual Instruction and Places of Worship in the Metropolis and in other Populous Districts in England and Wales, especially in tbe Mining and Manufacturing Districts and to consider the fittest means of meeting the Difficulties of the case, 18 June 1858* (London, 1858), 4.

29 Ibid. 67.

30 Ibid. 34.

31 *Bethnal Green Churches and Schools Fund Report 1854*, photocopy of an unpaginated letter of 25 April 1859 from the rector of St Matthew's, Bethnal Green, to Henry Mackenzie, vicar of St Martin-in-the-Fields, pasted into the back cover.

32 *Report of the Select Committee of the House of Lords*, 200.

changing attitudes to burial customs, anxieties about public health, and suspicions of successive governments' centralizing tendencies. Another seventeen years was required to achieve a solution, with which neither Anglicans nor Dissenters were entirely happy.

The Situation in the 1830s

In the rapidly growing metropolis, most people were buried near the communities in which they had lived, in their parish burial ground and amongst their neighbours, by their parish clergy. Incumbents received customary fees for conducting burials which, especially in London. formed a significant proportion of their incomes, enabling them to employ curates to undertake the very large number of funerals. For example, at St Giles-in-the-Fields there were 1,856 funerals in 1840, with funerals taking place most days, some days fifteen to eighteen, and occasionally more: on 20 December 1840 there were forty funerals, and on 27 December thirty-nine. Seven curates were employed, one of whom seems only to have taken funerals, sometimes burying seven or eight people a day but occasionally fifteen, eighteen or twenty.[33] Some Dissenting meeting houses, especially Quakers and Baptists, had their own burial grounds, and there was a large Dissenting burial ground at Bunhill Fields.[34] Otherwise Dissenters were buried in their parish burial grounds by parish clergy using the Prayer Book rite.[35] There were also some private commercial burial grounds, for example Samuel Sheen's New Burial Ground in Whitechapel.

In the late eighteenth and early nineteenth centuries, with rapid population growth, the churchyards of most central London parishes, and the vaults under churches for the better off, had been filled. Most parish vestries had acquired detached burial grounds beyond the built-up area, for example St James, Piccadilly, on Hampstead Road; St Giles-in-the-Fields adjoining St Pancras churchyard and St Marylebone at St John's Wood.[36] These burial grounds were

[33] LMA, P82/GIS/A/04/014–015, St Giles-in-the-Fields Burial Register, March 1838 – May 1840, May 1840 – August 1841.

[34] Bridget Cherry and Nikolaus Pevsner, *Buildings of England. London* 4: *North* (London, 1998), 607.

[35] Rugg, 'Origin and Progress of Cemetery Establishment', 111.

[36] St Marylebone's burial ground chapel survives as St John's Wood parish church.

provided with substantial chapels in which to conduct funeral services prior to burials, which also included burial vaults. The burial grounds were funded by parishes' church rates, payable by all property occupiers, including Dissenters. Only Anglican clergy were permitted by canon law to conduct funerals in these burial grounds, which had been episcopally consecrated, and only of baptized people. In the later 1830s some Anglican clergy, influenced by Tractarianism, became rigorous in their baptismal requirements for burials, resulting in a number of successful legal challenges by Dissenters to this interpretation of canon 68 and the Prayer Book rubric.

By the 1830s, most detached parochial burial grounds were surrounded by suburban residential developments. Customarily churchyards were buried over many times, with bones found when new graves were dug being deposited in a 'bone house'. London churchyards were usually reburied about every ten years. While urban churchyards had always been crowded, with continuing rapidly growing populations, high death rates and the arrival of cholera, the new burial grounds were becoming very full, and some were probably buried over too quickly, before the completion of the natural process of decay. Concerns were raised about the seemliness of too frequent reburying.[37]

Attitudes to death were also changing. The increase of the middling sort, able to afford doctors' fees, had led to a considerable growth in medical training and an increased need for bodies for dissection. The only legal source of such cadavers was executed criminals, which were in short supply. In consequence, an illegal trade in recently dead bodies stolen from burial grounds developed.[38] 'Body-snatching' and dissection, it was feared, threatened the hope of physical resurrection on the Day of Judgment, and there was also horror about desecration of bodies of loved ones. In the 1820s, therefore, urban burial grounds began to be defended with high walls and watch towers. Although the 1832 Anatomy Act rendered 'body snatching' redundant, anxiety about the security and integrity of interred bodies continued, and the practice of reburying over parochial burial grounds and depositing excavated bones in 'bone houses' became distasteful. People also seem to have become more conscious

[37] See Pinfold, 'Green Ground', 80–4.

[38] For 'body snatching', see Ruth Richardson, *Death, Dissection and the Destitute* (London, 1988).

of smells, and in the 1830s some doctors began associating decaying bodies with 'miasma', spread through the air, which was claimed to spread fevers and especially cholera.[39]

Since the late seventeenth century, the rich had sought burial in vaults in churches and burial grounds, and the growing London middle class also began seeking security of tenure in their graves. The expanding Dissenting population increasingly sought burial in their own grounds, unsullied by what they saw as superstitious and Romish episcopal consecration. From the 1820s, Dissenting elites in provincial towns and cities, such as Manchester, Liverpool, Leeds and Norwich began replacing their crowded burial grounds and vaults, and offering an alternative to parish burial grounds in the form of unconsecrated cemeteries, well defended from 'body snatchers' and established as joint-stock companies, on the outskirts of these centres.[40] Here their own ministers might conduct funerals, with no risk of Anglican clergy refusing to bury Baptist children and Unitarians. Dissenters considered the provision of new cemeteries an aspect of reforming 'old corruption' and promoting civic respectability in expanding towns, illustrating voluntarism in action. Reflecting the demography of Dissenting congregations, these new cemeteries tended to attract mostly middle-class burials.[41]

The Provision of Cemeteries in London

In London, where Dissenters were proportionately fewer than in major provincial cities, a proposal in the 1820s by George Frederick Carden for a joint-stock company landscaped cemetery failed.[42] However, in the 1830s a number of joint-stock cemeteries were established. Unlike in provincial towns, as Julie Rugg has pointed out, they were considered as investment opportunities, paying dividends to shareholders, who during the then financial boom were eagerly seeking investment opportunities. The major new

39 Laqueur, *Work of the Dead*, 217–27.

40 See Rugg, 'Rise of the Cemetery Company', 25–187; see also, for the establishment of a cemetery in a provincial town, Jim Morgan, 'The Burial Question in Leeds in the Eighteenth and Nineteenth Centuries', in Houlbrooke, ed., *Death, Ritual and Bereavement*, 95–104, at 96–9.

41 See Rugg, 'Rise of the Cemetery Company', 158–87.

42 Robert J. Moulder, 'Carden, George Frederick (1798–1874)', *ODNB*, online edn (2004), at: <https://doi-org.lonlib.idm.oclc.org/10.1093/ref:odnb/59472>.

suburban London joint-stock cemeteries at Kensal Green (1834), West Norwood (1836), Brompton (1837), Highgate (1839) and Nunhead (1840) were expensive projects with fashionable designs, intended to attract investors and pay dividends, and providing a luxury commodity permitting elite memorialization.[43]

These initiatives aroused anxieties among clergy and parish vestries, for, apart from losing their spiritual and pastoral role as ministers of the established church, clergy feared the loss of burial fee income which funded curates. At Christ Church, Spitalfields, fees provided nearly half the rector's income, from which he paid his curates' stipends.[44] It was also an issue for Dissenting ministers, who may have been even more reliant on income from burials in vaults under chapels.[45] These new London cemetery companies sought incorporation by Act of Parliament, securing which required mollifying the church interest, for Bishop Blomfield of London had successfully opposed an early cemetery bill in the Lords. However, a solution was achieved that partially remedied the growing Dissenting community's grievances about the provision of burial grounds while protecting the established church's interests. Although some leading London incumbents threatened opposition, Blomfield's support for the Kensal Green cemetery bill in 1832 was secured by establishing a precedent that cemetery companies should pay fees to incumbents, depending on the type of grave, for burying bodies from their parishes. Blomfield's concern for public health made him generally sympathetic to establishing cemeteries, providing land was consecrated, chapels provided and clergy recompensed for losing fees from their parochial burial grounds. He agreed to consecrate part of Kensal Green's land, stipulating only that an Anglican chapel should be built, thus making burial there acceptable for Anglicans. A chapel was also provided for Dissenters. An Anglican chaplain, licensed by the bishop, was appointed, paid £200 a year by the cemetery company. The investment for acquiring the land, landscaping it and

43 For London joint-stock cemetery companies, see Brookes, *Mortal Remains*, 11–29; Rugg, 'Rise of the Cemetery Company', 204–37. Rugg has pointed out that although London cemeteries have received the most attention from historians, they were exceptional in having a profit motive.

44 See James Stevens Curl, 'The General Cemetery Company 1833–1842', in idem, ed., *Kensal Green Cemetery*, 80–106; Rugg, 'Rise of the Cemetery Company', 185.

45 Jupp, 'Enon Chapel', 92–7; idem, *Dust to Ashes*, 26.

building classical-style chapels and vaults was very significant.[46] An alternative to the communal parochial burial ground was now available for London's better off, providing peace, security and seclusion in death, matching the conditions they were obtaining in life in the growing suburbs. However, business was initially slow. There were 84 interments in 1833, 197 in 1834, 360 in 1835, 427 in 1836, 677 in 1837, 787 in 1838, and thereafter about nine hundred a year.[47] By comparison, as we have seen, St Giles-in-the-Fields burial ground alone had 1,856 funerals in 1840.[48] Subsequently other London joint-stock cemeteries sought parliamentary incorporation and consecration of part of their sites to attract Anglican burials.

The exception was Abney Park, in the Dissenting stronghold of Stoke Newington, where all the trustees were Congregationalists. They did not seek parliamentary incorporation in order to avoid episcopal pressure for consecration of part of the land and fees payable to incumbents of parishes where the deceased lived. Abney Park Cemetery offered 'common' graves for paupers against the boundary wall,[49] and the City of London's Tower Hamlets Cemetery Company (1841) and the Victoria Park Cemetery Company (1845) also achieved financial success by aiming for the cheap end of the market, including the provision of common graves packed as densely as possible for pauper burials paid for by Poor Law guardians. However, the new cemeteries did not meet the need for burial grounds for the rapidly growing numbers of poor people amid a high death rate.[50]

Public Health Concerns about Burials

As we have noted, in the 1830s concerns began to arise about burial grounds as sources of infection arising from 'miasma' following London's first cholera outbreak in 1831–2. London burial grounds were extensively and melodramatically denounced by George Alfred

[46] Rugg, 'Rise of the Cemetery Company', 250–79,

[47] See Ruth Richardson and James Stevens Curl, 'George Frederick Carden and the Genesis of the General Cemetery Company'; Curl, 'The Architectural Competition of 1831–2 and its Aftermath'; and idem, 'General Cemetery Company', all in idem, ed., *Kensal Green Cemetery*, 22–46, 50–77, 80–106.

[48] LMA, P82/GIS/A/04/014–015, St Giles-in-the-Fields, Burial Registers, March 1838 – May 1840, May 1840 – August 1841.

[49] For Abney Park, see Cherry and Pevsner, *Buildings of London* 4, 536–7.

[50] Rugg, 'Rise of the Cemetery Company', 228.

Walker, a Quaker doctor living in Drury Lane, close to densely packed inner-city burial grounds at St Clement Danes and the Dissenting Enon Chapel. His lurid and sensationalist allegations in *Gatherings from Graveyards* (1839) and subsequent publications claimed that miasma arising from central London's forty-three burial grounds was a public health hazard. These claims were supported by some ambitious members of the as-yet unregulated medical profession in the newly launched *Lancet.*[51] How objective Walker's observations were is difficult to ascertain. Robert Bentley Todd, an Anglican and leading reforming surgeon at King's College Hospital in the Strand, which adjoined a burial ground denounced by Walker as particularly offensive and evil-smelling and an unhealthy place to live, in evidence to a select committee denied that offensive smells came from the burial ground and that it was an unhealthy place to live.[52] Also *The Builder*, in an article in 1846, noted St Giles-in-the Fields' burial ground, along with other parish burial grounds denounced by Walker, as 'well kept'.[53]

Walker's widely read exposés of parish burial grounds, and a steep rise in poor rates, led to a select committee on the health of the poorer classes in large towns, chaired by Robert Slaney MP, who was much concerned with the condition of the poor. Walker testified to the committee twice, alleging a coincidence of sickness among grave diggers working with decaying bodies. This influenced Edwin Chadwick, the driving force behind public health reform in the 1840s,[54] to regard cemetery provision as a major public health issue. Chadwick's *Report on the Sanitary Condition of the Labouring Population of Great Britain* (1843), revealing the filth and appalling health conditions in poor districts, led to a royal commission on the health of towns, which he assisted while completing a supplementary

[51] John Pinfold, 'Walker, George Alfred (1807–1884)', *ODNB*, online edn (2004), at: <https://doi-org.lonlib.idm.oclc.org/10.1093/ref:odnb/28484>. Only in 1858 was registration of medical practitioners established, but unqualified practice was not prohibited: see Christopher Lawrence, *Medicine in the Making of Modern Britain* (London, 1994), 16–25, 32–42.

[52] Pinfold, 'Green Ground', 84, quoting *House of Commons Select Committee Report*, Parliamentary Papers 1842, QQ. 1109–18, 2412–13, 2437–41.

[53] *The Builder* 4 (1846), 281, quoted in Curl, *Victorian Celebration of Death*, 135.

[54] For Chadwick, see Peter Mandler, 'Chadwick, Sir Edwin (1800–1890)', *ODNB*, online edn (2004), at: <https://doi-org.lonlib.idm.oclc.org/10.1093/ref:odnb/5013>.

report on metropolitan interments.[55] He recommended closing London's burial grounds, establishing new extra-urban, municipally controlled cemeteries and providing public mortuaries to avoid the health risk of poor people living alongside decaying relatives' bodies retained in their single-room dwellings, for fear of burying someone who was merely unconscious or while raising funds for a funeral. If a death occurred on a Wednesday or Thursday, the next Sunday (Sunday being the preferred day for poor people's funerals) was considered too soon for the funeral, and the body remained in the room with the family until the following Sunday. Sir John Simon, the City of London's medical officer of health, reckoned that at any moment there were probably thirty or forty bodies in single-room dwellings in the City awaiting burial.[56] Chadwick criticized joint-stock cemetery companies for commercializing burials and profiting from death, although this seems only to have been the case in London.[57] His recommendations, requiring extensive central government intervention, aroused much hostility at a time when state intervention in local matters was viewed with deep suspicion.

Legislation for Burials in London

Meanwhile the liberal conservative MP, William Mackinnon, a champion of the church,[58] achieved another select committee, to inquire into the evils arising from the interment of bodies in London and other large towns. Members included the leading Anglican evangelicals, Lord Ashley[59] and Sir Robert Inglis.[60] The

[55] *A Report on the Results of a Special Enquiry into the Practice of Interment in Towns, made at the Request of Her Majesty's Principal Secretary of State for the Home Department*, Parliamentary Papers 1843, vol. 12, col. 509.

[56] Sir John Simon, *City of London Medical Reports: Special Report on Intramural Interments* (1852), in E. Royston Pike, ed., *Human Documents of the Victorian Golden Age (1850–1875)* (London, 1967), 286–7.

[57] See Rugg, 'Rise of the Cemetery Company', 204–37.

[58] H. C. G. Matthew, 'Mackinnon, Sir William, baronet (1784–1870)', *ODNB*, online edn (2021), at: <https://doi-org.lonlib.idm.oclc.org/10.1093/ref:odnb/17619>.

[59] John Wolffe, 'Cooper, Anthony Ashley, seventh earl of Shaftesbury (1801–1885)', *ODNB*, online edn (2004), at: <https://doi-org.lonlib.idm.oclc.org/10.1093/ref:odnb/6210>.

[60] John Wolffe, 'Inglis, Sir Robert Harry, second baronet (1786–1855)', *ODNB*, online edn (2004), at: <https://doi-org.lonlib.idm.oclc.org/10.1093/ref:odnb/14406>; E. M. Forster, *Marianne Thornton, 1797–1887: A Domestic Biography* (London, 1956).

evidence confirmed that parish burial grounds were very overcrowded, although Blomfield claimed the evils were considerably exaggerated. Mackinnon focused on fees payable for burials, which revealed claims that many Dissenting ministers made more from the burial of the dead in chapel vaults than from their living congregations. Blomfield also claimed that clergy generally would be willing to 'make some sacrifice for the sake of effecting so great an improvement as is contemplated', although he recognized that they could not be expected willingly to surrender, in some cases, the greater part of their income 'arising from a practice that has hitherto not been complained of, without some compensation'. He complained that clergy experienced difficulties obtaining the statutory fees due to them from cemetery companies, themselves having to check cemetery companies' registers to identify such fees, and asserted that in twenty-three parishes clergy had experienced a six per cent decline in fee income between 1838 and 1840. He recommended that the government should take control of London's cemeteries and provide new cemeteries, while protecting clergy fees. The committee, however, recommended closing urban burial grounds, with vestries being permitted to establish new burial grounds funded from the rates, leaving some ground unconsecrated to provide for Dissenters.

The government failed to respond, so Mackinnon himself introduced a bill in the Commons in 1842 to close urban burial grounds and empower vestries to establish boards of health to provide cemeteries funded by church rates. Dissenters strongly objected to extending the powers of what they considered Anglican-controlled vestries, and also to the division of cemeteries into consecrated and unconsecrated ground and the fixing of fees for services conducted in cemeteries. They regarded these provisions as protecting Church of England interests. John Campbell, minister of Whitefield's Tabernacle, claimed that Mackinnon's bill endangered the future of Dissenting chapels by depriving ministers of income from fees for burials. The bill failed. Despite the publication of Chadwick's report, in the next parliamentary session Sir James Graham, the home secretary, indicated that he did not think a case had been made for legislation.[61]

Amidst Walker's continuing campaign against parish burial grounds, and increasing public health anxieties, in which Blomfield

[61] Jupp, *Dust to Ashes*, 26.

played a prominent part, new evidence emerged from statistical information in the registrar general's annual reports about London's very high death rate, especially among the young.[62] Lord John Russell, as home secretary, in 1847 secured the Cemetery Clauses Act which merely standardized provisions for private acts for cemeteries, generally following the outlines of Mackinnon's bill in protecting the church's interests. Private acts were required to provide for episcopal consecration of part of such cemeteries for Anglican use and an Anglican chapel, as well as a chapel 'for rites of any church or congregation other than the Church of England', and to appoint a chaplain licensed by the bishop, whose stipend was approved by the bishop. The bishop might object to any monumental inscription and procure its removal from any part of the cemetery. The act also provided for incumbents of parishes from which bodies came to be compensated for the loss of burial fees. It caused great offence to Dissenters and did nothing towards the continuing pressure on overcrowded metropolitan parochial burial grounds.[63]

In 1847, some London incumbents intervened, establishing a committee to consider the problem of burial grounds. They recommended legislation establishing unions of metropolitan parishes with boards of management with equal numbers of incumbents and laymen, empowered to raise funds for purchasing land for new extramural burial grounds, financed from fees. Parishioners would retain rights of burial as in existing burial grounds, with clergy conducting burials and approving inscriptions on gravestones. They also recommended providing mortuaries at cemeteries for bodies removed from 'small habitations', to be conveyed to burial grounds at fixed charges.[64]

Meanwhile the notorious fraudster Sir Richard Broun promoted the London Necropolis and National Mausoleum Company, proposing a National Mausoleum Church with a very large site for a burial ground on land acquired cheaply at Woking Common, sufficiently far from the metropolis to avoid infection from miasma arising

62 See Cullen, *Statistical Movement*, 39–41.

63 'An Act for consolidating in One Act certain Provisions usually contained in Acts authorizing the making of Cemeteries', 1847 (10 & 11 Vict., c. 65).

64 *Extramural Burial. The Three Schemes: I The London Clergy Plan. II The Board of Health or Erith Plan. III The Woking Necropolis Plan, with some General Remarks on the same* (London, 1850), 3–9.

from decaying bodies.[65] This Brookwood cemetery was to be connected by the London and South Western Railway to Waterloo Station, with mortuaries at Waterloo and two stations, one for Anglicans and one for Dissenters. It was proposed to serve all London.[66]

Against the background of the resurgence of Chartism in 1848, a severe cholera outbreak precipitated the Public Health Act 1848, steered by the devout Anglican Viscount Morpeth, responsible for public health as chief commissioner for woods and forests.[67] It established a General Board of Health, with Chadwick and Lord Ashley, with their long-standing interests in public health and the burial problem, as commissioners, and Thomas Southwood Smith, a Unitarian minister, physician, Benthamite and close associate of Chadwick in public health reform, as medical commissioner. It was empowered to create local boards of health, which might provide mortuaries and arrange burials, and inspect and close burial grounds. City of London parishes were excluded, despite their burial grounds being overwhelmed by cholera, increasing threefold the weekly rate of burial.[68]

Subsequently, to tackle the continuing problem of London's burial grounds, in April 1850 Sir George Grey, the devout evangelical Anglican and Whig home secretary,[69] noting that there had been meetings to consult clergy, successfully introduced the Metropolitan Interments Act to protect public health and 'the decency and solemnity of burial'.[70] It largely implemented Blomfield's recommendations to Mackinnon's select committee

[65] Anita McConnell, 'Broun, Sir Richard (1801–1858)', *ODNB*, online edn (2004), at: <https://doi-org.lonlib.idm.oclc.org/10.1093/ref:odnb/3595>.

[66] Clarke, *London's Necropolis*, 1–22. Clarke appears unaware of Broun's notoriety and his financial sharp practices.

[67] See Boyd Hilton, 'Whiggery, Religion and Social Reform: The Case of Lord Morpeth', *HistJ* 37 (1994), 829–59; R. K. Webb, 'Smith, (Thomas) Southwood (1788–1861)', *ODNB*, online edn (2004), at: <https://doi-org.lonlib.idm.oclc.org/10.1093/ref:odnb/25917>.

[68] Brookes, *Mortal Remains*, 43.

[69] David Frederick Smith, 'Grey, Sir George, second baronet (1799–1882)', *ODNB*, online edn (2004), at: <https://doi-org.lonlib.idm.oclc.org/10.1093/ref:odnb/11533>. When in London, Grey spent Sunday afternoons visiting the poor of St Giles-in-the-Fields.

[70] 'An Act to Make Better Provision for the Interment of the Dead in or near the Metropolis', 1850 (13 &14 Vict., c. 52).

and Chadwick's 1843 recommendations, establishing a Metropolitan Interment Commission empowered to close all urban burial grounds, take over existing joint-stock cemeteries and extend Kensal Green to serve West London, with a new cemetery for East London. The act protected Anglican interests, permitting the commission to provide mortuaries and consecrated ground for Anglicans, unconsecrated ground for non-Anglicans, and chapels, funded from the poor rate. Anglican chaplains were to be appointed, and incumbents retained the right to bury their parishioners and be compensated for loss of fees from new burial grounds. Noting that some form of fee formed nearly the whole of some incumbents' incomes, compensation would be continued beyond existing incumbencies, based on their average receipts from parish burial fees for the five years preceding the act. The bishop was authorized to oversee inscriptions on monuments. Parish clerks and sextons would be redeployed to the new cemeteries. To contain funeral costs and prevent exploitation by undertakers, the commission might seek tenders for contracts to undertake funerals in the cemeteries, and contract with railway and steamer companies for transporting bodies and mourners to cemeteries. Incumbents and non-Anglican ministers were to be paid the same fee for burials. It was envisaged that cemeteries would become self-financing from fees.[71] Many Dissenters objected strongly to having to pay rates to fund consecrated burial grounds and to compensate clergy for loss of fees, as well as paying fees for burials both to their own ministers and to Anglican clergy for what they considered should be a voluntary activity.[72]

During debates in the Commons, a leading critic of the established church, Sir Benjamin Hall, MP for Marylebone, fiercely criticized London clergy for making 'a traffic of their burial grounds', alleging abuses at the St Pancras burial ground of St Giles-in-the-Fields and claiming profiteering by the rector and malpractice by the sexton, who was allegedly ordained, acted as undertaker for funerals and solicited burials.[73] Lord Ashley, while defending the rector, admitted that inspection had shown that 'the system of pauper funerals was not

[71] See William Cunningham Glen, *The Metropolitan Interments Act 1850: With Introduction, Notes, and Appendix* (London, 1850); *Extramural Burial*, 27–34.

[72] Manning, *Protestant Dissenting Deputies*, 307.

[73] H. C. G. Matthew, 'Hall, Sir Benjamin (1802–1867)', *ODNB*, online edn (2004), at: <https://doi-org.lonlib.idm.oclc.org/10.1093/ref:odnb/11945>.

such as anyone could wish', but noted the rector was only one among many trustees managing the burial ground.[74] The act's centralizing principle was deeply disliked and Dissenters criticized it fiercely as a compromise with the established church. Moreover, the financial model for raising loans secured on income from rates proved unworkable; the Treasury successfully blocked finance for taking over cemeteries; and Chadwick was removed as a commissioner. Only Brompton Cemetery, where the trustees were in financial difficulties, was purchased by the Board of Health. The Metropolitan Interments Act proved a dead letter.[75]

The closure of inner London burial grounds enacted on health grounds placed the government under pressure to ensure that space was available for the burial of London's immense poor population, largely uncatered for by the joint-stock cemeteries. The Metropolitan Burial Act 1852, introduced by the devout Anglican Tory Lord John Manners as first commissioner of works,[76] in conjunction with other bills to reform London's sanitary arrangements, incorporated some elements from Mackinnon's bill and from the metropolitan clergy's recommendations. In contrast to the earlier act, localism prevailed, vestries being empowered to establish burial boards funded from the poor rate, to provide cemeteries or arrange for burials in existing cemeteries. The established church's interests were largely protected, for incumbents continued to chair vestries which elected burial boards. In new cemeteries ground might be consecrated for Anglican use and Anglican and Dissenting chapels provided, and parishioners continued to have a right of burial there with parish clergy officiating, who were entitled to receive fees. Bishops were authorized to approve inscriptions on monuments, for the erection of which clergy retained the right to receive fees. Boards might pay fees to clerks, sextons and churchwardens.[77] In the House of Lords, Lord Hardwicke explained that normally it was expected that a parish's own clergy would conduct funerals of

[74] See Parl. Deb. (3rd series), 15 April 1850 (vol. 110, cols 354–60), 3 June 1850 (vol 111, cols 677–710), 11 June 1850 (vol. 111, cols 1068–79), 14 June 1850 (vol 111, cols 1283–92).

[75] Brooks, *Mortal Remains*, 45–7.

[76] Jonathan Parry, 'Manners, John James Robert, seventh duke of Rutland (1818–1906)', *ODNB*, online edn (2004), at: <https://doi-org.lonlib.idm.oclc.org/10.1093/ref:odnb/17951>.

[77] 'Burial Act', 1852 (15 & 16 Vict., c. 85).

parishioners, while Dissenting ministers would conduct funerals in unconsecrated sections.[78] Government ministers resisted attempted amendments to permit Dissenting ministers to officiate in parish churchyards. Following amendment, the act was extended in 1853 to the rest of England and Wales.

Meanwhile the London Necropolis and National Mausoleum Company secured incorporation by Act of Parliament. Bishop Blomfield supported the bill in the Lords, although Lord Ashley, now seventh earl of Shaftesbury, objected that its distance from London would inconvenience the poor, and, if it were as successful as the promoters claimed, crowds of funerals would converge at Waterloo. He also claimed it would result in speculation in burial of the dead.[79] The cemetery company provided an 'all-in service' including mortuaries, transport to Brookwood in three different classes and refreshments after funerals. Space was allocated for parishes and community groups. An Anglican chaplain was appointed to conduct funerals and parish clergy were paid a fee of 6*s.* 2*d.* for burials from their parishes. Bishop Sumner of Winchester consecrated the Anglican section in 1854. However, although five parishes south of the river and six north of the river, including St Giles-in-the-Fields, St Anne's, Soho, and St Margaret's, Westminster, acquired sections, it had a slow start. The anticipated 10,000 burials a year, producing a ten per cent return for shareholders, was never achieved, the annual average for the first twenty years being 3,200.[80]

In 1853, Lord Palmerston as home secretary ordered 163 consecrated and 50 unconsecrated burial grounds to be closed, despite twenty-seven clergy petitioning against the closure of their parish's burial grounds.[81] Within three years, seven central London vestries, chaired by incumbents, established burial boards with cemeteries well outside built-up areas. The first was St Pancras where, although strong Dissenting representation on the vestry had resisted church rates for many years, the vicar laid the chapel foundation stone in 1853. Some parishes, as noted above, acquired sections at

78 Parl. Deb. (3rd series), 28 June 1852 (vol. 122, cols 1348–51).

79 'London Necropolis and National Mausoleum Bill', Parl. Deb. (3rd series), 8 June 1852 (vol. 122, cols 190–2). Lord Ashley succeeded to the earldom on his father's death in 1851.

80 For a detailed account of Brookwood's establishment, see Clarke, *London's Necropolis*, 1–15.

81 Wiggins, *Burial Acts*, 125–8.

Brookwood. Burial board cemeteries rendered new joint-stock companies financially unattractive investments. However, existing London joint-stock companies restored their finances by tendering to poor law guardians for burying paupers, usually in unmarked graves each taking ten coffins. Brookwood, exceptionally, buried paupers in private (although unmarked) graves, each reserved for one family. However, there, as elsewhere, paupers' funerals were, because of pressure of numbers, conducted en masse at the appropriate chapel prior to burial.[82]

The Impact of the Burial Legislation

Despite provision for incumbents to receive fees for burials from their parishes in new cemeteries, they complained of loss of income, and hence their capacity to pay curates, especially those largely employed in taking funerals. It was claimed the rector of St Clement Danes lost £150–200 from an income of £350–400 a year; the vicar of St Leonard's, Shoreditch, lost £300 a year and gave up a curate; and the rector of St Giles-in-the-Fields lost £700 from an income of £1,200.[83] The vicar of St Pancras noted that he had lost half his funeral fee income: the vestry having bought, jointly with Islington vestry, a cemetery in Finchley, he had retained half the fees, but had reduced his fee to compensate poor people for the expense of transporting bodies a much greater distance.[84] Overall about £30,000 a year was reckoned to have been lost to London clergy as a result of the Burial Acts.[85]

Conclusion

The evidence noted above given to the 1858 House of Lords select committee, and that gathered by Olive Anderson, Hugh McLeod and Sarah Williams for the late nineteenth century, suggests that the Church of England's rites of passage of baptism and marriage remained popular amongst poor Londoners at the end of the century. While the burial legislation had a much greater impact, in that it

82 Clarke, *London's Necropolis*, 16–22.
83 *Report of the Select Committee of the House of Lords*, vii.
84 Ibid. 200.
85 Ibid. 49.

separated the place of burial from the locality in which people lived, reducing the personal and communal aspect of funeral rites and burial, the religious element in burials, and especially that of the Church of England, was protected and preserved. Burial grounds, whether provided by incorporated joint-stock companies or vestry burial boards, continued to be required to secure episcopal consecration of a major part of their ground for Anglican burials, to provide an Anglican and a Dissenting chapel, and to appoint an Anglican chaplain licensed by the bishop. These pieces of legislation were achieved by ministers who themselves were Anglicans and sympathetic to the church, and sought solutions that protected church and clergy interests while seeking to ameliorate discrimination against Dissenters. These pieces of legislation did not lead to the Church of England's disestablishment, nor contribute to increasing secularization of English society.

The Early Nineteenth-Century Unitarian Campaign to change English Marriage Law

David L. Wykes*
Institute of Historical Research

The 1836 Marriage Act has received surprisingly little attention from historians of Dissent, despite its significance in permitting non-Anglicans to conduct legally recognized marriages according to their own ceremonies in Dissenting places of worship. The Clandestine Marriages Act (1753), better known as the Hardwicke Act, had limited valid marriages to the rites of the Church of England. Only Jews and Quakers were exempt. By the early nineteenth century the Anglican marriage service was objectionable to Unitarians because of the references to the Trinity. The struggle to change the Marriage Act was initiated by the Freethinking Christians, who engaged in a controversial and highly visible public protest during the marriage service. They successfully engaged the broader Unitarian movement in their campaign, who through the medium of the Unitarian Association undertook a remarkable, though largely fruitless, struggle to change the law until joined by the rest of Dissent in the early 1830s.

On Sunday 14 January 1827, at nine o'clock in the morning, Mr Lionel Trotter and Miss Agnes Campbell attended their parish church of St George the Martyr in Queen Square, Holborn, London, in order to be married. Trotter, his bride and the other members of the bridal party were Freethinking Christians. When the officiating minister, the Rev. John Holt Simpson, appeared at the altar, Trotter presented him with a paper of protest, stating that he and his bride were forced to submit to the marriage service of the Church of England, though 'contrary to their belief', as the only means of obtaining a legal marriage. Upon briefly glancing at the paper, Simpson said 'I refuse to marry the parties', and though called upon to perform his duty, left the altar. The wedding party

* Institute of Historical Research, Senate House, Malet St, London, WC1E 7HU. E-mail: wykesdl.history@gmail.com. I wish to thank Professor G. M. Ditchfield and the two anonymous referees for their helpful comments.

Studies in Church History 59 (2023), 289–311
doi: 10.1017/stc.2023.16

remained at the front of the church during the whole of the morning service. This, together with their refusal to take part, or, like the rest of the congregation, to wear mourning for the late Duke of York on conscientious grounds, made their behaviour even more striking.[1]

At the conclusion of the service, and before the administration of the sacrament, they were informed by the churchwardens that the legal hour for celebrating marriage had now passed. They were asked to attend the minister in the vestry, which they found filled with parish officers and members of the congregation. Among them was George Marriott, the well-known barrister and police magistrate. Trotter told Simpson that he had broken the law by his refusal. The person acting as the father to the bride likewise told Simpson: 'you have acted, Sir, unlawfully, in denying a civil right to these parties', and demanded to know whether Simpson would be willing to perform the service at ten on the following day. After what appears to have been a lengthy argument, Simpson was finally called upon for his decision. He deferred to Marriott, who confirmed that Simpson would be present to perform the service, provided that the bridal party was prepared to go through with it: 'to say all that other parties say, and not to say any thing that other parties do not say, and not to offer any obstruction'. Without agreeing to the conditions, the bridal party denied they had been obstructive and declared their intention of attending the next day.[2]

Presenting themselves the following morning at the vestry, they were accompanied by Samuel Thompson, who declared that he was the elder of the Freethinking Christian Church. They believed, he said, in 'one living and true God, and in his son, the *man* Jesus'. They had been 'compelled to act as they had done, in order to guard our consciences from violation'. He was interrupted by Marriott, and after Thompson had made a further statement about being persecuted for their faith, Marriott asked if the party would silently conform to the ceremony. Thompson replied that if the minister did his duty, they were 'prepared to act in the sight of God'.[3] The party then

[1] The incident was very widely reported, largely based on an account the Freethinking Christian Church provided. The following report is derived from 'Dissenters' Marriage', *Morning Chronicle*, 15 January 1827, 3; *Morning Post*, 16 January 1827, 4, *The Times*, 16 January 1827, 2–3. Simpson is not identified in the accounts, but see *Morning Advertiser*, 24 September 1835, 4.
[2] Ibid.
[3] *St James's Chronicle*, 16 January 1827, 3.

went into the church, where there was a considerable number present, both friends and others. On reaching the communion rail, Trotter offered another written protest to Simpson, stating the grounds on which they submitted to the law, but it accidentally fell to the ground where it remained unread. The service commenced, and continued uninterrupted until the bridegroom was told by the minister to repeat after him: 'In the name of the Father, and of the Son, and of the Holy Ghost'. Trotter at first refused. After Simpson insisted that he had to conform in every respect with the liturgy, he reluctantly repeated the words, protesting after saying 'in the name of the Son', and again after repeating 'in the name of the Holy Ghost'. Thompson also objected. Simpson paused, but after conferring with Marriott, continued. The bride, though encouraged to refuse by Thompson and her friends, appears to have complied with the rubric. When the minister was pronouncing the blessing, Thompson again interrupted the service, instructing the bridal party to turn their backs upon the altar, against which Simpson expostulated. Simpson told the party to kneel during the concluding prayers. They protested, saying that it was not required, whereupon Simpson stopped the service, and sat down by the altar. Marriott advised him simply to wait for the party to come to a better resolution. After a little while they did, expressing their wish to have the ceremony completed. The service was then concluded in the usual way, except that the bridal party turned their backs on the clergyman and the altar, 'in a disrespectful and unusual manner' when the Trinity was invoked during the final blessing. Afterwards Thompson expressed his regret that the law should inflict so unnecessary an injury upon all the parties concerned.[4]

The incident was widely reported. Not surprisingly the congregation and its supporters were outraged by the accounts of such irreverent, blasphemous behaviour, and the disrespect shown to the officiating clergyman. *The Times* denounced the hypocrisy of 'those who stickle for liberty of conscience', but did not allow it to others, and continued: 'Was ever absurdity like this? The bridegroom comes to demand the celebration of a rite, and at the same time protests against its celebration in the only way in which the clergyman has sworn and is bound to celebrate it. The clergyman has no option!'[5] The *St James's Chronicle* also condemned Trotter and his bride, who

[4] Ibid. See also *Morning Post*, 16 January 1827, 4.
[5] *The Times*, 16 January 1827, 2.

'thought their marriage a fit occasion to get up a scene in a crowded London church'. The cry of persecution had, indeed, been raised, but nobody forced Trotter and his bride into a marriage ceremony that they then spurned. They were told to seek 'the services of a Scotch blacksmith, or a French intendant'.[6]

The public protest by Trotter and his party was not an isolated case. There were at least another nine examples between 1814 and 1827, with more after this date. The written protests issued by couples (including Trotter and his bride) were careful to deny any intention of acting disrespectfully towards either the law or the officiating clergyman.[7] Both the Church of England clergy and those who objected to the Anglican service were in a hard place. The former had no choice. They were not at liberty to refuse to marry those who presented themselves, nor could they lawfully dispense with any part of the service, although it is clear that a number did do so to accommodate Unitarian objections. It was customary in any case to leave out most of the prayers.[8] On the other hand, being only human, some clergymen, having been challenged, were quite vindictive. The Rev. Hugh Jones, vicar of West Ham, Essex, not only went through the marriage service but, although he had pronounced the couple man and wife, insisted that they stayed as the ceremony was not yet over. He then went through all the prayers of the service at great length, the greater part of which it was the usual custom to omit.[9] For those with conscientious objections to the doctrine of the Trinity, there was no other means of obtaining a legal marriage in England after 1753.

The grievances of Dissenters, and in particular of Unitarians, were finally resolved after a long struggle by the Marriage Act of 1836. This provided an alternative to marriage in the Church of England, by allowing Dissenters to be married by their own ministers in their own places of worship, as well as permitting a civil ceremony before

[6] *St James's Chronicle*, 16 January 1827, 3.

[7] *The Examiner*, 19 June 1814, 16; 'Dissenters' Marriages', *Freethinking Christians' Quarterly Register* [hereafter: *Register*] 1 (1823), 267–316, at 292–3, 297–300, 302–4, 305–9; W. L., 'Protest against the Marriage Ceremony', *Monthly Repository* [hereafter: *MR*] 12 (1817), 570–1; 'Controversy on a Marriage Protest of "Freethinking Christians"', *MR* 20 (1825), 467–74; *The News*, 30 November 1817, 8; *The Times*, 30 May 1823, 3.

[8] *Register* 1, 293.

[9] Ibid. 306–9.

a registrar for those wishing to dispense with the religious element altogether. The 1836 Marriage Act, and in particular the campaign that led to it, has received surprisingly little attention from historians of Dissent, or from church historians more generally, despite its significance in permitting non-Anglicans to conduct legally recognized marriages according to their own ceremonies in places of worship registered for the purpose. It ended the Church of England's virtual monopoly on marriage. The history of the 1836 Act is of wider significance because it was closely tied to the 1836 Civil Registration Act.[10] The Act also forms the basis of modern English law on marriage. This article is concerned with the Unitarian campaign for reform of the marriage law before 1830.

English Dissenters were required to marry in the Church as a result of the 1753 Clandestine Marriages Act (26 Geo II c. 32), better known as the Hardwicke Act, which restricted valid marriages to the Church of England. Its purpose was narrow, to prevent clergymen from conducting clandestine marriages in the Fleet Prison, London. In the most comprehensive study of the Act and its consequences, Rebecca Probert has argued that it regularized what was already normal practice, and as a consequence was almost universally observed, even by religious Dissenters.[11] With the exception of a few foreign Protestant churches, and Quakers and Jews (who were exempt), Dissenters married in the Church of England until the law finally recognized their own marriages in 1836. It is also clear that Catholics and most Protestant Dissenters did not raise any formal objections as the Clandestine Marriages Bill passed through the two houses of parliament. Yet Dissenters and their representatives were not ignorant of the business of parliament, nor slow to raise objections to proposed legislation. In 1757, when the Militia Bill was being debated in the House of Commons, they petitioned successfully against the profanation of the Sabbath.[12] In contrast, the Society of Friends (or Quakers) lobbied parliament to be excluded from the terms of the 1753 Act. Jews were also exempt, probably by happenstance. The Jewish Naturalization Bill was introduced into the Lords while the

[10] The two Acts have consecutive statute numbers, 6 & 7 Wm IV c. 85 and 86: M. J. Cullen, 'The Making of the Civil Registration Act of 1836', *JEH* 25 (1974), 39–59.
[11] Rebecca Probert, *Marriage Law and Practice in the Long Eighteenth Century: A Reassessment* (Cambridge, 2009), 1–2, 5–6, 320–3.
[12] *JHC* 27, 717 (17 February 1757).

Marriage Bill was in committee.[13] As non-Christians, Jews were allowed to become citizens without taking the Anglican sacrament. Perhaps not surprisingly, the same concession was granted to them in the new Marriage Act.[14]

For the historian of Dissent, the silence, particularly by the sects, over the 1753 Act is surprising. Baptist and most Congregational or Independent churches shared with the Quakers a refusal to have anything to do with the Church of England and its sacraments. Members who failed 'to marry in the Lord', or who attended funerals, christenings and other acts of worship at the parish church, were regularly disowned in the decades before and after the 1689 Toleration Act. Yet the evidence suggests that they did marry in the Church of England.[15] Dissenters appear to have adopted a pragmatic approach. Marriage mattered. If the marriage was not recognized in law, then any issue of the marriage would be illegitimate and unable to inherit.[16] A couple who had not gone through a regular marriage in their parish church, but who cohabited, were also at risk of being prosecuted for fornication.[17]

Although most English Presbyterians refused to conform fully in 1662, because of their dislike of episcopacy and the use of the Common Prayer Book, they shared much of the same doctrine as the Church of England, and many practised partial conformity, attending that which they found acceptable in their parish church, while also resorting to the meeting-house. This was to change in the second half of the eighteenth century. As Presbyterians were influenced by rationalist ideas, they came to question the Trinity, original

[13] The 1753 Jewish Naturalisation Act (26 Geo. II c. 26) allowed Jews who lived in Great Britain or Ireland for three years to become citizens by act of parliament without taking the Anglican sacrament. It was repealed six months later.

[14] R. B. Outhwaite, *Clandestine Marriage in England, 1500–1850* (London, 1995), 35.

[15] See John Caffyn, *Sussex Believers: Baptist Marriage in the 17th and 18th Centuries* (Worthing, 1988), 128. I am grateful to the Rev. Stephen Copson, Secretary of the Baptist Historical Society, for his comments on this subject.

[16] Probert, *Marriage Law*, 140, 145.

[17] See, for example, E. Welch, 'The Origins of the New Connexion of General Baptists', *Transactions of the Leicestershire Archaeological and Historical Society* 49 (1995), 59–70, at 67; *A letter from the Rev. John Roe, Minister of the Protestant Dissenters at Calverton, near Nottingham, concerning the Imprisonment of their Wives, for Life, for Nonconformity to the Church of England, by Force of the Writ* excommunicato capiendo*: Addressed to the Rt. Hon. Ld. George Gordon, President of the Protestant Association* (Nottingham, 1789).

sin, atonement and other orthodox doctrines as unscriptural.[18] The term 'rational dissent' has been used to describe these changes. Not surprisingly, English Presbyterians found the Trinitarian formulas of the Anglican liturgy increasingly objectionable. As a consequence, they were unwilling to take the Anglican sacrament in order to qualify for political or crown office, thus ending the long-standing practice of occasional conformity.[19] It is less clear why this refusal to accept the Anglican sacraments did not extend to marriage in the Church of England.

Most of those who held anti-Trinitarian opinions in the eighteenth century were Arian: that is, they insisted on the worship of God the Father alone, regarding the Son as subordinate, although still divine. In the final decades of the eighteenth-century, as G. M. Ditchfield has shown, the earlier Arian form of anti-Trinitarian speculation was replaced by a more open and aggressive unitarianism, which, with its insistence on the humanity of Christ, was much more offensive to those who were orthodox.[20] Valerie Smith has recently identified the 1790s as a turning point in the evolution of rational Dissent. She also demonstrated a rise in orthodox attacks during the 1780s and 1790s on those holding anti-Trinitarian opinions.[21] Although many ministers and individuals had adopted unitarian ideas, it is not possible at this date to talk of unitarian congregations, both for reasons of nomenclature (the label 'unitarian' was not used by such congregations) and because a majority had not yet openly embraced unitarian opinions. When Thomas Belsham resigned as Theological Tutor of Daventry Academy in 1789, after adopting unitarian opinions, all but about six of the forty divinity students were said to share his views. One of them recalled that the prospects during the 1780s and 1790s for a young minister who had embraced unitarianism seeking a congregation were 'peculiarly disheartening'. The success of the Evangelical Revival in revitalizing Dissent had closed many churches to those who were not strictly orthodox. Only the congregations at

[18] For an account of this transformation, see C. Gordon Bolam et al., *The English Presbyterians: From Elizabethan Puritanism to Modern Unitarianism* (London, 1968), 134–40, 145–50.

[19] G. M. Ditchfield, 'Anti-Trinitarianism and Toleration in late Eighteenth-Century British Politics: The Unitarian Petition of 1792', *JEH* 42 (1991), 39–67.

[20] Ibid. 44.

[21] Valerie Smith, *Rational Dissenters in Late Eighteenth-Century England: 'An ardent desire of truth'* (Woodbridge, 2021), 140–52.

Kettering and Wellingborough in Northamptonshire, and the Great Meeting in Leicester, were willing to hear students from Daventry preach, or students from Northampton, where the academy moved in 1789.[22] The situation was to change rapidly in the first decades of the nineteenth century. By 1810, Charles Wellbeloved, principal of Manchester College, York, then the only academy openly preparing students for the Unitarian ministry, admitted that the demand for ministers completely outstripped the number being trained.[23]

The development of early nineteenth-century Unitarianism still has to be explained in detail, but undoubtedly the Unitarian Society, which assisted poor congregations and supported Unitarian missionaries, and the *Monthly Repository*, a publication dedicated to the advancement of Unitarianism, both founded in 1806, were important in helping to create a denominational focus. Moreover, constraints on the open avowal of unitarian views, proscribed until the passing of the Unitarian Relief Act in 1813 (53 Geo. III c. 160), had limited efforts to promote unitarianism. The establishment of the Association for the Protection of the Civil Rights of Unitarians in 1819, and the incorporation of the Association with the Unitarian Society and other bodies in 1825 to form the British and Foreign Unitarian Association, were important steps, particularly in the campaign for the removal of continuing penalties against Unitarians.

The doctrinal changes within English Presbyterianism lacked popular appeal, and there was significant loss of members, particularly in the countryside, to the Congregationalists. Only about a third of the congregations which had been Presbyterian in 1700 adopted unitarian opinions. Yet despite the decline in numbers, in most major towns by the end of the eighteenth century these congregations had become centres of great wealth and influence, often including members on the fringes of county society. By the early nineteenth century, Unitarianism was supported by some of the greatest

22 David L. Wykes, 'Rational Dissent, Unitarianism, and the Closure of the Northampton Academy in 1798', *Journal of Religious History* 41 (2017), 3–21, at 14, 18; A Daventry Student, 'Recollections of Mr Belsham, at Daventry', *Christian Reformer* 16 (1830), 102–3.

23 David L. Wykes, 'Educating Students for the Unitarian Ministry in the Early Nineteenth Century', *Transactions of the Unitarian Historical Society* 26 (2015), 79–98, at 82.

industrialists of the period.[24] Because of their social and political standing, Presbyterians, and later Unitarians, led the struggle for reform and provided the political leadership for Dissent until the 1832 Reform Act, which resulted in the return of large numbers of orthodox Dissenters to parliament representing many of the new urban constituencies. For more than twenty-five years, the Unitarian MP William Smith was the leading advocate for the Dissenters in the House of Commons until his retirement from parliament in 1830.[25]

Before 1814, most Unitarians, despite their opposition to the Trinity and other orthodox doctrines, voiced no apparent objections at having to marry in the Church of England and submit to a Trinitarian marriage ceremony. The Unitarian Association acknowledged in 1819 that Unitarians had not previously raised any formal objection to being married in the Church, and they admitted that before 1753 Dissenters largely conformed to the marriage rites of the Church of England. They gave several reasons: firstly, that for the most part English Presbyterians before the second half of the eighteenth century were still largely orthodox in matters of doctrine; secondly, the importance of having a marriage which was recognized as valid, and not at risk of challenge by the ecclesiastical courts. The Association accepted that the failure of Unitarians to challenge the law before 1819 was open to criticism, but they argued that until the Unitarian Relief Act 1813 gave them the same rights as other Dissenters under the 1689 Toleration Act, it was not appropriate for them to seek relief.[26] It is clear that their position changed, and the issue became of central importance to them, as a result of the efforts of the Freethinking Christians, whose militant objections to the Trinity and to any form of sacrament had long led them to object to the Anglican marriage service. Formed by a secession from the

24 John Seed, 'Gentlemen Dissenters: The Social and Political Meanings of Rational Dissent in the 1770s and 1780s', *HistJ* 28 (1985), 299–325, at 302–6; David L. Wykes, 'Sons and Subscribers: Lay Support and the College, 1786–1840', in B. Smith, ed., *Truth, Liberty, Religion: Essays Celebrating Two Hundred Years of Manchester College* (Oxford, 1986), 31–77, at 62–3, 67–8.

25 Richard W. Davis, *Dissent in Politics, 1780–1830: The Political Life of William Smith, M.P.* (London, 1971).

26 *Report of the Committee of the Unitarian Association for Protecting the Civil Rights of Unitarians to the General Meeting* (3 June 1819), [1]; *Short Statement of the Case of the Unitarian Dissenters, Petitioners for Relief from some parts of the Ceremony imposed by the Marriage Act* (n.pl., [after June 1819]), 2.

Universalists in Parliament Court, Bishopsgate, they first met on Christmas Day 1798, and elected Thompson as their elder. They at once announced their rejection of the Trinity, and the sacraments of baptism, marriage and the Lord's Supper, as well as public singing and prayer. The church developed rapidly, often by courting controversy.[27]

In 1808, the *Monthly Repository* published a letter in which the writer wrote that, after reading Theophilus Lindsey's *Conversations on Christian Idolatry* (1792), and examining the marriage service for himself, he had decided that it was 'utterly impossible' for a Unitarian, 'either tacitly or openly', conscientiously to go through the marriage service in the Church of England. For no Unitarian could 'join in the worship of the man Jesus, or to pronounce that he does all this, in the name of the Father, Son, and Holy Ghost, thereby giving a sanction to the absurd and idolatrous notion of the Trinity'. As a Unitarian he feared that he would not be able marry in the Church of England.[28] The letter received a reply from someone who signed himself 'an Unitarian Husband'. He claimed in the case of his own marriage to have used the words 'In the NAME of ALMIGHTY God', in the place of the Father, the Son and the Holy Ghost. He believed that because he was known to the clergyman conducting the service, his deviation from the liturgy was ignored.[29] Such an approach was impractical for most Unitarians. It is clear that clergymen generally were unwilling to be so accommodating, as the experience of Trotter and others demonstrates.[30]

The issue was not apparently raised again by Unitarians in any of their publications until 1812, when another letter, from a

[27] 'Free-thinking Christians', *MR* 4 (1809), 284–6; John Evans, *A Sketch of the Denominations of the Christian World* (London, 1814), 311–21 (by a member appointed by the society); 'A Brief Account of the Church of God known as Free-Thinking Christians', *Christian Teacher* n.s. 3 (1841), 284–6. Joan Christodoulou, 'The Freethinking Christians and the Millennium', *London Journal* 14 (1989), 148–59, is concerned with the links to other nineteenth-century radical groups, and only briefly mentions their marriage campaign.

[28] 'Unitarian Batchelors', *MR* 3 (1808), 377–8. The letter was by a leading member of the Freethinking Christian Church: see *Register* 1, 287–8. See also Candidus, 'On the Marriage Ceremony', dated Homerton, 11 December 1810, *Freethinking Christians' Magazine* 1 (1810–11), 33–7.

[29] 'An Unitarian Husband's Advice to an Unitarian Bachelor', *MR* 3 (1808), 470.

[30] See also 'The English Unitarians and the Marriage Question; a Conversation', *Christian Pioneer* 4 (1829), 86.

correspondent in Norfolk who was clearly a Unitarian, was published in the *Monthly Repository*. Why, the writer wrote, if Dissenters were permitted to baptize and bury according to their own religious forms, did they not have the same exemption enjoyed by Quakers to marry their own?[31] Although this suggests that Unitarians were beginning to think about the marriage ceremony, it did not amount to a campaign. The lack of progress led Freethinking Christians to seek an amendment to the Marriage Act themselves. When in March 1812, Griffin Wilson, MP for Great Yarmouth, gave notice in the Commons of motion to amend the 1753 Act, two members on behalf of the church sought his support to include relief for unitarians. Wilson, while apparently acknowledging the seriousness of their case, was unwilling to make any additions to his motion for fear of provoking opposition which might imperil his own proposal.[32]

The issue had become pressing for the church as a number of younger members were approaching an age when they wished to marry. The only solution involved taking a journey to Scotland, where the 1753 Act was not in force, but many could afford neither the time nor the expense. They were also conscious that marriage in Scotland offered 'to the world no public testimony against the injustice of the marriage ceremony, and could have no tendency to procure for us any relief from the Legislature'.[33] They therefore decided upon a common form of action for all members of the church who married in the Church of England. They were to draw up a written protest to give to the officiating clergyman at the altar before the ceremony (they had considered requiring the parties to read it out during the service) giving their objections, which they would afterwards publish in the newspapers. While some members feared that if the protest was presented at the altar the minister would refuse to marry them, they were advised that he could not refuse.[34] This plan was first carried out in June 1814 with the marriage of Thompson's eldest daughter, Mary Ann, to William Coates.[35]

31 T., 'Dissenters' Marriages', *MR* 7 (1812), 567–8. The reference to the right of Dissenters to baptize their children indicates that the correspondent was not a Freethinking Christian, since they rejected baptism.

32 *Register* 1, 290–1.

33 Ibid. 291–2; 'On Marriage', *Freethinking Christians' Magazine* 3 (1813), 513–20.

34 'Protest against the Marriage Ceremony', *Freethinking Christians' Magazine* 4 (1814), 326–36, at 327.

35 *The Examiner*, 19 June 1814, 16; 'A Protest against the Marriage Ceremony', *MR* 9 (1814), 354–6.

The Freethinking Christians were too few in number and lacking in influence to achieve any change in the legislation themselves. It was their success in engaging the general body of Unitarians which eventually led to the change in the law. In June 1814, they successfully lobbied the Unitarian Fund at its annual meeting in London. Thompson spoke at length about the lack of action by Unitarians and the urgent need to obtain relief through parliament. Afterwards he was assured that the committee would take up the issue.[36] From this date it is evident that Unitarians were increasingly troubled by the marriage question. In January 1815, a member of the Kent and Sussex Unitarian Association noted that Dissenters were now concerned about marrying in the Church of England. Unitarians, in particular, were 'apprehensive that they depart here from their great leading principle', since parts of the marriage service were undeniably Trinitarian. The correspondent thought the time opportune to seek relief from parliament, and suggested that the Unitarian MP William Smith should be approached for help.[37] In 1813, Smith had successfully persuaded parliament to remove the penalties against Unitarians. Before the Unitarian Relief Act the expression of anti-Trinitarian ideas had been unlawful; whilst the penalties were rarely enforced, the threat was there.[38]

The question of marrying according to the ceremony of the Church of England was raised publicly at the close of the annual meeting of the Kent and Sussex Unitarian Association in June 1815. It was represented 'as inconsistent with the doctrine of the Divine Unity, and with the supremacy of Christ in his church'.[39] The following month the newly established Devon and Cornwall Unitarian Society, at its first annual meeting, instructed the secretary to seek the support of similar Unitarian associations to obtain relief from the Anglican marriage service.[40] By late July 1816 the question was said to be 'agitating among different bodies of Unitarians', and

36 *Register* 1, 294. There is no record of Thompson's speech in the Unitarian accounts of the annual dinner.

37 'Marriage Service of the Established Church Trinitarian', *MR* 10 (1815), 80–1.

38 The Doctrine of the Trinity Act 1813 (53 Geo. III c. 160) amended the 1689 Toleration Act (1 Wm & Mary c. 18) to include non-Trinitarians and repealed the provisions of the 1697 Blasphemy Act (9 Wm III c. 35) against those who denied the Trinity.

39 [Thomas] P[ine], 'The Fourth Anniversary of the Kent and Sussex Unitarian Association and Tract Society', *MR* 10 (1815), 527.

40 'Mr Worsley on the Marriage Ceremony', *MR* 11 (1816), 208.

individual Unitarians were already in discussion with Smith about amending the 1753 Act to give relief.[41] It was essential that the issue was adopted by local Unitarian associations and congregations, since Unitarians at this date lacked an effective national body to organise a campaign.[42] In July 1817, a petition from Unitarian Christians in Kent and Sussex was presented in the Commons by Smith, and in the Lords by the Marquis of Lansdowne. It was said to have nearly five hundred signatures.[43] The Freethinking Christians complained that no further action in public was then taken by Unitarians for two years.[44]

It was not until the formation of the Association for the Protection of the Civil Rights of Unitarians in 1819, with the lawyer Edgar Taylor as secretary, that the first attempt was made in parliament by Unitarians to amend the 1753 Act. The contribution the Association made in organizing and sustaining the Unitarian campaign to change the marriage law was crucial. The survival of Taylor's papers makes it possible to see much more clearly his role and that of the Association.[45] There was some doubt amongst the committee about whether the Association should take direct action and lobby for a change in the law, but their hand was forced by 'a great number of our friends' in the country, 'bent on agitating the question'. The committee thought it essential that care be taken that no prejudice to the question should arise from any 'premature or imprudent introduction' of the Unitarian claim.[46] They therefore circulated a draft petition, stating the grounds on which the

[41] Consistianus, 'Unitarian Marriages', *Monthly Magazine* 42 (1816), 210.

[42] The various Unitarian national bodies were poorly supported: see H. L. Short, 'The Founding of the British and Foreign Unitarian Association', *Transactions of the Unitarian Historical Society: Supplement* (1975), 15s–16s.

[43] *JHC* 72, 466 (8 July 1817); *Morning Post*, 11 July 1817, 1; *Register* 1, 294.

[44] *Register* 1, 294–5.

[45] London, Parliamentary Archives, UAM/1–3, The Unitarian Association Marriage Law Petitioning Papers, 3 vols, 1819–37. The volumes are a rare example of a parliamentary agent's papers. Originally collected together by Edgar Taylor, they were given by Sharpe & Pritchard, the successors to his firm, to the British Record Association in 1965, who donated them to the House of Lords Record Office (now the Parliamentary Archives). I am grateful to Dr Mari Takayanagi, senior archivist, for information about the archive's provenance, and for granting permission on behalf of the Parliamentary Archives to cite and quote from the Unitarian Association's petitioning papers.

[46] Parliamentary Archives, UAM/1/5, Edgar Taylor to William Smith, 4 February 1819.

Unitarian case rested, for presentation to both the Lords and the Commons.[47]

From late May until late June congregations petitioned the two houses. The petitions reveal the depth and widespread nature of the grievances that had developed among Unitarians. There were petitions from major Unitarian congregations in Liverpool, Exeter, Bristol and Hackney, as well as from the Universalists at Parliament Court and the Freethinking Christians in Jewin Street. Smaller congregations at Newport (Isle of Wight), Gloucester, Framlingham (Suffolk), Thorne (near Doncaster), Lincoln, and Falmouth and Flushing (Cornwall) also presented petitions.[48] Marriage in the Church of England was an issue that concerned members of smaller and poorer congregations as much as those belonging to larger and wealthier ones. John Gaskell, minister at Thorne, reported that his congregation wanted their petition presented as soon as possible.[49]

Not every congregation was in favour of petitioning parliament, and there were doubts whether an application would succeed in the prevailing political climate, which was hostile to reform. There was a difference of opinion amongst the High Pavement congregation at Nottingham, where a considerable majority thought the time was wrong for an application. Despite this decision, James Tayler, the minister, wrote to Taylor a month later that 'the minority have, notwithstanding, prepared a petition to the House of Commons'.[50] Members of the Newport congregation, while wishing the committee success, were

> rather doubtful whether they will obtain their object on their own terms. The Unitarian body is now large & generally speaking is a wealthy body. The emoluments arising from the marriages among them are of course not in considerable [*sic*]. And the church & State have formed so strong a coalition & both watch over the pecuniary interests of the former with so much jealousy, that we fear our request may be

[47] 'Unitarian Association. Marriage Laws', *MR* 14 (1819), 125. In response to suggestions, a second version was issued: ibid. 198.

[48] 'Marriage Law', *MR* 14 (1819), 382–6, at 382.

[49] Parliamentary Archives, UAM/1/9, Gaskell to Taylor, 10 May 1819.

[50] Parliamentary Archives, UAM/1/15, 23, James Tayler (Nottingham) to Taylor, 23 May, 23 June 1819.

esteemed too extravagant for the Ministers to permit so great a source of profit to be taken from the clergy.[51]

The loss of fees by the parish clergy was to prove a major obstacle in gaining the support of some bishops for reform of the Marriage Act.

Care was taken to obtain as many signatures as possible, though this was not without difficulty when members were out of town, and local organizers were sensitive about the need to ensure that those who signed were respectable and entitled to vote. Doubtless because of the latter point, the decision was taken at Plymouth to canvass only male members.[52] Attention was also paid to who should present the petition in parliament. The campaign gave Unitarians an opportunity to demonstrate their political influence locally. It was generally accepted that Smith would present the petitions in the Commons, although a number of sympathetic MPs were also involved.[53] After being approached by Taylor, the Marquis of Lansdowne agreed to present any petitions in the Lords.[54] Lant Carpenter, in forwarding the petition for the Lewin's Mead congregation in Bristol, wrote: 'I take for granted you put those for the Commons in the hands of Mr Smith', but if the Association had no arrangement for the Lords, he suggested Lord Holland. 'I happened to have had some correspondence with him about Catholic Claims, and the Devonshire Election, and I think he would take pleasure in presenting it.'[55] The Plymouth congregation applied its influence, and the Lord Lieutenant, Lord Fortescue, agreed to present the petition in the Lords, and Sir William Congreve in the Commons.[56] Taylor attempted to enlist the support of the other Dissenting denominations, by canvassing the Ministers of the Three Denominations, although at this date without success.[57] The

[51] Parliamentary Archives, UAM/1/11, W. Stevens (Newport, Isle of Wight) to Taylor, 14 May [1819].

[52] Parliamentary Archives, UAM/1/12, J. Fullagar (Chichester) to Taylor; UAM/1/13, Lant Carpenter (Bristol) to Taylor, 17 May 1819; UAM/1/14, Israel Worsley (Plymouth) to Taylor, 28 May 1819.

[53] The Crediton congregation suggested the Whig politician Lord Ebrington, who sat in the Commons: Parliamentary Archives, UAM/1/10, G. Hinton (Crediton) to Taylor, 13 May 1819.

[54] Parliamentary Archives, UAM/1/17, Lansdowne to Taylor, 9 June 1819.

[55] Carpenter to Taylor, 17 May 1819.

[56] Worsley to Taylor, 28 May 1819.

[57] Parliamentary Archives, UAM/1/19, 21 Thomas Morgan (Dr Williams's Library) to Taylor, 17 June 1819.

petitioning by Unitarian congregations did, however, encourage some orthodox Dissenters to petition parliament.[58] Dissenters in Great and Little Broughton in Cumberland pointed out in their petition that Protestant Dissenters and Catholics in Ireland and Dissenters in Scotland (including the Episcopal Church) had the right to conduct their own marriages, and that it was 'an invidious and unmerited Distinction that the same Right should be withheld from them as Protestant Dissenters in England', except for Quakers and Jews.[59]

The committee not only organized the petitions to parliament, but it is clear that they were responsible for preparing the bill. After much consideration, they adopted the draft bill drawn up by Christopher Richmond, a parliamentary conveyancer and zealous Unitarian, who with Taylor was a member of Robert Aspland's congregation at Hackney.[60] Taylor had told Smith that the committee had no objection 'to the legal contract being perfected at the church if the ceremony were made unobjectionable or if persons scrupling the service or parts of it, were entitled to have it waived'. The committee thought the alternative, of Unitarians celebrating marriages in their own places of worship, was 'attended with many Inconveniences & not desirable', presumably because of problems over registration and in gaining the acceptance by the courts of the lawfulness of a ceremony conducted in a Dissenting chapel.[61] The Bill allowed for all the marriage service which was 'properly religious and devotional' to be omitted, leaving the priest as a registrar only, 'receiving his fee in that capacity', and making the parish church no more than a register office, the church being 'the most convenient and secure place for registration'.[62] The committee was aware that the draft Bill fell short of what some Unitarians wanted, who desired 'a complete separation of the marriage contract from the place as well as the officers, of the Established Church'. The committee was convinced such an object could not be achieved unless the general body of Dissenters united in support, and that it was better to gain 'relief from the chief, if not the whole, of the difficulties which at present exist'.[63]

58 *JHC* 74, 532, 597, 621 (14, 30 June, 6 July 1819).

59 Ibid. 621 (6 July 1819); see also Cockermouth, ibid. 597 (30 June 1819).

60 'Unitarian Association: Marriage Laws', *Christian Reformer* 5 (1819), 275–6, at 275; 'Marriage Law', 382. For Richmond, see 'Obituary', *MR* n.s. 6 (1832), 127.

61 Taylor to Smith, 4 February 1819.

62 'Unitarian Association', 275

63 'Marriage Law', 382; *Report of the Committee, 1819*, 1.

Taylor and the committee used the petitions to bring Unitarian grievances to the attention of both the Commons and the Lords, and to recite the arguments for reform. When introducing his motion in June 1819, Smith referred to the petitions, chiefly signed by Unitarians, and to the respectability of the petitioners. He gave the arguments which the Unitarian Association had in fact made earlier: that the Marriage Act was a civil contract and that a religious service was not necessary for it to be valid. His Bill authorized the clergyman to omit certain words at the request of the parties marrying. He claimed that it imposed no additional duties on the ministers; it proposed no reduction or loss of fees; it proposed no alteration of property; in short, it was to reconcile the scruples of the conscientious. Indeed, the clergyman would be relieved from the painful duty of enforcing what was offensive to others.[64] The Bill received a first reading on 29 June and a second the next day, and on 1 July Smith moved its commitment.[65] It was on the whole favourably received by the House, but Lord Castlereagh on behalf of the government asked for it to be postponed due to the lateness of the session. Because of the death of George III, the bill was not reintroduced in 1820, nor, because of the campaign for Catholic emancipation, in 1821.

In April 1822, Smith sent the archbishop of Canterbury, Charles Manners-Sutton, a copy of the draft Bill in the hope of engaging his support. The archbishop replied a week later, on 9 April, that the bishops were decidedly of the opinion that 'it is unreasonable to exact from the established Church for the purpose of removing the religious scruples of those who dissent from it, an alteration affecting an essential article of Faith, in the prescribed Form of Solemnization of Matrimony'.[66] Nonetheless, on 17 April, Smith reintroduced his measure 'to leave out the whole of that part of the ritual which stated opinions on which the petitioners dissented from the Church of England'.[67] The Editor of the *New Times*, while sympathetic to Smith's objects, pointed out that in seeking 'to relieve the consciences of *Dissenters*, a sore wound is given to the consciences of the *Established Clergy*'. They were being expected 'to perform a sacred

[64] 'Marriage Act Amendment Bill', HC Deb. (1st series), 16 June 1819 (vol. 40, cols 1200–1); 'Marriage Act', *The Times*, 17 June 1819, 2.

[65] *JHC* 74, 588, 598, 606–7 (29, 30 June, 1 July 1819).

[66] Parliamentary Archives, UAM/1/30, Archbishop of Canterbury to Smith, 9 April 1822.

[67] 'Marriages of Unitarian Dissenters', HC Deb., 17 April 1822 (vol. 6, col. 1462).

rite, in a manner which, to many of them, may appear little less than a renunciation of their faith.'[68] Because of the opposition from the Church of England, Smith withdrew his bill.

During February and March 1823, Taylor lobbied the House of Lords Committee which had been established to consider the state of the 1753 Marriage Act, 'with a view to frame one complete measure'. He asked Lansdowne and Lord Holland to present to the Committee petitions from Unitarians stating their grievances.[69] Holland thought the claim so reasonable that 'the only difficulty in Parliament is the mode of accomplishing your purpose'.[70] Unfortunately, securing the agreement of all the different interests over the best method of providing relief was to prove almost impossible, and vexed all attempts at obtaining relief for Dissenters generally or Unitarians in particular.

Smith's new Bill proposed to legalize Dissenting marriages conducted by their own ministers, as long as banns were published or a licence was obtained. Despite the earlier promise, Lord Ellenborough had to admit that the Committee was unwilling 'to embarrass' the intended bill by including all the various provisions necessary to guard against abuse, but there was 'no hostile feeling to the demands of the Unitarians', and the Lords 'would consider with a certain degree of favor' any bill introduced as a separate measure.[71] Taylor told Smith that the Unitarian Committee were 'decidedly of Opinion that they ought to embrace the sort of invitation held out' by the Lords' Committee. They thought it 'useless to pass a measure through the Commons' which would not meet the approval of the Lords. A draft Bill was then prepared and, as Taylor told the secretary of the Body of the Three Denominations, 'it has been settled by Counsel with the assistance of Lord Ellenborough and is considered to be in unison with the wishes of the Committee of the Lords'.[72]

[68] *New Times*, 20 May 1822, 3.

[69] Parliamentary Archives, UAM/1/43, copy of letters from Taylor to Lansdowne and Holland, 24 February 1823.

[70] Parliamentary Archives, UAM/1/44, 46, Holland to Taylor, 25 February 1823, Lansdowne to Taylor, 1 March 1823.

[71] Parliamentary Archives, UAM/1/47, 48, Lord Ellenborough to Smith, 8 and 15 March 1823.

[72] Parliamentary Archives, UAM/1/57, 58, 59, Taylor to Smith, 29 May, 5 June 1823, Taylor to Coates (Secretary of the Dissenting Ministers of the Three Denominations), 5 June 1823.

A Bill to extend to all Dissenters the privileges granted to Quakers and Jews in 1753 was introduced in the Lords by Lansdowne in June 1823. Unfortunately, the proposals were thought too wide, and there were concerns that they would open the door, in the Lord Chancellor Lord Eldon's words, to 'ranters, jumpers, and various other sects, of whose principles they knew nothing'. The Bill failed to obtain a second reading by 31 votes to 37.[73] As Smith later noted, the Lords' Committee 'seemed at first disposed to frame a very general Bill, leaving all classes of Diss[ente]^{rs} much to themselves – from this point they recede, to doing nothing in it, but professing to be ready to pass such Bill as shall be bro[ugh]t in by others'. He then expressed the frustration he and others felt over the behaviour of many in the Lords, always wanting something more, whatever was proposed. Even before the Bill was introduced by Lansdowne, Smith feared that 'the Bishops or some other Persons will contrive to extract arguments or rather Pretences against doing anything'.[74] Christopher Richmond, who had helped draft the Bill, feared 'they won[']t admit any class of Dissenters but upon application & upon narrow grounds'.[75] More generally, the Unitarian Committee was in an awkward situation. The Association had 'singly and unaided' campaigned for reform, but as Taylor told John Wilks, secretary of the Protestant Society, 'We have all along felt some difficulties, wishing on the one hand not to seek for ourselves alone, what was wanted by all; and on the other hand, fearing lest we should by making our measure quite general, be considered as taking too much on ourselves.'[76] Smith did not share such doubts, strongly believing that 'the Unitarians should not be prevented from obtaining any Relief which the L[or]^{ds} or the Gov[ernmen]^{t} may be disposed to grant them, even exclusively'.[77]

The following March, Lansdowne, after consulting Archbishop Manners-Sutton, told Taylor that he expected to be able to carry the Bill, although not without some amendments. The Bill, once again prepared by the Association, was introduced by Lansdowne to the Lords in April. It permitted marriages between parties who

[73] 'Dissenters Marriages Bill', HL Deb. (2nd series), 12 June 1823 (vol. 9, cols 969, 973).
[74] Parliamentary Archives, UAM/1/64, 65, Smith to Taylor, n.d. [early June 1823].
[75] Parliamentary Archives, UAM/1/[66], Richmond to Taylor, n.d.
[76] Parliamentary Archives, UAM/1/63, Taylor to Wilks, 11 June 1823.
[77] Parliamentary Archives, UAM/1/65, Smith to Taylor, n.d.

were both Unitarians, by their own ministers, in their own chapels, registered for the purpose. The archbishop believed that 'relief could only be given in one of two ways – either by enabling the Unitarians, under certain regulations, to intermarry in their own places of worship, or by an alteration of the form of the marriage ceremony in the church of England service.' He strongly objected to the latter, which simply transferred to the church the grievances which it sought to redress. 'The only mode of relief; then, was by this bill.' During the debate on the second reading, Lord Chancellor Eldon claimed to general surprise that despite the 1813 Act giving relief to Unitarians, according to common law it was still illegal to deny the doctrine of the Trinity. The bishop of Chester could not see what objections Unitarians might have to the words of the marriage ceremony, which were based on Scripture. 'The Unitarian was not bound to assent to the accuracy of those terms: he might affix to them what meaning he pleased. There was no force or compulsion upon him to induce him to acquiesce in them.' He also feared the loss of income by the clergy from marriages in the church. Lord Harrowby saw nothing in the Bill that would affect the dignity, honour or security of the church, and pointedly asked whether their Lordships would be satisfied with a marriage ceremony for themselves in which the name of Mahomet was adjured. The Bill received a second reading by 35 votes to 33.[78]

The *Leeds Mercury* was not sanguine that the Bill would proceed, because of the narrowness of the vote and because several who supported the principle of the Bill were hostile to its particular provisions. It continued: 'there is a party in the House of Lords, (which we fear will ultimately prove the majority,) with the Lord Chancellor at its head and a list of bishops in its ranks, which positively refuses any relief whatsoever to the Unitarians in this respect'.[79] When Lansdowne moved that the Lords resolved itself into a committee, the motion was again opposed by the bishop of Chester, who remained convinced that 'the Unitarians had no reasonable grounds for their objections to the marriage-ceremony of the Church of England'. He was supported by the bishops of St Davids and St Asaph. On the other hand, the archbishop of Canterbury could not

[78] 'Unitarian Marriage Relief Bill', HL Deb. (2nd series), 2 April 1824 (vol. 11, cols 75–6, 79, 82, 84, 95).
[79] *Leeds Mercury*, 10 April 1824, 2.

see that the strength of objection that they and others used on the church's behalf was justified. It was true that Unitarians denied the existence of the Trinity, and it was on that account they were entitled to be relieved from a ceremony which compelled them to appear to sanction that doctrine. Did the House wish 'to enforce a seeming acquiescence in the doctrines of the Established Church' from persons who so far dissented from them? The bishop of Exeter also thought that Unitarians were entitled to relief, 'that persons who did not believe in certain doctrines ought not to be compelled to join in ceremonies depending on those doctrines'. In turn, Lansdowne said that he could never suppose that any prelate of the Church of England would wish to impose an assent to doctrines which it was well known they came to church prepared to reject. 'To encourage equivocation was unworthy of a Christian and of a Protestant Christian.' When the House divided, the motion was lost by 105 votes to 66.[80] In 1825, the marriage bill passed the Commons but was lost in the Lords by two votes. Two years later, in May 1827, Smith introduced another Bill, which involved Dissenters having their banns for marriage called in their parish church and the marriage recorded in the parish register. This passed the Commons, and the bishop of Chester believed the clergy would not object to publishing the banns of Dissenters.[81] But it ran out of time. In fact, the clergy were against publishing 'banns in the church, affixing them to the church door, and the registering the marriage by the clergy', and petitioned strongly against it.[82] The Bill was reintroduced in 1828, but modified to exclude the involvement of the clergy. This failed too.

The campaign to amend the Marriage Act was then stalled by other campaigns for reform, in particular the Reform Bill, and above all weakened by the growing divisions between Unitarians and orthodox Dissenters, who deplored the religious beliefs of those who denied the Trinity. The preoccupation of the Dissenting Deputies with the repeal of the Test and Corporation Acts from 1827, and the determination of other Dissenters not to engage in

80 'Unitarian Marriage Bill', HL Deb. (2nd series), 4 May 1824 (vol. 11, cols 435–6, 446); 'Unitarian Marriages', *Morning Post*, 5 May 1824, 2.

81 'Dissenters' Marriages Bill', HL Deb. (2nd series), 29 June 1827 (vol. 17, col. 1427).

82 *The Standard*, 3 January 1828, 3; 10 January 1828, 4; 12 January 1828, 2; *Yorkshire Gazette*, 12 January 1828, 3.

what were seen as Unitarian causes, meant that the campaign for reform of the Marriage Act continued to be led by Unitarians.[83] Finally, after the passing of the Reform Bill in 1832, marriage relief became the second of the six major grievances published by Dissenters that year, civil registration being the first. In October, the Dissenting Deputies decided to act in concert with the Unitarian Association. They had concluded that reform of civil registration and reform of the Marriage Act had to go hand in hand. After Bills in 1832 and 1834 had failed, they were finally successful in 1836. The 1836 Act was far from perfect, but it was passed because the alternative was the failure of the whole Bill. Previous attempts to alter the liturgy or to give Dissenters the same exemption from the 1753 Act as Quakers had failed. The 1836 Act proved much broader. It removed the restriction that only marriage in the Church of England was a valid marriage, by allowing a registrar's certificate to be used in lieu of banns, either in an Anglican church or some other place of worship, and it introduced the option of civil marriage before the registrar in a register office.[84]

The struggle to amend the Marriage Act was initiated by the Freethinking Christians, who as a small and despised religious sect lacked the influence to achieve a change in the law themselves. They adopted the only means open to them, a controversial and highly visible public campaign of protest. They successfully engaged the broader Unitarian movement in their campaign. Unitarians, though losing influence to the much larger body of orthodox Dissent, still retained sufficient weight with the political establishment to undertake a campaign and to introduce a series of Bills in parliament. The papers of the Unitarian Association's parliamentary campaign reveal the remarkable efforts of the Association and of its secretary Edgar Taylor in undertaking an effective campaign while only representing a small denomination. Despite sponsoring a range of alternatives, it proved impossible to find a scheme acceptable to the Church of England. By 1827, when Trotter made his protest, five Bills had already failed, despite efforts to find an accommodation

[83] B. L. Manning, *The Protestant Dissenting Deputies* (Cambridge, 1952), 260–2, 272.

[84] For a detailed account of the final years of the campaign to change the law, see Cullen, 'Making of the Civil Registration Act', 40, 43, 48–9, 51–4; Rebecca Probert, *Tying the Knot: The Formation of Marriage 1836–2020* (Cambridge, 2021), 21–53; eadem, *Marriage Law*, 332–8.

with the Church of England; a further Bill introduced that year also failed. Whilst it is true that the Unitarian campaign did not directly result in the 1836 Act, it did establish general agreement in parliament that the Marriage Act needed to be reformed to accommodate the needs of Dissenters, and of Unitarians in particular. The campaign to amend the Marriage Act shows the importance of liturgy, both to the Church of England, for whom change was largely unacceptable, as well as to those protesting at being forced to go through a ceremony with a clergyman whose episcopal orders and ritual they rejected.

Rites and Wrongs: Anglican Ceremonies after Legal Weddings, 1837–57

Rebecca Probert*
University of Exeter

The Marriage Act 1836 marked an important change in the rites required for a valid marriage, allowing couples to marry in a register office or registered place of worship. For some, however, these unfamiliar rites did not constitute a marriage at all, and in the early 1850s a particular controversy emerged regarding Anglican clergymen who 'remarried' couples who had already been legally married under the 1836 Act. This article examines three cases of such 'remarriages' and how two of the clergymen involved subsequently found themselves facing prosecution. It analyses the circumstances in which a rite might become a 'wrong' in the eyes of the law and traces the impact of these cases on the development of a new provision governing when an additional religious ceremony could take place and, more unexpectedly, on the form of register office weddings.

Introduction

On the afternoon of 11 July 1856, a trial took place in Oxfordshire. The Rev. Richard Meux Benson, vicar of Cowley, was charged with conducting a ceremony of marriage in contravention of the Marriage Act 1823, banns not having been called nor a licence obtained to authorize it. The reason he had omitted these legal preliminaries was a simple one. The couple in question, Richard Pinnell Carey and Sarah Carey, were already married to each other, their legal wedding having taken place at the register office in Oxford in May 1852. Indeed, this earlier ceremony was the very reason that this prosecution was being brought. In the words of the counsel for the prosecution, conducting a second ceremony of marriage for couples who were already married was 'calculated to throw doubt' on the validity of the first ceremony 'and to create misgivings in the mind of those who previously had no doubt as

* School of Law, University of Exeter, EX4 4RJ. E-mail: r.j.probert@exeter.ac.uk.

Studies in Church History 59 (2023), 312–331
doi: 10.1017/stc.2023.14

to the soundness of their position'. The prosecution had therefore been 'instituted by the Attorney-General with a view to the purposes of public justice; and in order that the law might be established on a subject so important as that of matrimony'.[1]

This article examines why Benson (who was not the only Anglican clergyman to conduct such remarriages) found himself facing trial,[2] the outcome of the case and its legacy in determining the circumstances in which an Anglican ceremony could be performed after a legal wedding. To this end, it explains first how the option of getting married in a register office had been introduced by the Marriage Act 1836, along with that of being married in a non-Anglican place of worship, and how these new options were regarded by contemporaries. The second part then explores why the practice of 'remarrying' couples who had already been legally married under the 1836 Act emerged as a particular topic of controversy in the early 1850s. Along with Benson, two other examples of 'remarriage' attracted attention. These were ceremonies conducted by the Rev. William Bennett, vicar of Frome in Somerset, and the Rev. Alfred Lush, curate at Greywell in Hampshire. The accounts of these cases suggest that these men were conducting these ceremonies for religious reasons rather than because they had any doubts as to the legal validity of marriages conducted under the 1836 Act. For legal purposes, however, their motivations were less important than their actions and Lush (but not Bennett) also found himself facing prosecution. The third part examines the course of the proceedings against Benson and Lush and the outcomes in each case. The final part traces the impact of these cases on the inclusion of a specific provision in the legislation governing marriage, setting out when an additional religious ceremony may take place after a legal wedding, and the cases' unexpected impact on the form of the ceremonies that could be conducted in register offices. It concludes by considering the longer-term implications of this particular controversy, and the questions that it raises for future research into the religious allegiances of those who married in Dissenting places of worship and register offices.

[1] 'R *v.* Benson (Clerk)', *The Times*, 12 July 1856, 11.

[2] Somewhat surprisingly, there is no mention of the trial in M. V. Woodgate, *Father Benson: Founder of the Cowley Fathers* (London, 1953) or any of the essays in Martin L. Smith, ed., *Benson of Cowley* (Oxford, 1980), nor in Smith's *ODNB* entry on him (Martin L. Smith, 'Benson, Richard Meux [1824–1915]', *ODNB*, online edn [2004], at: < https://doi.org/10.1093/ref:odnb/30717>).

The Marriage Act 1836: Introducing Alternatives to the Anglican Rite

The Marriage Act 1836 had marked an important change in the rites required for a valid marriage. Previous legislation had required all marriages save those of Quakers and Jews to be solemnized according to Anglican rites.[3] From the early nineteenth century, however, there were objections from the Unitarians about the necessity of 'submission' to those rites,[4] and over the course of the next twenty years lawmakers sought to find a way of providing an acceptable alternative.[5] By 1833 the Protestant Dissenting Deputies had added their weight to the calls for reform, with 'compulsory conformity to the Rites and Ceremonies prescribed by the Book of Common Prayer for the Celebration of Matrimony' heading the list of their grievances.[6]

The solution eventually adopted in the 1836 Act was to provide two new ways of getting married. The first was the option of getting married in a certified place of worship that had been registered for weddings.[7] The second (and even more novel) option was that of getting married in the office of one of the new superintendent registrars.[8]

Both these options required a civil registrar to be present to register the marriage.[9] For a wedding in a register office a superintendent

[3] Clandestine Marriages Act 1753 (26 Geo. II c. 33), replaced by the Marriage Act 1823 (4 Geo. IV c. 76). See also Rebecca Probert, *Marriage Law and Practice in the Long Eighteenth Century: A Reassessment* (Cambridge, 2009).

[4] See, for example, the petition from 'several Unitarian Christians of Kent and Sussex' setting forth how such submission in essence acknowledged the authority of the established church 'to decree rites and ceremonies' and therefore violated the Unitarians' 'leading principle of dissent': *JHC* 72, 466 (8 July 1817). See also, in this volume, David L. Wykes, 'The Early Nineteenth-Century Unitarian Campaign to change English Marriage Law', 289–311.

[5] See Rebecca Probert, *Tying the Knot: The Formation of Marriage, 1836–2020* (Cambridge, 2021), 24–36.

[6] London, Guildhall Library, MS 03083, Minutes of the Protestant Dissenting Deputies, vol. 8, 15 March 1833, 156. A United Committee was appointed to consider these grievances which, in addition to representatives from each of the Protestant Dissenting Deputies, included the General Body of the Protestant Dissenting Ministers of the Three Denominations, the Protestant Society and the United Associate Presbytery of the Secession Church of Scotland: Guildhall Library, MS 03086, Minute Books of a committee called the United Committee appointed to consider the Grievances under which Dissenters now labour, vol. 1, 1834–5.

[7] Marriage Act 1836, §20.

[8] Marriage Act 1836, §21.

[9] Marriage Act 1836, §§20, 21.

registrar had also to be present, although the role they were to play was not specified.[10] Moreover, both options allowed for a wedding to be conducted either with or without any religious content. Weddings in a registered place of worship could be conducted 'according to such Form and Ceremony' as the parties saw 'fit to adopt'.[11] There was no legal requirement that this must be a religious ceremony, nor that it should be led by a Dissenting minister or a Catholic priest.[12] Conversely, there was no legal prohibition on religious content being included in a register office wedding, and contemporary evidence confirms that some were accompanied by prayers and Bible readings.[13] For both forms of ceremony, the only requirement was that certain prescribed words should be said.[14] While the prescribed declarations and vows were closely modelled on the Anglican marriage service, the excision of any references to a deity meant that there was nothing that would be objectionable to the parties, regardless of their religious allegiances or lack thereof.

For some, however, these unfamiliar and potentially entirely secular rites did not constitute a marriage at all. On 1 July 1837, the day that the new Act came into force, the *Yorkshire Gazette* inveighed against the fact that the pared-down rites required by the law contained no pledge by the parties to love and cherish each other or live together forever and argued that '[i]f such a contract be anything better than a gipsey marriage, which is but a mutual engagement for a brief term of years or during pleasure, it is at least proper that the parties entering into it should at the time be reminded of all its ties, duties, and responsibilities, by some explicit and impressive form of words'.[15] A couple of months later, *The Times* noted approvingly that the *Dorsetshire Chronicle* had 'adopted a very judicious mode of distinguishing these nondescript semi-marriages from the good old marriages proper' in its announcements columns, placing the former 'not in the ordinary list of "MARRIED", but in a separate paragraph, and

10 Marriage Act 1836, §21.
11 Marriage Act 1836, §20.
12 Cf. Lawrence Stone, *Road to Divorce: A History of the Making and Breaking of Marriage in England* (Oxford, 1995), 133, who mistakenly contrasts the possibility of marrying in 'a sacred religious ceremony conducted by a minister in holy orders in a church or chapel' with the 'purely secular contract' that was 'conducted by a state official in an office'.
13 See Probert, *Tying the Knot*, 73–4.
14 Marriage Act 1836, §20.
15 *Yorkshire Gazette*, 1 July 1837, 2.

under a more appropriate head, viz, "UNITED under the Act 6 and 7 William IV., c. 85".'[16] Reviewing the limited take-up of the new Act the following year, the *Halifax Guardian* rejoiced in the absence of demand for register office ceremonies in the town, commenting that 'the female who is united after such a *form* … is no more a wife than is one of the same sex in the less senseless and less licentious tribe of monkies'.[17]

Some Anglican clergymen preached sermons against the new Act and in particular against the idea of being married without religious rites. As the Rev. William Bennett, then minister of Portman Chapel, asked his hearers:

> When she, who is to be for ever the companion of our journey through life … is made ours, shall we be content to stand before man as the only witness, and thrust aside God? Shall we go before a magistrate, or a registrar, and despise the minister of the Lord Jesus Christ? Shall we send forth no aspirations to the throne of grace, that what is commenced in this world may have its reference and conclusion in the next? God forbid.[18]

More widely reported was the sermon preached by the rector of South Hackney, Henry Handley Norris. In arguing that marriage was a divine institution, Norris urged his hearers to shun the new forms that allowed 'holy matrimony' to be 'superseded by a coupling together which, upon scriptural principles, can be regarded only as a legalized concubinage'.[19]

While the new forms of marriage had their supporters,[20] given these objections it would have been natural for some of the couples marrying under the 1836 Act to feel a few qualms about the status of their union. After all, as Norris had reminded his hearers, the previous similar 'desecration' of the marriage rite – the introduction of civil

[16] *The Times*, 2 September 1837, 4.

[17] Reprinted in 'The Dissenters and the New Marriage Act', *Morning Post*, 14 September 1838, 2.

[18] William J. E. Bennett, *New Marriage Act: Three Sermons on Marriage, with Reference to its Divine Appointment* (London, 1837), quoted in the review in the *Church of England Quarterly Review* 1 (1837), 573–4, at 574.

[19] 'The Rector of South Hackney and the New Marriage Law', *Morning Chronicle*, 9 September 1837, 3; see also *Sheffield Independent*, 16 September 1837, 2.

[20] See, for example, *Bristol Mercury*, 5 August 1837, 4; *Sheffield Independent*, 16 September 1837, 2.

marriage during the Commonwealth – had lasted for only a brief period before being repealed.

Such qualms led some couples who had married in a register office or a non-Anglican registered place of worship to go through a second ceremony of marriage in an Anglican church. As early as 1842, Burn's *Ecclesiastical Law* noted that '[s]ince the passing of the Registration Acts, it has frequently happened that parties, united according to their provisions, have subsequently desired to be married according to the rites of the church', and set out the form of affidavit that had been adopted by the office of the Master of the Faculties to deal with this contingency. In this affidavit the husband swore that he had, in accordance with the Marriage Act 1836, 'contract[ed] and solemnize[d] marriage in a certain registered building … in the presence of the … registrar' but that 'to obviate all doubts which may arise touching the validity of such marriage, and for the greater facility of proof thereof, [they] are desirous of being re-married in the parish church'.[21] It hardly needs to be pointed out that this phrasing would have done little to reassure Dissenters that the Church of England respected their weddings.

When a Rite might become a Wrong

It is therefore somewhat surprising that it was only in the 1850s that any attempt was made to check this practice. A clue as to why remarriages became an issue at this point may lie in the fact that one of the clergymen involved, William Bennett, had become controversial for other reasons. As the incumbent of the church of St Barnabas in the parish of St Paul's, Knightsbridge, his adoption of certain high church rituals had generated controversy,[22] leading to riots, and he had been asked to resign.[23] His subsequent appointment as vicar of Frome St John had even prompted a lengthy debate in parliament.[24]

[21] Richard Burn and Robert Phillimore, *Ecclesiastical Law*, 9th edn, 4 vols (London, 1842), 2: 433.

[22] The rituals in question included 'chanting, genuflecting, bowing to the high altar, and the use of surplices': Dominic Janes, *Victorian Reformation: The Fight over Idolatry in the Church of England, 1840–1860* (Oxford, 2009), 66.

[23] See Walter Ralls, 'The Papal Aggression of 1850: A Study in Victorian Anti-Catholicism', *ChH* 43 (1974), 242–56.

[24] Parl. Deb. (3rd series), 20 April 1852 (vol. 120, cols 895–941).

In 1853, Bennett conducted an Anglican ceremony for William and Caroline Burton, who had previously married at Badcox Meeting House, a Baptist chapel in Frome.[25] The following year, a second couple, William and Elizabeth Dimmock, were also remarried at Frome St John, having previously married at Frome's Zion Chapel. The ceremony in this case was conducted by Bennett's curate. It was this latter remarriage that seems to have attracted public attention and criticism, with allegations being made that the couple in question had been pressurized into it.[26] A public meeting of Protestants 'of all denominations' was held,[27] at which it was resolved that 'the remarriage of persons already united in matrimony is a violation, or, at least, an evasion of the law of the land', and further that 'it forms part of a system designed to set up ecclesiastical arrogance against civil authority'.[28] Other commentators similarly made an explicit link between such remarriages and Bennett's propensity for the Oxford Movement, with the *Western Times* claiming that '[t]he Tractarians want to teach the people that marriage is a sacrament of the church, and that no marriage can be valid unless it be solemnized by a priest'.[29]

That, however, somewhat misrepresented Bennett's views. In his sermons he 'commends the freedom given in the case of those external to the Church, but points out that marriage has always been a religious matter, and speaks powerfully against *members of the Church* being married without her blessing'.[30] While there is scope for debate as to who counts as a 'member' of the Church of England,[31] it is worth noting

[25] It had been one of the first to be registered for weddings, in August 1837: *London Gazette*, 29 August 1837, 2284.

[26] According to the *Western Times*, 3 June 1854, 5, the 'chief agents' in this 'base business' were the 'Sisters of Mercy' who 'visit the houses of the poor Dissenters, charge them with not being married, that they are living in fornication, that their offspring are not legitimate, and that, if the children of such die unbaptized, they must go to hell.'

[27] 'Great Protestant Meeting at Frome', *Leeds Times*, 3 June 1854, 2.

[28] *Leicestershire Mercury*, 3 June 1854, 4.

[29] *Western Times*, 3 June 1854, 5.

[30] F. Bennett, *The Story of W. J. E. Bennett: Founder of St Barnabas', Pimlico, and Vicar of Froome-Selwood and of his Part in the Oxford Church Movement of the Nineteenth Century* (London, 1909), 257 (emphasis added).

[31] See, for example, Clive Field, *Periodizing Secularization: Religious Allegiance and Attendance in Britain, 1880–1945* (Oxford, 2019), 25, who calculates the Church of England community as being constituted by 'the vast residue of people left following subtraction from the whole population of the number of non-Anglicans: Dissenters, Roman Catholics, Jews, and what would now be termed religious "nones".'

that both the Burtons and Dimmocks went on to have their children baptized according to Anglican rites.[32] Indeed, at least five of the Dimmocks' children were baptized by Bennett himself, including their eldest daughter, Mary Jane, whose baptism took place just a few weeks after her parents' remarriage.

Nonetheless, the issue of the Dimmocks' remarriage was raised in parliament.[33] In the opinion of the ecclesiastical judge Dr Addams, however, Bennett had done nothing wrong and was indeed under a duty to conduct the marriage ceremony for any of his parishioners who, 'having scruples about the validity of their union before the registrar', applied to him 'to solemnize their marriage *facie ecclesiae*'.[34] There was, after all, nothing in the Marriage Act 1836 precluding the Church of England rite's being performed after a valid wedding in a registered place of worship or register office. Nor was there any scope for a prosecution to be brought in relation to the way in which the ceremony had been conducted, since all the regulations governing Church of England weddings had been punctiliously observed in both cases. Banns had been called in both cases, with the wife being given her married name rather than her maiden name.[35] The 'remarriages' had also been recorded in the parish register, and again, in each case, the wife had been recorded with her married name. Moreover, under the heading 'condition' the previous legal wedding had been noted, although here there was a small but telling difference between the two cases. While the Burtons were recorded as having been 'previously *married* at Badcox Meeting House',[36] the Dimmocks were described as 'previously *united* at Zion Meeting

[32] Taunton, Somerset Heritage Centre, Somerset Parish Records 1538–1914, D\P\fr.jo/2/1/10, Frome St John, Baptisms 1846–1864, 149 (Mary Jane [Dymock]), 168 (Joseph Burton), 285 (Walter Dimmock); D\P\fr.c.c/2/1/1, Frome Christ Church, Baptisms 1844–1863, 60 (William Dimmock); D\P\fr.h.t/2/1/3, Frome Holy Trinity, Baptisms 1853–1860, 97 (Emily and Albert Dimmock); D\P\fr.jo/2/1/11, Frome St John, Baptisms 1864–1889, 14 (Edward Dimmock), 45 (Bessie Dimmock), 67 (Lucy Dimmock), 98 (Minnie Dimmock), 136 (Arthur Dimmock).

[33] *Bristol Mercury*, 24 June 1854, 2; *Morning Chronicle*, 11 July 1854, 2. Unfortunately the discussion referred to does not appear in *Hansard*.

[34] Opinion of T. Addams, Doctors Commons, 8 June 1854, cited by the archdeacon of Cornwall and reported by the *Royal Cornwall Gazette*, 6 June 1856, 6.

[35] Somerset Heritage Centre, Somerset Parish Records, D\P\fr.jo/2/2/4, Frome St John, Banns Book, 1837–1856, nos 586, 615.

[36] Ibid., D\P\fr.jo/2/1/25, Frome St John, Marriage Register, 1852–1866, 39 (no. 78; emphasis added).

House'.[37] The use of the word 'united' sidestepped the question of whether this constituted a marriage and may explain why the Dimmocks' case had generated a more hostile reaction than that of the Burtons. Nonetheless, it provided no ground for a prosecution.

Without any means of proceeding against Bennett, those who wished to emphasize the legitimacy of marriages conducted under the 1836 Act had to look elsewhere. It was against this backdrop that the actions of Benson attracted attention. Benson was a far less well known (and certainly less controversial) figure than Bennett.[38] At the time of the events in question he was in his early thirties, having been ordained in 1849 and appointed as vicar of Cowley in 1850. The ceremony that was to lead to his prosecution had taken place on 3 May 1855. As noted in the introduction, Richard and Sarah Carey had been married at the Oxford register office some three years earlier. The reason for this relatively belated remarriage was that Sarah had asked to be churched after the birth of her children. Benson, according to the subsequent court case, had 'objected to perform the ceremony on the ground that the way in which she had been married was not right in the sight of God, and not in accordance with the religion of the Church of England'.[39] As Sarah herself later told the court, Benson had told her that the register office wedding 'was perfectly legal, but that it was a right and proper thing to have the blessing of the church upon our union, and that that was the object of reading the service in church'.[40]

It was understandable that Benson might take the view that there was no need to call banns or for the parties to obtain a licence if the Anglican rite was being performed purely for religious purposes. It was equally clear that the Registrar-General, George Graham, was keen to make an example in order to dispel any doubts anyone might have about the status of ceremonies conducted under the

[37] Ibid., no. 110 (emphasis added).

[38] While Benson has attracted scholarly attention (see the sources in n. 2 above), the focus has been on his later life and work, in particular his role in founding the Society of St John the Evangelist, his advocacy of retreats and his missionary work: Mark Gibbard, 'R. M. Benson, the Founder of SSJE', *Theology* 69 (1966) 194–201; John Tyers, 'Not a Papal Conspiracy but a Spiritual Practice: Three Early Apologists for the Practice of Retreat', *Journal of Anglican Studies* 8 (2010), 165–83; Rowan Strong, 'Origins of Anglo-Catholic Missions: Fr Richard Benson and the Initial Missions of the Society of St John the Evangelist, 1869–1882', *JEH* 66 (2015), 90–115.

[39] 'R *v.* Benson (Clerk)', *The Times*, 12 July 1856, 11.

[40] Ibid.

1836 Act. In a letter of 10 January 1856, he stated that he had received many complaints that Anglican clergy were in the habit of informing couples who had married in a register office that their marriage was not binding. Noting that since the passage of the 1836 Act nearly six hundred thousand persons would have been married according to its terms, he added: 'It appears to me very reprehensible that clergymen, because the marriages have not been solemnized in Parish Churches according to the rites of the Established Church to which they belong, should be so bigoted as to consider it right thus to disturb the minds of parties so married, inducing them to doubt whether they have not been living in fornication and whether their issue be illegitimate.'[41] To address this, he suggested that Benson should be prosecuted under the 1823 Act, which continued to govern the conduct of Church of England weddings. This Act had provided that if any person solemnized a marriage 'without due publication of banns' or the grant of a licence, 'every Person knowingly and willfully so offending, and being lawfully convicted thereof, shall be deemed and adjudged guilty of Felony, and shall be transported for the Space of Fourteen Years.'[42]

The Protestant Dissenting Deputies were also on the look-out for a possible case to prosecute, specifically one in which an Anglican ceremony had taken place after a ceremony in a registered place of worship. On 7 February 1856, at their annual meeting in London, it was reported that '[t]here had been several instances of clergymen re-marrying parties who had been married under the new act – one at Frome, one in Wiltshire, one in Oxfordshire, and one in the north of England.' Having sought legal advice as to the case in Wiltshire, the committee had been advised that it was 'an indictable offence entailing the penalty of fourteen years transportation'.[43]

It seems likely that the case they had in mind was that of the Rev. Alfred Lush.[44] Lush was the curate of St Mary's Church in Greywell, a small chapelry annexed to the living of Odiham (Hampshire), with a population of around three hundred. In 1855, he had conducted a ceremony of marriage for Francis Freeman and Sarah Rogers, who

[41] Kew, TNA, HO45/6357.
[42] Marriage Act 1823, §21.
[43] *Daily News*, 8 February 1856, 6.
[44] While Lush was based in Hampshire, not Wiltshire, all other facts fit and no Wiltshire case has been traced.

had married in the Independent chapel in the district the year before. His explanation (and excuse) was that the couple had asked to be remarried in church following doubts expressed by neighbours about the validity of their marriage.[45] He also pointed out that they were both regular communicants and had only married in the Independent chapel to escape the notice of nineteen-year-old Sarah's parents. Nonetheless, as with Bennett, his actions seem to have occasioned some ill-feeling locally, and in December it was reported that Dissenters in Greywell had 'got up a public meeting to censure the conduct of the Rev. Mr. Lush'.[46]

The legal case against Lush was slightly different from that against Benson. While Benson had conducted a ceremony without first calling banns, Lush had called the banns for the remarriage of Francis and Sarah Freeman. The issue was that they had been called in the maiden name of the wife rather than her married name. For Dissenters, this was tantamount to ignoring the existence of the first marriage and, as the *Berkshire Chronicle* reported, they had 'expressed their grievances in very audible terms'.[47] Legally, the key point was that it could be argued that there had not been 'due' publication of banns if they had not been called in the wife's true name. As a result, Lush was charged with the same offence as Benson and faced the same potential penalty. The second charge against him also related to the names that had been used, in that the marriage had been registered in the wife's maiden name and the parties had been described as 'bachelor' and 'spinster'.[48] He was therefore charged also with making a false entry in the marriage register, potentially an even more serious offence, carrying the penalty of transportation for life.[49]

The Legal Outcomes

Preliminary steps were taken against both Lush and Benson in the early months of 1856. Lush appeared at the petty sessions in Odiham in February, where the charges against him were read and

[45] 'The Re-Marriage Case at Greywell', *Berkshire Chronicle*, 1 December 1855, 6.
[46] *Manchester Courier and Lancashire General Advertiser*, 8 December 1855, 5.
[47] 'Re-Marriage Case at Greywell'.
[48] Ibid; see also *Morning Post*, 13 February 1856, 4; *Berkshire Chronicle*, 16 February 1856, 6.
[49] Marriage Act 1823, §29.

he was committed for trial.[50] A true bill was returned against him at the Hampshire Spring Assizes but the trial was removed to the Queen's Bench by a writ of certiorari.[51] Benson, meanwhile, was committed for trial at the Oxford Assizes.[52]

However, Lush's case never came to trial. As the *Berkshire Chronicle* subsequently reported, the case against him had been withdrawn by the prosecution upon his making a full apology for his actions, the terms of which it reprinted for the benefit of its readers:

> To the Committee of the Deputies of Protestant Dissenters of the Three Denominations, Presbyterian, Independent, and Baptist, appointed to protect their Civil Rights. GENTLEMEN, Prosecution has been instituted against me for having by my proceedings in the Re-marriage Case at Greywell, cast a doubt upon the validity of Marriages before the Superintendent Registrar, or, as in the particular case at Greywell, before the Registrar in a dissenting place of worship, registered for solemnizing marriages therein.
>
> I consider that in a religious point of view all Church people ought to receive the blessing of the Church upon their marriages, and I acted honestly and conscientiously in carrying out that view, and certainly had no intention or idea of violating the two Acts of Parliament under which I have been indicted.
>
> I however, now, after taking the advice and counsel of those whose opinions I most highly value, am persuaded that I erred in re-marrying those parties as if the previous marriage were not valid, and so gave just cause of offence, which I much regret.
>
> I think now and hereby declare for your satisfaction, that Marriages before the Registrar in a dissenting place of worship registered for solemnizing marriages therein, or before the Superintendent Registrar, are not only legally valid (which I never questioned), but also binding in the sight of the Church.
>
> I am, Gentlemen, your obedient Servant, ALFRED LUSH. Greywell, 1st July, 1856.[53]

[50] *Morning Post*, 13 February 1856, 4.
[51] *Berkshire Chronicle*, 8 March 1856, 4–5; *Reading Mercury*, 8 March 1856, 8.
[52] *Morning Post*, 25 February 1856, 6.
[53] *Berkshire Chronicle*, 23 August 1856, 5.

Ten days later, Benson's trial at the Oxford Assizes took place. Yet despite the confident assertion of counsel for the prosecution that this was a matter of considerable public importance, it was difficult for him to identify any convincing reasons as to why it was problematic that the preliminaries had not been observed in this case. While he urged the importance of the banns being properly published to enable parents or guardians to prevent 'improper' marriages, this had no application to a couple who were already married. Even more tenuous was his argument that the certificate of the later marriage might be used in a court of law as evidence that the children born after the first ceremony but before the second were in fact illegitimate and 'so might lose the property which would otherwise be secured to them'. His argument that matters of property might also be at stake if it were to turn out that the first marriage was in fact invalid for some reason could be seen as an argument *for* remarriages rather than against them.[54]

In Benson's defence, it was simply argued that the case was not within the 'mischief' of the statute, for the simple reason that it referred to a marriage being 'solemnized', and a marriage could not be solemnized between parties who were already married to each other.[55]

The sympathies of the presiding judge, Baron Alderson, were clear from the outset. Indeed, he appears to have treated the case as something of a joke. The account of the trial in *The Times* is punctuated by notes of the laughter in court in response to his wisecracks. Upon the superintendent registrar giving evidence that the notice of the original register office marriage had been displayed in his office for twenty-one days, Alderson sarcastically commented '[a]nd the office is shut all the time', and later suggested that it would be no bad thing if the registrar was to be transported for fourteen days. He accepted the argument of the defence that Benson had not actually 'solemnized' a marriage within the terms of the 1823 Act:

> When it said that, if any person should solemnize matrimony, without due publication of ban[n]s, he should be guilty of felony, the meaning was, that if any person should do an act which changed the status of the parties from being unmarried to that of being married, and did that

[54] 'R *v.* Benson (Clerk)', *The Times*, 12 July 1856, 11.
[55] Ibid.

> without the due publication of ban[n]s or license, he should be guilty of felony, and transported for 14 years. … In the present case Mr. Benson read the service between two persons who were already man and wife, and he could not marry them clandestinely, so that the act had no application to him.[56]

As he joked, if Benson 'had read *Chevy Chase* over to them, it would have had the same legal effect, though the effect upon their consciences would have been different'. Yet at the same time he also made it clear that he did not endorse Benson's conduct, noting tartly that '[i]f Mr. Benson had consulted his wisdom he would have applied to his bishop' and in so doing would have 'received a strong remonstrance against his unwiseness'.[57]

The Legal Legacy

If Benson was acquitted, and Lush was never prosecuted, did that mean that there was nothing wrong in conducting an Anglican ceremony of marriage for a couple who were already validly married under the Marriage Act 1836? Here matters get a little more complicated.

At the same time that the charges against Lush and Benson had been made, parliament had been considering a bill to reform the law of marriage and address various grievances identified by the Protestant Dissenting Deputies.[58] There was nothing about remarriages of this kind in the original drafts of any of the bills that led up to the 1856 Act. On the third reading of the 1856 bill, however, a clause was added that seemed to have the cases of Lush and Benson in mind.

The third reading of the bill took place in the early hours of the morning of 1 July 1856. This can be ascertained because the time was recorded in the *Journals of the House of Commons*.[59] Ascertaining what was said is more of a challenge. No report of the debate appeared in the newspapers, and no debate was recorded in

[56] Ibid.

[57] Ibid. The bishop in question was Samuel Wilberforce, bishop of Oxford. For an account of Wilberforce's lack of sympathy with the Tractarians, see Standish Meacham, *Lord Bishop: The Life of Samuel Wilberforce, 1805–1873* (Cambridge, MA, 1970).

[58] Probert, *Tying the Knot*, 85–91.

[59] *JHC* 111, 310 (1 July 1856).

Hansard. Nonetheless, in the version of the bill that was sent to the House of Lords later that day there was a new clause. It provided that the parties 'to any Marriage contracted before the Registrar' could, if they so wished, have a religious ceremony afterwards but that 'nothing in the Reading or Celebration of such Service shall be held to supersede or invalidate any Marriages previously contracted'.[60]

The reference to weddings 'before the Registrar' covered those in registered places of worship as well as those in the register office. While the clause was couched in permissive terms, it was clearly intended (and seen) as a rebuke to individuals such as Bennett, Benson and Lush. This can be seen from the reaction in the Liberal *Bradford Observer*, which exulted that it put 'an effectual stop ... to the re-marriages by which the Tractarian clergy have striven to cast a slur upon the civil contract and upon marriages lawfully solemnized in registered buildings'.[61] The message was that clergy should not cast any doubt on the validity of marriages that had been duly solemnized under the Marriage Act 1836.

It is unlikely to be a coincidence that it was on that very same day, 1 July, that Lush penned his apology for his actions. By 1856, lines of communication were well established and swift: a letter bearing word of the new clause, posted in London on the morning of 1 July, would have reached Greywell by the afternoon; alternatively, though more costly, a telegram could have been sent via Odiham Post Office. It was subsequently reported that the case against Lush had been withdrawn.

It also seems unlikely that it was a coincidence that it was on 11 July that the Select Committee appointed to consider the bill met. The date was that of Benson's trial; the time, an hour earlier. As a result, there was no risk that the outcome of one could influence the other. Again, no report of any debate appears to exist, so the story has to be followed through the Minutes of the House of Lords and the various drafts of the bill. The committee revised the new clause so that it referred only to the possibility of having a religious ceremony after a wedding *in the register office*, rather than after *any* wedding before a registrar.[62] This suggests that they were aware of

[60] Marriage and Registration Acts Amendment Bill, 1 July 1856 (no. 205), cl. 12.
[61] *Bradford Observer*, 28 August 1856, 6.
[62] The Select Committee sat at 1 p.m.: *House of Lords Minutes of Proceedings*, 11 July 1856, 853. For the version of the bill as amended by the Select Committee, see

Lush's apology and felt that there was no longer any need for the clause to include marriages in registered places of worship within its scope.

Had this provision in the 1856 Bill merely been intended to allow clergy to conduct a religious ceremony after a wedding in the register office, the outcome in Benson's case would have shown that it was unnecessary: he was, after all, acquitted of wrongdoing in exactly such an instance. But once it is understood as conferring permission to conduct a subsequent religious ceremony only in certain defined circumstances, and as an implied rebuke to any who might deny the validity of the earlier wedding, it still had a role to play. A further amendment clarified that any subsequent religious ceremony should not be entered in the marriage register.[63]

The final version of the Marriage and Registration Act 1856 provided that it was perfectly legitimate for any clergyman or minister of any persuasion to conduct a religious ceremony for a couple who had married in a register office as long as it was clear that it was the register office wedding that constituted the legal marriage. As it set out:

> If the Parties to any Marriage contracted at the Registry Office … shall desire to add the Religious Ceremony ordained or used by the Church or Persuasion of which such Parties shall be Members to the Marriage so contracted, it shall be competent for them to present themselves for that Purpose to a Clergyman or Minister of the Church or Persuasion of which such Parties shall be Members, having given Notice to such Clergyman or Minister of their Intention so to do; and such Clergyman or Minister, upon the Production of their Certificate of Marriage before the Superintendent Registrar, and upon the Payment of the customary Fees (if any), may, if he shall see fit, in the Church or Chapel whereof he is the regular Minister, by himself or by some Minister nominated by him, read or celebrate the Marriage Service of the Persuasion to which such Minister shall belong … but nothing in the Reading or Celebration of such Service shall be held to supersede or invalidate any Marriage so previously contracted, nor shall such

Marriage and Registration Acts Amendment Bill (no. 236). The committee included both the archbishop of Canterbury, John Bird Sumner, and the bishop of Oxford, Samuel Wilberforce.

[63] Marriage and Registration Acts Amendment Bill (no. 236).

> Reading or Celebration be entered as a Marriage among the Marriages in the Parish Register.[64]

All this was clear enough, so far as it went. But the fact that the relevant section of the Act only said that those who had married in a register office could have a further religious ceremony raised the question of whether it was also permitted to conduct a further religious ceremony for a couple who had already had a religious ceremony in a registered place of worship. The ongoing discussion of Lush's case meant that this question was swiftly answered.

In January 1857, the newspapers reported that Lush's case had been discussed at the Annual Meeting of Protestant Dissenters, noting that the prosecution had been withdrawn on him making a full and public apology and paying the costs.[65] The necessity for the apology, or the formal withdrawal of the prosecution, baffled one reader, who wrote to the *Justice of the Peace* to ask: 'Now, Sir, how can this be? Has the judgment of Mr. Baron Alderson in Reg. v. Benson, Clerk, been overruled, or is it to be supposed that the attorney-general and also Mr. Lush's counsel were ignorant of that judgment?'[66] One obvious answer to this might be that Lush had made his apology before Benson's case, even if the formal withdrawal of the prosecution had happened afterwards. But the answer given in the *Justice of the Peace* was that the 1856 Act had altered the law. The reasoning was that the express permission to perform a subsequent religious ceremony where the marriage had been conducted at the register office 'tends to show that the performance of it in any other case would be unlawful'.[67]

This might seem to be a somewhat tenuous inference to draw. However, a further piece of evidence suggests that the redrafting of the clause on 11 July was indeed intended to exclude the option of conducting a second religious ceremony after a religious wedding in a registered place of worship. A subsequent addition to section 12 stipulated that 'at no Marriage solemnized at the Register Office of any District shall any Religious Service be used'. Again, there is no report of any debate on this change, but its addition to that specific section

64 Marriage and Registration Act 1856, §12.

65 *Morning Chronicle*, 10 January 1857, 3.

66 *The Justice of the Peace, and County, Borough, Poor Law Union, and Parish Law Recorder* 21 (1857), 90 (7 February 1857).

67 Ibid.

only makes sense if the drafters were assuming that having two religious ceremonies was not an option. The option of marrying in a religious ceremony in a register office needed, logically, to be done away with, so that a distinct line could be drawn so far as the lawfulness of any subsequent religious ceremony was concerned. Had this option not been removed, there would have been the oddity of a subsequent religious ceremony being barred where the legal wedding had taken place in a registered place of worship but not where the couple had married in a register office with religious rites.

With a single stroke this recast marriage in the register office as a purely secular rite. No longer was it possible for a wedding to be celebrated in the register office with prayers or readings from Scripture, or even, in the account of one vicar, with a 'God bless you' from the registrar.[68] Given that many chapels remained unregistered, there would also have been many Dissenters who were unable to marry in their own place of worship but were opposed to the idea of marrying in a Church of England church. The effect of the new prohibition on religious content was to prevent them from having a wedding in the register office that reflected their beliefs, removing much of the flexibility that the 1836 Act had originally offered.[69] It was a hugely significant change.

Conclusion

The fact that action was taken against Benson and Lush, but not against Bennett, illustrated how the available criminal provisions were a very poor means of dealing with the particular harm of which the Registrar-General and the Protestant Dissenting Deputies complained. Focusing on whether the Anglican ceremony had been properly performed diverted attention from the motivations of the cleric performing the ceremony: performing a ceremony for a couple who had asked for the Anglican rite was very different from persuading a couple that they needed to go through a second religious ceremony, but in legal terms it was irrelevant to the issue to be decided.

[68] *Report of the Royal Commission on the Laws of Marriage*, Cm 4059 (London, 1868), Appendix, 20.

[69] See Rebecca Probert, 'Sacred or Secular? The Ambiguity of "Civil" Marriage in the Marriage Act 1836', *Journal of Legal History* 43 (2022), 136–60.

The Marriage and Registration Act 1856 made it clear that there was nothing wrong in conducting a subsequent religious ceremony for couples who had married in a register office. Nonetheless, by framing this in permissive terms it left much else uncertain. As noted above, commentators inferred from its terms that couples could not have a subsequent religious ceremony after a religious wedding. However, it was a step too far to infer that the person conducting the ceremony was thereby guilty of a criminal offence without this being explicitly stated. Just seven years later, when Sir Morton Peto asked the government whether they would take action against a clergyman who had remarried a couple in church eight days after they had married in an Independent chapel, the response was that no offence had been committed.[70]

Similarly, although the 1856 Act had laid down particular conditions under which a religious ceremony could take place after a register office wedding, it had not said what the consequences would be if clergy failed to observe those conditions. One very obvious breach occurred when Archibald Primrose, fifth earl of Rosebery and future prime minister, married Hannah de Rothschild: their register office wedding was followed by a second ceremony at an Anglican church that was entered into the register, in apparent contravention of the terms of the 1856 Act.[71] The Registrar-General – doubtless influenced by the fact that the witnesses who had signed the register included the prime minister, the Prince of Wales and the duke of Cambridge – quickly came up with an explanation to counter any suggestion of wrongdoing.[72]

It is tempting to speculate on how things might have turned out had Lush not penned his letter of apology. It seems clear that he, like Benson, would have been acquitted of any offence under the 1823 Act on the basis that he too was not 'solemnizing' a marriage.[73] If he had not apologized, would the Select

[70] Parl. Deb. (3rd series), 27 July 1863 (vol. 172, cols 1465–6).

[71] 'Lord Rosebery's Marriage', *The Times*, 22 March 1878, 11.

[72] His explanation was that since both ceremonies took place on the same morning, they 'would be held to constitute one marriage', and so 'the officiating minister did nothing illegal in registering the marriage in the usual way': 'Church News', *The Graphic*, 6 April 1878, 347.

[73] The reasoning in Benson's case would also apply to the charge of making a false entry in the register, since the relevant section referred to this being done with '[i]ntent to elude the Force of this Act': Marriage Act 1823, §29.

Committee have left the clause as originally drafted, with its reference to marriages before the registrar? Had they done so, it would have been clear that it was perfectly acceptable to have a further religious ceremony after a religious wedding and there would have been no need to add the prohibition on the use of religious content in weddings in a register office. The experiences of subsequent generations of couples marrying in the register office – and, later, on approved premises – would have been very different.[74]

Finally, it is worth reflecting on the couples whose remarriages were conducted by Bennett, Benson and Lush. Their stories raise some difficult questions about the religious affiliations of those who married in Nonconformist chapels or in register offices during the mid-nineteenth century. As we have seen, the Burtons and the Dimmocks had their children baptized in the Church of England; the Freemans had married in an Independent chapel for tactical reasons; and Sarah Carey told the court that she and her husband 'were always members of the church of England'.[75] The puzzle in this last case is not why they went through with the Anglican ceremony but why they married in the register office in the first place. Even more importantly, their case casts doubt on whether it is valid to draw wider inferences about the rejection of religion from the popularity of register office weddings.[76] At the very least, we should be open to the possibility that it was the second, legally ineffective religious ceremony that was the more meaningful rite for some couples.

[74] On the restrictive nature of the current law, see Stephanie Pywell and Rebecca Probert, 'Neither Sacred nor Profane: The Permitted Content of Civil Marriage Ceremonies', *Child and Family Law Quarterly* 30 (2018), 415–36.

[75] Their son William was baptized in St James, Cowley, in August 1853: Oxford, Oxfordshire Family History Society, Anglican Parish Registers, BOD75_c_2, Cowley St James, Baptisms 1853–1892, 35.

[76] On which, see Olive Anderson, 'The Incidence of Civil Marriage in Victorian England and Wales', *P&P* 69 (1975), 50–87; Roderick Floud and Pat Thane, 'Debate: The Incidence of Civil Marriage in Victorian England and Wales', *P&P* 84 (1979), 146–54; Olive Anderson, 'The Incidence of Civil Marriage in Victorian England and Wales: A Rejoinder', *P&P* 84 (1979), 155–62. For more recent analysis of the range of reasons why couples might marry in a register office, see Rebecca Probert 'Interpreting Choices: What can we infer from where our Ancestors Married?', *Journal of Genealogy and Family History* 5 (2021), 75–84.

SPCK Tracts and Rites of Passage in the Long Nineteenth Century

Frances Knight*

University of Nottingham

This article investigates how the SPCK, the Church of England's major nineteenth-century publishing house, encouraged what it saw as correct participation in church-administered rites of passage, by the mass production of tracts. SPCK's elaborate editorial policy meant that the tracts provide a rare glimpse into what can be assumed to be the Church of England's officially sanctioned voice, giving the tracts a significance beyond their survival as ephemeral religious literature. The article discusses tracts relating to marriage, baptism, churching and confirmation, the audience for which was mainly, although not exclusively, working-class adherents of the Church of England. It highlights the tangle between theological ideas and social expectations, as well as the echoes of some other theorists – from Malthus to Freud – which found their way into the Church of England's thinking at different times during this period.

Introduction

A whole retinue of ideas clustered around the rites of passage celebrated by the Church of England in the long nineteenth century. Some were theological: baptismal regeneration, confirmation as the renewal of baptismal vows by the instructed baptized, marriage as an analogy of the union between Christ and his Church, churching as thanksgiving and reincorporation, burial as a prelude to judgment and eternal life. An even larger retinue of social and cultural practices surrounded the ceremonies. Although liturgical language smoothed over differing circumstances and perspectives, creating the impression of a shared understanding, and of a goal jointly achieved, it is obvious that the participants often engaged in these rites with very different expectations. When church ended, a domestic ritual usually took

* E-mail: frances.knight@nottingham.ac.uk.

Studies in Church History 59 (2023), 332–358
doi: 10.1017/stc.2023.15

over – a wedding reception, a baptismal family celebration, a confirmation party in a pub, a funeral tea – which created further layers of meaning, and the *communitas* which Victor Turner, anthropologist and interpreter of Arnold van Gennep, identified as arising from rites of passage.[1] Kinship networks were strengthened by merging families and by creating what were often the reciprocal ties of godparenthood,[2] or they were fractured by death or strained by controversial marriage choices. The presence of family, friends and sometimes the wider community was usually seen as adding to the efficacy of the event, although sometimes the participants wished for privacy, and to keep others at a distance. For several centuries, the Church of England's rites of passage had provided the pivots and scaffolding for a myriad of personal crises and celebrations. But as people came to its churches for these ceremonies, it looked on nervously. It wanted everyone to participate, but it wanted them to do so in what it considered to be the right way. In an attempt to improve correct participation, it adopted a strategy typical of religious organizations and movements in the long nineteenth century: it issued tracts. The idea was that supporters would buy them in bulk and give them to people in their parishes.[3]

These tracts were published by the Society for Promoting Christian Knowledge (SPCK), beginning shortly after 1689 and ending only in the 1950s. Over one million SPCK tracts were described as 'in circulation' in 1817, and the figure had risen to over six million in 1887.[4] As Nicholas Dixon has pointed out, SPCK 'constituted a crucial component of normative Anglican identity', particularly in the years before the revivals of the convocations of Canterbury and York

[1] Victor Turner wrote extensively about *communitas*, particularly in *The Ritual Process: Structure and Anti-Structure* (New York, 1969). For a useful summary, see Victor and Edith Turner, 'Religious Celebrations', in Victor Turner, ed., *Celebration: Studies in Festivity and Ritual* (Washington DC, 1982), 201–9. For more on Victor Turner, see Fiona Bowie, *Anthropology of Religion*, 2nd edn (Oxford 2006), 153–66. See also Douglas J. Davies, *Anthropology and Theology* (Oxford, 2002), 120, 129. Davies argues that 'the priest does well to enter into the spirit of those occasions, fostering *koinonia* amidst *communitas*'.

[2] Naomi Tadmor, 'Early Modern English Kinship in the Long Run: Reflections on Continuity and Change', *Continuity and Change* 25 (2010), 15–48.

[3] The biographers of Archbishop Secker claimed that he had distributed thirty thousand SPCK tracts during his primary visitation of the Canterbury diocese in 1758: Richard Sharp, 'Review of R. W. Greaves and John S. Macauley, *The Autobiography of Thomas Secker: Archbishop of Canterbury*', *Anglican and Episcopal History* 61 (1992), 92–4.

[4] W. O. B. Allen and Edmund McClure, *Two Hundred Years: The History of the Society for Promoting Christian Knowledge* (London, 1898), 197.

in 1852 and 1861 respectively. The society was sanctioned and supported by all the English bishops and large numbers of clergy and laypeople. For many years, it represented the mainstream of Church of England opinion, and was not identified with any particular party, proclaiming itself to be as equally 'Against Enthusiasm' as it was 'Against Popery'.[5] By the early Victorian period, however, the sharpening of party identities caused SPCK to be criticized from both the Tractarian and the evangelical wings of the church,[6] but although it found it harder to retain its position in the Anglican centre ground, it remained a very important vehicle for promoting officially sanctioned ecclesiastical opinion. This article examines a selection of the tracts issued by SPCK relating to marriage, baptism, churching and confirmation during the long nineteenth century. The SPCK tract collection, in the care of the Cambridge University Library since 1998, has much to tell us about the behaviours that the church wanted to instil, particularly in its working-class members, and about the practices that it wanted to stamp out. The tracts reveal the church attempting to uphold traditional social and class conventions, amid changing social and legal realities. Rooted in a rural mindset, they reveal a church struggling to adjust to the urban world.

With growing levels of literacy and a shortage of simple reading materials, SPCK started tract production when it began its publishing activities in the late seventeenth century, with *A Tract on Confirmation* by Josiah Woodward, and *Pastoral Advices to those who are Newly Confirmed* amongst its earliest publications.[7] The society formed a specific tract committee only in 1834, the year after the beginning of the Oxford *Tracts for the Times*. This may have been an attempt to provide an episcopally sanctioned counterblast to the Tractarians. It certainly provided a rival to the influential evangelical Religious Tract Society, founded in 1799.[8] The approval process for

[5] Nicholas Dixon, 'The Activity and Influence of the Established Church in England *c.*1800–1837' (PhD thesis, Cambridge University, 2018), 238, 256–7. His chapter on 'The Society for Promoting Christian Knowledge and the Press' (ibid. 238–93) contains much useful material on the SPCK in the earlier nineteenth century.

[6] Ibid. 289–91.

[7] Allen and McClure, *Two Hundred Years*, 168–9. These publications appeared shortly after SPCK was founded, in 1698.

[8] For the Religious Tract Society, see Joseph Stubenrauch, 'Silent Preachers in the Age of Ingenuity: Faith, Commerce, and Religious Tracts in Early Nineteenth-Century Britain', *ChH* 80 (2011), 547–74.

publication was convoluted and slow, producing works which were designed to be inoffensive to the largest number of SPCK supporters, who needed to be willing to buy and distribute them. First, a new manuscript had to be recommended by four SPCK members, and then referred to the tract committee via the society's standing committee. It was read by members of the tract committee, and then set in type, with proofs sent to five episcopal referees. Only once they had given approval and the author had agreed to any required changes was the revised document sent back to the standing committee, which authorized its onward progress to the society's board. Then, at least until 1838, there followed the most surprising part of the editorial process: a final decision on whether it should be published was settled by a ballot of the members attending each monthly board. The ballot presumably came to be regarded as too unpredictable (and perhaps too democratic), and after 1838, the decision was placed in the hands of the seven-member tract committee, with a final sanction of approval provided by the episcopal referees.[9]

Yet despite these challenges, there were plenty of authors who were prepared to write tracts. The work was well paid and being published by SPCK was useful as a guarantee of one's orthodoxy. The peak years of tract production were in the period from 1850 to 1890. In a representative year, 1859, one hundred and twelve new titles were issued. They were very specifically targeted.[10] The society's 1874 report

[9] W. K. Lowther Clarke, *A Short History of the SPCK* (London, 1919), 47; idem, *The History of the SPCK* (London, 1959), 172–81; Allen and McClure, *Two Hundred Years*, 191. Close supervision from a panel of bishops continued into the twentieth century. Various high churchmen were critical of SPCK's policy: John Keble, preaching at the annual meeting of the Winchester District Committees of the Societies for Propagating the Gospel, and Promoting Christian Knowledge on 31 May 1838, criticized the SPCK's willingness to admit anyone as a subscriber, without enquiry as to whether they lived a sober and religious life. He believed that this was a fearful accommodation to the spirit of the world: John Keble, *Sermons Academical and Occasional* (Oxford, 1847), 249. Equally, many of the SPCK tracts did not find favour with evangelicals: Isabel Rivers, 'The First Evangelical Tract Society', *HistJ* 50 (2007), 1–22.

[10] Target groups identified by other scholars include prisoners and emigrants. Rosalind Crone provides an interesting exploration of the work of John Field, chaplain at Reading Gaol in the 1840s and 1850s, who wrote SPCK tracts for prison inmates, including 'Friendly Advice to a Prisoner' and 'A Chaplain's Word at Parting': Rosalind Crone, 'The Great "Reading" Experiment: An Examination of the Role of Education in the Nineteenth-Century Gaol', *Crime, History and Societies* 16 (2012), 47–74. Rowan Strong identified an anonymous female tract writer from Plymouth, who wrote a children's tract, 'The Young Emigrants', around 1850: Rowan Strong, 'Pilgrims, Paupers or

indicates some of the categories of people that they were aiming to reach with specific tracts: 'self-educated persons of average ability', 'semi-educated persons', 'imperfectly educated persons', 'infidels', 'deists', 'very plain people', 'untidy wives', those with 'itching ears'.[11] The largest category comprised tracts for 'general distribution'.[12] This targeted approach can be seen in the tracts relating to rites of passage, which frequently address themselves to a specific social class or gender. There are, unsurprisingly, tracts on marriage aimed at young men, and others aimed at young women: there are those intended for middle-class couples, and those for the working class (which are sometimes alarmingly explicit about the prevalence of domestic violence). The tract committee avoided any concessions to modern scholarship. B. F. Westcott on the resurrection was turned down by Bishops Sumner of Winchester, Jackson of Lincoln and Ollivant of Llandaff in 1868, and in 1864 Henry Alford was criticized for attempting his own translation of some verses in the Bible, which was seen as a slur on the Authorized Version.[13]

There were two main formats. There was the narrative form, most popular in the second half of the nineteenth century, which was designed to stimulate the interest of those in search of a short story. There was also the simple theological treatise, which was usually blended with practical instructions on how to conduct oneself at the ceremony being discussed. They varied in length, but typically were in the range of ten to twenty pages and published in a small format similar to the modern A6 international paper size (105 mm x 148 mm). The shortest I found was a single sheet printed on one side listing six do's and don'ts for a woman coming to a churching ceremony (including the instruction that she should enjoy it).[14] Most of the tracts were anonymous, although the tract collection also contains some relevant longer works by named individuals, for example Edward Berens's *Explanatory Observations on the Occasional Offices of the Church of England* (1843). The society seems to have been willing to place the author's name on

Progenitors: Religious Constructions of British Emigration from the 1840s to the 1870s', *History* 100 (2015), 392–411.

[11] Those who wandered between places of worship because their ears itched for something different: see 2 Tim. 4: 3.

[12] Lowther Clarke, *History*, 173.

[13] Ibid. 176.

[14] Anon, *A Word on the Churching of Women* (London, 1876).

the title page when the work was considered particularly good, and when a bishop or archdeacon wrote, he appears to have done so under his own name. Far fewer tracts were produced in the early twentieth century, and after the First World War they turned into longer and more informative pamphlets, written in short chapters or clear sections. The story form, which by the 1890s must have seemed old-fashioned and patronizing, was abandoned.

Of course, none of these tract writers would have known the phrase 'rites of passage'. They saw themselves as writing about the occasional offices. It is to Arnold van Gennep that we owe the language and theory of rites of passage. Van Gennep published *Rites de passage* in 1909: it was not translated into English until 1960, after which, slowly but surely, it began to make an impact.[15] Part of van Gennep's enduring significance comes from his having identified a three-fold pattern to the moments of transition in people's lives: separation, transition and incorporation. He saw these three states together as the schema of the rites of passage. The late John Bossy was probably the first modern ecclesiastical historian to adopt the terminology, and van Gennep's theory, in his ground-breaking book *The English Catholic Community* (1975).[16] Bossy realized the significance of rites of passage in delineating the boundaries of separation for a community which felt itself under threat. He returned to rites of passage more generally in his *Christianity in the West* (1985).

The SPCK tracts provide some insights into the expectations surrounding these moments of transition. It is evident that clergy and participants were often seeking different meanings within the ceremonies themselves,[17] and were layering legal, theological, social and cultural meanings, although these were to some extent concealed by the liturgical assumption that all Christians should be treated in a similar way. There were plenty of contradictions and tensions, but these ceremonies would not have been functioning in van Gennep's sense as rites of passage if this had not been so.

[15] Arnold van Gennep, *The Rites of Passage*, 2nd edn (Chicago, IL, 2019).

[16] John Bossy, *The English Catholic Community 1570–1850* (London, 1975), 132–44.

[17] Davies, *Anthropology and Theology*, 120.

Marriage

For the whole of the long nineteenth century, marriage was seen as one of the great public institutions on which the stability of society rested.[18] The era after Lord Hardwicke's 1753 Marriage Act emphasized that it was a contract creating legal certainty, apportioning responsibility for children and safeguarding property and inheritance rights. SPCK's tract writers tried to instil a sense of the enormous spiritual risks and responsibilities that marriage entailed. Marriage was consistently treated as the least predictable and most hazardous rite of passage, because it involved two souls in a complex relationship, in which one could drag the other into perdition. Until the early twentieth century, it was presented as having profound implications for one's fortunes in the next life, yet it lacked the compelling eschatological promises associated with baptism and confirmation. This sense of the serious risks involved is one of the tracts' frequently recurring themes. George Davys in a narrative tract commented that the seriousness of marriage was such that 'the happiness of this world, and probably the next' depended upon it.[19] Edward Berens, writing for SPCK in 1843, urged married couples 'not only to live together in this life in mutual love, but to have a hope of meeting together again in the life everlasting'.[20] While the tract writers emphasized the gospel teaching that the risen dead will be as angels, 'neither married nor given in marriage', they promised that those who had had holy marriages could expect to be 'in a closer union, absorbed in each other, and both in Eternal Love'.[21]

Selecting the most suitable partner was therefore paramount, and the tract writers delivered much advice about the qualities to look for. Working men should look for 'a good housekeeper' who would shop

[18] Josef Ehmer, 'Marriage', in David I. Kertzer and Marzio Barbagli, eds, *Family Life in the Long Nineteenth Century* (New Haven, CT, 2002), 282–321, at 285. For more on the background, see Erica Harth, 'The Virtue of Love: Lord Hardwicke's Marriage Act', *Cultural Critique* 9 (1988), 123–54; David Lemmings, 'Marriage and the Law in the Eighteenth Century: Lord Hardwicke's Marriage Act of 1753', *HistJ* 39 (1996), 339–60; Ginger S. Frost, *Living in Sin: Cohabitation as Husband and Wife in Nineteenth-Century England* (Manchester, 2008), 9–28.

[19] George Davys, *Village Conversations* (London, 1850), 35.

[20] Edward Berens, *Explanatory Observations on the Occasional Offices of the Church of England* (London, 1843), 31.

[21] Anon, *Tracts on Practical Subjects addressed to the Working Classes*, No. 2: *Marriage* (London, 1860), 24; see also Mark 12: 25; Matt. 22: 30; Luke 20: 34–6.

well, cook well and sew well, 'a neat, tidy, bright little woman to sit opposite to you and chat to you'.[22] Working-class girls should look for a young man who had been a good son. If no one was suitable, they should stay single, rather than risk a perilous marriage.[23] Marrying someone from the same church was also considered highly desirable, presumably meaning someone of the same denomination, rather than restricting one's choice to worshippers at the parish church. Beilby Porteous, writing in 1781, was particularly candid about the risks associated with intermarriage between Catholics and Protestants, which resulted, he believed, in a 'shipwreck of faith' with the Church of England partner usually the one sunk.[24] Much of the advice was predictable and timeless: Berens urged people intending to marry to consider the disposition and habits of their partner when 'the first warmth of passion has subsided'.[25]

The continuing influence of the political economy theories of Thomas Malthus is seen late into the nineteenth century, with couples urged to delay marriage for as long as possible, using the lengthy engagement to save money, and also to limit their fertility.[26] A writer addressing a tract on 'reckless marriage' to church workers expressed it bluntly: a bride of seventeen might have had six children by the age of twenty-five. The author noted callously: 'Happily, owing to the inexperience and neglect of these girl-mothers, many of these unfortunate children early end their sufferings in death, but a sufficient number of them linger on, a misery to themselves and a burden to the State.'[27] Seventeen-year-olds who wanted to marry should be told to wait for eight years. If work was short, the young man should seek work in the colonies, and send for his bride when ready. This writer regretted that the clergy could not enforce this policy, but were legally obliged to marry couples if no one objected when the banns were called. Another tract against early marriage, this one addressed to the mothers of teenagers, suggested that marriage could be delayed by settling girls as residential servants in respectable homes, and encouraging

22 Anon, *Three Questions about getting Married: A Tract for Young Men* (London, 1885).

23 Anon, *On Marriage: A Letter to Young Girls* (London, 1873).

24 Beilby Porteous, *A Letter to the Clergy of the Diocese of Chester containing Precautions respecting the Roman Catholics* (London, 1781), 9.

25 Berens, *Explanatory Observations*, 25

26 Ibid.; Anon, *Three Questions*; Anon, *About Marriage: Thoughts for Young People* (London, 1889).

27 Anon, *About Reckless Marriage: to Church Workers* (London, 1888).

boys to lodge at YMCAs with restaurants, rather than looking for a young bride to cook and mend.[28]

There are echoes of the changing legal framework surrounding marriage. The ability to marry in a register office, or a registered religious building belonging to another denomination, which was granted under the 1836 Marriage Act, made it clear that matrimony was no longer seen as having exclusively religious overtones, and yet it was still far from being a civil partnership between equals.[29] As late as 1880, SPCK issued a tract aiming to clarify the legal and ecclesiastical position on civil marriage. 'There seems no doubt that a marriage by a Registrar is lawful; and however strongly we Christian churchmen must regret the adoption of such a mode of marriage, we are not justified in treating people married by a Registrar as if they were not "man and wife" or their children as if they were not legitimate.' Nothing should be done which seemed to 'treat the law of the land with contempt'.[30] However, if a civilly married couple decided that they would afterwards like to come to church, they were entitled to have the full Prayer Book marriage service, with the omission of the publication of banns, and the register signing.[31] Rebecca Probert's article in this volume discusses in detail the questions surrounding Anglican ceremonies that were held after register office weddings in the period from 1837 to 1857. But the SPCK tracts show that the question of the ecclesiastical status of civil marriages was far from settled even in the late nineteenth century.

The 1857 Matrimonial Causes Act moved divorce from the ecclesiastical to the civil courts, whilst still making it extremely difficult to obtain. The legal position of married women under English law was also evolving, as they began to be seen as retaining some level of independence, instead of being entirely absorbed into the legal entity of their husband. This was expressed in the Married Women's Property Acts of 1870 and 1882.[32] SPCK remained unsympathetic to these developments: 'Too often people think that when they weary of each other, they can separate – but this is one of the greatest sins against God.' Furthermore, stated the same tract writer, evidently

[28] Anon, *On Marriage: Address to Mothers* (London, 1890).
[29] Lloyd Bonfield, 'European Family Law', in Kertzer and Barbagli, eds, *Family Life*, 109–54, at 115.
[30] Anon, *Marriage by a Registrar: Or, Where shall I be Married?* (London, 1880), 5.
[31] Anon, *Marriage by a Registrar*, 3.
[32] Bonfield, 'European Family Law', 121–4.

addressing a male readership: 'God has given you dominion over the woman; your superior strength of mind and body entitle you to this rule. … The first duty of a wife is obedience, and she should readily submit, even if she is better educated or has a stronger intellect than her husband.'[33] A tract writer in 1890, who identified herself as a middle-class mother and a 'lady', stated bluntly that many, in all classes of society, would regret their choice of marriage partner, but there was 'nothing to be done about it' beyond trying to prevent the same fate being perpetuated in the next generation, by counselling against early and reckless marriages.[34] The SPCK material was very typical of much nineteenth-century writing on marriage in attempting to link together the claim of male dominance with the concept of companionate marriage based on mutual respect and affection.[35]

In contrast with the material on baptism, churching and confirmation, which tends to be more ecclesiastically focussed, the tracts on marriage tell us relatively little about the conduct that tract writers desired to see at the wedding ceremony itself: the overwhelming amount of material relates to choosing a partner, and then surviving in the married state. When weddings are discussed, emphasis is placed on ensuring a serious demeanour among bride and groom, and sometimes also the guests. A reference to bad behaviour among those who came 'to see a wedding' indicates that the convention of wedding services being attended only by invited guests had not yet been established:

> It is the people that go to the wedding that generally behave the worst. There are some idle gossips … who are sure to be at every wedding, though they perhaps seldom are at Church at any other time; and then there is often a noise, and a going in and out, and a clattering of pattens, so as to raise a very great disturbance in the Church, and to make every thing quite different from what it ought to be.[36]

Laughing when the banns were announced and gathering in alehouses before and after a wedding were also condemned. The emphasis was on having the bride and groom exhibit seriousness

33 Anon, *Tracts on Practical Subjects: Marriage*, 1.
34 Anon, *On Marriage: Address to Mothers* (London, 1890), 1.
35 Ehmer, 'Marriage', 286.
36 Davys, *Village Conversations*, 32.

and 'religious reverence' in the face of all the public interest and carousing.

Baptism

When the SPCK tract writers wrote about baptism, they concentrated mainly on three issues. The first was upholding and defending the doctrine of baptismal regeneration, and the second was emphasizing the duties and responsibilities of godparents. The third related to the performance of the rite, and the need to distinguish adequately between the civil registration of births and the sacrament of baptism, and to counsel against informal naming practices, which, even though theologically valid, were seen as inferior to publicly celebrated baptisms.

Baptismal regeneration had long been a contentious issue, with varying theologies arising from the differing emphases in the liturgy, rubrics and canons. SPCK had, however, been making the case for baptismal regeneration decades before it became an issue for the Tractarians or the subject of the infamous Gorham judgment in 1850.[37] Samuel Bradford's *A Discourse concerning Baptismal and Spiritual Regeneration*, first published by SPCK in 1709, was a staple on their list throughout the eighteenth century. It was reissued in 1771 and, in anticipation of bulk sales, was advertised at twelve shillings and sixpence for a hundred copies. Bradford, an early eighteenth-century bishop of Rochester, and not a high churchman, referred repeatedly to baptism as 'the washing of regeneration'.[38] A similar theology was expressed in *Christian Directions and Instructions for Negroes*, published in 1789. This took the form of ten dialogues imagined between a presumably enslaved man and a clergyman. The instruction was that one man should read one dialogue per week 'to as many other negroes as he can gather together' returning to the first dialogue after week ten and continuing with that pattern 'until your dying day'. The eighth dialogue, on baptism, indicated that faith and repentance were required of adult converts, and

[37] E. B. Pusey offered the Tractarian view of baptismal regeneration in Tracts 67, 68 and 69. For Gorham, see John Wolffe, 'Gorham, George Cornelius (1787–1857)', *ODNB*, online edn (2004), at: <https://doi.org/10.1093/ref:odnb/11099>.

[38] Samuel Bradford, *A Discourse concerning Baptismal and Spiritual Regeneration* (London, 1771), 8, 10, 15.

assumed that adult baptismal candidates would be the majority in the context of a slave plantation, but it also implied the full efficacy of infant baptism.[39]

The material addressed to godparents provides an insight into the social effort required as a child was incorporated into the local community through baptism. Two godmothers and one godfather were required for a female child, and two godfathers and one godmother for a male. Acting as a godparent was, as Edward Berens remarked, 'an act of neighbourly kindness ... of Christian charity. It is an office which neighbours ought to undertake for each other, from their obligation to do as they would be done by.' Neighbours who refused to act as godparents put the parents of a child who needed to be baptized 'to most serious inconvenience'.[40] The church required godparents 'for greater security', and to step in, in the event that the parents were ignorant or inattentive or died prematurely, when they were 'to stand proxy for the child, to covenant in its name, and to engage for its Christian education'.[41] The rubrics required them to be present at a baptism, but the concern was that not everyone took on the task with sufficient seriousness, with neighbours sometimes making hasty arrangements before the service to take turns in standing godparent for each other's children. A tract of 1838 reminded godparents that they too had once been baptized at 'the font of regeneration', and others had made promises on their behalf. Now it was their turn: the eternal welfare of their godchildren rested in their hands, until the time that the young person was confirmed. Godparents were urged to intervene if the parents seemed to be neglecting the child's religious education, and they should persuade them to send the child to the local National or parochial school.[42] After his rather stark recital of the weighty obligations of the office in the earlier tract, Berens shifted into a notably more pastoral tone, inviting those 'who kindly undertake the office of sponsors' to inform themselves beforehand of the answers the baptismal liturgy required them to make and requesting 'that those who can read would bring their Prayer Books with them to the font'.[43] He also sought to reassure godparents, in a manner which

[39] Anon, *Christian Directions and Instructions for Negroes* (London, 1789), 74–86.
[40] Berens, *Explanatory Observations*, 11.
[41] Ibid. 7.
[42] Anon, *Address to Godfathers and Godmothers* (London, 1838).
[43] Berens, *Explanatory Observations*, 7–8.

softened slightly the expectations imposed in the 1838 tract, that they were not required to ensure that their godchild grew up to be virtuous, merely that he or she was instructed in religion. Berens maintained that godparents were still necessary in the event of adult baptism 'as witnesses to their engagement', even though adults made answers at the font for themselves.[44]

George Davys's *Village Conversations* tract on baptism began with a discussion of godparenthood. Thomas asked William to be godfather to his latest child, and expressed regret that with his older children, he had failed to take the matter seriously, relying on 'any of our relations, or anybody we could get'. These godparents had been predictably useless: 'not one word of Christian advice had any of them ever given the children'.[45] Thomas and William's discussion proceeded to model the desirable attitudes to godparenthood: they pointed out that asking after the children's progress was not the same as interfering, and that a 'scrupulous religious person' should not be deterred from the office by the fear of doing it wrong. In a manner typical of these narrative tracts, the two men are described settling down together to read through the baptismal service, to check their understanding.

The promotion of public baptism, sometimes also linked with public churching, was a further topic of concern to the tract writers. Thomas admitted to another of his failings as a father: he had arranged for his older children to be baptized at home, almost as soon as they were born 'for fear that they should die, as they say, *without a name* ... *Named*, or as some people call it *half-baptised*'.[46] Whether anyone besides the tract writers referred to naming as 'half-baptism' is unclear, particularly as there was printed in the Prayer Book a shorter form authorized for the 'private baptism of children in houses'. The popularity of 'naming', a swift private baptism which conferred a name and thus an identity on a child, as well as guaranteeing Christian burial, is well attested in the mid-nineteenth century.[47] Naming was certainly a valid form of baptism, and some poorer parents saw it as having the additional benefit of not requiring

[44] Ibid. 14.
[45] Davys, *Village Conversations*, 4.
[46] Ibid. 7 (italics original).
[47] Frances Knight, *The Nineteenth-Century Church and English Society* (Cambridge, 1995), 86–9.

godparents, who might expect to be 'treated' and invited to a social gathering afterwards. Higher status parents, or those with a sick baby, sometimes expected the clergyman to call on them, and conduct a private baptism in the home, which would use a shortened form of the rite. The child was then supposed to be brought to the church to be publicly received once its health had improved.[48] Berens warned that '[i]n no case does the Church allow the service of Public Baptism [i.e., the full service – FK] to be used in a private room.'[49]

The ideal was full public baptism with godparents present, incorporated into the service after the second lesson during Morning or Evening Prayer, on a Sunday or holy day, but this was only practical when the numbers of babies were small. Unsurprisingly, naming had its defenders amongst the hard-pressed urban clergy. In the 1840s, George Wilkins, archdeacon of Nottingham and vicar of St Mary's, Nottingham, named the many children that were brought to him in the vestry, sprinkling them with water, using the baptismal formula, saying a couple of prayers and then registering them as the son or daughter of the person whom the bearer stated.[50] For the SPCK tract writers, such a practice would have been lamentable, although they never explained how full public baptism was supposed to work in heavily populated urban parishes, or where parents were unable or unwilling to find sponsors. Wilkins also pointed out that the civil registration of births, which had been enacted in 1836, coming into effect in the following year at the same time as the civil registration of marriages, had had a detrimental effect on the numbers of babies being brought for baptism. Before that time, a baptism certificate had been seen as essential, functioning in much the same way that a birth certificate did subsequently, and many children of non-church members had been brought to the font to ensure the creation of their legal identity.

A tract of 1860 tackled the issue of people thinking that civil registration had done away with baptism; it is interesting that this was evidently still seen as a problem over twenty years after the legislation

[48] W. M. Jacob, *The Clerical Profession in the Long Eighteenth Century, 1680–1840* (Oxford, 2007), 194–5.

[49] Berens, *Explanatory Observations*, 13.

[50] Knight, *Nineteenth-Century Church*, 87–8. He appears to have been using the Prayer Book's service for the Private Baptism of Children in Houses. Perhaps this was why he chose to perform the baptisms in the vestry, rather than in the main body of the church. It probably also speeded up the issuing of the baptismal certificate.

had been passed. It was written as a dialogue between John (a new father) and a clergyman. The clergyman hoped that John's baby would soon be brought to church for baptism. John replied that he had no plans to do this: 'I was very glad when the registration was brought in, and did away with Baptism altogether.' He explained further that 'if you want to get [the baby's] certificate, and know all about him, you can get it from the office'.[51] The clergyman responded that although the birth certificate would do for this world, it would not be adequate for entry into the next world, an argument which seemed to place all the emphasis on the eschatological significance of baptism, rather than the more immediate issue of entry into the Christian community of the church. This baptism tract, together with the 1880 marriage tract considered earlier, indicate just how destabilizing the arrival of civil registration had been for the Church of England's traditional role as the supervisor of these rites of passage. The full significance of the 1836 Act seems to have dawned on the clergy only slowly.

Churching

David Cressy and others have provided extensive discussion of the issues surrounding churching in early modern England.[52] Less evidence survives for the nineteenth century, although some of the old debates, for example over the wearing of white veils, made a reappearance. SPCK claimed in 1876 that 'the duty of coming to Church to give thanks after childbirth is one that, happily is but seldom omitted',[53] and the relatively small number of tracts issued on the subject could suggest either that it was so uncontroversial as to require little additional promotion, or that it was beginning to be seen as something of a lost cause. Yet we know that it continued well into the twentieth century, particularly in

[51] Anon, *Infant Baptism, or, Hath this Child been already Baptized?* (London, 1860), 3.
[52] David Cressy, 'Purification, Thanksgiving and the Churching of Women in Post-Reformation England', *P&P* 141 (1993), 106–46; idem, *Birth, Marriage and Death: Ritual, Religion, and the Life-Cycle in Tudor and Stuart England* (Oxford, 1997), 197–229; William Coster, 'Purity, Profanity and Puritanism: The Churching of Women 1500–1700', in W. J. Sheils and Diana Wood, eds, *Women in the Church*, SCH 27 (Oxford, 1990), 377–87; Donna K. Ray, 'A View from the Child-Wife's Pew: The Development of Rites around Child-Birth in the Anglican Communion', *Anglican and Episcopal History* 69 (2000), 443–73.
[53] Anon, *The Churching of Women* (London, 1876).

working-class communities, and, as Sarah Williams and Margaret Houlbrooke have shown, that it became a private ceremony performed in church or (as the number of hospital births increased) in hospital. It was seen as spiritually significant by some participants, but also hedged around with family pressures and concerns about bad luck and impurity.[54] Writing in the early 1970s, the Anglican sociologist Bill Pickering noted the continued persistence of churching in the North of England.[55] A rite for churching did not, however, appear in the Church of England's *Alternative Service Book*, published in 1980.

The 1662 liturgy, following the revision of 1552, provided the woman with an opportunity to give 'hearty thanks' for having safely survived the great dangers of childbirth, and it did not hint at Levitical concerns about post-partum uncleanness. Indeed, the only Levitically-derived requirement was in the rubric that she should 'offer accustomed offerings' which by the nineteenth century had become a financial offering, which was presumably retained by the minister, or directed to church expenses.[56] Nevertheless, it is evident that ideas about new mothers being tainted and sources of ill-luck had not disappeared, and a common feature of the SPCK tracts was to hammer home the point that the service was a form of thanksgiving, and not a cleansing from ritual pollution or a means of securing good luck. Edward Berens declared that 'this part of the Jewish ritual as well as the notion of legal pollution or defilement was entirely

[54] S. C. Williams, *Religious Belief and Popular Culture in Southwark* c.*1880–1939* (Oxford, 1999), 87–104; see also Sarah Williams, 'Urban Popular Religion and Rites of Passage', in Hugh McLeod, ed, *European Religion in the Age of Great Cities 1830–1930* (London, 1995), 216–36; Margaret Houlbrooke, *Rite Out of Time: A Study of the Churching of Women and its Survival into the Twentieth Century* (Donington, 2011). Some of the women that Houlbooke interviewed looked back on the experience positively, but others expressed anger or disgust that they had been pressured to undergo a ritual that they barely understood.

[55] W. S. F. Pickering, 'The Persistence of Rites of Passage: Towards an Explanation', *British Journal of Sociology* 25 (1974), 63–78; see also Michael Young and Peter Willmott, *Family and Kinship in East London* (London, 1957), 56–7. They noted that in Bethnal Green in the 1950s, forty-one out of a sample of forty-five mothers had been churched after the birth of their most recent child.

[56] See Lev. 12 for the biblical origins of the churching rite. Unlike baptism, marriage and burial, there was no set fee for a churching, although the woman was expected to make an offering based on what she could afford. A tract in 1890 suggested that 'a rich lady might give a pound, or five pounds' whereas the poorest were only expected to give a penny: Anon, *The Churching of Women* (London, 1890).

done away with by our blessed Saviour.'[57] Nonetheless, people evidently wondered why the church provided a special thanksgiving for women who had survived childbirth, but not for those who had overcome other personal crises. Berens implied that friends and neighbours should use the churching service to join in a general sense of thankfulness for their own deliverances. Other writers felt that the only justification needed was that there was such a service in the Prayer Book. To promote this idea, George Davys penned a dialogue between Mrs Brown who had just had a baby, and her friend Mrs Walker, with the women making alternating speeches on the duty of post-partum thankfulness, and the beauty of the liturgy which would be the vehicle for the thanksgiving.[58]

The other much-repeated theme was the importance of the churching service's taking place in the context of public Sunday worship, something which it seems was increasingly widely ignored. The BCP rubric did not presuppose the presence of a congregation, which made enforcement tricky. The desire for privacy in relation to baptism, particularly amongst elite families, is well documented,[59] and this extended naturally to a desire for privacy concerning the churching of the new mothers. Citing words which he had directly taken from the eighteenth-century liturgist Charles Wheatly, Berens railed against what he described as the 'ridiculous solecism' of being 'churched at home'. 'For with what decency or propriety can the woman pretend "to pay her vows in the presence of all God's people, in the courts of the Lord's house" when she is only assuming state in a bed-chamber or parlour, and perhaps only accompanied by her midwife or nurse?'[60] A tract of 1856 instructed that a woman should attend the churching ceremony 'as soon as her feet can carry her beyond her own threshold', advice which perhaps only served to reinforce the popular belief that an unchurched woman was a source

[57] Berens, *Explanatory Observations*, 56.

[58] Davys, *Village Conversations: Churching*, 53–4.

[59] James Woodforde, *The Diary of a Country Parson 1758–1802*, ed. John Beresford (Oxford, 1978), entries for 1 October 1777, 11 April 1779, 29 January 1780, 22 September 1780; see also Jacob, *Clerical Profession*, 194–6.

[60] Berens, *Explanatory Observations*, 57, citing Charles Wheatly, *A Rational Illustration of the Book of Common Prayer* (London, many editions), 596; originally published as *The Church of England Man's Companion … or, A Rational Illustration of the Book of Common Prayer* (London, 1710).

of contamination.[61] The writer added that the woman had a further cause for gratitude if the child had survived, which underlines the point that the ceremony was intended to be a thanksgiving for the survival of the mother, and all about the woman, irrespective of what had happened to the baby.

The clerical insistence on public churching clashed with various social conventions. In 1808, the Anglican priest-poet George Crabbe had pointed out the incongruity of the 'amorous dame':

> For Rite of Churching soon she made her way,
> In dread of scandal, should she miss the day;
> Two matrons came! With them she humbly knelt,
> Their action copied and their comforts felt.[62]

Presumably the possibility of one's wife having to kneel down in public beside the local 'amorous dame' was one of the reasons why men as well as women could be critical of the clerical expectation for public churching: the ceremony created a worrisome level of equality among new mothers of different social stations. In 1850, H. R. Harrison of Elston, Nottinghamshire, announced that the only time that he was prepared to church women was immediately before the general thanksgiving during the Sunday service, at the same time that babies were brought for baptism. This led to a row with the patron of his living, whose wife wished to avoid the 'novelty and publicity' to which she would be exposed by such a procedure.[63] It appears that he took her elsewhere, to be churched on a weekday. Another priest-poet, John Keble, in his poem 'The Churching of Women', which was part of his best-selling *Christian Year* collection, drew on the medieval tradition advocating the veiling of women, which had been revived in the early seventeenth century as a marker of high church ceremonial.[64] He saw this as having the double benefit of being a return to an ancient custom and making the woman less identifiable and largely inaudible:

[61] Anon, *Advice to Cottagers* (London, 1859).

[62] George Crabbe, 'The Parish Register, Part 1: Baptisms', in *The Poetical Works of the Revd George Crabbe*, vol. 2 (London, 1834), 159.

[63] Lincoln, Lincolnshire Archives, Cor B5/8A/3, Elston Papers, June 1850; see also Knight, *Nineteenth-Century Church*, 89–91.

[64] Cressy, *Birth, Marriage and Death*, 216–22.

Slight tremblings only of her veil declare
Soft answers duly whispered to each soothing prayer.[65]

Keble provided a footnote in which he cited Wheatly as his authority that for the woman coming to church after her delivery 'decently apparelled' meant 'in a white covering or veil', although in fact whilst Wheatly had acknowledged the ancient veiling custom, he had declared that it was in 1710 obsolete and that 'the woman's apparel should be left entirely to her own discretion'.[66] Percy Dearmer, at the end of the nineteenth century, alluded to the ancient veiling custom in the earliest editions of *The Parson's Handbook* almost as a historical curiosity, but advocated it in the enlarged edition that he produced in 1902.[67] He advised that the verger should keep a clean veil, and hand it to each woman as she came to be churched, which was an admission that women would not arrive at the ceremony already veiled. In characteristic Dearmer style, he was precise about the details: the veil should be hemmed and about four feet square, of very thin linen, so that it could be placed over the bonnet. In those twentieth-century communities where pressure was exerted for women to be churched, the veil was probably only a minor issue, although Houlbrooke hints that old veils were being cleared out of vestry cupboards along with service cards, and suggests that this may have taken place much later than is generally supposed.[68] She shows that in many areas of England the rite remained widely observed until the 1950s.[69]

In the 1928 Prayer Book, the rubrical reference to 'decent apparel' was dropped and replaced with the instruction that the husband should also attend, 'if he so desire'. This hinted rather strongly that the ceremony was now understood to be a private one. Houlbrooke's evidence confirms that this was indeed the case, and that women attended either

[65] John Keble, 'The Churching of Women', in *The Christian Year* (London, 1827), 255–6.

[66] Wheatly, *Rational Illustration*, 598. As Cressy has shown, Keble could have drawn on an older body of high Anglican sources to support the use of the veil, as it had been a heavily contested issue: Cressy, 'Churching', 132–40.

[67] Percy Dearmer, *The Parson's Handbook* (London, 1899), 192; idem, *Parson's Handbook*, 2nd edn (London, 1902), 417.

[68] Houlbrooke, *Rite Out of Time*, 104, 133. About one-third of her sample had covered their heads, or worn special clothes, and a similar proportion remembered sitting or kneeling in a special 'churching' place. The example that she gives of a vestry clear-out occurred in 2002.

[69] Ibid., e.g. 125–38.

alone, or with their mother or mother-in-law; husbands were almost never present.[70] Another intriguing alteration in 1928 was the replacement of the word 'priest' with 'minister'. Whilst this meant that the rite could now be performed by deacons, around this time there was discussion of extending the duties of deaconesses to include churching, and this was recommended at the Lambeth Conference in 1930,[71] although not apparently widely adopted. But it signalled, whether consciously or not, a return to the situation which had pertained in early modern England, in which churching had been a ceremony that the new mother had celebrated with her midwife and with other female friends, and which also contained an important occasion for all-female socializing.[72]

SPCK issued a small flurry of churching tracts in the 1870s; there was, it seemed, so much about churching that had to be explained and defended. Why, for example, did it not take place in the Church of Scotland? This question was tackled by Susanna Warren in *Mrs Angus's Thanksgiving* (1873). Did it bring good luck and did the absence of it bring bad luck? Could a new mother leave the house and go to town, if unchurched? What happened to the money that the woman offered? Why was the fee not fixed? These and other matters were discussed in what appears to have been the final SPCK tract on the subject, in 1890, which helpfully illustrated a broad range of popular understandings.[73] It was perhaps evident to the tract committee that churching had been recast in the realm of folk religion, and this provides a context for Dearmer's attempt to resuscitate its historic Anglican credentials at the end of the decade.

Confirmation

The Church of England's rite of confirmation retained its popularity into the 1960s, particularly among young women and girls. In that

[70] Ibid. 104.

[71] Lambeth Conference Resolutions Archive, 1930, Resolution 70, 'The Ministry of the Church – The Ministry of Women', online at: <https://www.anglicancommunion.org/media/127734/1930.pdf>. Whether or not a deaconess could officiate at churchings was left to the discretion of each bishop: Timothy Willem Jones, *Sexual Politics in the Church of England 1857–1957* (Oxford, 2013), 102, 115.

[72] Cressy, 'Churching', 113–15, 143. He suggests that in some places, midwives and other women were excluded from their special seats after the Restoration.

[73] Anon, *The Churching of Women* (London, 1890).

decade, there was a rapid drop in candidates of both sexes. The number of female confirmation candidates per thousand of population in the age range 12–20 halved in the period from 1961 to 1974, from 39.3 in 1961 to 19.6 in 1974. Numbers of male confirmation candidates followed a similar trend.[74] Before that, however, it was popular with the youth of both sexes. It was the traditional point of entry into full adult participation in the church, as the candidates 'confirmed' their faith for themselves, but as a rite of passage its cultural significance was probably more important than its varied theological meanings.[75] At some point early in the twentieth century, confirmation ceased to be inextricably linked to catechizing.[76] Before that, children were expected to commit to memory the whole catechism, which began with the simple 'What is your Name?' and rapidly moved into much more complex territory. It required specific answers concerning the meaning of sacraments, the essential components of Christian conduct and the duty towards neighbours, as well as the accurate recital of the Apostles' Creed, the Ten Commandments and the Lord's Prayer. It also assumed the existence of godparents. A rubric in the Prayer Book stated that 'all fathers, mothers, masters and dames shall cause their children, servants and apprentices to come to church at the time appointed … until such time as they have learned all that is here appointed for them to learn'.[77] The idea was that clergy and teachers would drill young people in the catechism until they had it off by heart, although effective catechizing was seen as involving far more than parrot repetition. In this way, the intergenerational transfer of religious knowledge would be assured.

[74] Robert Currie, Alan Gilbert and Lee Horsley, *Churches and Churchgoers: Patterns of Church Growth in the British Isles since 1700* (Oxford, 1977), 167; Callum Brown, *The Death of Christian Britain: Understanding Secularisation 1800–2000* (London, 2001), 191–2.

[75] See Phillip Tovey, *Anglican Confirmation 1662–1820* (London, 2014) for a comprehensive study of confirmation in the long eighteenth century. His chapter on 'Theologies of Confirmation' is particularly helpful in outlining the range of traditional understandings which may have informed some of the tract writers: ibid. 7–29.

[76] The evangelical James Packer, writing in 1961, commented however that 'few clergy now make confirmation candidates learn it' and that it had been neglected over the previous fifty years: James Packer, 'The Revised Catechism', *The Churchman* 75 (1961), 107–18, at 110.

[77] The catechism was printed between the orders of service for baptism and confirmation in the Book of Common Prayer. SPCK published a range of teaching aids, often known as 'Broken Catechisms', that were intended to assist with catechetical instruction.

SPCK published around a hundred and eighty tracts on confirmation, about one hundred more than were produced for either marriage or baptism. Presumably it regarded confirmation candidates as a captive market, sufficiently literate and, as they prepared for the service, open to religious influence. It may also have anticipated that a tract would make a suitable confirmation gift. Probably the most frequently repeated theme was that the grace conferred at confirmation, when properly received, gave the recipient the power to resist the impulses of youth, as they entered upon the period when they were 'beset with temptation' and no longer under the watchful protection of their parents.[78] In a narrative tract from 1891, one boy tells another that the purpose of confirmation was to give the strength to resist temptation, and that fact that so many returned from the ceremony apparently unchanged was a sign that they had thrown the gift away.[79] Bishop John Kaye, in a tract aimed at 'young ladies' after their confirmation, made much of the dangers to which they would be exposed in the 'world of gaiety and amusement' in the years before they entered upon their duties as wives and mothers.[80] As well as being seen as a vaccination against succumbing to temptation, confirmation was regarded as a gateway, with entry limited to those who passed the test: 'the great requisite is a competent knowledge of the Church Catechism',[81] wrote Berens. For those who achieved a pass, the way was opened up to admission to holy communion, although, as a writer in 1888 noted, 'many who are confirmed never come to Holy Communion'.[82] Another stressed that although confirmation was not itself a sacrament, its sacramental promise of 'inward and spiritual grace' was 'strongly implied'. Furthermore, it had been instituted by the apostles only a very short time after Christ's ascension, making it even more nearly sacramental. He also implied that confirmation could function as a 'break clause' for those who no longer wished to be associated with Christianity: 'if we neglect this … we show that we no longer wish to be considered members of the

[78] William Grey, *A Village Clergyman's Address to his Parishioners on an Approaching Confirmation* (London, 1850), 7. The understanding of confirmation as a vaccination against temptation was a theme proposed by Jeremy Taylor: Tovey, *Confirmation*, 10.

[79] Anon, *Confirmation* (London, 1888).

[80] John Kaye, *Advice to Young Ladies after their Confirmation* (London, 1849), 10.

[81] Berens, *Explanatory Observations*, 17.

[82] Anon, *Confirmation.*

Christian body'.[83] This was a softening of the harsher message conveyed by a tract writer of the late eighteenth century, who had declared that their religious welfare was now no longer the responsibility of their parents and godparents: 'Eternity is before you, and it is left to your own choice whether to be happy or miserable forever … . It will therefore be your own fault, if you bring [God's] curse upon you and not a blessing'.[84]

The tract writers' comments about candidates' behaviour during and after the confirmation service suggests that they were only too aware of what could happen when large numbers of young people were brought together.[85] Riotous behaviour had been reported following confirmations in various Lincolnshire parishes in the 1830s and 1840s. Perhaps these young people linked confirmation with other more boisterous rites of passage into full adulthood, such as drinking to excess, dancing with 'lewd women' and generally noisy behaviour in which they asserted their new status. The clergy were expected to police the proceedings and to lay on treats for the candidates, no doubt partly to dissuade them from the public houses.[86] Tovey, however, stresses that eighteenth-century conduct was often described as pious and well-mannered, and that 'confirmation seemed to hold a festal part in society as a whole'.[87] It typically took place between the ages of fourteen and nineteen, and the huge gatherings of young people – over a thousand were confirmed in Bedford in 1829 – certainly generated their own momentum of excitement and festivity. Many parishes produced high numbers of candidates, and this, coupled with the fact that the tract writers warned against repeat confirmations, suggests that some people did indeed go forward more than once, although efforts were made to prevent this.[88] In 1838, Amersham produced 126 candidates out of a population of 2,816, and Milton Keynes produced 30 out of a population of 334.

83 Grey, *Village Clergyman*, 2, 6–7.

84 Anon, *Pastoral Advice to Young Persons before Confirmation* (London, 1799), 5.

85 On the numbers of candidates presented at eighteenth-century confirmations in England, see Tovey, *Confirmation*, 107–36.

86 Knight, *Nineteenth-Century Church*, 92.

87 Tovey, *Confirmation*; 110, 171.

88 Anon, *The Order of Confirmation: With Instructions for them that come to be Confirmed and Prayers to be used before and after Confirmation* (London, 1800), 13; Anon, *Pastoral Advice*, also stressed that confirmation should only be undertaken once.

In the other Buckinghamshire parishes, typically between 1 and 7 per cent of the population were confirmed in 1838.[89]

George Davys used a dialogue tract between his village characters, George and Thomas, to reflect on confirmation practices in 1850 and in the earlier generation. When Thomas's son is due to be confirmed, Thomas reflects on his own confirmation, presumably back in the 1830s: they had been taken to the service in the churchwarden's wagon, he remembers, and laughed the whole way. When the service was over, they went to the alehouse for bread and cheese and beer, 'and we all thought it was nothing else but a fine holiday'. The pious William speaks up for the warden, who had arranged the wagon so that they did not arrive hot and weary, and who had taken them to the alehouse because they needed some refreshment. If Thomas had behaved badly, or had improper thoughts, it was nobody's fault but his own. After reflecting on all this, Thomas decides that he will give up a day's work, in order to take his son to the confirmation so 'that he might stand a better chance of keeping out of harm's way'.[90] This seems to be an admission that, even in the fictionalized rural parish imagined by Davys, rowdy confirmation could be imagined as a problem. It was partly for these reasons that in the second half of the nineteenth century, candidates were sometimes segregated by gender and class.[91] Public school boys began to be separated from farm boys and apprentices, and young ladies separated from kitchen maids. This assisted in achieving the reformers' objective of making the ceremonies smaller. It also suggested confirmation preparation could be tailored to particular groups, and SPCK's material provided for this possibility.

Conclusion

What is the significance of the SPCK tract material? Firstly, it provides a relatively rare glimpse into the Church of England's officially

[89] Knight, *Nineteenth-Century Church*, 93, citing Lincoln, Lincolnshire Archives Office, CorB5/9/1–14, Confirmation Papers. The largest confirmation service that Tovey discovered was for over five thousand candidates in Manchester in 1787: Tovey, *Confirmation*, 107.

[90] Davys, *Village Conversation: Confirmation*, 29.

[91] Anthropologists see gender separation in puberty rites as normal: Barbara Myerhoff, 'Rites of Passage: Process and Paradox', in Turner, ed., *Celebration*, 109–35, at 122–6. Segregation by gender may also have been usual in the earlier period: Tovey, *Confirmation*, 109.

sanctioned collective voice. The extremely cumbersome editorial processes, and the heavy episcopal involvement, give the tract collection a status which extends beyond its significance as a survival of once widely distributed, but ephemeral, popular religious literature. The teaching in the SPCK tracts remained fairly consistent over the nineteenth century. As is often typical of religious literature, it continued to imagine a world that was rapidly passing away. The seemingly unreflective tangle of theological ideas with contemporary social and economic theories is itself very revealing.

Secondly, the tracts provide further evidence of the centrality to the Church of England of the Book of Common Prayer. We know that as the Church of England's only authorized liturgy the Prayer Book was vitally important to nineteenth-century Anglicans, but the tracts emphasize this again. Arguments end in a simple appeal to its authority, and in the narrative tracts a much-repeated trope is the production of a well-thumbed Prayer Book from the pocket of the more knowledgeable character, who goes through the relevant service with the character who needs to be instructed. In this way, Anglican doctrine is portrayed as being passed on among the literate working classes. 'Beautiful' is perhaps the word used most frequently to describe it, and the Prayer Book is mentioned much more frequently than the Bible.

Thirdly, the tracts give an insight into the generally dismal fare served up at this period for the instruction of the tens of thousands of people who lived within the Anglican tradition. The teaching may be roughly summarized as follows: the significance of public baptism needed to be regularly restated in the face of those who wanted a quick 'naming' ceremony, or worse still, thought that the issuing of their baby's birth certificate had made baptism unnecessary. Confirmation, rather than being the opportunity to publicly assert adult faith, or receive a spiritual gift, was rather crudely a vaccine against temptation, and if the vaccine appeared not to take, then to hell one might go. An unwise marriage would likely lead in the same direction. For new mothers, there were multiple pressures to get to the churching pew, and a fair amount of mixed messaging. Of course, there is scant evidence for how the advice in the tracts was received; we may assume that for people of all classes, including tract readers, baptisms, confirmations, weddings and safe recoveries from childbirth remained occasions for personal and communal celebration and festivity. But at a time when many of the Church of England's leading thinkers were adopting a more incarnational theology, there was a noticeably lengthy time lag before there is evidence of change in SPCK's popular messaging.

After the First World War there was, however, a very discernible change. The tracts were replaced with small-format pamphlets, and there was a revolution in content, as well as in style. Gone were the references to the Prayer Book as a source whose authority was beyond question, and the need for obedience to church teaching in order to secure the heavenly reward. The content became more Catholic – the two dominical sacraments were augmented to create the full seven – and also more biblical, with more frequent references to Scripture. Two examples from the 1930s were astonishingly different from anything produced earlier. In 1932, F. H. Hulme produced *Enlisted and Armed: Instructions for Confirmation Candidates*, which began with an energizing series of exclamations: 'We are alive! God made us for a purpose! God made me to live as his child! God became man!' The sixty-eight-page booklet then developed as a confirmation course, with the emphasis upon confirmation as a form of ordination into Christian service for the laity, for 'in the ship of the church, there are no passengers, all are crew'. Hulme, who was archdeacon of Bloemfontein, went further:

> You have been ordained to serve God in prayer, public and private, to receive the sacraments, assist in missionary work, to give alms … to serve your fellow man irrespective of his nationality, position or colour, to maintain the indissolubility of marriage, to work and pray for the reunion of Christendom … you must never cease to fight against class, race and colour prejudice.[92]

In 1936, SPCK published *In Preparation for Marriage* by Lindsay Dewar, which was revised and reissued on several occasions up until 1958. At only twenty pages, it conformed to the tract format, and it seems to have been SPCK's final, much republished, tract on this subject. It was set within a hinterland of psychology and sexology, far removed from the earlier material; gone was the once familiar language about marriage as the preparation for the heavenly realm. The engaged couple were urged to get themselves checked by a doctor, to ensure that they would be capable of having sex, and they were urged

[92] F. H. Hulme, *Enlisted and Armed: Instructions for Confirmation Candidates* (London 1932), 64–5. A note stamped on the front indicates that it was not to be reprinted after December 1941.

to find out what it involved, by consulting a doctor, a clergyman or a book. Sexual intercourse should always be by mutual consent: there were no conjugal 'rights'. Men were warned that if women nagged, it was likely that this had a psychological cause: they were feeling ignored or imposed upon. Dewar observed that 'women have been treated as inferior for so long that this has a bad effect on many of them, giving them an inferiority complex'.[93] For this reason, the 'obey' clause in the marriage service should always be omitted, when the bride wished this, for marriage was 'a joint achievement'. He went further: a couple would have learned much from the behaviour of their own parents; a man would unconsciously think of his wife in terms of his mother, and a woman, 'deep down', would think of her husband in terms of her father.

There had clearly been a revolution at the SPCK tract committee, and the society's publishing programme appeared to be developing in some intriguing new directions. The SPCK remains significantly under-researched. This is perhaps surprising, in view of its central importance in the history of Christianity in Britain and overseas over a period of three hundred years, and the fact that its archives are now in a major research library. The relative paucity of SPCK's twentieth-century tract material makes generalizations on the basis of Hulme and Dewar unwise, but a useful avenue for further research might be to examine more widely SPCK's mid-twentieth-century popular publications, to see if they share the progressive sentiments of these authors. For most of the period covered in this article, SPCK showed itself to be the cautious, conservative mouthpiece of the Church of England, but it may turn out that by the middle years of the twentieth century, it was in the vanguard of driving religious change. These final tracts provide a revealing glimpse into the revolutions in popular Christian thought that were then occurring.

[93] Lindsay Dewar, *In Preparation for Marriage*, 2nd edn (London, 1947), 8–9.

'Does God Mind?': Reshaping Chinese Christian Rites of Passage, *c.*1877–1940

Tim Yung*

The University of Hong Kong

Chinese Anglicans and missionaries wrestled with the relationship between Christian rituals and culture. Missionaries entered China with preconceived notions about rites of passage, but quickly realized the difficulties of implementation. For example, with the backdrop of Western imperialism, clergy reported 'unworthy adherents' misusing their certificates of admission to churches only to gain extraterritorial legal privileges. Another question was how far traditional Chinese wedding customs could be integrated into Christian marriage. Students at Anglican schools wondered whether God would 'mind' if they believed Jesus in their hearts, but did not receive baptism because of parental opposition, because, to them, both faith and filial piety mattered. The complexity of the Chinese social and cultural context made it impossible to prescribe set formats for rites of passage. Instead, clergy and Chinese Anglicans reshaped rites of passage by referring to loosely formulated guidelines, using case-by-case discretion, and adjusting to their surroundings.

At the landmark 1877 General Conference of Protestant Missionaries in China, over 120 missionaries representing nineteen missionary societies gathered to discuss shared problems in their ministry. In addition to questions about missions and church government, rites of passage were discussed.[1] In their proceedings, delegates attempted to prescribe the ideal standard for Chinese Christian baptism,

* 10.63, 10/F Run Run Shaw Tower, Centennial Campus, The University of Hong Kong, Hong Kong SAR. E-mail: timyung@connect.hku.hk.

1 M. T. Yates, R. Nelson and E. R. Barrett, eds, *Records of the General Conference of the Protestant Missionaries of China, held at Shanghai, 10–24 May 1877* (Shanghai, 1878), i–iii, 1–9.

Studies in Church History 59 (2023), 359–382
doi: 10.1017/stc.2023.13

confirmation, marriage and funerals. They afterwards published and circulated their findings in order to unify practice around the country and, in so doing, establish clear guidelines on how Christian ceremonies could – and could not – incorporate Chinese culture.

Sixty years later, far from conforming to clear guidelines, Chinese Christian rites of passage remained in question. Lee Eng-choon, a graduate from an Anglican girls' school in Hong Kong, had been betrothed by her parents at the age of eighteen. The groom was a graduate from an Anglican boys' school. Although both newly-weds considered themselves Christians, the parents on both sides had opted for a traditional Chinese wedding. Lee's teacher, Mary Baxter, witnessed the occasion in the school hall. A Chinese master of ceremonies, dressed in black satin and donning a round cap, officiated at the wedding. The formalities were completed when the newly-weds bowed to each other three times. Baxter then noticed the Rev. Victor Halward leading the couple to St John's Cathedral nearby. Five minutes later, the couple hopped into a taxi to go on their honeymoon. Baxter felt disturbed at this, knowing that the newly-weds could not be married in a church because neither of them had been baptized due to parental opposition. While confronting Halward, she received his reassurance that he had only given the couple his blessing. Although the couple could not undergo a Christian wedding ceremony out of respect for their parents, they nevertheless had every intention of entering into married life as active Christians, as far as they were able.[2]

Evidently, Christian rites of passage were entangled with the Chinese cultural context. Existing research has explored Chinese Roman Catholic rites of passage and those traditional rites that came under scrutiny during the Chinese Rites Controversy (*c.*1643–1724).[3] However, there are relatively few historical studies

[2] Birmingham, Cadbury Research Library [hereafter: CRL], CMS/ACC821/F4, Mary Baxter, 'Lee Eng Choon's Modern Wedding and the Rev. Victor Halward', *c.*1930–40.

[3] For studies in Chinese Roman Catholic religious culture, see Ji Li, *God's Little Daughters: Catholic Women in Nineteenth-Century Manchuria* (Seattle, WA, 2017); Richard Madsen, *China's Catholics: Tragedy and Hope in an Emerging Civil Society*, Comparative Studies in Religion and Society 12 (Berkeley, CA, 1998); David E. Mungello, *The Spirit and the Flesh in Shandong, 1650–1785* (Lanham, MD, 2001); Nicolas Standaert, *The Interweaving of Rituals: Funerals in the Cultural Exchange between China and Europe* (Seattle, WA, 2008). For further reading on the Chinese Rites Controversy, see 李天纲 [Li Tiangang], 中国礼仪之争：历史、文献和意义 [*Zhongguo liyi zhizheng: lishi wenxian he yiyi*; *The Chinese Rites Controversy: History,*

that specifically address rites of passage among Chinese Protestants in the nineteenth and twentieth centuries.[4] Existing studies focus more on major debates in Chinese Protestantism in other realms, such as theology and politics.[5] Consequently, this study uses Chinese Anglican rites of passage to further research on the religious culture of Chinese Protestantism.

The majority of sources addressing rites of passage are conference records, church periodicals (both Chinese and English), or missionary letters. Some address Chinese Protestants more generally, while others are specific to Chinese Anglicans. There are very few first-hand accounts from Chinese Anglicans that explore rites of passage in great detail, except for commentaries in *The Chinese Churchman*, a monthly periodical circulated nationally by the Chung Hua Sheng Kung Hui (Chinese Anglican Church; hereafter: CHSKH). However, this does not mean that Chinese voices were silent in the reshaping of rites of passage. A close examination of the positions articulated by missionaries and Chinese church leaders reveals a sophisticated awareness of social and cultural norms at all levels of Chinese society. The

Documents, Significance] (Shanghai, 1998); Nicolas Standaert, 'Chinese Voices in the Rites Controversy: The Role of Christian Communities', in Ines G. Županov and Pierre Antoine Fabre, eds, *The Rites Controversies in the Early Modern World*, Studies in Christian Mission 53 (Leiden, 2018), 50–67. Views on the start and end dates of the Chinese Rites Controversy vary. In 1643, the Dominican missionary Juan Bautista Morales arrived in Rome and reported to the papacy about problems concerning Chinese rites. In 1724, the Yongzheng emperor issued an imperial edict to proscribe Christianity.

[4] Examinations of Chinese Protestant religious culture tend to be embedded within a wider study, such as Melissa Wei-Tsing Inouye, *China and the True Jesus: Charisma and Organization in a Chinese Christian Church* (Oxford, 2018), 250–8; Carl S. Kilcourse, *Taiping Theology: The Localization of Christianity in China, 1843–64*, Christianities of the World 10 (New York, 2016), 134–9; Jessie G. Lutz, *Mission Dilemmas: Bride Price, Minor Marriage, Concubinage, Infanticide, and Education of Women*, Yale Divinity School Library Occasional Publications 16 (New Haven, CT, 2002), 5–8, 17–18.

[5] For example, see Yangwen Zheng, ed., *Sinicizing Christianity*, Studies in Christian Mission 49 (Brill, 2017), which contains case studies on the interaction between Christianity and Chinese culture in architecture, music and theology. For in-depth studies of Chinese Christian theology, see Chloë Starr, *Chinese Theology: Text and Context* (New Haven, CT, 2016); Alexander Chow, *Chinese Public Theology: Generational Shifts and Confucian Imagination in Chinese Christianity* (Oxford, 2018). For a recent study addressing Christianity in the twentieth-century Chinese social and political context, see Thomas H. Reilly, *Saving the Nation: Chinese Protestant Elites and the Quest to Build a New China, 1922–1952* (Oxford, 2021).

ensuing compromises by the mid-twentieth century were the result of ongoing dialogue with church members.

Over time, both missionaries and Chinese Anglicans became aware of the manifest difficulties in defining set forms for baptism, confirmation, marriage and funerals. However, this did not hinder them in their quest to define Chinese Anglican rites of passage that could incorporate aspects of Chinese culture while remaining distinctly Christian. As they encountered a wide variety of situations and exceptions, their solution was to exercise discretion regarding rites of passage on a case-by-case basis while holding to a general set of principles, rather than adhere to overly rigid specifications.[6]

The earliest recorded attempts to regulate Chinese Christian rites of passage date back to the third advent of Christianity in China with Roman Catholic missionaries in the 1600s and 1700s, during the late Ming and Qing dynasties. Debates over ancestral veneration, civic ceremonies and whether Chinese Christians should be permitted to participate in community festivals became known as the 'Chinese Rites Controversy'. In the 1640s, Spanish missionaries arriving in China disagreed with how Jesuit missionaries had allowed Chinese Roman Catholics to honour their ancestors. Unlike the Jesuits, they thought that such activities had religious implications. Influential missionaries from the Society of Foreign Missions of Paris, especially Charles Maigrot, vicar apostolic of Fujian from 1684, also opposed the Jesuit view on Chinese rites. This led Pope Clement XI to issue a decree in 1704 that decisively ruled against all 'non-Christian' activities. The Kangxi emperor responded by issuing an imperial decree in 1707 that required all foreign missionaries in China to obtain certification. Only those who followed Matteo Ricci and the Jesuit way of allowing participation in Confucian ceremonies would be issued a certificate. His successors, the Yongzheng and Qianlong emperors, perceived Christianity as subversive towards Chinese culture and values, and thus increased legal restrictions on Christianity. The dispute over rites eventually led to the expulsion

[6] Certain source materials in this article overlap with those in Tim Yung, 'Crafting and Communicating Theology in the Chung Hua Sheng Kung Hui, 1849–1949', in Chloë Starr, ed., *Modern Chinese Theologies*, 1: *Heritage and Prospect* (Minneapolis, MN, 2023). Parts are also based on Tim Yung, 'Forming Chinese Anglican Identity: South China Anglicanism, 1849–1951' (PhD thesis, The University of Hong Kong, 2021).

of most European priests, though some remained by going underground.[7]

The matter of Chinese Christian rites of passage resurfaced during the next advent of Christianity in China, when Protestant missionaries arrived with mid-nineteenth-century foreign imperialism and were granted access into China via the Treaty of Nanjing (1842). With only a few exceptions, such as the American Presbyterian missionary, John Nevius (1829–93), or the founder of the China Inland Mission, Hudson Taylor (1832–1905), the general assumption among missionaries was that China needed not only Christ, but also Western culture.[8] They attempted to refashion the lives of Chinese Christians along Western lines.[9] However, after roughly thirty years of work among Chinese Christians, it became clear that the shaping of Chinese Christianity would require significant mediation. For instance, prospective plans to introduce Christian Western learning did not have the desired effect of mass conversion and the adoption of Western culture.[10] The most extreme instance of unmediated Christian ideas causing unintended consequences was Hong Xiuquan's 'Taiping Heavenly Kingdom' (1851–64). After his encounter with Congregationalist tracts and preaching, Hong came to believe that he was the brother of Jesus and had been given a heavenly mandate to liberate China from its socio-economic grievances through military conquest. Almost one million 'God worshippers' joined Hong's Taiping movement throughout the 1850s, until its eventual defeat in 1864 by a coalition of Qing and Western forces.[11]

With this troubled past in mind, Protestant missionary representatives at the 1877 General Conference conscientiously sought to reconcile Christianity with the Chinese context. Many subjects were discussed, including suitable arrangements for admission to holy

[7] R. Po-chia Hsia, 'Imperial China and the Christian Mission', in idem, ed., *A Companion to the Early Modern Catholic Global Missions*, Brill's Companions to the Christian Tradition 80 (Leiden, 2018), 344–66, at 359–64.

[8] Daniel Bays, *A New History of Christianity in China* (Malden, MA, and Oxford, 2012), 70–2.

[9] Peggy Brock et al., eds, *Indigenous Evangelists and Questions of Authority in the British Empire 1750–1940*, Studies in Christian Mission 46 (Leiden, 2015), 4.

[10] Tim Yung, 'Visions and Realities in Hong Kong Anglican Mission Schools, 1849–1941', in Charlotte Methuen, Alec Ryrie and Andrew Spicer, eds, *Inspiration and Institution in Christian History*, SCH 57 (Cambridge, 2021), 254–76, at 256–60.

[11] Jonathan D. Spence, *God's Chinese Son: The Taiping Heavenly Kingdom of Hong Xiuquan* (New York, 1996), xxvi, 64, 118, 178, 316–32.

communion, confirmation, weddings and funerals. Concerning admission to holy communion and confirmation, the Rev. J. W. Lambuth of the American Southern Methodist Episcopal Mission highlighted the 'great importance' of Chinese disciples' gaining knowledge of God. This was not to be demonstrated through reciting creeds or observing rites, but through 'a thorough change of a spiritual and religious character'. Candidates were to be examined before baptism and would be granted full membership only after six months' probation, in line with the practice in North America. Crucially, members would need to respect the Sabbath, give up opium and demonstrate the absence of covetousness.[12] Concerning weddings, delegates agreed that certain cultural features should be retained but others removed. For instance, the red sedan chair for the bridal procession could be kept because it was more of a fashion statement than a superstitious practice. However, payment for brides or petitioning heaven and earth for blessings ought to be abandoned. Equally, they agreed that introducing 'foreign exotic observances' from the West was unnecessary. Joining the hands of the bridegroom and bride during the wedding often brought 'unnecessary ridicule' from guests.[13] Funerals were less straightforward. One major question was whether Chinese Christians could attend 'heathen' funerals. On the one hand, delegates argued that Chinese Christians ought to refrain from complicity with such ceremonies for fear of idolatrous practices. On the other hand, some noted that the absence of Chinese Christians at funerals could be perceived as demonstrating a lack of sympathy. In the end, there was disagreement between those delegates who suggested that individuals could exercise discretion while attending non-Christian funerals, and others who desired a clear set of guidelines for Chinese Christian funerals.[14]

The 1877 General Conference was followed by a similar meeting in 1890, and subsequently the 1907 Centenary Conference.[15] Foreign missionaries and Chinese clergy continued their attempts to demarcate the acceptable boundaries of Chinese Christian rites of passage while investigating cultural nuances further. The Morrison Society was formed in Guling in 1903 to enable younger

[12] Yates, Nelson and Barrett, eds, *Records of the General Conference*, 241–50.
[13] Ibid. 387–90.
[14] Ibid. 391–8.
[15] Bays, *New History*, 70–1.

missionaries to study problems relating to missions in China. Frederick Graves, Anglican bishop of Kiangsu (Jiangsu) diocese, stated that the society's aim was to secure all that was essential in the Christian ceremony without condemning what was innocent in the Chinese rites. In practice, this meant circulating publications on religious culture. One volume discussed the subject of Chinese Christian marriage. It affirmed aspects of the pre-existing Chinese system, such as betrothal via a go-between, betrothal cards, the sending of gifts and the wedding reception being hosted at the bridegroom's house. However, it rejected 'heathen' customs such as 'drinking to excess and the playing of rough pranks in the bridal chamber', or an understanding of marriage as 'a mere contract between families'. The booklet added that it would be 'an excellent plan' if, in future, parents consulted their children before betrothing them.[16]

Among Chinese Anglicans, more concerted efforts to regulate Chinese Christian ceremonies took place from 1897, when bishops representing different Anglican missionary societies working in China convened for the first time. Previously, these agencies from England and America had arrived at different times and had different priorities. From England, for instance, the Church Missionary Society worked in the south, while the Society for the Propagation of the Gospel worked in the north, and the American Church Mission focused on areas along the Yangtze river.[17] At these meetings, the bishops took concrete steps towards organizing a general synod. At the same time, they passed various resolutions that addressed church order and rites of passage.[18] For instance, at their 1899 meeting, they distinguished between hearers and catechumens at different stages of preparation for baptism. They also resolved that marriages in church should require both newly-weds to be baptized Christians. In addition, ten resolutions were passed on discipline. If an offender was found to have committed 'grievous and notorious sin', they could be

[16] Hong Kong, Sheng Kung Hui Archive [hereafter: HKSKH], 2138/37, Morrison Society Papers 2, 'Marriage in the Chinese Church', December 1903, 1–3, 8–15.

[17] G. F. S. Gray with Martha Lund Smalley, *Anglicans in China: A History of the Zhonghua Shenggong Hui*, The Episcopal China Mission History Project (New Haven, CT, 1996), 5. The Canadian Church began work in Henan Province in 1907.

[18] For further information about the meetings, see Tim Yung, 'Keeping up with the Chinese: Constituting and Reconstituting the Anglican Church in South China, 1897–1951', in Rosamond McKitterick, Charlotte Methuen and Andrew Spicer, eds, *The Church and the Law*, SCH 56 (Cambridge, 2020), 383–400.

permitted to return to church services after public confession, but would be suspended from holy communion for a period stipulated by the bishop. Those unwilling to confess their sin should be openly excommunicated, with their name posted on the door of the church.[19] In the diocese of Victoria (Hong Kong), Bishop Joseph Charles Hoare implemented these resolutions by suspending from holy communion those who were caught gambling, smoking opium, stealing, taking a concubine or marrying a 'heathen'. More serious offences resulting in excommunication included 'idolatrous practices', fornication, adultery, 'dealings with a prostitute' and, in one instance, 'notorious villainy'.[20]

Notably, Chinese Anglican attempts to regulate rites of passage were consistent with efforts among Anglicans worldwide. As missions expanded to all parts of the world in the second half of the nineteenth century, the regular gathering of Anglican bishops at the Lambeth Conference, initiated in 1867 and convened roughly every ten years, became a platform to restore 'union among the churches of the Anglican Communion', especially with respect to 'diversities in worship' resulting from increasingly complicated cultural encounters.[21] Specific resolutions from successive Lambeth Conferences addressed baptism and marriage, though resolutions were issued to Anglican churches worldwide only for 'consideration' and did not have legislative authority.[22]

After positions were articulated at both Lambeth and CHSKH conferences, publications and periodicals were disseminated to inform clergy and church members about proper procedure. The

[19] Hong Kong, Public Records Office [hereafter: HKPRO], HKMS94/1/5/60A, 'Letters and Resolutions of the Conference of the Bishops of the Anglican Communion in China, Hong Kong, and Corea, held at Shanghai', 14–20 October 1899, 3–8.

[20] HKPRO, HKMS95/1/24, Diocesan Register, 161–7.

[21] Robert W. Prichard, 'The Lambeth Conference', in Ian Markham, J. Barney Hawkins IV and Leslie Steffensen, eds, *The Wiley-Blackwell Companion to the Anglican Communion* (Chichester, 2013), 91–104, at 94–6, 101. The quotation is from Recommendation 7 of the *1878 Lambeth Conference Recommendations*, online at: <http://www.anglicancommunion.org/structures/instruments-of-communion/lambeth-conference.aspx>, last accessed 20 February 2020.

[22] For example, Resolution 5 from the 1888 Lambeth Conference addresses polygamy, and Resolutions 48 and 49 from the 1897 Conference address baptism. Resolution 3 from the 1897 Conference explains the consultative, rather than legislative nature of the conferences: online at: <http://www.anglicancommunion.org/structures/instruments-of-communion/lambeth-conference.aspx>, last accessed 18 June 2021.

CHSKH monthly periodical, *The Chinese Churchman*, was introduced in 1908. Extended articles and commentaries from both missionary and Chinese writers gave theological and practical guidance on organizing rites of passage. For instance, two articles in the November 1916 edition of *The Chinese Churchman* addressed marriage. Zhang Yaoxiang, a postgraduate at Columbia University who later set up the first experimental psychology laboratory at Peking Normal College, emphasized that children of church members should not be betrothed to non-Christians. The instruction in 1 Corinthians 7 was very clear about husband and wife becoming one flesh, implying that Christians marrying non-Christians would defile both spouses. This was especially the case for women in Chinese society, who were expected to adopt the religious beliefs of their husband. Marrying a non-Christian would 'violate their religious freedom' and was therefore 'a must not, ten thousand times'. Furthermore, such marriages would lead to their children being brought up under non-Christian instruction.[23]

Huai Xin's article on upholding certain standards for Christian marriage referred to resolutions from the 1915 CHSKH General Synod concerning marriage. While it is not possible to locate his biographical information, details in his article (which provide more information than the meeting minutes) suggest he may have been one of the lay delegates who attended the synod. Huai also referred to the Bible, citing 1 Corinthians 9: 5, 2 Corinthians 6: 14 and Hebrews 13: 4 as clearly asserting that marriage with non-Christians was not permissible under any circumstances. However, Huai explained the practical difficulties of applying these instructions in China. Men significantly outnumbered women in the CHSKH, which compelled many to seek a wife outside the CHSKH and in other churches. Moreover, the cultural practice of betrothal at a young age through parental arrangement meant that it was difficult for young believers to marry according to biblical instruction.[24]

23 張耀翔 [Zhang Yaoxiang], '教會子女與教外人結婚問題解决之一法' ['Jiaohui zinü yu jiaowairen jiehun wentijiejue zhiyifa'; 'The Sole Resolution to the Dilemma of Betrothing Children to Non-Christians'], 中華聖公會報 [*Zhonghuashenggonghui bao*; *The Chinese Churchman*] 9/11 (1916), 17–20.

24 懷新 [Huai Xin], '論基督徒與非基督徒通婚' ['Lun jidutu yu feijidutu tonghun'; 'Treatise on Christians Marrying Non-Christians'], 中華聖公會報 [*Zhonghuashenggonghui bao*; *The Chinese Churchman*] 9/11 (1916), 20–3.

In February 1918, an article by Li Yaoting, who later became a priest in the CHSKH, discussed Chinese Christian funerals, and the compromises and complications surrounding them. Li explained how local churches should go about funeral rites, from how to support an individual at the end of life to commemorative practices. Certain biblical teachings were recommended as especially important; a number of traditional practices were deemed tolerable; but certain customs were labelled unacceptable. For example, the pastor was encouraged to visit and pray for the one in need, as mentioned in James 5. However, during the visit, there was to be no negative talk of death, this being a taboo subject in Chinese culture. The Chinese Christian justification for this was that Jesus had avoided negative language during his visit to Jairus's daughter (Mark 5: 21–43). At the time of death, expressions of grief were acceptable, but Bible readings were to replace the 'superstitious' songs that were traditionally sung to cast away demons. Although the family could acknowledge friends and relatives who offered support, there was to be no kneeling before the dead, as this would constitute a form of idolatry. The funeral procession could take place on any day except Sundays, Christmas Day or during the Easter Triduum. After burial, an upright gravestone was permitted to indicate the year of birth and death of the deceased, and might include a suitable Bible verse to indicate hope of resurrection at Jesus's second coming. However, a level horizontal stone which might be used for 'sacrificial offerings' was strictly forbidden. Instead of participating in the annual Chinese tomb-sweeping festival (Qingming Festival), church members were encouraged to visit the graves of their deceased on All Souls' Day. Rather than providing food and burnt offerings for the deceased (as was the common practice in the Qingming Festival), they could sing hymns and share testimonies. The fact that the Qingming Festival and All Souls' Day were in April and November respectively would have created differentiation from non-Christians. Finally, recognizing the many grey areas that remained, the writer encouraged readers to discuss further issues with their fellow church members as required.[25]

Just as *The Chinese Churchman* addressed Chinese readers, in 1899 Bishop Hoare initiated a new English periodical, *From Month to*

[25] 李耀廷 [Li Yaoting], '喪事規禮' ['Sangshiguili'; 'Rules for Funerals'], 中華聖公會報 [*Zhonghuashenggonghui bao*; *The Chinese Churchman*] 11/2 (1918), 12–16.

Month, to address English readers in his diocese. In its inaugural edition, Hoare explained that the primary intention was to raise awareness of localized perspectives of theology, which included defining the reasonable scope for Chinese Anglican rites of passage.[26] For instance, in the May 1902 edition, Hoare described a Chinese Anglican funeral in the town of Shiu Hing. The article appraised aspects of Chinese culture that were consistent with Christianity, while condemning unacceptable practices. One tradition that was deemed acceptable was the wearing of 'a length of white calico' by the widow and four children of the deceased as a sign of mourning. However, gongs, firecrackers, burnt paper offerings and 'extravagant wailing' were absent, for these items and practices indicated fear that the dead would come back to haunt living relatives.[27]

Another platform used by Bishop Hoare to communicate the ideal standard of baptism was his annual pastoral letter to the clergy and laity of the diocese. In 1901, Hoare noted that although the two thousand confirmations in the past year were commendable, he frequently observed discrepancies between baptismal registers and the actual number of attendees at Sunday services. In one instance, thirty-eight were registered but only seven maintained their connection with the church. In another church, sixty-six were registered but only nine kept in touch. Hoare attributed this 'leakage' to individuals' decision either to attend other churches or to leave the faith altogether, and he exhorted clergy to exercise greater caution when administering baptism. Furthermore, Hoare introduced procedures in the admittance of catechumens, in which church registers would be divided into 'hearers', who attended regularly for at least three months; 'catechumens', who attended regularly for at least six months; and 'church members' who attended regularly. Only catechumens were to be given cards of admission and could become eligible for baptism the following year, but would have their card confiscated if they were not baptized within the year.[28]

Nevertheless, there were limitations in the quest for a definitive statement on Chinese Anglican rites of passage. No publication or

[26] CRL, CMS/H/H5/E1/Ch2/3, *From Month to Month* 1, October 1899, 1.

[27] CRL, CMS/H/H5/E1/Ch2/3, Kathleen Hipwell, 'A Chinese Christian Funeral at Shiu Hing', *From Month to Month* 24, May 1902, 3–4.

[28] HKPRO, HKMS94/1/5/59, 'A Pastoral Letter to the Clergy and Laity of the Diocese from the Bishop of Victoria', Hong Kong, August 1901, 3–6.

set of conference proceedings addressed practical realities comprehensively. To begin with, the very process of drawing up such guidelines presented challenges, partly because conferences lacked time to hold adequate discussions. For example, the 1907 Anglican conference, the first bishops' meeting to involve Chinese representatives, organized a committee to investigate the adaptation of church practices to local circumstances.[29] Although it was intended to examine a broad range of issues, when the eventual report was presented at the 1909 Anglican bishops' conference, the committee had only had enough time to focus on church architecture, marriage customs and burial rites.[30] Even then, they fell short of conclusive statements regarding weddings and funerals. Although they could agree that wedding invitations should be sent to guests and family earlier so that objections could be raised if needed, there was no agreement on whether the traditional crossing of wine cups (when the newlyweds took a sip from their wine cup, exchanged with the other, then finished drinking as a symbol of their union) should be replaced by holy communion.[31] Harder questions about polygamy were avoided completely. Concerning burial rites, only two resolutions were achieved. First, the Chinese custom of exorcism for the critically ill was to be replaced with clergy visitation, prayers and holy communion. Second, it was recommended that the dead be laid in an inner coffin which could then in turn be placed within another, larger, outer coffin, the use and size of which was widely acknowledged to be a sign of filial piety. The smaller inner coffin was needed to fit into the church hall for the funeral service.[32] The use of two coffins was intended as a way of maintaining traditional displays of filial piety while incorporating a Christian funeral. The report avoided discussing more contentious issues such as ancestral veneration.

[29] HKPRO, HKMS94/1/6/34, 'Report and Resolutions of the Conference of the Anglican Communion in China and Hong Kong held in Shanghai, 15–20 April 1907', 11.

[30] HKPRO, HKMS/94/1/6/33, 'Report of the Committee on "Local Adaptation" presented to the Conference of the Anglican Communion held in Shanghai, 27 March – 6 April 1909', 1–4.

[31] This rite is derived from the Book of Rites, a classical Chinese text believed to have been written during the late 'Warring States' period (*c.*500–221 BCE). For further information, see 周兵 [Zhou Bing], '喝交杯酒的由来' ['He jiaobeijiu de youlai'; 'The Origins of Crossing Wine Cups'], 文苑 [*Wenyuan*] 4 (2008), 56.

[32] Report of the Committee on "Local Adaptation"', 2–9.

Even after the constitution of the CHSKH in 1912, the General Synod voted in 1915 that it was 'inexpedient' to discuss certain questions about church order. The synod instead devoted most of its time to more pressing issues, such as the appointment of committees, church literature and developing a constitution for the General Synod.[33] It comes as no surprise, then, that Huai Xin was unable to take an authoritative stance in *The Chinese Churchman* on how the 1915 General Synod viewed marriage.[34] Lack of time was a recurring issue at every meeting. At the 1921 General Synod, the question of including a canon on betrothal, marriage and divorce was referred to a special committee, and effectively postponed until the 1924 meeting.[35] Even in 1928, the canon on marriage and divorce was still being deferred 'owing to pressure of business' and 'inability to give the proposed canon on marriage and divorce adequate consideration'.[36] Astonishingly, the 1931 General Synod was again compelled to defer the marriage canon due to a lack of time.[37]

Logistical challenges were not unique to Chinese Anglicans. At the seventh annual meeting of the China Continuation Committee in 1919, a gathering that sought to survey the state of all Chinese Protestants, convenors struggled to gather responses from the various churches across China. As a result, they were unable to produce a conclusive report about ancestral veneration, marriage and burial services.[38] At meetings of the National Christian Council of China, an interdenominational organization formed in 1922 to discuss shared problems in mission work, matters relating to faith, order and doctrine were constitutionally excluded from discussion (due to the Fundamentalist-Modernist controversy) in favour of other topics, such as medical and educational work. By 1937, various church representatives at the National Christian Council highlighted

33 London, LPL, MS 2447, CHSKH General Synod House of Bishops Meeting Minutes, 14–22 April 1915, fols 6–30.

34 Huai, 'Treatise on Christians Marrying Non-Christians', 20–3.

35 CHSKH General Synod House of Bishops Meeting Minutes, 18–25 April 1921, fol. 85.

36 Ibid. 21–28 April 1928, fol. 148.

37 Ibid. 25 April–2 May 1931, fol. 160.

38 CRL, CMS/G/GZ2/2, *Proceedings of the Seventh Annual Meeting of the China Continuation Committee, Shanghai, 25–30 April 1919* (Shanghai, 1919), 39–44.

the need to deliberate over faith and order in addition to Christian life and work.[39]

Beneath these logistical challenges lay the fact that rites of passage were entangled with political, social and cultural issues in ways that made it exceptionally difficult to define appropriate procedures. For instance, admission to the catechumenate was mired in legal complications. Between 1842 and 1943, becoming affiliated with a church brought with it additional legal protection because foreign missionaries were granted extraterritorial privileges under the 'unequal treaties' signed between the Qing government and Western countries throughout the nineteenth century. With extraterritoriality, foreign citizens were placed under the jurisdiction of their consular authorities instead of the Qing law.[40] As a result, Chinese magistrates were reluctant to prosecute lawbreakers who claimed to be Christian because foreign missionaries would come to their aid using extraterritorial privileges. Paul Cohen highlights various cases in the 1860s and 1870s when Chinese subjects took advantage of their relationship with French Roman Catholic missionaries, resisting paying taxes and trumping up false legal charges. One particularly infamous incident involved a cash-strapped blacksmith in Suzhou who travelled around the area, threatening non-Christian families with the wrath of Roman Catholicism unless they paid him vast sums of money.[41] At the 1903 Anglican bishops' conference, the bishops discussed what to do about 'unworthy adherents attracted by the prospect of obtaining worldly advantages', who reputedly obtained certificates of admission to the catechumenate in order to use them for legal protection in local courts.[42]

What made matters even more complicated were instances of Chinese clergy and missionaries genuinely using their extraterritorial privileges to protect the underprivileged. Between 1912 and 1920, the Rev. Mok Shau-tsang, an Anglican priest in South China, used his foreign connections to help the Ng clan in Nanbo village,

[39] Ronald Rees, *Christian Cooperation in China as illustrated by the Biennial Meeting* (Shanghai, 1937), 11.

[40] Bays, *A New History*, 47–8.

[41] Paul Cohen, *China and Christianity: The Missionary Movement and the Growth of Chinese Antiforeignism, 1860–1870*, Harvard East Asian Series 11 (Cambridge, MA, 1963), 133–5.

[42] HKPRO, HKMS94/1/5/56, 'A Pastoral Letter to the Clergy and Laity of the Diocese from the Bishop of Victoria', Hong Kong, August 1903, 4.

which had recently become Christian. On one occasion, two clans from neighbouring villages decided to hold a Taoist procession that cut through land belonging to the Ng clan. Arguments broke out which then led to fights. The outnumbered Ng clan had much of their property vandalized, which included damage inflicted upon their church hall. Mok subsequently sought restitution from the prefectural government on their behalf and was praised by contemporaries for taking action.[43] A similar encounter took place with the Chow clan in Lo-A-Shan village, which had become Christian and affiliated themselves with Chinese Anglicans in the area. The Chow clan had an ongoing rivalry with the Lau clan in the neighbouring village of Shixia. The Lau clan once allegedly stole oxen in order to incite a fight, leading Mok to take the issue to the prefectural government, since the Chows were under his pastoral care. The Laus attempted, in turn, to seek protection from Dr John Fisher of the American Presbyterian Mission, who agreed to represent them in court. However, Mok clarified the matter privately with Fisher, who promptly chose not to represent them. This led the Laus to leave Fisher and the Presbyterian Church, before losing the case to Mok and the Chows.[44] Mok's biographer, a Chinese priest writing in 1972, extolled his intervention in these two cases, explaining that such legal intervention demonstrated faith by caring for the oppressed and seeking social justice.[45] There was no straightforward way of defining right and wrong regarding admission because the main problem was not the accompanying legal protection itself, but the context in which individuals chose to avail themselves of such protection.

An equally complicated problem was the intertwining of baptism with filial piety. In Confucian teaching, filial piety is a highly esteemed virtue as it shows that a person remembers their beginnings and gives due credit to heaven, as well as to their parents.[46] However, this teaching could cause tension if the convert's parents were not Christian. Edna Atkins, headmistress of St Stephen's Girls' College in Hong Kong, explained in her annual letters to the CMS

[43] 鍾仁立 [Zhong Renli], 莫壽增會督傳 [*Moshouzeng huiduzhuan*; *Life of Bishop Mok Shau Tsang*] (Hong Kong, 1972), 20–1.
[44] Ibid. 22–3.
[45] Ibid. 78–80.
[46] Huiliang Ni, 'Sinicizing Jesus in the First Half of the Twentieth Century – How Chinese Christians Understood Jesus' (PhD thesis, Claremont Graduate University, 2008), 18, 45–54.

Secretary of the South China Mission in London that family affairs were always given priority in Chinese culture.[47] Many students attending Anglican schools who considered themselves Christians in their heart opted not to receive baptism due to their parents' opposition. This accounted for one of Atkins's students from Borneo whose parents threatened to cut off their support if she were to be baptized.[48] Another student, who died of illness in 1936, had been reportedly 'a very fine Christian at heart, but not baptized', the reason being that her family was unwilling. Even on her deathbed, she opted not to receive baptism because she was afraid it would distress her mother. Her missionary teacher, Mary Baxter, approved of this decision.[49] One of Baxter's students went so far as to ask, 'Does God mind if we don't go to church and have prayers and all the ceremonious things?' Her thinking was that, although she believed in Jesus, she knew her parents would not grant her permission to receive baptism. Another student said, 'Perhaps our parents will not let us be Christians because Jesus said we were to love Him more than them.'[50] Even opposition from parents-in-law was enough to deter students from baptism. Atkins mentioned a former student in Beijing who ran a Christian kindergarten, but never received baptism because of her mother-in-law's opposition.[51] A similar encounter took place with a graduate who wanted to be baptized and had her parents' support, but was unable to receive baptism because her fiancé's parents refused permission for either of them to be baptized.[52]

On rare occasions, filial piety could work in the opposite direction in promoting baptism. Several missionaries recorded the case of Mrs Cheung Wing-kui, the headmistress of Fairlea, another Anglican girls' school in Hong Kong. In July 1932, on his deathbed, her father finally rescinded his opposition to his children becoming Christians. Cheung's sisters-in-law received baptism in December that year after receiving approval from their mothers as well.[53] In a separate instance, three boarders who were sisters received baptism on Easter Sunday of

[47] CRL, CMS/1917–1934/G1/AL/A–BA, Edna Atkins Annual Letter, November 1926.
[48] CRL, CMS/1935–1939/G1/AL/A–BA, Edna Atkins Annual Letter, 16 August 1935.
[49] Ibid., Mary Baxter Annual Letter, 23 August 1936.
[50] CRL, CMS/1917–1934/G1/AL/A–BA, Mary Baxter Annual Letter, 13 August 1934.
[51] CRL, CMS/1935–1939/G1/AL/A–BA, Edna Atkins Annual Letter, 3 August 1937.
[52] CRL, CMS/1917–1934/G1/AL/A–BA, Edna Atkins Annual Letter, 18 July 1933.
[53] Ibid.

1940 alongside their six other siblings, their mother and father.[54] Mary Baxter fondly recalled how the father and one of the daughters were confirmed the following year. After the ceremony, the father took his entire family out for ice cream, together with the church staff.[55] Filial piety played a central role in shaping baptism and confirmation. Jessie Lutz goes so far as to argue that filial piety even shaped proselytism among Chinese Christians, who had a tendency to rely more on family and kinship networks than public preaching and religious instruction.[56] Consequently, as with admission, it is difficult to make a clear statement about the relationship between baptism and filial piety because, for some, it worked in favour of baptism, while for others it worked against.

Illiteracy was another feature of Chinese society that compelled missionaries and clergy to reshape baptism and confirmation in the CHSKH. In early twentieth-century China, many were unable to read and write. For instance, during a visit to the street gospel halls in Kowloon, Bishop and Mrs Duppuy felt that some of the newly confirmed women had 'a very superficial knowledge of the gospel' and encouraged them to attend Sunday afternoon Bible classes.[57] Nonetheless, illiterate Chinese Christians often adopted a simplified version of Christian beliefs, although they did not always realize this.[58] At Holy Trinity Church in Hong Kong, one of the baptism classes was taught by a blind, older Christian who could not read and had such limited Bible knowledge that all she could do was retell Bible stories.[59] In another instance, a women's worker conducting a confirmation class came across a seventy-year-old nicknamed 'Granny Comfort' who had spent over two hours learning the Lord's Prayer but, by the end, could only remember the first line.[60] Over the ensuing year, she eventually managed to learn the entirety of the Lord's

[54] CRL, CMS/G1/CH1/e7, Far East Committee Minute on St Stephen's Girls' College, 4 June 1940.

[55] CRL, CMS/ACC821/F8, Mary Baxter's Letter to Friends, 28 July 1941.

[56] Jessie G. Lutz, 'China and Protestantism: Historical Perspectives, 1807–1949', in Stephen Uhalley Jr and Xiaoxin Wu, eds, *China and Christianity: Burdened Past, Hopeful Future* (Armonk, NY, 2001), 179–94, at 181–2.

[57] CRL, CMS/1917–1934/G1/AL/HA–HO, S. L. Hollis Annual Letter, 29 August 1928.

[58] See Yung, 'Crafting and Communicating Theology'.

[59] CRL, CMS/1917–1934/G1/AL/HA–HO, S. L. Hollis Annual Letter, 18 October 1918.

[60] Ibid.

Prayer. At her confirmation, she and the twelve other candidates were asked by Bishop Duppuy to explain the sacraments and to repeat parts of the catechism. However, when it came to 'Granny Comfort', Duppuy asked her specifically to say the Lord's Prayer. After the Rev. Isaac Blanchett had to shout Duppuy's request again due to her hearing difficulties, she repeated the Lord's Prayer flawlessly. She was then confirmed. Afterwards, she confessed that her heart was filled with comfort, because she had only been able to memorize the Lord's Prayer and nothing else.[61] Rather than feeling disdain towards such believers, missionaries and clergy in the CHSKH – even Bishop Duppuy – accepted this simpler pattern of faith and adapted the requirements of theological knowledge for baptism and confirmation.[62]

In more extreme cases, certain Chinese Christians in rural areas did not have the same regard for rites of passage, preferring alternative markers of faith. Deaconess Lucy Vincent, who was eventually put in charge of religious education in her diocese, observed that many Christian villagers had limited Bible knowledge. As she administered a short course on Jesus and the life of Moses, she eventually diverted her focus to teaching simple prayers, as well as introducing her hearers to easy newly published books. She was startled by the number of those content with having 'a Christian household' without receiving baptism. To this community, the absence of traditional religion, rather than baptism, was the defining marker of a Christian village.[63] Moreover, it was logistically difficult to conduct baptisms and confirmations because senior clergy were spread so thinly across their dioceses, and journeying inland was not straightforward.[64] Theologian Simon Chan argues that one should view such expressions of faith as creative adaptation, based on 'grassroots' experiences of

[61] Ibid., 27 November 1919.

[62] HKSKH, 2756/3, Minutes of the Tenth Meeting of the Diocesan Synod, 'Bishop's Charge: Diocesan Development', 3–5 September 1931, 9–13.

[63] CRL, CMS/1917–1934/G1/AL/ST–V, Lucy Vincent Annual Letter, 9 August 1933. For further reading on Chinese markers of faith, see Simon Chan, *Grassroots Asian Theology: Thinking the Faith from the Ground Up* (Downers Grove, IL, 2014); Hwa Yung, *Mangoes or Bananas? The Quest for an Authentic Asian Christian Theology*, 2nd edn (New York, 2014).

[64] For instance, Bishop Duppuy was only able to visit certain parishes once per year. See HKPRO, HKMS94/1/7/1920–1921, Bishop's Schedule, November 1920 – December 1921, 19–73. Journeys by land and by river were also complicated by widespread banditry and piracy. See Bays, *A New History*, 131.

Christianity that focus more on protection and prosperity, as opposed to 'elitist' understandings that focus on salvific principles.[65] Within the context of widespread illiteracy and folk religion in rural communities, some Chinese Anglicans went so far as to re-examine the place of baptism and confirmation in their view of Christian commitment.

However, most Chinese Anglicans and foreign missionaries continued to place great emphasis on baptism and confirmation as the primary rites of passage in the profession of faith. Annual letters from missionaries meticulously recorded the number of baptisms each year and did not neglect their essential purpose.[66] Statistical tables published by the CHSKH General Synod carefully counted the number of church members in each diocese. In 1918, there were 52,689 across the twelve dioceses, including 23,165 baptized non-communicants, 19,871 communicants and 9,220 catechumens.[67] In 1933, the total number of baptized members grew to 58,665.[68] Even after the Second World War, the CHSKH continued counting the number of baptism candidates and communicants in each diocese, which totalled 66,651.[69] The existence of such detailed statistics suggests that church leaders and members recognized the importance of baptism and confirmation as rites of passage, despite the effects of extraterritoriality, filial piety, illiteracy and folk religion.

For funerals, complications with regard to tradition persisted. The general approach adopted by the CHSKH found expression in a book about ancestral veneration by James Thayer Addison, an Episcopal minister under the CHSKH who taught at Boone University in Wuhan. That the Literature Committee of the General Synod published Addison's book suggests that its contents were endorsed by the CHSKH as a whole. Addison encouraged readers to be sympathetic towards Chinese customs, so that Chinese believers could discover for themselves what was 'both truly Chinese and truly Christian'. First,

65 Chan, *Grassroots Asian Theology*, 59–61.

66 For example, CRL, CMS/1917–1934/G1/AL/HA–HO, S. L. Hollis Annual Letter, 27 November 1919; CMS/1917–1934/G1/AL/A–BA, Edna Atkins Annual Letter, 18 July 1933.

67 New Haven, Yale Divinity School Library [hereafter: YDSL], HR114, Montgomery Throop, *General Statistics for the Chung Hua Sheng Kung Hui for the Year of our Lord 1918* (Shanghai, 1918), 3.

68 YDSL, Montgomery Throop, *General Statistics for the Chung Hua Sheng Kung Hui for the Year of our Lord 1933* (Shanghai, 1933), 5.

69 中華聖公會年鑑 [*Zhonghua shenggonghui nianjian*; *CHSKH Yearbook*] (Shanghai, 1949), 23.

this meant understanding the tradition of ancestral veneration as regulating social relationships, rather than as mere heathenism. Moreover, Addison explained that, although the historical origins of ancestral veneration could be found in classical texts – namely, the *Shijing* 詩經 (*Classic of Poetry*) and the *Liji* 禮記 (*Book of Rites*) – practices had evolved over the centuries and, by the 1900s, there were countless regional variations. By the time Addison was writing in the early 1920s, sacrificial rites did not necessarily have a particular basis or rationale in the Chinese cultural context, but were implemented simply because the same rites had been performed 'as far back as memory and tradition could reach'. Addison also noted how churches had become increasingly accommodating towards Chinese ancestral veneration, from the Rites Controversy in the seventeenth century, to the national Protestant missionary conferences of 1877, 1890 and 1907. He concluded that after accommodating for culture and tradition in funerals, readers ought to focus on devising Christian substitutes for filial piety, such as having memorial services in churches, selecting different days to commemorate ancestors annually, and keeping family trees in Bibles instead of on inscription tablets.[70] In other words, it would be more helpful to suggest what to do, rather than merely instructing what not to do. The debate about accommodating funeral traditions was ongoing. There were no fixed guidelines, partly because ancestral veneration practices were not themselves fixed according to classical texts, but shifted in parallel with changing fashions, ruling authorities and social and cultural norms. Addison believed that the same shifting parameters applied to the relationship between ancestral veneration and Christianity.

Finally, marriage was the most complicated rite of passage for clergy and church members because it was deeply entangled with the widespread practice of concubinage. In late imperial Qing society, patriarchy and patrilineage were social norms. Taking a concubine was considered to be a display of wealth, prestige and sexual prowess. Men over the age of forty without a son were permitted, by law, to take a concubine in order to produce a male heir.[71] This caused

[70] James Thayer Addison, *Chinese Ancestor Worship: A Study of its Meaning and its Relations with Christianity* (Peking, 1925), 4–5, 20–2, 29–49, 61–8, 74–6, 82–4, online at: <http://anglicanhistory.org/asia/china/addison_ancestor1925/>, last accessed 19 February 2021.

[71] Lisa Tran, *Concubines in Court: Marriage and Monogamy in Twentieth-Century China* (Lanham, MD, 2015), 9.

problems among churches as early as 1862, when the Basel Mission in Guangdong found itself wrestling with the question of polygamy, which it understood to be contrary to biblical teaching. Their evangelist, Zhang Fuxing, was the lineage elder in the village of Wuhua. However, his only son had died and, due to a chronic illness, his wife could no longer bear children. To maintain his position as lineage elder, he was required to take a second wife in order to produce a male heir. One of the main reasons Zhang wished to retain this position was that it enabled him to protect the fledgling Christian community. To justify his action, he cited the example of Abraham producing a male heir through Hagar (Genesis 16). Moreover, his second wife said she would not have been accepted back into her family. After much deliberation, the Basel Home Committee recommended that Zhang be excommunicated. However, missionaries in the field had compassion on Zhang and decided not to implement the recommendation. As a compromise, they dismissed him from his role but allowed him to attend church services.[72] The Qing legal code remained in use for civil matters until 1929, even after the establishment of the republic in 1911, meaning that polygamy remained an issue for Chinese Christians well into the 1920s.[73]

Within the CHSKH, Bishop Frederick Graves of Shanghai noted that Chinese Christian marriage was treated 'very leniently' because clergy and missionaries alike understood the difficulties of handling the deeply entrenched practice of concubinage. In his diocese, a man would not be forced to put away either his wife or his concubine, lest he inflict hardship on a woman who was 'innocent of wrongdoing' without a say in her situation, and merely a victim of Chinese law and custom. Graves's solution for church members in Shanghai was for husbands to attend church services and be admitted as catechumens, provided they had a good reputation. However, baptism would not be administered until either their wife or concubine died, since it would otherwise suggest that polygamy was given official recognition in the Christian community.[74] Bishop William Banister of Kwangsi-Hunan (Guangxi-Hunan) observed that whenever other Nonconformist churches admitted men with concubines to baptism,

[72] Lutz, *Mission Dilemmas*, 5–7.
[73] Tran, *Concubines in Court*, 22.
[74] HKSKH, 2138/39, Graves to Duppuy, 17 October 1921.

this always had a 'bad effect' on the church.[75] Nevertheless, most Anglican bishops in China were supportive of allowing wives, concubines and children to be baptized, since there was no resolution from the Lambeth Conference explicitly advising against family members of 'polygamists' being baptized.[76] CHSKH leaders were especially keen to baptize children because this would ensure their upbringing in the faith by affiliating them with the church.[77] Bishop John Hind of Fukien (Fujian) summarized the situation, stating that, due to the complexity of the situation, there was simply no uniformity in the CHSKH, nor was there a canon on marriage and divorce. Instead, clergy were advised to assess how far individual family members in such situations were committed to the Christian faith on a case-by-case basis before taking corresponding action.[78] The worry was that creating a canon with strict limitations would lead to the false implication of innocent church members in exceptional cases.

Case-by-case discretion was exercised in other unusual marriage situations. In another instance in Hong Kong in 1928, a church member asked his vicar whether he was permitted to marry his deceased wife's sister.[79] The vicar wrote to Bishop Duppuy, who searched extensively for answers. Resolutions from the Lambeth Conference noted that, although such a union was prohibited by the canons of the Church of England, it was now permitted by civil law.[80] This implied that the marriage would be legal but 'ecclesiastically irregular' if performed in the Church of England. However, the marriage in question was under the CHSKH, not the Church of England. Duppuy then consulted other bishops. Bishop Mandell Creighton of London referred to his speech at the 1898 Convocation of Canterbury, which focused on whether the individuals themselves believed, in conscience, that they were permitted by the Bible to marry.[81] Bishop Handley Moule of

[75] HKSKH, 2138/41, Banister to Duppuy, 17 October 1921.
[76] See Resolutions 39–40 of the 1908 Lambeth Conference Resolutions, online at: <http://www.anglicancommunion.org/structures/instruments-of-communion/lambeth-conference.aspx>, last accessed 18 June 2021.
[77] HKSKH, 2138/42, Molony to Duppuy, 5 October 1921.
[78] HKSKH, 2138/43, Hind to Duppuy, 10 October 1921.
[79] HKSKH, 2138/46, Duppuy to Tsang, 8 May 1928.
[80] This had been permitted by civil law in England through the Deceased Wife's Sister's Marriage Act of 1907. Discussions about the more recent Deceased Brother's Widow's Marriage Act of 1921 demonstrated that the matter was still a live question amongst English bishops.
[81] HKSKH, 2138/47, Creighton to Duppuy, 23 November 1927.

Durham wrote an article in 1917 explaining that the Bible did not explicitly forbid such unions, nor did it commend them. Moule urged all parties to exercise careful consideration before entering into the covenant of marriage, and suggested that the parish priest commit the matter to their conscience and judgment.[82] Without a clear ruling or precedent, Duppuy informed the vicar that he should decide the matter since he knew the circumstances best.[83]

Chinese Anglican baptism, confirmation, marriage and funerals were entangled with confusing and ever-changing social and cultural norms, meaning that clearly articulated positions could not be made once and for all. Chinese Anglicans and foreign missionaries had carefully and continuously to navigate through issues of extraterritoriality, filial piety, illiteracy and concubinage in order to, as Bishop Frederick Graves put it, secure all that was essential in the Christian ceremony without condemning what was innocent in the Chinese rites.[84] With regard to Chinese theology, Chloë Starr argues that it is impossible to understand the Chinese church 'without first grasping something of China's complex relationship with itself as a nation and as a people', especially with respect to the historical, intellectual, social and cultural context.[85] The same must be said of understanding the shape of Chinese Christian rites of passage.

Over time, clergy and missionaries in the CHSKH learned to assess the sincerity and inner posture of individuals on a case-by-case basis, rather than making sweeping judgments based on the external qualities of the ceremonies themselves. Between 1877 and 1940, Chinese Anglicans and missionaries came to realize that rites of passage could not simply be prescribed at conferences, and through periodicals and publications, but had to accommodate the reality of life on the ground.[86] Fixing forms in writing would have been a near-impossible

[82] HKSKH, 2138/52, Extracts from Resolutions and Letters on Divorce, 1867–1928.
[83] HKSKH, 2138/46, Duppuy to Tsang, 8 May 1928.
[84] HKSKH, 2138/37, Morrison Society Papers 2, 'Marriage in the Chinese Church', December 1903, 10–11.
[85] Chloë Starr, 'Maintaining Faith in the Chinese World', in Joel Cabrita, David Maxwell and Emma Wild-Wood, eds, *Relocating World Christianity: Interdisciplinary Studies in Universal and Local Expressions of the Christian Faith*, Theology and Mission in World Christianity 7 (Leiden, 2017), 213–37, at 214.
[86] For a more general study of Christian living in non-Christian cultures, see K. K. Yeo, 'Biblical Interpretation in the Majority World', in Mark P. Hutchinson, ed., *The Oxford History of Protestant Dissenting Traditions*, 5: *The Twentieth Century: Themes and Variations in a Global Context* (Oxford, 2018), 131–69, at 140.

undertaking since there existed an infinite number of possible scenarios.[87] Among Chinese Protestants, rites of passage in the nineteenth and twentieth centuries varied immensely. Bishop Handley Moule of Durham rightly observed that even the Bible left certain questions open, but invited readers to examine their consciences.

The journey of reshaping Chinese Anglican rites of passage fits with W. M. Jacob's broader description of the Anglican Communion as a network of dioceses and provinces 'without fixed structures and systematic theologies', evolving from the Henrician Reformation to the North American Episcopal Church, and then to British – and American – imperial dioceses and independent provinces. The global expansion of Anglicanism led to increasingly complex interactions with other denominations and the non-Christian world.[88] The CHSKH and other non-Western churches had to negotiate the meaning and practice of rites of passage within their respective social and cultural contexts. They became 'self-theologizing' in addition to self-supporting, self-governing and self-propagating.[89] 'Self-theologizing' was not unique to Chinese Anglicans.[90] As for the CHSKH in the early twentieth century, their solution was to have resolutions from their General Synod and from the Lambeth Conference as reference points, but also flexibility and openness when confronted with social and cultural dilemmas. This constituted part of the broader quest for the convergence of faith and life, of Scripture and reason.

[87] For instance, the 1949 CHSKH yearbook makes no mention of rites of passage when summarizing the history of the CHSKH. Instead, it focuses on more defined aspects of Anglican identity, such as church polity, evangelism, finance, unity, women's work and religious education. See 中華聖公會年鑑 [*Zhonghua shenggonghui nianjian*; *CHSKH Yearbook*] (Shanghai, 1949).

[88] W. M. Jacob, *The Making of the Anglican Church Worldwide* (London, 1997), 299–300.

[89] This term is adopted from Justo L. González, *Mañana: Christian Theology from a Hispanic Perspective* (Nashville, TN, 1990), and mentioned in Yeo, 'Biblical Interpretation in the Majority World', 135–7.

[90] For instance, see Aminta Arrington, *Songs of the Lisu Hills: Practicing Christianity in Southwest China* (University Park, PA, 2020); Lian Xi, *Redeemed by Fire: The Rise of Popular Christianity in Modern China* (New Haven, CT, 2010); Xin Yalin, *Inside China's House Church Network: The Word of Life Movement and its Renewing Dynamic* (Lexington, KY, 2009).

'First' or 'Solemn' Communion Images in France, 1885–2021

Françoise Deconinck-Brossard*
Université Paris Nanterre, France

Arguably, the 'first' or 'solemn' communion, later also called 'profession of faith', was a rite of passage for generations of French eleven- or twelve-year-old children. It remained virtually unchanged, under these different names, until the early 1970s, when it gradually fell into decline. Friends, relatives, and even state school teachers, were customarily given small religious images with a commemorative inscription on the reverse, stating the communicant's name as well as the date and place of the ceremony. This article analyses a small private collection of such 'popular' objects and discusses the evolution in their representations of lived religion in a secular country where a strong Roman Catholic tradition has given way to a post-Christian society.

For generations of French children, 'making their communion' (*faire sa communion*) was arguably a rite of passage, combining religious ceremonies with profane feasting. Communicants and their parents customarily presented friends, relatives and even their state school teachers with small illustrated commemorative cards. That the gift was usually accompanied by small bags of sugared almonds (*dragées*) exemplifies the intertwining of the sacred and the secular in this event.[1] These religious images were meant to be used as bookmarks in the recipients' missals or Bibles, but people who did not own

* 22 Rue de Berri, Boîte 1407, 75008 Paris, France. E-mail: fadeco@parisnanterre.fr.

[1] This combination is confirmed by Yann Raison du Cleuziou, in 'Penser les images de dévotion à partir des hypothèses de Serge Bonnet sur le catholicisme populaire', in Dominique Lerch et al., eds, *Les Images de dévotion en Europe XVIe–XXIe siècle. Une Précieuse Histoire* (Paris, 2021), 87–111, at 94. The greater part of this article was written before the publication of Lerch's volume, which deals with many categories of devotional religious images and has no specific chapter about communion cards. Communion cards are only a subcategory of a much larger genre. Lerch discusses many possible approaches to the production, publication, dissemination, history, ideology, iconography and diversity of these small religious images, not only in France, but also in other continental countries.

Studies in Church History 59 (2023), 383–410
doi: 10.1017/stc.2023.17

a prayer book also treasured these 'precious souvenirs' (Figure 1), keeping them, for instance, in a cupboard with the family archives, in a wallet, or tucked into a poetry book.[2] The standard size of these holy cards, predominantly vertical in format, is roughly 60 x 110 mm. The recto typically includes a picture, often with a caption consisting of an aphorism, a short prayer or a quotation. In the nineteenth century, the image was sometimes surrounded by a border of delicate paper lace called *canivet* (Figure 1). A minority of religious cards imitate the layout of medieval illuminated manuscripts, with the illustration being placed in the margin, and the text given pride of place (Figure 2). An inscription on the verso usually includes at least the date and place of the ceremony, as well as the communicant's name. Depending on the family's wealth or religious commitment, these details could be printed, typewritten, calligraphed by an adult or handwritten by the child. Occasional traces of old adhesive tape suggest that some may have been displayed, perhaps on a wall or in a notebook. That some cards were intended for such display may be discerned in their layout, with a thin gold outline and a white space emulating the frame and mount traditionally used to enhance the visual appeal of a picture. Other signs of wear and tear, even fingerprints, are visible on some of these fragile objects (Figure 3).

This article will analyse a small private collection of such 'popular' items, which can be divided into two subsets. The original collection includes 240 holy cards, collected, used and treasured over the course of a century (1885–1991) by four generations of three related branches of my family, predominantly in the Paris area. The second group comprises 150 devotional pictures used more recently (1944–2009) by a single family of practising Roman Catholic friends, with a more provincial bias and a culture of education in private Roman Catholic schools, who kindly offered to lend me their personal collection.[3] With 390 images overall, this represents a very modest assortment compared to the hundreds of thousands of such items

[2] This last example, given to a young woman in the 1960s, was provided in an e-mail from Brigitte Friant-Kessler, dated 28 February 2021.

[3] The original owners of the cards, and the names of communicants, are anonymized throughout the article. Dates given are of when cards were used, rather than of publication.

Figure 1. 'A precious souvenir of first communion' (1885), image n° 2460, Bouasse-Lebel, Paris. Private collection. 78 x 121 mm. Photograph credit: Françoise Deconinck-Brossard. © The author.

Figure 2. 'Rejoice with me for I have received my God. Souvenir' (1888), image n° 859, Bouasse-Lebel, Paris. Private collection. 77 x 119 mm. Photograph credit: Françoise Deconinck-Brossard. © The author.

Figure 3. 'He took bread and broke it' (1937), image n° 2177, Morel, Paris. Private collection. 66 x 109 mm. Photograph credit: Françoise Deconinck-Brossard. © The author.

held by libraries such as the Bibliothèque du Saulchoir (Paris)[4] and the print room of the Bibliothèque nationale de France (Paris).[5]

[4] Michel Albaric estimates that the collection held by this Dominican library amounts to perhaps 200,000 or 250,000 items: 'La Collection d'images de piété de la Bibliothèque du Saulchoir', in Lerch et al., eds, *Les Images de dévotion,* 45–62, at 50. I am very grateful to the staff of the library for their assistance. At a crucial stage in the research for this article, Isabelle Séruzier provided extremely helpful information.

[5] The Bibliothèque nationale holds deposit copies of 'almost 20,000 small images' produced between 1830 and the Second World War: C[atherine]. R[osenbaum].-[Dondaine], 'L'Imagerie de piété du XIXe siècle au Département des Estampes de la Bibliothèque Nationale', in Michel Albaric, Catherine Rosenbaum-Dondaine and Jean-Pierre Seguin,

While commemorative cards were given to mark other religious events, the vast majority of images in this small private collection commemorate admission to communion. Indeed, of the other rites regarded as sacraments by Roman Catholics (and which could similarly be considered rites of passage), only ten baptisms, five confirmations[6] and one ordination are memorialized. Marriage is not represented, though the collection includes two jubilee cards, one of which is in thanksgiving for a golden wedding anniversary.[7] Penance and extreme unction do not appear at all,[8] perhaps unsurprisingly considering both the confidential nature of confession and the context of emergency in which extreme unction was sought and administered.

Such visual memorabilia deserve attention and study before they fall into oblivion or are discarded. Were it not for the relatively recent interest in popular art and traditions,[9] these humble objects might

eds, *L'Image de piété en France, 1814–1914. Musée-galerie de la SEITA* (Paris, 1984), 179–82, at 179. The chronological order in which they have been catalogued highlights production issues, and reveals how manufacturing processes, as well as religious and aesthetic taste, changed over time.

6 For many young Protestants, confirmation is the rite of passage that holds a significance comparable to the 'first communion' or 'solemn communion' in Roman Catholic families. For the history of confirmation, see Freddy Sarg, *La Confirmation en Alsace* (Strasbourg, 1981). The Musée de l'image populaire in Pfaffenhoffen (Alsace) holds an archive of commemorative confirmation images that could be paralleled with their Catholic equivalents: see online at <https://commune-valdemoder.fr/culture-loisirs/musee-de-l-image-populaire>, last accessed 22 September 2021. I owe this information to Brigitte Friant-Kessler. On small Protestant commemorative confirmation images, see also Gustave Koch, 'Y a-t-il une Image de dévotion protestante? Les Petites Images bibliques protestantes', in Lerch et al., eds, *Les Images de dévotion*, 317–26. The confirmation souvenirs analysed by Dominique Lerch are much larger documents (200 x 250 mm), similar to the certificates sometimes received by Roman Catholic youngsters after their first communion: 'Un Aspect de l'activité pastorale. Les Souvenirs de confirmation aux XIXe et XXe siècles', *Bulletin de la Société d'histoire du protestantisme français* (1978), 67–83.

7 Jean-Claude Schmitt comments that he has not come across any holy card for marriage: 'Conclusion', in Lerch et al., eds, *Les Images de dévotion*, 521–9, at 527.

8 At least one souvenir of first confession prior to private communion is known to have existed elsewhere: Michel Mallèvre, 'Trois Générations de missels et leurs images', in ibid. 113–29, at 126.

9 The *Religions et traditions populaires* exhibition by the Musée national des arts et traditions populaires (Paris) in 1979–80 was a pioneer in this respect: see the sections on 'Les Images de dévotion' and 'La Communion solennelle' in the eponymous exhibition catalogue: ed. Jean Cuisenier, Françoise Lautman and Josselyne Chamarrat (Paris, 1979), 181–6, 217–22 respectively.

easily have been overlooked. They are particularly interesting as a means to explore how the representation of lived religion in a secular country with a once strong Roman Catholic tradition has changed over time. As this article focuses on usage rather than production, the dates mentioned refer to the ceremonies, rather than to the years of publication. It will consider how changes in the representation of first and solemn communion, as exemplified in these popular objects from the 1880s to the early 2020s, reflect a broader evolution in French religious culture.

First communion has a long history.[10] The earliest descriptions of a particular celebration to mark first reception of holy communion in the Roman Catholic Church date back to the early seventeenth century, while its main features had been established by the mid-eighteenth century.[11] In the seventeenth and eighteenth centuries, first communion took place at Eastertide, but after the French Revolution it became customary in France to schedule the celebration in May or June, at the end of the school year and before the harvest season.[12]

The question of the age at which first communion was made emerged in the early twentieth century. In 1910, Pope Pius X allowed younger children to receive the sacrament once they had reached 'the age of discretion, … that is about the seventh year, more or less'.[13] Pointing to the gospel accounts of Jesus's willingness to welcome all children, Pius X sought, in *Quam singulari*, to combat what he viewed as 'abuses' in the French church, namely 'the growing custom … of postponing the First Communion of children until more mature years', that is, until they were older than twelve.[14] What was at stake was whether or not 'a full and perfect knowledge of Christian doctrine' was necessary for the child to be admitted to confession and communion. Pius X wanted the children to 'be obliged to learn gradually the entire Catechism' after their first communion.

[10] Jean Delumeau, ed., *La Première Communion. Quatre Siècles d'histoire* (Paris, 1987), 9–10.

[11] Louis Andrieux, *La Première Communion. Histoire et discipline. Textes et documents. Des Origines au XXe siècle* (Paris, 1911), 282.

[12] Andrieux, *La Première Communion,* 288.

[13] Pope Pius X, *Decree of the Sacred Congregation of the Discipline of the Sacraments on First Communion* (1910), online at: <https://www.papalencyclicals.net/pius10/p10quam.htm>, last accessed 18 July 2021.

[14] Ibid.

The French clergy, on the other hand, knew from experience that many would never attend religious instruction if it was not a compulsory requirement for admission to communion.[15] Although the rite is to be found elsewhere in the francophone world, for instance in Belgium, Québec or Switzerland,[16] and in other countries with large Roman Catholic communities, only France and Alsace (which at that time was annexed to the German Empire) were explicitly mentioned in the papal decree.

From then on, first communion received at an early age was deemed to be 'private' and could be an event focused on an individual child during a normal eucharistic service, whereas the collective rite for cohorts of twelve-year-olds was renamed 'solemn communion' (*communion solennelle*) or – especially after the Second World War – 'profession of faith' (*profession de foi*). However, the inscriptions in our collection of images show that it took a generation for the phrase 'solemn communion' to be regularly used to describe what remained the major rite of passage: the first such usage is dated 1937. Moreover, despite what the Church advocated, the term 'private communion' never caught on. It only appears thirteen times altogether in our collection, with all instances occurring after 1952. In post-Second World War circles of practising Roman Catholics, the distinction between 'private communion' and 'solemn communion' (or 'profession of faith') became very clearly marked, although the latter remained the significant rite of passage.[17] With its tripartite rhythm of mass, lunch and vespers, the special clothing, photography, the distribution of images and the reception of gifts, it was a popular, day-long feast, in contrast with the much more low-key 'private' communion that only involved attendance at mass. A quarter of the inscriptions do not name the occasion. The omission could perhaps be explained by a desire to save the expense and labour of writing an extra line. Before 1910, there

[15] In the early twentieth century, there was already a considerable drop-off in church attendance after the first communion. The trend continued throughout the period under review. A 1967 opinion poll, quoted in Serge Bonnet and Augustin Cottin, *La Communion solennelle. Folklore païen ou fête chrétienne* (Paris, 1969), 244, revealed that one third of the sample said that after their first or solemn communion they immediately stopped going to church; one third continued to attend mass for a few years; and only one third continued to practise their religion regularly and longer term.

[16] Bonnet and Cottin, *La Communion solennelle*, 247.

[17] Dominique Lerch, *Imagerie populaire en Alsace et dans l'Est de la France* (Nancy, 1992), 234.

would have been no ambiguity, but after that date the meaning was implicit.

The rites of both 'first communion' and 'solemn communion' remained virtually unchanged until the early 1970s. As late as 1967, the Institut français d'opinion publique (IFOP) found that 87% of a representative sample of French adults had formally made their communion.[18] The permanence of these rites may have derived from the fact that they both manifested the three phases – or rather, the three different categories of rites – initially identified by Arnold van Gennep in his tripartite scheme: preliminary separation, liminality, and incorporation or aggregation.[19] Neither van Gennep nor Victor and Edith Turner include 'first communion' or 'solemn communion' in their lists of religious ceremonies that might be identified as rites of transition.[20] However, we can confidently accept the Gennepian invitation to apply the tripartite scheme to our own subject matter, as will become apparent.[21]

After a religious retreat which included, among other activities, a question-and-answer examination designed to verify that the creed and main prayers had been learnt properly during the period of religious instruction,[22] and which ended with auricular confession, the youngsters publicly ('solemnly') partook of the eucharist.[23] The retreat temporarily separated the youngsters from their usual

[18] Sylvie de La Baumelle, '[L'Éducation religieuse des catholiques] Résultats d'ensemble', *Sondages. Revue française de l'opinion publique* 29/2 (1967), 19–40, at 19, 32.

[19] Arnold van Gennep, *Les Rites de passage. Étude systématique des rites de la porte et du seuil, de l'hospitalité[,] de l'adoption, de la grossesse et de l'accouchement[,] de la naissance, de l'enfance, de la puberté[,] de l'initiation, de l'ordination, du couronnement[,] des fiançailles et du mariage[,] des funérailles, des saisons, etc.* (Paris, 1909).

[20] Victor Turner and Edith Turner, *Image and Pilgrimage in Christian Culture: Anthropological Perspectives* (Oxford, 1978), 2–4.

[21] 'Je crois … ma démonstration suffisante, et prie le lecteur de s'en assurer en appliquant le Schéma des Rites de Passage aux faits de son domaine personnel d'étude' ('I believe that my demonstration is sufficient, and I invite the reader to check it by applying the Scheme of the Rites of Passage to data in his / her own field of study'): Van Gennep, *Rites de passage*, ii.

[22] In the seventeenth and eighteenth centuries, children were catechized several times a week during Lent: Andrieux, *La Première Communion*, 285. Since the nineteenth century, the 'first communion' or the 'solemn communion' (or 'profession of faith') has been the culmination of three years of weekly catechism classes.

[23] Sylviane Grésillon, 'De la Communion solennelle aux fêtes de la foi', in Delumeau, ed., *La Première Communion*, 217–53, at 234. There would be no auricular confession among Protestants, but Sarg identifies similar stages in the preparation for Protestant confirmation (catechism classes, examination, retreat and the ceremony itself), to which he explicitly applies

environment, their schoolfellows of other faiths and none, and their families.[24] It may therefore be regarded as the preliminary stage in the rite of passage, or even as the first rite of separation. The retreat usually lasted for three days, although some were up to a week in length.[25] A small leaflet with the programme of 'hymns and prayers' for a five-day retreat, followed by two days of 'first communion', confirmation and a thanksgiving mass in an unspecified parish in May 1914, shows a combination of 'instruction', attendance at religious services and a rehearsal including prayers, hymns, a procession and baptismal vows.[26] In 1937, Jean B.'s small retreat notebook (80 x 110 mm), handwritten in pencil, began with the statement that the purpose of the retreat was 'communion and the Christian life that begins more personally'.[27] Paradoxically, in the French context of *laïcité*[28] – the result of the 1905 French law on the separation of the churches and the state – the children's absence from secularized state schools whilst they were on retreat was de facto tolerated.[29] In his memoirs, the country vicar Bernard Alexandre (1918–90) explained how, in his Normandy parish, the children thoroughly enjoyed the extra-ordinary experience of spending three 'full' days 'together', 'differently', away from school.[30] When the school-leaving age was raised – initially to fourteen in 1936, and more significantly

the Gennepian scheme: *La Confirmation en Alsace*, 9. However, he also underlines the fact that there have been many variations within this broad outline: ibid. 17.

[24] Jean Mellot, 'Rite de passage et fête familiale. Rapprochements', in Delumeau, ed., *La Première Communion*, 171–96, at 174.

[25] The practice and custom of three days of 'pious exercises', far from being specific to France, was encouraged in Italy, the USA and South America from 1855, 1866 and 1899 respectively: Jean Pirotte, *Images des vivants et des morts. La Vision du monde propagée par l'imagerie de dévotion dans le Namurois 1840–1965* (Bruxelles, 1987), 149 n. 2; Andrieux, *La Première Communion*, 283–4. On longer retreats, see Mellot, 'Rite de passage et fête familiale', 174.

[26] Paris, Bibliothèque du Saulchoir, box VI 2–8, 'Communion des enfants', n° 5, 'Communion (Documents Paroisses)'.

[27] 'Le but de la retraite e[s]t la communion ou la vie chrétienne qui commence plus personnellement': Private collection.

[28] I have never found an adequate English translation for this word, but 'secularism' is one possibility.

[29] Bonnet and Cottin, *La Communion solennelle*, 197.

[30] 'La retraite va durer trois jours pleins. Trois jours sans école: les enfants sont radieux, ils ont l'impression d'être en vacances et surtout de vivre ensemble …"autrement", ce qui n'arrive quasiment jamais' ('The retreat will last for three full days. Three days without school: the children are beaming with joy, they have a feeling that they are on holiday

to sixteen in 1959 – high school chaplaincies, rather than parishes, took over the ceremonies, even in state-run institutions, such as the Lycée Pasteur in Neuilly-sur-Seine on the outskirts of Paris. Indeed, an inscription on the verso of one communion card reads: 'Bernard L. … 27 mai 1955 Lycée Pasteur – St Pierre de Neuilly', demonstrating how some ceremonies were taking place in the church to which the chaplaincy was attached, rather than the parish where the family worshipped.

As co-education was only gradually introduced after 1959, and more generally in 1975–6, this meant that the ceremony could end up being a single-sex experience, unlike in the parishes, where all the boys and girls in a particular age group would have taken their first communion together, albeit in segregated areas of the church or at separate altar rails. This probably explains why gendered representations of communicants are to be found on commemorative images until the mid-1960s. The most extreme example is a pair of sepia monochrome images used in 1949 and 1951, in which a boy and a girl kneel on the same altar step and receive communion from the same angel, with the same landscape in the background (Figures 4 and 5). In producing both these images, the publishers were targeting two separate markets, depending on the gender of the individual communicants, whether or not they had actually taken part in single-sex celebrations.

Between mass and vespers, the communicants were treated to a festive family meal, often with Pantagruelian menus.[31] Alexandre recalled that the timing of the two religious services had to allow at least four hours for the lunch: this could be considered the second, liminal, Gennepian stage of the rite.[32] The youngsters received

and especially that they are living together … "differently", which hardly ever happens'): Bernard Alexandre, *Le Horsain. Vivre et survivre en Pays de Caux* (Paris, 1988), 358.

31 For instance, the menu for Jacques F.'s communion in 1934, headed with a picture similar to many a first communion card, included seven or eight courses. Three years later, the menu for Jean B.'s communion ended with the traditional pyramid of choux pastry at the top of which stood the small figure of a male communicant that has been kept to this day. Cf. Cuisenier, Lautman and Chamarrat, eds, 'La Communion solennelle', in *Religions et traditions populaires*, 217–22, at 221, according to whom neither the lavishness of the meal, nor the care with which the menu was kept, were exceptional.

32 '[M]esse à 10 heures, vêpres à 16 heures (il faut bien compter quatre heures pour le repas)' ('mass at 10 a.m., vespers at 4 p.m. [you must allow a good four hours for the meal]'): Alexandre, *Le Horsain*, 358.

Figure 4. 1949. Private collection. 55 x 98 mm. Photograph credit: Françoise Deconinck-Brossard. © The author.

presents to mark their coming of age and their entry into the adult world. From that day onwards, they would be regarded as grown-ups, which often meant that their first communion would also be their last communion, or one of very few.[33] In the nineteenth-century working class environment described in Émile Zola's most famous

[33] Not only was there a significant fall in religious practice after first or solemn communion, as mentioned above – hence the clergy's recurrent emphasis on the need to 'persevere' – but even regular churchgoers rarely partook of the eucharist; frequent communion was only encouraged from the 1960s: see Delumeau, ed., *La Première Communion*, 240.

Figure 5. 1951. Private collection. 55 x 98 mm. Photograph credit: Françoise Deconinck-Brossard. © The author.

naturalistic novel, *L'Assommoir* (1877), the French author explicitly connected the young Nana's entry into adulthood with her having made her first communion. He described how Nana and her friend Pauline 'by now … ought to know how to cook, to darn socks, and to run a house'.[34] During the first communion meal, the diners arranged

[34] Émile Zola, *L'Assommoir*, transl. Atwood H. Townsend (New York, 1962), 359. This is given in the original as 'elles devaient désormais savoir faire la cuisine, raccommoder des chaussettes, conduire une maison' (Émile Zola, *L'Assommoir* [Paris, 1964; first publ.

for Nana to start work 'the next morning' (*dès le lendemain*).[35] In the following century, Bernard Alexandre's catechumens looked forward to being allowed to help themselves to food at the family table once they had made their communion. In Gennepian terms, they had reached the stage of 'incorporation' into the adult word. The retired vicar cogently commented that 'here the religious act still ha[d] a social impact.[36]

In exchange for the profane and religious gifts that they received, the youngsters distributed commemorative cards to guests. They also presented images to their teachers the following week and exchanged them with their schoolfriends, which explains the great variety in styles that can be found among cards from a single child. For instance, eight different images, with a wide range of aesthetic and religious styles, commemorating Jean B.'s communion in Paris on 23 May 1937 are extant. They include not only monochrome rectangular pictures with simple frames (Figure 3), but also more sophisticated cards with deckle or feathered edges, and a composition showing a frame within a frame, a technique traditionally used in the visual arts to draw the spectator's attention to the subject. Three of these items represent Jesus Christ, and the Virgin Mary appears in five images, although not always as the central character. The captions are as varied as the pictures. Contrary to the common belief that Roman Catholic laypeople were long kept ignorant of the Bible, a gospel quotation (Matthew 19: 14) is illustrated by a black-and-white picture with a classical three-distance composition showing Christ surrounded by several children.[37] Even though the chapter and verse

1877], 369). A few lines earlier, the English translation for 'Nana et Pauline étaient des femmes, maintenant qu'elles avaient communié' (369) reads 'Nana and Pauline were women now that they had been confirmed' (transl. Townsend, 359), implicitly comparing the significance of the Roman Catholic rite with that of confirmation in Protestant communities, and acknowledging the difficulty of finding an equivalent for 'first communion' or 'solemn communion' in the British context.

[35] Zola, *L'Assommoir*, 368 (transl. Townsend, 359).

[36] 'L'acte religieux garde encore ici un impact social. Après sa communion, Jean pourra se servir à table, comme les grands' ('The religious rite still has a social impact here. After making his communion, Jean will be allowed to serve himself at table, like the grown-ups'): Alexandre, *Le Horsain*, 143 Mellot and Delumeau mention many other activities that would become accessible to the youngsters after their 'first communion' or 'solemn communion'.

[37] Dominique Lerch's claim that from the 1960s biblical quotations appeared and replaced mawkish prayers needs qualification: *Imagerie populaire en Alsace*, 234.

are not explicitly identified, there would have been no doubt about the source of the text. This is not at all an isolated case in the collection. Two other quotations are attributed to Ignatius of Loyola (1491–1556) and the prelate and apologist Louis-Gaston de Ségur (1820–81), son of the famous children's author, the Comtesse de Ségur. Some of the other captions include prayers and maxims.

A generation later, communion cards continued to be varied in style. François P. had at least three images, again in completely different styles, for his 'solemn communion' in Rouen on 6 May 1964. They range from a sepia monochrome portrait of the Madonna by the Italian Renaissance painter Bastiano Mainardi (1466–1513) to contemporary religious art with simplified outlines. Here, a young Jesus is depicted, with a limited palette, as he blesses the bread and wine, with his right hand raised in a benediction gesture reminiscent of Byzantine art, icons or medieval statues. Étienne P. had no fewer than eleven cards for his profession of faith in a private school in Rouen on 14 May 1966, the majority comprising black-and-white photography, with two very simplified imitations of a manuscript. Even though it would be far beyond the scope of this article to address the complex issues of marketing and supply,[38] the variety suggests that communicants' parents were able to select a range of images that appealed to them (or to their children), and which characterized their religious and artistic tastes. There must have been plenty of choice, as the collections under discussion contain very few instances of duplication. One exception is the reproduction of Leonardo da Vinci's *Last Supper* (*c.*1495–8) with its horizontal format, unusual for these commemoration cards (Figure 6). This image was used by two different families thirty years apart (1907 and 1937), which suggests that it had lasting appeal.[39] As well as reproductions of popular artworks, a number of motifs recur, such as a candle, a reminder of the communicants' renewal of their baptismal vows (with the lighting of a candle) at vespers, which took place after the celebratory meal. Vespers

[38] The market was huge. Lerch reckons that in Alsace alone, in the year 1962, with a population of approximately one million Roman Catholics, there would have been about fifty thousand communicants at 'first communion' and 'solemn communion' in total; at the rate of a dozen or more commemorative images per child, the figure could well have been near the one million mark for that year alone: ibid. 236.

[39] Lerch has found that, through both Roman Catholic and Protestant imagery, Leonardo's painting has become the standard reference for the Last Supper: 'Un Aspect de l'activité pastorale', 77.

Figure 6. 'The Last Supper' (1907, 1937), image n° 2.500, Morel, Paris. Private collection. 111 x 67 mm. Photograph credit: Françoise Deconinck-Brossard. © The author.

often ended with a prayer known as an 'act of consecration to the holy Virgin' in which the communicants 'offered their hearts' to Mary and asked for her guidance and 'motherly protection' in order to remain faithful to their commitment to follow Jesus and 'persevere in their love of God'.[40] This may partly explain the large number of representations of the Virgin in the collection under discussion.

Confirmation sometimes took place the following day, or even on the same day. To some extent, the summary of the religious experience of Jean-Marie D. (born in November 1946), printed on the reverse of his holy card, exemplifies the post-1910 distinction between private

[40] 'PRENDRE MARIE POUR GUIDE et pour protectrice. ACTE DE CONSÉCRATION A LA SAINTE VIERGE: Très Sainte Vierge ..., les enfants que vous voyez ici ... viennent réclamer votre maternelle protection. Nous vous offrons notre cœur; ... avec votre protection nous persévérerons dans l'amour de Dieu' ('TAKE MARY AS YOUR GUIDE and protector. ACT OF CONSECRATION TO THE HOLY VIRGIN: Most Holy Virgin ..., the children you see here ... come to claim your motherly protection. We offer you our hearts ... with your protection we will persevere in the love of God'): Église catholique, *Missel pour les jeunes et pour tous ceux qui veulent prier ensemble* (Sèvres, 1953; first publ. 1946), 237 Andrieux (born in 1877) seemed to consider that this prayer had become standard, but noted that in the mid-eighteenth century it had not yet been included in the celebration: *La Première Communion,* 302.

and solemn communion: 'The great days of my life: BAPTISM 6 May 1947 — PRIVATE COMMUNION 13 April 1952 — Profession of Christian faith and Confirmation 1 May 1958.'[41] Holy cards usually only included the date of a single ceremony on their verso. This particular card is unusual in including several. The wording of the inscription, with its use of the first-person singular pronoun, shows that devotional pictures were meant to be kept as souvenirs, not only by friends and family, but also by the communicants themselves. The use of capital letters suggests that, in this devout family, the first private communion (at the very early age of five and a half in this particular case) was regarded as more momentous, from a religious point of view, than the later profession of faith, even though it was the latter which remained the major rite of passage, as has been seen above.

Over time, the only major change in the rite was in the communicants' traditional clothes, which are repeatedly depicted on these holy cards. Before the Second World War, girls' communion outfits resembled an elaborate wedding dress, albeit slightly shorter, with a long veil held in place by a tulle cap and / or a flower crown, together with a small white purse, an adult's missal, rosary beads and a candle (Figure 7). The garments would sometimes be hired, and professional photography arranged to commemorate the event. At other times, however, these items would be part of the gifts for the occasion, as portrayed by Zola:

> The thought of the white communion dress made Nana dance with joy. The Lorilleuxs as godparents had promised to provide the dress, a gift which they advertised throughout the building. Mme Lerat was to give the veil and cap, Virginie the purse, Lantier the prayer book, with the result that the Coupeaus could look forward to the ceremony without much to worry about.[42]

Boys' clothes represented a smaller outlay. Male communicants wore trousers (rather than shorts) for the first time in their lives, a symbol

[41] 'Les grands jours de ma vie: BAPTÊME le 6 mai 1947 — COMMUNION PRIVÉE le 13 avril 1952 — Profession de foi Chrétienne et Confirmation le 1er mai 1958.'

[42] 'Nana dansait de joie en pensant à la robe blanche. Les Lorilleux, comme parrain et marraine, avaient promis la robe, un cadeau dont ils parlaient dans toute la maison; Mme Lerat devait donner le voile et le bonnet, Virginie la bourse, Lantier le paroissien; de façon que les Coupeau attendaient la cérémonie sans trop s'inquiéter': Zola, *L'Assommoir*, 364 (transl. Townsend, 354).

Figure 7. 'Souvenir of first communion' (1904). Private collection. 67 x 123 mm. Photograph credit: Françoise Deconinck-Brossard. © The author.

of their entry into the world of adulthood. On the left sleeve of the jacket, an armband knotted with a long white ribbon symbolized the purity of the communicant's soul as he approached the sacrament.

Along with the candle, the armband and knotted ribbon became visual shorthand for male communion in pre-Second World War devotional pictures.

However, after the Second World War, these quasi-wedding garments were gradually replaced by unisex albs that were supposed to mask social inequality, since all the communicants now wore the same clothes, which the parish or chaplaincy church often arranged to hire at a reasonable price. At first, girls still had to cover their heads, usually with short veils or small caps, even though they now wore the same robes as the bare-headed boys. The new fashion soon found its way onto holy cards,[43] where the alb now represented the 'solemn communion' or 'profession of faith'. As white prevailed in the depiction of the central subject, whether male or female, the traditional pictorial order of colours continued to be reversed, with a dark background remaining a widespread feature (Figure 8).

In some places, the images themselves were blessed by the priest at the end of the mass, ahead of their distribution to friends and family.[44] Although the rite was the communal experience of a specific age group, until the 1950s these devotional images portrayed the act of communion as a highly individual religious experience. Only a handful show several communicants or groups of children. In some of these rare instances, the youngsters are not even wearing the traditional communicants' clothes. However, even if depicted alone, the child was understood to be part of a community: the text printed on the recto often emphasizes the child's intercession for family and friends, for whom the communicant acts as a mediator (Figure 9). Moreover, the fact that the images were circulated as gifts highlights their significance as signs of identity and of belonging to a community of Roman Catholic believers, however intermittently the members of that community may have practised their religion. Beyond the earthly community, the communicants were also assisted, in turn, by the mediation of the communion of saints. Many images used until the early 1950s show the youngsters being either led to the altar for communion, or brought in front of the tabernacle for adoration, by one or several angels (Figure 7), the Virgin Mary or, more

[43] Grésillon draws an interesting parallel between the widespread adoption of affordable solemn communion albs from the 1950s and the development of ready-to-wear fashion: 'De la Communion solennelle aux fêtes de la foi', 240.

[44] Rosenbaum-Dondaine and Seguin, eds, *L'Image de piété en France,* 166.

Figure 8. 'To unite myself with Jesus Christ and walk in his light' (1966), image n° 73, © Carmel de Montélimar, Montélimar, now at Develier, Switzerland. Private collection. 70 x 112 mm. Photograph credit: Françoise Deconinck-Brossard.

rarely, a saint such as St Joseph or St Bernadette, often accompanied by other angels or cherubim. The communicant was not alone in his or her approach to the sacrament. The sense of awe generated by Christ's real presence was emphasized visually. Drawing on a variety of pictorial techniques borrowed from classical painting, artists designed devotional pictures that focused on Christ, or the host

EJP
T.C.
Seigneur, en ce beau jour,
Bénissez ceux que j'aime,

Figure 9. 'Lord, on this beautiful day, bless those whom I love' (1959), É[tablissement] J[acques] P[etit], [Angers]. Private collection. 60 x 104 mm. Photograph credit: Françoise Deconinck-Brossard. © The author.

and chalice.[45] In some of these images, a leading line in the foreground diagonally guided the communicants' eye to the hand from

[45] I am greatly indebted to Marie-Madeleine Martinet for all her technical explanations in this respect.

which they were receiving communion, or to the host in a monstrance or tabernacle, while accompanying angels and saints modestly remained in the background or in the second part of the foreground (Figures 7 and 9). Moreover, the classical rules of perspective were applied in such a way as to direct the viewer's eye to the central figure. For instance, the step on which the communicant knelt out of reverence towards the sacrament, together with any floor tiles, provided convenient vanishing lines (Figures 4, 5 and 7).

Paradoxically, the emphasis on transubstantiation often led artists to replace the celebrant with Christ himself, with many pre-1960s pictures showing boys and girls receiving communion directly from him. In one instance, Christ is even wearing clerical vestments (Figure 10).[46] Such an identification visually represents the doctrine defined in the Decree for the Armenians (1439) at the Council of Florence (1438–45), which stated that the priest makes this sacrament *in persona Christi*.[47] Arguably, such a representation of two simultaneous modes of Christ's presence, one physical and one sacramental, may be interpreted as 'a negation' of the Roman Catholic belief that the real presence of Jesus Christ in the eucharist differs from the mode of his presence during his life on earth.[48] Similarly, the representation on some of the cards of the infant Jesus distributing communion to young children, or having his Last Supper with them, was perhaps intended to appeal to youngsters, but seems to

[46] In a smaller collection of 65 twentieth-century images used in Alsace (1914–54), more than half represent Jesus wearing clerical vestments when distributing communion to youngsters: Lerch, *Imagerie populaire en Alsace*, 234.

[47] Henri Denzinger and Adolf Schönmetzer, eds, *Enchiridion symbolorum definitionum et declarationum de rebus fidei et morum*, 32nd edn (Freiburg im Breisgau, 1963; first publ. 1854), 335, §698: 'sacerdos ... in persona Christi loquens hoc conficit sacramentum' (translated as 'The priest speaking in the person of Christ effects this sacrament', in Norman P. Tanner, ed., *Decrees of the Ecumenical Councils*, 2 vols [Washington DC, 1990], 1: 546). In contrast, Gervais Dumeige translates the term *in persona Christi* as 'au nom du Christ' ('in the name of Christ'): *La Foi catholique. Textes doctrinaux du magistère de l'Église* (Paris, 1961), 407, §732. Thanks are due to Laurent Chauvin for drawing my attention to this doctrine.

[48] Elisabeth Oberson, 'La Grâce d'être humain: un savoir du cœur. Essai de dialogue avec le corpus d'images de piété Saint-sulpiciennes de la maison Desgodets-Lorthioir', 3 vols (PhD thesis, Institut catholique de Paris, 2001), 1: 231. I am grateful to Isabelle Séruzier for drawing my attention to this work. Compare also Les évêques de France, *Catéchisme pour adultes. L'Alliance de Dieu avec les hommes* (Paris, 1991), 253: 'La présence de Jésus ainsi réalisée n'est pas celle des jours de sa vie sur la terre.' ('The presence of Jesus thus effected is not that of the days of his life on earth.')

Figure 10. 'Souvenir of first communion' (1912), A. & M. B. [unidentified], n.pl. Private collection. 47 x 102 mm. Photograph credit: Françoise Deconinck-Brossard. © The author.

deny the eucharistic memorial of the life and resurrection of Jesus Christ. One rare instance, used in 1963, shows a communicant wearing an old-fashioned armband; a window in the background refers to the transfiguration or the resurrection, a combined reference to the depiction of an elevated Christ with both arms raised in Raphael's famous painting of *The Transfiguration of Christ* (1516–20) and to the panel of the Resurrection on the Isenheim altarpiece (1512–16) by Matthias Grünewald, as if the transfigured Christ had borrowed the red cloak of the risen one (Figure 11).

The reception of communion from the hands of angels (Figures 4 and 5) might appear even more unorthodox, were it not for the traditional description, until at least 1960, of the eucharistic host as 'the bread of angels'.[49] The phrase dates back to Thomas a Kempis's *Imitation of Christ*, with a reference to Psalm 78: 25 and John 6: 33–51: 'Thou givest unto me the meat of heaven and the bread of angels which is the bread of life.'[50] Likewise, one would search Scripture in vain for a reference to the recurrent theme of the holy Virgin receiving communion from the hands of St John, presented as a model of sanctity. This popular scene is inspired by the revelations of seventeenth-century mystic Mary of Jesus of Ágreda regarding the life of the Virgin Mary.[51]

From the early 1960s,[52] that is to say before, during and immediately after the Second Vatican Council (1962–5), and before the events of May 1968, the landscape changed radically, both from an aesthetic and spiritual point of view. Gone were the three-dimensional representations based on Renaissance practice, which gave depth to the scenes and borrowed artistic techniques from classical art. These gave way to simplified images without backgrounds, silhouette-style drawing and flat, two-dimensional colour poster style. The act of communion lost all its mediators: angels and saints disappeared from religious cards. However, images relating to Marian devotion remained widespread. Mary was sometimes represented as the central figure, particularly with several different representations of 'Our Lady of all Joy' (*Notre-Dame de toute joie*). However, she was more often invoked as a mediator and intercessor. For instance, the caption of an image used in 1986, showing male and female communicants gathered around a large thick candle near a statue of the

[49] This is the central theme of a rather spectacular image on a communion card used in 1960.

[50] Thomas a Kempis, *The Imitation of Christ* (London and Toronto, 1916), 236; *De Imitatione Christi*, ed. Friedrich Eichler (Munich, 1966), 4.3.16: 'Tu mihi dare vis caelestem cibum; et panem angelorum ad manducandum'.

[51] I am indebted to Thomas O'Loughlin for this reference.

[52] Hugh McLeod suggests that the period 'between about 1958 and 1962' might be termed 'the early 1960s': *The Religious Crisis of the 1960s* (Oxford, 2009), 60.

Figure 11. 1963. Private collection. 56 x 96 mm. Photograph credit: Françoise Deconinck-Brossard. © The author.

Virgin, reads 'O Mother of LIGHT, hear our prayer' (*Ô mère de LUMIÈRE entends notre prière*). On another image, used in 1960, a female communicant addressed the Virgin in words attributed to St

Bernadette: 'Virgin Mary, keep my heart for Jesus and Jesus in my heart' (*Vierge Marie gardez mon cœur à Jesus et Jésus dans mon cœur*). References to the eucharist became more allusive or symbolic, although quotations on the recto of images included excerpts from the liturgy, especially the rite of peace or the invitation to behold 'the Lamb of God'. Both colour and black-and-white photography were introduced and widely used. Images sometimes showed the portrait of a boy or girl wearing an alb, whether the actual communicant or a posing model. Other photographs showed religious statues, church buildings, beautiful landscapes, liturgical moments, or a close-up shot of the act of communion itself against an unidentified, neutral background. In the increasingly secularized world of the late twentieth and early twenty-first century, communion and 'profession of faith' images have often become general statements of faith, rather than specific references to the eucharist.

In the 1960s and 1970s, the rite of 'first communion' was much criticized for being 'pagan folklore', rather than a Christian feast.[53] In response to such objections, and in the quest of spiritual authenticity, it was abolished in many parishes. Even where it survives, some of its traditional features have been altered. The profession of faith and solemn communion now take place during mass, and the communicants are not expected to attend vespers. The retreat will often be organized out of school hours, shortly but not immediately before the event. In addition, the social context has changed radically. Practising Roman Catholics now represent less than 5% of the French population,[54] to the extent that they may be said to belong to a minority church. With the post-Vatican II liturgical reforms, especially the widespread use of vernacular language, most laypersons now consider it unnecessary to own a proper missal, with some subscribing to ephemeral monthly or yearly missals. As a result, sales of pious bookmarks (including holy cards) have plummeted.[55] The number of young communicants has dwindled, and the tradition of solemn communion and profession of faith has lost much of its impact on the local economy. The 2020

[53] Cf. the title of a book by Serge Bonnet and Augustin Cottin: *La Communion solennelle. Folklore païen ou fête chrétienne* (quoted above).

[54] Guillaume Cuchet, *Comment Notre Monde a cessé d'être chrétien. Anatomie d'un effondrement* (Paris, 2018), 16. 'Practising Catholics' is to be understood in the strict sociological definition of believers attending Sunday mass every week, so the figure may be slightly exaggerated.

[55] Lerch, *Imagerie populaire en Alsace*, 10.

Figure 12. 'Go and tell all your brethren, that God exists and that he loves us' (2021), image n° 427, 70 x 120 mm. © Ateliers de l'Abbaye de Jouarre, Jouarre, reproduction interdite.

lockdown cancelled or delayed most ceremonies. In 2021, with restrictions aiming at reducing the spread of COVID-19, cohorts of communicants had to be split into smaller groups in order to abide by government regulations regarding the number of people allowed to be seated indoors at any one time. In at least one semi-rural parish in the Paris area, a series of pious images designed and produced by the Benedictine monastery of Jouarre (Île-de-France) found a new use. These were glued onto large decorative boards prepared by the youngsters during their retreat in order to decorate the church on the day of their 'profession of faith'. None of these images focuses on the act of communion, but they include short prayers as well as excerpts from the liturgy, especially the Lord's Prayer, including the petition to 'give us this day our daily bread', illustrated with two green fishes and three loaves of bread,[56] as well as a confession that 'he is risen CHRIST our Hope'.[57] The final image shows a group of communicants holding their candles, with the text 'Go and tell all your brethren that God exists and that he loves us'.[58] The words 'God exists' and 'loves' are highlighted through the use of different colours, and a cross in the background specifies the Christian context (Figure 12).

One may conclude that, over the course of the past century and a half, French commemorative communion images have evolved to mirror the changes within French society. Earlier images focussed on a personal and intimate communion with God in the eucharist, represented by an emphasis on transubstantiation, along with Marian devotion. Later images, more allusive and symbolic in nature, capture the move away from a clearly defined Roman Catholic religious culture towards the more diffuse apologetics of a post-Christian world.

[56] Jouarre, Ateliers de l'Abbaye de Jouarre, image n° 454.

[57] '[I]l est r[e]ssuscité le CHRIST notre Espérance': ibid., image n° 398.

[58] '[A]llez dire à tous vos frères, que Dieu existe et qu'il nous aime': ibid., image n° 427.

The Sick Call and the Drama of Extreme Unction in Irish Folklore

Salvador Ryan*

Saint Patrick's Pontifical University, Maynooth

This article examines the priest's sick call in Irish folklore. The sick call normally involved the hearing of the dying person's confession; the administration of extreme unction, the last sacrament that a Roman Catholic was expected to receive; and (if possible) the reception of holy communion, viaticum, *food for the journey. Drawing from the large body of stories in the Schools' Collection (gathered in 1937–8), the article shows how the greatest concern in the popular mindset was ensuring that the priest arrived in time to perform his duties. However, all manner of difficulties awaited him in the exercise of this ministry, from diabolical apparitions to the wiles of other humans, including other priests, who purposefully attempted to thwart his path. In this sense, Irish folk tales dramatize the administration of this sacrament into a rite of passage.*

> It is 'a very grievous sin', says the Catechism of the Council of Trent, 'to defer the holy unction until, all hope of recovery now lost, life begins to ebb, and the sick person is sinking into insensibility'. It is obvious that if administered whilst the mental faculties are yet unimpaired and the sick man 'can bring to its reception sentiments of faith and devotion, this circumstance must contribute very much to enable him to partake more abundantly of the graces of the sacrament'.[1]

This salutary observation appears in the section on extreme unction in *Notes on the Rubrics of the Roman Ritual*, by the Rev. James O'Kane (1825–74), senior dean, St Patrick's College, Maynooth, which was first published in 1867. The work would go on to be highly influential, being revised and updated, and appearing on seminary

* Faculty of Theology, St Patrick's Pontifical University, Maynooth, County Kildare, Ireland. E-mail: salvador.ryan@spcm.ie.

[1] James O'Kane, *Notes on the Rubrics of the Roman Ritual: Regarding the Sacraments in General, Baptism, the Eucharist, and Extreme Unction, with an Appendix on Penance and Matrimony* (New York, 1883), 533.

Studies in Church History 59 (2023), 411–432
doi: 10.1017/stc.2023.18

curricula up to the 1950s. Despite its title, O'Kane's 'Notes' are, in fact, quite comprehensive, and seek to address all aspects of the administration of the last rites, including even the most unexpected of cases. While speaking of the anointing of the hands of the dying person, for instance, it presents the following scenario: 'Should the person have redundant members, e.g. a third hand, then those are to be anointed that have been most in use, or that are nearest to the natural position'.[2] However, as important as being prepared for such unlikely occurrences might be, the most crucial element in attending to the dying was surely the matter of timing. The excerpt from O'Kane's work with which this article opens clearly underlines this. Extreme unction should not be delayed until the person's mental faculties have begun to slip away; it is always best that the recipient can welcome the last sacrament with full knowledge of its import, and with an appropriately faith-filled response. That said, the element of timing, however crucial it might be, was not the only consideration for the priest administering the sacrament.

Works such as O'Kane's were necessarily detailed in their discussion of what needed to be done once the priest arrived in the room of the dying person. What was paramount for the majority of Roman Catholic men and women in O'Kane's Ireland, and indeed in the decades immediately following his death, was that a priest be present and that the sacrament be administered. In this case, timing was, literally, everything. It is of little surprise, then, that the curse '*Bás gan sagart ort!*' ('May you die without a priest!') was reserved for one's most detested enemies, as the consequences of such a wish might well be eternal punishment, should the individual die in his or her sin. This article examines popular concerns regarding the timely administration of the last rites in late nineteenth- and early twentieth-century Ireland. It does so by exploring stories of the priest's sick call to the dying as recounted in Irish folklore, most specifically in a body of folklore known as the 'Schools' Collection', which was collected in 1937–8. Although these stories were gathered and written down in the 1930s, many of them reflect an earlier period when the priest travelled on horseback to the dying, hastening to their side before death could snatch them away from the grace of the sacrament. Some tales name specific individuals who had only recently died, or whose dates can otherwise be established. What is noteworthy is that,

[2] Ibid. 408.

contrary to the preoccupations of O'Kane in his *Notes on the Rubrics of the Roman Ritual*, most of the stories are concerned with the drama of the priest's journey to the dying person, rather than what happens once he gets there. Indeed, many accounts simply end once the priest has safely arrived at his destination, the relief in the narrative being almost palpable. By discussing some examples of these tales, this article offers a window, albeit an imperfect one, onto how the importance of this rite of passage *in extremis* was conveyed in the Irish folk tradition, and why the timing of the priest's arrival remained the predominant concern for those who told them. First, however, some words of introduction to the Schools' Collection itself, and its genesis, are warranted.

The Schools' Collection, 1937–8

The schools' scheme of 1937–8 was a project spearheaded by the newly-founded Irish Folklore Commission under the direction of Séamus Ó Duilearga, a native of Antrim and lecturer in Irish at University College Dublin, and Seán Ó Súilleabháin, a national school teacher from County Kerry. It enlisted the assistance of Irish schoolchildren to record local folklore from their parents, grandparents, older relatives and neighbours. School time usually devoted to composition was now reassigned to recording in their copybooks the material that the children had collected. To avoid repetition, some children, or teachers, would then transcribe a selection of this material into the official notebooks provided by the Department of Education, which were subsequently deposited in the Irish Folklore Archives. By the close of the project, more than 50,000 children from 5,000 schools in the Irish Free State had contributed to the scheme, resulting in 1,128 volumes, not counting some 40,000 of the children's original copybooks.[3] In the foreword to the scheme's guidebook, senior pupils were invited to 'participate in the task of rescuing from oblivion the traditions which, in spite of the vicissitudes of the historic Irish nation, have, century in, century out, been preserved

[3] Mícheál Briody, *The Irish Folklore Commission, 1935–1970: History, Ideology, Methodology* (Helsinki, 2007), 261. The Schools' Collection has been digitized in recent years and can be found online at: <www.duchas.ie>. For a comprehensive introduction, see especially Patricia Lysaght, 'Collecting the Folklore of Ireland: The Schoolchildren's Contribution', *Folklore* 132 (2021), 1–33.

with loving care by their ancestors'.[4] Séamus Ó Duilearga regarded these traditions as no less than 'the State Papers of a forgotten and neglected people'.[5] While the scheme set out a wide variety of themes to explore, religious folk tales are particularly well represented and, within them, the figure of the Roman Catholic priest features prominently.[6]

A word of caution is nonetheless in order. While the Schools' Collection remains a fascinating repository, historians who use it should be aware that the material they encounter has already been significantly mediated in its transmission. To begin with, the scheme covered twenty-six of the thirty-two counties on the island, and its principal focus was on rural Ireland (while some city schools did participate, they were, on the whole, under-represented). Likewise, the schools which featured were predominantly Roman Catholic, although there was some representation from other denominations. Given that the 'collectors' were schoolchildren, and their 'informants' adults, the stories they collected were largely recounted in an age-appropriate fashion (although there are occasional surprises here too). When individual students returned to school with their material, the contents of their copybooks were further filtered, with only a selection of material transferred to the official notebooks, usually transcribed by the students with the neatest handwriting or, as noted, by the teachers themselves. Duplicate material was often omitted from the official notebooks (different versions of stories, songs, and so on). Historians are advised, where possible, to also examine the original copybooks of the children (the rough drafts, as it were), although these were not always returned along with the official notebooks. What we are left with in the official notebooks (which can now be viewed online) does not fully represent all the material that was originally collected; rather, it comprises what individual teachers

[4] Diarmuid Ó Giolláin, *Locating Irish Folklore: Tradition, Modernity, Identity* (Cork, 2000), 134.

[5] S. Ó Duilearga, 'An Untapped Source of Irish History', *Studies: An Irish Quarterly Review* 25 (1936), 399–412, at 399. See also Mary E. Daly, '"The State Papers of a Forgotten and Neglected People": The National Folklore Collection and the Writing of Irish History', *Béaloideas* 78 (2010), 61–79.

[6] For a broader discussion of the portrayal of the priest in Irish folklore, see Pádraig Ó Héalaí, 'Cumhacht an tSagairt sa Bhéaloideas', *Léachtaí Cholm Cille* 8 (1977), 103–91, and more recently, Salvador Ryan, '"Begorra, Paddy, the Clergy have the Power Yet": Priests of the Province of Armagh and their Portrayal in the Folklore of the Schools Collection (1937–38)', *Seanchas Ard Mhacha* 28 (2020–1), 56–81.

deemed appropriate, and sufficiently interesting, to include.[7] These considerations present real methodological issues for the historian attempting a detailed analysis of this source, not least the question of the extent to which these stories are a product of a purely oral culture, or whether they have also been influenced by print culture filtering back into 'folklore'. This is a difficult question, but it is not our immediate focus here. Furthermore, invaluable as the digitization of the Schools' Collection has been, there is also another large folklore collection in existence, the very substantial Main Manuscript Collection of the former Irish Folklore Commission, amassed by adult collectors using *A Handbook of Irish Folklore* by Seán Ó Súilleabháin. This collection, which has not yet been digitized, consists of 2,400 bound and paginated volumes, containing approximately 700,000 pages of material.[8] It would be of interest to compare and contrast the content of both collections to obtain further insight into the image of the priest on the sick call, and the drama of extreme unction in Irish folklore. However, again, this must await future study.

The Hunted Priest and the Sick Call

One of the most iconic portrayals in the tales found in the Schools' Collection is that of the priest during the 'penal times', with a price on his head, hunted down and risking his life so that his people could have access to the sacraments.[9] A number of stories concern priests setting out on, or returning from, sick calls in this period.[10] One tale from Ballindaggan, Co. Wexford, relates how:

[7] Lysaght, 'Collecting the Folklore of Ireland', especially 5–10.

[8] See <https://www.duchas.ie/en/info/cbe> for a fuller description of the Main Manuscript Collection.

[9] Strictly speaking, the Penal Laws can be dated to the late seventeenth and eighteenth centuries. For a reassessment of their severity, see Thomas Bartlett, 'The Penal Laws against Irish Catholics: Were they too good for them?', in Oliver Rafferty, ed., *Irish Catholic Identities* (Manchester, 2013), 154–70.

[10] When stories from the Schools' Collection are quoted here, I have inserted some basic punctuation for clarity, and have occasionally corrected misspellings. I have also clarified some words or expressions which may be unfamiliar to readers by adding either an equivalent word in square brackets or an explanatory note. I have not otherwise amended the text.

> Fr. Hickey was killed on the bridge of Killcumney one night when he was coming home from a sick-call. The soldiers knew that Fr. Hickey was out on a call. They put a rope across the bridge and tightened it well. Fr. Hickey was coming quickly, and the horse tripped over the rope and fell, and Father Hickey fell also. The soldiers beheaded him, and they put his head up on a pike for all the people to see it. Ever since that time everyone who goes leaves a stone in the place where the priest was killed.[11]

In contrast to the periodizing tendencies of historians, the 'penal days' was quite an elastic concept in Irish folklore and could be used to refer to a variety of oppressive measures experienced by Roman Catholics, from the sixteenth through to the nineteenth centuries. A tale from Baunreagh, Co. Carlow, relates how priests setting out on sick calls would sometimes disguise themselves to evade capture:

> When Cromwell's soldiers were in Ireland, a poor Franciscan Friar was going to a sick call … He dressed himself in a pedlar's suit, put a bag on his back, and set off across the fields … He met the soldiers and one of them said: 'This is a Popish Friar.' Another said: 'Don't you see he is a pedlar?' 'What have you in your bag?' 'Sure, my pack. Will you buy?' 'No, we buy nothing in this damn country.' The Friar took a piece of lace from his bag. He gave it to one of the soldiers who said: 'This will do my fiancée, she is a dear old pet.' And so they passed away.[12] The Friar went to the sick call.[13]

Meanwhile, assistance to priests in danger often came from seemingly unlikely quarters. A story collected from the Mercy Convent in Kinsale relates how in 1710:

> While a Carmelite was attending a sick call in Cork Street, he was surprised by soldiers known as 'Buffs and Blues'. Escaping from the house, the priest ran through Market Lane … Passing a shop owned by a Protestant named John Heard, he appealed for help. He was invited in, and was directed to lie on the floor under a heap of sacking …
>
> A few hours later, in the darkness of the night, John Heard had the priest conveyed on a car [cart] from his house to a place of refuge in

[11] Dublin, National Folklore Collection, The Schools' Collection [hereafter: NFCS], Ballindaggan, Co. Wexford, vol. 892, 300–1.
[12] That is, 'passed on their way'.
[13] NFCS, Baunreagh, Co. Carlow, vol. 907, 149–51.

> West Cork. John Heard became very prosperous after this incident. He lived until the year 1742.
>
> The house in which we now live was the one where the priest found shelter.[14]

Other tales relate how the sick call itself was used as a ruse to trap a priest. A tale from Wexford town recounts how a priest was called out on a bogus sick call before being accosted by two men who jumped out from behind a wall with guns. The priest lashed the first with his horsewhip across the face (prompting the storyteller to say 'The mark of the whip is said to be on his descendants'), while the second 'ran his bayonet through the priest's heart and his blood began to drop onto the bridge where, it is claimed, it can still be seen to this day'.[15] A story from Ballyshannon, Co. Donegal, meanwhile, related that at the site of a similar decoy where a priest on his way to administer the last rites was shot dead, 'no grass has been known to grow on that spot since'.[16] A tale from Aglish in Co. Tipperary, again set vaguely in 'the Penal Times', relates how a Protestant family called Smith convinced a Roman Catholic man to feign illness and send for the priest in order to capture him. When he arrived, they made him prisoner and hanged him on a tree. Predictably, there were consequences:

> The tree withered, and was there till some years ago. Before he died, the priest cursed the place, saying that the rooks would fly in through the broken windows and grass would grow on the doorstep. Also, that no one of the name Smith would live there afterwards. The man who pretended he was sick was found dead in bed.[17]

A tale of feigned illness from Terryglass, Co. Tipperary, is more graphic in its denouement. When the captured priest is told that the man was not sick, but pretending, the priest challenges the soldiers to 'Come with me to the house and you will see he is sick': 'and when the party arrived at the sick man's house, they found him not alone sick, but dead, with all sorts of beetles continually

[14] NFCS, Mercy Convent, Kinsale, Co. Cork, vol. 319, 377–9.
[15] NFCS, Scoil na mBráthar, Co. Wexford, vol. 880, 434.
[16] NFCS, Ballyshannon, Co. Donegal, vol. 1028, 7.
[17] NFCS, Aglish, Co. Tipperary, vol. 532, 20. The implication, of course, is that this Roman Catholic man died without a priest, or the consolation of the last rites.

coming out of his ears, nose and mouth. The soldiers feared the priest and let him pass.'[18] Cautionary tales regarding those who would feign fatal sickness, either to trap or mock a priest, were not just the stuff of folklore. In the same year in which the schools' scheme was under way, a story appeared in the *Kilkenny People* newspaper under the title 'Letter from Rome' which recounted how 'some days ago, *L'Osservatore Romano* published details about a young man to whose bedside a priest was called to administer the Last Sacraments'. It related that as soon as the priest reached the sick man's room, 'the invalid jumped up and hurled all kinds of insults at the priest'. The story continued:

> A group of companions explained that the sick call was only a joke, but the priest with much indignation told the young man that he had committed the greatest sin that he could commit. And while they were speaking the false invalid breathed his last.[19]

The threat of priest-hunters could be eliminated before a priest was captured, occasionally through the intercession of a local saint. A story from Lombardstown, Co. Cork, tells of how a priest on a sick call was followed, and then overtaken, by a priest-hunter, but was soon released from his predicament when he prayed to St Abbey (Abigail) who arranged that a highwayman in hiding should, at that moment, appear and shoot the priest-hunter dead.[20]

Stories concerning the historic heroism of priests are common in the Schools' Collection. It was important to have such reminders to ensure that future generations would not forget the priest's sacrifice. Such reminders often took the form of impressions on the physical landscape, much as early Irish saints were believed to have left imprints on the rocks where they prayed. But absences could also function as reminders (the erasure of a family name from a locality, for instance). While the most familiar stories concern priests apprehended while celebrating mass, those detailing efforts to thwart a priest from administering the last rites are also common, underlining the significance of this sacrament in the popular mindset.

18 NFCS, Terryglass, Co. Tipperary, vol. 530, 311.
19 'Letter from Rome', *Kilkenny People*, 5 June 1937, 3.
20 NFCS, Glantane, Lombardstown, Co. Cork, vol. 363, 19–20.

Diabolical Ruses to Delay a Priest from Attending a Sick Call

The most common sick call stories recount how diabolical forces attempted to hinder priests on their journey, with the intention that an individual would be found dead (and worse, unshriven, that is, having not confessed their sins) by the time the priest arrived. These demonic interventions could come in various guises. A story from Ahane, Co. Limerick, relates how a priest hired a man with a sidecar to go out on a night call.[21] When they came to a certain place on the road:

> the horse stop[ped] up on the road and would not go any farther. The priest saw a white man on the road, and the man [he was with] could see nothing. The man was beating the horse and the horse wouldn't pass it. They turned back and went another road. The priest got a fright. When they went to the house, the person was dead.[22]

A story from Co. Leitrim concerning a certain Fr Galligan relates how 'when he was going along the road, a black dog came out before him, with flames of fire coming out of his mouth, and the horse would not go on'. The story continues:

> The priest put on the stole on his neck and began to read, and he worked bit by bit until he came to the gate of the house, and there the dog made a bad attack at him.[23] When the priest went into the house, the woman was above in the room with the door bolted, and the man below with a crow-bar trying to break the door to kill the woman. Then the priest put the stole round his neck and began to read, and the man stopped it. The woman came down, and they got the man into the bed, and the priest gave him confession.[24]

In an account from Rahavanig, Co. Kerry, a certain Fr O'Connor 'met a sow which attacked him and tried to stop him, but the priest persevered and after a long struggle passed it, and attended the dying

[21] A sidecar, or jaunting car, was a two-wheeled carriage for a single horse, popular in Ireland from the early nineteenth century. Most commonly, it had seats for two to four people, who were seated back-to-back.

[22] NFCS, Ahane, Co. Limerick, vol. 523, 426.

[23] The placing of the stole around the priest's neck is a significant moment, often leading to the banishment of the diabolical force, or the revelation of the true identity of some demon in disguise. On the significance of the stole in the administration of extreme unction, see O'Kane, *Notes on the Rubrics of the Roman Ritual*, 389.

[24] NFCS, Tullaghan, Co. Leitrim, vol. 190, 180.

person. About five minutes after the priest leaving, the person died.'[25] A tale from Co. Meath, meanwhile, gives an exact year for the strange occurrence, relating how, in November 1860, the parish priest of Ballivor, Fr Halligan, was called from a dinner at a wealthy farmer's house to go on a sick call (the aside here, which would not have been lost on the story's hearers, is revealing: 'It was a custom at that time for a priest to dine out with his well-to-do parishioners regularly'). The priest mounts his horse and departs on his journey until, at one point, the horse stops suddenly, its eyes transfixed by what was on the road ahead. The priest can see nothing, but after donning his stole and praying:

> he saw a headless turkey-cock walk towards him. He at once knew him for what he was – the Devil. He therefore said prayers to drive him back to Hell again and, as he said them, the turkey cock began to fade away. The priest then knew that the Devil had full possession of the dying man's soul (to whom he had been called to attend), and was trying to prevent him from going to attend him in his last agonies.[26]

However, it was not always something potentially terrifying that delayed a priest on a sick call. In other instances, it was quite the reverse. A story from Co. Limerick relates how:

> One night there was a person dying, and the priest was sent for. When the priest was coming along the road, he heard two people inside the wall singing a song, called 'An Cailin Deas Crudaithe na Mbo'.[27] It was the grandest singing the priest ever heard. So he waited until the song was finished. When it was finished, he went over, and looked in over the wall, and saw it was two dogs that was after singing the song.[28]
>
> The priest journeyed on towards the house, where the sick person was living. When he came to the house, the person was dead. The priest said that the two dogs were two devils, and that they wanted to delay the priest, so that they could get the person's soul. The priest

[25] NFCS, Rahanavig, Co. Kerry, vol. 400, 36–7.

[26] NFCS, Killyon, Co. Meath, vol. 692, 320–1.

[27] A more accurate spelling, in this case, is 'Cailín Deas Crúidhte na mBó' ('The Pretty Girl who milked the Cows').

[28] The implication is that it was two dogs that had been singing the song. The 'after' perfect in Hiberno-English can be used to express the perfect tense, using the word 'after' to indicate that something occurred in the immediate, or very recent, past.

> cursed the song they were singing, and from that day to this, it is considered wrong to sing it.[29]

Meanwhile, an informant from Drogheda, Co. Louth, related a tale which he claimed to have heard fifty years earlier from the very priest to whom it had happened. In this case, while out on a sick call, the priest was waylaid by two nuns who were inordinately eager to chat with him, and accompanied him home, whereupon they blew their cover by turning into two large dogs. The priest concluded: 'The two Nuns were the Devil; he thought I would delay and stand and talk to them and keep me late from the dying woman. But God was with me.'[30] Moreover, priests were thought to have their own powers which helped them circumvent those who would wish to keep them from administering the sacraments. The following tale from Connagh, Co. Cork, is particularly striking:

> One day a priest was going on a sick call. He was stopped by a Protestant named Gilman. He wanted to know where the priest was going, and he wanted to take the Holy Oils from him.[31] Then the priest came out of the car [cart], and he asked the man to go dancing with him. He did so, and after a while the priest went into his car again, and Gilman remained dancing until the priest returned again. Gilman asked the priest to stop him dancing again, and the priest did so.[32]

But delays might not always be the work of the devil. Sometimes accidents simply happened. The following account from Co. Mayo is fascinating in another respect:

> In the olden times there was an old woman who had charms and cures. The priest who lived in the same place was against her. One day this priest was going on a sick call on horseback. When he was going along a certain place on the road, his horse fell under him and he could not rise. A few men came to him and they mentioned about this old woman who had the charms. At first the priest would not hear tell of her. But, at last, he told them to go for her. So she came and she spat on the horse three times, and then told the priest to strike the horse with

[29] NFCS, Lurga, Patrick's Well, Co. Limerick, vol. 527, 89.

[30] NFCS, St Mary's, Drogheda, Co. Louth, vol. 680, 486.

[31] According to O'Kane (quoting De Herdt), 'The vessel of oil should be fastened around the neck, and carried under the surplice, so as not to appear': O'Kane, *Notes on the Rubrics of the Roman Ritual*, 368.

[32] NFCS, Connagh, Co. Cork, vol. 306, 257–8.

> his gown. So the horse rose up and the priest jumped into the saddle and went off.[33]

Here we have the meeting of two authority figures, one representing the institutional church and (presumably) orthodoxy, the other representing folk belief, heterodoxy and, indeed, female authority. In this case, it is to be inferred that the timely administration of the last rites by the former depended wholly on the latter.

Stories which describe the supernatural obstacles that priests faced in administering the last rites are a reminder that the priest-figure was understood to contend not only with earthly powers bent on obstructing his ministry, but also with diabolical forces which, sometimes, cooperated with human agents and, at other times, intervened directly themselves. Moreover, in a similar vein to some parables in the New Testament, neither hindrance nor help are always found in the places where you might expect them to appear.

When the Priest arrives late through his own Fault

Sometimes priests arrived late, not on account of some malign distraction, but rather owing to their own negligence. Instances such as these were treated with the utmost seriousness. A story from Mullinavat, Co. Kilkenny, recalls how:

> a poor travelling woman was dying, and she sent someone for the priest, but the priest did not answer the call at the time. He came in the morning, but the woman was dead, and there were seven candles lighting [burning] around her corpse and, when the priest went in, all the candles quenched, and when he went out, they all lit again. When the priest heard this, he knew he did wrong by not answering the call sooner.[34]

A similar story was told in Gusserane, Co. Wexford:

> One night in winter a woman named Mrs Doyle was dying, and the priest was sent for. The priest did not come for about three hours after he [was] getting word. He came about one o'clock in the night, and there were twins sitting up in a cradle, and the mother was dead in the bed beside them. The twins had two blessed candles in their hands.

33 NFCS, Lankill, Co. Mayo, vol. 137F, 32.
34 NFCS, Mullinavat, Co. Kilkenny, vol. 850, 107.

When the priest went in, the two candles went out, and when the priest would go out again, the candles would light.[35]

The importance placed upon the prompt arrival of a priest to a death-bed, and the backlash from a grieving relative that might follow such a dereliction of duty, can be keenly observed in a story from Dunlavin, Co. Wicklow. In this account, a priest arrives late for a man's death and is met in the yard by the man's wife who promptly hits him in the face with a can of buttermilk. Despite the circumstances, to strike a priest was regarded as a serious offence, and the story continues with the priest jibing that 'You might want a priest yet!'. It concludes by noting how 'ever after, a priest was never got in time for one of the family.'[36] Stories such as these may have given voice to Roman Catholics disappointed with the negligence of their parish clergy, but this last tale also sets clear limits on how legitimate grievances against poorly performing priests should be addressed.

The Curse of 'May you die without a Priest!'

Given the significance attached to the priest's sick call, it is little wonder that the curse '*Bás gan sagart ort!*' ('May you die without a priest!') had such potency. The wish might be made in general terms, but those who wished this upon their enemies might also play a more active part in its fulfilment. A story from Killeen, Co. Mayo, is an example of one such case:

> Once upon a time a priest was on a sick call and he did not know the way too good. He went into a house to find the way. The man of the house was not great with the people of the house to which the priest was going.[37] So he told the priest the wrong way. The priest came back again to the house, and he put the man sitting on a chair, and the man tried to get up, but he could not get up. The chair was stuck to him and, wherever the man would go, the chair would be after him.[38] The

[35] NFCS, Gusserane, Co. Wexford, vol. 872, 163.

[36] NFCS, Baile Dáithí, Dunlavin, Co. Wicklow, vol. 914, 467.

[37] For 'not great', read 'not very friendly'.

[38] Allusions to priests having the power to 'stick' people to things, most often to the ground, are plentiful in Irish religious tales. I first heard of this tradition from Maynooth ecclesiastical historian, Mgr Patrick Corish, in a lecture delivered in September 1992. He recounted the tale of how a priest, who was travelling on horseback to a sick call at night, handed the reins of his horse over rather gruffly to a stable boy.

> priest said to him if he told him the truth he would leave him all right. The man told him the right way, and the priest left him all right again.[39]

But one could also bring the curse of dying without a priest upon oneself by certain loathsome behaviours. One of these was contempt for the poor. The following cautionary tale from Kilruane in Co. Tipperary is a good example:

> Once upon a time, there was a woman who was very 'tight'.[40] She would never help the poor. One day, about a week before Christmas, a poor man came to her door, but she sent him away without giving him anything. The next day he came again, but got nothing. He came again in Christmas Night just as the woman was cutting the cake, and when she saw him she said, 'How dare you come in to a decent respectable house like this, get away for yourself,' and the man went away.
>
> Now the woman's husband was looking on, and when he saw what was done, he got a couple of cuts of bread, buttered them, and went after the man. The poor man said: 'I do not want that bread at all. I am one of God's angels. I was sent down to your wife, but she would not give me anything. On the Twelfth of January your wife will be dead.'
>
> So, on the Twelfth of January, the woman was dying. The priest and doctor were there, and she had a blessed candle in her hand. But she let the candle fall, and the room filled up with smoke. The priest nor people could not see at all, so the woman died without Extreme Unction.[41]

The curse of death without a priest might also be employed by a priest who had been slighted in some way. A tale from Tullogher, Co. Kilkenny, recalls how there was once a 'silenced' priest who was forced to resort to the workhouse in New Ross, Co. Wexford, for sustenance. When one of his fellow inmates, a farmer, complained that the priest was being treated with greater solicitude than the others, he

---

When the priest barked, 'Hold that horse for me while I go inside!', the stable boy grunted reluctantly, precipitating the priest's sharp and more insistent retort: 'Hold that horse for me, or I'll stick you to the ground!' This prompted the stable boy to quip, 'In that case, why don't you stick your horse to the ground?'

39 NFCS, Killeen, Co. Mayo, vol. 140, 574–5.

40 That is, who was mean or lacked generosity.

41 NFCS, Kilruane, Co. Tipperary, vol. 533, 318–19.

became angry and vowed that 'this man would be roaring for a priest yet, and that nobody would hear him'. The story went on to relate that, sometime later, the same farmer was killed when he got caught under a reaper and binder machine when the other workmen had gone to dinner. The account concludes with the observation that, 'the strangest thing was that the man was calling loudly for help, and for a priest likely, because people at the far side of the river heard him: they could never forget his roars, they said'.[42] Meanwhile, in the following account from Hospital in Co. Limerick, there can be found a slight, but effective, twist on the malediction of 'May you die without a priest!':

> Long ago there lived a judge named O'Grady. He lived in Baggotstown. One day there was a priest up in court. The judge came and he examined his case, and he put him to prison for six months. When the priest was going into prison he said to the judge, 'That you may never die without a priest!' When the judge got old he got very sick, but he could not die. He was in pain and suffering for a very long time because the priest would not come to him. It was said that the devil appeared to him. Then the priest came to him and he died.[43]

In this case, we find a curse wrapped in what appears to be a blessing; and, indeed, one that was aimed at ensuring the maximum physical suffering for the intended victim before he was finally (presumably) relieved of his punishment. To die without a priest was to risk dying in a state of sin, and without the saving grace of penance, *viaticum* and the administration of the holy oils of extreme unction; in short, it was to risk eternal damnation. This is what gave the curse of 'May you die without a priest!' its potency. It is also what gave tales recounting a priest's race to get to a deathbed on time such dramatic effect.

A Messenger brings a Priest to a Dying Person

By contrast, to die having been attended to by a priest was regarded as a great blessing, and many stories survive of heavenly messengers sent to ensure a priest was notified of the impending death of those

[42] NFCS, Tullogher, Co. Kilkenny, vol. 846, 442–3.
[43] NFCS, Scoil na mBráthar, Hospital, Co. Limerick, vol. 514, 393.

considered deserving of his presence. A tale from Ballymahon, Co. Longford, which closely resembles a medieval *exemplum*, relates how a boy who had promised his mother that he would never go to bed without saying a 'Hail Mary', went to America for eight years and then returned home in 1921, only to die three years later. Just before his death:

> The priest was out on [another] sick call when he was stopped by a masked man and brought along a road to the dying man's house. The road was never seen since or before. The priest was five miles away when he was stopped; so the man had not died without the priest because he had kept his promise to his mother.[44]

The account goes on to relate how the priest in question was a Fr McCabe, who 'is at present Canon of the Parish of Ardagh'.[45] Meanwhile, a tale from Co. Wexford relates how, one night:

> a priest was coming home from a sick call when he met a woman on the road. She told him that her son was dying in the quarry in Ballygarven, and she told him to go to the quarry and anoint him. When he reached the quarry, this James O'Connor was lying unconscious. James asked the priest who [had] sent him to that quarry, and he told him that his mother [had] told him. The boy told the priest that the woman [was] dead twenty year before that.[46]

Stories of individuals returning from the dead to perform such works of mercy were relatively common in Irish folklore. A further example from Camross in Co. Laois recounts how:

> One night a priest got a sick call. He was to go to a man who was dying. He got out his horse and started from the house. When he went to the house there was no one inside, only the sick man. When he went into the room, he saw a picture of a man on the wall. It was the man who went for him, and he had been dead for a great many years.[47]

In other instances, it is St Joseph himself, patron of the dying, who acts as the heavenly messenger. A story from the Presentation

44 NFCS, Ballymahon, Co. Longford, vol. 751, 266.
45 Ibid.
46 NFCS, Gusserane, Co. Wexford, vol. 872, 162–3.
47 NFCS, Camross, Mountrath, Co. Laois, vol. 826, 436.

Convent, Lucan, Co. Dublin, which has more than a little confessional edge to it, relates how:

> In one of the Crescent Houses, there lived a man in No. 4. He was Protestant, and lived a very bad life. He had a girl attending on him. She was a Catholic. Now he was Mr. O'Toole and he hated Christianity and priests, and would not let one inside his door.[48]
>
> One day the girl became very ill, and she wished to have a priest. One night a man with a long beard knocked at the priest's door, and asked him to come to the girl as she was very ill. He led the way to the girl's room. They passed through a room where there were men playing cards and drinking. The priest passed through, and the old man with him, and no one saw them (they were made invisible). When they reached the door, the old man disappeared, and when the priest entered the room the girl asked him who told him she had been ill, because no one knew that she was ill.
>
> The priest then asked her if she had ever said any special prayer to any saint, and she said that she had promised her mother to say the little prayer, 'Jesus, Mary and Joseph,' no matter what happened. Then she made a good Confession, and received Holy Communion. The priest said that it must have been St. Joseph who brought him to the girl.[49]

Other tales of obstacles encountered by those wishing to receive the sacrament played on memories of proselytism in the nineteenth century. The following story from Moyard in Co. Galway is a particularly good example:

> There was an old hedge school in Cleggan about [a] hundred years ago; it was called the Jumper school.[50] Many poor people went to it, to be educated. All the people that went got a cup of soup at noon daily. The

[48] It is noteworthy that, in this tale, 'Christianity' appears to be solely equated with Roman Catholicism.

[49] NFCS, Presentation Convent, Lucan, Co. Dublin, vol. 794, 20–1. The Schools' Collection contains many prayers to St Joseph as patron of the dying.

[50] The term 'Jumper' was used to describe Irish Roman Catholics who, in the period of the Great Hunger (the Irish Famine), were prepared to accept religious instruction from Protestant societies in return for material relief. This might come in the form of the provision of soup, from which the related term 'Souper' derives. Accusations against individuals and families who had 'taken the soup' would be long-lasting in the cultural memory of Irish Catholicism. See also Deirdre Nuttall, *Different and the Same: A Folk History of Protestants in Independent Ireland* (Dublin, 2020).

> first day they went, they got a flannel coat. One man, whose name was Tommy Heaney, went two days; as soon as he got a flannel coat, he never went to it again.
>
> There was a girl named Sally Tierney [who] was a Jumper for part of her life. She was very ill one day. The minister that was in Moyard went to the Jumper school, and brought her over to the school house in Moyard. She was crying for the priest. Mrs Nee was passing the road; she heard her crying [for] the priest. Mrs Nee ran to Letterfrack to tell the priest. The priest came at once; he went to the school house. The minister was inside the door, but the priest said he would break the door. The minister opened the door at once. The priest gave her the sacrament of Extreme Unction.
>
> The priest got a man, and ass and cart, and they brought her up to Moyard, and she died there.[51]

A priest at one's deathbed might be regarded as a blessing for any Roman Catholic, but there were some individuals who were rewarded in even greater abundance, such as a certain man who defended a priest at a mass rock during the penal times,[52] as recounted in another Co. Wexford story. Upon commending him for his bravery, the priest enquired as to what the man would like him to ask God for in return. The man simply answered, 'To have a priest beside me at the hour of my death', to which the priest replied, 'You will not only have a priest … but you will have seven priests with you.' When the time eventually came for the man to take ill and draw near to death:

> No priest could be got for him in this parish … Someone said there was a great dinner going on at Lamberts of Cornagh and there would surely be priests there. A messenger was sent. Seven priests were at the dinner. When the sick call was announced, each priest sprang to his feet, and so the seven priests went to the dying man.[53]

[51] NFCS, Moyard, Co. Galway, vol. 6, 121. For the wider historical context, see Miriam Moffitt, *Soupers and Jumpers: The Protestant Missions in Connemara, 1848–1937* (Dublin, 2008).

[52] A rock, usually located in a remote area, which was used as an altar for the clandestine celebration of mass during the period of the Penal Laws in the seventeenth century.

[53] NFCS, San Leonard, Ballycullane, Co. Wexford, Volume 871, 76. Of course, the throwaway lines in such stories are often more interesting than the main plot lines themselves. The subversive subtext here might be that you will never find priests too far from a dinner table! Such subtle references, encompassing a gently critical jibe at the lifestyle of

In other instances, the desire of some to receive the last sacrament could summon a priest from beyond the grave. A tale from Querrin in Co. Clare relates how an old woman on an island off Loop Head was dying and called for a priest. As there were no priests on the island, one had to be found on the mainland. As the priest was making his way to the woman, he was drowned at sea; nevertheless, his ghost proceeded to visit the woman and give her the last rites. Next day the priest's body was 'washed in on the shore'.[54]

The significance placed on the presence of a priest at one's deathbed made this the *sine qua non* of a happy death in many of the stories found in the Schools' Collection. Those who prayed fervently for such a favour might be rewarded by the intercession of a heavenly figure, such as St Joseph, patron saint of the dying. Alternatively, the prayers of a deceased loved one could be instrumental in summoning a priest just in time. What is evident in these tales is that for those who sufficiently desired the sacrament, and were suitably disposed, the necessary assistance would be provided, even from beyond the grave.

Performing one's Sacramental Duties with Due Care

Although most of the tales examined here do not concern themselves with the types of questions that the Rev. James O'Kane dealt with in his *Notes on the Rubrics of the Roman Ritual*, that is not to say that the Schools' Collection does not exhibit any interest in procedural propriety. The following story, from Borris in Co. Carlow, is a good example of the scruples of a conscientious priest:

> One night a priest was on a sick call. When he heard her confession, the priest forgot to bless her. He went home and went to bed. He could not sleep. He woke up about a quarter to three, and then he thought that he did not bless the girl. He went over to a drawer and took out a prayer book, and he gave the blessing.

the clergy, were not uncommon in Irish folklore, acting as release valves of sorts for the laity. These instances deserve further scholarly attention, and I hope to explore the topic further in a future article.

[54] NFCS, Querrin, Co. Clare, vol. 632, 78–9.

> He slept soundly that night, and the next morning when he woke up he went back to the dying girl's house. The people of the house told him that she died about three o'clock. The priest remembered that it was three o'clock when he jumped into bed. They told him that she saw a priest standing next to her and he blessed her. Then she saw the priest no more. She asked the people where did he go. They said they saw no priest.[55]

By contrast, there are also stories of priests who, for various reasons, chose to cut corners in their ministry to the dying. One colourful example from Carniska, Co. Roscommon, concerns a 'very tasty' priest called Fr Kane who 'hated to see any dirty house'. It relates how, 'when he used to come to anoint any old person, he would not go near them, only stand at the room door and say "Shout them [their sins] out to me, old warrior!"'[56]

There were many other elements that a priest needed to remember when administering the last rites to those who were sick in order that the proper understanding and use of the sacrament were preserved. This often involved reminding people that extreme unction could only be administered once for each grave illness. Nonetheless, that did not stop some individuals from receiving the sacrament multiple times. In the case of an example from Ardfield in Co. Cork, it is not clear whether the marvel is that the man in question received extreme unction so many times, or that he had so many distinct grave illnesses. The reference concerns a certain Michael Footman, who owned a shop in Dunowen. It was said of him that 'He was married and had seven children. He received the Sacrament of extreme unction twenty-five times before he died.'[57]

Conclusion

Tales of the priest's sick call are plentiful in Irish folklore. The examples from the Schools' Collection surveyed here do not concern themselves so much with the mechanics of administering the sacrament, and therefore are not preoccupied with correct procedure in the way a publication such as the Rev. James O'Kane's was. Nor should

55 NFCS, Borris, Co. Carlow, vol. 904, 328.
56 NFCS, Carniska, Co. Roscommon, vol. 253, 118–19.
57 NFCS, Ardfield, Co. Cork, vol. 317, 8.

they have been, given that O'Kane's work was designed for consultation by clergy in the practice of their profession, whereas the stories we have been examining were predominantly told by lay people, most often in informal, casual settings, even if preachers might have also occasionally peppered their sermons with such stories as salutary reminders of what was, ultimately, essential: that the priest arrive to the bed of the dying person on time, and that the person receiving the priest be properly disposed. While this article has introduced, in broad brushstrokes, some of the most prominent categories of tales relating to the sick call, many elements within these stories merit much closer examination, not least the occasional hints of clerical critique. The dramatic tension that accompanies these tales, which so often involve a race against time (and malign forces), underlines the significance of this last sacrament. In this respect, then, what we have been examining are not so much tales about a rite of passage, but about (safe) passage to a rite. After all, extreme unction was often simply considered as a matter of eternal life, or eternal torment. For many, the relief of the sacrament was worth hanging onto life for. There can surely be no better example of this than the following account from Co. Tipperary:

> There is a story told about a place called Tubberdoney where the huntsmen saw a fox run in through the briars; they cut away the briars and found a hole, they looked in and saw inside with the fox two old women.
>
> There was a priest in the hunt, who said he would find out for himself. What did he find but a cosy little kitchen and a nice turf fire and a kettle hanging over it and the two women and they chatting about a sermon they had heard preached last Sunday.
>
> He asked what the priest said at Mass and they told him. When he went home he found that the priest they told him of was dead with [for] three hundred years. He then went back to the hole and anointed the two old women and they died off. They had waited all that time for a priest.[58]

Despite the prominence of clergy in the cultural memory of Irish Roman Catholicism, it is surprising, perhaps, that Irish

[58] NFCS, Curraghcloney, Co. Tipperary, vol. 572, 31.

historiography still awaits a comprehensive study of the depiction of the Roman Catholic priest in Irish folklore. The above account, concerned with one aspect of priestly ministry, the sick call, hints at the richness of the material available, and the possibilities for future historians.

From Necrology to Eulogy? A Preacher memorializes his Father-in-Law

Clyde Binfield*
University of Sheffield

Whether death is a passage or a terminus, an obituary can be an important accompaniment for the survivors. Victorian funerals were improved by sermons setting the deceased in the eye of eternity. Today's funerals prefer eulogies. The Congregational City Temple's Joseph Parker (1830–1902) was second only to the Baptist Metropolitan Tabernacle's Charles Haddon Spurgeon (1834–92) in popular estimation. Parker's father-in-law, Andrew Common (1815–96), bank manager, chapel deacon and active Liberal, was a type found nationwide. Parker and Common are placed in context, with Parker's commemoration of Common in the Evangelical Magazine *as a prime focus for this article, balanced by his earlier extempore graveside appreciation of Common's kinsman Robert Teasdale (1809–83). What might be gleaned about their attitudes to life and death? Were these particular instances representative? Was the piece in the* Evangelical Magazine *a sermon slipping insensibly into eulogy, the occupational hazard of any preacher at such a moment?*

Is death a passage or a terminus? Whatever rites mark a death, an obituary can be an important accompaniment for those who survive. A funeral is the culmination of a life. Victorian funerals were improved by sermons which set the deceased in the eye of eternity. Today's funerals prefer eulogies to sermons; these may recreate a life but keep well away from eternity.[1]

The Congregational City Temple's Joseph Parker (1830–1902) was second only to the Baptist Metropolitan Tabernacle's Charles Haddon Spurgeon (1834–92) in popular estimation. Parker's father-in-law, Andrew Common (1815–96), was a Sunderland banker, a Congregational deacon and an active Liberal. His was a

* E-mail: noreenbinfield@gmail.com.
[1] I acknowledge the help during a long gestation of Irene, James and Ruth Common, Barbara Dainton, Geoffrey E. Milburn, Geoffrey F. Nuttall, Patricia J. Storey and E. Tinker (City of Sunderland Community and Cultural Services).

Studies in Church History 59 (2023), 433–445
doi: 10.1017/stc.2023.20

type found nationwide. Parker's commemoration of Common, as published in the *Evangelical Magazine*, is the prime focus for this article.[2]

What might be gleaned from it about Parker, Common and their attitudes to both life and death? Was this instance, particular to that preacher and his family but shared with the readers of the *Evangelical Magazine*, at all representative? Was it more sermon than eulogy, or was the former slipping insensibly into the latter, the occupational hazard of any preacher at such a moment? Some scene-setting is necessary: who and what were Parker and Common?

The Preacher

Joseph Parker was a pulpit phenomenon.[3] He was a Congregationalist who in early life had a Methodist phase. Between 1853 and 1901 he held three contrasting Congregational pastorates in equally contrasting parts of England.[4] Each was locally influential but the third and longest allowed for an influence beyond both national and Nonconformist bounds. This was in the City of London, at a cause dating from the 1640s which in Parker's time moved from Poultry to Holborn Viaduct. There, taking full advantage of the adjacent railway station, Poultry Chapel (which had been advantageously sold to what became the Midland Bank) was rebuilt as the City Temple. Its façade was a display of architectural good manners verging on arrogance, for it suggested the west front, judiciously pared down, of St Paul's Cathedral. Given the City's steadily and irreversibly declining population it was in all respects a bold venture.

Nothing about this passionate Congregationalist fitted a Congregational template. He had not trained for ministry at a

[2] For Parker and Spurgeon, see R. Tudur Jones, 'Parker, Joseph (1830–1902)' and Rosemary Chadwick, 'Spurgeon, Charles Haddon (1834–1892)', both *ODNB*, online edn (2004), at: <https://doi.org/10.1093/ref:odnb/35386> and <https://doi.org/10.1093/ref:odnb/26187>, respectively; for Common, see *Sunderland Daily Echo*, 14 February 1896, 4; Joseph Parker, 'Andrew Common, J.P.', *Evangelical Magazine* 3rd series 39 (1897), 17–23, at 17.

[3] The following account is largely drawn from Joseph Parker, *A Preacher's Life*, 5th edn (London, 1903); *Congregational Year Book* [hereafter: *CYB*] 1903, 208b–e; Albert Clare, *The City Temple 1640–1940: The Tercentenary Commemoration Volume* (London, 1940), 76–137.

[4] Banbury (1853–8); Cavendish Chapel, Manchester (1858–69); City Temple, London (1869–1901).

theological college. His pastorates were manifestly successful but his model of Congregational ministry exemplified an autocracy in which the essence of Congregationalism, its church members' and deacons' meetings, was ignored. It is characteristic that when the *Congregational Year Book* began to publish denominational statistics, church by church, the City Temple's were left blank. Was there a fear that they would not bear comparison with those of the Metropolitan Tabernacle?[5]

In fact, Parker was more than a pulpit autocrat. He was twice chairman of the national Congregational Union (only one other man achieved that before 1901) and he had a statesmanlike and accurate grasp of where Congregationalism's future lay. There was, moreover, little doubt as to his evangelical orthodoxy, although, like Spurgeon's, his was a strikingly capacious orthodoxy and in one respect it was a strained orthodoxy: death and immortality. In the words of his admiring friend, W. Robertson Nicoll: 'Death was to him the most formidable of foes … but much was dark to him on that side. He viewed the life after death for long with hesitations and tremors … The unknown and untried regions which the spirit enters when it is severed from the flesh daunted him.'[6] Nicoll also quoted Parker: 'When I come to die do not preach to me, do not exhort me – leave me with myself and with God.'[7]

Parker's publications were prolific without being memorable. His fame as a man of words and the Word depended on his mastery of speech. This is best illustrated by two of his most famous interventions, each delivered in the City Temple, as recalled by Alexander

[5] In 1893, the Metropolitan Tabernacle seated 4,880, with a further 4,050 in its 19 mission stations and 25 Sunday and Ragged schools. It had 5,179 members, 8,034 scholars and 611 Sunday school teachers: *Baptist Handbook* 1894, 227. In 1898, the first year for which the *CYB* published such statistics, the City Temple seated 3,000; no figures were given for membership but 225 scholars and 25 teachers were listed: *CYB* 1899, 288. In 1901, no figures were given beyond the 3,000 sittings: ibid. 1902, 206.

[6] W. Robertson Nicoll, *Princes of the Church*, 4th edn (London, ?1921), 181–2.

[7] Ibid. 181. Leaving Parker with himself and God is something that historians cannot do. Parker's pivotal, indeed posthumous, influence on Congregationalism informs Alan Argent, *The Transformation of Congregationalism 1900–2000* (Nottingham, 2013), especially 1–9. He figures significantly in D. W. Bebbington, *The Nonconformist Conscience: Chapel and Politics, 1870–1914* (London, 1982); James Munson, *The Nonconformists: In Search of a Lost Culture* (London, 1991); M. R. Watts, *The Dissenters*, 3: *The Crisis and Conscience of Nonconformity* (Oxford, 2015).

Gammie, journalist and sermon-taster, and J. D. Jones, the next man to be twice chairman of the Congregational Union.

The first was more speech than sermon. The occasion was an evening meeting held during the Congregational May Meetings for 1897. The intention was to celebrate the queen's diamond jubilee by reviewing the 'progress of civil and religious liberty during Her Majesty's reign' in the form of addresses on 'The Relation of the Free Churches to the Hanoverian Dynasty', 'Some Notable Religious Movements of the Reign', 'The Development of the Social Idea in the Reign of Victoria' and 'Pastors and Teachers who represented Congregationalism in the early part of Her Majesty's Reign'.[8] It was a thoroughly worthy occasion and, given the inescapable sense of time passing, it was more commemoration than celebration. It was, in preview, a national rite of passage as observed by some of the nation's Nonconformists. Parker took full advantage of it.

His was the fourth address, on 'Pastors and Teachers', but he swept his hearers from England in the 1830s and 1840s to present-day Turkey and the failure of the Powers to restrain its sultan, Abdul Hamid. There could be no doubt as to his answer to that failure: '"I believe in another King, Our Jesus, whom Paul affirmed to be *alive*." He shot that word *alive* out like a thunderbolt. It left the audience literally stunned and speechless. People scarcely realized that the speech was finished … Then such a tumult of applause broke out'. It was 'a tremendous passage' in a speech aflame in every sentence 'with the fire of genius'.[9] It was also a perfect example of oratorical sleight of hand. Parker repeated it two years later.

On 25 April 1899 he preached from Ezra 9.3 (KJV): 'And when I heard this thing, I rent my garment and my mantle, and plucked off the hair of my head and of my beard, and sat down astonied.'[10] The occasion for this sermon was the tercentenary of Oliver Cromwell's birth and the text's preceding verse, so applicable to the Stuarts – 'yea, the hand of the princes and rulers hath been chief in this trespass' – allowed for a switch to contemporary princes and rulers. Parker's hearers always expected the unexpected but the effect was startling. He seized on a recent reference to Abdul Hamid as the

8 *CYB* 1898, 5–6.
9 J. D. Jones, *Three Score Years and Ten* (London, 1940), 67–8.
10 R. Tudur Jones, *Congregationalism in England 1662–1962* (London, 1962), 324.

friend of the emperor of Germany: 'He may have been the Kaiser's friend, but in the name of God, in the name of the Father and the Son and the Holy Ghost – speaking of the Sultan not merely as a man, but speaking of him as the Great Assassin – I say, "God damn the Sultan!"'[11] The words could not have been simpler or more direct but it was the timing – the pause between 'God' and 'damn' – which made them electrifying.[12]

There was more. Years later Alexander Gammie of the *Glasgow Citizen* emphasized the appearance (the massive figure, leonine head, shaggy locks, gleaming eyes and sweeping gestures), the voice (its 'constantly changing inflexion … at one moment like a roar of thunder and the next soft as a whisper'), the orthodoxy ('I preach the love of Christ, the power of the Cross, the One Priesthood of the One Priest') and the discipline ('Apparently free from rule, it was unconsciously obedient to the great principles of art'),[13] but it was a quotation in the *Congregational Year Book* obituary which best summed him up, in a sequence of Parker-like paradoxes: 'so deep and so shallow, so brusque and sarcastic and bitter, so gentle and tender and lovable, so rugged in his independence and self-esteem, so absolute in his dependence on the sympathy and goodwill of those about him, so full of inconsistencies of all sorts'.[14]

However outsize his pulpit presence, a Congregational minister's position depended on his credibility. Parker's was rock solid. He was a Northumbrian stonemason's son with farming links on his mother's side. As the minister of increasingly eligible churches, a professional man with a position to enhance, he expressed social mobility at its most admirable. In London he moved from Highbury New Park to Hampstead. His houses were comfortable without ostentation, his household ran to three servants, and he left £27,000.[15] His marriages, both of them happy, confirmed the credibility. His first wife, Ann Nesbit (d. 1863), a Methodist farmer's daughter, was of a similar age and background to his own. His second wife, Emma Jane

[11] Alexander Gammie, *Preachers I have heard* (London, 1945), 40.

[12] So Dr Ernest A. Payne (1902–79), whose father was in the congregation, told the present writer.

[13] Gammie, *Preachers*, 40–1.

[14] *CYB* 1903, 208e.

[15] According to the 1881 census return, the household at North Holme, Highbury Park, included cook, housemaid and assistant cook: RG11/0255/113/27; Clare, *City Temple*, 128.

Common (1845–99), also came from the north-east but she was fifteen years younger, well connected and financially secure.

That Parker was touchingly aware of his good fortune is illustrated by the reminiscence of a young cousin of Emma Jane's, a medical man who in 1898 called one Saturday evening on the Parkers:

> I saw very little of him as he was preparing his Sunday sermons. She was a good-looking woman and he was a plain man, and they went by the name of 'Beauty and the Beast.' Dr. Parker had sufficient humour to accept this, but he complained that whilst he had no objection to being called a beauty he did really object to his wife's being designated a beast![16]

That story, with its engaging flash of egotism, did the rounds. It is with the Beauty that we come to her Beast's father-in-law, Andrew Common.

The Father-in-Law

His stock was farming and Scottish, all Commons claiming descent from the Red Comyn,[17] but this Common left the Lowlands and agriculture for England's north-east and banking in York, Darlington and Sunderland, latterly with the Quaker Backhouses. He worked his way from inspecting their branch banks to opening, managing and then rebuilding their Sunderland branch. His success was undoubted. He was a man to be reckoned with.

That was as clear from his appearance, his shock of red hair and beard whitening with age, as from the range of his interests. He was a lifelong Congregationalist, a lay preacher, a deacon for over thirty years and church treasurer for nearly as long at The Grange Congregational Church, Sunderland. He was a political Dissenter, a vocal opponent of church rates which he 'hated with the perfect hatred of a Nonconformist and a lover of religious fair play'.[18] He was an educationalist and it cannot have been wholly coincidental

16 Charles Herbert Melland, 'Memoirs Part I' (typescript, 1950–1; in possession of the Melland family when I consulted it in 1974), 142–3; for Melland (1872–1953), see *Who Was Who 1951–1960* (London, 1961), 756.

17 For John Comyn (d. 1306), see Alan Young, 'Comyn, Sir John, lord of Badenoch (*d.* 1306)', *ODNB*, online edn (2004), at: <https://doi.org/10.1093/ref:odnb/6046>.

18 'Mr. Andrew Common, JP: His Separation from Sunderland. Biographical Sketch', *Sunderland Daily Echo*, 8 February 1895, 3.

that his church's new school buildings were widely admired for the way they appropriated and improved on 'the American plan of Sunday-schools'.[19] His secular politics were Liberal. In 1865, he chaired the election committee of John Candlish, the Radical who sat for Sunderland from 1866 to 1874.[20] In the 1870s he presided over Sunderland's Liberal Political Union; for rather longer he was a vice-president of one or other of the Liberal organizations which succeeded it; and he was an unfailing presence on Liberal election platforms. It followed that he was a JP and that he was elected to the board of guardians. It also followed that he had married appropriately.

His wife, Ann Kipling, was a Darlington woman, two years her husband's senior. Her family – Kiplings, Teasdales, Middletons and Mellands – were chiefly Methodists, originally Wesleyan but latterly Free Methodist, with a Congregational admixture. In Darlington they were tanners and carpet manufacturers, the sort to serve as guardians or Improvement and Inland Revenue commissioners or to sit on the local board of health. One of them was Darlington's mayor in 1869, two years after his town's incorporation. Their network reached Manchester, where one of them married a future Liberal home secretary and prime minister, H. H. Asquith, although she died the year before he achieved front-bench eminence. In Sunderland the future seemed assured for the next generation of Commons: the banker's iron merchant son, the London solicitor son, the accountant son-in-law and the ship-owning grandson with a war-time knighthood ahead of him.[21]

There was, however, one mortal caveat: health. Andrew Common's health was poor; his wife predeceased him by many years; two sons and a son-in-law died in their thirties; a third son survived into his fifties and then committed suicide. That their world

[19] *CYB* 1882, 408.

[20] For Candlish (1816–74), see Michael Stenton, *Who's Who of British Members of Parliament*, 1: *1832–1885* (Hassocks, 1976), 65.

[21] Ann (Kipling) Common's brother, Edward Kipling (1807–80), was mayor of Darlington in 1869; her great-nephew, Charles Herbert Melland, was the young medical student who called on the Parkers in 1898; his much older half-sister, Helen Melland (1854–91), was H. H. Asquith's first wife; Ann's ship-owning grandson was Sir Lawrence Common (b. 1889), director of the Ship Management Division of the Ministry of War Transport, 1940–6. I have not been able to verify the relationship which the Darlington Kiplings claimed with the Nidderdale Kiplings, also Methodists, of whom Rudyard Kipling was the best-known scion.

was not quite their oyster was evident in Andrew Common's own career.

For all his platform prominence, Andrew Common, quintessential Nonconformist in a strongly Nonconformist town, was a background figure. He was a banker, but as a manager rather than a Backhouse. He never achieved the eminence of the Baptist John Candlish, the Congregational Sir Edward Gourley or the Free Methodist Samuel Storey, each of them a local MP.[22] He was a guardian for only one year, he failed to be elected to Sunderland's school board and his Liberal activism was less seamless than it appeared to be. Were Nonconformity's local differences too hot to handle? Was it his ill-health at critical moments? Or were there quirks of character? It is time to turn to his ministerial son-in-law's memorial assessment.

Commemoration

Joseph Parker was closer in age to his father-in-law than to his wife. The two men shared much in outlook and personality. Parker was not a man who found friendship easy and his wife's family, her siblings all much younger than her husband, met that need. This made it the more natural that her father should move in the last year of his life to be with Joseph and Emma Jane; their Tynehome, in Hampstead, was a north-eastern outpost. There he died, on 14 February 1896. Five days later he was buried in Bishopwearmouth Cemetery, following a service in The Grange Church.[23] A year later, in May 1897, Parker's memoir of Common appeared in the *Evangelical Magazine.*[24]

Its status is unclear. As a memoir it is rounded but relatively brief. Its rhythms are those of the spoken word, crisp, clear and direct. It is not a sermon, for it takes no biblical text. Is it the distillation of what

[22] For Sir Edward Temperley Gourley (1828–1902), see *Who Was Who 1897–1916* (London, 1920), 288; for Samuel Storey (1840–1925), see *Who Was Who 1916–1928* (London, 1929), 1004. For their religious context, see Geoffrey E. Milburn, *Religion in Sunderland in the Mid-Nineteenth Century*, Occasional Paper 3, Department of Geography and History, Sunderland Polytechnic (Sunderland, 1983). I must acknowledge the meticulous help of Patricia J. Storey in navigating Sunderland's political history and in alerting me to the *Sunderland Daily Echo*, of which her forebear was proprietor.

[23] 'Death of Mr. A. Common, J.P.: A Sketch of His Career', *Sunderland Daily Echo*, 14 February 1896, 4.

[24] Parker, 'Common', 17.

was said (perhaps extempore) at the graveside or (perhaps more likely) at the unveiling of the windows which Emma Jane Parker gave to the City Temple in memory of her parents? Whatever its genesis, it is vintage Parker, turbocharged with passion and affection, as expressive of the speaker as it is of his subject.

Its structure flows naturally. First, the necessary details: birth, death, marriage, children, denomination and political affiliation:

> You may know all that, and yet know nothing about the spirit and character of Andrew Common. You may even know that in dignity of carriage, in loveliness of expression, in majestic type of head, he would be noticeable in any assembly of men, and yet you would have no conception of his noble personality. In his very soul Andrew Common was spiritual and heavenly-minded.[25]

First you must confront what 'affected the whole life and thought of the man', his 'fiery enthusiasm':

> ... it extinguished all frivolity, and kept even humour at bay. He made no jokes; he told no stories; he asked no riddles. It was emphatically true ... that he had no 'small talk'. He did not converse, he lectured; he discussed subjects, he did not gossip about individuals. His very food he ate with the impatience of a man who wanted to get on without hindrance with some higher service. When he visited us, I always gave him the work of carving for the whole company, and even then he was done first, and he would look round for his work, his book, his paper ...[26]

That is the cue for Common's next enthusiasm: reading, that essentially solitary passion:

> During the closing years of his life he read, so to say, voraciously, ... He was never so little alone as when alone ... If it is possible to be enthusiastic in silence, Mr. Common would be first in that line. I never knew so silent a man. He could read in his papers about shipwrecks, collisions, explosions, earthquakes, and conflagrations, and never 'let on' that he knew anything about them. As I have said, he lectured, he did not chatter.[27]

[25] Ibid.
[26] Ibid.
[27] Ibid.

He was knowledgeable, he knew where he stood, he was vocal on the platform and in the pulpit, and he was 'popular and efficient' in both: 'With what eager rapidity he spoke! How furiously he carried the war into the enemy's camp! And yet when he preached upon "He was a man of sorrows, and acquainted with grief," or "There remaineth a rest for the people of God," what tenderness!'[28] He was, of course a businessman.

> Through and through his life, the enthusiasm glowed and quivered, in business, ... in all manner of consecrated service ... he was daily in business, yet daily above it ... He made no bargains; he never underbade a tradesman; he never boasted that he got an article worth thirty pounds for little more than thirty shillings. In such transactions he took no delight.[29]

By his own account Parker had been close to Common for thirty-five years; he was well placed to judge the integrated Christian citizenship of his friend and father-in-law. He praised his generosity. Here was a man whose 'mind naturally turned to religion, to politics, to social advancement, to public responsibility, to personal stewardship, and beneficence', who tithed his income, 'often, indeed, he gave away a third', on occasion even a half. 'I never knew so conscientious and so bountiful a giver.'[30] Parker stressed his discretion:

> But surely, as a man of business, he would talk about banking, and discounts, and loans, and exchanges, and new enterprises? Never – literally never – on his own motion. If others inquired, he would answer, but never to my knowledge did he introduce the subject or prolong the conversation. He did not reside on the premises; he lived away on the sunny green hills that sloped up to heaven ... .[31]

And how conscientiously he shouldered the consequences:

> How he was trusted, consulted, waited for! Wherever he went he cleared a space for himself, and walked, as if by right, to the presidency and the casting vote. At one period he did a great deal of book-keeping at home, but it was book-keeping for the church. As the treasurer, he

28 Ibid. 19.
29 Ibid.
30 Ibid.
31 Ibid. 20.

weekly opened hundreds of envelopes, and entered the amounts in the church-books … .[32]

Parker had a gift for introducing the humdrum and the domestic and investing it with spiritual significance. Such things gave credence to his remembrance and to his picturing of mortality, for Andrew Common was mortal: 'I never knew any man suffer so continuously and so distressingly … he would say that for five-and-forty years he had never been wholly free from pain'. Yet there is no death-bed scene in Parker's account, no glimpse or gleam of immortality such as a good death might provide. Parker keeps this side of the veil. It had been enough to recapture a vital humanity that surely could not be extinguished. Hence, perhaps, the significance of a swift last word-picture to bring his old friend and father-in-law home, of the sort to which Victorian preachers, fired by memories of Alpine visits, were irresistibly drawn. It conveyed the Christian hope: 'The yellow hair which adorned the head of his youth expressed the hopefulness of his temperament, and the Jungfrau-like snow that transformed it into the lustre of a Silberhorn signified that his hope in God was unsullied by a stain.'[33]

Postscript – and Envoi?

Almost thirteen years earlier, 9 August 1883, Joseph Parker was in Darlington for the funeral of a Common connection, Robert Teasdale. Teasdale, tanner, bank director, guardian, Inland Revenue commissioner, Liberal and Free Methodist, had been a business partner as well as kinsman of Ann Common's brother, Edward Kipling.[34] The weather fitted the moment. It was 'rather unpropitious, a cold wind blowing, and threatening clouds hanging overhead during the morning'. There was, nonetheless, an 'exceedingly large' attendance and the procession from Westfield, the Teasdale house, to the West Cemetery was impressive. It was headed by Durham County Constabulary's Darlington Division, followed by 'several magistrates', the trustees of two Free Methodist chapels, the mayor and corporation, the town clerk and the local MP. There were five

32 Ibid.
33 Ibid.
34 For Robert Teasdale (1809–83), see Julie Nichol, 'Aspects of Public Health in Darlington' (Undergraduate dissertation, University of Sheffield, 1986), 42.

mourning carriages. Andrew Common was in the second and Joseph Parker was in the fifth, along with three ministers. One was Darlington's Congregational minister, one was the principal of the Free Methodist Theological Institute, and one was Marmaduke Miller, a past minister of Robert Teasdale's Paradise Chapel and long a leading man in Free Methodism.[35]

Miller conducted the service, and asked Parker to speak. Parker had not expected this. He rose, of course, to the occasion. Only ten days earlier he had been a guest at Westfield. Teasdale, whom he had known for nearly twenty years, had been in good spirits: 'The grip of his hand … was strong; his voice had no faltering.' Parker began modestly: 'Yet, even here, I am stopped by a wholesome fear, as if our friend were himself present, for I know how critical he was as to every eulogium that is passed upon human life and conduct. Our friend was so honest in this matter'. But modesty was not really Parker's style and he got into his stride: 'Yet, it is the delight of love to exaggerate. Love cannot be content with bare measure; it says it must be good measure, pressed down, heaped up, running over. So would we now speak of our neighbour, and friend, and Christian brother.'[36] So Parker spoke of him as 'a business man, a reading man, a Christian evangelist, a teacher who gathered around him many young and devoted disciples who loved to hail him as their guide, philosopher, and friend'. Parker's words were striking and appropriate but hardly unexpected:

> The occasion, however, would be lost upon us, would sink into commonplace, if it did not remind every man who is here, the strongest and bravest, that there is but a step between him and death. It is on these occasions that I personally feel the grandeur, the sublimity, the infinite helpfulness of the Divine Word. These are times characterised by a mocking godlessness … but when we look into the out ground and see the blank pit, and feel the great farewell has been spoken, we do instinctively look about us with a serious and anxious inquiry … .[37]

[35] *Northern Echo*, 10 August 1883, 3. The MP was from a local Quaker dynasty: (Sir) Theodore Fry (1836–1912), MP for Darlington 1880–95. Marmaduke Miller (1827–89), who ministered in Darlington from 1862–6, held positions of national responsibility in Free Methodism from 1858–83.

[36] *Northern Echo*, 10 August 1883, 3.

[37] Ibid.

Did these words lift the veil for Parker and his hearers as together they looked into the out ground and the blank pit?

Parker's friendship with Teasdale began, it would seem, at the time of his marriage to Emma Jane Common. Emma Parker died in January 1899, and her husband was inconsolable. His own health began to fail in the autumn of 1901. He dated this from the time of his autumnal chairman's address to the Congregational Union on 15 October; the place was Manchester's Free Trade Hall, and his theme was 'The United Congregational Church'. His illness, he said, was 'a mystery even to his physicians'. Nonetheless, in March 1902, he became president of the National Free Church Council and by September he was sufficiently recovered to resume preaching 'with unabated power'. On 28 September he preached his last sermon.[38] On 28 November, at teatime, he died, cared for by his brother-in-law, Francis Common, the Sunderland iron merchant. Francis was prone to depression and his depression increased after Parker's death. He returned to Sunderland and shot himself on the morning of 10 October 1903.[39]

What conclusions are to be drawn from this? Parker was *sui generis.* That is not to downplay his role in contemporary Congregationalism or his posthumous influence. He was a Free Churchman of national note and was long remembered as such, but he was not to be pigeon-holed. His re-creation of his friend and father-in-law, so particular to their family, was bound to resonate among those with whom he shared it because it was so characteristic of him. It could not be other than a sermon slipping insensibly into eulogy. Even so, the question with which I began hangs in the air. For the Christian death is a passage; for the historian it is a terminus extended by memory; and for the Christian historian? Here more attention might be paid to that word shot like a thunderbolt to stun that audience gathered so worthily in the City Temple to commemorate the Queen's Diamond Jubilee: 'I believe in another King, Our Jesus, whom Paul affirmed to be *alive*.' There was more to that than pulpit pyrotechnics but it was a word for this world and not the next – or was it?

[38] Jones, 'Parker, Joseph (1830–1902)'; Nicoll, *Princes*, 170; *CYB* 1902, 9–10.

[39] *Sunderland Daily Echo*, 12 October, 6; ibid. 13 October 1903, 6. Francis Common (1847–1903) was a trustee and deacon of the Royalty Union Congregational Church, Sunderland, and treasurer of the Parker Memorial Home for Girls, founded in memory of his sister, Emma Jane Parker.

'To our earthly view Dietrich is dead': George Bell's Eulogy for Dietrich Bonhoeffer

Dan D. Cruickshank*
University of Glasgow

This article considers the eulogy given by George Bell, then bishop of Chichester, at the London remembrance service held in July 1945 for Dietrich Bonhoeffer. Bell's eulogy offers a unique form of marking a death. On the one hand he presented a traditional biography of Bonhoeffer, whilst at the same time he depicted Bonhoeffer's life as not over, but as having moved into a stage of glorified martyrdom. The article explores how Bell argued that Bonhoeffer's death offered the potential for life to a post-war Europe, raising issues with van Gennep's understanding of the relationship between the living and a dead person who had had no proper funerary rites. The article thus seeks to explain how Bell marked Bonhoeffer's death by presenting him as a man, a potential assassin and a martyr, in an attempt to secure an eternal earthly legacy for a man Bell believed had offered the world life through his death. The article is followed by an edition of the text of Bell's eulogy in full.

It was a mild summer evening in London when on 27 July 1945 a congregation gathered at Holy Trinity, Kingsway, to mark the death of Dietrich Bonhoeffer.[1] Those in the church were joined by those listening to the service as it was broadcast by the BBC, probably via the European Service.[2] According to Bonhoeffer's biographer

* Theology and Religious Studies, No. 4 The Square, University of Glasgow, G12 8QQ. E-mail: dan.cruickshank@glasgow.ac.uk. This work was supported by the Arts and Humanities Research Council, grant no. AH/R012717.

[1] Weather data obtained from the Met Office, 'DWR_1945_07', online at: <https://digital.nmla.metoffice.gov.uk/io_4e6f2851-384e-4933-8a3b-74560f6d9bdc/>, accessed 14 September 2021.

[2] Bethge recorded that the service was broadcast on the BBC. However, it was not broadcast on the Home Service and is not listed in their programming for the day: see BBC, 'Programme Index', online at: <https://genome.ch.bbc.co.uk/schedules/service_home_service/1945-07-27>, accessed 20 September 2021. The fact that Bonhoeffer's parents

Studies in Church History 59 (2023), 446–470
doi: 10.1017/stc.2023.19

Eberhard Bethge, 'the Church was packed to the doors with English people and German emigrants, theologians, and laypeople, including Bonhoeffer's twin sister and her family'.[3] The service began with the congregation singing 'For all the saints, who from their labours rest' before Bell offered a 'prayer of supplication and thanksgiving'.[4] A sermon was preached on Matthew 10: 17–42, most probably by either Franz Hildebrandt or Julius Rieger, both former associates of Bonhoeffer in the Confessing Church who had moved to England in the 1930s.[5] After the choir from Bonhoeffer's former London congregation had sung *Mir nach, spricht Christus, unser Held*, Bell rose to deliver a eulogy for his friend.[6]

Bell and Bonhoeffer had first become acquainted in Geneva in August 1932 at the meeting of the working committee of the World Alliance for International Friendship through the Churches.[7] Although the ecumenical world had first brought these two men together, it was the time which Bonhoeffer spent in London between 1933 and 1935, as the pastor of two German-speaking congregations, which would cement their friendship.[8] The two would work together to ensure the Confessing Church would have a place in the ecumenical movement, most famously at the Life & Work conference at Fanø, Denmark, in 1934.[9] After Bonhoeffer's return to Germany in 1935, the two men kept in contact as much as they could until war broke out in 1939. During the war they

---

seem to have listened to the service in Berlin suggests it was broadcast on the BBC European Service, for which programming information does not survive. Bonhoeffer was, of course, not that well known a figure within Britain at that time and, as Bethge comments, for the BBC to broadcast a memorial service for a German so soon after hostilities with that country had ended was rather unusual, so for these reasons it seems it was not broadcast in Britain: Eberhard Bethge, *Dietrich Bonhoeffer: A Biography*, transl. Eric Mosbacher et al., rev. edn (Minneapolis, MN, 2000), 930.

[3] Ibid. 930–1.

[4] Sabine Leibholz-Bonhoeffer, *The Bonhoeffers: Portrait of a Family* (London, 1971), 188.

[5] Ibid. For more information on these two men and their time in London see Amos S. Cresswell and Maxwell G. Tow, *Franz Hildebrandt: Mr Valiant-for-Truth* (Leominster, 2000), 84–6.

[6] Leibholz-Bonhoeffer, *The Bonhoeffers*, 188.

[7] Bethge, *Bonhoeffer: A Biography*, 249.

[8] For an account of this time, see ibid. 356–72.

[9] Ibid. 372–92; Andrew Chandler, *George Bell, Bishop of Chichester: Church, State, and Resistance in the Age of Dictatorship* (Grand Rapids, MI, and Cambridge, 2016), 55–6.

would meet only once more, when Bonhoeffer surprised Bell by travelling to meet him during a trip to Stockholm in 1942. This meeting would lead to months of Bell's attempting to persuade the British Government to support Bonhoeffer's resistance circle in Germany, with no success.[10] As the Third Reich collapsed, Bonhoeffer's friends and family waited to hear his fate after the failure of the 20 July 1944 assassination plot, in which they believed he had been closely involved.[11] News of Bonhoeffer's death was slow to emerge, and in Germany the news only reached his friends and family in June and July, with Bonhoeffer's parents receiving confirmation of his death perhaps days before the memorial service.[12] Bell was in New York in May or June 1945 when he received a telegram, probably from the leading ecumenist Willem Visser't Hooft, informing him that Bonhoeffer had been executed in Flossenbürg in April.[13] On his return to Britain, Bell set about organizing a memorial service for his friend.[14]

[10] For an account of this period, see Andrew Chandler, 'The Patronage of Resistance: George Bell and the "Other Germany" during the Second World War', in idem, ed., *The Church and Humanity: The Life and Work of George Bell, 1883–1958* (Farnham, 2012), 89–107, at 98–102. For an account that puts Bell's actions into the wider context of 'peace feelers', see Rainer A. Blasius, 'Waiting for Action: The Debate on the "Other Germany" in Great Britain and the Reaction of the Foreign Office to German "Peace-Feelers", 1942', in Francis R. Nicosia and Lawrence D. Stokes, eds, *Germans Against Nazism: Nonconformity, Opposition and Resistance in the Third Reich. Essays in Honour of Peter Hoffmann*, rev. edn (New York and Oxford, 2015), 279–304.

[11] The 20 July 1944 plot was a failed attempt to assassinate Hitler through a bomb planted at Wolf's Lair. Although the bomb exploded, it failed to injure Hitler seriously, and the plotters' plan to seize control of Berlin in the aftermath likewise failed. Bonhoeffer had links to those who planned the 20 July plot, but was already in prison before it took final form in the autumn of 1943. For more information on the plot, see Richard J. Evans, *The Third Reich at War* (London, 2008), 762–80. In the draft obituary Bell wrote for *The Times*, he claimed that Bonhoeffer was 'deeply involved in the Hitler plot of July 1944'. However, the obituary that appeared in *The Times* had been edited to say that 'he was deeply involved in the early stages of the plot to destroy Hitler, which failed in July, 1944'. The printed version thus better reflected the fact Bonhoeffer had been imprisoned since 5 April 1943. See, respectively, London, LPL, Bell Papers 42, fol. 87, G. K. A. Bell, 'Pastor Dietrich Bonhoeffer: The Bishop of Chichester writes'; idem, 'Pastor D. Bonhoeffer', *The Times*, 25 July 1945, 7.

[12] Bethge, *Bonhoeffer: A Biography*, 930.

[13] Leibholz-Bonhoeffer includes in her account a transcript of the letter of condolence she received from Bell upon his return to Chichester; in this he mentions receiving the telegram but does not say from whom. Bethge states that Visser't Hooft informed Bell and Leibholz-Bonhoeffer of Bonhoeffer's death by telegram on 30 May 1945, but Leibholz-Bonhoeffer recounts that it was in fact Julius Rieger who informed her of the news: Leibholz-Bonhoeffer, *The Bonhoeffers*, 186; Bethge, *Bonhoeffer: A Biography*, 930.

[14] Leibholz-Bonhoeffer, *The Bonhoeffers*, 187.

The memorial service for Bonhoeffer, and in particular Bell's eulogy at the service, can be seen as a rite of passage. They marked, for those in Britain, the death of Bonhoeffer, and, as this article will explore, Bell's eulogy attempted to define the transition Bonhoeffer had undergone by dying. Bell's eulogy has formed a staple part of Bonhoeffer biographies since Bethge published his landmark account of the life of his friend in 1967.[15] Bethge had in fact first published the memorial service as a small pamphlet, including Bell's eulogy, in 1947.[16] In his biography of Bonhoeffer, Bethge included only a small section of Bell's eulogy, and it is this section, or extracts from it, which is found in the majority of Bonhoeffer biographies that mention the eulogy.[17] For a recent example, Ferdinand Schlingensiepen's biography of Bonhoeffer quotes from Bethge's work when discussing the eulogy.[18] However another independent source for the eulogy also exists. This is found in perhaps the most infamous recent biography of Bonhoeffer, that by Eric Metaxas.[19] Metaxas's source for

[15] Eberhard Bethge, *Dietrich Bonhoeffer: Theologe, Christ, Zeitgenosse. Eine Biographie* (Munich, 1967).

[16] G. K. A. Bell, *Bonhoeffer Gedenkheft*, ed. Eberhard Bethge (Berlin, 1947).

[17] Bethge, *Bonhoeffer: Theologe, Christ, Zeitgenosse*, 1041–2. The extract, which was reproduced by Bethge in English, reads: 'His death is a death for Germany – indeed for Europe too. … his death, like his life, marks a fact of the deepest value in the witness of the Confessional Church. As one of a noble company of martyrs of differing traditions, he represents both the resistance of the believing soul, in the name of God, to the assault of evil, and also the moral and political revolt of the human conscience against injustice and cruelty. He and his fellows are indeed built upon the foundation of the Apostles and the Prophets. And it was this passion for justice that brought him, and so many others …, into such close partnership with other resisters who, though outside the Church, shared the same humanitarian and liberal ideals. … For him and Klaus … there is the resurrection from the dead: for Germany redemption and resurrection, if God pleases to lead the nation through men animated by his spirit, holy and humble and brave like him: for the Church, not only in that Germany which he loved, but also the Church Universal, which was greater to him than nations, the hope of a new life.' These excerpts are identical with the text of the eulogy found in the Bell papers (London, LPL, Bell Papers 42, fols 81–3; see also the appendix to this article).

[18] Ferdinand Schlingensiepen, *Dietrich Bonhoeffer, 1906–1945: Martyr, Thinker, Man of Resistance*, transl. Isabel Best (London and New York, 2012), 380–1.

[19] Metaxas mistakenly has the service taking place not at Holy Trinity, Kingsway, but at the now much more famous Holy Trinity, Brompton: Eric Metaxas, *Bonhoeffer: Pastor, Martyr, Prophet, Spy. A Righteous Gentile vs. the Third Reich* (Nashville, TN, 2012), 537. His biography has been criticized from many angles. Victoria J. Barnett in her review highlighted Metaxas's 'very shaky grasp of the political, theological, and ecumenical history of the period' and found that 'the book is a polemic, written to make the case that Bonhoeffer was in reality an evangelical Christian'. Clifford Green places the biography in the context

the eulogy is Bonhoeffer's twin sister Sabine Leibholz-Bonhoeffer, specifically her book on the Bonhoeffer family. However, the eulogy presented by Leibholz-Bonhoeffer is completely different to that presented by Bethge. Leibholz-Bonhoeffer included the following excerpt from Bell's eulogy:

> He was quite clear in his convictions, and for all that he was so young and unassuming, he saw the truth and he spoke it out with absolute freedom and without fear. When he came to me all unexpectedly in 1942 at Stockholm as the emissary of the Resistance to Hitler, he was, as always, absolutely open and quite untroubled about his own person, his safety. Wherever he went and whoever he spoke with – whether young or old – he was fearless, regardless of himself and, with it all, devoted heart and soul to his parents, his friends, his country as God willed it to be, to his Church and to his Master.[20]

As Leibholz-Bonhoeffer provided neither references nor a bibliography, it is impossible to know the source of this text, or whether,

---

of Metaxas's political views and those of right-wing American Evangelicals in the Obama era. Stephen R. Haynes in 2019 examined Metaxas's use of Bonhoeffer in support for his political causes, and as a justification of why Christians 'must' vote for Donald Trump in 2016. Metaxas's use of Bonhoeffer for his support of Trump increased after the 2020 election. In an interview with *The Atlantic* in February 2021, when asked about his comments in a November 2020 podcast when talking to Donald Trump that he would 'die' in support of Trump's claims that the 2020 presidential election had been the victim of widespread fraud, Metaxas replied, 'When you believe liberty is being threatened; when you believe elections are being threatened; when you believe that any of these things are being threatened—people have died for these things. When you say something like that, what you're saying is: I would, like Dietrich Bonhoeffer … stand up for what I think is right and true. I am not just going to go with the crowd.' See, respectively, Victoria J. Barnett, 'Review of Eric Metaxas, Bonhoeffer: Pastor, Martyr, Prophet, Spy: A Righteous Gentile vs. the Third Reich', 1 September 2010, *ACCH Quarterly* 15 (2010) [online journal], at: <https://contemporarychurchhistory.org/2010/09/review-of-eric-metaxas-bonhoeffer-pastor-martyr-prophet-spy-a-righteous-gentile-vs-the-third-reich/>, accessed 22 September 2021; Clifford Green, 'Hijacking Bonhoeffer', *Christian Century*, 4 October 2010, online at: <https://www.christiancentury.org/reviews/2010-09/hijacking-bonhoeffer>, accessed 22 September 2021; Stephen R. Haynes, 'Readings and Receptions', in Philip G. Ziegler and Michael Mawson, eds, *The Oxford Handbook of Dietrich Bonhoeffer* (Oxford, 2019), 472–85, at 478–82; Emma Green, 'Eric Metaxas believes America is creeping toward Nazi Germany', *The Atlantic*, 21 April 2021, online at: <https://www.theatlantic.com/politics/archive/2021/02/eric-metaxas-2020-election-trump/617999/>, accessed 22 September 2021.

[20] Leibholz-Bonhoeffer, *The Bonhoeffers*, 188–9.

having attended the service in person, she was simply writing from memory.[21]

A third source also exists: the Bell papers include a copy of the eulogy as prepared by Bell. The Bethge extracts from the eulogy appear in this text, whereas the text quoted by Leibholz-Bonhoeffer does not. It seems clear that Leibholz-Bonhoeffer was not using either a copy of Bell's eulogy as written or the published version prepared by Bethge and quoted within his biography. However, Leibholz-Bonhoeffer was present at the service, and although her quotations from the eulogy do not align with the source material we have, her other recollections of the contents do. Apart from the 'quoted' section of text, Leibholz-Bonhoeffer wrote that in the eulogy Bell 'also paid tribute to the memory of our brother Klaus and our brothers-in-law, Rüdiger Schleicher and Hans von Dohnanyi, whose fate had been revealed to us only at a later stage'.[22] All three were indeed mentioned in the eulogy that exists in the Bell Papers, suggesting that there were definitely intersections between the eulogy Leibholz-Bonhoeffer remembered hearing and this written text.[23] It is possible that Leibholz-Bonhoeffer conflated what was said in the sermon and what was said by Bell in the eulogy. As biographers of Bonhoeffer have relied on these earlier biographies, two distinct and to some extent contradictory versions of the eulogy have been passed on. Returning to the archival source material, and the original eulogy as found in Bell's papers, indicates that it is the more widespread tradition, sourced from the Bethge material, that aligns with the eulogy as originally drafted by Bell.

Bell's eulogy has struggled to find a place within studies of Bell himself. In Ronald Jasper's biography of Bell, neither the eulogy nor the memorial service for Bonhoeffer is mentioned.[24] Peter Raina, whilst recognizing that Bonhoeffer's death inspired much of Bell's enthusiasm for reconstruction in post-war Europe, also does not mention either the memorial service or Bell's eulogy, despite the eulogy's being perhaps Bell's clearest exposition of how

[21] Ibid.
[22] Ibid. 189.
[23] LPL, Bell Papers 42, fols 78–83, G. K. A. Bell, 'Pastor Dietrich Bonhoeffer: Holy Trinity Church, Kingsway: July 27th, 1945', at fol. 81. For an edition of this text, see the appendix to this article.
[24] Ronald C. D. Jasper, *George Bell: Bishop of Chichester* (London, 1967).

Bonhoeffer's death should inspire a post-war Europe.[25] Andrew Chandler quoted a brief section of the eulogy as found in the Bell Papers in his biography of Bell, also pointing the reader to where it could be read in full.[26] Building on Chandler's invitation, this article will offer a closer reading of the eulogy to examine how Bell envisaged the importance of Bonhoeffer's life and death in almost immediate response to the news of his death.

As Bell began his eulogy, there could be no doubt about his views on Bonhoeffer: 'In this church, hallowed by many memories of Christian fellowship in wartime, we gather now in memory of Dietrich Bonhoeffer, our most dear brother and a martyr of the Church.'[27] Straight away Bell was explicitly calling Bonhoeffer 'a martyr of the Church'. This was to be a most unusual eulogy. Lucy Bregman has presented a comprehensive overview of Protestant funeral sermons in the United States of America from the nineteenth century until the present day.[28] Although Bregman's work is the most extensive overview of funeral sermons in the twentieth century, Bell's eulogy does not fit neatly into any of the trends identified by Bregman, who argued that sermons developed from being mainly concerned with convincing mourners to come to Christ in the face of death and the hope of eternal life, to the more modern form of using biography and anecdotes related to the deceased to comfort the bereaved.[29] This suggests either that those trends were predominantly American, or that Bell's eulogy demonstrated unique characteristics.

The eulogy can be understood as consisting of two main sections: in the first, Bell presented a biography of Bonhoeffer, followed by a second in which Bell presented a meditation on the meaning of Bonhoeffer's death to the world he had seemingly left.[30] We should not see these sections as completely distinct: rather the biographical

[25] Peter Raina, *Bishop George Bell, the Greatest Churchman: A Portrait in Letters* (London, 2006), 284–7.

[26] Chandler, *George Bell*, 126–7.

[27] Bell, 'Pastor Dietrich Bonhoeffer', fol. 78.

[28] Lucy Bregman, *Preaching Death: The Transformation of Christian Funeral Sermons* (Waco, TX, 2011).

[29] Ibid., especially 17–182.

[30] For a brief overview of the biographical nature of eulogies, as opposed to other forms of funeral oration, and their basis in ancient Greek oratory, see John Allyn Melloch, 'Homily or Eulogy? The Dilemma of Funeral Preaching', in David Day, Jeff Astley and Leslie J. Francis, eds, *A Reader on Preaching: Making Connections* (London and New York, 2016), 204–7, at 206–7.

material served the claims Bell would make in the second section about the implications of Bonhoeffer's death. Evidence of this is that Bell did not wait until after the biographical section to call Bonhoeffer a martyr; he made the claim in his first sentence. Bregman, surveying mainly American preacher's handbooks from the first half of the twentieth century, noted that they discouraged a focus on biographical information when preaching at the funerals of clergymen.[31] The fact that Bell did focus on Bonhoeffer's biography in his eulogy might further suggest the uniqueness of this eulogy. There is a sense in which the biography of Bonhoeffer served in the eulogy as hagiography. It did so not in the pejorative sense of the word as often employed today, but rather in a more literal sense. Bell, through his biography of Bonhoeffer, would demonstrate not only that Bonhoeffer was a martyr, but also that his whole life had been a path towards martyrdom. Petra Brown places Bell's eulogy as the first in a line of statements and claims within 'the English-speaking world' about Bonhoeffer as a martyr.[32] As Brown underscores, this claim was not made in the decades after his death, but only 'three months after Dietrich Bonhoeffer was killed on charges of conspiracy against the state'.[33] Even more startlingly, it was merely weeks after Bell had discovered that Bonhoeffer was dead.

Bell began the biographical section of the eulogy by stressing that Bonhoeffer had been born 'to a family which claimed not a few eminent divines, judges, and artists in its ranks in previous generations'. This, then, was a family at the apex of German culture, providing Bonhoeffer the opportunity to accomplish great things within that realm; as Bell pointed out, 'Dietrich himself achieved distinction in his own field of theology as a young man.'[34] Within the first two paragraphs, Bell placed the listener on first-name terms with Bonhoeffer. Undoubtedly there would have been many in the congregation at Holy Trinity, Kingsway who would have known Bonhoeffer personally. However, since the BBC was broadcasting the service, they would also be joined by potentially thousands who had never met him. In his obituary for *The Times*, Bell had only referred to

[31] Lucy Bregman, 'Funeral for a Homeless Vagrant? Religious and Social Margins', *Religions* 12 (2021), 1–10, at 2.
[32] Petra Brown, *Bonhoeffer: God's Conspirator in a State of Exception* (Cham, 2019), 2.
[33] Ibid. 2.
[34] Bell, 'Pastor Dietrich Bonhoeffer', fol. 78.

Bonhoeffer by his last name or as 'Pastor Bonhoeffer'.[35] Now, in his eulogy, Bell was suggesting that through his death, those who had not known him in life could truly know who this Dietrich was, and approach him on first-name terms. Bell would return to the idea of Bonhoeffer's privileged lineage, explaining how Bonhoeffer, like his ancestors, could have claimed a place in the upper echelons of German culture. 'There was no doubt,' Bell claimed, 'humanly speaking, of the high position which would have been justly his in the realm of theological scholarship and teaching had God willed that his qualities should be thus used.'[36] Bell was suggesting here that God had called Bonhoeffer to higher things, beyond the human heights of a permanent academic post and a scholarly reputation. Bonhoeffer also 'loved life' and was a 'man in whose company, because of his charm, his humour, his character and his gifts it was a delight to be', yet these things were mere background to Bell's biography.[37] Bonhoeffer had a deep love of life, yet Bell was presenting a biography of a man whose life had found purpose in death.

Against this background and that of Bonhoeffer's path to human greatness, Bell presented the ascension of Adolf Hitler to the chancellorship of Germany as the great interruption: Bonhoeffer 'was not quite 27 on January 30th, 1933, when one whom history will surely judge as the source of Germany's greatest shame and ruin became Chancellor of the Reich. But it was that event which was to determine the course of the rest of Dietrich's life.'[38] In the structure of the eulogy it is at this point that Bonhoeffer's life seems to really begin and to take meaning. 'Young as he was', Bell claimed, Bonhoeffer 'immediately and instinctively perceived the significance of the National Socialist revolution.'[39] Nothing in Bell's previous exposition of Bonhoeffer's upbringing provided an explanation of Bonhoeffer's immediate understanding of the 'significance of the National Socialist revolution'.[40] Bell had so far shown his audience a young man, from a respected and cultured family, who seemed to be finding a place for

[35] G. K. A. Bell, 'Pastor Dietrich Bonhoeffer: The Bishop of Chichester writes', London, LPL, Bell Papers 42, fols 87–9; idem, 'Pastor D. Bonhoeffer', *The Times*, 25 July 1945, 7.
[36] Bell, 'Pastor Dietrich Bonhoeffer', fol. 78.
[37] Ibid., fols 87–9.
[38] Ibid., fol. 79.
[39] Ibid.
[40] Ibid.

himself in the world of theological academia. Now he presented a man who had immediately understood the crisis facing Germany. Bell claimed that this was because Bonhoeffer recognized the importance of National Socialism's 'annihilation of all human rights, and its repudiation of God'.[41] Bonhoeffer 'understood as few others understood that the attack on the Jews was an attack on Christ, as well as an attack on man'.[42] However, and intriguingly, Bell's retrospective presentation of Bonhoeffer's views in 1933 from the point of view of 1945 does not align with Bell's own attitudes in that same period. The question of National Socialism's religious views, and to what extent it was anti-Christian, had exercised some English Christians from the beginning of the regime, but Bell was a later convert to the view he attributed to Bonhoeffer.[43] In fact, Bell initially engaged with the National Socialist regime as a Christian regime that was being led astray by a fringe extreme of pagans.[44] Likewise, for much of the pre-war period Bell's defence of Jews against attacks and discrimination was focused almost exclusively on the plight of 'Non-Aryan Christians', that is Christians whom the National Socialist regime deemed to have Jewish heritage. Bell took the view that Jews would care for Jews, and the concern for non-German Christians should be helping non-Aryan Christians.[45] Bell himself, then, had at the time not 'understood as few others understood that the attack on the Jews was an attack on Christ'.[46] Consciously or not, Bell presented Bonhoeffer as a corrective to Bell's own pre-war understanding; a martyr who understood from the beginning the true nature of the regime in a way that Bell himself only came to understand as the regime developed or perhaps even after it had collapsed.

Bell depicted Bonhoeffer's part in opposing the policies and goals of the National Socialist authorities as part of a much larger struggle. In the context of the Third Reich Bonhoeffer had sought how he

41 Ibid.
42 Ibid.
43 See Dan D. Cruickshank, 'The Church of England and The Third Reich: A Case Study in Church-State Relations' (PhD thesis, University of Glasgow, forthcoming).
44 See Cruickshank, 'The Church of England and The Third Reich'; compare also Andrew Chandler, 'The Church of England and Nazi Germany' (PhD thesis, University of Cambridge, 1990), 25–31; Daphne Hampson 'The British Response to the German Church Struggle, 1933–1939' (DPhil thesis, University of Oxford, 1973), 23, 30, 47–55.
45 See Cruickshank, 'The Church of England and The Third Reich'.
46 Bell, 'Pastor Dietrich Bonhoeffer', fol. 79.

'could best serve God and the Church in the fight against Hitler'.[47] The fight against Hitler was not a mere political fight; rather Bonhoeffer sought to comprehend 'how he could save Germany's soul from the demons which were assailing it on every side'.[48] Bell thus portrayed the Third Reich not only as an arena of political struggle, but as the latest battlefield in the cosmic struggle between the forces of God and those of Satan. For Bell, Bonhoeffer had clearly positioned himself on the side of God and sought how better to overcome the enemies of God, as personified by Hitler and his regime. However, Bell had to acknowledge that Bonhoeffer had left Germany at the end of 1933 and spent two years in London. How could a man who had recognized so early on the dangers National Socialism posed to Germany have left the country at its hour of need? Bell passed over this period in a sentence, saying that during this time, whilst Bonhoeffer was 'endearing himself to his two German congregations', he also 'saw much of British friends, and helped them at least to begin to see the inwardness of the German Church struggle'.[49] Bell seems here to be smoothing out the trajectory of Bonhoeffer's life, so that it was all in service of Bonhoeffer's final witness in death. Bonhoeffer's sojourn in London did not fit easily into that narrative, but Bell was able to emphasize this period as a time when Bonhoeffer brought the *Kirchenkampf* to international attention. This is not to suggest that Bonhoeffer did not indeed do such work in this period, but rather to highlight that it was not the sole or even primary focus of his ministry in London; he was there as a pastor to two congregations, not as a link between English Christians and the German churches.[50] This latter aspect, however, was the aspect of his life in London that best aligned with Bell's narrative of a life that led inevitably to martyrdom, and it was the part of Bonhoeffer's life in London that had most affected Bell himself, and this is probably why it was the aspect Bell emphasized.

On Bonhoeffer's return to Germany, he began 'playing an active, militant part in the opposition to Hitler, and in the resistance to the barbarities of his regime'.[51] This activity, Bell noted, continued until

[47] Ibid.
[48] Ibid.
[49] Ibid.
[50] For more information on Bonhoeffer's time in London, see Bethge, *Bonhoeffer: A Biography*, 328–34.
[51] Bell, 'Pastor Dietrich Bonhoeffer', fol. 79.

the outbreak of war through Bonhoeffer's principalship of 'an illegal Confessional Church Training College in Pomerania', which was 'interspersed with visits to America and England'.[52] Throughout this period he was also 'giving aid and direction to the pastors within the Confessional Church'.[53] Bell thus placed Bonhoeffer at the heart of the Confessing Church, training its pastors, while also providing it with international links in the English-speaking world. This Bonhoeffer was a man of action, working in practical ways to oppose the National Socialist regime.

Bell was clear that Bonhoeffer 'hated war'. He recalled his 'last memory but one of Dietrich': 'a long talk at Chichester in the summer of 1939, when he was convinced that war was inevitable, on what his own duty should be if called up'.[54] Bell particularly remembered 'the horror with which [Dietrich's] conscience rejected any service under Hitler'. Fortunately, 'he was in fact spared the ordeal of serving in the army; and devoted his whole strength to his work for the Confessional Church, and to aiding the underground political opposition planning the overthrow of the Fuehrer'. Whilst not completely clear about what this involvement had entailed, Bell was aware that Bonhoeffer, during the war, was not solely involved in church opposition, but had involved himself in resistance groups actively working to overthrow Hitler. Bell was more confident about what had been involved in Bonhoeffer's work in the Confessing Church during the war, of how his seminary was dissolved in 1940 and his 'travels through the country, visiting parishes for the Confessional Church'.[55] Then Bonhoeffer 'at the end of 1940 … was prohibited by the Gestapo from preaching and speaking'.[56] In light of this prohibition, Bell highlighted that Bonhoeffer became 'engaged on his book on Christian ethics, and in preparing memoranda for the brethren's councils'.[57] Bell was also not entirely certain how Bonhoeffer managed to be practically involved both in political and ecclesiastical opposition during the war, merely saying that he gave 'his evenings to political activities'.[58] Bell seems to have been quite astounded at

52 Ibid.
53 Ibid.
54 Ibid., fols 79–80.
55 Ibid.
56 Ibid.
57 Ibid.
58 Ibid.

how active Bonhoeffer was and how he managed to fit so much work into the time given him. The uncertainty on Bell's part of what Bonhoeffer's resistance work had entailed should not be seen as obfuscation about what resistance meant, but as genuine lack of knowledge of what it had actually entailed, understandable at this point of time, just months after the collapse of the Third Reich.

Bell's knowledge of Bonhoeffer's work amongst resistance circles was only really clear when it had involved Bell himself. In his eulogy, Bell recalled their last meeting: Bonhoeffer's surprise appearance in Sigtuna, Sweden, in 1942 while Bell was visiting on behalf of the Ministry of Information to help build stronger links with the Swedish churches.[59] Bonhoeffer had travelled to Sweden, Bell emphasized, 'at risk of his life, to give me information of the utmost importance about the movement of the opposition in Germany, to eliminate Hitler and all his chief colleagues, and to set up a new government which should repeal the Nuremberg Laws, undo Hitler's deeds so far as they could be undone, and seek peace with the Allies'.[60] Bell had been impressed by Bonhoeffer and the plans of his resistance circles, and had attempted without success to get the British government to support those circles.[61] Bell did not mention these attempts in the eulogy, perhaps sensitive to revealing such information so soon after the end of the war. However, whether the resistance circles in which Bonhoeffer was involved were as determined as Bell suggested in his eulogy to do away completely with the National Socialist regime, and specifically its anti-Semitism, is debatable.[62] Bell's portrayal of Bonhoeffer and the resistance circles in which he was involved fits into a common theme for Bell during the war, that of the 'other Germany'. Chandler has written of how during the war Bell became a 'patron' of resistance circles in Germany, bringing them to the attention of the British government and in some ways

[59] The Ministry of Information was attempting to help thaw relations between the British and Swedish governments. For an account of Bell's three-week mission to Sweden to help reinvigorate links between the Church of England and the Church of Sweden, see Jasper, *George Bell*, 266–9.

[60] Bell, 'Pastor Dietrich Bonhoeffer', fol. 80.

[61] For an account of this, see Chandler, 'Patronage of Resistance', 98–102.

[62] Whilst some in the resistance circles linked to the 20 July Plot felt the genocide of the European Jews led them to resistance, others were involved in the genocide, and the plans drawn up for the reconstruction of Germany after the assassination involved anti-Semitic elements: Evans, *Third Reich at War*, 766–7.

that of the public also.[63] In doing so, Bell 'stepped out from the centre of a powerful national consensus and into a difficult and even dangerous fringe'.[64] In all this work he was inspired by the image of 'another Germany': one with citizens who saw German ideals and culture as in conflict with National Socialism, and struggled to rid themselves of their National Socialist rulers. It was this Germany that Bell believed to be the majority, with the National Socialist regime a minority that had forced its rule upon the other.[65] After the war, as Tom Lawson has shown, this view would lead to Bell's opposition to war trials, and to his interventions on behalf of those involved in war crimes and the Holocaust, as he was unable – or unwilling – to conceive that anyone apart from the elite leadership of the National Socialists had been involved in these atrocities.[66] In the eulogy, we see Bell halfway between these positions. Bonhoeffer was presented as part of this 'other Germany', taking concrete action to overthrow National Socialism, part of a wider group of people willing to risk their lives to do so. However, Bell was not yet linking people like Bonhoeffer with figures such as Eberhard von Mackensen, one of the perpetrators of the Ardeatine massacre, on whose behalf Bell would later intercede during von Mackensen's trial for war crimes.[67] There was at this stage still a distinction in Bell's mind between those who had clearly been involved in attempts to overthrow National Socialism, and those who after its downfall would plead unease with the actions they had undertaken. The 'other Germany' of which Bell positioned Bonhoeffer as part in his eulogy was still that which Bell had envisioned during the war.

Although Bonhoeffer was 'deeply committed … to the plan for elimination, he was not altogether at ease as a Christian about such a solution'.[68] Bell was aware from their meeting in 1942 that the resistance circles in which Bonhoeffer was involved were planning the assassination of Hitler. The eulogy reveals also that at that meeting Bell had learned something of Bonhoeffer's inner life and his

[63] Chandler, 'Patronage of Resistance', 89–107.
[64] Ibid. 107.
[65] Tom Lawson, 'Bishop Bell and the Trial of German War Criminals: A Moral History', in Andrew Chandler, ed., *The Church and Humanity: The Life and Work of George Bell, 1883–1958* (Farnham and Burlington, VT, 2012), 129–48, at 134.
[66] Ibid.
[67] Ibid. 135–8.
[68] Bell, 'Pastor Dietrich Bonhoeffer', fols 80–1.

theological wrestling with the issue of tyrannicide.[69] In his eulogy Bell repeated Bonhoeffer's explanation to him from 1942 of how he could reconcile his Christian ethics with his involvement in an assassination plot. '"There must be punishment by God," he said. "We do not want to escape repentance." The elimination itself, he urged, must be understood as an act of repentance. "Oh we have to be punished. Christians do not wish to escape repentance or chaos, if God wills to bring it on us. We must endure this judgement as Christians."'[70] Using Bonhoeffer's own words, Bell related Bonhoeffer to the national story of Germany. This was a nation that had sinned before God by allowing Hitler and National Socialism to rise to power, and now the nation was being judged and needed to repent of this sin. For Bonhoeffer, and apparently also for Bell, this repentance started with the killing of Hitler. Bell did not comment on how Germany was to repent now that Hitler was dead by his own hand and the Third Reich had collapsed. This claim of a need for repentance also causes problems for our understanding of Bell's view of the 'other Germany', for why did the 'other Germany' need to repent of the acts of the National Socialist Germany? The simplest explanation would be that all had Germany had, in some way, shared in the guilt of the evil committed by National Socialism. Bell's actions after the war, however, and his interventions on behalf of those who had committed war crimes and been involved in the Holocaust, do not fit with this reading. Again, then, Bell's eulogy for Bonhoeffer seems to show Bell at a liminal stage, somewhere between his wartime thoughts and his post-war thoughts. At this time he envisioned a need for national repentance, even if he was not entirely clear about what that entailed.

The biographical section of Bell's eulogy ended with a brief summary of Bonhoeffer's final years, his arrest and his death. Bell said Bonhoeffer was tried in 'the People's court … for his share in the events of July 20th, 1944', which was the official reason given at Bonhoeffer's trial.[71] However, this is inaccurate; Bell was understandably still quite confused about the events surrounding Bonhoeffer's death at this point, just over a month after he had learned of it. In fact, Dietrich Bonhoeffer was never tried in the People's Court,

[69] For an overview of Bonhoeffer's theological wrestling with tyrannicide, see Larry L. Rasmussen, *Dietrich Bonhoeffer: Reality and Resistance* (Louisville, KY, 2005), 127–48.
[70] Bell, 'Pastor Dietrich Bonhoeffer', fol. 81.
[71] Ibid.

although his brother Klaus was.[72] Bell said in his eulogy that 'through the death of the judge in an air raid the sentence could not be carried out', a reference to the death of the judge president of the court, Roland Freisler, in an American air raid on 3 February 1945.[73] However, Friesler's death had no effect on Bonhoeffer, as he was never brought before the People's Court; instead he was tried by an SS court at Flossenbürg on 8 April 1945, the day before his execution.[74] Where Bell's account again meets the historical narrative is in his presentation of Bonhoeffer's death: 'Dietrich and Klaus were both murdered in Flossenburg Concentration camp only a few days before the Americans came to liberate the prisoners.'[75]

'And now Dietrich is gone.'[76] With these words Bell began his meditation on Bonhoeffer's death. 'He died, with his brother, as a hostage.'[77] This was definitive. Bonhoeffer was dead; he was no longer amongst the living. So far this seemed a standard rite of passage, marking Bonhoeffer's passing from the community of the living to the community of the dead, and having the community of the living recognize this. But Bell quickly troubled this simple understanding: 'Our debt to them, and to all others similarly murdered, is immense.'[78] Now he claimed that the living owed something of their existence to the dead person, but he would go further than this vague claim. 'His death is a death for Germany – indeed for Europe too.'[79] Bell, who had already linked Bonhoeffer's life to the national story of Germany, thus connected his death not only to Germany, but to the wider continent. Bell argued that Bonhoeffer was conscious of his role in the German national story, for 'he made the sacrifice of human prospects, of home, friends, and career because he believed in God's vocation for his country, and refused to follow those false leaders, who were the servants of the devil'.[80] Bonhoeffer, in Bell's view, had freely given up all he could have attained in the world to fight against the powers of evil which had

[72] Bethge, *Bonhoeffer: A Biography*, 914.
[73] Bell, 'Pastor Dietrich Bonhoffer', fol. 81; see also Nikolaus Wachsmann, *Hitler's Prisons: Legal Terror in Nazi Germany* (New Haven, CT, and London, 2004), 321.
[74] Bethge, *Bonhoeffer: A Biography*, 927.
[75] Bell, 'Pastor Dietrich Bonhoeffer', fol. 81.
[76] Ibid.
[77] Ibid.
[78] Ibid.
[79] Ibid., fols 81–2.
[80] Ibid., fol. 82.

overtaken Germany. Bell also believed that Bonhoeffer saw a 'vocation' for Germany, given by God, to which it was failing to attain. Bonhoeffer in this 'was inspired by his faith in the living God, and by his devotion to truth and honour. In this way Bonhoeffer's death, like his life, marks a fact of the deepest value in the witness of the Confessional Church.'[81] Bell here offered perhaps the first image of Bonhoeffer as the ultimate personification of the Confessing Church, a view that lingers to the present day.

It was now that Bell tried to explain how Bonhoeffer's death served those still living. Firstly, it gave support to the Confessing Church and its opposition to the regime's ecclesiastical policies.[82] Bell then went once again beyond the vague and into the bold. 'As one of a noble company of martyrs of differing traditions, he represents both the resistance of the believing soul, in the name of God, to the assault of evil, and also the moral and political revolt of the human conscience against injustice and cruelty.'[83] Bell's use of the present tense – Bonhoeffer 'represents', rather than 'represented' – seems to have been a conscious choice to emphasize the message of the eulogy. Though dead, he was still active, and still stood as a witness to the will of God against the powers of hell. In his actions, Bell argued, Bonhoeffer 'built upon the foundation of the Apostles and Prophets'.[84] Bonhoeffer's struggle against National Socialism, and his involvement in the plot to assassinate Hitler, had thus represented a biblical Christianity, showing the judgment of God against National Socialist Germany as God had shown through the prophets his judgment on Judah and Israel. 'It was this passion for justice,' which, Bell argued, was the same passion which had fuelled the prophets and apostles, 'that brought him, and so many others in the Confessional Church who were in agreement with him, into such close partnership with other resisters who, though outside the Church, shared the same humanitarian and liberal ideals.'[85] Although others involved in the plot to assassinate Hitler had not been within the fold of the church, Bell believed that Bonhoeffer, and those who likewise joined it from the Confessing Church, had been able to link their sacred cause with those who agreed with the

81 Ibid.
82 Ibid.
83 Ibid.
84 Ibid.
85 Ibid.

principle of assassinating Hitler, bringing all involved in the political struggle into the wider, and for Bell more important, religious struggle. Bell was sacralizing the history of the resistance movements within the Third Reich, demonstrating how, knowingly or unknowingly, they had been following the will of God.

Bell ended his eulogy with his boldest claims, suggesting that Bonhoeffer's death was part of the power of God to bring about new life. 'Our Lord said, "Except a corn of wheat fall into the ground and die, it abideth alone; but if it die, it bringeth forth much fruit. He that loveth his life shall lose it, and he that hateth his life in this world shall keep it unto life eternal."'[86] Bell had initially painted Bonhoeffer as a man who loved life, and yet he had now lost it; Bell had then added to that picture an image of a man at odds with the life of Germany as it existed in his time. Bell was here arguing that this tension could only be resolved by Bonhoeffer's death. Once again, Bell reiterated Bonhoeffer's mortality, for 'to our earthly view Dietrich is dead'.[87] Yet this was not the finality it seemed to be. It was, after all, only in our 'earthly view' that he was dead.[88] 'Deep and unfathomable as our sorrow seems, let us comfort one another with these words. For him and Klaus, and for the countless multitudes of their fellow victims through these terrible years of war, there is resurrection from the dead.'[89] This resurrection was not limited to the human dead, though; there was also the possibility 'for Germany [of] redemption and resurrection'.[90] This possibility was for Bell tied up with the death of Bonhoeffer, for the resurrection of Germany could only happen 'if God pleases to lead the nation through men animated by his [Bonhoeffer's] spirit, holy and humble and brave like him'.[91] As Bell had already intimated, Bonhoeffer's death gave wider hope outside Germany, offering the possibility of 'redemption and resurrection' 'for the church, not only in that Germany which he loved, but also the Church Universal, which was greater to him than nations, the hope of a new life'.[92] If the wider church could be animated by the spirit of Bonhoeffer, it

[86] Ibid.
[87] Ibid.
[88] Ibid.
[89] Ibid., fols 82–3.
[90] Ibid., fol. 83.
[91] Ibid.
[92] Ibid.

could manifest 'the hope of a new life' which Bonhoeffer had seen in it.[93] In death, then, Bell saw Bonhoeffer calling Germany, its church, and the church universal to greater and greater things, moving closer and closer to the 'Living God' who had so animated him. In his death, then, was life, and the potential for new life throughout the world. By dying in opposition to National Socialism, Bonhoeffer offered those left behind the chance to build a new world that would also stand as the opposite of the ideals of National Socialism.

Bell ended his eulogy by quoting Tertullian, telling those listening in Holy Trinity, Kingsway, and over the wireless that 'the blood of the martyrs is the seed of the Church'.[94] Bonhoeffer had imitated his Lord, following his call even unto death, and his blood shed could provide water for new life across the world. This was no typical rite of passage, for the man who had died was one who was giving new life to those still living. The Bonhoeffer Bell presented in his eulogy was a man whose life found true meaning and purpose in death. In death, Bonhoeffer's life blood could be shared across the world. He was in a very true sense for Bell still living, if not in our 'earthly view', then in a heavenly one. Bell's eulogy had not been entirely in service of Bonhoeffer, to mark his passage from life to death. Instead, Bell had been speaking to the living, highlighting the new life which could be found in Bonhoeffer's death, calling them to take up the hope of resurrection and new life given by the death of Bonhoeffer.

Van Gennep, in his study of rites of passage, claimed that:

> [P]ersons for whom funeral rites are not performed are condemned to a pitiable existence, since they are never able to enter the world of the dead or to become incorporated in the society established there. These are the most dangerous dead. They would like to be reincorporated into the world of the living, and since they cannot be, they behave like hostile strangers toward it.[95]

Bell's eulogy for Bonhoeffer challenges this notion. No funeral was held for Bonhoeffer, and his remains were cremated immediately after his execution at Flossenbürg.[96] The memorial service in

[93] Ibid.
[94] Ibid.
[95] Arnold van Gennep, *The Rites of Passage*, transl. Monika B. Vizedom and Gabrielle L. Caffee (Oxford and New York, 2010), 160.
[96] Schlingenspiepen, *Dietrich Bonhoeffer*, 378.

London was the closest thing to a funeral held for Bonhoeffer. Nevertheless, there is no sense in Bell's eulogy of Bonhoeffer's being among the restless dead. He is not presented as a dangerous member of the dead, but rather as one who is dead and in death offers the living more blessings. Where van Gennep's work might help us understand Bell's eulogy is in his consideration of rites of incorporation in funeral practices. Considering 'the meals shared after funerals and at commemoration celebrations', van Gennep wrote that 'their purpose is to reunite all the surviving members of the group with each other, and sometimes also with the deceased in the same way that a chain which has been broken by the disappearance of one of its links must be rejoined'.[97] Bell used his eulogy to enact such a rite of incorporation. But, to use van Gennep's metaphor, instead of merely reforming the chain after the loss of one link, Bell was attempting to show those still living that in reality the link had not been lost at all. Bonhoeffer was dead in an earthly sense, and yet Bell stressed in his eulogy time and time again that in that death was life. In death, Bonhoeffer's life had found its fulfilment, and in losing his life in our limited understanding of life, he had truly gained life. Consequently his life now took on a meaning far more universal than it had when he had been alive only in the earthly realm.

The work of Douglas J. Davies may also help us to understand Bell's eulogy, specifically his thesis of 'words against death'. Davies sees language as the vital part of death rites as 'it is precisely because language is the very medium through which human beings obtain their sense of self-consciousness that it can serve so well as the basis of reaction to the awareness of death'.[98] Davies claims that 'death rites are a means of encouraging a commitment to life despite the fact of death'.[99] In this process, he sees a unique place for 'verbal rites to express human triumph over death'.[100] Thus these verbal rites become 'words against death'.[101] Such words are reliant on 'the content of the words which does the work against death. It is their rhetoric – their power to persuade, to state a case in defiance of the fact of death – through which mourners' beings and identities are

[97] Van Gennep, *Rites of Passage*, 164–5.
[98] Douglas J. Davies, *Death, Ritual and Belief: The Rhetoric of Funerary Rites*, 2nd edn (London and New York, 2002), 1.
[99] Ibid., 6.
[100] Ibid.
[101] Ibid. 7.

transformed.'[102] Bell's eulogy was intended to have such an effect, to show how Bonhoeffer's death allowed the meaning of his life to be imbued into the life of those still living. It allowed them to continue the work that Bonhoeffer had begun, and thus to give his life a new global significance.

Bell's eulogy highlights a limitation of the concept of rites of passage. When it comes to rites of passage for the dead, they assume that the relationship to be reformed is between those who remain living in the mortal world, with the deceased forever removed from that community. This is not the claim of many religious traditions, especially Christianity. Bell was consciously emphasizing the link between the living and the dead, maintaining that Bonhoeffer still had gifts to impart to those left in mortality. The living and the dead were, in Bell's eulogy, in constant dialogue with each other, and the dead, especially those righteous dead who could be called martyrs, strengthened and encouraged the living to follow their example and continue the fight for the cause of God. Thomas G. Long, identifying what he sees as the fundamentals of a Christian funeral sermon, called such sermons 'faithful storytelling'.[103] This is the task in which Bell was engaged, constructing a story about Bonhoeffer's life that served to remind its audience 'that death changes, but does not destroy, the communion with this saint'.[104] Through this eulogy Bell attempted not only to bring comfort to those who had known Bonhoeffer in life, but to bring him onto an international stage. He presented the narrative of one whose life that found true fulfilment in the struggle against National Socialism, and his resultant death. Bell then affirmed that Bonhoeffer's death offered life to war-torn Europe, and the chance for Germany to rebuild itself based on the truer and purer traditions of the 'other Germany' Bell had so long championed. Through all this, it seems staggering to remember that Bell thought of Bonhoeffer as a friend. Bell presented to Europe the power that the death of his friend held, the opportunity that his friend's death gave them. To Bell's 'earthly view Dietrich is dead', but through this eulogy Bell began a quest to ensure that his friend's death would bring new life across a war-torn continent.

[102] Tara Bailey and Tony Walter, 'Funerals against Death', *Mortality* 21 (2016), 149–66, at 154.
[103] Thomas G. Long, *Accompany them with Singing: The Christian Funeral* (Louisville, KY, 2009), 182.
[104] Ibid.

Appendix

London, LPL, Bell Papers 42, fols 78–83, 'Pastor Dietrich Bonhoeffer: Holy Trinity Church, Kingsway: July 27th, 1945'.[105]

<78> Pastor Dietrich Bonhoeffer
Holy Trinity Church, Kingsway: July 27th, 1945

In this church, hallowed by many memories of Christian fellowship in wartime, we gather now in memory of Dietrich Bonhoeffer, our most dear brother and a martyr of the Church.

He was born in Breslau on February 4th, 1906, the son of a famous physician, and belonging to a family which claimed not a few eminent divines, judges, and artisans in its ranks in previous generations. Dietrich himself achieved distinction in his own field of theology as a young man. After pursuing his studies not only in Germany but in Barcelona, Rome and New York, he became a lecturer in Systematic Theology in Berlin University in 1930, and was ordained in 1931. Before the war he had published at least five books, and in these last years was engaged on a work on Christian ethics. There was no doubt, humanly speaking, of the high position which would have been justly his in the realm of theological scholarship and teaching had God willed that his qualities should be thus used. He was also a man who loved life, and rejoiced in human ties and human pleasures, in home and friendship, in literature, and music and art; a man in whose company, because of his charm, his humour, his character and his gifts it was a delight to be.

<79> He was not quite 27 on January 30th, 1933, when one whom history will surely judge as the source of Germany's greatest shame and ruin become Chancellor of the Reich. But it was that event which was to determine the course of the rest of Dietrich's life. Young as he was, he immediately and instinctively perceived the significance of the National Socialist revolution, its annihilation of all human rights, and its repudiation of God. He understood as few others understood that the attack on the Jews was an attack on Christ as well and an attack on man. From the very first he sought both how

[105] Thanks are due to Lambeth Palace Library for permission to reproduce a complete transcription of the text of Bell's eulogy.

he could best serve God and the Church in the fight against Hitler; and how he could save Germany's soul from the ~~devils~~ demons which were assailing it on every side. For two years he ~~served~~ ministered in London as a German pastor, and, while beyond doubt endearing himself to his two German congregations, he saw much of British friends, and helped them at least to begin to see the inwardness of the German Church struggle. He went back to Germany in 1935, and directed an illegal Confessional Church Training College in Pomerania; and from 1935 to the outbreak of war, interspersed with visits to America and England, he was giving aid and direction to the pastors within the Confessional Church, and playing an active, militant part in the opposition to Hitler, and in the resistance to the barbarities of his regime. He hated war, and my last memory but one of Dietrich is of a long talk, at <80> Chichester in the summer of 1939, when he was convinced that war was inevitable, on what his own duty should be if called up, and of the horror with which his conscience rejected any service under Hitler.

He was in fact spared the ordeal of serving in the army; and devoted his whole strength to his work for the Confessional Church, and to aiding the underground political opposition planning the overthrow of the Fuehrer. His illegal Training College was dissolved for the second time in 1940. He then ~~went~~ travelled through the country, visiting the parishes for the Confessional Church. At the end of 1940 he was prohibited by the Gestapo from preaching and speaking. In 1941 and 1942 he was engaged on his book on Christian ethics, and in preparing memoranda for the brethren's councils, while giving his evenings to political activities.

It was in May, 1942 that I had my last sight of him in Stockholm, when, altogether unexpected, he came from Berlin, at the risk of his life, to give me ~~much~~ information of the utmost importance about the movement of the opposition in Germany, to eliminate Hitler and all his chief colleagues, and to set up a new government which should repeal the Nuremberg Laws, undo Hitler's deeds so far as they could be undone, and seek peace with the Allies. Of those solemn last talks I had with Dietrich I will say nothing further ~~but~~ than this: deeply committed as he was to the plan for elimination, he was not altogether at <81> ease as a Christian about such a solution. "There must be punishment by God", he said. "We do not want to escape repentance". The elimination itself, he urged, must be understood as an act of repentance. "Oh we have to be punished. Christians do not wish to escape repentance or chaos, if God wills to bring it on us. We must endure this judgement as Christians." Very moving was our talk: very moving our farewell. And the last letter I had from him, just before he returned to Berlin, knowing what might well await him there, I shall treasure for the whole of my life.

Not many months after his return he was arrested. For a long time he was kept in prison or concentration camp. Early this year he was tried in the "People's Court" for his share in the events of July 20th, 1944, and sentenced to death, with his brother Klaus, and his brother-in-law, Professor Schleicher. Another brother-in-law, Professor v. Donanyi [*sic*], was arrested at the same time, and fell ill in the concentration camp. Though through the death of the judge in an air raid the sentence could not then be carried out, and we hoped so much that he might be saved for the future of Germany, Dietrich and Klaus were both murdered in Flossenburg Concentration camp only a few days before the Americans came to liberate the prisoners.

And now Dietrich ~~has~~ is gone. He died, with his brother, as a hostage. Our debt to them, and to all others similarly murdered, is immense. His death is a death for Germany – indeed for <82> Europe too. He made the sacrifice of human prospects, of home, friends, and career because he believed in God's vocation for his country, and refused to follow those false leaders, who were the servants of the devil. He was inspired by his faith in the living God, and by his devotion to truth and honour. And so his death, like his life, marks a fact of the deepest value in the witness of the Confessional Church. As one of a noble company of martyrs of differing traditions, he represents both the resistance of the believing soul, in the name of God, to the assault of evil, and also the moral and political revolt of the human conscience against injustice and cruelty. He and his fellows are ~~indeed~~ built upon the foundation of the Apostles and the Prophets. And it was this passion for justice that brought him, and so many others in the Confessional Church who were in agreement with him, into such close partnership with other resisters who, though outside the Church, shared the same humanitarian and liberal ideals.

Our Lord said, "Except a corn of wheat fall into the ground and die, it abideth alone; but if it die, it bringeth forth much fruit. He that loveth his life shall lose it, and he that hateth his life in this world shall keep it unto life eternal." To our earthly view Dietrich is dead. Deep and unfathomable as our sorrow seems, let us comfort one another with these words. For him and Klaus, and for the countless multitudes of their <83> fellow victims through these terrible years of war, there is the resurrection from the dead: for Germany redemption and resurrection, if God pleases to lead the nation through men animated by his spirit, holy and humble and brave like him: for the Church, not only in that Germany which he loved, but also the Church Universal, which was greater to him than nations, the hope of a new life. "The blood of the martyrs is the seed of the Church."

E. L. Mascall and the Anglican Opposition to the Ordination of Women as Priests, 1954–78

Peter Webster*

Chichester

This article examines the grounds on which the Anglican philosopher and theologian Eric Mascall opposed the ordination of women, in a series of influential publications from the 1950s to the 1970s. It explores their basis in Mascall's understanding of the Church, the Incarnation and the ontological status of the sexes. It also considers the particular atmosphere of the Anglo-Catholicism of the period, convulsed by ecumenical advance at the Second Vatican Council and (as Anglo-Catholics understood it) the danger of moves towards the Protestant denominations in England. Whilst Mascall allowed that women priests might one day be embraced by the worldwide church, acting together, the peculiar atmosphere of the period seemed to make it the least auspicious time to make what would be a unilateral and far-reaching decision. The article also situates Mascall's interventions in the context of a wider realignment of conservatives, both evangelicals and Anglo-Catholics, within the Church of England.

The period from the late 1960s until the early 1980s was a time in which several strands of conservative Christian opinion turned decisively against the trends of the previous few years, both in England and elsewhere. Hugh McLeod characterized the decade to 1975 as one of acute crisis for Christian churches in many countries, while at the same time conservative churches were relatively buoyant.[1] In part this was a retreat to older certainties in a time of disruption. Such a retreat might have entailed a re-establishment of older party divisions within churches. However, the pattern in the Church of England was different, and significant in the longer term, as conservative Anglo-Catholics and conservative evangelicals, previously divided over matters of doctrine and ritual, began to find common

* E-mail: peter@websterresearchconsulting.com. Thanks are due to Andrew Atherstone, Grace Heaton, Ian Jones, John Maiden, Charlotte Methuen, Margery Roberts and Julia Stapleton for comments on various drafts of this article, or on the issue at large.

[1] Hugh McLeod, *The Religious Crisis of the 1960s* (Oxford, 2007), 188–212.

Studies in Church History 59 (2023), 471–491
doi: 10.1017/stc.2023.22

cause against developments within the Church of England that both groups opposed.[2] A straw in the wind was the collaboration in the late 1960s and early 1970s between conservatives on both sides in opposition to the scheme to reunite the Church of England and the Methodist Church.[3] There was also shared concern over the liberal direction in which academic theology seemed to be heading, in publications such as *The Myth of God Incarnate* (1977), edited by John Hick and *Christian Believing*, the 1976 report of the Doctrine Commission of the Church of England.[4]

Born in 1905, Eric Mascall established his reputation as a theologian and philosopher in the catholic and Thomist tradition with a series of substantial works in the 1940s and 1950s. Although ordained as a priest, he worked out his vocation primarily in institutions of teaching and research: Lincoln Theological College (as subwarden); Christ Church, Oxford, from 1945; and King's College London, where he was professor of historical theology from 1962 until 1973.[5] Although his reputation rests principally on his substantive books, he was also a tireless reviewer and critic of the work of others, a theological popularizer, and a trenchant polemicist on a range of issues. As such, he came to be an unofficial theologian-in-chief to conservative catholics in the Church of England, and increasingly overseas. As a result, Mascall was drawn into several of the disputes of the period on the conservative side. He was one of the authors – with the catholic Graham Leonard and the evangelicals Colin Buchanan and J. I. Packer – of the dissenting report on Anglican-Methodist reunion, *Growing into Union* (1970).[6] He was also a prominent critic of trends in liberal theology for over two

[2] On this development, see John Maiden, 'Evangelical and Anglo-Catholic Relations, 1928–1983', in Andrew Atherstone and John Maiden, eds, *Evangelicalism and the Church of England in the Twentieth Century: Reform, Resistance and Renewal* (Woodbridge, 2014), 136–61, at 148–57.

[3] Andrew Atherstone, 'A Mad Hatter's Tea Party in the Old Mitre Tavern? Ecumenical Reactions to *Growing into Union*', *Ecclesiology* 6 (2010), 39–67. This is to be read along with Atherstone's article, 'Evangelical Dissentients and the Defeat of the Anglican-Methodist Unity Scheme', in Jane Platt and Martin Wellings, eds, *Anglican-Methodist Ecumenism: The Search for Church Unity, 1920–2020* (Abingdon, 2022), 118–34.

[4] Peter Webster, 'Eric Mascall and the Responsibility of the Theologian in England, 1962–77', *International Journal for the Study of the Christian Church* 21 (2021), 250–65.

[5] On Mascall's understanding of his vocation as scholar and priest, see ibid. 252.

[6] Colin Buchanan et al., *Growing into Union: Proposals for forming a United Church in England* (London, 1970).

decades. By the late 1970s, Mascall was convinced that the theology then being produced in England was misdirected in terms of its subject matter, inattentive to the tradition on which it should have been based and irresponsible in its expression. His critique found many echoes in evangelical concerns of the same period.[7] Writing his memoir in the early 1990s, Mascall noted the growing alignment of evangelical and catholic voices, of which he had been part, on the side of revelation and the supernatural over against the kind of liberalism that had, he thought, come to dominate both church and academy.[8]

Conservative evangelicals and traditionalist Anglo-Catholics also found themselves in unfamiliar and unstable coalitions with others who owned neither label. Opposition hardened during the 1970s to liturgical reform and the supposed 'abandonment' of the Book of Common Prayer, and the adoption of the Alternative Service Book in 1980.[9] There was increasing disquiet over the reforms of the law that had weakened the influence of parliament in the running of the Church of England, in favour of the General Synod.[10] In the early 1970s there were signs of increasing conservative opposition to the permissive legislation of the 1960s: a sense that even qualified church support for those reforms had had ill effects, both foreseen and not, notably in the case of abortion.[11] Other critics charged the established church with having been captured by a kind of left-wing politics, and of concentrating on the kingdom on earth to the exclusion of the main issue, entry into the kingdom in

7 Webster, 'Eric Mascall and the Responsibility of the Theologian', 261.

8 E. L. Mascall, *Saraband: The Memoirs of E. L. Mascall* (Leominster, 1992), 380–1.

9 See, for instance, the essay by the conservative evangelical Roger Beckwith, 'Doctrine and Devotion in the Book of Common Prayer', in David Martin and Peter Mullen, eds, *No Alternative: The Prayer Book Controversy* (Oxford, 1981), 73–9. On the critique of the direction of travel within the church from a non-aligned perspective, see Peter Webster, '"Poet of church and state": C. H. Sisson and the Church of England', in Victoria Moul and John Talbot, eds, *C. H. Sisson Reconsidered* (Basingstoke, 2022), 159–82.

10 Peter Webster, 'Parliament and the Law of the Church of England, 1945–74', in Tom Rodger, Philip Williamson and Matthew Grimley, eds, *The Church of England and British Politics since 1900* (Woodbridge, 2020), 181–98, at 198.

11 On a shift in evangelical engagement with 'permissiveness', see Matthew Grimley, 'Anglican Evangelicals and Anti-Permissiveness: The Nationwide Festival of Light, 1971–1983', in Atherstone and Maiden, eds, *Evangelicalism and the Church of England*, 183–205. More generally, see also Andrew Atherstone, 'The Keele Congress of 1967: A Paradigm Shift in Anglican Evangelical Attitudes', *Journal of Anglican Studies* 9 (2011), 175–97, at 185–6.

heaven.[12] A prolific essayist, Mascall was a frequent contributor to collections drawn together by others which addressed these themes.[13] Mascall's contribution to one 1983 volume was typical. His essay was a reprise of his familiar critique of liberal theology, but the volume also contained essays on the various supposed ills of the established church, including the ordination of women.[14]

The philosophical theologian Brian Hebblethwaite in the *Oxford Dictionary of National Biography* described Mascall's apologetic works of the 1960s as 'polemical conservatism at its best'; 'less appealing', however, 'were his extraordinary arguments against the ordination of women'. A similar note, of faint incomprehension attended by the whiff of moral failure, has tended to be struck in the wider literature on the position of women within the Anglican churches. For Wendy Fletcher-Marsh, such 'bizarre' and illogical arguments were those of the Gramscian traditional intellectual, 'who resists change in a self-protective desire to preserve the privilege of his or her own position in the old order society'.[15] The accusation was made at the time, and has been echoed in the literature since, that opposition to the ordination of women was grounded in complex and deep-seated feelings of sexual inadequacy, and a fear of female sexuality, in the same male clergy.[16] Both of these may well have influenced at least some of the opponents, although the degree of such influence is hard to determine. In general, however, the opponents of the ordination of women have rarely been treated in their own terms, and placed in their fullest historical context.

[12] See, for instance, Edward Norman's Reith Lectures for 1978, published as *Christianity and the World Order* (Oxford, 1979).

[13] See, for instance, Mascall's preface to a collection of essays on abortion, from the evangelical Paternoster Press: J. H. Channer, ed., *Abortion and the Sanctity of Life* (Exeter, 1985), 7–12.

[14] Anthony Kilmister, ed., *When will ye be wise? The State of the Church of England* (London, 1983).

[15] Wendy Fletcher Marsh, *Beyond the Walled Garden* (Dundas, ON, 2005), 209–15, quotation at 209. Similar, though more measured, is the account in Sean Gill, *Women and the Church of England from the Eighteenth Century to the Present* (London, 1994), 232–67; on an earlier period, see Timothy Jones, '"Unduly conscious of her sex": Priesthood, Female Bodies, and Sacred Space in the Church of England', *Women's History Review* 21 (2012), 639–55, particularly 640; idem, *Sexual Politics in the Church of England, 1857–1957* (Oxford, 2013), 93–130.

[16] Fletcher Marsh, *Beyond the Walled Garden*, 212–13; Gill, *Women and the Church of England*, 259–60; Rupert E. Davies, *The Church of England Observed* (London, 1984), 50.

Leaving aside their intrinsic appeal, or lack of it (in Hebblethwaite's terms), this article examines the grounds on which Mascall opposed the ordination of women, expressed in a series of influential publications from the late 1950s to the 1970s. It explores their basis in Mascall's understanding of the Church, the Incarnation and the ontological status of the sexes. It considers the particular atmosphere of the Anglo-Catholicism of the period, convulsed both by ecumenical advance at the Second Vatican Council and (as Anglo-Catholics understood it) the danger of moves towards the Protestant denominations in England. It also situates the opposition to the ordination of women in the context of shifting patterns of cooperation between Anglican evangelicals and Anglo-Catholics. Mascall was far from alone among Anglican Catholics of the period in expressing such opposition.[17] However, his interventions form a useful case study. They were among the most extensive and the most noticed writings on the subject, expressing the substantial parts of the Anglo-Catholic objection at their strongest, while largely eschewing the more flimsy objections which were also heard.[18]

The movement towards women's ordination was an international one, with different parts of the Anglican Communion making decisions at their own speed. Mascall kept a keen eye on developments, as he did with most international trends, both ecumenical and theological. The 1968 Lambeth Conference was unable to reach a conclusive view on the question, and asked the various provinces of the Communion to consider the issue.[19] The meeting of the Anglican Consultative Council in 1971 decided (by 24 votes to 22) that if

[17] Other notable statements included the contribution of V. S. Demant, Regius Professor of Moral and Pastoral Theology in the University of Oxford, to the report *Women and Holy Orders* (London, 1966), entitled 'Why the Christian Priesthood is Male': ibid. 96–114. Often cited was an essay by C. S. Lewis, 'Priestesses in the Church?', first published in 1948, and included in Lesley Walmsley, ed., *Essay Collection and other Short Pieces* (London, 2000), 398–402. In the 1970s, the Church Literature Association published a series of pamphlets, including reprints of Demant's essay, and another by Mascall himself.

[18] Examples of Mascall's arguments being cited in later discussion include Susan Dowell and Jane Williams, *Bread, Wine and Women: The Ordination Debate in the Church of England* (London, 1994), 23; from a Methodist point of view, Davies, *Church of England Observed*, 41–2.

[19] Resolutions 34 and 35, in *The Lambeth Conference 1968: Resolutions and Reports* (London, 1968), 39.

the diocese of Hong Kong (where the deaconess Florence Li Tim Oi had been ordained priest in 1944, but later surrendered her licence, although not her orders), and any others that might follow suit, should decide to ordain women, the decision would be 'acceptable to this Council', which would 'use its good offices to encourage all provinces of the Anglican Communion to continue in communion with these dioceses'.[20] Thus each province could follow its own path, and the central organs of the Communion would try to manage whatever tensions that might cause, both within the Communion and in its global relations with other churches. By 1978 women had been ordained to the priesthood in Hong Kong, Canada, New Zealand and the USA.[21]

The story in England ended much later, but had begun earlier, not least due to campaigners such as Maude Royden between the world wars.[22] The debate began to intensify in the 1950s, and a series of reports were issued, most notably that on *Women and Holy Orders* (1966). Unable to resolve anything in the Church Assembly in 1967, the Church of England continued to deliberate. In response to the request from the Anglican Consultative Council, there was a period of consultation between 1973 and 1975; in July 1975 a majority in the General Synod agreed that there were no barriers in principle to the ordination of women, but did not act to remove the barriers that existed in fact. In 1978 the matter came once again to the synod, which debated a motion to remove those barriers. Carried by the laity and the bishops, it was heavily defeated in the House of Clergy.[23] The movement in favour of women's ordination continued to gather momentum, however, and in 1984 the synod returned to the question, agreeing this time to bring forward legislation to ordain women to the diaconate. Finally, in 1992 the vote on the ordination of women to the

[20] Resolution 28, in *The Time is Now: Anglican Consultative Council, First Meeting, Limuru, Kenya* (London, 1971), 34–5, 38–9.

[21] For an overview, see Cordelia Moyse, 'Gender Perspectives: Women and Anglicanism', in Jeremy Morris, ed., *The Oxford History of Anglicanism*, 4: *Global Western Anglicanism,* c.*1910–Present* (Oxford, 2017), 68–92.

[22] See Gill, *Women and the Church*, 234–42; Brian Heeney, *The Women's Movement in the Church of England, 1850–1930* (Oxford, 1988), 116–38.

[23] The motion was defeated in the House of Clergy by 149 votes to 94. The bishops accepted it by 32 votes to 17, and the laity by 120 votes to 106. See Paul A. Welsby, *A History of the Church of England, 1945–1980* (Oxford, 1984), 258.

priesthood was won, and the first women were ordained as priests in 1994.[24]

It is not quite clear when Mascall first began to take note of the issue, although the range of his reading on most other subjects suggests that it might well have been between the wars. He certainly knew the book by Charles Raven, *Women and Holy Orders: A Plea to the Church of England*, first published in 1928 when Mascall was a highly engaged young Anglican Catholic and reading voraciously.[25] He also read a reprinted essay by the former MP and Anglican laywoman Edith Picton-Turbervill, which appeared in 1953 under the auspices of the Society for the Equal Ministry of Men and Women in the Church; other books that came to his notice included a 1949 study by the evangelical R. W. Howard.[26] His first intervention was in the journal *Theology* in 1954 in response to the New Testament scholar Margaret Thrall, later one of the first women ordained in the Church in Wales.[27] Thrall subsequently expanded her case into a short book, which appeared in 1958.[28] Mascall was for a time a member of the theological committee of the Church Union, the conservative catholic society, and produced private reports on various issues. His report on the ordination of women was written in 1959, presumably as a response to the renewed discussion, and published shortly after; it dealt with Thrall's case at some length.[29]

[24] For a summary account of the process to 1980, see ibid. 255–8; Ivan Clutterbuck, secretary of the Church Union between 1966 and 1974, covers it at length, if more partially, in his *Marginal Catholics: Anglo-Catholicism, a further Chapter of Modern Church History* (Leominster, 1993), 240–55.

[25] Although Mascall cites a later edition, it seems likely that he would have been aware of the book, or at least the debate, at the time of its first publication.

[26] Edith Picton-Turbervill, *Should Women be Priests and Ministers?* (London, 1953); this consisted of two chapters first published in B. H. Streeter and Edith Picton-Turbervill, *Woman and the Church* (London, 1917). See also R. W. Howard, *Should Women be Priests?* (Oxford, 1949).

[27] Eric Mascall, 'The Ministry of Women' [letter to the editor], *Theology* 57 (1954), 428–9; Jenny Watts, 'Margaret Thrall: Obituary', *The Guardian*, 21 December 2010, online at: <https://www.theguardian.com/theguardian/2010/dec/21/the-rev-margaret-thrall-obituary>, accessed 12 December 2021.

[28] M. E. Thrall, *The Ordination of Women to the Priesthood: A Study of the Biblical Evidence* (London, 1958).

[29] A typescript dated September 1959 is at London, LPL, CU 104/2/2. It was published as Eric Mascall, *Women and the Priesthood of the Church* (London, 1959); citations are of the published edition.

It became widely cited as a summary of the catholic dissenting position.[30]

Mascall laid out his case again in three publications in the 1970s. Two of them appeared in 1972. One was a pamphlet published by the Church Literature Association, the publishing arm of the Church Union.[31] The second, a reprinting of his 1959 report, appeared in a volume of essays that emerged from circles overlapping with those that had opposed Anglican-Methodist reunion. It had originated as a project involving catholics alone, but became a collaboration with evangelicals, led by Michael Bruce, vicar of St Mark's, North Audley Street, in central London, and his evangelical counterpart in the Church Assembly, Gervase Duffield. The book contained an essay by J. I. (James) Packer, a co-author with Mascall of *Growing into Union*, who occupied a position among conservative evangelicals analogous of that of Mascall among Anglo-Catholics. Much of the editorial work was done by Roger Beckwith, librarian of Latimer House in Oxford, of which Packer had been warden. The publisher was Duffield's own Marcham Manor Press.[32] Mascall returned to the fray in 1978 in another collection of essays, this time with contributions from Orthodox, Roman Catholic and Jewish authors, as well as from Roger Beckwith (again); it also included vivid reports of divisions caused by recent decisions to ordain women in both the Church of Sweden, and (within the Anglican Communion) the Episcopal Church in the USA.[33]

As a young man, Mascall had not imagined himself heading towards ordination. He read not theology but mathematics in the mid-1920s and then spent some years as a schoolmaster, before entering Ely Theological College. It was also a surprise to find himself, as one without any formal theological training, responsible for teaching ordinands the subject from 1937, as sub-warden of Lincoln Theological College. Despite the professional status that he achieved

[30] Demant, 'Why the Christian Priesthood is Male', 112; see also the repeated citations in the 1972 report by the Advisory Council on the Church's Ministry, *The Ordination of Women to the Priesthood* (London, 1972), 39–44.

[31] Eric Mascall, *Women Priests?* (London, 1972).

[32] Eric Mascall, 'Women and the Priesthood of the Church', in Michael Bruce and Gervase Duffield, eds, *Why not? Priesthood and the Ministry of Women* (Appleford, 1972), 95–120. The work went into a second edition, significantly expanded, in 1976.

[33] Eric Mascall, 'Some Basic Considerations', in Peter Moore, ed., *Man, Woman and Priesthood* (London, 1978), 9–26.

within the discipline, throughout his career he retained a sense of distance from it; a feeling that his approach – logical, philosophical, rigorous – was not shared by many others.[34] As I show elsewhere, his entire project of synthesis and exposition was founded on a sense that, in principle at least, reason would confirm revelation; indeed, it could do no other without contradicting the nature of God himself.[35] An almost aesthetic sense of the beauty and orderliness of doctrine was accompanied in Mascall by an impatience with those who seemed to see things less clearly, and a kind of righteous anger at those who seemed consciously to sidestep inconvenient questions. The scheme for Anglican-Methodist reunion had been based, for Mascall, on an unacceptable ducking of the crucial issue; a rather disreputable dodge to avoid the inconvenience of derailing a process that was already in motion.[36] So, too, did some advocates of women priests seem to capitulate to a kind of institutional pragmatism that ignored the questions it could not answer. It was not enough to act, he thought, and hope that a theological rationale might follow. Leslie Houlden, principal of Ripon College Cuddesdon, argued that, as the ecclesiastical past was no longer normative for the present, then it was a matter to be settled by 'common sense': 'if social institutions point that way, if there is need, if there is desire, let not "theology" be falsely involved … It is a matter of expediency for the Church, no more, no less'.[37] This kind of argument Mascall could not accept. Soon after the Movement for the Ordination of Women was formed in 1979, its leaders were challenged (by a supporter) to put aside arguments based on emotion, and to apply themselves to the theology of the matter.[38] This Mascall would surely have welcomed.

Although he paid close attention to the proceedings of both, Mascall seems never to have considered standing for election to the Church Assembly or its successor, the General Synod. Why this

[34] Mascall, *Saraband*, 378–9.

[35] Peter Webster, 'Eric Mascall and the Making of an Anglican Thomist, 1937–46', *Journal for the History of Modern Theology* (forthcoming).

[36] Peter Webster, 'Theology, Providence and Anglican-Methodist Reunion: The Case of Michael Ramsey and E. L. Mascall', in Platt and Wellings, eds, *Anglican-Methodist Ecumenism*, 101–17, at 110–11.

[37] As quoted by Eric Mascall, *Theology and the Gospel of Christ: An Essay in Reorientation* (London, 1977), 37.

[38] The recollection of Judith Maltby from 1980 or 1981, as recorded in eadem, 'One Lord, One Faith, One Baptism, but Two Integrities?', in Monica Furlong, ed., *Act of Synod – Act of Folly?* (London, 1998), 42–58, at 42.

was is unclear, but the issue of women priests showed, in Mascall's view, that such quasi-democratic bodies were unsuited to dealing with certain kinds of questions. 'There will always', he argued, 'be possible courses of action that are constitutionally and canonically legal but are either morally or theologically wrong, abhorrent as the fact is to the administrative mind.'[39] Despite assertions to the contrary, the 1975 Synod vote had not settled the theological justification for the ordination of women, but had merely shown that a majority of delegates thought there was one to be found. How, he asked, could such a body be competent to decide when its members needed only to be resident in a parish, and named on its electoral roll?[40] Mascall also doubted both the competence of the Anglican Consultative Council to rule as it had done in 1971, and the status of its ruling. He was similarly critical of the grounds on which the Lambeth Conference of 1968 had reasoned.[41] But Mascall's understanding of the Church placed the greatest importance on the worldwide and historic body of bishops as makers of such decisions, even if some of them seemed content to delegate the task to their local synodical assemblies.[42] The precipitous action of the American and Canadian churches in ordaining women (he later reflected) might have been avoided had there been a greater consciousness among the American and Canadian bishops of their membership in a worldwide episcopate of all the bishops of historic catholic Christendom: Roman, Orthodox and Old Catholic, as well as Anglican.[43]

There were, however, more substantial disagreements in play. As in relation to Anglican-Methodist unity, Anglo-Catholic and conservative evangelical opposition to the ordination of women was on related but not identical grounds. Evangelical opposition tended to start and end with a reading of Scripture, and the Pauline epistles in particular. The issue was not so much about the sacraments as it was about authority in the congregation. As such, some evangelicals, such as James Packer, were content (though unenthusiastic) to see

[39] Mascall, 'Some Basic Considerations', 18.
[40] Ibid. 17–18.
[41] Mascall, *Women Priests?*, 6–9, 13–14
[42] See, for instance, Eric Mascall, *The Recovery of Unity: A Theological Approach* (London, 1958), 170–93.
[43] In an unpublished manuscript, dating from late 1984: Oxford, Pusey House Library, Mascall Papers, Box 4B, 'The Overarching Question: Divine Revelation or Human Invention?', fol. 101.

women at the altar and in the pulpit so long as they were not exercising headship over the whole congregation.[44] Mascall did make some use of the analogy of the headship of God the Father over the Son, Christ as the head of the Church, and the Genesis account of man as head of woman.[45] However, his use of it was not central to his argument; the specifically historical and biblical arguments that Mascall deployed, along with other Anglo-Catholic critics, were related but distinct.

It was not enough (Mascall thought) to read the record of the early church as merely determined by the cultural context of the first century; to argue, in effect, that Christ could just as easily have been incarnated as woman, and appointed female apostles, but was not and did not in order that the reception of the gospel be made easier. Jesus, after all, had hardly shied away from controversy, and the opening of the sacraments to male and female alike was in itself a radically equalizing act. In view of the counter-cultural emphasis that Christ had put on the equality of men and women otherwise, Mascall argued, it was not accidental that Christ was incarnated male, and that all the apostles were men: 'is it not natural to assume that there must be some very deep and significant reason in the nature of things for this restriction?'[46]

That deep and significant reason, for Mascall, lay in the given nature of the Church. Mascall observed that the ministry of women posed different issues to catholic churches than to Protestant ones. Protestant churches, as Mascall understood them, tended to view their ministers primarily as laypeople with a particular training, authorized in various ways to perform certain functions. Apart from that authorization, there was no essential difference in character between clergy and laity; nothing in a person's nature changed at ordination.[47] In books such as *Christ, the Christian and the Church* (1946) and *Corpus Christi* (1953, 2nd edn 1965), Mascall had worked out a doctrine of the Church, the body of Christ, the eucharist and the priesthood which was perhaps as elaborate and rarefied as an Anglican could produce. The common

44 See, for instance, James Packer, 'Thoughts on the Role and Function of Women in the Church', in Colin Craston, ed., *Evangelicals and the Ordination of Women* (Nottingham, 1973), 22–26.

45 Mascall, *Women and the Priesthood*, 17, 33–4.

46 Ibid. 12.

47 Ibid. 15–16.

Protestant focus on the priesthood of all believers – male and female, but individuals – was, in his view, correct but slightly out of focus. This priesthood was only secondarily individual in nature; the 'priesthood of the Body' (as he preferred to call it) was corporate, and 'is seen in its fullest exercise when the Church is assembled together, with all its members playing their several and interrelated parts in one organic and coherent activity of praise and offering, for the celebration of the Eucharist, the rite which day by day recreates the Church and gives it its life'.[48] However, there was a ministerial priesthood, quite distinct from the corporate priesthood exercised by all Christians together, that was in the hands of the priest himself: 'in his sacerdotal acts Christ's priesthood is, as it were, channelled or focused to a point and made operative by the words and gestures of one particular man'.[49] Within the body, the very manifestation of Christ on earth, the clergy did not act merely as representatives, or even as agents, but as 'the very organs through whom [Christ] himself acts'; there was an 'essential identity' between Christ's personal ministry on earth and that which he now exercised in the Church. As such, it was 'highly congruous that the manhood through which he acts is male as he is male'.[50]

For some catholic Anglicans, then, an exclusively male priesthood contained an important symbolic fact, and there was a loss entailed by its discontinuation. At stake was what two later commentators (and supporters of the ordination of women) described as a 'particularly dense and satisfying sacramental framework'.[51] But even if the ordination of women was undesirable, was it feasible nonetheless? The bishop of Ripon, John Moorman, a vigorous opponent of the Anglican-Methodist reunion scheme, while thinking the ordination of women inexpedient, held that there were no fundamental objections: a position not unlike that of Michael Ramsey, archbishop of Canterbury from 1961 until 1974.[52] For Mascall the issue was not that women were in some way temperamentally unsuited to the

[48] Ibid. 18.

[49] Ibid. 22.

[50] Mascall, *Women Priests?*, 16.

[51] Dowell and Williams, *Bread, Wine and Women*, 23.

[52] Michael Manktelow, *John Moorman: Anglican, Franciscan, Independent* (Norwich, 1999), 77–8. On Ramsey, see Owen Chadwick, *Michael Ramsey: A Life* (Oxford, 1990), 278–84.

work of a priest, although some campaigners did take this line. Neither was the issue that the presence of female bodies in such a visible position would pose too great a distraction from their prayers to heterosexual male worshippers, although such an argument had also been made, and by eminent men.[53] From Mascall's understanding of the metaphysics of the human person flowed certain unavoidable, and drastic, conclusions about women priests, that went beyond considerations of symbolic richness and congruity. It was at this point that his thought was most distinctive, and most speculative.

In the heat of the debate in England, it was suggested that it was no more possible to ordain a woman as a priest than one could a dog, a monkey or a pork pie.[54] All the evidence of Mascall's character suggests that he could not possibly have used such an expression, in print or in person. Nonetheless, it starkly expressed the heart of the catholic objection at its very strongest, a position that Mascall held right from the start of his public involvement in the issue and which he continued to elaborate throughout. The very nature of a woman made it not undesirable that she be a priest, but *impossible*. Mascall held a high view of fundamental human rights; there was a specificity to human nature, that distinguished the human from the other animals, derived from the Incarnation.[55] However, Mascall could not regard the exclusion of women from the priesthood as a form of discrimination analogous to racism, as some critics did. For Mascall the very nature of the human person was fundamentally binary, organized around a division into male and female. Beneath all the racial, temperamental and cultural differentiations of human beings, there was not, for Mascall, a single human nature, common to male and female but sexless in nature. At the most fundamental ontological level, there was no essential human being, only men and women. 'Humanity is, so to speak, essentially binary; it exists only in the two modes of masculinity and femininity'. It did not exist partly in one and partly in the

[53] Such a view had been expressed in 1938 by N. P. Williams, the Lady Margaret Professor of Divinity in the University of Oxford. Mascall concluded that it would bear little weight: Mascall, *Women and the Priesthood*, 6–11.

[54] The recollection of Judith Maltby, prominent in the Movement for the Ordination of Women, as given in eadem, 'One Lord', 42.

[55] Mascall, 'Some Basic Considerations', 21; on Mascall's understanding of human rights, see Peter Webster, 'Eric Mascall and the Rise, Fall and Rise of "Christian Sociology", *c.*1935–1985', *International Journal for the Study of the Christian Church* 23 (2023).

other: 'under a difference in mode it is fully in each'.[56] Since the priest was the 'agent and instrument through which [Christ] is exercising *his* priesthood, he too must be male … Christ exercises his priesthood in the Church through human beings who possess human nature in the same sexual mode in which he possesses it.'[57] Mascall admitted that this could not easily be fitted within the Aristotelian logic on which his work usually rested, but it pertained both to the redemptive order and to nature. Sex differentiation was not merely read off from the existence of the human body: in the words of C. S. Lewis, in an essay often quoted (including by Mascall), 'we are dealing with male and female not merely as facts of nature but as the live and awful shadows of realities utterly beyond our control and largely beyond our direct knowledge'.[58]

It was not coincidental that the Christian churches that had retained an exclusively male priesthood – the Roman Catholic Church and the Orthodox – were also those with the highest view of the person of Mary. Writing in 1959, Mascall thought that the demand that the roles of men and women in the church be identical stemmed from an almost complete neglect of Mariology in the Church of England.[59] Mascall, along with other opponents, sought to separate out the priesthood from the other professions to which women sought access (rightly, in his view), since to treat them in the same way was to make a category error. The particular cultural pressures of the time made it difficult for any argument based on the obedient Mother of God to be heard. However, Mascall wanted always to speak not in terms of the sexes being inferior or superior to each other, but different. Although men and women had been made equally members of the body of Christ, it had been to a woman that the highest possible honour had been given: to give birth to the incarnate Christ. For Mascall, there was a tight theological intertwining of Mary as *theotokos*, the permanent incarnation of Christ, and the existence of the Church as his body, into which all were incorporated.[60] As he told a 1949 symposium of Anglicans and Orthodox, 'Mary is

[56] Mascall, 'Some Basic Considerations', 20–1. Mascall was to elaborate his thinking on the absolute binary division of sex, based on a reading of contemporary genetics, in *Whatever happened to the Human Mind?* (London, 1980), 131–8.

[57] Mascall, 'Some Basic Considerations', 22–3.

[58] Lewis, 'Priestesses in the Church?', as quoted by Mascall, *Women Priests?*, 17.

[59] Mascall, *Women and the Priesthood*, 26.

[60] Mascall, 'Some Basic Considerations', 23–4.

our mother and we are her children, by adoption into her Son. This is not an exuberance of devotion, but a fact of theology; it can be denied only by denying the Catholic doctrine of the Incarnation.'[61] Mascall's sense of the dogma concerned was largely unchanged by the time he expounded it again in 1968, to a meeting of the newly formed Ecumenical Society of the Blessed Virgin Mary, but he had been encouraged in particular by the treatment of Mary in relation to the church in the decrees of the Second Vatican Council, which seemed to chime with his own.[62] Here was part of the ecumenical balance that was threatened by the ordination of women, to which I shall return shortly.

There were other arguments, based on grounds not of principle but of the position of the Church of England: just one part, if an important one, of a communion which even as a whole represented perhaps only one in twenty of the world's Christians, by Mascall's reckoning.[63] As the 'canon' of Vincent of Lerins – the widely-used threefold test of catholicity – had it, it was for the catholic church to hold to those things 'which hath been believed everywhere, always and by all men'; it was a matter of 'universality, antiquity and consent'.[64] The catholicity of the Church of England was central to Mascall's concerns throughout his career, and from it flowed his opposition to successive ecumenical schemes, from the Church of South India in the 1940s and 1950s to Anglican-Methodist reunion in the 1960s.[65] The whole body of the church, in all its separated parts, had for nineteen centuries maintained the apostolic practice of an exclusively male priesthood. Should it not be a matter of great seriousness, then, to alter it? A sense of history alone ought to impart a certain circumspection. It was possible, he conceded, that the worldwide church might, after the requisite reflection, agree

[61] Eric Mascall, 'The Dogmatic Theology of the Mother of God', in idem, ed., *The Mother of God: A Symposium* (London, 1949), 37–50, at 43–4.
[62] Later published as 'The Mother of God', in Alberic Stacpoole, ed., *Mary's Place in Christian Dialogue* (Slough, 1982), 91–7. Mascall was referring to the eighth chapter of *Lumen Gentium*, properly titled the Dogmatic Constitution on the Church. See also his 'Theotokos: The Place of Mary in the Work of Salvation', in H. S. Box and E. L. Mascall, eds, *The Blessed Virgin Mary: Essays by Anglican Writers* (London, 1963), 12–26.
[63] Mascall, 'Some Basic Considerations', 26.
[64] Ibid. 11; on the issue at large, see Andrew Chandler, '*Catholicity*: Anglicanism, History and the Universal Church in 1947', *International Journal for the Study of the Christian Church* 18 (2018), 236–51.
[65] Webster, 'Theology, Providence and Anglican-Methodist Reunion', 104–10.

that a fuller understanding of ecclesiology and Christology demanded a priesthood of men and women. Particularly in times of such theological turbulence, however, the most searching examination of the issues was required, lest the church commit itself to an 'irreversible course of action that future generations will condemn as reflecting the ephemeral and unsubstantial prejudices of the latter part of the twentieth century'.[66]

Mascall had often intervened in the movements towards unity between Anglican and Protestant churches. Such interventions indicated not opposition to ecumenism as such, but where his priorities lay: with the Roman Catholic Church and the Orthodox East. Mascall had been involved in the Fellowship of St Alban and St Sergius from the late 1920s onwards, editing its journal and symposia, and thus helping to bring together Anglican and Orthodox.[67] Ecumenical progress with the Orthodox had been slow; rather more had been achieved with the Old Catholic churches, with the entry into full communion in 1931. The change in theological atmosphere after the Second Vatican Council came as an astonishment to Anglican Catholics of Mascall's generation, and there seemed to be a prospect of real advance.[68] The Anglican-Roman Catholic International Commission (ARCIC) began work in 1970, as did an equivalent enterprise between Anglican and Orthodox in 1973.[69] Just as prospects for real progress among the catholic churches seemed to be brighter than ever before, the ordination of women threatened to destroy them.[70] Meanwhile, after a second rebuff from the Church of England in 1972, the Methodist Church in England had decided in 1974 to go ahead with the ordination of women.[71] Writing in 1972, Mascall thought it unwise to take the apparently lively discussions within the Roman church as an indication of imminent change in

[66] Mascall, *Women Priests?*, 25.

[67] Aidan Nichols, *Alban and Sergius: The Story of a Journal* (Leominster, 2018), 21–3; Mascall, *Saraband*, 80–4.

[68] For more on this context, see Webster, 'Theology, Providence and Anglican-Methodist Reunion', 104–6.

[69] ARCIC built on the work of a preparatory commission set up in response to a joint declaration by Michael Ramsey and Pope Paul VI in 1966: ARCIC, *The Final Report* (London 1982), 1–4; Welsby, *Church of England*, 272.

[70] This was the feeling of Peter Moore, editor of one of the collections in which Mascall's work appeared: 'Introduction', in Moore, ed., *Man, Woman and Priesthood*, 1–8, at 1.

[71] Jane Platt and Martin Wellings, 'Introduction', in eidem, eds, *Anglican-Methodist Ecumenism*, 1–10, at 7.

relation to women priests, and certainly not as an invitation to other churches to change their practice.[72] By 1978, it had become clear to him how damaging such a move might be. After its vote in 1975, the General Synod had asked Donald Coggan, archbishop of Canterbury from 1974 to 1980, to consult with other worldwide churches in order to gauge their likely reactions. The responses came in different ways but all were resoundingly negative, from the Orthodox churches, the Vatican and the Old Catholic bishops; for a time the idea seemed even to jeopardize the ongoing ecumenical exchanges with the Orthodox churches.[73] The reaction was expressed not only in private; *Inter insigniores*, the declaration issued by the Vatican in October 1976, was clearly negative, in terms congruent with Mascall's.[74] The recent experience of the Episcopal Church in the USA had been both disorderly and divisive.[75] In the light of all these reactions, Mascall wondered why the matter seemed to be of 'such immediate and compulsive urgency' to its proponents 'that literally nothing … can be allowed to stand in its way'.[76]

As noted already, Mascall was prepared to accept that it was at least conceivable that, together, the whole worldwide church might one day embrace women priests. The shape of his whole theological output suggests that he should have accepted the fact; his view of the authority of Christ in his church would most likely have outweighed his scruples.[77] However, Mascall thought the social and cultural ferment of the period to be another reason for caution. Mascall was far from alone in detecting in English society a much more fundamental questioning of traditional Christian understandings of sex, gender, marriage and the family that brought together conservatives of all

[72] Mascall, *Women Priests?*, 4–5. Mascall noted the lack of precedent in Roman Catholic history in a review of Haye van der Meer, *Women Priests in the Catholic Church?*, *Religious Studies* 12 (1976), 394–5.

[73] Welsby, *Church of England*, 257–8; Margaret Pawley, *Donald Coggan* (London, 1989), 234–5.

[74] 'Declaration on the Question of Admission of Women to the Ministerial Priesthood', 1976, online at: <https://www.vatican.va/roman_curia/congregations/cfaith/documents/rc_con_cfaith_doc_19761015_inter-insigniores_en.html>, accessed 11 January 2022.

[75] Mascall was in the United States for several weeks early in 1977, months after the General Convention of the Episcopal Church had authorized the ordination of women as priests, and it is highly likely that the subject was discussed: see Mascall, *Saraband*, 337–43.

[76] Mascall, 'Some Basic Considerations', 13–14.

[77] Ibid. 25–6.

kinds.[78] No sound understanding of the sexes and their relation could, he thought, be discerned when sex itself was trivialized and commercialized, and detached from its place in the order of creation.[79] The long history of women's suffrage, and the changing patterns of employment catalyzed by the two world wars, made it perhaps inevitable that equality of access to the profession of priest should be caught up in the same questioning. 'It is unfortunately true', Mascall wrote some years later, 'that we live in a society whose public structure was mainly devised by men for men'. However, the efforts of secular feminism, as he saw it, were misdirected: 'a really healthy society will not be one which offers women increased facilities for imitating men, but one which makes it easier and more natural for them to be themselves'.[80]

The question of social status was made sharper in the Church of England which, when compared to the Free Churches, was relatively clerical in its unspoken assumptions. The priesthood was bound up with questions of status and power, made sharper again by the particular social standing that establishment conferred. James Packer, though he could imagine women ministering in a team of clergy under male headship, thought that it would be an unkindness to those women to ordain them while withholding what many reflexively felt to be the 'minimum sign of clerical adequacy', that is, to be 'a sole incumbent [holding] a parish freehold with the degree of independence of the bishop that this gives'.[81] The real underlying issue was, for Packer, the kind of clericalism that caused people to focus on the stipendiary clergy in isolation, rather than the many ministries of clergy and laity, exercised together. Until the Church of England had a clearer theology of ministry, the time was not right to think about women's ordination. Mascall had himself never been a parish incumbent but only a curate, in the early 1930s. But it was, he thought, possible to separate the issues of authority and sacramental competence: he could imagine a situation, theologically coherent if perhaps somewhat inconvenient, in which the government of the church was in lay hands but the

[78] On the issues at large, see Nigel Yates, *Love now, pay later? Sex and Religion in the Fifties and Sixties* (London, 2010), 22–37; Peter Webster, *Archbishop Ramsey: The Shape of the Church* (Farnham, 2015), 65–90.
[79] Mascall, 'Some Basic Considerations', 20.
[80] Mascall, in the preface to Channer, ed., *Abortion*, 11–12.
[81] Packer, 'Thoughts on the Role and Function of Women', 26.

sacramental function remained in the hands of the male priesthood he desired.[82]

Conclusion

Read superficially, and without the context of his metaphysics and understanding of the person, Mascall's view perhaps seemed indistinguishable from the patriarchal discrimination that campaigners were trying to dismantle; indeed, he himself was conscious that it might be so read.[83] One can only speculate how Mascall's attempt to rescue the word 'subordinate' from negative connotation would have been received, or his suggestion that the unique privilege granted to Mary as mother placed women *above* men both in nature and in the scheme of redemption;[84] as Sean Gill has noted, the sheer force of changing language and culture made such resistance quaintly Canute-like in its futility.[85] A reviewer in the *Times Literary Supplement* was blunt: 'whatever Professor Mascall says, androcentrism of the kind he expresses is now no more morally tolerable than racial discrimination or slavery'.[86] That many of those arguing against women's ordination were, like Mascall, ordained men – and, again like Mascall, unmarried too – made it harder for their case to be heard. But the kinds of argument that Mascall made, 'important worries ... about the theological significance of the particular, the concrete historicity of God's speech with us in Jesus', were enough to keep a theologian of the subtlety and openness of Rowan Williams from supporting the cause for several years, although by the early 1980s his mind had changed.[87] If this article has placed the early opponents of the ordination of women in a more secure historical context, and shown the internal logic (if not necessarily the persuasiveness) of the catholic objections, it will have achieved its aim.

[82] Mascall, *Women and the Priesthood*, 17.
[83] Mascall, 'Some Basic Considerations', 23.
[84] Mascall, *Women and the Priesthood*, 17, 33–4; idem, 'Some Basic Considerations', 22–4.
[85] Gill, *Women and the Church of England*, 262.
[86] 'Reverend Madam', *Times Literary Supplement*, 17 November 1972, 1399.
[87] Rowan Williams, 'Women and the Ministry: A Case for Theological Seriousness', in Monica Furlong, ed., *Feminine in the Church* (London, 1984), 11–27, at 19, referring to Mascall specifically.

This article covers the period until 1978, although the story of the Anglican ordination of women was far from over. But the defeat in the Church of England's General Synod at the hands of the clergy in that year was a marker of a kind, of the point by which all the negative arguments that were to be heard had been thoroughly aired, and the two sides firmly entrenched. Mascall was never to be reconciled to the idea of women priests; the evangelical George Carey, who as archbishop of Canterbury presided over the final vote in 1992, came to regret the pain the matter had caused Mascall in his old age.[88] Mascall continued to correspond with opponents, including his long-time friend the bishop of London, Graham Leonard, and Margaret Hood, one of the leaders of Women Against the Ordination of Women; he also wrote letters to both the national and the church press.[89] 1978, however, marks the end of the sequence of his writings on the issue directly; he was in his seventy-third year, and although he continued to write, the rate of production was already slowing significantly.

Yet the objections persisted, until (and after) the ordination of the first women to the priesthood in the Church of England in 1994 and beyond, forming a persistent dividing line within both catholic and evangelical constituencies, and a bond between conservatives on both sides, both in England and around the Anglican Communion. Many on the evangelical side, from the 1960s onwards growing in numbers in the Church of England where Anglo-Catholics were not, were able from that position of strength to come to a more accommodating position.[90] But evangelical opposition continued, not least from the campaign group Reform, founded in 1993.[91] On the Anglo-Catholic side, the resistance remained stronger, although far from universal; Forward in Faith stood against the ordination of women from its formation in 1992. Continued co-operation between evangelical and Anglo-Catholic was evident in the Association for

[88] George Carey, *Know the Truth: A Memoir* (London, 2004), 61–2. Carey was archbishop of Canterbury from 1991 until 2002.

[89] The correspondence with Hood is at Pusey House Library, Mascall Papers, Box 13. See also ibid., Box 2, File 3, fol. 188, Graham Leonard to Mascall, 8 May 1984. Mascall's letters to the editor of *The Times* were published on 12 February 1982 (p. 11) and 12 June 1986 (p. 15); draft letters to the *Church Times* and *The Tablet* from February 1986 are in Mascall Papers, Box 2, File 3, fols 4–5.

[90] For example, by 1986 Colin Craston had become fully and vocally supportive: *Biblical Headship and the Ordination of Women* (Nottingham, 1986).

[91] See, from within the orbit of Reform, Douglas Spanner, 'Men, Women and God', in Melvin Tinker, ed., *The Anglican Evangelical Crisis* (Fearn, 1995), 72–93.

the Apostolic Ministry, formed in 1985, which numbered among its early members James Packer, by that time resident in Canada, and Roger Beckwith.[92]

The issue was fundamentally one of the relationship between the Bible and Catholic tradition on the one hand, and the ongoing work of the Spirit in the churches, and the salience of culture, on the other. Conservative evangelicals and conservative Anglican Catholics could agree that the balance was threatened, even if they disagreed on the precise relationship of Scripture and tradition. The point at issue was succinctly expressed in 1972 by Benedict Green, vice-principal of the Anglo-Catholic theological college at Mirfield, while reviewing both *Why not?* and *Women Priests?* Despite all the arguments, he suggested, there had to be more that catholic Anglicans could say to those women who felt a call to ordained ministry than *non possumus*. 'At some point,' he continued, referring to the joint evangelical-catholic symposium, 'collaboration becomes collusion; the fundamental question that both sides dodge is (as put to evangelicals) "has the Lord yet more light and truth to break forth from his holy Word?", or (as put to catholics) "is the Holy Spirit still leading the Church into all truth or has it already got there?"'[93] Mascall, in contrast, used a formulation of the same problem to which he was to return several times in his later years. The most salient division among Christians was fast becoming that between 'those who believe in the fundamentally revealed and given character of the Christian religion and those who find their norms in the outlooks and assumptions of contemporary secularised culture and are concerned to assimilate the beliefs and institutions of Christianity to it'.[94] Mascall's readers may have thought this a false dichotomy, but it was along these lines that other conflicts in the Church of England and the Anglican Communion have often been configured since.

[92] Gill, *Women and the Church of England*, 254. In 1986 Beckwith was listed as one of the two joint secretaries of the Association: Mascall Papers, Box 2 File 3, fol. 202, Arthur Leggatt to Mascall, 10 February 1986.

[93] Benedict Green, review of *Why Not?* and *Women Priests?*, *C.R.* [the journal of the Community of the Resurrection] 279 (1972), 46–7.

[94] Mascall, *Women Priests?*, 24; on the same lines, see idem, 'Some Basic Considerations', 26; (much later) idem, *Saraband*, 380.

Negotiating Dissonance between the Religious, the Civil and the Legal in Anglican Same-Sex Weddings

Rémy Bethmont*
Université Paris 8 Vincennes-Saint-Denis

With the adoption of same-sex marriage or marriage-like schemes by civil authorities on both sides of the North Atlantic, Anglican same-sex couples in England, Scotland and the United States have had to negotiate various forms of dissonance between the religious celebration and the legal or civil status of their unions. This often translates into couples having multiple celebrations of their unions in order to bring together the legal and the religious creatively. These multiple ceremonies evidence the grip exercised by the tradition of a single wedding ritual that is both religious and legal on the imagination of Anglican same-sex couples. Enduring attachment to this tradition has given rise to particular LGBTQ ways of relating the celebration of a union to time, thus contributing to the unravelling of a rigidly legal Anglican understanding of the marriage rite.

Since the rise of the gay liberation movement in the late 1960s on both sides of the Atlantic, local clergy from various denominations or in so-called gay churches have offered same-sex couples the possibility of celebrating their relationship liturgically. Some of these clergy have been Anglican. In the 1970s, 1980s and 1990s, religious same-sex ceremonies were more often than not the only way by which same-sex couples could celebrate their commitments in as public a way as local and denominational circumstances would allow. These ceremonies accompanied the rise of an Anglican LGBT-affirming movement, which led to the multiplication of local congregations and sometimes dioceses in which, whatever the position of the national church, same-sex couples could feel valued. The absence of any state-sanctioned recognition of these couples, however, meant that the church ceremonies were purely symbolic, religious events and understandably left a bitter-sweet taste of incompleteness

* E-mail: remy.bethmont@univ-paris8.fr.

Studies in Church History 59 (2023), 492–512
doi: 10.1017/stc.2023.23

in the mouths of many. This initial discrepancy between the symbolic capital conferred by these same-sex ceremonies and the civil rights that the couples wanted gave way to new forms of dissonance, at least initially, when marriage-like schemes and same-sex marriage appeared as legal realities on both sides of the Atlantic.

In the decade preceding the US Supreme Court's 2015 ruling on same-sex marriage and the Episcopal Church's decision that year to make its marriage canon gender-neutral, a number of US states legalized same-sex marriage, although some dioceses would only solemnize such marriages in liturgies that did not make use of marital terminology. In a somewhat different vein, in the Scottish Episcopal Church between 2007 and 2014, it was the new gender-neutral marriage service that progressive clergy who blessed civil partnerships felt it natural to use, introducing what might be called a prophetic dissonance. In both these churches, dissonance between the religious and the civil meaning of the relationship went hand in hand with the necessity, whether imposed by the law of the land or by the church, of staging two ceremonies, or at the very least one ceremony with two distinct, separate parts, one religious and one legal. In the Church of England, the terminology and spirit of ceremonies for same-sex couples have usually reflected the status of the relationship in law, but since the implementation of the Civil Partnership Act 2004, the norm resulting from legal rules and denominational discipline has also been to plan for two separate events, one civil and one religious. Church of England same-sex couples have often introduced subjective meaning into both that jars with the status of the civil ceremony and sometimes also of the religious one. Although this regime of imposed, multiple celebratory events disappeared in the American and Scottish Episcopal Churches when they changed their marriage canons in 2015 and 2017 respectively, it remains the rule in the Church of England.

The various forms of dissonance that accompany these double same-sex weddings[1] highlight enduring LGBTQ attachment to the British and American tradition of a single wedding ritual that is both religious and legal. Same-sex couples' desire for one wedding

[1] This article will use the term 'wedding' in a loose sense, as it is used by many same-sex couples, to refer to more than just ceremonies that celebrate the entry into state-sanctioned marriage. A wedding may therefore also be the name of a civil partnership ceremony or even of a liturgy to which no legal recognition of the relationship is attached.

– which is striking for this author, who comes from a country in which the norm for all religious couples is to have two weddings – has often given rise to rituals that acknowledge in some way or other the queer chronology of their stories. The resulting time-bending experiences contribute to the unravelling of a rigidly legal Anglican understanding of the marriage rite.

Recent Debates, Sources and Methodology

A significant number of studies, many of them in the United States, have focused on the celebration of same-sex weddings. Most examine these weddings within a historical context in which no legal recognition of the couple attaches to the ceremony and religious same-sex weddings are not particularly singled out. Consequently there is little discussion of the way in which couples relate to the religious tradition in which they celebrate their union.[2] Mark Jordan has filled a gap in that respect with his book on blessing same-sex unions, in which, among other things, he studies the religious genealogies of same-sex wedding liturgies in the context of American culture and interprets them through the lens of queer theory.[3] Jordan, however, was writing before most of the recent developments giving legal recognition to same-sex unions in the United States. In England, a few scholars have focused on the impossibility or difficulty of religiously registering a civil partnership or solemnizing a marriage for same-sex couples in various denominations.[4] They have paid attention to the possibility of there being some importation by same-sex couples of religious elements into civil ceremonies[5] or underlined the legal risks that

[2] See for instance, Ellen Lewin, *Recognizing Ourselves: Ceremonies of Lesbian and Gay Commitment* (New York, 1999); Kathleen E. Hull, *Same-Sex Marriage: The Cultural Politics of Love and Law* (Cambridge, 2006).

[3] Mark D. Jordan, *Blessing Same-Sex Unions: The Perils of Queer Romance and the Confusions of Christian Marriage* (Chicago, IL, 2005), in particular ch. 5, pp. 128–55.

[4] A useful overview of the legal regulations within which English churches have to operate has been offered by Paul Johnson and Robert M. Vanderbeck, 'Sacred Spaces, Sacred Words: Religion and Same-Sex Marriage in England and Wales', *Journal of Law and Society* 44 (2017), 228–54.

[5] Peter W. Edge and Dominic Corrywright, 'Including Religion: Reflections on Legal, Religious, and Social Implications of the developing Ceremonial Law of Marriage and Civil Partnership', *Journal of Contemporary Religion* 26 (2011), 19–32. Edge and Corrywright do not, however, document the importation of religious elements into civil ceremonies and call for a systematic ethnographic study that would fill this gap.

liturgical creativity may represent for Church of England celebrants.[6] This article attempts to study the way in which same-sex weddings relate to both the legal and ecclesiastical contexts in which they take place. By taking into consideration the stories of same-sex couples from different Anglican provinces, I seek to understand better how the legal and ecclesiastical parameters interact with one another locally and shape different kinds of experiences.

The Church of England and the Episcopal Church in the USA are among the first in global Anglicanism to have started a debate on homosexuality in the 1970s, and have been unrivalled in the qualitative and quantitative importance and influence of Anglican resources produced by their members, with or without institutional church support, on homosexuality in general and on same-sex unions in particular, in the form of theological and liturgical writings. Institutionally, however, they differ starkly. The US Episcopal Church has been a pioneer for marriage rights within Anglicanism, whilst the Church of England as an institution has been among the most reluctant provinces in the Anglican global North to move away from a conservative status quo.

The relative ease with which same-sex marriage was adopted in the Scottish Episcopal Church, with a minimum amount of controversy and drama in a comparatively short period of time,[7] makes it an attractive candidate as a counterpoint to the study of the Church of England and the US Episcopal Church.

There is little scholarship bearing on same-sex commitment ceremonies in Anglicanism and still less that focuses on the interplay between the religious and the legal. In the United States, Heather White's study of the blessing of same-sex unions in the Episcopal diocese of New York and the subsequent threats of prosecution by local civil authorities focuses on the early 1970s.[8] Baptiste Coulmont has

[6] Charlotte Smith, 'The Church of England and Same-Sex Marriage: Beyond a Rights-Based Analysis', *Ecclesiastical Law Journal* 21 (2019), 153–78.

[7] Although the quietly relaxed attitude towards homosexuality that prevailed in the Scottish Episcopal Church gradually found a more public voice and manifestation from the 1980s, there was no institutional discussion of LGBTQ matters at General Synod level until the early 2000s.

[8] Heather R. White, 'Gay Rites and Religious Rights: New York's first Same-Sex Marriage Controversy', in Kathleen T. Talvacchia, Michael F. Pettinger and Mark Larrimore, eds, *Queer Christianities: Lived Religion in Transgressive Forms* (New York, 2014), 79–90.

written about the religious celebration of civil unions and includes the analysis of an Episcopalian ceremony but does not discuss the denominational context.[9]

In England, a recent article by Silvia Falcetta, Paul Johnson and Robert Vanderbeck studies the experience of same-sex couples marrying in places of worship registered for same-sex marriage in view of the provisions of the Marriage (Same-Sex Couples) Act 2013, which excludes Church of England churches. Their study adopts a similar approach to mine and shares some of the same concerns, but its focus on registered buildings excludes most of the ceremonies intended for Anglican same-sex couples, except the minority who choose to marry in another denomination.[10]

A smaller Anglican province like the Scottish Episcopal Church, the second in world Anglicanism, after the US Episcopal Church, to change its marriage canon to include same-sex couples in marriage, has, to my knowledge, attracted no scholarly interest beyond Charlotte Methuen's brief presentation of the theological logic of the 2017 decision.[11]

By and large, the history of Anglican celebrations of same-sex unions is yet to be written. In this history the relation between the religious and the legal deserves more attention. The creativity displayed by same-sex couples and celebrants in navigating the dissonance between the civil

[9] Baptiste Coulmont, 'Do the Rite Thing: Religious Civil Unions in Vermont', *Social Compass* 52 (2005), 225–39.

[10] Silvia Falcetta, Paul Johnson and Robert M Vanderbeck, 'The Experience of Religious Same-Sex Marriage in England and Wales: Understanding the Opportunities and Limits created by the Marriage (Same Sex Couples) Act 2013', *International Journal of Law, Policy and the Family* 35 (2021) [online journal], at: <https://doi.org/10.1093/lawfam/ebab003>, last accessed 13 September 2022. Their 2017 publication on the subject, which examined a large sample of buildings registered for same-sex marriage, estimated that the number of same-sex couples who marry in a different denomination from their own (because it is not allowable there) 'is likely small': Paul Johnson, Robert Vanderbeck, and Silvia Falcetta, 'Religious Marriage of Same-Sex Couples: A Report on Places of Worship in England and Wales registered for the Solemnization of Same-Sex Marriage', *SSRN Electronic Journal* (2017) [online journal], §6.16, at: <http://dx.doi.org/10.2139/ssrn.3076841>, last accessed 13 September 2022. My own experience of interviewing committed Anglican same-sex couples leads to the same tentative conclusion. Most would not contemplate marrying in a congregation that is not their own, let alone another denomination.

[11] Charlotte Methuen, 'Ehe, gleichgeschlechtliche Partnerschaften und Kirchengemeinschaft: Überlegungen zum anglikanischen Kontext', in Andreas Krebs and Matthias Ring, eds, *Mit dem Segen der Kirche: Die Segnung gleichgeschlechtlicher Partnerschaften in der theologischen Diskussion* (Bonn, 2018), 99–109, at 107–9.

and religious meanings of same-sex weddings is a challenge to the institutional churches' understanding of marriage, inherited from the time when there was a seamless partnership between church and state in the business of marriage. The recognition in civil law of same-sex unions has destroyed this seamlessness and given rise to ritual experiences which call for a different approach to what it is that the church does when it celebrates the union of a couple.

From within British and American culture the institutional church's instinct is to see one single ceremony as the beginning of a marriage, which aligns with the moment in time when the couple are legally recognized as spouses. Any subsequent, non-legal ceremony cannot therefore be termed a wedding. It was this approach that made possible the compromise solution reached by the Church in Wales in 2021; same-sex couples can have their marriage blessed but not solemnized in church. Taking stock of the lack of the required two-thirds majority in its governing body for a change in the doctrine of marriage,[12] the Church in Wales allowed the blessing of civil marriages, apparently considering that these church celebrations would not be actual weddings. No same-sex marriages would thereby be created; the church would merely bless relationships that happen to be part of its life.

The institutional logic which sees the blessing as essentially different from the wedding because, the church insists, it does not change the fabric of reality, is part of the history of the three Anglican churches on which this article focuses. This logic, however, is out of tune with the flexibility with which many same-sex couples experience religious ritual in their marriage histories. In the interstices between religious and legal performance of wedding ceremonies, committed Anglican same-sex couples and their celebrants have found new opportunities to enhance the transformative power of Anglican marriage rituals. For these couples the marriage liturgy is a vital source and resource to give meaning to their individual histories and to change the fabric of reality in ways that the power of law alone cannot. This article therefore identifies an area in which Anglican liturgical performance of marriage acquired new life and significance at the very moment when the diminished partnership

[12] 'Church in Wales issues draft Bill on Same-Sex Blessings', *Church Times*, 18 December 2020, online at: <https://www.churchtimes.co.uk/articles/2020/18-december/news/uk/church-in-wales-issues-draft-bill-on-same-sex-blessings>, accessed 18 May 2022.

between church and state over marriage may have led some to believe that this liturgical performance was becoming increasingly irrelevant.

This article is based primarily on forty oral history interviews across all three churches with Anglican same-sex couples and Anglican clergy who have officiated at same-sex ceremonies. Initial respondents were recruited from 2015 through personal contacts or LGBTQ Christian networks. Some of these respondents then provided further introductions to other clergy or same-sex couples. Whereas the stories collected in the Scottish and American Episcopal Churches about multiple same-sex wedding celebrations are firmly situated in the past, however recent, those originating from the Church of England provide material for what is literally a history of the present, as they witness to experiences induced by an institutional church context that has continued unchanged since the 2013 Marriage (Same-Sex Couples) Act.[13] These oral sources grant an insight into the recent history of same-sex ritual experience which textual sources alone do not.

Strategies to unite the Legal and the Religious

For the committed Anglican couples I interviewed, as for the clergy who supported them, their union, whether or not it was called marriage, was something in which faith was indissolubly intertwined with their participation in state-defined institutions. The idea of going through two ceremonies in order to fully validate the relationship from a legal as well as a religious point of view was unwelcome for most of them and somehow jarred with their understanding of the unity of life. This was an acute problem for the couples I interviewed in England, where a stark distinction between religious and civil paths to marriage is enshrined in the law of the land.

On both sides of the Atlantic many of the couples and officiants I interviewed had found creative ways of bringing together the legal and the religious. This creativity took different paths according to

[13] The situation of same-sex couples in the Church of England will be changed by the decision of the House of Bishops, confirmed by General Synod, in February 2023 (while this article was going to press) to authorize 'New prayers to celebrate committed relationships between two people.' These will create a situation for English same-sex couples similar to that in the Church in Wales. See *Living in Love and Faith: A Response from the Bishops of the Church of England* (GS 2289), online at: <https://www.churchofengland.org/media/29241>.

the legal and ecclesiastical contexts, evidencing the vastly different, context-related questions raised by the liturgical celebration of same-sex unions from one Anglican province to another. One recurring feature of this creativity was the challenge it represented to a merely legal, rigidly linear understanding of time in those rites of passage that publicly recognize and validate a couple. This creativity highlights what is effected by the religious dimension of such rites of passage. It has the potential to not just create a 'before' and 'after' but also to infuse the 'before' with the transformative quality of the present and sometimes the present with the transformative quality of a hoped-for future.

Many of the stories I collected on both sides of the Atlantic bear witness to the enduring power of the tradition of a single wedding ceremony which is at one and the same time religious and legal. The ingenuity with which English couples smuggled religious elements into their civil ceremonies was equalled by some of the Americans' determination that a ceremony whose purpose was to be purely legal should be celebrated by a member of clergy.

Different strategies were adopted by the couples, depending on the local legal context. The legal impossibility for same-sex couples to register their civil partnership or to get married in the Church of England makes it inevitable that the legal wedding should always be a civil wedding, either at the register office or on approved premises. Church of England same-sex couples who want a religious ceremony must therefore have it separately. This, at least, is the theory. In practice, one observes a great variety of practices which often betray the couple's desire to overcome what they see as an unwelcome, forced separation of the religious and the legal. None of the couples I interviewed saw the ceremony presided over by a registrar as purely civil and in their different ways, they endeavoured to make their subjective experience of the ceremony religious.

One strategy was to circumvent the legal prohibition on the use of religious language or texts into the civil ceremony by introducing religious elements that were not recognized as such by the registrar or whose marginal rewriting was seen to make them acceptable. One male couple, for example, used the marriage vows from the American Book of Common Prayer, from which explicit references to God had been expunged. The two men had tried unsuccessfully to use the vows from the English Book of Common Prayer but, even without any explicit mention of God, the register office had recognized the text and forbidden it. It did not, however, recognize the American Episcopal version, in spite of its close resemblance to the English version (at least, the official who looked at the text, who may not have been the same person as previously, deemed it acceptable).

Another strategy was adopted by a female couple, Deborah and Sarah,[14] in 2016. They planned their civil wedding in a hotel lounge so that they would have more creative freedom than at the register office. The registrar arrived for the legal ceremony which was devoid of any religious connotations, in line with English law. He left when his part of the ceremony was completed, but it did not end. Now led by one of the couple's friends, it continued with a Bible reading and two traditional hymns. The reading (Ephesians 3: 14–21) was particularly remarkable in that it read like a blessing of the couple, to which the first hymn, in the form of a prayer, was the couple's response of dedication to God. The whole ceremony, civil and religious, was presented as one in the order of service that was distributed to the guests.

Deborah and Sarah did this, even though a liturgical celebration of their marriage in church a few months later had been planned with their parish priest. For the two women, both ceremonies were equally important and in their different ways testified to the unity of the civil and religious dimensions of their marriage.

> Sarah: We thought of getting married in a Unitarian church or with the Quakers, but it would have been meaningless because we aren't part of these communities. So in the end we opted for a civil wedding. … But we wanted God to be present in our civil wedding. I feel we were brought together by God. … We found our way to God together. We wanted to acknowledge that on our wedding day, even though Deborah's parents and most of our friends are not religious.[15]

Although Sarah and Deborah decided against getting married in another denomination, other couples sometimes chose this path.[16] Robin and Patrick, for example, who were committed members of an inclusive Church of England parish, took advantage of their

[14] All first names given without surnames are pseudonyms. Depictions of interviewees' experiences have been checked with them for accuracy prior to submission of this article for publication.

[15] Interview with Sarah and Deborah, October 2019.

[16] Several such stories can be found in Falcetta, Johnson and Vanderbeck, 'Experience of Religious Same-Sex Marriage'.

personal friendship with a Unitarian minister to register their civil partnership religiously in her church in 2012, shortly after the ban on the use of religious buildings for registering civil partnerships was lifted by the Cameron government in November 2011. 'We wanted something in church, but there were so many restrictions. It was too much hassle. We were working on a project at the time and were in touch with a Unitarian minister. She invited us to have a ceremony at her church.'[17] The minister was happy for Robin and Patrick to write their service of commitment themselves and she did not mind the trinitarian language they wanted. The service may not have been strictly Anglican, but it certainly was not Unitarian.[18] It was in fact the expression of Robin and Patrick's theological understanding of their relationship, drawing on, among other resources, liturgies that had been rediscovered from an LGBTQ perspective, such as the rite of *adelphopoiesis* as analysed by John Boswell.[19] Robin underlines that 'the liturgy was almost [their] sermon'.

These English stories testify to the impossibility for the couples I interviewed to conceive of their union in a way that did not give primacy of place to its religious dimension and meaning. The category of civil as distinct from religious did not make any sense. The paradoxical practice, made possible by English law,[20] of the *religious* registration of Robin and Patrick's *civil* partnership is telling in that respect. From their own perspectives, the couples engaged in *legal* ceremonies which happened to be labelled *civil* but whose meaning in their eyes was primarily *religious*.

American stories of same-sex ceremonies also exemplified the unwillingness to separate the civil from the religious dimensions of same-sex unions, but the flexibility of American marriage laws also allowed all kinds of conflations between religious and legal which

17 Interview with Robin, February 2021.

18 Such flexibility for same-sex couples from another denomination than the one where the marriage is solemnized has been analysed at greater length in Falcetta, Johnson and Vanderbeck, 'Experience of Religious Same-Sex Marriage', 19–22.

19 John Boswell, *The Marriage of Likeness: Same-Sex Unions in Pre-Modern Europe*, 2nd edn (London, 1996).

20 The possibility of registering civil partnerships in religious buildings also indicates that the state itself does not have a clear understanding of how the civil relates to the religious. For details regarding the legal construct allowing a strictly civil ceremony to take place in a religious registered building, see Johnson and Vanderbeck, 'Sacred Spaces, Sacred Words', 242.

would be impossible in either the Church of England or to a large extent in the Scottish Episcopal Church.

English law defines as one of the legal paths to marriage that which is solemnized 'according to the rites of the Church of England'.[21] It is therefore the conformity to the rites and rules of the Church of England that gives an Anglican wedding ceremony its legal weight. The content of the ceremony and its venue are matters that affect the validity of the marriage. In Scotland, the state has no interest in the venue of the wedding ceremony, and for those 'prescribed' religious bodies (like the Scottish Episcopal Church) which enjoy an automatic right to solemnize marriages,[22] the state has no particular requirements concerning the wording of the marriage service.[23] However, Scots law specifies that ministers of prescribed religious bodies must solemnize marriages 'in accordance with a form of ceremony recognised by the religious body' to which they belong.[24] There is therefore little leeway in the wording of the authorized nuptial liturgies for individual creativity.[25]

American marriage laws, on the other hand, allow huge flexibility regarding the wording and venue of a wedding ceremony. Other than the prescribed legal paperwork demanded by the state in which the marriage is registered, legal requirements about what is said and done in the ceremony never go beyond demanding that there should be some declaration of intent by the couple and, in most states, a

[21] Marriage Act 1949, §5.

[22] Marriage (Scotland) Act 1977, §8(1)(a)(ii).

[23] This point was made clear to the Episcopal Church's Liturgy Committee working on a new marriage service when they enquired of the Scottish civil authorities in 2001, at a time when not even civil partnership existed, whether the complete omission of the mention of 'husband and wife' in the new liturgy might endanger the legal validity of a marriage thus celebrated. The answer was a resounding no: 'Parliament, when drawing up the Marriage (Scotland) Act 1977, dealt with certain religious bodies differently. There are those bodies, such as the Episcopal Church in Scotland, that have an automatic authority to solemnize marriages … The Registrar General is not involved in the registering of the celebrants and it is up to each religious body to decide what form of marriage ceremony is appropriate for their celebrants to use. The 1977 Act does not stipulate any form of words that have to be used by such bodies': General Synod Office, Edinburgh, Liturgy Committee Minutes and Documents, e-mail from Kathleen F. O'Donnell on behalf of the General Register Office for Scotland to Elspeth Davey, 22 November 2001, unpaginated.

[24] Marriage (Scotland) Act 1977, §14(a). Scottish Episcopal celebrants do sometimes make small alterations to the marriage service but they are understood to be the kinds of changes that the bishop would not object to.

[25] National Records of Scotland, 'Marriage Celebrants: National Records of Scotland Policy on Authorisation', online at: <https://www.nrscotland.gov.uk/files//registration/nrs-marriage-authorisation-policy.pdf>, accessed 12 January 2022.

pronouncement by the officiant. American weddings are the superimposition of a state-sanctioned ceremony, in which the celebrant acts as an agent of the state, on a religious ceremony, whose content and compliance with ecclesiastical rules is of no interest to the state, in which the same celebrant acts as a representative of the church. The religious content of the ceremony therefore depends exclusively on what the individual celebrant is ready to countenance. Consequently, there is considerable freedom when it comes to bringing together the legal and the religious. This can be seen in services tailored to the needs of a particular couple as well as in institutional searching for compromise solutions.

The US Episcopal Church first officially authorized a same-sex commitment liturgy for experimental use in 2012. *The Witnessing and Blessing of a Lifelong Covenant* eschewed marital terminology, as the name of the service indicates. On the face of it, in those states where same-sex marriage was legal, it would have made sense to use it only in order to bless a civil marriage, since the liturgy was not in fact a marriage service. But the general reluctance to separate the civil from the religious allied to the flexibility of American marriage laws led to the frequent use of the 2012 liturgy to solemnize same-sex marriages whenever the bishop allowed it. None of the couples I interviewed who used this liturgy to get married in one single ceremony were in any way troubled by the absence of marital terminology. The fact that it was used to solemnize their legal marriage made the language of covenant equivalent to that of marriage in their eyes.[26]

It was the officiating clergy who sometimes felt the dissonance most acutely because they were much more aware of the fact that the avoidance of marital terminology had been a concession to a relatively conservative House of Bishops and therefore expressive of a refusal to acknowledge the full interchangeability of the notion of covenant in the liturgy with that of marriage. As one priest in Portland, Oregon told me in 2014, using the 2012 liturgy was bewildering because the civil and ecclesiastical roles of the officiant were slightly at odds with each other. What in weddings of straight couples had always been an invisible, seamless superimposition of a civil ceremony on a religious one had now become a visible superimposition

[26] As the story of one couple I interviewed suggests, they were sometimes helped by the officiant who told them ahead of the ceremony that a lifelong covenant could only mean marriage in her eyes.

in which the officiating priest was doing one thing on behalf of the church and something called by a different name on behalf of the state.[27] Because of the legal need to make clear that a marriage was being solemnized, the officiant had to add a sentence including marital terminology, while signalling that the sentence in question only took care of the legal, non-religious aspect of the ceremony, as in this Californian example: 'In as much as N. and N. have exchanged vows of love and fidelity in the presence of God and the church, I now pronounce that they are bound to one another in a holy covenant, as long as they both shall live, and according to the laws of the state of California are married.'[28]

This dissonance played a part in encouraging progressive clergy to demand the replacement of 'covenant' by 'marriage' ahead of the 2015 General Convention, which turned the 2012 liturgy into a gender-neutral marriage service. The 2012 rite prophetically declared the equivalence of marriage and lifelong covenant.

Time-bending Ritual Experiences

When, however, personal history and diocesan discipline allied to make a single ceremony impossible, the American same-sex couples I interviewed were as resourceful as their English counterparts. They also benefited from the freedom given by the American legal context to create unique ceremonies which could bring together not only the legal and the religious but also the past and present of the couple's inscription in both state and church.

Joy and Judy had their 'illegal wedding', as they call it, in their parish church in Iowa in 1999, ten years before they would make it legal in a second ceremony after the law changed in their state. The two women wanted the 2009 legal ceremony to be religious. The diocesan bishop, however, would not allow the solemnization of a same-sex marriage in church but only the blessing of a civil marriage. They

[27] Although not as jarring, the visible superimposition of civil and religious ceremonies was already something that could be observed in some religious civil union ceremonies. Coulmont mentions a homily during an Episcopalian civil union ceremony in Vermont in which the officiant talked of a 'Holy and Civil Union': Coulmont, 'Do the Rite Thing', 235.

[28] Tom Bauer, 'Tom and Nilo's Wedding July 4, 2014, Christ Episcopal Church, Sausalito, CA', 2014, wedding video, 24:57–25:19, online at: <https://www.youtube.com/watch?v=kT0Z_5vJSMQ>, accessed 14 February 2022.

therefore asked their priest to preside over the legal ceremony, assisted by the deacon, in the home of a friend of the couple, using a liturgy that the two women drafted for the occasion. The service started by a reaffirmation of the vows the two women had exchanged ten years earlier without marital terminology in accordance with the bishop's instructions at that time. This reaffirmation of vows was followed by questions by the celebrants and marriage vows borrowed from the New Zealand Prayer Book. The priest then declared them married 'in the presence of God and in this company, by the power vested in me by the State of Iowa' and the licence was signed. Not only did the service unite the religious and the legal, even though a blessing of the 'civil' marriage was planned in the church two days later, but it also harked back to the 1999 ceremony, uniting the two events which had taken place ten years apart. The opening of the service made this very clear:

> Ten years ago, Joy and Judy had what they called a Covenant service at … In every sense but legal this was the beginning of their marriage. Now the State of Iowa has made it possible for them to marry legally; so, in a sense, today, we will be completing the service that happened 10 years ago. It was important to them then, and is important to them now, that these services take place in a context that integrates their faith and their relationship.[29]

The service therefore legally validated an existing marriage which had been celebrated without marital terminology ten years earlier. From the two women's perspective, the meaning of the two services was therefore one: the 1999 ceremony anticipated what the 2009 service looked back to. The two services were conflated in every possible way: not only were the 1999 vows repeated, but the officiants were the same priest and deacon in both ceremonies and the two Bible readings were intentionally identical. The two women then had their marriage blessed two days later during the ordinary Sunday service, using the liturgy for the blessing of a civil marriage. Although that liturgy explicitly blessed the legal marriage that had occurred the preceding Friday, the subjective conflation of that event with the 1999 service

[29] Archives of the Episcopal Church, Digital Archive for General Convention Resolution 2009-C056, Standing Commission on Liturgy and Music, 'The Marriage of N. and N.', 5 June 2009, online at: <https://www.episcopalarchives.org/sites/default/files/sclm-c056/liturgies/099_Liturgy_2009.pdf>, accessed 14 February 2022.

also turned the Sunday service into an echo of the church ceremony that had taken place ten years before. The kind of change effected by the marriage rite in the life of the couple is thus far more complex that dividing their history into before and after a particular moment in time. The religious rite is not constrained by linear time.

A slightly different kind of time-bending experience appears to have taken place in the Scottish Episcopal Church. Between 2007 and 2014 a number of civil partnership celebrations in church, which had to be separate from the legal event, had the peculiar quality of expanding for a hoped-for future the meaning and status of the relationship. A great many Scottish same-sex couples, like many of their English counterparts,[30] tended to see civil partnership as marriage in everything but name. Therefore the terminology that was used informally about the ceremony was often that of marriage. However, I would argue that Scottish liturgical resources also had the potential, infinitely more than English liturgies, to impress on a civil partnership all the Christian qualities of a marriage by giving the couple and the wedding party a prophetic view of what the Scottish liturgical understanding of marriage meant for same-sex celebrations.

The 2007 Scottish marriage service contains multiple options to cater for different kinds of couples and the consistent selection of option A allows one to devise a gender-neutral marriage service. This was officially presented at the time as the promotion of gender equality in marriage: option A did not prescribe the order in which the bride and bridegroom would take their vows or answer the celebrant's questions, eschewing the sexist liturgical custom of having the man always speak first. But with civil partnerships coming onto the British political agenda from about 2002, the Scottish liturgy commission drafted the new service in a context in which same-sex couples were inevitably on their minds.[31] As Greg, a gay priest I

[30] Rémy Bethmont, 'Blessing Same-Sex Unions in the Church of England: The Liturgical Challenge of Same-Sex Couples' Demand for Equal Marriage Rites', *Journal of Anglican Studies* 17 (2019), 148–67.

[31] Indeed, in a recorded interview with a representative of the US Episcopal liturgical commission, the Rev. Ian Paton, who then chaired the Scottish Liturgy Committee, declared that same-sex marriage was evoked quite early on during a residential conference of the liturgy committee before it was 'even on the political horizon': Interview with Ian Paton by Drew Keane on behalf of the Standing Commission on Liturgy and Music of the [US] Episcopal Church, transcript, 2017, 3, online at: <https://liturgyandmusic.files.wordpress.com/2017/11/interview-with-ian-paton.pdf>, accessed 14 February 2022).

interviewed, told me: 'Most of the liturgy group members were gay or at least gay friendly. There's no doubt that some of them were thinking about what could happen with the liturgy, that it could be used for same-sex couples.'[32] When the adoption of the new marriage service was accompanied by an encouragement to experiment with it and use it for other pastoral occasions, such as a wedding anniversary, a number of LGBTQ and LGBTQ-friendly clergy saw this as licence to use it to bless civil partnerships. All that was needed was to substitute 'partnership' for the word 'marriage'.

The trend towards using the 2007 marriage service to bless civil partnerships was also strengthened by a quietly liberal atmosphere on the issue. Only three years earlier, in 2004, the Scottish College of Bishops had expressed 'the hope that within existing provision, clergy and laity will be able to minister sensitively and pastorally to each other regardless of issues of sexuality or gender'.[33] Unlike the Church of England, there was never any official ban on the blessing of same-sex relationships in the Scottish Episcopal Church.

Greg, who between 2007 and 2014 officiated at about ten same-sex ceremonies after a civil partnership, using the new marriage service, says that people in attendance saw the ceremony as a wedding: 'Relatives of the couple would come to me and say: "It's incredible how much it looks like a wedding! It is a wedding!" It was an epiphany. They suddenly realized that it *was* a wedding.'[34] The discrepancy between the legal status of the relationship and the marriage service did not seem to trouble anybody, neither the priest nor the wedding party. On the contrary, in a similar way to what the US Episcopal liturgy of 2012 effected, some couples may have been able to experience the liturgy as prophetic of what they truly were in the eyes of God, if not in the eyes of the law. Greg mentions a Roman Catholic male couple whose civil partnership he blessed in 2007 using the new marriage liturgy. After the Scottish Episcopal Church changed its marriage canon, Greg contacted them and asked whether they wanted 'to do everything again'. But the couple

[32] Interview with Greg, July 2018.

[33] Scottish Episcopal Church, College of Bishops, 'A Response from the College of Bishops to Submissions made as a Result of Discussion of the Publication *Human Sexuality: A Study Guide*', Virtue Online, February 2004, at: <https://ec2-54-88-218-0.compute-1.amazonaws.com/scotland-scottish-episcopal-church-responds-sexuality-issues>, accessed 14 February 2022.

[34] Interview with Greg, July 2018.

answered that they had considered themselves married for ten years. 'They just converted their civil partnership but didn't feel the need to celebrate it.' The Scottish nuptial liturgy, even without marital terminology, had done its job of marrying them.

Similar stories can also be heard in England by couples looking back to their civil partnership ceremony and seeing it as their entry into marriage, but the Scottish use of a nuptial liturgy that did not need adapting to fit same-sex couples sent what was at the time a unique message about gender not being part of the essence of marriage. Since, by and large, the distinction between civil partnership and marriage revolved exclusively around gender, the use of the Scottish marriage service in the blessing of a civil partnership could be heard as a prophetic declaration about the inclusion of same-sex couples in marriage even though back then it was on the institutional agenda of neither state nor church. The capital of sacramental marriage was already being granted to these couples, uniting the present of the celebration with the future time when, one hoped, the church would draw all the relevant conclusions from its developing understanding of marriage.

In the cases I have mentioned, the legal timeline is unambiguous: there is a precise moment in time when the couple starts to enjoy their civil rights as a couple who has entered into a particular state-sanctioned institution. The religious timeline, however, often appears to be no timeline at all. In their subjective experience, many couples conflate separate events that may sometimes lie years apart, as in the case of Joy and Judy in Iowa. Their multiple ceremonies were partly due to the fact that they lived through years of changing possibilities for them as a couple. The religious ceremony on offer for them in 1999 excluded anything legal, while what was available ten years later did not allow the religious ceremony they would have wanted: the solemnization of their legal marriage in their church. But their three ceremonies, the 'illegal marriage', as they call it, the legal marriage and the blessing of their marriage, were united in a sacramental time that was essentially different from legal, linear time. The two 2009 ceremonies did not only change the present (as the first one did legally) but they also transformed the past by functioning as a source of authenticity for marking the 1999 ceremony with the seal of marriage, endowed with all its sacramental and legal capital.

Time-bending is not always part of the experience of those same-sex couples who have several wedding ceremonies. In the case of Sarah and Deborah in England, it was enough for the two women to give a religious dimension to the civil ceremony. When they had their second ceremony in their local church, they were very clear that the two events were quite separate and they made sure that the church ceremony would not be seen as their actual wedding. In their minds it was nothing other than a church-community celebration of a marriage that had already been contracted and they intentionally did not wear their wedding dresses in church.

Nonetheless, a non-linear relationship to time in same-sex weddings is evident in most of the stories featuring a separate civil and religious ceremony, including in the Church of England. Natalie and Patricia, for example, first married at the register office in a civil ceremony to which only their closest family members were invited. It took place far away from where they lived because they 'wanted to get away from everybody'.

> Patricia: We wanted the *church* to be the celebration.
>
> Natalie: In my mind, the church wedding was going to be big. In the end there were eighty people. … I like the idea of a celebration rather than a blessing, because you can be blessed elsewhere than in church. We felt blessed at the civil ceremony. I had a Bible in my pocket at the register office. It was a way of bringing God into the civil ceremony. … The church celebration was the fulfilment of all the things I had imagined. We walked down the aisle together after showing a video of the civil ceremony. We wanted people to have a sense of what had happened before.[35]

The desire to conflate the two events into one is clear enough. One might say that just as the Bible in Natalie's pocket transformed the first wedding – which meant a lot more than a mere bureaucratic formality – into an anticipation of the second, the video in the church ceremony united it with the civil event. There was a single legal point in time when the two women began to be treated as spouses, and by a similar kind of religious time-bending as in Joy and Judy's story the two ceremonies were subjectively made one.

[35] Interview, October 2019.

Same-Sex Liturgical Experience and the Revision of Anglican Marriage Rites

The not-so-uncommon subjective experience of time-bending in same-sex weddings challenges a unidimensional understanding of the chronology of marriage with an objectively identifiable beginning in linear time. Insurance companies or the tax office must of course be able to identify objectively when the couple begins to enjoy spousal rights. However, conferring legal rights is far from being the only thing that couples expect from a wedding,[36] especially a religious wedding in which couples want to be blessed in the specificities of their histories, so that new meaning may be injected into their past and new hopes entertained for the future.

The almost universal practice of cohabitation before marriage in the heterosexual population in the last half-century has already presented the church with the question of what it is exactly that a church wedding celebrates. Is it the entry into marriage or the blessing of a marriage which in more ways than one, at least from the subjective perspective of the couple (and sometimes of their families and friends), already exists? Authorized marriage services have struggled to come to terms with this kind of question.

The 2007 Scottish service acknowledges this major shift in the practice of marriage. One of the three possible introductions to the service, presenting the ceremony as one of many 'cairns at the roadside' in the couple's journey, is an invitation, whenever appropriate, to interpret the religious wedding as a decisive moment in a marriage-like relationship that started long before.[37] But the same introduction continues in a way that tends to align with legal, linear time and shies away from offering the option of retroactively naming as marriage the months or years of cohabitation: 'N. and N.'s relationship is a great journey that, in different ways, we have travelled and will continue to travel with them. Today we pause along the way to gather at a decisive and important moment for us all. They are to be married.'[38]

In the United States, the Standing Commission on Liturgy and Music's intentional focus on LGBTQ couples when they drafted

[36] Kathleen Hull's work shows this very well about same-sex weddings which took place at a time when there was no state recognition of the couples: see in particular *Same-Sex Marriage*, 26–77.

[37] Marriage Liturgy 2007, 2.A.

[38] Ibid. A more open formulation of the last sentence might have been proposed, such as: 'They are celebrating their marriage.'

the new inclusive liturgy for marriage in the run-up to the 2015 General Convention challenged the US Episcopal Church to go further than the Scottish Episcopal Church in that respect, indeed further than most authorized marriage services allowed across global Anglicanism, with the exception perhaps of New Zealand.[39] The 2015 liturgy offers an introduction to be used specifically by 'those who have previously made a lifelong commitment to one another', as the rubric makes clear. However, the draft version of the introduction varies from the text that was eventually adopted by the General Convention. The revised text appears to betray some discomfort with a non-linear understanding of the chronology of marriage, although one may also interpret the revision as resulting from an attempt to make the formulation suitable for those couples who, for various reasons, had had a civil marriage prior to the church ceremony, but who did not want the liturgy of blessing of a civil marriage to be used.[40]

> We have come together today with N. N. and N. N.
> to witness the sacred vows they make this day
> *draft version*: as they solemnize their marriage / *amended version*: as they are married
> [according to the laws of the state or civil jurisdiction of X],
> and reaffirm their commitment to one another.
> Forsaking all others,
> they will renew their covenant of mutual fidelity and steadfast love,
> remaining true to one another in heart, body, and mind,
> as long as they both shall live.[41]

[39] The third form of the marriage service in the 1989 New Zealand Prayer Book offers a consistently open formulation that allows the wedding party to understand the ceremony as the celebration of a marriage that is already in existence. However, in contrast to the draft 2015 American liturgy, this option is never explicitly presented as applying to couples who already consider themselves married in some way or other.

[40] Although in theory marriage services are reserved for the solemnization of marriage, they have also been used in many instances for the church wedding of couples who had legally contracted a marriage in a prior ceremony.

[41] The draft version is to be found in Standing Commission on Liturgy and Music, 'Reports to the 78th General Convention: Supplemental Materials; Appendices of the Report of the Standing Commission on Liturgy and Music' (Episcopal Church, 2015), 89, online at: <https://extranet.generalconvention.org/staff/files/download/13068>, accessed 14 February 2022; the authorized version can be found in *Liturgical Resources 1: I will bless you and you will be a Blessing*, revised and expanded (New York, 2015), online at: <https://www.churchpublishing.org/products/liturgicalresources1>, accessed 14 February 2022.

'As they solemnize their marriage' offers the possibility to understand that an existing marriage is now being solemnized. The problem is that the solemnization of marriage is commonly understood to mean a religious ceremony that makes a marriage legal. The revisers of the draft version may have felt that it would not be suitable in those cases where the ceremony is devoid of legal content, as in a number of Episcopal churches outside the United States, in civil jurisdictions where a religious ceremony cannot by law make a marriage legal.[42] Moreover, there may also have been some resistance to the naming of the existing relationship, prior to the celebration, as a marriage. The idea of celebration, of which the New Zealand Prayer Book makes great use,[43] might have easily replaced that of solemnization. In any case, the text that was finally authorized for use creates the same effect as the 2007 Scottish liturgy and implies that a 'proper' marriage is what the ceremony inaugurates.

Whatever their timidity, however, Scottish and American engagement with the question of extra-legal marital chronology has created a liturgical environment that is better able to take seriously or reflect the experience of many same-sex couples, especially those who have lived through the years of the LGBTQ marriage rights campaigns. It is also an environment that is probably more in tune with the variety of contemporary histories of marriage in the heterosexual population. By contrast, the absence of any engagement with this kind of question in the latest revisions of the English marriage service is one among several elements that have marginalized same-sex couples in the Church of England and also, perhaps, those straight couples whose subjective interpretation of their histories does not sit well with the legal objectivity of the English liturgy. The specifics of LGBTQ ritual experience may well constitute a significant reference point for Anglican attempts to offer marriage services that speak to contemporary couples, irrespective of their sexual orientation.

[42] Most of the countries covered by the Convocation of the Episcopal Church in Europe are a case in point.
[43] 'Marriage Liturgy: Third Form', *A New Zealand Prayer Book*, 1989 (New York, 1997), 790–1.